S0-BTB-248

Beginning Transact-SQL
with SQL Server 2000 and 2005

Beginning Transact-SQL
with SQL Server 2000 and 2005

Paul Turley with Dan Wood

WILEY

Wiley Publishing, Inc.

Beginning Transact-SQL with SQL Server 2000 and 2005

Published by
Wiley Publishing, Inc.
10475 Crosspoint Boulevard
Indianapolis, IN 46256
www.wiley.com

Copyright © 2006 by Wiley Publishing, Inc., Indianapolis, Indiana

Published simultaneously in Canada

ISBN 10: 0-7645-7955-X

ISBN 13: 978-0-7645-7955-4

Manufactured in the United States of America

10 9 8 7 6 5 4 3 2 1

1MA/QW/RQ/QV/IN

Library of Congress Cataloging-in-Publication Data: Available from the publisher.

No part of this publication may be reproduced, stored in a retrieval system or transmitted in any form or by any means, electronic, mechanical, photocopying, recording, scanning or otherwise, except as permitted under Sections 107 or 108 of the 1976 United States Copyright Act, without either the prior written permission of the Publisher, or authorization through payment of the appropriate per-copy fee to the Copyright Clearance Center, 222 Rosewood Drive, Danvers, MA 01923, (978) 750-8400, fax (978) 646-8600. Requests to the Publisher for permission should be addressed to the Legal Department, Wiley Publishing, Inc., 10475 Crosspoint Blvd., Indianapolis, IN 46256, (317) 572-3447, fax (317) 572-4355, or online at http://www.wiley.com/go/permissions.

LIMIT OF LIABILITY/DISCLAIMER OF WARRANTY: THE PUBLISHER AND THE AUTHOR MAKE NO REPRESENTATIONS OR WARRANTIES WITH RESPECT TO THE ACCURACY OR COMPLETENESS OF THE CONTENTS OF THIS WORK AND SPECIFICALLY DISCLAIM ALL WARRANTIES, INCLUDING WITHOUT LIMITATION WARRANTIES OF FITNESS FOR A PARTICULAR PURPOSE. NO WARRANTY MAY BE CREATED OR EXTENDED BY SALES OR PROMOTIONAL MATERIALS. THE ADVICE AND STRATEGIES CONTAINED HEREIN MAY NOT BE SUITABLE FOR EVERY SITUATION. THIS WORK IS SOLD WITH THE UNDERSTANDING THAT THE PUBLISHER IS NOT ENGAGED IN RENDERING LEGAL, ACCOUNTING, OR OTHER PROFESSIONAL SERVICES. IF PROFESSIONAL ASSISTANCE IS REQUIRED, THE SERVICES OF A COMPETENT PROFESSIONAL PERSON SHOULD BE SOUGHT. NEITHER THE PUBLISHER NOR THE AUTHOR SHALL BE LIABLE FOR DAMAGES ARISING HEREFROM. THE FACT THAT AN ORGANIZATION OR WEBSITE IS REFERRED TO IN THIS WORK AS A CITATION AND/OR A POTENTIAL SOURCE OF FURTHER INFORMATION DOES NOT MEAN THAT THE AUTHOR OR THE PUBLISHER ENDORSES THE INFORMATION THE ORGANIZATION OR WEBSITE MAY PROVIDE OR RECOMMENDATIONS IT MAY MAKE. FURTHER, READERS SHOULD BE AWARE THAT INTERNET WEBSITES LISTED IN THIS WORK MAY HAVE CHANGED OR DISAPPEARED BETWEEN WHEN THIS WORK WAS WRITTEN AND WHEN IT IS READ.

For general information on our other products and services please contact our Customer Care Department within the United States at (800) 762-2974, outside the United States at (317) 572-3993 or fax (317) 572-4002.

Trademarks: Wiley, the Wiley logo, Wrox, the Wrox logo, Programmer to Programmer, and related trade dress are trademarks or registered trademarks of John Wiley & Sons, Inc. and/or its affiliates, in the United States and other countries, and may not be used without written permission. All other trademarks are the property of their respective owners. Wiley Publishing, Inc., is not associated with any product or vendor mentioned in this book.

Wiley also publishes its books in a variety of electronic formats. Some content that appears in print may not be available in electronic books.

About the Authors

Paul Turley (Seattle, WA) is a Senior Consultant for Hitachi Consulting, where he architects and develops business reporting solutions and database systems for many high-profile business clients. He has been developing database solutions since 1991 for companies such as Hewlett-Packard, Boise Cascade, Disney, and Microsoft. He has been a Microsoft Certified Professional and Trainer since 1996 and currently holds his MCDBA, MCSD, MSF Practitioner, IT Project+, and A+ certifications.

Paul designed and maintains www.Scout-Master.com, a web-based service that enables Boy Scouts and their leaders to manage their own unit web sites, membership, and advancement records on-line using SQL Server and ASP.NET. Paul has been a contributing or lead author on *Professional SQL Server Reporting Services* (1st and 2nd editions), *Beginning Access 2002 VBA*, *Professional SQL Server 2000 Data Warehousing with Analysis Services,* and *Professional Access 2000 Programming* from WROX Press.

Dan Wood (Silverdale, WA) is the Operations Manager, Database Administrator, and SQL Server Trainer for Netdesk Corporation, a Microsoft Gold Certified Partner for Learning Solutions in Seattle where he manages and develops database solutions as well as trains database professionals from organizations throughout the Northwest. He has been a Microsoft Certified Professional and Trainer since 1999 and currently holds his MCDBA, MCSD, and MCSE certifications.

Credits

Acquisitions Editor
Bob Elliott

Development Editor
Marcia Ellett

Production Editor
Angela Smith

Copy Editor
Kim Cofer

Editorial Manager
Mary Beth Wakefield

Vice President & Executive Group Publisher
Richard Swadley

Vice President and Publisher
Joseph B. Wikert

Production Coordinator
Michael Kruzil

Graphics and Production Specialists
Carrie A. Foster
Denny Hager
Joyce Haughey
Alicia South
Ron Terry
Julie Trippetti

Quality Control Technicians
David Faust
John Greenough
Leeann Harney

Proofreading and Indexing
TECHBOOKS Production Services

For my daughter, Sara

Who doesn't care much about SQL but has been a source of incredible strength and inspiration. You're a fighter and a champion! — P. T.

Contents

Contents

Contents

Contents

Contents

Contents

Acknowledgments

Thanks to my wife, Sherri, and our kids for their support during a turbulent year; to my parents, Mark and Carol Turley, for their ever-present love and support; to Sharon Simpson for coming to the rescue.

Props to Dan Wood, my supporting author, for his dedication and perseverance. He did an awesome job of picking me up, slapping me around, and saying "what were you thinking?!" at just the right time; and thanks to the entire Wood family for allowing me talk him into this. My appreciation goes to Gregg Shipler for his assistance, friendship, and instruction. Thanks to everyone at Hitachi Consulting, a truly amazing organization and stellar group of professionals; and thanks to many students and consulting clients, without whom none of this would be possible.

Thanks to the folks at Wiley Publishing: Marcia Ellett, Bob Elliott, and Joe Wikert. You are professionals and great people with a genuine sense of what's really important. Thanks to my daughter, Rachael, for a great job managing my screen shot files.

Foreword

Data has been an integral part of business for decades. But the advent of the Internet, the increasing rate of innovation in technology, and the emergence of corporate governance has placed data center stage in the new Millennium. The Internet opened a new window to the world. It broke down barriers and dissolved national and geographic boundaries. As people established ways to leverage the Internet for business, companies found themselves competing in a new arena. Enterprises realized that they no longer had a corner on the market "in their area." The Internet did away with areas and dissolved the advantage of location for many sectors of the economy. A customer could easily reach across the world to a competitor with the click of a hyperlink. This phenomenon catapulted business into a new generation of fierce competition: Competition ripe with the need for competitive advantage over rivals. Out of this, data emerged as the new golden asset within corporations. What companies know about their customers, vendors, supply chain, operations, and markets is often the single most advantageous factor they can bring to bear as they strive for success over their competitors.

Unfortunately, it came to light recently that others were willing to go beyond the rules in their effort to win out over their competition. Scandals made front page news, investors demanded change, and governments responded with legislation. These new bills and regulations have intensified the spotlight on the data within a company. Laws now dictate that data must be available and must meet new levels of accuracy, quality, and integrity. Data must be verifiable and it must be recoverable. Technology has responded to support these new requirements. Faster and more robust hardware and software continue to be produced at an ever-increasing rate. But technology in and of itself is a double-edge sword. While it has provided the means to meet much of the requirements this new global marketplace requires, technology has also introduced new challenges. Because of technology innovations, data can now be produced and stored at staggering speeds. Long gone are the days when a data analyst could review a spreadsheet of data visually and find an error. The data volumes of today freeze the analysts of old in their tracks. What they would have thought a large volume of data can now be stored on a small handheld device and may have been generated in the blink of an eye. The amount of data that must be captured, manipulated, and retrieved each day within companies has reached terabytes and even petabytes in certain scientific sectors. Those responsible for this data, and the data systems, are faced with the challenge of safekeeping what may be an enterprise's most valuable asset.

Fortunately, tools exist for meeting this challenge head-on. One such tool has been at the heart of my professional career; Transact-SQL, or T-SQL. Woven throughout data's lifecycle is the need to transact business and capture data-states, to build data structures, to store data, to retrieve it, sort it, manipulate it, aggregate it, present it . . . on and on. T-SQL provides a means to meets these needs and has sustained itself as a powerful and robust language for data definition and data manipulation. The book you have in your hands holds the key to starting down the path of T-SQL use. I encourage you to do more than read this book; study it. If you do, you will undoubtedly find many of the uses for T-SQL that I have. T-SQL has provided me with the means to create the databases that have been core to applications I've developed. It has provided me with the means to create tools for managing hundreds of other databases across the U.S., the UK, and Japan. And it has provided core functionality for transactional and analytical applications supporting some of the top sites on the Internet. There is a lot of power in the T-SQL language. I hope you find the spark of interest to work through this book in its entirety and add T-SQL to your set of skills. It will help equip you to meet the ever-increasing demands of today's data professionals and will help your company be successful in the new era where data is key to success.

—Matt Estes
Enterprise Information Architect,
The Walt Disney Internet Group

Beginning Transact-SQL
with SQL Server 2000 and 2005

Introducing Transact-SQL and Data Management Systems

Welcome to the world of Transact-Structured Query Language programming. Transact-SQL, or T-SQL, is Microsoft Corporation's implementation of the Structured Query Language, which was designed to retrieve, manipulate, and add data to Relational Database Management Systems (RDBMS). Hopefully, you already have a basic idea of what SQL is used for because you purchased this book, but you may not have a good understanding of the concepts behind relational databases and the purpose of SQL. This first chapter introduces you to some of the fundamentals of the design and architecture of relational databases and presents a brief description of SQL as a language. If you are brand new to SQL and database technologies, this chapter will provide a foundation to help ensure the rest of the book is as effective as possible. If you are already comfortable with the concepts of relational databases and Microsoft's implementation, specifically, you may want to skip on ahead to Chapter 2, "SQL Server Fundamentals," or Chapter 3, "Tools for Accessing SQL Server." Both of these chapters introduce some of the features and tools in SQL Server 2000 as well as the new features and tools coming with SQL Server 2005.

> *Another great, more in-depth source for SQL 2000 and SQL 2005 programming from the application developer's perspective are the Wrox Press books authored by Rob Viera:* Professional SQL Server 2000 Programming, Beginning SQL Server 2005 Programming, *and* Professional SQL Server 2005 Programming. *Throughout the chapters ahead, I will refer back to both the basic concepts introduced in this chapter and to areas in the books mentioned here for further clarification in the use or nature of the Transact-SQL language.*

Transact-Structured Query Language

T-SQL is Microsoft's implementation of a standard established by the American National Standards Institute (ANSI) for the Structured Query Language (SQL). SQL was first developed by researchers at IBM. They called their first pre-release version of SQL "SEQUEL," which stood for **S**tructured **E**nglish **QUE**ry Language. The first release version was renamed to SQL, dropping the

English part but retaining the pronunciation to identify it with its predecessor. Today, several implementations of SQL by different stakeholders are in the database marketplace, and as you sojourn through the sometimes-mystifying lands of database technology you will undoubtedly encounter these different varieties of SQL. What makes them all similar is the ANSI standard to which IBM, more than any other vendor, adheres to with tenacious rigidity. However, what differentiate the many implementations of SQL are the customized programming objects and extensions to the language that make it unique to that particular platform. Microsoft SQL Server 2000 implements ANSI-92, or the 1992 standard as set by ANSI. SQL Server 2005 implements ANSI-99. The term "implements" is of significance. T-SQL is not fully compliant with ANSI standards in its 2000 or 2005 implementation; neither is Oracle's P/L SQL, Sybase's SQLAnywhere, or the open-source MySQL. Each implementation has custom extensions and variations that deviate from the established standard. ANSI has three levels of compliance: Entry, Intermediate, and Full. T-SQL is certified at the entry level of ANSI compliance. If you strictly adhere to the features that are ANSI-compliant, the same code you write for Microsoft SQL Server should work on any ANSI-compliant platform; that's the theory, anyway. If you find that you are writing cross-platform queries, you will most certainly need to take extra care to ensure that the syntax is perfectly suited for all the platforms it affects. Really, the simple reality of this issue is that very few people will need to write queries to work on multiple database platforms. These standards serve as a guideline to help keep query languages focused on working with data, rather than other forms of programming, perhaps slowing the evolution of relational databases just enough to keep us sane.

T-SQL: Programming Language or Query Language?

T-SQL was not really developed to be a full-fledged programming language. Over the years the ANSI standard has been expanded to incorporate more and more procedural language elements, but it still lacks the power and flexibility of a true programming language. Antoine, a talented programmer and friend of mine, refers to SQL as "Visual Basic on Quaaludes." I share this bit of information not because I agree with it, but because I think it is funny. I also think it is indicative of many application developers' view of this versatile language.

The Structured Query Language was designed with the exclusive purpose of data retrieval and data manipulation. Microsoft's T-SQL implementation of SQL was specifically designed for use in Microsoft's Relational Database Management System (RDBMS), SQL Server. Although T-SQL, like its ANSI sibling, can be used for many programming-like operations, its effectiveness at these tasks varies from excellent to abysmal. That being said, I am still more than happy to call T-SQL a programming language if only to avoid someone calling me a SQL "Queryer" instead of a SQL Programmer. However, the undeniable fact still remains; as a programming language, T-SQL falls short. The good news is that as a data retrieval and set manipulation language it is exceptional. When T-SQL programmers try to use T-SQL like a programming language they invariably run afoul of the best practices that ensure the efficient processing and execution of the code. Because T-SQL is at its best when manipulating sets of data, try to keep that fact foremost in your thoughts during the process of developing T-SQL code.

Performing multiple recursive row operations or complex mathematical computations is quite possible with T-SQL, but so is writing a .NET application with Notepad. Antoine was fond of responding to these discussions with, "Yes, you can do that. You can also crawl around the Pentagon on your hands and knees if you want to." His sentiments were the same as my father's when I was growing up; he used to make a point of telling me that "Just because you can do something doesn't mean you should." The point here is that oftentimes SQL programmers will resort to creating custom objects in their code that are inefficient as far as memory and CPU consumption are concerned. They do this because it is the easiest and quickest way to finish the code. I agree that there are times when a quick solution is the best, but future performance must always be taken into account. This book tries to show you the best way to write T-SQL so that you can avoid writing code that will bring your server to its knees, begging for mercy.

What's New in SQL Server 2005

Several books and hundreds of web sites have already been published that are devoted to the topic of "What's New in SQL Server 2005," so I won't spend a great deal of time describing all the changes that come with this new release. Instead, throughout the book I will identify those changes that are applicable to the subject being described. However, in this introductory chapter I want to spend a little time discussing one of the most significant changes and how it will impact the SQL programmer. This change is the incorporation of the .NET Framework with SQL Server.

T-SQL and the .NET Framework

The integration of SQL Server with Microsoft's .NET Framework is an awesome leap forward in database programming possibilities. It is also a significant source of misunderstanding and trepidation, especially by traditional infrastructure database administrators.

This new feature, among other things, allows developers to use programming languages to write stored procedures and functions that access and manipulate data with object-oriented code, rather than SQL statements.

Kiss T-SQL Goodbye?

Any reports of T-SQL's demise are premature and highly exaggerated. The ability to create database programming objects in managed code instead of SQL does not mean that T-SQL is in danger of becoming extinct. A marketing-minded executive at one of Microsoft's partner companies came up with a cool tagline about SQL Server 2005 and the .NET Framework that said "SQL Server 2005 and .NET; Kiss SQL Good-bye." He was quickly dissuaded by his team when presented with the facts. However, the executive wasn't completely wrong. What his catchy tagline could say and be accurate is "SQL Server 2005 and .NET; Kiss SQL Cursors Good-bye." It could also have said the same thing about complex T-SQL aggregations or a number of T-SQL solutions presently used that will quickly become obsolete with the release of SQL Server 2005.

Transact-SQL cursors are covered in detail in Chapter 10, so for the time being, suffice it to say that they are generally a bad thing and should be avoided. Cursors are all about recursive operations with single or row values. They consume a disproportionate amount of memory and CPU resources compared to set operations.

With the integration of the .NET Framework and SQL Server, expensive cursor operations can be replaced by efficient, compiled assemblies, but that is just the beginning. A whole book could be written about the possibilities created with SQL Server's direct access to the .NET Framework. Complex data types, custom aggregations, powerful functions, and even managed code triggers can be added to a database to exponentially increase the flexibility and power of the database application. Among other things, one of the chief advantages of the .NET Framework's integration is the ability of T-SQL developers to have complete access to the entire .NET object model and operating system application programming interface (API) library without the use of custom extended stored procedures. Extended stored procedures and especially custom extended stored procedures, which are almost always implemented through unmanaged code, have typically been the source of a majority of the security and reliability issues involving SQL Server. By replacing extended stored procedures, which can only exist at the server level, with managed assemblies that exist at the database level, all kinds of security and scalability issues virtually disappear.

Database Management System (DBMS)

A DBMS is a set of programs that are designed to store and maintain data. The role of the DBMS is to manage the data so that the consistency and integrity of the data is maintained above all else. Quite a few types and implementations of Database Management Systems exist:

- ❑ **Hierarchical Database Management Systems (HDBMS)** — Hierarchical databases have been around for a long time and are perhaps the oldest of all databases. It was (and in some cases still is) used to manage hierarchical data. It has several limitations such as only being able to manage single trees of hierarchical data and the inability to efficiently prevent erroneous and duplicate data. HDBMS implementations are getting increasingly rare and are constrained to specialized, and typically, non-commercial applications.

- ❑ **Network Database Management System (NDBMS)** — The NDBMS has been largely abandoned. In the past, large organizational database systems were implemented as network or hierarchical systems. The network systems did not suffer from the data inconsistencies of the hierarchical model but they did suffer from a very complex and rigid structure that made changes to the database or its hosted applications very difficult.

- ❑ **Relational Database Management System (RDBMS)** — An RDBMS is a software application used to store data in multiple related tables using SQL as the tool for creating, managing, and modifying both the data and the data structures. An RDBMS maintains data by storing it in tables that represent single entities and storing information about the relationship of these tables to each other in yet more tables. The concept of a relational database was first described by E.F. Codd, an IBM scientist who defined the relational model in 1970. Relational databases are optimized for recording transactions and the resultant transactional data. Most commercial software applications use an RDBMS as their data store. Because SQL was designed specifically for use with an RDBMS, I will spend a little extra time covering the basic structures of an RDBMS later in this chapter.

- ❑ **Object-Oriented Database Management System (ODBMS)** — The ODBMS emerged a few years ago as a system where data was stored as objects in a database. ODBMS supports multiple classes of objects and inheritance of classes along with other aspects of object orientation. Currently, no international standard exists that specifies exactly what an ODBMS is and what it isn't. Because ODBMS applications store objects instead of related entities, it makes the system very efficient when dealing with complex data objects and object-oriented programming (OOP) languages such as the new .NET languages from Microsoft as well as C and Java. When ODBMS solutions were first released they were quickly touted as the ultimate database system and predicted to make all other database systems obsolete. However, they never achieved the wide acceptance that was predicted. They do have a very valid position in the database market, but it is a niche market held mostly within the Computer-Aided Design (CAD) and telecommunications industries.

- ❑ **Object-Relational Database Management System (ORDBMS)** — The ORDBMS emerged from existing RDBMS solutions when the vendors who produced the relational systems realized that the ability to store objects was becoming more important. They incorporated mechanisms to be able to store classes and objects in the relational model. ORDBMS implementations have, for the most part, usurped the market that the ODBMS vendors were targeting for a variety of reasons that I won't expound on here. However, Microsoft's SQL Server 2005, with its XML data type and incorporation of the .NET Framework, could arguably be labeled an ORDBMS.

SQL Server as a Relational Database Management System

This section introduces you to the concepts behind relational databases and how they are implemented from a Microsoft viewpoint. This will, by necessity, skirt the edges of database object creation, which is covered in great detail in Chapter 11, so for the purpose of this discussion I will avoid the exact mechanics and focus on the final results.

As I mentioned earlier, a relational database stores all of its data inside tables. Ideally, each table will represent a single entity or object. You would not want to create one table that contained data about both dogs and cars. That isn't to say you couldn't do this, but it wouldn't be very efficient or easy to maintain if you did.

Tables

Tables are divided up into rows and columns. Each row must be able to stand on its own, without a dependency to other rows in the table. The row must represent a single, complete instance of the entity the table was created to represent. Each column in the row contains specific attributes that help define the instance. This may sound a bit complex, but it is actually very simple. To help illustrate, consider a real-world entity, an employee. If you want to store data about an employee you would need to create a table that has the properties you need to record data about your employee. For simplicity's sake, call your table Employee.

For more information on naming objects, check out the "Naming Conventions" section in Chapter 4.

When you create your employee table you also need to decide on what attributes of the employee you want to store. For the purposes of this example you have decided to store the employee's last name, first name, social security number, department, extension, and hire date. The resulting table would look something like that shown in Figure 1-1.

Figure 1-1

The data in the table would look something like that shown in Figure 1-2.

LastName	FirstName	SSN	Dept	Extension	HireDate
Flintstone	Fred	123456789	Operations	9876	11/12/2000
Slate	George	987654321	Management	3456	4/14/1999

Figure 1-2

Primary Keys

To efficiently manage the data in your table you need to be able to uniquely identify each individual row in the table. It is much more difficult to retrieve, update, or delete a single row if there is not a single attribute that identifies each row individually. In many cases, this identifier is *not* a descriptive attribute of the entity. For example, the logical choice to uniquely identify your employee is the social security number attribute. However, there are a couple of reasons why you would not want to use the social security number as the primary mechanism for identifying each instance of an employee. So instead of using the social security number you will assign a non-descriptive key to each row. The key value used to uniquely identify individual rows in a table is called a *primary key*.

The reasons you choose not to use the social security number as your primary key column boil down to two different areas: security and efficiency.

When it comes to security, what you want to avoid is the necessity of securing the employee's social security number in multiple tables. Because you will most likely be using the key column in multiple tables to form your relationships (more on that in a moment), it makes sense to substitute a non-descriptive key. In this way you avoid the issue of duplicating private or sensitive data in multiple locations to provide the mechanism to form relationships between tables.

As far as efficiency is concerned, you can often substitute a non-data key that has a more efficient or smaller data type associated with it. For example, in your design you might have created the social security number with either a character data type or an integer. If you have fewer than 32,767 employees, you can use a double byte integer instead of a 4-byte integer or 10-byte character type; besides, integers process faster than characters.

You will still want to ensure that every social security number in your table is unique and not NULL, but you will use a different method to guarantee this behavior without making it a primary key.

Keys and enforcement of uniqueness are detailed in Chapter 11.

A non-descriptive key doesn't represent anything else with the exception of being a value that uniquely identifies each row or individual instance of the entity in a table. This will simplify the joining of this table to other tables and provide the basis for a "Relation." In this example you will simply alter the table by adding an EmployeeKey column that will uniquely identify every row in the table, as shown in Figure 1-3.

Figure 1-3

With the EmployeeKey column, you have an efficient, easy-to-manage primary key.

Each table can have only one primary key, which means that this key column is the primary method for uniquely identifying individual rows. It doesn't have to be the only mechanism for uniquely identifying individual rows; it is just the "primary" mechanism for doing so. Primary keys can never be NULL and they must be unique. I am a firm believer that primary keys should almost always be single-column keys, but this is not a requirement. Primary keys can also be combinations of columns. If you have a table where two columns in combination are unique, while either single column is not, you can combine the two columns as a single primary key, as illustrated in Figure 1-4.

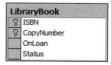

Figure 1-4

In this example the LibraryBook table is used to maintain a record of every book in the library. Because multiple copies of each book can exist, the ISBN column is not useful for uniquely identifying each book. To enable the identification of each individual book the table designer decided to combine the ISBN column with the copy number of each book. I personally avoid the practice of using multiple column keys. I prefer to create a separate column that can uniquely identify the row. This makes it much easier to write JOIN queries (covered in great detail in Chapter 5). The resulting code is cleaner and the queries are generally more efficient. For the library book example, a more efficient mechanism might be to assign each book its own number. The resulting table would look like that shown in Figure 1-5.

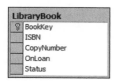

Figure 1-5

A table is a set of rows and columns used to represent an entity. Each row represents an instance of the entity. Each column in the row will contain at most one value that represents an attribute, or property, of the entity. Take the employee table; each row represents a single instance of the employee entity. Each employee can have one and only one first name, last name, SSN, extension, or hire date according to your design specifications. In addition to deciding what attributes you want to maintain, you must also decide how to store those attributes. When you define columns for your tables you must, at a minimum, define three things:

- ❑ The name of the column
- ❑ The data type of the column
- ❑ Whether or not the column can support NULL

Column Names

Keep the names simple and intuitive. For more information see Chapter 11.

Data Types

The general rule on data types is to use the smallest one you can. This conserves memory usage and disk space. Also keep in mind that SQL Server processes numbers much more efficiently than characters, so use numbers whenever practical. I have heard the argument that numbers should only be used if you plan on performing mathematical operations on the columns that contain them, but that just doesn't wash. Numbers are preferred over string data for sorting and comparison as well as mathematical computations. The exception to this rule is if the string of numbers you want to use starts with a zero. Take the social security number, for example. Other than the unfortunate fact that some social security numbers (like my daughter's) begin with a zero, the social security number would be a perfect candidate for using an integer instead of a character string. However, if you tried to store the integer 012345678 you would end up with 12345678. These two values may be numeric equivalents but the government doesn't see it that way. They are strings of numerical characters and therefore must be stored as characters rather than numbers.

When designing tables and choosing a data type for each column, try to be conservative and use the smallest, most efficient type possible. But, at the same time, carefully consider the exception, however rare, and make sure that the chosen type will always meet these requirements.

The data types available for columns in SQL Server 2000 and 2005 are specified in the following table.

Data Type	Storage	Description
Bigint	8 bytes	An 8-byte signed integer. Valid values are -9223372036854775808 through +9223372036854775807.
Int	4 bytes	A 4-byte signed integer. Valid values are -2,147,483,648 through +2,147,483,647.
SmallInt	2 bytes	A double-byte signed integer. Valid values are -32,768 through +32,767.
TinyInt	1 byte	A single-byte unsigned integer. Valid values are from 0 through 255.
Bit	1 bit	Integer data with either a 1 or 0 value.

Data Type	Storage	Description
Decimal	5 – 17 bytes	A predefined, fixed, signed decimal number ranging from -1000000000000000000000000000000000000001 ($-10^{38}+1$) to 99999999999999999999999999999999999999 ($-10^{38}-1$). A decimal is declared with a precision and scale value that determines how many decimal places to the left and right are supported. This is expressed as decimal[(precision,[scale])]. The precision setting determines how many total digits to the left and right of the decimal point are supported. The scale setting determines how many digits to the right of the decimal point are supported. For example, to support the number 3.141592653589793 the decimal data type would have to be specified as decimal(16,15). If the data type was specified as decimal(3,2), only 3.14 would be stored. The scale defaults to zero and must be between 0 and the precision. The precision defaults to 18 and can be a maximum of 38.
Numeric	5 – 17 bytes	Numeric is identical to decimal so use decimal instead. Numeric is much less descriptive because most people think of integers as being numeric.
Money	8 bytes	The money data type can be used to store -922,337,203,685,477.5808 to +922,337,203,685,477.5807 of a monetary unit. The advantage of the money data type over a decimal data type is that developers can take advantage of automatic currency formatting for specific locales. Notice that the money data type supports figures to the fourth decimal place. Accountants like that. A few million of those ten thousandths of a penny add up after a while!
SmallMoney	4 bytes	Bill Gates needs the money data type to track his portfolio, but most of us can get by with the small-money data type. It consumes 4 bytes of storage and can be used to store -214,748.3648 to +214,748.3647 of a monetary unit.
Float	4 or 8 bytes	A float is an approximate value (SQL Server performs rounding) that supports real numbers between -1.79×10^{308} and 1.79×10^{308} sdff.
Real	4 bytes	Real is a synonym for a float.

Table continued on following page

Data Type	Storage	Description
DateTime	8 bytes	Datetime is used to store dates from January 1, 1753 through December 31, 9999 (which could cause a huge Y10K disaster). The accuracy of the datetime data type is 3.33 milliseconds.
SmallDatetime	4 bytes	Smalldatetime stores dates from January 1, 1900 through June 6, 2079 with an accuracy of 1 minute.
Char	1 byte per character. Maximum 8000 characters	The char data type is a fixed-length data type used to store character data. The number of possible characters is between 1 and 8000. The possible combinations of characters in a char data type are 256. The characters that are represented depend on what language, or collation, is defined. English, for example, is actually defined with a Latin collation. The Latin collation provides support for all English and western European characters.
VarChar	1 byte per character. Maximum 8000 characters	The varchar data type is identical to the char data type with the exception of it being a variable length type. If a column is defined as char(8) it will consume 8 bytes of storage even if only three characters are placed in it. A varchar column only consumes the space it needs. Typically, char data types are more efficient when it comes to processing and varchar data types are more efficient for storage. The rule of thumb is: use char if the data will always be close to the defined length. Use varchar if it will vary widely. For example, a city name would be stored with varchar(167) if you wanted to allow for the longest city name in the world, which is Krung thep mahanakhon bovorn ratanakosin mahintharayutthaya mahadilok pop noparatratchathani burirom udomratchanivetmahasathan amornpiman avatarnsathit sakkathattiyavisnukarmprasit (the poetic name of Bangkok, Thailand). Use char for data that is always the same. For example, you could use char(12) to store a domestic phone number in the United States: (123)456-7890.
Text	1 byte per character. Maximum 2,147,483,648 characters (2GB)	The text data type is similar to the varchar data type in that it is a variable-length character data type. The significant difference is the maximum length of about 2 billion characters (including spaces) and where the data is physically stored. With a varchar data type on a table column, the data is stored physically in the row with the rest of the data. With a text data type, the data is stored separately from the actual row and a pointer is stored in the row so SQL Server can find the text.

Data Type	Storage	Description
nChar	2 bytes per character. Maximum 4000 characters (8000 bytes).	The nchar data type is a fixed-length type identical to the char data type with the exception of the amount of characters supported. Char data is represented by a single byte and thus only 256 different characters can be supported. Nchar is a double-byte data type and can support 65,536 different characters. The cost of the extra character support is the double-byte length, so the maximum nchar length is 4000 characters or 8000 bytes.
nVarChar	2 bytes per character. Maximum 4000 characters (8000 bytes).	The nvarchar data type is a variable length identical to the varchar data type with the exception of the amount of characters supported. Varchar data is represented by a single byte and only 256 different characters can be supported. Nvarchar is a double-byte data type and can support 65,536 different characters. The cost of the extra character support is the double-byte length, so the maximum nchar length is 4000 characters or 8000 bytes.
nText	2 bytes per character. Maximum 1,073,741,823 characters	The ntext data type is identical to the text data type with the exception of the amount of characters supported. Text data is represented by a single byte and only 256 different characters can be supported. Ntext is a double-byte data type and can support 65,536 different characters. The cost of the extra character support is the double-byte length, so the maximum ntext length is 1,073,741,823 characters or 2GB.
Binary	1 – 8000 bytes	Fixed-length binary data. Length is fixed when created between 1 and 8000 bytes.
VarBinary	1 – 8000 bytes	Variable-length binary data type identical to the binary data type with the exception of only consuming the amount of storage that is necessary to hold the data.
Image	Up to 2,147,483,647 bytes	The image data type is similar to the varbinary data type in that it is a variable-length binary data type. The significant difference is the maximum length of about 2GB and where the data is physically stored. With a varbinary data type on a table column, the data is stored physically in the row with the rest of the data. With an image data type, the data is stored separately from the actual row and a pointer is stored in the row so SQL Server can find the data. Image data types are typically used to store actual images, binary documents, or binary objects.

Table continued on following page

Data Type	Storage	Description
TimeStamp	8 bytes	The timestamp data type has nothing to do with time. It is more accurately described as a row version data type and is, in fact, being replaced by a data type called rowversion. In SQL Server 2000, rowversion is provided as a synonym for the timestamp data type and should be used instead of timestamp. What timestamp actually provides is a database unique identifier to identify a version of a row.
UniqueIdentifier	32 bytes	A data type used to store a Globally Unique Identifier (GUID).
Sql_Variant	Up to 8016 bytes	The sql_variant is used when the exact data type is unknown. It can be used to hold any data type with the exception of text, ntext, image, and timestamp.

SQL Server supports additional data types that can be used in queries and programming objects, but they are not used to define columns. These data types are listed in the following table.

Data Type	Description
Cursor	The cursor data is used to point to an instance of a cursor.
Table	The table data type is used to store an in-memory rowset for processing. It was developed primarily for use with the new table-valued functions introduced in SQL Server 2000.

SQL Server 2005 Data Types

SQL Server 2005 brings a significant new data type and changes to existing variable data types. New to SQL Server 2005 is the XML data type. The XML data type is a major change to SQL Server. The XML data type allows you to store complete XML documents or well-formed XML fragments in the database. Support for the XML data type includes the ability to create and register an XML schema and then bind the schema to an XML column in a table. This ensures that any XML data stored in that column will adhere to the schema. The XML data type essentially allows the storage and management of objects, as described by XML, to be stored in the database. The argument can then be made that SQL Server 2005 is really an Object-Relational Database Management System (ORDBMS).

LOBs, BLOBs, and CLOBs!

SQL Server 2005 also introduces changes to three variable data types in the form of the new (max) option that can be used with the varchar, nvarchar, and varbinary data types. The (max) option allows for the storage of character or variable-length binary data in excess of the previous 8000-byte limitation. At first glance, this seems like a redundant option because the image data type is already available to store binary data up to 2GB and the text and ntext types can be used to store character data. The difference is in how the data is treated. The classic text, ntext, and image data types are Large Object (LOB) data types and can't typically be used with parameters. The new variable data types with the (max) option are Large Value Types (LVT) and can be used with parameters just like the smaller sized types. This brings a myriad of opportunities to the developer. Large Value Types can be updated or inserted without the need of special handling through *STREAM* operations. STREAM operations are implemented through an application programming interface (API) such as OLE DB or ODBC and are used to handle data in the form of a Binary Large Object (BLOB). T-SQL cannot natively handle BLOBs, so it doesn't support the use of BLOBs as T-SQL parameters. SQL Server 2005's new Large Value Types are implemented as a Character Large Object (CLOB) and can be interpreted by the SQL engine.

Nullability

All rows from the same table have the same set of columns. However, not all columns will necessarily have values in them. For example, a new employee is hired, but he has not been assigned an extension yet. In this case, the extension column may not have any data in it. Instead, it may contain NULL, which means the value for that column was not initialized. Note that a NULL value for a string column is different from an empty string. An empty string is defined; a NULL is not. You should always consider a NULL as an unknown value. When you design your tables you need to decide whether or not to allow a NULL condition to exist in your columns. NULLs can be allowed or disallowed on a column-by-column basis, so your employee table design could look like that shown in Figure 1-6.

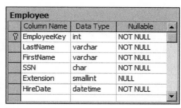

Figure 1-6

Relationships

Relational databases are all about relations. To manage these relations you use common keys. For example, your employees sell products to customers. This process involves multiple entities:

- ❑ The employee
- ❑ The product
- ❑ The customer
- ❑ The sale

To identify which employee sold which product to a customer you need some way to link all the entities together. These links are typically managed through the use of keys, primary keys in the parent table and foreign keys in the child table.

As a practical example you can revisit the employee example. When your employee sells a product, his or her identifying information is added to the Sale table to record who the responsible employee was, as illustrated in Figure 1-7. In this case the Employee table is the parent table and the Sale table is the child table.

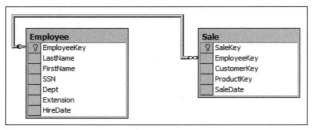

Figure 1-7

Because the same employee could sell products to many customers, the relationship between the Employee table and the Sale table is called a *one-to-many relationship*. The fact that the employee is the unique participant in the relationship makes it the *parent* table. Relationships are very often *parent-child relationships*, which means that the record in the parent table must exist before the child record can be added. In the example, because every employee is not required to make a sale, the relationship is more accurately described as a one-to-zero-or-more relationship. In Figure 1-7 this relationship is represented by a key and infinity symbol, which doesn't adequately model the true relationship because you don't know if the EmployeeKey field is nullable. In Figure 1-8, the more traditional and informative "Crows Feet" symbols are used. The relationship symbol in this figure represents a one-to-zero-or-more relationship. Figure 1-9 shows the two tables with a one-to-one-or-more relationship symbol.

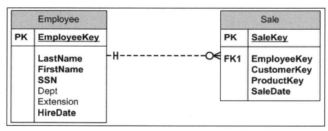

Figure 1-8

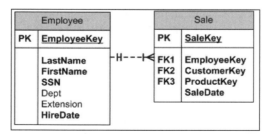

Figure 1-9

Relationships can be defined as follows:

❑ One-to-zero or many

❑ One-to-one or many

❑   One-to-exactly-one

❑   Many-to-many

The many-to-many relationship requires three tables because a many-to-many constraint would be unenforceable. An example of a many-to-many relationship is illustrated in Figure 1-10. The necessity for this relationship is created by the relationships between your entities: In a single sale many products can be sold, but one product can be in many sales. This creates the many-to-many relationship between the Sale table and the Product table. To uniquely identify every product and sale combination, you need to create what is called a *linking table*. The Order table manages your many-to-many relationship by uniquely tracking every combination of sale and product.

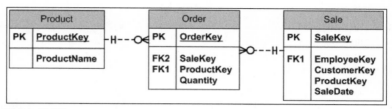

Figure 1-10

These figures are an example of a tool called an Entity Relationship Diagram (ERD). The ERD allows the database designer to conceptualize the database design during planning. Microsoft and several other vendors provide design tools that will automatically build the database and component objects from an ERD.

As an example of a one-to-one relationship, suppose that you want to record more detailed data about a sale, but you do not want to alter the current table. In this case, you could build a table called SaleDetail to store the data. To ensure that the sale can be linked to the detailed data, you create a relationship between the two tables. Because each sale should appear in both the Sale table and the SaleDetail table, you would create a one-to-one relationship instead of a one-to-many, as illustrated in Figures 1-11 and 1-12.

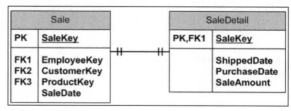

Figure 1-11

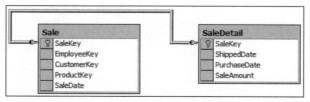

Figure 1-12

RDBMS and Data Integrity

The RDBMS is designed to maintain data integrity in a transactional environment. This is accomplished through several mechanisms implemented through database objects. The most prominent of these objects are as follows:

- Locks
- Constraints
- Keys
- Indexes

Before I describe these objects in more detail two other important pieces of the SQL architecture need to be understood: connections and transactions.

Connections

A connection is created anytime a process attaches to SQL Server. The connection is established with defined security and connection properties. These security and connection properties determine what data you have access to and, to a certain degree, how SQL Server will behave during the duration of the query in the context of the query. For example, a connection can specify which database to connect to on the server and how to manage memory resident objects.

Transactions

Transactions are explored in detail in Chapter 8, so for the purposes of this introduction I will keep the explanation brief. In a nutshell, a SQL Server transaction is a collection of dependent data modifications that is controlled so that it completes entirely or not at all. For example, you go to the bank and transfer $100.00 from your savings account to your checking account. This transaction involves two modifications, one to the checking account and the other to the savings account. Each update is dependent on the other. It is very important to you and the bank that the funds are transferred correctly so the modifications are placed together in a transaction. If the update to the checking account fails but the update to the savings account succeeds, you most definitely want the entire transaction to fail. The bank feels the same way if the opposite occurs.

With a basic idea about these two objects, let's proceed to the four mechanisms that ensure integrity and consistency in your data.

Locks

SQL Server uses locks to ensure that multiple users can access data at the same time with the assurance that the data will not be altered while they are reading it. At the same time, the locks are used to ensure that modifications to data can be accomplished without impacting other modifications or reads in progress. SQL Server manages locks on a connection basis, which simply means that locks cannot be held mutually by multiple connections. SQL Server also manages locks on a transaction basis. In the same way that multiple connections cannot share the same lock, neither can transactions. For example, if an application opens a connection to SQL Server and is granted a shared lock on a table, that same application cannot open an additional connection and modify that data. The same is true for transactions. If an application begins a transaction that modifies specific data, that data cannot be modified in any other transaction until the first has completed its work. This is true even if the multiple transactions share the same connection.

SQL Server utilizes six lock types, or more accurately, six resource lock modes:

- ❏ Shared
- ❏ Update
- ❏ Exclusive
- ❏ Intent
- ❏ Schema
- ❏ Bulk Update

Shared, Update, Exclusive, and Intent locks can be applied to rows of tables or indexes, pages (8-kilobyte storage page of an index or table), extents (64-kilobyte collection of 8contiguous index or table pages), tables, or databases. Schema and Bulk Update locks apply to tables.

Shared Locks

Shared locks allow multiple connections and transactions to read the resources they are assigned to. No other connection or transaction is allowed to modify the data as long as the Shared lock is granted. Once an application successfully reads the data the Shared locks are typically released, but this behavior can be modified for special circumstances. Shared locks are compatible with other Shared locks so that many transactions and connections can read the same data without conflict.

Update Locks

Update locks are used by SQL Server to help prevent an event known as a deadlock. Deadlocks are bad. They are mostly caused by poor programming techniques. A deadlock occurs when two processes get into a stand-off over shared resources. Let's return to the banking example: In this hypothetical banking transaction both my wife and I go online to transfer funds from our savings account to our checking account. We somehow manage to execute the transfer operation simultaneously and two separate processes are launched to execute the transfer. When my process accesses the two accounts it is issued Shared locks on the resources. When my wife's process accesses the accounts, it is also granted a Shared lock to the resources. So far, so good, but when our processes try to modify the resources pandemonium ensues. First my wife's process attempts to escalate its lock to Exclusive to make the modifications. At about the same time my process attempts the same escalation. However, our mutual Shared locks prevent either of our processes from escalating to an Exclusive lock. Because neither process is willing to release its Shared lock, a deadlock occurs. SQL Server doesn't particularly care for deadlocks. If one occurs SQL Server will automatically select one of the processes as a victim and kill it. SQL Server selects the process with the least cost associated with it, kills it, rolls back the associated transaction, and notifies the responsible application of the termination by returning error number 1205. If properly captured, this error informs the user that "Transaction ## was deadlocked on x resources with another process and has been chosen as the deadlock victim. Rerun the transaction." To avoid the deadlock from ever occurring SQL Server will typically use Update locks in place of Shared locks. Only one process can obtain an Update lock, preventing the opposing process from escalating its lock. The bottom line is that if a read is executed for the sole purpose of an update, SQL Server may issue an Update lock instead of a Shared lock to avoid a potential deadlock. This can all be avoided through careful planning and implementation of SQL logic that prevents the deadlock from ever occurring.

Exclusive Locks

SQL Server typically issues Exclusive locks when a modification is executed. To change the value of a field in a row SQL Server grants exclusive access of that row to the calling process. This exclusive access prevents a process from any concurrent transaction or connection from reading, updating, or deleting the data being modified. Exclusive locks are not compatible with any other lock types.

Intent Locks

SQL Server issues Intent locks to prevent a process from any concurrent transaction or connection from placing a more exclusive lock on a resource that contains a locked resource from a separate process. For example, if you execute a transaction that updates a single row in a table, SQL Server grants the transaction an Exclusive lock on the row, but also grants an Intent lock on the table containing the row. This prevents another process from placing an Exclusive lock on the table.

Here is an analogy I often use to explain the Intent lock behavior in SQL programming classes: You check in to room 404 at the SQL Hotel. You now have exclusive use of Room 4 on the fourth floor. No other hotel patron will be allowed access to this room. In addition, no other patron will be allowed to buy out every room in the hotel because you have already been given exclusive control to one of the rooms. You have what amounts to an Intent Exclusive lock on the hotel and an Exclusive lock on Room 404. Intent locks are compatible with any less-exclusive lock, as illustrated in the following table on lock compatibility.

	Existing Granted Lock				
Requested Lock Type	**IS**	**S**	**U**	**IX**	**X**
Intent Shared (IS)	Yes	Yes	Yes	Yes	No
Shared (S)	Yes	Yes	Yes	No	No
Update(U)	Yes	Yes	No	No	No
Intent Exclusive (IX)	Yes	No	No	Yes	No
Exclusive (X)	No	No	No	No	No

SQL Server and Other Products

Microsoft has plenty of competition in the client/server database world and SQL Server is a relatively young product by comparison. However, it has enjoyed wide acceptance in the industry due to its ease of use and attractive pricing. If our friends at Microsoft know how to do anything exceptionally well, it's taking a product to market so it becomes very mainstream and widely accepted.

Microsoft SQL Server

Here is a short history lesson on Microsoft's SQL Server. SQL Server was originally a Sybase product created for IBM's OS/2 platform. Microsoft Engineers worked with Sybase and IBM but eventually withdrew from the project. Microsoft licensed the Sybase SQL Server code and ported the product to work with Windows NT. It took a couple of years before SQL Server really became a viable product. The SQL Server team went to work to create a brand new database engine using the Sybase code as a model. They eventually rewrote the product from scratch.

When SQL Server 7.0 was released in late 1998, it was a major departure from the previous version, SQL Server 6.5. SQL Server 7.0 contained very little Sybase code with the exception of the core database engine technology, which was still under license from Sybase. SQL Server 2000 was released in 2000 with many useful new features, but was essentially just an incremental upgrade of the 7.0 product. SQL Server 2005, however, is a major upgrade and, some say, the very first completely Microsoft product. Any vestiges of Sybase are long gone. The storage and retrieval engine has been completely rewritten, the .NET Framework has been incorporated, and the product has significantly risen in both power and scalability.

Oracle

Oracle is probably the most recognizable enterprise-class database product in the industry. After IBM's E.F. Codd published his original papers on the fundamental principles of relational data storage and design in 1970, Larry Ellison, founder of Oracle, went to work to build a product to apply those principles. Oracle has had a dominant place in the database market for quite some time with a comprehensive suite of database tools and related solutions. Versions of Oracle run on UNIX, Linux, and Windows Servers.

The query language of Oracle is known as Procedure Language/Structured Query Language (PL/SQL). Indeed, many aspects of PL/SQL resemble a C-like procedural programming language. This is evidenced by syntax such as command-line termination using semicolons. Unlike Transact-SQL, statements are not actually executed until an explicit run command is issued (preceded with a single line containing a period.) PL/SQL is particular about using data types and includes expressions for assigning values to compatible column types.

IBM DB2

This is really where it all began. Relational databases and the SQL language were first conceptualized and then implemented in IBM's research department. Although IBM's database products have been around for a very long time, Oracle (then Relational Software) actually beat them to market. DB2 database professionals perceive the form of SQL used in this product to be purely ANSI SQL and other dialects such as Microsoft's T-SQL and Oracle's PL-SQL to be more proprietary. Although DB2 has a long history of running on System 390 mainframes and the AS/400, it is not just a legacy product. IBM has effectively continued to breathe life into DB2 and it remains a viable database for modern business solutions. DB2 runs on a variety of operating systems today including Windows, UNIX, and Linux.

Informix

This product had been a relatively strong force in the client/server database community, but its popularity waned in the late 1990s. Originally designed for the UNIX platform, Informix is a serious enterprise database. Popularity slipped over the past few years, as many applications built on Informix had to be upgraded to contend with year 2000 compatibility issues. Some organizations moving to other platforms (such as Linux and Windows) have also switched products. The 2001 acquisition of Informix nudged

IBM to the top spot over Oracle as they brought existing Informix customers with them. Today, Informix runs on Linux and integrates with other IBM products.

Sybase SQLAnywhere

Sybase has deep roots in the client/server database industry and has a strong product offering. At the enterprise level, Sybase products are deployed on UNIX and Linux platforms and have strong support in Java programming circles. At the mid-scale level, SQLAnywhere runs on several platforms including UNIX, Linux, Mac OS, Netware, and Windows. Sybase has carved a niche for itself in the industry for mobile device applications and related databases.

Microsoft Access

Access was partially created from the ground up but also leverages some of the query technology gleaned from Microsoft's acquisition of FoxPro. As a part of Microsoft's Office Suite, Access is a very convenient tool for creating simple business applications. Although Access SQL is ANSI 92 SQL–compliant, it is quite a bit different from Transact-SQL. For this reason, I have made it a point to identify some of the differences between Access and Transact-SQL throughout the book.

Access has become the non-programmer's application development tool. Many people get started in database design using Access and then move on to SQL Server as their needs become more sophisticated. Access is a powerful tool for the right kinds of applications, and some commercial products have actually been developed using Access. Unfortunately, because Access is designed (and documented) to be an end-user's tool rather than a software developer's tool, many Access databases are often poorly designed and power users learn through painful trial and error about how *not* to create database applications.

Access was developed right around 1992 and is based on the JET Database Engine. JET is a simple and efficient storage system for small to moderate volumes of data and for relatively few concurrent users, but falls short of the stability and fault-tolerance of SQL Server. For this reason, a desktop version of the SQL Server engine has shipped with Access since Office 2000. The Microsoft SQL Server Desktop Engine (MSDE) is an alternative to using JET and really should be used in place of JET for any serious database. Starting smaller-scale projects with the MSDE provides an easier path for migrating them to full-blown SQL Server later on.

MySQL

MySQL is a developer's tool embraced by the open-source community. Like Linux and Java, it can be obtained free of charge and includes source code. Compilers and components of the database engine can be modified and compiled to run on most any computer platform. Although MySQL supports ANSI SQL, it promotes the use of an application programming interface (API) that wraps SQL statements. As a database product, MySQL is a widely accepted and capable product. However, it appeals more to the open source developer than to the business user.

Many other database products on the market may share some characteristics of the products discussed here. The preceding list represents the most popular database products that use ANSI SQL.

Summary

Microsoft SQL Server 2000 remains a very capable and powerful database management server, but I am more than just a little excited about the upcoming release of SQL Server 2005. SQL Server 2005 takes T-SQL and database management a huge step forward. Having worked with "Yukon" since its first beta release, I have witnessed the emergence of a world-class database management system that will undoubtedly strike fear in the heart of its competitors.

The coming chapters explore all the longstanding features and capabilities of T-SQL and preview some of the awesome new capabilities that SQL Server 2005 brings to the field of T-SQL programming. So sit back and hold on; it's going to be an exciting ride.

If the whole idea of writing T-SQL code and working with databases doesn't thrill you like it does me, I apologize for my overt enthusiasm. My wife has reminded me on many occasions that no matter how I may look, I really am a geek. I freely confess it. I also eagerly confess that I love working with databases. Working with databases puts you in the middle of everything in information technology. There is absolutely no better place to be. Can you name an enterprise application that doesn't somehow interface with a database? You see? Databases are the sun of the IT solar system.

In the coming months and years you will most likely find more and more applications storing their data in a SQL Server database, especially if that application is carrying a Microsoft logo. Microsoft Exchange Server doesn't presently store its data in SQL, but it will. Active Directory will also reportedly move its data store to SQL Server. The Windows file system itself is likely to be moved to a SQL-type store in a future release of the Windows operating system. For the T-SQL programmer and Microsoft SQL Server professional the future is indeed bright.

SQL Server Fundamentals

Where does SQL Server fit in the grand scheme of business applications? At one time, this was a simple question with a simple answer. Today, SQL Server is at the core of many different types of applications and business solutions large and small. Just last week I was fortunate enough to attend a developers' conference on the Microsoft Corporate Campus in Redmond, Washington, and sit at the feet of the Chairman and Chief Architect of Microsoft, Bill Gates. He spoke of his vision for the next generation of products. He said that the current evolution of software technologies is as significant to the industry as was the first generation of Windows. He talked about the importance of XML web services, smart clients, and the pieces that make them all work together. The new generation of servers and operating systems will blend file storage and document and data management in a seamless, uniform approach; and at the core of all of this Microsoft technology is SQL Server. Under the hood, this is not the same SQL Server as it was in years past. SQL Server 2005 is a complex, multipurpose data storage engine, capable of doing some very sophisticated things. This new-and-improved SQL Server can manage complex binary streams, hierarchies, cubes, files, and folders in addition to text, numbers, and other simple data types. Mr. Gates didn't have a perfect answer to every question posed but he certainly had a clear vision for the future of Microsoft products and related technologies — and that future includes SQL Server playing a major role.

For the purposes of this book we're only concerned with using SQL Server to store and manage *relational* data. This is what it was designed for years ago — and what it does even better today. However, SQL Server 2005 can also be used to store and manage application objects in the form of XML. On the surface, SQL Server 2005 and SQL Server 2000 behave much the same way for the same Transact-SQL statements. For our purposes, the most significant differences are simply the tools that you use, not the statements you use to perform operations. The SQL part of SQL Server has evolved some over the years but fundamentally is not so different.

Who Uses SQL Server?

Not very long ago, enterprise databases were hidden away on large servers that were never visible to the casual business computer user. Any interaction with these systems was performed only by members of the elite order of database administrators. These highly revered professionals worked in large, noisy, sealed server rooms on special consoles and workstations. Even after many companies migrated their database systems from mainframe and mid-range computer platforms to PC-based servers, the databases were still hands-off and carefully protected from all but a select few.

A generation of smaller-scale database products evolved to fill the void left for the casual application developer and power user. Products such as the following became the norm for department-level applications because they were accessible and inexpensive:

- ❏ dBase
- ❏ FoxPro
- ❏ Paradox
- ❏ Clipper
- ❏ Clarion
- ❏ FileMaker
- ❏ Access

The big databases were in another class and were simply not available outside of formal IT circles. They were complicated and expensive. Database administrators and designers used cumbersome command-line script to create and manage databases. It was a full-time job; DBAs wrote the script to manage the databases and application developers wrote the code for the applications that ran against them. Life was good. Everyone was happy. However, there is only one real constant in the IT world and that is change. In the past five years, there have been significant changes in the world of application development, database design, and management.

I recall attending the launch event for SQL Server 7.0. Steve Ballmer, the President of Microsoft Corporation, was on the road to introduce this significant product release. After demonstrating several simple, wizard-based features, he asked for all of the career database administrators to stand up. There were probably 1500 people in the audience and 100 or so DBAs came to their feet. He said, "I'd like to do you all a favor and give you some career advice." He paused with a big smile before he continued, "Learn Visual Basic." Needless to say, there were several uneasy DBAs leaving the launch event that day. Steve's advice was evidence of the harsh reality of changing times. Today, SQL Server (and other related Microsoft products) represents a toolkit in the hands of a different kind of business IT professional; not a full-time DBA, specialized Business Analyst, or single-minded Application Developer, but a Solution Architect who creates a variety of software solutions consisting of all these pieces. From the initial requirement gathering and solution concept to the database design, component architecture, and user-interface construction, the Database Solution Developer often covers all these bases. Just a quick note to help clarify Mr. Ballmer's point: What do SQL Server and Visual Basic have to do with one another? Chapter 14 answers this question more completely by showing you some examples of complete application solutions. In short, solving business problems requires the use of multiple tools, SQL and programming languages working together to solve complex business problems.

Although we have certainly seen a lot of recent change in the database world, I won't be so naïve to say that traditional database servers are going away. On the contrary, most large companies have centralized most of their data on large-scale servers and the largest corporate databases are now in the ballpark of 10–20 terabytes in size. In just the past few years, these volumes have been doubling about every three years. There are really two separate trends: Corporate, mission-critical data is growing more than ever, stored on large-scale (albeit physically much smaller) servers, managed by full-time database administrators. The other trend is that small-scale, regional data marts (relatively small, reporting databases) and data silos (specialized, departmental databases) have emerged. Unlike the ad-hoc, desktop databases of the past decade, these are stored on department-level database servers. They are managed and used primarily by business unit power users, rather than career IT folks.

A new class of SQL Server user has recently emerged. Computer power users now have access to SQL Server using a variety of tools. Bill Gates refers to these individuals as the "knowledge worker" of the twenty-first century. Desktop applications such as Microsoft Excel and Access can easily be used as front-ends for SQL Server. In fact, Access gives users the ability to create and manage database objects much like an administrator would using SQL Server Enterprise Manager and Management Studio. This means that more casual users have the ability to create and utilize these powerful databases that were available only to highly trained professionals a few years ago. Of course, this also means that untrained users can use these powerful tools to make a big mess. Yes, this means that more users now have the tools to create poorly designed databases, more efficiently than ever before.

Hopefully, your organization has standards and policies in place to manage production database servers and to control access to sensitive data. With a little guidance and the appropriate level of security access, SQL Server can be a very useful tool in the hands of new users who possess some fundamental skills.

SQL Server Editions and Features

A brief comparison of the various editions of SQL Server 2000 and SQL Server 2005 follows.

SQL Server 2000

Two editions of SQL Server 2000 exist that may be used for production databases: *Standard* and *Enterprise*. The Standard Edition is a more economical investment for most small businesses. It is full-featured, but lacks some scalability and availability features that make the Enterprise Edition more attractive for very large-scale business environments and servers, such as supporting a larger number of processors and more memory, as well as a few database objects specifically targeted toward the large enterprise. The *Developer Edition* IS the Enterprise Edition — that's right, it is actually the same code with some specific adaptations. The Developer Edition will run on a desktop operating system, such as Windows 2000 Professional and Windows XP, and is limited to 10 concurrent connections. With these exceptions, all SQL Server features in the Developer Edition should behave like the Enterprise Edition. Keep this in mind if you plan to implement the Standard Edition that doesn't support a few advanced features available in the Developer Edition.

SQL Server 2005

Several new features and capabilities have been added to SQL Server 2005. Some of the most notable features include native XML storage and query support, and integration with the .NET Common Language Runtime. The comparative editions of this version of SQL Server haven't really changed much. In addition to the Standard, Developer, and Enterprise editions, there is a variety of the product called the SQL Server 2005 Express Edition. This is essentially the replacement for the SQL Server 2000 Desktop Engine (MSDE) that shipped with versions of Office and Access in the past. It's a lightweight version of the SQL Server engine, intended to run on a desktop computer with a limited number of connections. As our friends at Microsoft continue to gently nudge users away from the Access JET database engine and toward SQL Server, their products will continue to become more aligned and standardized. Like the more serious editions, SQL Server Express can be managed from within Access, Visual Studio, or the SQL Server client tools.

The SQL language has been enhanced in a few places but is generally unchanged. Because Transact-SQL conforms to the industry standard ANSI SQL standard, you will find only a few minor additions to the supported syntax in SQL Server 2005.

Relational Database Engine

Big differences exist between a true RDBMS Relational Database Management System (RDBMS) and a file-based database product. Although a true RDBMS product, such as SQL Server, does store its data in files managed by the file system, the data in these files cannot be accessed directly. The concepts of relational integrity have been applied to file-based databases for several years. Programmers wrote these rules into their program code. The difference is that the RDBMS system contains this code to enforce business rules and doesn't allow a user or developer to work around them once a database has been designed with certain rules applied.

The language used to access nearly all relational database products is SQL. The dialect of SQL used in Microsoft SQL Server is called Transact-SQL. Using SQL is the front door to the data in a database and the administrative objects of the database server. Specialized programmatic interfaces also exist that developers can use to access a database with the appropriate security clearance. Unlike file-based databases, RDBMS systems are designed so there is no "back door" to a database.

Semantics

The words used to describe data concepts are often different, depending a great deal upon the context of the discussion. Data lives in tables. Usually, a table represents some kind of business entity, such as a *Product* or *Customer*, for example. Each item in a table is called a *row* or *record*. For our purposes, these mean the same thing. I may use these words interchangeably throughout the book. Envision several rows in an Excel worksheet representing different products. Each product has a manufacturer, supplier, packaging quantity, and price. In Excel, these values would be contained in different cells. In a table, separate values are referred to as a *column* or *field*. As far as we're concerned, these words have the same meaning as well. How do you decide how data should be organized into tables and columns? That is the fine art of database design and is often no easy task. To arrive at an optimal database design, you must first have a thorough understanding of the business process and the how data will be used.

So, what is data, really? We often hear the words *information* and *data* used to mean the same thing. In reality, they are very different concepts. We, as humans, generally concern ourselves with meaningful information we can use day-to-day. Information has a context — it makes sense to us. If my wife were to give me a call and ask that I stop by the store on the way home from work and pick up eggs and milk, I should have enough information to accomplish this simple task. I have a few informational items to contend with in this scenario: the store, eggs, and milk. If we were to ask some people in the database business about these simple things, we might get some interesting (or not so interesting) answers. For example, my friend Greg, a city geographic information systems (GIS) expert employed by the city government, might point out that in his database, the *store* is a building with an address, property plot number, city zoning record, water, sewer, and electrical service locations. It has latitude and longitude coordinates, a business license, and tax record. If we were to talk to someone in the grocery business, they might tell us that *eggs* and *milk* exist in a *products* table in their point of sale and inventory management database systems. Each is assigned a product record ID and UPC codes. The product supplier, vendors, shipping companies, and the dairies likely have their own systems and deal with these items in different ways. However, as a consumer, I'm not concerned with such things. I just need to stop by the store and pick up the eggs and milk.

Here's the bottom line: data is just numbers and letters in a database or computer application somewhere. At some point, all of that cryptic data was probably useful information until it was entered into the database. For the database designer or programmer, these values may be meaningful. For the rest of us, it isn't useful at all until it gets translated back into something we understand — information.

Changing Terminology

One of the greatest challenges in our relatively new world of technology is how we use common language to communicate both technical and non-technical concepts. Even when dealing with the same system, terminology often changes as you progress through the different stages of the solution design and construction. These stages are generally as follows:

❑   Conceptual or Architectural Design

❑   Logical Design

❑   Physical Design

Conceptual Design

As you approach the subject of automating business processes through the use of databases and software, one of the first and most important tasks is to gather business requirements from users and other business stakeholders. Beginning with non-technical, business, and user-centric language, you must find terms to describe each unit of pertinent information to be stored and processed. A complete unit of information is known as an *entity*. Business entities generally represent a whole unit that can stand on its own. For example, a *customer* and a *product* are examples of entities. Another conceptual unit of information is an *attribute*. This unit of information describes a characteristic of an entity. An attribute may be something as simple as the color or price of a product. It could also be something more complex such as the dimensions of a package. The important thing during conceptual design is to deal with the simple and conceptual aspects and not all of the implementation details. This way you leave your options open to consider creative ways to model and manage the data according to your business requirements.

In most processes, different terms may be used to describe the same or similar concepts. For example, in an order processing environment, the terms *customer, shopper,* and *purchaser* could mean the same thing. Under closer evaluation, perhaps a *shopper* is a person who looks for products and a *customer* is a person who actually purchases a product. In this case, a *shopper* may become a *customer* at some point in the process. In some cases, a *customer* may not actually be a person. A *customer* could also be an *organization*. It's important to understand the distinction between each entity and find agreeable terms to be used by anyone dealing with the process, especially non-technical users and business stakeholders. Conceptual design is very free-form and often takes a few iterations to reveal all of the hidden requirements.

Along with the entity and attribute concepts, another important notion is that of an *instance*. You may have 100,000 customers on record, but as far as your database system is concerned, these customers don't really exist until you need to deal with their information. Sure, these people do exist out in customer land, but your unfeeling database system couldn't care less about customers who are not currently engaged in buying products, spending money, or updating their billing information. Your system was designed to process orders and purchase products — that's it. If a customer isn't involved in ordering, purchasing, or paying, the system pays no attention. When a customer places an order, you start caring about this information and your order processing system needs to do something with the customer information. At this point, your system reaches into the repository of would-be customers and activates an instance of a specific customer. The customer becomes alive just long enough for the system to do something useful with it and then put it back into cold storage, moving on to the next task.

Logical Design

This stage of design is the transition between the abstract, non-specific world of conceptual design and the very specific, technical world of physical design. After gaining a thorough understanding of business requirements in the language of users, this is an opportunity to model the data and the information flow through the system processes. With respect to data, you should be able to use the terms *entity*, *attribute*, and *instance* to describe every unit of data. Contrasted with conceptual design, logical design is more formalized and makes use of diagramming models to confirm assumptions made in conceptual design. Prototyping is also part of the logical design effort. A quick mock-up database can be used to demonstrate design ideas and test business cases. It's important, though, that prototypes aren't allowed to evolve into the production design. As Fredrick P. Brooks said in his book, *The Mythical Man Month*, "Plan to throw one away. You will do that, anyway. Your only choice is whether to try to sell the throwaway to customers." When you finally happen upon a working model, throw it out and start fresh. This gives you the opportunity to design a functional solution without the baggage of evolutionary design. In logical design, you decide what you're going to build and for what purpose.

In particular, logical database design involves the definition of all the data entities and their attributes. For example, you know that a customer entity should have a name, a shipping location, and a line of credit. Although you realize that the customer's name may consist of a first name, middle initial, and last name, this is unimportant in this stage of design. Likewise, the customer's location may consist of a street address, city, state, and zip code; you also leave these details for the physical design stage. The point during this stage is to understand the need and recognize how this entity will behave with other data entities and their attributes.

Physical Design

One of the greatest reasons to have a formal design process is to find all of the system requirements before attempting to build the solution. Requirements are like water. They're easier to build on when they're frozen. An attempt to define requirements as you go along will inevitably lead to disastrous results. Ask any seasoned software professional. I guarantee their response will be preceded with either a tear or a smile.

Physical design is like drawing the blueprints for a building. It's not a sketch or a rough model. It is the specification for the real project in explicit detail. As your design efforts turn to the physical database implementation, entities may turn into tables and attributes into columns. However, there is not always a one-to-one correspondence between conceptual entities and physical tables. The value of appropriate design is to find similarities and reduce redundant effort. You will likely discover the need for more detail than originally envisioned.

In a recent project, I needed to design a database system to manage a youth activity. The requirements specified both youth and adult entities. Due to the similarities between these entities, I created a single table of *members* with a flag to indicate the member type as either an adult member or youth member.

Relationships

Although I briefly discussed entity relationships in Chapter 1, I want to devote a little more time expounding on the concepts to add clarity to the current topic of design. The purpose of nearly all database systems is to model elements in our physical world. To do this effectively, you need to consider the associations that exist between the various entities you want to keep track of. This concept of an item or multiple items being related to a different item or multiple items is known as *cardinality* or *multiplicity*. To illustrate this concept, just look around you. Nearly everything fits into some kind of collection or set of like objects. The leaves on a tree, the passengers in a car, and the change in your pocket are all examples of this simple principle. These are sets of similar objects in a collection and associated with some kind of container or attached to some type of parent entity. Relationships can be described and discovered using common language. As you describe associations, listen for words such as is, have, and has. For example a customer has orders. Now turn it around: an order has a customer. By looking at the equation from both sides, you've discovered a *one-to-many relationship* between customers and orders.

Relationships generally can be grouped into three different types of cardinality:

- ❏ One-to-one
- ❏ One-to-many
- ❏ Many-to-many

The one-to-one and one-to-many relationships are fairly easy to define using a combination of foreign key and unique constraints, but many-to-many relationships cannot actually be defined using two tables. To reduce redundancy, minimize data storage requirements, and facilitate these relationships, you apply standard rules of normalization (the rules of normal form), which are described briefly in this section.

Primary Keys

According to the first rule of normal form (1NF), which says that each column contains a single type of information, a single value, and there are no repeating groups of data, it is imperative that each row (or record) be stamped with a unique key value. This key could either be a meaningful value that is useful for other reasons, or a surrogate key, a value generated only for the sake of uniqueness. The uniqueness of a record depends entirely on the primary key. Be very cautious and think twice (or three times) before choosing to use non-surrogate key values. I've designed more than a few database systems where it seemed to make sense to use an intelligent value for the primary key (for example, social security number, address, phone number, product code, and so on) and later wished I had just generated a unique value for the key. Most experienced database folks have horror stories to share about such experiences.

I'll briefly share an experience of my own. A few years ago, I was asked to design a database solution for a large fire department to manage the wellness and immunization records of their employees. They had some existing data and used social security numbers to identify each person in their personnel table. Trying to avoid problems and accommodate future requirements, I asked the project sponsor if every one of their employees would always have an SSN on file. She said that this was absolute—every employee would always have an SSN and that this could always be used as an identifier for an employee. I made the SSN the primary key of the Person table and constructed an entire application around it. A year later the client called me on the phone with a problem. She explained that they had been contracted by the volunteer fire department in a small town to manage their health wellness records and that when she entered new volunteer firefighters the system was throwing an error (something about a primary key violation). I asked about social security numbers and she told me that these were unavailable for volunteer personnel. As I began to remind her of our earlier conversation, she interrupted me and repeated our exchange word-for-word: "You asked me if all of *our* employees had social security numbers. These aren't our employees." I had not asked if they would be managing personnel records other than their own employees. Lesson learned: Use surrogate keys or have a very good reason not to.

Two common forms of surrogate key values exist. An *identity* key type is simply an integer value that is automatically incremented by the database system. This will serve as a unique value as long as all data is entered into a single instance of the database. In distributed systems consisting of multiple, disconnected databases, it can be a bit challenging to keep these values unique. The other type of automatically generated key uses a special data type called a *unique identifier* or globally unique identifier (GUID). This SQL data type is equipped to store a very large numeric value automatically generated by the system. A complex algorithm is used to produce a value, partially random and partially predictable. The result is what I call a *big ugly number*, guaranteed to be unique—any time and anywhere. The chances of this value being duplicated are astronomically improbable.

Foreign Keys

One purpose for keys is to relate the records in one table to those in another table. A column in the table containing related records is designated as a *foreign key*. This means that it contains the same values found in the primary key column(s) of the primary table. Unlike a primary key, a foreign key doesn't have to be unique. Using the Customer/Order example, one customer can have multiple orders but one order only has one customer. This describes a one-to-many relationship. The primary key column of the Customer table is related to the foreign key column of the Order table through a relationship known as a *foreign key constraint*. Later, in Chapter 6, you see how this relationship is defined in Transact-SQL.

Normalization Rules

Because this is not a book about database design, I will not engage in a lengthy discussion on the background behind these rules. Volumes have been written on these subjects. On the surface, a short discussion on database design is an important prerequisite to using the Transact-SQL language. The problem with this is that it's nearly impossible to engage in a short discussion on a topic that is so conceptual and subject to individual style and technique. Like so many "simple" concepts in this industry, this one can be debated almost endlessly. Having written and rewritten this section a few times now, I have decided not to walk through an example and align this with the true rules of normal form, as so many books on this subject do. Rather, I'll briefly present the definitions of each rule and then walk you through an example of distilling an unnormalized database into a practical, normalized form without the weighty discussion of the rules.

Unless you have a taste for mathematical theory, you may not even be interested in the gory details of normalized database design. Throughout this book, I discuss query techniques for normalized and denormalized data. It would be convenient to say that when a person designs any database, he should do so according to certain rules and patterns. In fact, a number of people do prescribe one single approach regardless of the system they intend to design. Everyone wants to be normal, right? Well, maybe not. Perhaps it will suffice to say that most folks want their data to be normal. But, what does this mean in terms of database design? Are different values stored in one table or should they be stored in multiple tables with some kind of association between them? If the latter approach is taken, how are relationships between these tables devised? This is the subject of a number of books on relational database design. If you are new to this subject and find yourself in the position of a database designer, I would recommend that you pick up a book or research this topic to meet your needs. This subject is discussed in greater detail in Rob Viera's books on SQL Server programming, mentioned at the beginning of the previous chapter. I'll discuss some of the fundamentals here but this is a complex topic that goes beyond the scope of the SQL language.

In the early 1970s, a small group of mathematicians at IBM proposed a set of standards for designing relational data systems. In 1970, Dr. Edger (E. F.) Codd wrote a paper entitled "A Relational Model of Data for Large Shared Data Banks" for the Association of Computing Machinery. He later published 12 principles for relational database design in 1974. These principles described the low-level mechanics of relational database systems as well as the higher-level rules of entity-relation design for a specific database. Dr. Codd teamed with others who also wrote papers on these subjects including Chris (CJ) Date and Raymond F. Boyce. Boyce and Codd are now credited as the authors of relational database design. Codd's original 12 principles of design involved using set calculus and algebraic expressions to access and describe data. One of the goals of this effort was to reduce data redundancy and minimize storage space requirements. Something to consider is that, at the time, data was stored on magnetic tape, paper punch cards, and, eventually, disks ranging from 5 to 20 megabytes in capacity. As the low-level requirements were satisfied by file system and database products, these 12 rules were distilled into the five rules of normal form taught in college classes today.

In short, the rules of normal form, or principles of relational database design, are aimed at the following objectives:

- ❑ Present data to the relational engine that is set accessible

- ❑ Label and identify unique records and columns within a table

- ❑ Promote the smallest necessary result set for data retrieval

- ❑ Minimize storage space requirements by reducing redundant values in the same table and in multiple tables

- ❑ Describe standards for relating records in one table to those in another table

- ❑ Create stability and efficiency in the use of the data system while creating flexibility in its structure

To apply these principles, tables are created with the fewest number of columns (or fields) to define a single entity. For example, if your objective is to keep track of customers who have ordered products, you will store only the customer information in a single table. The order and product information would be stored their own respective tables.

The idea behind even this lowest form of normalizations is to allow straightforward management of the business rules and the queries that implement these rules against data structures that are flexible to accommodate these changes.

The real purpose of first normal form is to standardize the shape of the entity (relation) — to form a two-dimensional grid that is easily accessed and managed using set-based functions in the data engine.

It's really quite difficult to take a table and apply just one rule. One of the tenets of all the rules of normal form is that each rule in succession must conform to its predecessor. In other words, a design that conforms to second normal form must also conform to first normal form. Also, to effectively apply one, you may also be applying a subsequent rule. Although each of these rules describes a distinct principle, they are interrelated. This means that generally speaking, normalization, up to a certain level, is kind of a package deal.

First Normal Form — 1NF

The first rule of normal form states that an entity shouldn't contain duplicate types of attributes. This means that a table shouldn't contain more than one column that represents the same type of non-distinct value.

To convert flat data to First Normal Form, additional tables are created. Duplicate columns are eliminated and the corresponding values are placed into unique rows of a second table. This rule is applied to reduce redundancy along the horizontal axis (columns).

Second Normal Form — 2NF

This rule states that non-key fields may not depend on a portion of the primary key. These fields are placed into a separate table from those that depend on the key value.

To meet Second Normal Form, you must satisfy First Normal Form and decompose attributes that have partial dependencies to the key attribute.

Without a composite key or by correcting a partial dependency by constructing a new entity with its Reference Key, you arrive at Second Normal Form. Then move to the transitive dependencies of Third Normal Form.

Third Normal Form — 3NF

The first rule states that rows are assigned a key value for identification. This rule takes this principle one step further by stating that the uniqueness of any rule depends entirely upon the primary key. My friend Rick, who teaches and writes books on this topic, uses a phrase to help remember this rule: "The uniqueness of a row depends on the key, the whole key, and nothing but the key; so help me Dr. Codd."

In some cases it makes sense for the primary key to be a combination of columns. Redundant values along multiple rows should be eliminated by placing these values into a separate table as well. Compared with First Normal Form, this rule attempts to reduce duplication along the vertical axis (rows).

Fourth and Fifth Normal Form

Boyce and Codd built their standards — Boyce-Codd Normal Form (BCNF) — on earlier ideals that recognized only those discussed thus far. You must satisfy First and Second and Third Normal Form before moving on to satisfy subsequent forms. In fact, it is the process of the First, Second, and Third Normal Forms that drives the need for BCNF. Through the decomposition of attribute functional dependencies, many-to-many relationships develop between some entities. This is sometimes inaccurately left in a state where each entity involved has duplicate candidate keys in one or more of the entities.

Attributes upon which non-key attributes depend are candidate keys. BCNF deals with the dependencies within candidate keys. The short version of what could be a lengthy and complex discussion of mathematical theory is that fourth and fifth normal forms are used to resolve many-to-many relationships. On the surface this seems to be a simple matter — and for our purposes, we'll keep it that way. Customers can buy many different products and products can be purchased by multiple customers. Concerning ourselves with only customers and products, these two entities have a many-to-many relationship. The fact is that you cannot perform many-to-many joins with just two tables. This requires another table, sometimes called a bridge or intermediary table, to make the association. The bridge table typically doesn't need its own specific key value because the combination of primary key values from the two outer tables will always be unique (keep in mind that this is not a requirement of this type of association but is typically the case). Therefore, the bridge table conforms to third normal form by defining its primary key as the composite of the two foreign keys, each corresponding to the primary keys of the two outer, related tables. Fifth normal form is a unique variation of this rule, which factors in additional business logic, disallowing certain key combinations. For our purposes, this should suffice.

Other Normal Forms

A number of disciplines and conceptual approaches to data modeling and database design exist. Among others, these include Unified Modeling Language (UML) and Object Role Modeling (ORM). These include additional forms that help to manage special anomalies that might arise to describe constraints within and between groups or populations of information. The forms that qualify these descriptions usually move into user-defined procedures added to the database and not the declarative structures that have been addressed so far.

Transforming Information into Data

In the real world, the concepts and information you deal with exist in relationships and hierarchies. Just look around you and observe the way things are grouped and associated. As I write this, I'm sitting on a ferry boat. The ferry contains several cars, and cars have passengers. If I needed to store this information in a relational database, I would likely define separate tables to represent each of the entities I just mentioned. These are simple concepts but when applied at all possible levels, some of the associations may take a little more thought and cautious analysis. At times the business rules of data are not quite so straightforward. Often, the best way to discover these rules (and the limits of these rules) is to ask a series of "what if" questions. Given the ferry/car/passenger scenario, what if a passenger came onto the ferry in one car and left in another? What if she walked on and then drove off? Is this important? Do we care? These questions are not arbitrarily answered by a database designer but through the consensus of designers and system stakeholders.

At some point you will need to decide upon the boundaries of your business rules. This is where you decide that a particular exception or condition is beyond the scope of your database system. Don't treat this matter lightly. It is imperative to define specific criteria while also moving quickly past trivial decision points so that you can move forward and stay on schedule. This is the great balancing act of project management.

When you attempt to take this information and store it in a flat, two-dimensional table as rows and columns, you can't help but create redundant or repeating values. Take a look at a simple example using data from the Northwind sample database. The table in Figure 2-1 shows employee records. Each employee has a name and may have two addresses and two phone numbers. Most employees also have a supervisor. This is the way this data might appear in a simple spreadsheet.

EmployeeName	Title	Address1	CityLine1	Address2	CityLine2	HomePhone	WorkPhone	SupervisorName
Nancy Davolio	Sales Representative	507 - 20th Ave. E.	Seattle, WA 98122	<NULL>	<NULL>	(206) 555-9857	(425) 555-1101	Andrew Fuller
Andrew Fuller	Vice President, Sales	908 W. Capital Way	Tacoma, WA 98401	9317 Clear Creek Ln	Vashon Is, WA 98070	(206) 555-9482	(425) 555-1100	<NULL>
Janet Leverling	Sales Representative	722 Moss Bay Blvd.	Kirkland, WA 98033	<NULL>	<NULL>	(206) 555-3412	(425) 555-1119	Andrew Fuller
Margaret Peacock	Sales Representative	4110 Old Redmond Rd.	Redmond, WA 98052	<NULL>	<NULL>	(206) 555-8122	(425) 555-1108	Andrew Fuller
Steven Buchanan	Sales Manager	14 Garrett Hill	London, SW1 8JR	9035 Pike Place	Olalla, WA 98367	(71) 555-4848	(425) 555-1123	Andrew Fuller
Michael Suyama	Sales Representative	Coventry House	London, EC2 7JR	<NULL>	<NULL>	(71) 555-7773	(425) 555-1103	Steven Buchanan
Robert King	Sales Representative	Edgeham Hollow	London, RG1 9SP	<NULL>	<NULL>	(71) 555-5598	(425) 555-1132	Steven Buchanan
Laura Callahan	Inside Sales Coordinator	9317 Clear Creek Ln	Vashon Is, WA 98070	<NULL>	<NULL>	(206) 555-1189	(425) 555-1114	Andrew Fuller
Anne Dodsworth	Sales Representative	7 Houndstooth Rd.	London, WG2 7LT	<NULL>	<NULL>	(71) 555-4444	(425) 555-1124	Steven Buchanan

Figure 2-1

The <NULL> text is SQL Server's way of telling you that there is nothing in that field. Each employee has a name, title, one or two residence locations, a home and work phone number, and a supervisor. This data is easy to read in this form but it may be difficult to use in a proper database system.

Applying Normalization Rules

Using the previous Employees table, look for violations of the first rule of normal form. Is there more than one column containing information about the same type of attributes? Beginning with the numbered Address and CityLine fields, each "location" consists of a column for the address and another column for the city, state, and zip code. Because there are two pairs of these columns, this may be a problem. Each phone number is a single column, designated as either the home or work phone. How would I make a single list of all phone numbers? What happens if I need to record a mobile phone for an employee? I could add a third column to the table. How about a fourth? How about the Title column? The Supervisor column may be viewed as a special case but the fact is that the EmployeeName and Supervisor columns store the same type of values. They both represent employees.

I can move all of these columns into separate tables but how do I keep them associated with the employee? This is accomplished through the use of keys. A key is just a simple value used to associate a record in one table to a record in another table (among other things). To satisfy the first rule of normal form, I'll move these columns to different tables and create key values to wire up the associations. In the following example, I have removed the address and city information and have placed it into a separate table.

I have devised a method to identify each employee with a six-character character key, using part of their last and first names. I chose this method because this was once a very popular method for assigning key values. This allows me to maintain the associations between employees and their addresses. In this first iteration (see Figure 2-2), I use this method to make a point. This is a relatively small database for a small company and I don't have any employees with similar first and last names, so this method ought to work just fine, right? Hold that thought for now.

EmployeeKey	EmployeeName	Title	SupervisorName
DAV_NA	Nancy Davolio	Sales Representative	Andrew Fuller
FUL_AN	Andrew Fuller	Vice President, Sales	<NULL>
LAV_JA	Janet Leverling	Sales Representative	Andrew Fuller
PEA_MA	Margaret Peacock	Sales Representative	Andrew Fuller
BUC_ST	Steven Buchanan	Sales Manager	Andrew Fuller
SUY_MI	Michael Suyama	Sales Representative	Steven Buchanan
KIN_RO	Robert King	Sales Representative	Steven Buchanan
CAL_LA	Laura Callahan	Inside Sales Coordinator	Andrew Fuller
DOD_AN	Anne Dodsworth	Sales Representative	Steven Buchanan

Figure 2-2

I do the same thing with the new Addresses table (see Figure 2-3). Each address record is assigned an EmployeeKey value to link it back to the Employees table.

EmployeeKey	AddressLine	CityLine
DAV_NA	507 - 20th Ave. E.	Seattle, WA 98122
FUL_AN	908 W. Capital Way	Tacoma, WA 98401
LEV_JA	722 Moss Bay Blvd.	Kirkland, WA 98033
PEA_MA	4110 Old Redmond Rd.	Redmond, WA 98052
BUC_ST	14 Garrett Hill	London, SW1 8JR
SUY_MI	Coventry House	London, EC2 7JR
KIN_RO	Edgeham Hollow	London, RG1 9SP
DOD_AN	7 Houndstooth Rd.	London, WG2 7LT
CAL_LA	9317 Clear Creek Ln	Vashon Is, WA 98353
FUL_AN	9317 Clear Creek Ln	Vashon Is, WA 98353
BUC_ST	9035 Pike Place	Olalla, WA 98367

Figure 2-3

I have lost a significant piece of information in doing this. I've flattened the address information so I no longer have one address designated as either primary or secondary for an employee. I'll get to this later. For now, I'm only concerned with adhering to the first rule of normal form. Besides, does the information in the old Address1 and CityLine1 columns imply that this is the employee's primary residence? Did I have a complete understanding of the business rules when I began working with this data? Unfortunately, in most ad-hoc projects, it is more often a case of making things up as we go along.

For the phone numbers I'll do the same thing as before, move the phone number values into their own table and then add the corresponding key value to associate them with the employee record. I'm also going to add a column to designate the type of phone number this represents (see Figure 2-4). I could use this as an argument to do the same thing with the addresses, but I'll hold off for now.

EmployeeKey	PhoneNumber	PhoneType
DAV_NA	(206) 555-9857	Home
FUL_AN	(206) 555-9482	Home
LAV_JA	(206) 555-3412	Home
PEA_MA	(206) 555-8122	Home
BUC_ST	(71) 555-4848	Home
SUY_MI	(71) 555-7773	Home
KIN_RO	(71) 555-5598	Home
CAL_LA	(206) 555-1189	Home
DOD_AN	(71) 555-4444	Home
DAV_NA	(425) 555-1101	Work
FUL_AN	(425) 555-1100	Work
LAV_JA	(425) 555-1119	Work
PEA_MA	(425) 555-1108	Work
BUC_ST	(425) 555-1123	Work
SUY_MI	(425) 555-1103	Work
KIN_RO	(425) 555-1132	Work
CAL_LA	(425) 555-1114	Work
DOD_AN	(425) 555-1124	Work

Figure 2-4

Now that I have three tables with common column values, do I have a relational database? Although it may be true that this is related data, it's not a fully relational database. The key values only give me ability to locate the related records in other tables, but this does nothing to ensure that my data stays intact. Take a look at what I have done so far (see Figure 2-5). The presence of the same key value in all three of these tables is an implied relationship. There is currently no mechanism in place for the database to prevent users from making silly mistakes (such as deleting an employee record without also removing the corresponding address and phone information, for example). This would create a condition, common in early database systems, called orphaned records.

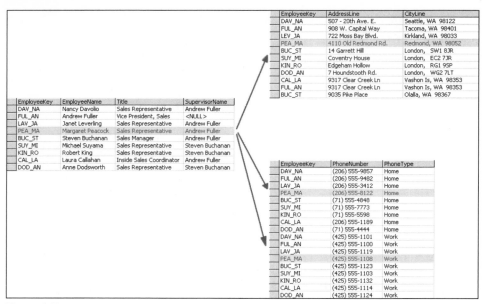

Figure 2-5

Before continuing, I must correct a horrible indiscretion. I told you that this business of using parts of different field values (such as the first and last name) to form a meaningful unique key was once a common practice. This is because database system designers in the past often had to create a system where users had to provide a special number to look up a record. To make this easier, they would come up with some kind of intelligent, unique value. It might include characters from a customer or patient's name, or perhaps a series of numbers with digits in specific positions representing an account type or region. For example, when was the last time you called the bank or the telephone company and was asked for your account number? This happens to me all the time. It amazes me that the companies in possession of the most sophisticated, state-of-the-art technology on the planet require me to memorize my account number. How about looking up my account using my name, address, phone number, mother's maiden name, or any of the other information they required when I set up my account?

Using this simple name-based key may have seemed like the right thing to do at the time but the fact is that it will likely get me into a whole lot of trouble down the road. I worked for a company that used this approach in a small, commercial application. The program even appended numbers to the end of the keys so there could be nearly a hundred unique key values for a given last name/first name combination. What they didn't anticipate was that their product would eventually become the most popular medical billing software in the country and would be used in business environments they couldn't possibly have imagined. Eventually this got them into trouble and they had to completely re-architect the application to get around this limitation. One customer, a medical office in the Chicago area, had so many patients with the same or similar names, that they actual ran out of key values.

Thinking Ahead

I'll resolve the EmployeeKey issue by changing it to an auto-sequencing integer called an *identity* (see Figure 2-6). This is known as a surrogate key, which simply means that key values are absolutely meaningless as far as the user is concerned. The database assigns numbers that will always be unique within this column. The purpose of the key is to uniquely identify each row, not to give employees or users something to memorize.

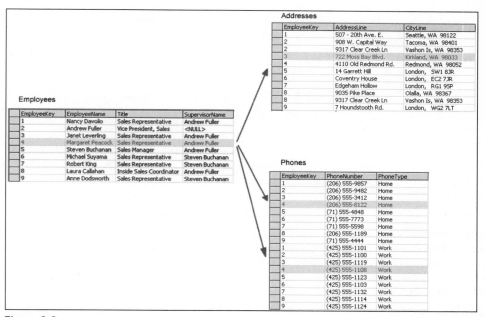

Figure 2-6

The next step is to designate the EmployeeKey in the Employees table as a primary key and the related keys as foreign keys. The foreign key constraints cause the database engine to validate any action that could cause these relationships to be violated. For example, the database would not allow an employee record to be deleted if there were existing, related address or phone records. Related tables are often documented using an entity-relation diagram (ERD). The diagram in Figure 2-7 shows the columns and relationships between these tables.

There is still work to do. The SupervisorName is also a violation of first normal form because it duplicates some employee names. This is a special case, however, because these names already exist in the Employees table. This can be resolved using a self-join, or relationship on the same table (see Figure 2-8).

The supervisor designation within the Employees table is now just an integer value referring to another employee record.

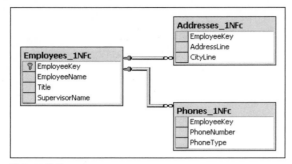

Figure 2-7

EmployeeKey	EmployeeName	Title	SupervisorEmployeeID
1	Nancy Davolio	Sales Representative	2
2	Andrew Fuller	Vice President, Sales	<NULL>
3	Janet Leverling	Sales Representative	2
4	Margaret Peacock	Sales Representative	2
5	Steven Buchanan	Sales Manager	2
6	Michael Suyama	Sales Representative	5
7	Robert King	Sales Representative	5
8	Laura Callahan	Inside Sales Coordinator	2
9	Anne Dodsworth	Sales Representative	5

Figure 2-8

The Title column is also in violation of first normal form and could be moved into its own table, as well. A title isn't uniquely owned by an employee, but each employee only has one title. To discern this relationship, you must look at it from both directions:

❑ One employee has one title

❑ One title can have multiple employees

This is a one-to-many relationship from the title to the employee. Resolving this is a simple matter of placing one instance of each title value in a separate table, identified by a unique primary key. A similar column is added to the Employees table as a non-unique foreign key (see Figure 2-9).

You should see a pattern developing. This is an iterative process that will typically send you in one of two directions in each cycle. You will either continue to move these values into related tables with related keys or you will find discrepancies between your business rules and the data, and then head back to the drawing board to correct the data and table structure.

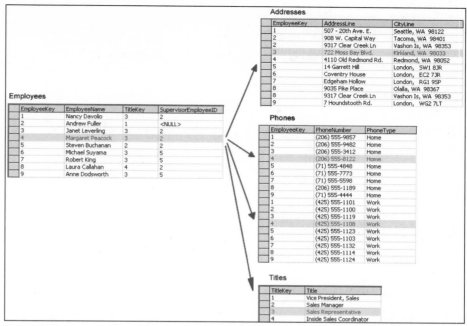

Figure 2-9

Multiple Associations

I know that a title can be associated with more than one employee, but what happens if an address is shared by more than one individual? This is a problem in the current database model. I can't use one primary key value and have multiple associations going in both directions. The only way I can do this is to create a primary key that includes two separate values: one for the employee key and one for the address key. However, I can't do this using either of these two tables. If I add the EmployeeKey to the Addresses table, I'm back to the original problem, where I would have duplicate address rows. Because a record in the Addresses table will no longer be directly tied to a record in the Employees table, I must remove the EmployeeKey and create a new primary key for this table and remove the duplicate values. Now the Addresses table conforms to first normal form and third normal form.

Many-to-many relationships are solved using a separate table, often called a *join* or *bridge* table. Often, this table contains no user-readable values, only keys to bridge one table to another. However, you may recall that we have a missing bit of information. Remember when I moved the address information from the Address1/CityLine1 columns and Address2/CityLine2 columns into the Address table? I said that we had no way to trace these back to their roots and recall which location was the employee's primary residence? I can now resolve this within the bridge table by adding an additional column (see Figure 2-10).

The new AddressType column is used to indicate the type of residence. This allows employees to share addresses while eliminating redundant address records. Does the AddressType column violate first normal form? Technically, yes. This could be an opportunity to optimize the database even more by creating yet another table for these values. It looks like there would only be three address type records related to the nine employees (see Figure 2-11).

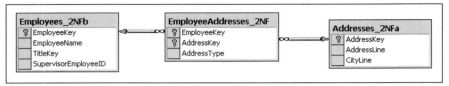

Figure 2-10

EmployeeKey	AddressKey	AddressType
1	1	Primary Home
2	2	Primary Home
2	10	Weekend Home
3	3	Primary Home
4	4	Primary Home
5	5	Primary Home
5	11	Vacation Home
6	6	Primary Home
7	7	Primary Home
8	10	Primary Home
9	9	Primary Home

Figure 2-11

A simple query is used to obtain detail information about employees at a common address:

```
SELECT    EmployeeName, AddressLine, CityLine, AddressType
FROM      Employees
  INNER JOIN EmployeeAddresses
        ON Employees.EmployeeKey = EmployeeAddresses.EmployeeKey
  INNER JOIN Addresses
        ON EmployeeAddresses.AddressKey = Addresses.AddressKey
WHERE     Addresses.AddressKey = 10
```

It looks like the Vice President of Sales and the Inside Sales Coordinator share a residence only on weekends (see Figure 2-12).

	EmployeeName	AddressLine	CityLine	AddressType
1	Andrew Fuller	9317 Clear Creek Ln	Vashon Is, WA 98353	Weekend Home
2	Laura Callahan	9317 Clear Creek Ln	Vashon Is, WA 98353	Primary Home

Figure 2-12

Multi-valued Columns

The last issue with which I must contend is that of having multiple values stored in a single column. There are quite a few examples in these tables. For example, the EmployeeName column in the Employees table contains both the first and last name, the AddressLine column in the Addresses table includes all parts of a street address, and the CityLine contains the city name, U.S. state, and zip code/postal code. Before I just willy-nilly start parsing all the values into separate columns, it's important for me to consider how this data will be used and the advantages and disadvantages of breaking it into pieces. Here are some sample questions that could help to define these business requirements:

❑   Will the employee first name and last name ever be used separately?

❑   Will I ever need to sort on one single value (such as last name)?

❑   Does every employee have a first name and last name? Do they only have a first name and last name (middle names/initials, hyphenated names, and so on)?

❑   Is there any value or need in separating parts of the address line (will I need a list of streets, and so on)?

❑   If I separate parts of the AddressLine or CityLine into separate columns, do I need to accommodate international addresses?

Apparently I do need to consider addresses in at least two locales because I have locations in the UK and the U.S., so I will need to think beyond only one style of address. So, suppose that I have consulted my sponsoring customer and have learned that it would be useful to store separate first names and last names and we don't care about middle names or initials. We also don't plan to accommodate anyone without a first and last name. We have no need to break up the address line. This practice is highly uncommon outside of specialized systems and would be very cumbersome to maintain. We would benefit from storing the city, postal code or zip code, and state or province. It would also be useful to store the country, which is currently not included. Storing geographic information can be tricky due to the lack of consistency across international regions. This may require that you devise your own synonyms for different regional divisions (such as city, township, municipality, county, state, province, and country). In distributing these values into separate columns, you may find even more redundancies. Should these be further normalized and placed into separate tables? Does this ever end? I'll site one example where the city, state, and zip code is normalized. I maintain a system that stores U.S. addresses and stores only the zip code on the individual's record. A separate table contains related city and state information obtained from the U.S. Postal Service.

I won't bore you will the mechanics of separating all of these fields. The process is quite straightforward and very similar to what's already been done. Figure 2-13 shows the completed data model, based on the original flat table.

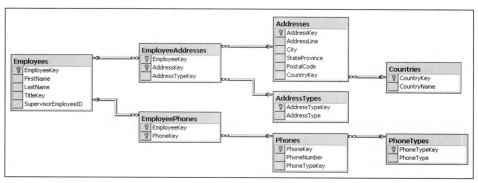

Figure 2-13

To Normalize or to De-normalize?

Depending on how a database is to be used (generally, it will be used for data input or for reporting), it may or may not be appropriate to apply all of the rules just presented. The fact of the matter is that fully normalized databases require some gnarly, complex queries to support reporting and business analysis requirements. To fully comply with all of the rules of normal form often adds more overhead to the application. Without going into detail, here's something to think about: If you are designing a new database system to support a typical business process, you will usually want to follow these rules completely and normalize all of your data structures. After a time, when you have a large volume of data to extract and analyze through reports and business intelligence tools, you may find it appropriate to create a second database system for this purpose. In this database, you will strategically break the rules of normal form, creating redundant values in fewer, larger tables. Here's the catch: Only after you fully understand the rules of normal form will you likely know when and where you should break them.

Question Authority

You should ask yourself an important question as you encounter each opportunity to normalize: "Why?" Know why you should apply the rules and what the benefits and cost are. One of the challenges of applying normalization rules is to know just how far to go and to what degree it makes sense to apply them. At times it just makes sense to break some of the rules. There are good arguments to support both sides of this issue and without a complete understanding of business requirements I would be hard pressed to make a general statement about how data elements (such as phone numbers, titles, or addresses) should always be managed. In short, you need to understand the business requirements for your application and then apply the appropriate level of database normalization to reach that goal. If ever in doubt, it's usually best to err on the side of keeping the rules.

Client/Server Processes

SQL Server is a true client/server database. This means that application logic is processed both on the application client computer and the database server. The client process is typically encapsulated within an application that needs to submit or access data. In addition to the standard operating system and network protocols, a set of special components is installed on both the client and server computers, allowing the client to send requests and receive results. Server-side components enable SQL Server to receive and respond to the client requests, as illustrated in Figure 2-14.

The Mechanics of Query Processing

To drive a car, it's not essential to understand how the engine works. However, if you want to be able to drive a car well (and perhaps maintain and tune it for optimal performance), it's helpful to have a fundamental understanding of the engine mechanics and to know what's going on inside. Likewise, it's possible to use SQL Server without fully understanding its mechanics, but if you want to create queries that work efficiently, it will help to understand what goes on within the relational database engine and the query processor.

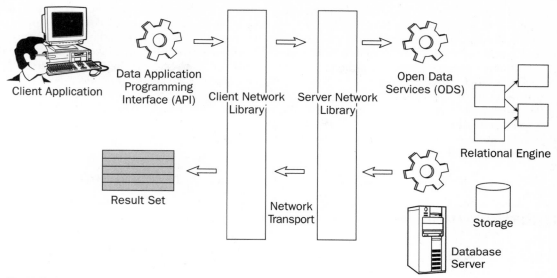

Figure 2-14

When a SQL statement is presented to the database engine, it begins to analyze the request and break it down into steps. Based on characteristics of the data stored in tables, decisions are made resulting in the selection of appropriate operations. Many factors are considered including the table structures, existence of indexes, and the relative uniqueness of relevant data values.

It would be inefficient for the query-processing engine to analyze all of the data prior to each query, so SQL Server gathers statistical information it uses to make these decisions. In essence, SQL Server learns from previous query executions and adapts as the data changes (see Figure 2-15). In theory, queries will continue to be optimized and updated as time goes on.

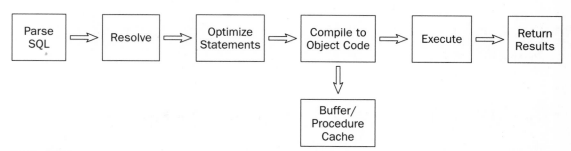

Figure 2-15

Complex queries are broken down into individual steps — smaller queries — that process granular operations. This list of steps and operations is known as an *execution plan*. The query's syntax may actually be rewritten by the query optimizer into a standard form of SQL. SQL Server doesn't actually execute SQL — that's just how we talk to it. Before SQL Server can send instructions to the computer's processor, these commands must be compiled into low-level computer instructions, or object code. The optimized, compiled query is placed into an in-memory cache. Depending on how the query is created (for example, it may be saved as a view or stored procedure), the execution plan and cache are saved with that object in the database, called *procedure cache*. Even ad-hoc queries may benefit from this process. The cached compiled query and execution plan is held into memory as *buffer cache* and reused until the user and client application's connection is closed. This way, if the same query is executed multiple times, it should run faster and more efficiently after the first time. In SQL Server 2005, the same mechanism is used to manage both buffer cache and procedure cache. Here's a closer look at this process, also illustrated in Figure 2-16:

1. First the query text is flat-lined and translated into a standardized form of SQL.

2. Objects and then permissions are resolved, replacing object names with data-specific numeric identifiers and security context. These identifiers streamline conversations between the relation and storage engine.

3. The query is semantically translated from SQL to Tabular Data Stream (TDS), the native language of the SQL Server net libraries. In this translation, operations are simplified and optimized. More than 300 possible semantic operations exist.

4. Compiled version of the plan and call are placed into the buffer.

5. The relational engine spawns threads for calling logical and physical I/O and operational execution. Database object locks are placed and managed by the transactional engine.

Figure 2-16

The Adventure Works Cycles Database

Through the remainder of the book, you'll be working with the Adventure Works Cycles sample database. This is a new sample database included with SQL Server 2005. There have actually been several different versions of this database as it evolved from the first edition in 2004 and then through the SQL Server 2005 beta test period. The version that installs with SQL Server 2005 is a little more complex than deemed appropriate for this book, so I decided to use the SQL Server 2000 version for the examples. It will work with both SQL Server 2000 and SQL Server 2005.

You can download and install the AdventureWorks2000 sample database from the support site for this book at Wrox Press. You will find this at http://www.wrox.com/go/begintransact-SQL. To install the sample database, follow these steps:

1. Click the Download button and then click Open in the File Download dialog and follow the directions in the InstallShield Wizard.

2. Double-check that the AdventureWorks2000 database has been added to the list of available databases on your server. Right-click the Databases node and choose Refresh.

3. If the new database is not displayed on the database tree, the database file may need to be attached manually. This is easy to do using the following steps:

    a. For SQL Server 2000, in Enterprise Manager, right-click the Databases node and select All Tasks ⇨ Attach Database. In the Attach Database dialog, click the small ellipsis (...) button and then browse for the file. The AdventureWorks2000_Data.MDF file should be at C:\Program Files\Microsoft SQL Server\MSSQL\Data. Select the file and click OK.

    b. For SQL Server 2005, the procedure is similar. Right-click the database server node in the SQL Server Management Studio object browser and select Attach Database. Browse to the database file and then click OK.

The AdventureWorks2000 database is also an optional installation component with SQL Server Reporting Services for SQL Server 2000. An evaluation version of Reporting Services is available for download from Microsoft.

Summary

SQL Server is a product widely used by a lot of different people in many different ways. At its core is the relational database engine, and sitting on this foundation are a wealth of features and capabilities. The way that SQL Server databases are designed and administered has changed as the client applications have improved and been integrated into Microsoft's suite of solution development tools. SQL Server is now accessible to business users in addition to technical professionals.

You read about the conceptual, logical, and physical phases of solution design and how they apply to designing a database. A relational database stores data in separate tables, associated through primary key/foreign key relationships that implement the rules of normal form. You saw how flat, spreadsheet-like data is transformed into a normalized structure by applying these rules. Normalizing data structures is not an absolute necessity for all databases and it sometimes is prudent to ignore the rules to simplify the design. Both normalizing and de-normalizing a database design come at a cost that must be carefully considered and kept in balance with the business rules for the solution. These business rules and the user's requirements ultimately drive the capabilities and long-term needs of a project.

You also learned about the client/server database execution model and how SQL Server uses both client-side and server-side components to process requests and to execute queries. The execution and procedure cache allow SQL Server to optimize performance by compiling execution plans for ad-hoc queries and prepared stored procedures.

Tools for Accessing SQL Server

It's said that a craftsman's work is only as good as his tools. To some degree, I agree that this principle applies to SQL Server. However, many database professionals from the old school choose not to use sophisticated tools, just as many craftsmen use tools (chisels, carving knives, and so on) to do the work that is often simplified through automation. Many would even argue that the results are different, perhaps even better, when you remove automation from the equation. Regardless of the ideals to which you subscribe, a number of tools and applications are available that you can use to create and debug queries. What tools do you need? This depends a great deal on what you need to do.

Here's a breakdown of some of the common tasks you may need to perform with SQL Server:

- ❑ Administrative Tasks
    - ❑ Creating databases
    - ❑ Creating and managing server logins and database roles and users
    - ❑ Granting and managing security permissions
    - ❑ Scheduling backups
    - ❑ Auditing and error checking
    - ❑ Diagnosing failures and application errors
    - ❑ Performance tuning
    - ❑ Configuring data replication
    - ❑ Managing disk space and data files
- ❑ Database Management Tasks
    - ❑ Adding and managing tables, views, stored procedures, and functions
    - ❑ Creating indexes

❏ Creating views, stored procedures, and functions

❏ Importing, exporting, or transforming data

❏ Data Operations

❏ Inserting, updating, and deleting records

❏ Supporting application features

❏ Defining business rules

❏ Selecting records from a table or multi-table join

Whether you are using SQL Server 2000 or SQL Server 2005, this chapter walks you though similar exercises for each version of the product. I'm assuming that you have SQL Server installed on your local computer with all of the server and client tools. This is the default setting when you run the setup. If your database server is on another computer, you will need to install the client tools on your local computer to follow these directions. I am also assuming that you are using Integrated Windows authentication and that your Windows account has sufficient permissions to create objects and run queries against the database server. If you have installed SQL Server on your local computer with default options, this should be the case.

If you are working with a remote database server, you should talk to your system administrator and make sure you have the client tools correctly installed and that you have the appropriate permissions to run queries. As you work through these exercises, the only difference will be that you will be connecting to a remote server rather than the local server.

Tools for SQL Server 2000

If you have installed the client tools for SQL Server on your computer, the Microsoft SQL Server menu will appear on your Start menu with some or all of the shortcuts shown in Figure 3-1.

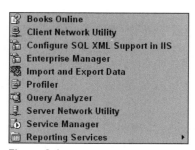

Figure 3-1

The following table provides a brief overview of these tools, and then you'll take a look at those related to Transact-SQL in detail.

Menu Option	Description
Books Online	SQL Server Books Online (BOL) is the online help system for all SQL Server tools and features. Books Online opens in a separate window with options to search keywords and browse the index of topics. To launch Books Online from within a SQL Server tool, press F1. Context-sensitive help is available from within Query Analyzer when you highlight a keyword and then press Shift+F1.
Configure SQL XML Support in IIS	This option will only be available if you have Internet Information Services installed. It allows a SQL Server database to be configured as a web folder, accessible through HTTP requests. Data may be queried using a URL and through a variety of XML-based techniques. Data is typically returned as XML to be used within a web page or an XML transform script.
Enterprise Manager	Database server administrators and database developers use Enterprise Manager to perform a variety of useful tasks. This is the central management interface for most database management activity.
Import and Export Data	This shortcut launches the Data Import/Export Wizard. This is actually a simplified interface for creating and running Data Transformation Services (DTS) packages and tasks. It can be used to copy and move practically any database objects and data from and to most any standard data source (including text files, dBase, FoxPro, Excel, Access, Paradox, SQL Server, and other ODBC-compliant sources).
Profiler	The SQL Server Profiler is an extensive troubleshooting and optimization tool. It can be used to monitor a broad range of database activity, or to pinpoint specific events. Operations can be captured and recorded for later playback. Events and activities can be recorded as scripts or logs to text files or to a database.
Query Analyzer	This ad-hoc query utility is the tool of choice for most SQL-savvy database users. It gives database designers, developers, and administrators an unconstrained free-form environment to test and run SQL script in a multi-window interface, connected to multiple database servers. SQL scripts can be generated for nearly all database objects from the object browser. Commands can be saved to script files and can be used to build database objects in different databases and on different servers.
Server Network Utility	The client and server network utilities are used to install and configure database network libraries, which provide low-level, network protocol-specific connectivity to database servers.
Service Manager	This simple utility provides a convenient tool for managing the Windows services, which comprise the features of SQL Server. It is also accessible from the Windows System Tray, in the lower-right corner of the desktop.
Reporting Services	SQL Server Reporting Services is an add-on, server-based, enterprise reporting product from Microsoft that integrates with SQL Server. It is freely available to licensed owners of SQL Server to be used on the same server and requires a separate installation. This shortcut leads to another menu with Reporting Services features.

Enterprise Manager

This is the administrative console for SQL Server 2000. It's actually a snap-in for the Microsoft Management Console (MMC) so it may look familiar if you have worked with other Windows administrative tools. Later, you'll see how to customize the MMC so you can have all of your tools in one place.

To open Enterprise Manager, select the shortcut from the start-up menu by clicking the Start button and then select All Programs ➪ Microsoft SQL Server ➪ Enterprise Manager (see Figure 3-2).

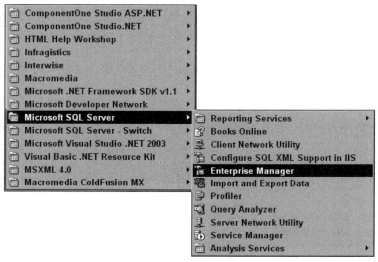

Figure 3-2

Assuming that you have the appropriate level of security access to get to your databases, it's just a simple matter to drill down to the database on your registered server. Here's a quick tour to get you started. On the left side of the window, you will see a tree view pane that lets you navigate through various nodes and folders that represent feature areas and server and database objects. You can resize this pane as needed. The right pane shows items related to the selection on the left. This view can be modified to show more or less detail by using options on the View menu. Figure 3-3 shows the initial view after opening Enterprise Manager. Note that on my system, I have groups and registrations for several servers and databases. You will only see those that have been set up on your system. The demonstrations here will be using only the local database server. If you have installed the client tools on your local computer and SQL Server is on a different computer, you will need to create a registration for the remote server. You can easily do this by right-clicking the node labeled SQL Server Group and selecting New SQL Server Registration.

One anomaly of this tool is that it opens with one window inside the other. For simplicity, I recommend that you maximize the inner snap-in window so it fills the console window. To do this, click the rectangular-shaped icon in the upper-right corner of the smaller window.

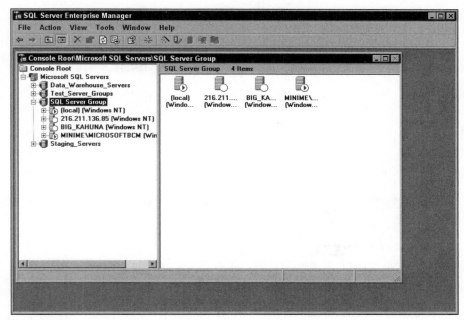

Figure 3-3

In the left pane, click the tree node labeled Microsoft SQL Servers. This will display groups used to organize remote connections to any SQL Server database servers available to you. The default group is called
SQL Server Group. If you click the little plus sign icon next to any item in the tree, it will expand to show
related items under that node. Expand the SQL Server Group to show any registered servers. Your local
server should be registered by default. You can also add registrations for additional servers by right-
clicking the group and choosing New Server Registration. The local server will either be labeled (local)
or with the name of the SQL Server 2000 instance specified during installation. Expand this node to
reveal databases and administrative items for this server. Expand the Databases node and select the
AdventureWorks2000 sample database.

Enterprise Manager is not a query-editing tool, but it contains some features that use or generate
Transact-SQL script. You can use Transact-SQL in a few different ways in the Enterprise Manager. You
can enter the Transact-SQL Query Designer by choosing to create a new view or to return records from a
table. For writing complex queries containing multi-table joins and groupings, this is a very useful technique even if you don't plan to save the script as a view.

You can also create stored procedures and user-defined functions from Enterprise Manager and just type
the SQL directly into the related editor window.

You learn how to create these database objects in Chapter 10.

Using Query Designer Window

This section takes a brief look at the Query Designer tool. I haven't discussed the components of SQL
statements yet but I want to show you the mechanics of this tool. This tool is available in several different Microsoft products including Visual Studio 6, Visual Studio.NET, SQL Server Reporting Services,
and Microsoft Access Data Projects.

1. Using Enterprise Manager, expand the nodes in the left pane. If you haven't done so already, start with Microsoft SQL Servers ⇨ SQL Server Group ⇨ (local). Note that this node may also be labeled (local) (Windows NT) depending on the operating system.

2. The next node to expand is Databases. Expand the AdventureWorks2000 database and right-click the icon labeled Views.

3. From the right-click Action Menu, select New View.

Now you should be looking at a new window that contains four panes arranged vertically. This is the Query Designer window. Figure 3-4 shows the initial view before you add tables.

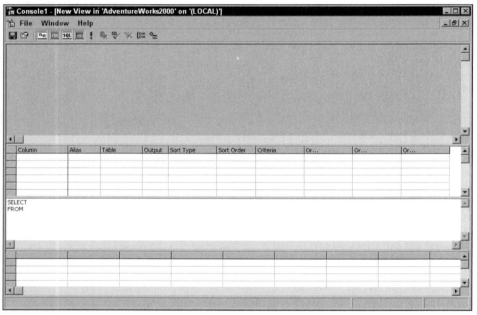

Figure 3-4

How It Works

The Transact-SQL Query Designer is actually a utility (separate from Enterprise Manager) that can be called from a few different places within Enterprise Manager, including the Database Diagram tool and on the Action menu in the Tables node of Enterprise Manager. The easiest way to open the Query Designer window without actually having to retrieve data from a table is to choose the option to create a new view. You don't have to save the expression as a view. In fact, this is one of the most convenient techniques to use when you just need to quickly create a SQL expression to copy and paste into another tool or window. In the following Try It Out, you use this technique to create a simple multi-table query. After you build the query, I will show you a few of the features and toolbar options.

The Query Designer contains four panes that can be resized and scrolled individually. Each of these panes can be hidden and shown using buttons on the toolbar. The top area is the diagram pane. It graphically displays tables and views included in the query. Joins are depicted as lines between each table window.

The second pane is the grid pane and is for managing the columns for the tables in the query. The grid pane allows you to specify column aliases, calculations and expressions, output, and sorting options.

The third pane is the SQL pane. SQL syntax will be generated automatically from selections and settings in the tables and columns panes and placed in the SQL pane. SQL expressions can also be typed or changed directly in the third pane. As long as the SQL syntax is supported by the graphical view, the tables and columns pane content will be updated to reflect these changes. There are a few expressions that the Query Designer can't represent graphically. These include unions and some types of subqueries. Query Designer is a very smart tool and, with these few exceptions, will handle almost anything else you can throw at it.

On the toolbar, the right-most icon is used to add tables to the query. Click this icon to open a window listing all of the tables in the AdventureWorks2000 database. The same dialog can be accessed by right-clicking the diagram pane and selecting Add Table from the resultant Action Menu. For future reference, note that this dialog (shown in Figure 3-5) can be used to add views and functions as well.

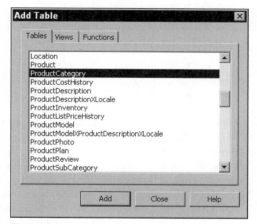

Figure 3-5

Now add the Product and ProductSubCategory tables to this query. Click ProductSubCategory to select it from the list and click the Add button. Now, do the same for the Product table — select it from the list and click Add. Both of these tables should have been added to the top-most pane in the Query Designer and a thick line intersected by a diamond should be visible, as shown in Figure 3-6.

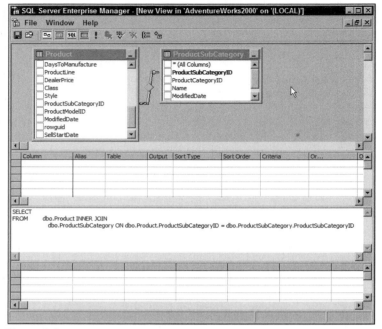

Figure 3-6

The line between the two tables represents a join. The Query Designer assumes there should be a join between these tables because a relationship was designated between these tables when the database was created. If you need to, you can use the mouse to move the tables and resize them in the designer for clarity. This won't actually affect anything other than your ability to see what's going on. The line end on the ProductSubCategory table side shows a key icon because this table contains the primary key column in the join. The ProductSubCategoryID column is used to ensure that there can be only one subcategory with a particular CustomerID value. The little infinity symbol on the Product table end of the line means that for one ProductSubCategory there can be many products (usually based on tables having a one-to-many relationship). The ProductSubCategoryID column in the Product table is a foreign key. Its value may be duplicated but a related ProductSubCategoryID must exist in the ProductSubCategory table. The diamond shape indicates that this is an inner join. This means that related records must exist in both of the tables participating in the join. In other words, subcategories that don't have products won't be included in the query's result set. If it were permissible in the design of this database, products without related subcategories also would not be included. Due to a foreign-key constraint that the database designer used to define this relationship, this condition isn't allowed.

The next step is to choose the columns you'd like to output from the query. Use the check boxes in each of the table windows. Check the Name, ProductNumber, Color, and ListPrice columns for the Product table and the Name column for the ProductSubCategory table. Note that this places these column names into the grid in the second pane, or column list.

You will notice that because the Name column has been selected in both tables, the Query Designer has created an Alias for the Name column from the ProductSubCategory table. The Query Designer does this automatically any time a duplicate name appears in the column list for a SELECT statement. The Alias that the Query Designer chooses, "Expr1," is probably not what you want. This is easy to correct. Either in the SQL pane or the Column pane, change Expr1 to SubCategory. The other columns can also be aliased as desired to make the column headers more intuitive for anyone who runs this query in the future. For this query, alias the Name column from the Product table as well as to Product.

In the third pane, you will see the actual SQL expression. The fact is that the SQL expression is the only thing you're building. Everything else in this designer is derived from this expression. Figure 3-7 shows the designer window thus far.

Notice the text in the Alias column for the Name field in the Product table. Because this field name is the same as the Name field in the ProductSubCategory table, an alias should be defined to make these column names more readable. You can address this by defining a meaningful alias for both the product name and the subcategory name. Place the cursor in the alias column on the first row, representing the ProductSubCategory Name field, and type **SubCategoryName**. This will be the name of this field. Now do the same for the second row, representing the Name field for the Product table: replace the text Expr1 with ProductName. The Query Designer also allows you to change the sort order for your result list by specifying a Sort Type and Sort Order. For your query you want the results ordered by the ProductSubCategory, Product, and ListPrice in that order, but you want the ListPrice to be sorted from the most expensive to the least expensive. The resultant query designer should look like that shown in Figure 3-8.

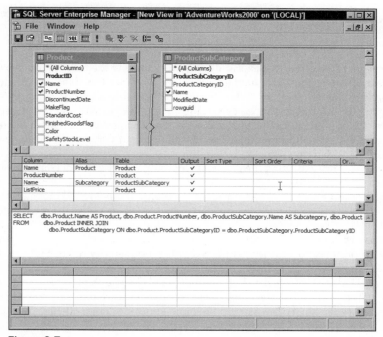

Figure 3-7

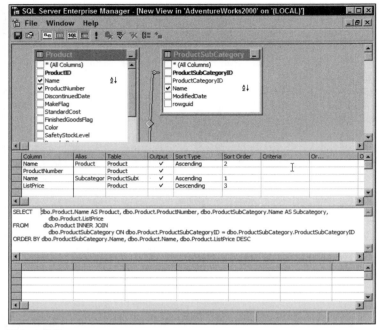

Figure 3-8

The Query Designer also allows for executing the query to view the results. You can do this by clicking the dark red exclamation point icon on the toolbar. This executes the query and displays records in the results pane grid at the very bottom of the Query Designer window. An important aspect of this particular feature to keep in mind is that when executing a query in Query Designer you are actually opening an updateable cursor to the underlying data objects. Any changes to the data in the results pane are immediately applied to the underlying tables. This may sound very useful, but in reality it is quite dangerous and has the added downside of consuming very large amounts of server resources. I would strongly recommend not executing the query in Query Designer. Instead, copy the query to Query Analyzer or the query window in SQL Server Management Studio and execute it there. The results window in these latter tools does not hold any locks or create cursors to hold the data. Figure 3-9 shows the Query Designer with the results pane populated (which again, is not recommended).

If you leave this window open and have a large number of rows returned from a query, you may be prompted by the designer to clear these results and free up memory on the SQL Server.

To finish this short tour of the Query Designer tool, take a look at the toolbar to see some additional features. First of all, you can launch the Query Designer in a few different ways. Further in this section, you open a table and use the Query Designer to filter and sort rows. Figure 3-10 shows the Query Designer toolbar.

Because the Query Designer is a multipurpose tool that has been incorporated into different products for different reasons, some of these features may not be enabled. For example, Cancel Filter isn't enabled in this environment. In some applications, buttons may be added or hidden. In Microsoft Access, sorting buttons are added to the toolbar. On the toolbar (as with most Microsoft products), if you hover the mouse pointer over a button, a pop-up tooltip displays a short caption describing the button's feature.

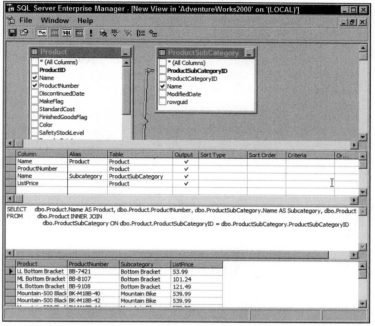

Figure 3-9

Figure 3-10

The toolbar options are described in the following table.

Icon	Toolbar Button	Description
	Save	Save SQL expression to a script file
	Properties	View the properties dialog to specify advance query options and query parameters
	Diagram Pane	Toggle show/hide diagram pane
	Columns Pane	Toggle show/hide columns pane
	SQL Pane	Toggle show/hide SQL pane
	Results Pane	Toggle show/hide results pane

Table continued on following page

Icon	Toolbar Button	Description
!	Execute	Execute the query and display results
	Cancel Execution	Cancel query execution if in process
SQL	Verify SQL	Check the SQL expression for errors
	Cancel Filter	Not used in Enterprise Manager
	Group By	Add the Group By SQL clause and aggregate functions to the expression
	Add Tables	Open the Add Table dialog to add tables and views to the diagram pane

Using the Query Designer to View a Table

There are a few different ways to use features of the Query Designer. Another method, in Enterprise Manager, is to view records from a table in a grid. Simply right-click any table and choose Open Table from the menu. Selecting any of the three submenu options (Return All Rows, Return Top, or Query) will show the Query Designer window in a customized view. Remember, however, that returning data with the Query Designer does not come without risk or cost.

Try It Out

Using Enterprise Manager, drill down to the Product table in the AdventureWorks2000 database. Right-click the table icon and, from the pop-up window, choose Open Table. A new menu option is displayed. From this menu, select Return All Rows. Figure 3-11 shows the results pane filled with product records.

For simplicity and to avoid redundancy, this section doesn't step you through the same exercise just used. In this case, you will modify a SQL expression and then view the outcome in the columns pane. Click the SQL Pane toolbar button (the one on the left labeled SQL). The SQL pane is displayed above the results grid and contains the following expression:

```
SELECT        *
FROM          Product
```

Spaces and carriage returns are ignored so don't be concerned with these. The designer makes it a point to format expressions and try to make them more readable. This isn't a concern right now. For this example, this expression reads as follows:

```
SELECT * FROM Product
```

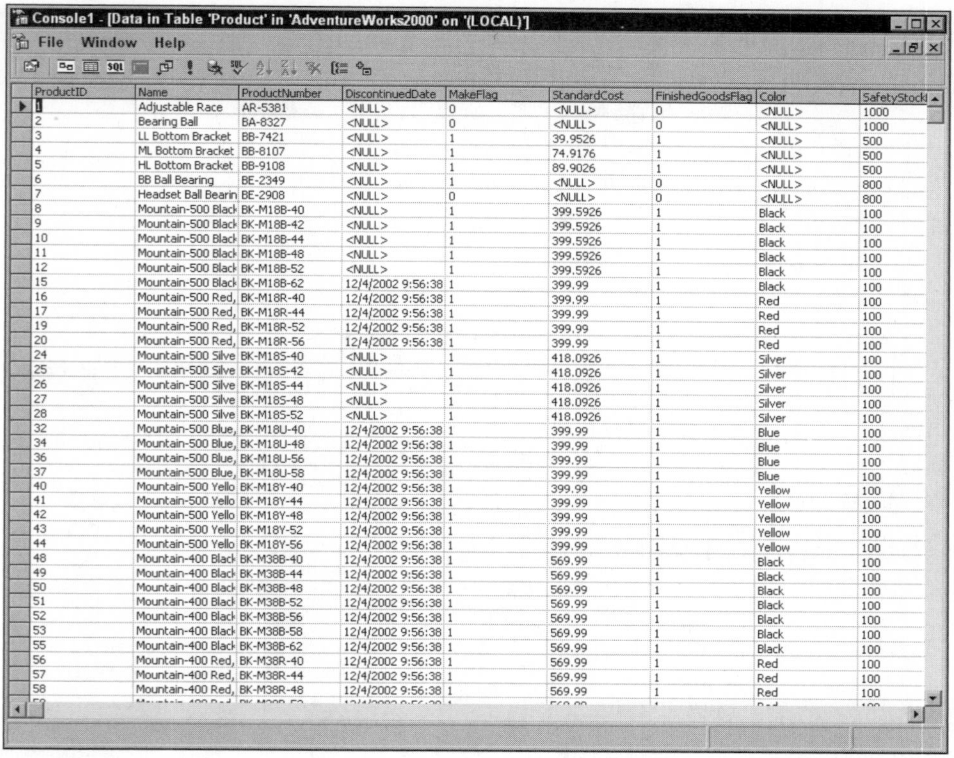

ProductID	Name	ProductNumber	DiscontinuedDate	MakeFlag	StandardCost	FinishedGoodsFlag	Color	SafetyStockl
1	Adjustable Race	AR-5381	<NULL>	0	<NULL>	0	<NULL>	1000
2	Bearing Ball	BA-8327	<NULL>	0	<NULL>	0	<NULL>	1000
3	LL Bottom Bracket	BB-7421	<NULL>	1	39.9526	1	<NULL>	500
4	ML Bottom Bracket	BB-8107	<NULL>	1	74.9176	1	<NULL>	500
5	HL Bottom Bracket	BB-9108	<NULL>	1	89.9026	1	<NULL>	500
6	BB Ball Bearing	BE-2349	<NULL>	1	<NULL>	0	<NULL>	800
7	Headset Ball Bearin	BE-2908	<NULL>	0	<NULL>	0	<NULL>	800
8	Mountain-500 Black	BK-M18B-40	<NULL>	1	399.5926	1	Black	100
9	Mountain-500 Black	BK-M18B-42	<NULL>	1	399.5926	1	Black	100
10	Mountain-500 Black	BK-M18B-44	<NULL>	1	399.5926	1	Black	100
11	Mountain-500 Black	BK-M18B-48	<NULL>	1	399.5926	1	Black	100
12	Mountain-500 Black	BK-M18B-52	<NULL>	1	399.5926	1	Black	100
15	Mountain-500 Black	BK-M18B-62	12/4/2002 9:56:38	1	399.99	1	Black	100
16	Mountain-500 Red,	BK-M18R-40	12/4/2002 9:56:38	1	399.99	1	Red	100
17	Mountain-500 Red,	BK-M18R-44	12/4/2002 9:56:38	1	399.99	1	Red	100
19	Mountain-500 Red,	BK-M18R-52	12/4/2002 9:56:38	1	399.99	1	Red	100
20	Mountain-500 Red,	BK-M18R-56	12/4/2002 9:56:38	1	399.99	1	Red	100
24	Mountain-500 Silve	BK-M18S-40	<NULL>	1	418.0926	1	Silver	100
25	Mountain-500 Silve	BK-M18S-42	<NULL>	1	418.0926	1	Silver	100
26	Mountain-500 Silve	BK-M18S-44	<NULL>	1	418.0926	1	Silver	100
27	Mountain-500 Silve	BK-M18S-48	<NULL>	1	418.0926	1	Silver	100
28	Mountain-500 Silve	BK-M18S-52	<NULL>	1	418.0926	1	Silver	100
32	Mountain-500 Blue,	BK-M18U-40	12/4/2002 9:56:38	1	399.99	1	Blue	100
34	Mountain-500 Blue,	BK-M18U-48	12/4/2002 9:56:38	1	399.99	1	Blue	100
36	Mountain-500 Blue,	BK-M18U-56	12/4/2002 9:56:38	1	399.99	1	Blue	100
37	Mountain-500 Blue,	BK-M18U-58	12/4/2002 9:56:38	1	399.99	1	Blue	100
40	Mountain-500 Yello	BK-M18Y-40	12/4/2002 9:56:38	1	399.99	1	Yellow	100
41	Mountain-500 Yello	BK-M18Y-44	12/4/2002 9:56:38	1	399.99	1	Yellow	100
42	Mountain-500 Yello	BK-M18Y-48	12/4/2002 9:56:38	1	399.99	1	Yellow	100
43	Mountain-500 Yello	BK-M18Y-52	12/4/2002 9:56:38	1	399.99	1	Yellow	100
44	Mountain-500 Yello	BK-M18Y-56	12/4/2002 9:56:38	1	399.99	1	Yellow	100
48	Mountain-400 Black	BK-M38B-40	12/4/2002 9:56:38	1	569.99	1	Black	100
49	Mountain-400 Black	BK-M38B-44	12/4/2002 9:56:38	1	569.99	1	Black	100
50	Mountain-400 Black	BK-M38B-48	12/4/2002 9:56:38	1	569.99	1	Black	100
51	Mountain-400 Black	BK-M38B-52	12/4/2002 9:56:38	1	569.99	1	Black	100
52	Mountain-400 Black	BK-M38B-56	12/4/2002 9:56:38	1	569.99	1	Black	100
53	Mountain-400 Black	BK-M38B-58	12/4/2002 9:56:38	1	569.99	1	Black	100
55	Mountain-400 Black	BK-M38B-62	12/4/2002 9:56:38	1	569.99	1	Black	100
56	Mountain-400 Red,	BK-M38R-40	12/4/2002 9:56:38	1	569.99	1	Red	100
57	Mountain-400 Red,	BK-M38R-44	12/4/2002 9:56:38	1	569.99	1	Red	100
58	Mountain-400 Red,	BK-M38R-48	12/4/2002 9:56:38	1	569.99	1	Red	100

Figure 3-11

You can add text to a new line or just append it to the existing text on the same line as long as there is at least one space between each word. Modify this statement so it reads as follows:

```
SELECT *
FROM Product
WHERE StandardCost > 100
```

Click the Run button (the exclamation mark) on the toolbar and the results should be updated to show only products with a cost greater than $100. Figure 3-12 shows these results.

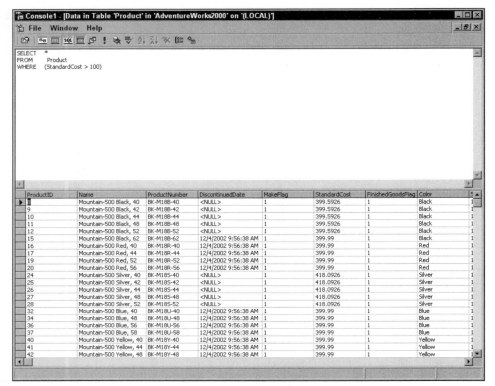

Figure 3-12

The Query Designer did a couple of things. The first thing it did was reformat the query text, placing parentheses around the text following the word WHERE. Don't be concerned with this. The Query Designer is just trying to be helpful. The results were also refreshed to show only records where the StandardCost field values met the criteria.

The last step is to modify the SQL expression (see Figure 3-13) by adding the ORDER BY clause to the end, and then click the Run button on the toolbar.

You can see that the designer added parentheses. This was actually not necessary in this simple query but it doesn't hurt anything. You can leave these on or off for the next step.

For a little variety, close the inner console window and right-click the Product table again. Choose the Open Table menu as before, but this time choose Query from the submenu, as shown in Figure 3-14.

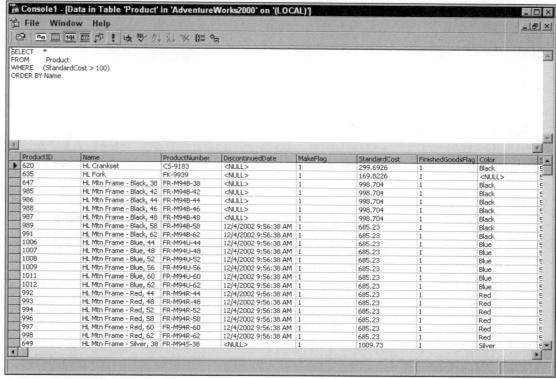

Figure 3-13

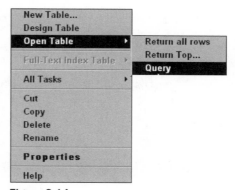

Figure 3-14

You should see the Query Designer window with four panes displayed.

Now add one more bit of text to the expression that will sort the list by the ProductNumber column. Again, add text to the expression so it looks like this:

```
SELECT        *
FROM          [dbo].[Product]
ORDER BY ProductNumber
```

Click the Run button to view the results. Figure 3-15 shows the records sorted by the product number.

Finally, take a look at the query from another viewpoint. Click the Diagram Pane (second toolbar button) and the Column Pane (third toolbar button) and you will see that the Query Designer is able to decipher your SQL expression into a graphical form. Granted, this is a very simple expression but later in the book you will see how this tool can be used to work with more complex, multi-table queries — which will save you a lot of time and effort. Figure 3-16 shows the Query Designer with all of the panes visible.

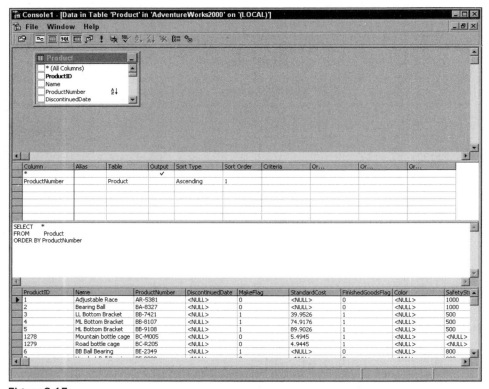

Figure 3-15

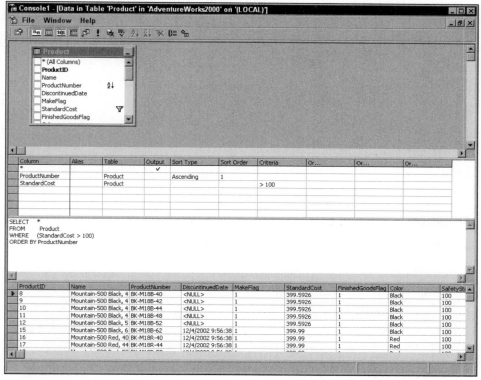

Figure 3-16

How It Works

Using the toolbar, you can show any combination of the diagram pane, columns pane, and/or SQL pane. If you were to show the SQL pane after displaying a table's rows in this manner, you would see that the expression, SELECT * FROM (table name), had been executed for you. To sort or filter the rows for this table, you can use the Query Designer options as if you were creating a query from scratch.

Note how the Query Designer represents the WHERE clause and the ORDER BY clause in the columns grid. The placement of these expressions in the columns criteria grid can be very useful when working with complex operations. The SQL WHERE clause can often be a little difficult to read without a lot of practice. The Query Designer makes it a point to add sets of parentheses to separate logical expressions (even in cases where you might not choose to use them). As you work with complex WHERE conditions, you may find it beneficial to copy and paste queries into the designer window to see how the designer parses and interprets the logic.

Query Analyzer

This tool has evolved and matured as SQL Server has grown up over the years. Previously known as the ISQL Windows Client, Query Analyzer is the main console for talking to SQL Server 2000.

To launch Query Analyzer, you can either choose SQL Query Analyzer from the Tools menu in Enterprise Manager or Query Analyzer from the Microsoft SQL Server program group on the Windows Start menu.

Although the look and feel is much like Enterprise Manager, Query Analyzer is not a snap-in for the MMC. A query window is opened by default and, like Enterprise Manager, is not maximized inside the main application window. Multiple query windows can be opened and each can be used to open or save to a script file.

Here's a quick tour. The main menu bar and toolbar gives you access to all of Query Analyzer's features. Again, the purpose here isn't to undertake a comprehensive discussion of these features, but you should be familiar with this application. This section lists each feature as it is arranged on the main menu bar.

On the File menu, you will find options to manage connections to database servers. If you initially open Query Analyzer from the Start menu, you will be prompted to connect to a server. Choosing the menu option to create a new connection will open the same dialog window. You will also find options to open and save SQL script files. A script file is a text file containing SQL commands and expressions.

On the Edit menu, you will find the standard clipboard options: Cut, Copy, and Paste. These features are useful when working with text and can also be accessed using the right-click menu and standard keyboard shortcuts. Below the standard edit features are Find, Replace, Go to line, and Bookmark features that are invaluable when debugging or editing large SQL scripts. The Edit menu also contains two template options. The first one inserts template syntax into the query window and the second gives you the ability to replace template placeholders with appropriate values. Templates are useful to give designers a standard starting place. For example, you may establish a standard template for creating stored procedures that include a block header and corporate contact information. Templates are stored as text files with the .TQL extension and can be created and saved from Query Analyzer. Several standard templates come installed with SQL Server.

The Query menu includes options to change the active database for a connection, execute, or just parse the active query window. Results can be output to unformatted text, to a grid, or to a text file. The text option uses a monospaced font. Variable-length columns are formatted in columns to use their maximum width. The Display Estimated Execution Plan or Show Execution Plan translates individual query operations into graphical icons, depicting the precedence order and data flow between each step. The Current Connection Properties menu option allows you to set query behavior options that will be applied only to the current connection.

On the Tools menu, you can manage indexes, statistics, and set program options. The Manage Indexes option allows you to create and drop indexes. The Manage Statistics option is used to create, update, or delete column statistics. The query optimizer uses statistics to construct the execution plan when a query is executed. The statistics managed by this option are not index statistics, but column statistics. Index statistics are created by SQL Server to determine whether an index is useful for a particular query. Column statistics can be created by the database administrator or automatically by SQL Server if the Auto Create Statistics database option is turned on. These column statistics help the query optimizer create optimal query plans without the overhead incurred by an index. For more information on this particular feature check out Books Online under the topic "statistical information, creating."

SQL Script and Batch Conventions

Query Analyzer can execute SQL in two ways. With either method SQL expressions are simply typed directly into the query window. You can then either execute all script in the window or select part of the script and execute only the selected statements.

You are going to use Query Analyzer to write and execute the same query as you did using the Query Designer in the previous exercise. After opening the Query Analyzer, you will connect to the local database server and then designate Northwind to be the active database. In the following Try It Out you'll enter a couple different queries and then execute them, one at a time and then all at once.

Try It Out

Open Query Analyzer from the Windows Start menu. You should find the shortcut in the Microsoft SQL Server group. You will be prompted to connect to a database server. If your database server is not installed locally, select or type the server name and then indicate whether you are using Integrated Windows security or supply a username and password. The connection dialog window is shown in Figure 3-17. To connect to your local server using integrated security you can simply type a period in the SQL Server drop-down list and then select the Windows authentication option under the Connect using option. Note that in the drop-down list labeled SQL Server, there is a default entry. At first it may not be apparent but a single period (.) signifies the local database server. This has the same meaning as (local) and LocalHost on most systems. If your SQL Server is installed locally, make no changes to these settings and click OK.

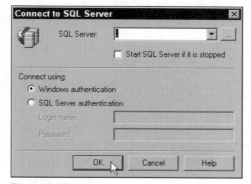

Figure 3-17

Query Analyzer is a multi-document interface, which means that the larger parent window contains one or more child windows. As you can see in Figure 3-18, the inner query window is freestanding and can be repositioned within the parent window space. This is useful if you need to manage multiple queries or different database connections. For this example, maximize this window so it occupies all of the available space. To do this, click the small rectangular maximize button in the top-right corner of the smaller window.

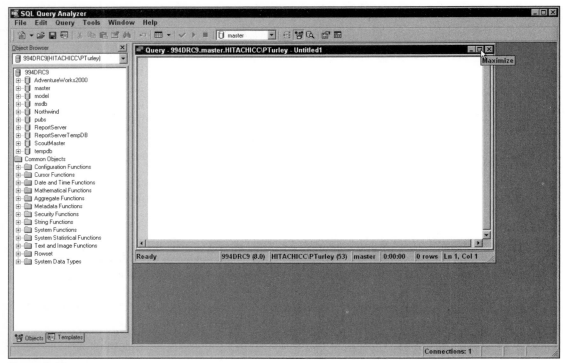

Figure 3-18

In the middle of the toolbar, you will see a drop-down list. If you drop it down, you'll see that it has a yellow drum icon next to each database name. Don't do anything with this. I just want you to know where it is. Notice that it shows that you are currently using the Master database.

Two ways exist to indicate the database with which you want to work. One method is to select the database from this drop-down list and the other is to execute the SQL statement USE *(database name)*. In the database window, type the following text:

```
USE AdventureWorks2000
GO
```

One database is always active. This code changes the active database to AdventureWorks2000. The GO statement means all of the previous statements must finish executing before any more statements can run. This is known as a *batch directive*. SQL code before or after a batch directive is called a batch. There will be more on this later.

Add some more text to the query window. Enter a carriage return and then the following SQL text:

```
SELECT * FROM Product WHERE StandardCost < 4
```

Note the various colors applied to the text. Blue text represents key words and commands that Query Analyzer recognizes. Object names are in gray text, and red text is used for literal text values. These colors are selected by default, but they can be changed to anything you want from the Options dialog on the Tools menu. On the toolbar, just to the left of the current database drop-down list, you will find a green arrow. The pop-up tip should display Execute Query (F5). Click this button or press F5 to execute the query. You will see a results grid displayed at the bottom of the Query Analyzer window.

Add another GO statement and then another SELECT statement. The entire query window content should now look like this:

```
USE AdventureWorks2000
GO
SELECT * FROM Product WHERE StandardCost < 4
GO
SELECT LocationID, Name FROM Location
GO
```

Because you've already executed the first set of SQL statements, you'll see that the current database is now AdventureWorks2000. Therefore, it's not necessary to run this again. Highlight the last SELECT line only and click the Execute button again. The results are shown in Figure 3-19.

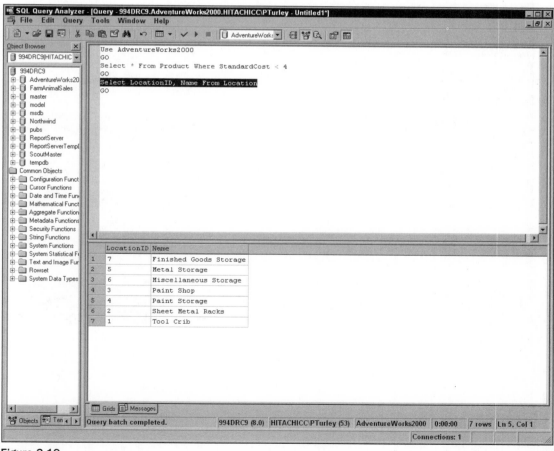

Figure 3-19

As you can see, only the highlighted expression was executed. Now deselect the highlighted text by clicking anywhere else in the query window and click the Execute button again. As Figure 3-20 shows, without any query text highlighted, both queries are executed and the results are displayed in separate result panes at the bottom of the Query Analyzer window.

Query Analyzer is where I live. After I've opened it once, I leave it open because I'm going to go back. In my opinion, the only query functionality missing from Query Analyzer is the Query Designer you looked at in Enterprise Manager. If you would like to create a query in the Query Designer and then analyze and massage the script in Query Analyzer, this is easy enough to do. Create the query in Enterprise Manager using the previous technique and then copy and paste the SQL into the query window in Query Analyzer.

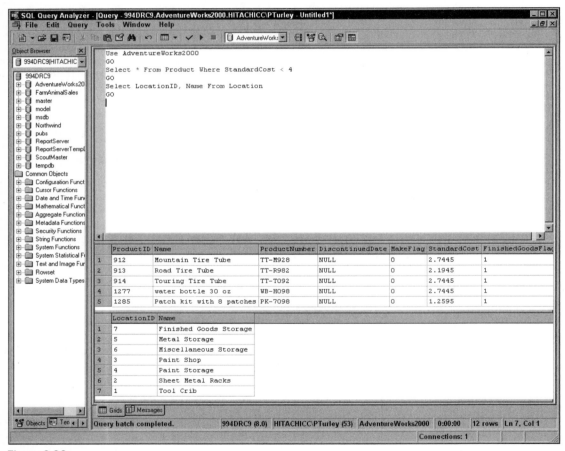

Figure 3-20

Object Browser

The most recent addition to Query Analyzer, since SQL Server 7.0, is the object browser. If you are an application developer and you have worked with Microsoft development tools, you should know that this has nothing to do with the object browser in Visual Studio or Visual Basic for Applications. However, it's a very useful feature that will provide a lot of help and save you a significant amount of work.

The object browser can be used to find practically any database object in both the system catalog and any user databases. If you need help with a system function, view, or stored procedure, this is a convenient way to learn about the input arguments and data types you will need to call or use these objects. You can also generate the calling script for any object.

Let's step through a few scenarios. These are not complete walk-through exercises, just simple examples.

Hypothetically, say that I know my database contains a table with a name containing the word "sales." I could search the system tables if I knew how they were structured and what columns to look at. Fortunately, this isn't necessary. Located in the Master database is a set of system views with names prefixed with INFORMATION_SCHEMA. Using the object browser, I drill down into the Master database and browse through the views. I know that the Information Schema views are used to return easy-to-read metadata about various database objects. I find the INFORMATION_SCHEMA.TABLES view and expand this node to see the columns. This tells me that the name of the table can be found in the Table_Name column. Armed with this information, I type a query expression into Query Analyzer: SELECT * FROM INFORMATION_SCHEMA.TABLES WHERE Table_Name LIKE '%sales%'. The results show any tables with a name including the word "sales" and their associated properties.

I would like to insert rows into the Products table but I don't know all of the column names. I use the object browser to find the Products table in the appropriate database, right-click the table name, and select Script Object to Clipboard as Insert from the pop-up menu. This generates SQL script and places it on the in-memory clipboard. Next, I place the cursor in the query window and use the keyboard shortcut, Control+V, to paste the script into the query window. The script includes placeholders for the literal values I replace to perform the insert operation.

Using Books Online

Books Online is the user documentation and help system for SQL Server 2000. From the graphical tools for SQL Server, such as Enterprise Manager or Query Analyzer, just press the F1 key to open Books Online. In Query Analyzer, you can also highlight key words in your SQL script and press Shift+F1 to navigate to the specific help topic related to the key word.

Here's a little-known secret: Books Online was updated extensively after the release of SQL Server 2000 and is not updated along with the service packs. To update Books Online you must download the latest version from the Microsoft SQL Server web site at www.microsoft.com/sql. If you don't have the update, I recommend that you download and install it. The updated version has corrected many inconsistencies and added a very large amount of new data, especially about the extended XML capabilities that have been added to SQL Server 2000.

OSQL Command-line Utility

The OSQL utility is a command-line interface used to run scripts and queries for SQL Server 2000. This program can be used at a command prompt in any folder. Like most command-line utilities, it is self-documenting. To run OSQL, open a command prompt window. One way to do this is to click the Windows Start button and then select Run from the program menu. In the Run dialog, type **CMD** and click OK. A list of all command-line options can be displayed by using the -? Switch (type **OSQL -?**). Figure 3-21 shows the complete help listing.

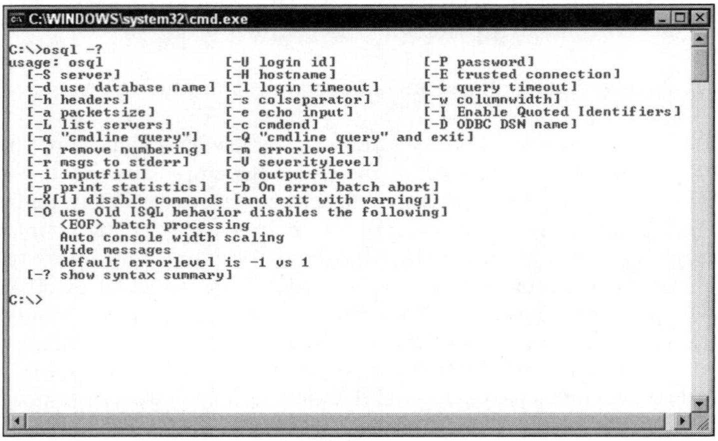

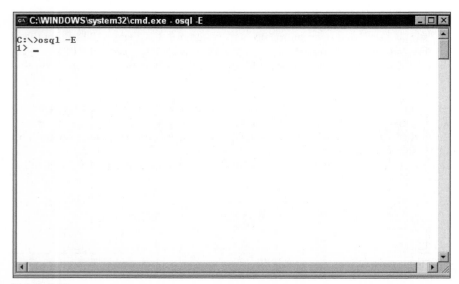

Figure 3-21

To execute a query, first create a connection to the local SQL Server using Windows integrated security with the command **OSQL –E**. The E stands for Enterprise security, which means the same thing as Windows integrated security. This returns a numbered batch prompt. This is OSQL's way of saying "First command, please." You can see this in Figure 3-22.

Figure 3-22

Each prompt will be enumerated until you issue a GO command. At this point, all commands in the preceding batch will be executed and then a new batch begins at line 1. Any SQL statements may be executed at the OSQL prompt. It is necessary to set the current database before working with data. This is done with the USE statement, followed by the GO command, as shown in Figure 3-23.

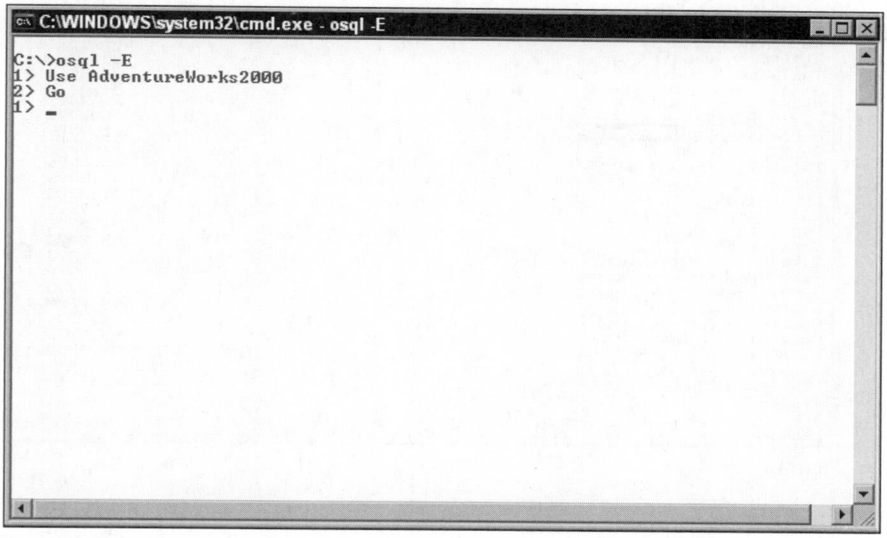

```
C:\WINDOWS\system32\cmd.exe - osql -E

C:\>osql -E
1> Use AdventureWorks2000
2> Go
1> _
```

Figure 3-23

Note how the batch line numbers start over after the GO command is issued. This example uses a simple SELECT statement so you can see the return values from a query. The command window before I press Enter is shown in Figure 3-24.

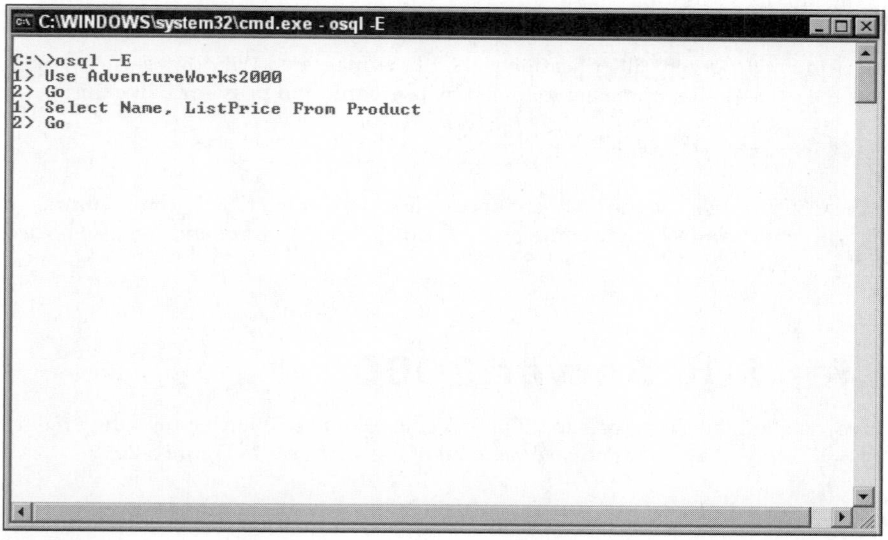

```
C:\WINDOWS\system32\cmd.exe - osql -E

C:\>osql -E
1> Use AdventureWorks2000
2> Go
1> Select Name, ListPrice From Product
2> Go
```

Figure 3-24

Figure 3-25 shows the command window after I enter the second GO command and press the Enter key.

```
C:\WINDOWS\system32\cmd.exe - osql -E
Full-finger Gloves, M                                    47.4875
Full-finger Gloves, L                                    47.4875
Classic Vest, S                                          79.3750
Classic Vest, M                                          79.3750
Classic Vest, L                                          79.3750
AWC logo cap                                             11.2375
Hydration pack -70oz                                     68.7375
Taillights - battery powered                             17.4875
Headlights - dual-beam                                   43.7375
Headlights - weatherproof                                56.2375
water bottle 30 oz                                        6.2375
Mountain bottle cage                                     12.4875
Road bottle cage                                         11.2375
Patch kit with 8 patches                                  2.8625
Sport-100 helmet, Blue                                   43.7375
Cable lock                                               31.2500
Mini-pump                                                24.9875
Mountain pump                                            31.2375
Hitch rack - 4 bike                                     150.0000
Bike wash - dissolver                                     9.9375
Touring-Panniers, large                                 156.2500
Fender set - mountain                                    27.4750
All-purpose bike stand                                  198.7500
Sport-100 helmet, Red                                    43.7375
Sport-100 helmet, Black                                  43.7375
HL Road Frame - Red, 58                                1789.3750

(999 rows affected)
1> _
```

Figure 3-25

As you see, this is a no-frills environment. It's not as elegant as the Query Analyzer but it's also very simple and uncluttered. System and database administrators often go to the command prompt to run scripted maintenance tasks. Executing a script file is quite easy. As you've seen, scripts are most easily created from Enterprise Manager and Query Analyzer. You could also use Notepad to create a script file. After saving the SQL text to a script file, simply execute OSQL and pass the script file as a parameter, like this:

```
OSQL -E -I C:\MyScript.sql
```

If you are using SQL Server authentication rather than Integrated Windows security, the command line would use the –U and –P parameters followed by username and password, like this:

```
OSQL -Uusername -Ppassword
```

To close the OSQL utility, use the EXIT command. If you executed OSQL from a command prompt window, this will return control to the command prompt. The EXIT command can also be used to close this window.

Tools for SQL Server 2005

If you have installed the client tools for SQL Server 2005, you will have a cascading menu on the Start menu for SQL Server 2005 containing some or all of the shortcuts in Figure 3-26.

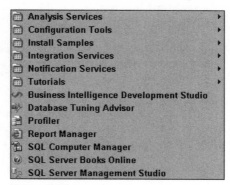

Figure 3-26

Some of these items are installed with optional SQL Server components. We're concerned only with the iconized shortcuts in the lower section of this menu. These are described in the following table.

Menu Option	Description
Business Intelligence Development Studio	This tool uses a set of project templates in the Microsoft Development Environment (the same interface as Visual Studio.NET 2005). It is used to create and manage database queries and objects, Reporting Services reports, Analysis Services cubes, and Integration Services packages (formerly called DTS).
Database Tuning Advisor	The Tuning Advisor is the successor to the Index Tuning Wizard in SQL Server 2000. It takes the features of the SQL Server Profiler to the next level by actively monitoring database sessions. These sessions are analyzed and then the Advisor suggests configuration changes and enhancements to improve database efficiency and performance. The new interface simplifies the complex process of running workload query scripts and profiler traces to test, among other elements, index usage, execution plan efficiency, caching, and I/O costing.
Profiler	The SQL Server Profiler is an extensive troubleshooting and optimization tool. It can be used to monitor a broad range of database activity, or to pinpoint specific events. Operations can be captured and recorded for later playback. Events and activities can be recorded as scripts or logs to text files or to a database.
Report Manager	This is the main web browser interface for Reporting Services. It is used for both report and folder management and for viewing reports. Report server administrators use this application to define security and server configuration settings. Users can browse and view reports, create subscriptions and report snapshots, and export reports in various formats.

Table continued on following page

Menu Option	Description
SQL Computer Manager	This management console replaces several utilities in earlier SQL Server versions. With it, administrators can configure network libraries, services, and maintenance tasks.
SQL Server Books Online	SQL Server Books Online (BOL) is the online help system for all SQL Server tools and features. Books Online opens in a separate window with options to search keywords and browse the index of topics. To launch Books Online from within a SQL Server tool, press F1. Context-sensitive help is available from within Query Analyzer when you highlight a keyword and then press Shift+F1.
SQL Server Management Studio	Management Studio combines the best features of Enterprise Manager, Query Analyzer, and Analysis Services Manager with the new capabilities of SQL Server 2005. This is the central management and design interface for all SQL Server, databases, objects, and various types of queries.

SQL Computer Manager

The SQL Computer Manager combines the functionality of the Server Network Utility, Client Network Utility, and Service Manager from SQL Server 2000 into one central tool. With this Microsoft Management Console (MMC) snap-in, the database administrator can start, stop, and pause any SQL Server–related service without having to scroll through the huge list of services that are presented with the standard Windows Services management console. The SQL Computer Manager can also be used to manage server and client network libraries by enabling and disabling supported libraries and specifying the individual settings for the libraries such as TCP port assignments and IP listeners.

The SQL Computer Manager is a very straightforward interface. Each SQL Server–related service and network configuration is listed in the tree view, as shown in Figure 3-27, and can be controlled using right-click menu selections.

SQL Server Management Studio

The Management Studio is specifically used for SQL Server and offers more functionality and greater flexibility than Enterprise Manager did in earlier versions. The Microsoft Management Console interface, used by Enterprise Manager and several other administrative utilities, is a very generic approach to system management that has been outgrown by an application as robust as SQL Server.

When you open the Management Studio, you are prompted to connect to a server. When working with the local server using standard Windows security, you can simply leave the default settings and connect with the Connect button.

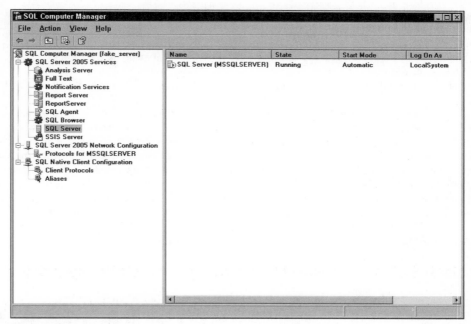

Figure 3-27

The Amazing Floating, Docking, Hiding Tool Windows

At first glance, this interface looks a bit like Visual Studio (with dockable tool windows that can auto-show and hide themselves, and can be pinned down using the familiar thumbtack icons). That's because Microsoft has designed the Management Studio to use the Visual Studio 2005 shell. SQL Server 2005 and Visual Studio 2005 have been jointly developed so that there is seamless interaction between the two environments. This new developer-centric view of database management comes as quite a shock to many database administrators who have considered themselves more of an engineer than a developer. However, once the initial shock wears off, most have learned to love the new interface for the amount of control and flexibility it brings to database administration. When you open the Microsoft SQL Server Management Studio in the default view, you will see two tool windows docked on the left side. These can be undocked, moved, and hidden as you please. Note the three little icons in the top-right corner of each window (see Figure 3-28):

❑   **Down arrow** — If you click the down arrow, the pop-up menu will display options for working with this window.

❑   **Thumbtack** — The thumbtack is used to pin the window down (when the tack is positioned vertically). If a window is unpinned, it will auto-hide when the mouse pointer is moved away, leaving a small icon on a vertical tab. To show a hidden window, simply hover the mouse pointer over the tab. I generally will pin a window down if I'm going to use it frequently and then unpin to hide it when I need the screen space for other things. With a little practice, I think you'll find that this can be a convenient feature, especially if you are working on a small monitor.

❑   **X** — The familiar X icon will close the tool window entirely. Rather than closing windows, I recommend that you use the auto-hide feature so you can easily show the window when you need it in the future.

If you do close a window, or you need one of the windows that is not shown in the designer by default, these can be opened from the View menu.

To reposition a tool window, you can also just grab it by the title bar using the mouse pointer, and then drag to undock and move it around the design surface. Something interesting happens when you do this. Before showing you how to use the docking tools, allow me to provide some context for this feature.

Between 1997 and 2001, I spent a good deal of my time traveling around the United States teaching programming classes at Microsoft certified training facilities. Visual Basic had become wildly popular and I taught five or six Visual Basic courses on a regular basis. One particular course, the introductory-level VB course, became very routine for me. On the first day of the class, I would introduce the Visual Studio Integrated Development Environment and walk students through some exercises to get them accustomed to the interface. I explained that the various tool windows could be undocked by dragging them around with the mouse. When you dragged the window close to the edge of the container window, it would stick to that edge of the window. It took about 2 minutes to show the students how to do this and then another 20 minutes to go around the room and help everyone put everything back. It was a little difficult to get the windows to stick back in their original location.

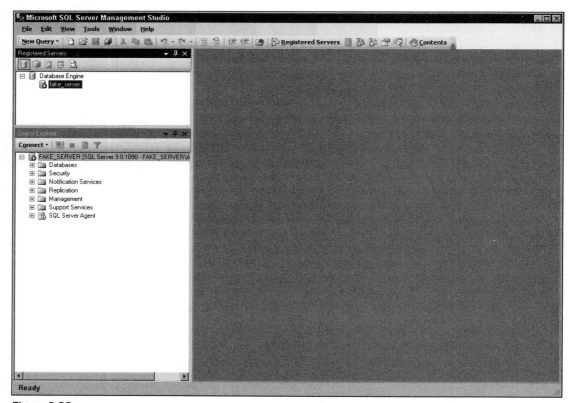

Figure 3-28

When a window is undocked and you drag it around the main window, guide diamonds are displayed — like points of a compass — to assist with the docking window placement (see Figure 3-29). When you hover over one of the guide diamonds, the docking target area of the window is designated with a translucent shaded rectangle.

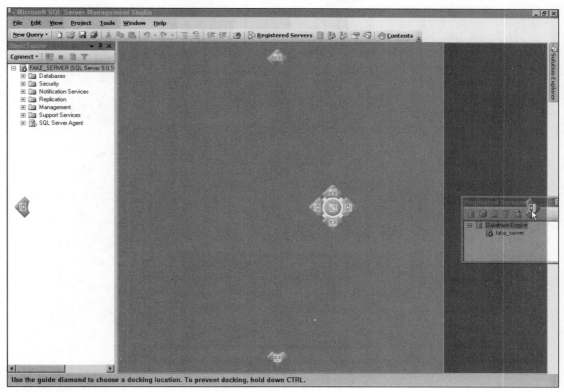

Figure 3-29

As you see in Figure 3-30, you can also use the guide diamonds in the center cluster of the window. If a window is already docked in that area, using the center guide will dock your window adjacent to the existing window.

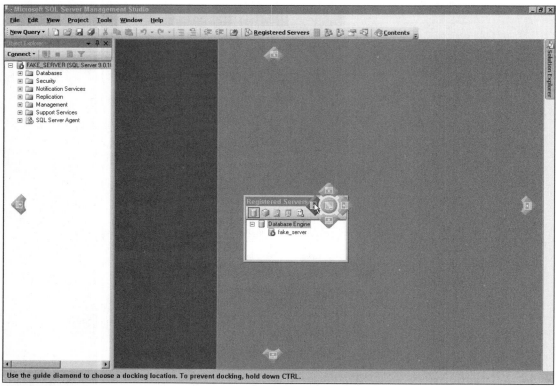

Figure 3-30

The result of the previous docking selection is shown in Figure 3-31.

Figure 3-31

If you hover over an existing docked window, a separate set of guides will appear, allowing you to dock within this space or to create tabbed documents where the windows share screen real estate with other windows in the same space (see Figure 3-32).

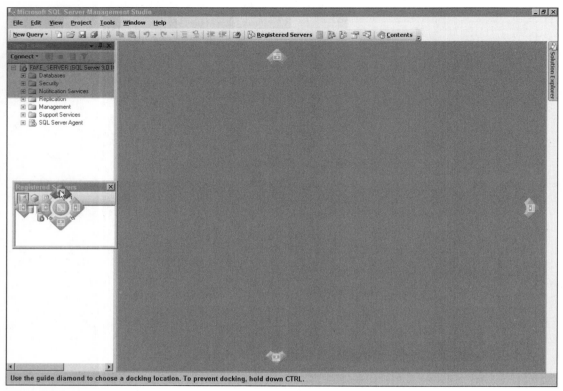

Figure 3-32

Now my tool windows are back where they started (see Figure 3-33). If you get into trouble and can't place a window where you want it, click to set focus to the window and then use the Window menu on the standard menu bar to toggle the window back to either Floating or Dockable. This should allow you to reposition the window however you wish.

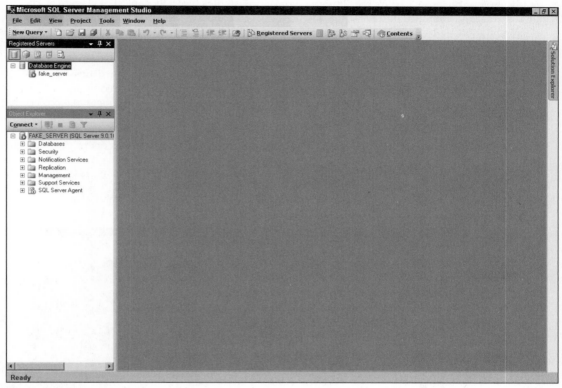

Figure 3-33

What's in a Project?

The project and solutions paradigms have become commonplace among application developers using Microsoft programming tools. These same concepts are now extended into the database design space. These concepts are actually quite simple. A project is simply a collection of files that support a common application or purpose. In the programming world, project files typically consist of class files, code modules, forms, and configuration files. In a database project, common files can include scripts, diagrams, documentation, and Integration Services packages. The project is simply the glue that binds all of these files together.

A solution is simply a catalog of one or more projects. Often, an application is constructed in different phases and there may be multiple designers or developers in charge of different components, perhaps even different versions of the same application or database. Each of these may equate to a project that rolls-up into a larger solution.

You can create a new project by selecting New ⇨ Project from the File menu. This opens the New Project dialog shown in Figure 3-34. Select the icon to create a SQL Server Scripts project, give the project a name, and either verify or change the path. I typically keep all of my projects in a special folder on a network share. By default, files are saved in folders created under My Documents\SQL Server Management Studio\Projects\.

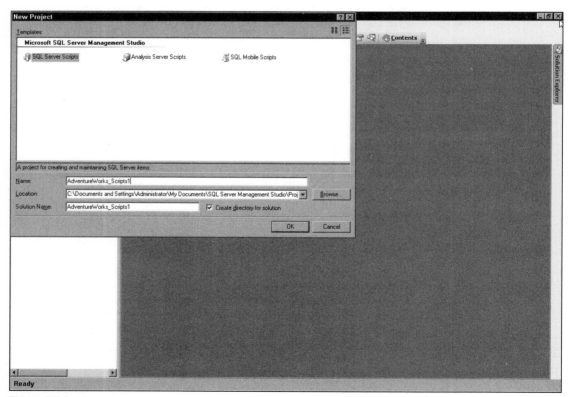

Figure 3-34

It's important to note that this path is user profile–specific. In other words, if another user were to log in to the same computer, these files would not be available at the same path. If you plan to share projects between users, it's advisable to use a network share or common folder.

Object Explorer

This window displays a tree view of database objects, somewhat similar to the Enterprise Manager for SQL Server 2000. Connections can be made to multiple database servers and each server is displayed at the root level of the tree with a small icon to indicate the state of the server. In Figure 3-35, the small arrow (green on screen) indicates that SQL Server is running. Folders represent groups of like objects or special features. Click the plus sign icon to expand a folder to view the items in this container. Expanding a specific database folder reveals folders representing the related Tables, Views, and other objects. Right-click any folder to create an object of that type and right-click any object for options related to that object.

If you continue to expand, drilling down to a table and then the columns for that table, you will see that summary information is displayed for each column (see Figure 3-36).

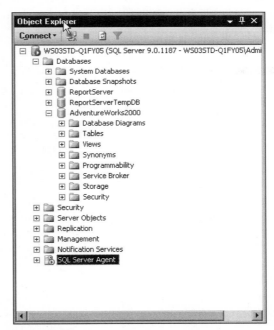

Figure 3-35

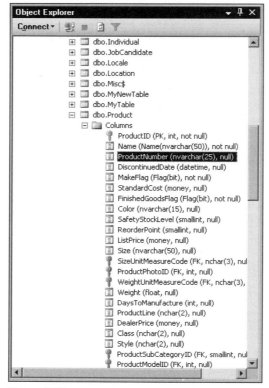

Figure 3-36

Detailed information is available for the selected column as well as for a variety of other objects. Right-click the item in the tree view to see all of the related options (see Figure 3-37). Select the Properties menu item to view and modify the properties. With a little experience, you should find this interface very intuitive and easy to use.

Writing Queries

A number of different types of queries are used to return results from different types of data sources and data structures. Each of these specialized query types is now brought into one tool. This includes the following:

❑ Database Engine Queries in Transact-SQL

❑ Analysis Services queries using Multi-Dimensional Expressions (MDX)

❑ Analysis Services Mining Model queries using Data Mining Expressions (DMX)

❑ Analysis Services configuration scripts using XML for Analysis (XMLA)

Creating a query in SQL Server Management Studio involves defining a connection to a data source and providing a design window. A query can be saved to a script file or simply used as a temporary workspace. To create a new SQL query, use the New Query drop-down button. From the menu, select Database Engine Query, as shown in Figure 3-38.

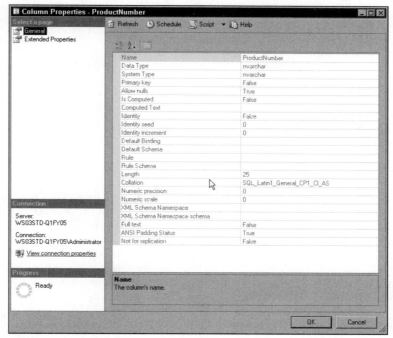

Figure 3-37

Figure 3-38

This opens another connection dialog for the query. Even if you intend for the query to run against the same data source that you specified earlier for the main Management Studio interface, you are prompted for this information when creating a new query.

With the new query window open, you must specify the database you would like to use. You can do this can in one of two ways. With a query window open, the SQL Editor toolbar is displayed with a drop-down list of available databases from the current data source (server). Drop this list down and select the database. All of the examples in this book for SQL Server 2005 use the AdventureWorks2000 database (see Figure 3-39). Using the database drop-down list has the same effect as typing the SQL command **USE (***database name***)**.

Figure 3-39

Now for a simple query: To list all of the columns in all of the rows in the Product table, type the following SQL expression:

```
SELECT * FROM Product
```

Go ahead and type this text into the query window and click the Execute button on the SQL Editor toolbar. That's the button with the red exclamation mark. When you do this, your computer will go to work and look up about 500 product records. You'll probably see the hard disk light come on for a few seconds while SQL Server performs this action. While the query is running, a small, animated icon of a spinning world is displayed in the status bar at the bottom of the window. When it's done, summary information will be displayed with the running time and the number of records returned. The first few rows are displayed in a new window pane at the bottom of the Management Studio window, as shown in Figure 3-40.

Anything else that you would do to retrieve data will likely be an extension of this simple exercise.

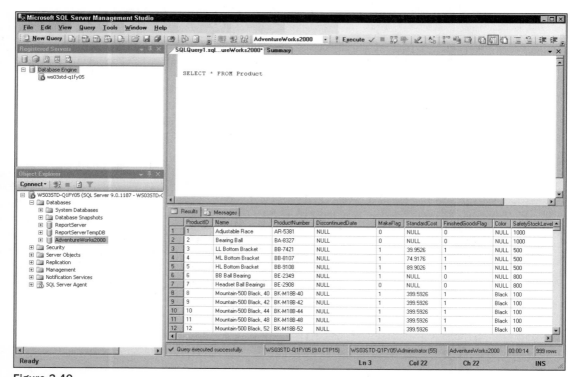

Figure 3-40

Scripting Options

SQL statements can be very verbose and often require a lot of typing. Much of this work can be minimized by letting the Management Studio do the work for you. Most common actions can be scripted automatically using a few simple menu selections. There are several different methods for scripting a query and many actions to perform so I'm not going to demonstrate them all. The menu selections are self-explanatory for the most part. The following Try It Out should get you started.

Try It Out

Using the Object Explorer, expand the AdventureWorks2000 database and then the Tables folder. Under this folder, you will see a list of all of the tables in the database. You want to generate script to return all of the columns in the Contact table. Scroll down until you see dbo.Contact. Right-click this item and navigate through the menus, as you see in Figure 3-41. You want to generate a SELECT statement to read and return rows from the table. You also want to display the script in a new query window, so choose New Query Editor Window.

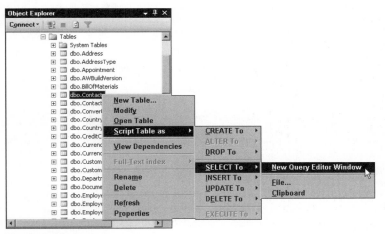

Figure 3-41

The SELECT statement is generated and displayed in a new window (see Figure 3-42). You should know that many options when using SQL can affect the way a query looks on the screen, but don't matter that much to SQL Server. The automated script is formatted to make it easy to read. You should note a couple things about the format of this SQL script. First of all, the square brackets containing column names are optional. This is done so SQL Server can use names containing spaces. There are none here so it really doesn't matter. Also, take a look at the last line starting with the word FROM. The script includes the database name, schema name, and then the table name separated by periods. The database name is optional when you have elected to set this as a current database. Auto-generated script is generally very descriptive.

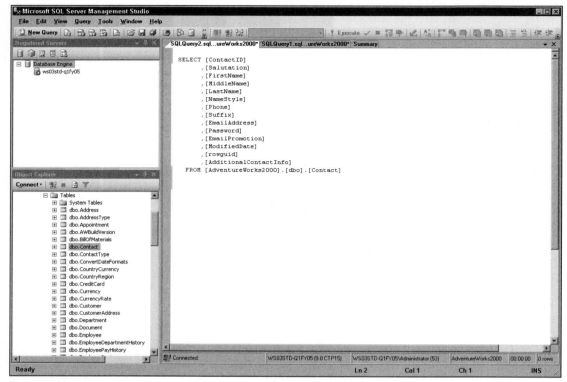

Figure 3-42

Finally, execute this query using the Execute button on the SQL Editor toolbar. After a few seconds, results will be displayed in a grid at the bottom of the window. Look at the status bar in Figure 3-43: nearly 20,000 contact rows were returned in about 2 seconds. Of course, the time it takes to run a query will depend on several factors, so your results may be different from mine.

Using the Graphical Query Designer

The single-table queries written so far are fairly simple. Now you can start building a more complex query. To use the graphical query designer, right-click the query window and choose Design Query in Editor... from the menu. If you need to edit existing query text, you can highlight the SQL and use this same technique to make changes using the query builder. Another method for invoking the graphical query designer is to start creating a new view. You won't actually save your query as a view. If you read the previous section about the SQL Server 2000 design tools, I'm going to repeat myself a bit here. The following Try It Out demonstrates building a query using the AdventureWorks sample database, but the mechanics of this tool are identical to those used in Enterprise Manager with some minor enhancements. For consistency, I'll use the first technique in the following example.

Try It Out

Using the Object Explorer, right-click the Views folder under the AdventureWorks2000 database. On the pop-up menu, select New View, as shown in Figure 3-44.

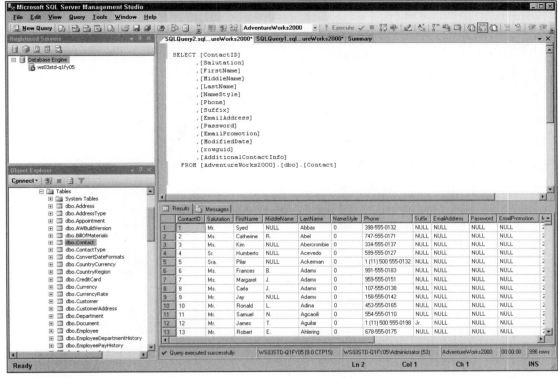

Figure 3-43

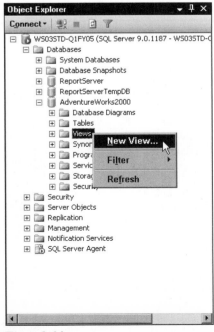

Figure 3-44

The query window changes to a window split into four different panes. I'll explain how each of these panes is used as you continue. On top of the new designer window, the Add Table dialog (shown in Figure 3-45) is displayed to prompt you for the tables to be used in this query. Note that the schema names are displayed in parentheses following the table names. This is of little consequence since all of the tables in the AdventureWorks2000 database are in the dbo schema. You can either double-click each table one at a time or hold down the Ctrl key and click to select multiple tables. For this exercise, choose the Product, ProductCategory, and ProductSubCategory tables to be added to this query. Click the Add button to add these tables to the query and then click Close when you're done.

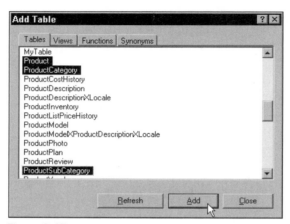

Figure 3-45

Four panes in the designer window, each represents the query in a different way:

❑   Diagram pane .

❑   Columns pane

❑   SQL pane

❑   Results pane

The first three panes are synchronized, and changes made to the query in any one of these panes will be reflected in the others. A window graphically representing each table is placed into the top-most diagram pane of the designer. The graphical query designer draws lines from column names in each of these tables, with a diamond on each. This represents an inner join derived from the existence of corresponding relationships that exist in the database design. For example, in the definition for the ProductCategory table, a relationship, or foreign key constraint, is defined between the ProductCategoryID column and the ProductCategoryID column in the ProductSubCategory table. The Query Designer is smart enough to translate this relationship into a join statement, between these tables. The diamond tells you that this is an inner join and that records will only be returned if corresponding values exist in the joined columns for both of these tables.

One thing that can be a little confusing when discussing your interaction with the columns pane is the use of the word Columns. Each column that is to be returned from the query is displayed as a row in the columns pane grid. It would be convenient if they could be referred to as fields rather than columns;

however, the tool makes reference to "Columns" in the first column of the grid. This means that in our conversations regarding this interface, we are left to distinguish the columns (or fields) of the query from the columns in the grid, which represent attributes or characteristics to the query columns.

The View Designer toolbar is displayed above this window. If you have used the graphical query designer in Enterprise Manager, Access, or earlier versions of Visual Studio, you'll probably notice that the toolbar icons have been given a facelift and that a new button has been added. The right-most button will add a derived table expression. You'll learn about derived tables and subqueries in Chapter 6. The View Designer toolbar is shown in Figure 3-46.

Figure 3-46

Hover the mouse pointer over each button to show a pop-up tooltip and display a short caption describing the button's feature. The toolbar options are described in the following table.

Icon	Toolbar Button	Description	
	Diagram Pane	Toggle show/hide diagram pane	
	Criteria Pane	Toggle show/hide criteria pane (previously called the columns pane)	
	SQL Pane	Toggle show/hide SQL pane	
	Results Pane	Toggle show/hide results pane	
	Execute	Execute the query and display results	
	Verify SQL	Check the SQL expression for errors	
	Group By	Add the Group By SQL clause and aggregate functions to the expression	
	Add Table	Open a dialog to add tables, views, or user-defined functions to the query	
	Add New Derived Table	Add a derived table/subquery expression to the query	

To choose columns to be returned, check the boxes in the table windows in the order that they appear in Figure 3-47. As you do this, these column names will be added to the columns pane and to the SELECT clause in the SQL pane. Note that there are three different Name columns between the three tables. Because the column names in a query must be unique, the designer creates aliased names for the ProductSubCategory and ProductCategory Name columns as Expr1 and Expr2. This satisfies this rule but the aliases' names aren't exactly optimal.

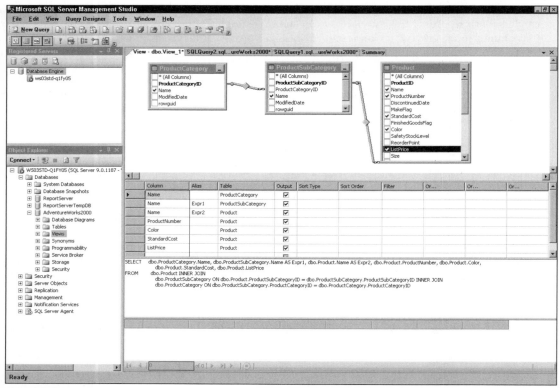

Figure 3-47

I'd prefer to use more intuitive names for the three Name columns. In the columns pane (second section of the designer), add or replace the text with the alias names from Figure 3-48. Call the ProductCategory.Name Category. The ProductSubCategory.Name is SubCategory, and the Product.Name will be known as ProductName. Also, under the Sort Order column, type or select the values 1, 2, and 3 for these three columns.

	Column	Alias	Table	Output	Sort Type	Sort Order	Filter	Or...	Or...	Or...
	Name	Category	ProductCategory	☑	Ascending	1				
	Name	SubCategory	ProductSubCategory	☑	Ascending	2				
▶	Name	ProductName	Product	☑	Ascending	3				
	ProductNumber		Product	☑						
	Color		Product	☑						
	StandardCost		Product	☑						
	ListPrice		Product	☑						

Figure 3-48

The query is now ready to return data. The Execute button has a red exclamation mark icon. You can also use keyboard shortcuts: Ctrl+E or the F5 key. Click the Execute button and you should see rows returned in the grid in the fourth pane of the designer window (see Figure 3-49).

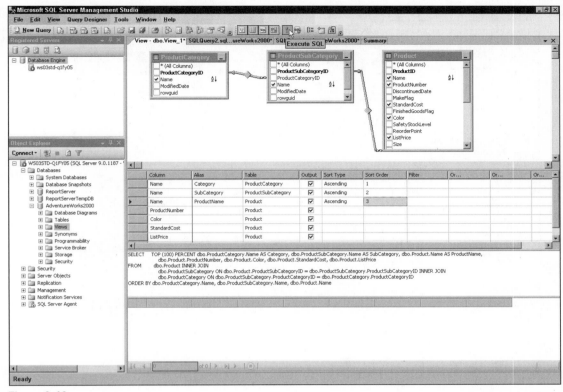

Figure 3-49

The query results are displayed in the Results grid, in the fourth section of the designer window (see Figure 3-50). If you leave this window open and have a large number of rows returned from a query, you may be prompted by the designer to clear these results and free-up memory on your workstation.

You can experiment by adding and removing columns and changing the sort order and alias names. I didn't intend to save this query as a view or script file so if you close the query window, just indicate that you don't want to save changes. Remember that to get to the graphical query designer, you told the SQL Management Studio that you wanted to create a view.

Views and other database programming objects are discussed in Chapter 10.

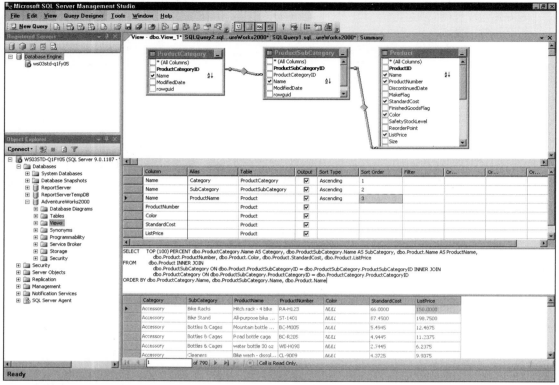

Figure 3-50

Using Templates

Unless you have a perfect memory, there will be many times in your journey with SQL Server that you will need some assistance. I'd say that about ninety-eight percent of the SQL I write is from memory because the vast majority of the time, I need to do fairly common things: Select, Insert, Update, Delete, and so on. The rest of the time, I'll either need to jog my memory or learn to use a command I haven't had to use before. I have enough trouble just remembering the names of my kids let alone how to rebuild an index with a specific fill-factor. So, I'll either need to look this up in Books Online and/or go find an example. Most of the time, it's more helpful to just to see the script than it is to learn about the command and exactly how it affects the mechanics of the database engine.

Script templates simply provide a starting point for queries. A template is really just a piece of script saved to a file that you open in the SQL Query Designer and then modify to suit your needs. The Templates Explorer window is optional. Use the View menu or Templates Explorer button on the toolbar to enable this window if it isn't already visible (see Figure 3-51). Templates are organized into categories. Simply expand the folder icons on the tree view to find the template you are looking for.

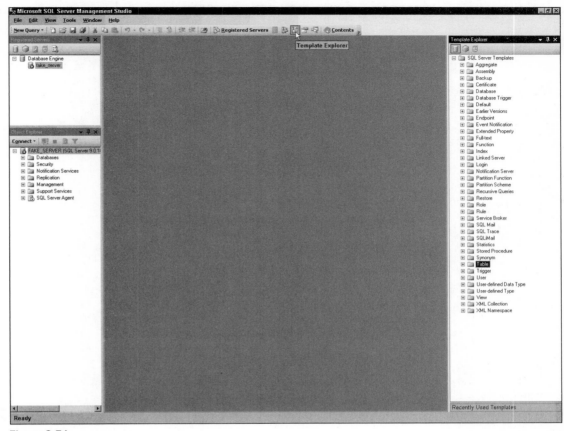

Figure 3-51

Now, create a query to add columns to an existing table. This is easy to do using a template. Find the folder for table-related templates, expand it, and then find the template labeled Add Column. Right-click this item to display the pop-up menu and select Open to use the template in a new query, as shown in Figure 3-52.

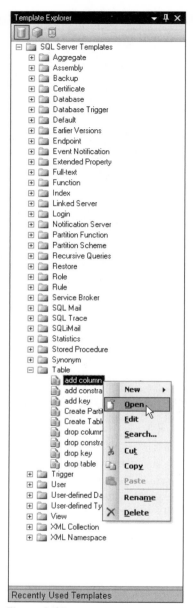

Figure 3-52

This action opens a new query editor window with a copy of the template. Note the color-coding used to help distinguish keywords, commands, and comments in the SQL text (see Figure 3-53). With the skeleton of the query written for you, it's a fairly simple matter to replace the generic placeholders with your own text and then execute the query.

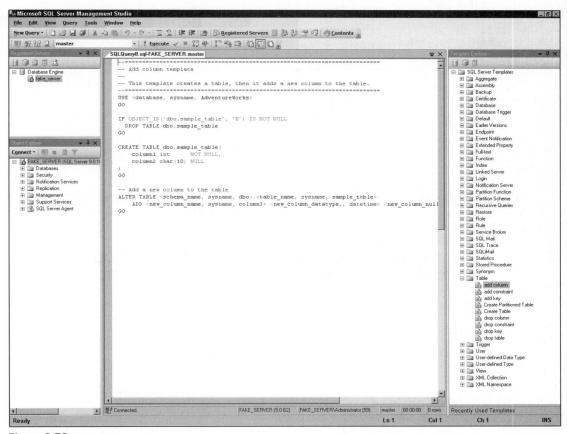

Figure 3-53

Business Intelligence Development Studio

SQL Server 2005 offers one more tool in its arsenal of design and solution development applications. This one is the granddaddy of them all and represents the final merger of database administration and software development tools. Whereas the Management Studio is implemented in a Visual Studio shell, the Business Intelligence Studio is an actual instance of Microsoft Visual Studio and is a very robust application used by application developers to create desktop software, web site solutions, and business components. So, what's it doing in the suite of tools installed with SQL Server? To answer this question effectively, you need to understand Microsoft's vision for the present and future state of business solutions. Since the inception of Microsoft Visual Basic in the very early 1990s, Bill Gates has promoted the notion of making software development capabilities accessible to just about anyone who could drive a computer mouse. He has evangelized empowering the information worker by bringing advanced design and development capabilities to the desktop and making them intuitive and easier to use. In the latter part of the last decade (and century) we saw disparate programming language tools merge into toolkit suites such as Visual Studio, for use by many types of application developers. Now we see the same tool being placed into the hands of database professionals.

I think that this stage in the evolution of this tool is, in large part, a reflection of our changing industry. Not long ago, the lines between programmer, architect, and database administrator were well defined. We stayed out of each other's way and didn't tread on another's turf. The IT industry shakedowns following the dot com bust and economic recession, along with maturing technology, have redefined professional roles. Now we wear more hats and are driven to do more with less. I'd submit that we have the opportunity to do more with more: more information, more computing power, better-utilized talent, and, yes; more bandwidth. We all have more bandwidth to move information around but we're expected to use more of our mental bandwidth to take on more and get more done more effectively than before. Regardless of the reasons, here we are and the industry demands tools that let us do it all from our desktops.

What can you do with this amazing tool? Just about anything related to designing and developing software and database solutions. In a standard installation of SQL Server 2005, you will have the Business Intelligence Projects item you see in the left-most pane of Figure 3-54. After installing SQL Server 2005, I also installed Visual Studio, which has added additional project type templates to the integrated development environment.

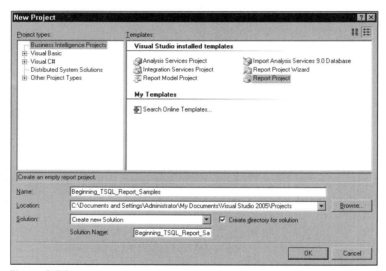

Figure 3-54

You have several opportunities to apply your SQL skills in application development and data presentation solutions that you create using this environment. One such opportunity is to design reports with SQL Server Reporting Services. Reports can use parameterized queries to filter data and provide advanced reporting features (see Figure 3-55). The report designer contains an integrated SQL query designer that will enable you to create, debug, and test queries for reporting.

Chapter 12 leads you, step-by-step, through the process of creating a report in the Business Intelligence Studio. This is an effective means to quickly take the results of a query and present them to users in the right format (see Figure 3-56). Reporting Services enables you to transform data into useful information, delivered to a user's web browser, desktop, and Office applications. Reports may be viewed on demand or by automated e-mail or file share subscriptions.

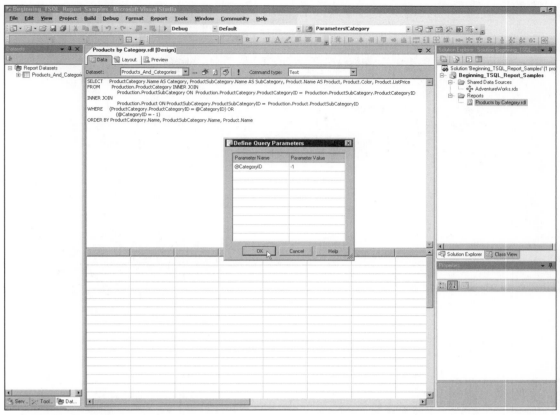

Figure 3-55

SQLCMD Command-line Utility

There are times when a system administrator just needs to get the job done and execute SQL script without the frills of a desktop user interface. SQL Server 7 and 2000 had this capability in a simple command-line utility called OSQL. OSQL also ships with SQL Server 2005 for backward compatibility and is part of the standard installation package. However, OSQL doesn't support some of the new capabilities introduced in SQL Server 2005. The recommended tool for command-line scripting is now called SQLCMD. This can be executed in a command prompt window for any folder on your database server. This is most definitely the old-school method for executing SQL, but sometimes it's actually easier than using newer, more sophisticated tools.

To use SQLCMD, open a command prompt window. One way to do this is to click the Windows Start button and select Run from the program menu. In the Run dialog, type **CMD** and click OK. It doesn't matter what path you see at the command prompt. To see the list of available commands, just type **SQL-CMD -?** and press Enter (see Figure 3-57). Although the SQLCMD command itself is not case-sensitive, the switches used with it are; for example, the switch "-e" specifies that the SQLCMD commands should be echoed back, but the switch "-E" indicates using trusted security.

Chapter 3

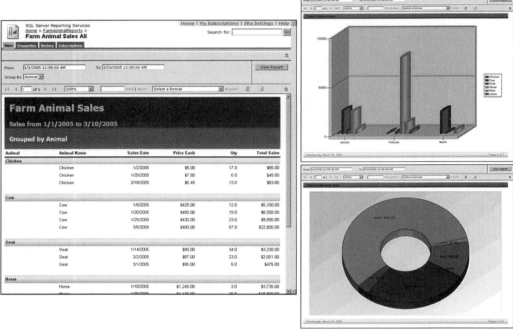

Figure 3-56

```
C:\>sqlcmd -?
Microsoft (R) SQL Server Command Line Tool
Version 9.00.1090 NT INTEL X86
Copyright (C) 2004 Microsoft Corporation.  All rights reserved.

usage: Sqlcmd            [-U login id]          [-P password]
  [-S server]            [-H hostname]          [-E trusted connection]
  [-d use database name] [-l login timeout]     [-t query timeout]
  [-h headers]           [-s colseparator]      [-w screen width]
  [-a packetsize]        [-e echo input]        [-I Enable Quoted Identifiers]
  [-c cmdend]            [-L[c] list servers[clean output]]
  [-q "cmdline query"]   [-Q "cmdline query" and exit]
  [-m errorlevel]        [-V severitylevel]     [-W remove trailing spaces]
  [-u unicode output]    [-r[0|1] msgs to stderr]
  [-i inputfile]         [-o outputfile]        [-z new password]
  [-f <codepage> | i:<codepage>[,o:<codepage>]] [-Z new password and exit]
  [-k[1|2] remove[replace] control characters]
  [-y variable length type display width]
  [-Y fixed length type display width]
  [-p[1] print statistics[colon format]]
  [-R use client regional setting]
  [-b On error batch abort]
  [-v var = "value"...] [-A dedicated admin connection]
  [-X[1] disable commands[and exit with warning]]
  [-x disable variable substitution]
  [-? show syntax summary]

C:\>_
```

Figure 3-57

Just about any SQL command can be executed using this utility, but it's typically used to execute batch scripts for system maintenance. Here's a quick example of a SELECT query to show how results are returned.

Because SQLCMD isn't a particularly interactive environment, some actions must be performed using a single-line command. When you launch SQLCMD, you must provide login information—either a user-name and password for SQL Server authentication, or a switch to indicate that you want to use integrated Windows security. This example uses integrated security by using the –E switch (this stands for Enterprise security.) Note that the documentation for the –E switch shows that this means *trusted connection*. When you press Enter, a new prompt is displayed:

```
1>
```

This indicates that you are now working in the SQLCMD environment rather than at the command prompt. It also lets you know that this is the first line in a batch process. SQLCMD runs all commands in batch mode and doesn't actually execute any commands until you explicitly tell it to, using the GO command. I'll continue to enter SQL commands and then type **GO** when I'm ready to execute the entire batch (see Figure 3-58).

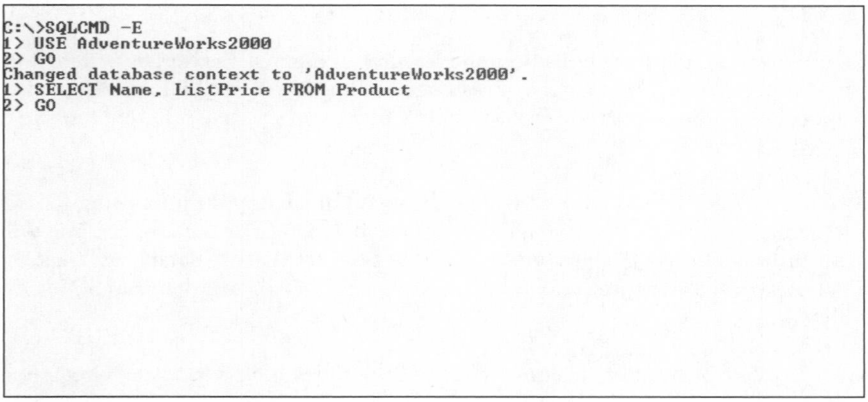

```
C:\>SQLCMD -E
1> USE AdventureWorks2000
2> GO
Changed database context to 'AdventureWorks2000'.
1> SELECT Name, ListPrice FROM Product
2> GO
```

Figure 3-58

In the SQL SELECT command, I only asked to return two columns and the results used up most of my screen real estate. Each character type column will use the maximum number of allocated characters. This means that if you have a column defined as VarChar(255), even if the actual data doesn't take up this much space, this column will require 255 characters of screen space, not allowing much room for anything else (see Figure 3-59). Another drawback to using this interface for returning data is that little of the result set is held in memory after the query runs. You can scroll the command window up to view some text but this is very limited.

The EXIT command is used to leave SQLCMD and return to a command prompt. Type **EXIT** again to close the command prompt window.

```
Touring-3000 Blue, 44                                    742.3500
Touring-3000 Blue, 50                                    742.3500
Mountain-400-W Silver, 38                                769.4900
Mountain-400-W Silver, 40                                769.4900
Mountain-400-W Silver, 42                                769.4900
Mountain-400-W Silver, 46                                769.4900
Mountain-500 Silver, 40                                  564.9900
Mountain-500 Silver, 42                                  564.9900
Mountain-500 Silver, 44                                  564.9900
Mountain-500 Silver, 48                                  564.9900
Mountain-500 Silver, 52                                  564.9900
Mountain-500 Black, 40                                   539.9900
Mountain-500 Black, 42                                   539.9900
Mountain-500 Black, 44                                   539.9900
Mountain-500 Black, 48                                   539.9900
Mountain-500 Black, 52                                   539.9900
LL Bottom Bracket                                         53.9900
ML Bottom Bracket                                        101.2400
HL Bottom Bracket                                        121.4900
Road-750 Black, 44                                       539.9900
Road-750 Black, 48                                       539.9900
Road-750 Black, 52                                       539.9900

(504 rows affected)
1>
```

Figure 3-59

Summary

I could have written a complete book about the features of the SQL Server 2005 client and management tools. In this chapter you learned what you will need to know to write SQL queries and choose the best tool for the job. Depending upon your role and objectives, you will use different tools to do different things.

If you are a database administrator, you will likely spend much of your time using the SQL Computer Manager to configure servers and manage the services that comprise SQL Server. You will likely spend most of your time using the SQL Server Management Studio to secure databases, create, monitor, and tune various database objects, and you may use the SQLCMD utility to run SQL scripts on the command line.

If you are an architect or solution designer, you may use the SQL Server Management Studio to diagram and generate database objects and the SQL Query Editor to create stored procedures, functions, and views to optimize database access. You may also use Microsoft Visio and the advanced solution design tools in Visual Studio and the Business Intelligence Studio to design and manage database projects.

If you are an application developer, you will likely spend most of your time developing software and creating integrated stored procedures and views in the Visual Studio integrated database design environment, and using SQL Server Management Studio to create and manage database objects. You may also use these tools to design and deploy reports using SQL Server Reporting Services.

It's often difficult to draw a clear distinction between these roles anymore. This is why these tools are tightly integrated and contain overlapping features and capabilities. Fortunately, they have been designed to work together and provide a consistent user experience. Once you have mastered the Management Studio, for example, you should be able to open the Business Intelligence Studio and work comfortably with the menus, toolbars, tool windows, and similar features.

As you read on, I will make reference to some of these tools but you will spend most of your time using the SQL Server Management Studio for SQL Server 2005 and the Query Analyzer for SQL Server 2000. To use the Transact-SQL language, you don't need to be concerned about the features of a particular design application, but you will find these features useful when you go to design entire database solutions, debug queries, and tune database objects.

Exercises

The exercises for this chapter and Chapter 4 provide numbered, step-by-step instructions. The solutions for these exercises are the final query, commands, or result. The exercises for subsequent chapters provide less-detailed instructions. You should use the material in each chapter to determine the appropriate steps and to find the solutions.

Exercise 1

1. Using Enterprise Manager or SQL Server Management Studio, create a new view in the AdventureWorks2000 database. You won't actually save the view, but use this option to open the graphical query designer.

2. Add the Product table to the designer.

3. Select the ProductID, Name, and ListPrice columns by checking the corresponding boxes in the table window.

4. Sort the results by the Name column in ascending order using the Sort Type option.

5. Check the SQL expression in the third pane of the graphical query designer with the solution.

Exercise 2

1. Using Enterprise Manager or SQL Server Management Studio, create a new view in the AdventureWorks2000 database as you did in Exercise 1.

2. Add two tables: the Product table and the ProductSubCategory table.

3. For the ProductSubCategory table, select the Name column and create an alias for it as SubCategory. For the Product table, select the Name column and create an alias for it as ProductName. Also select the ListPrice column from this table.

4. Sort the query by the ProductSubCategory Name column and then the Product table Name column, both in ascending order.

5. Execute the query and scroll through the results using the fourth pane in the designer. Check the SQL expression displayed in the third pane of the designer with the solution.

Exercise 3

Write a simple query using the query editor window in Query Analyzer or the SQL Server Manager Studio using the following steps:

1. Open Query Analyzer or SQL Server Management Studio.

2. If you are using Query Analyzer for SQL Server 2000, you will be prompted for connection information. Enter **localhost** for the server name or the name of your server if connecting remotely. If you are using SQL Server 2005, create a new query and provide this same connection information.

3. Select the AdventureWorks2000 database from the database selection list in the toolbar.

4. Enter the following SQL script in the query window:

```
SELECT * FROM Product WHERE ListPrice > 4000
```

5. To find out how many products have a list price greater than $4000, execute this query and check the row count in the status bar.

Exercise 4

Execute a simple query using command-line utilities:

1. If you are using SQL Server 2000, open a command prompt and execute the OSQL utility to utilize Windows Integrated (Enterprise) security. If you are using SQL Server 2005, use the SQL-CMD utility to utilize Windows Integrated (Enterprise) security. Each statement should be followed by a batch delineation command.

2. Indicate that you want run statements using the AdventureWorks2000 database.

3. Execute the following SQL statement and view the results:

```
SELECT ProductCategoryID, Name FROM ProductCategory
```

4. Exit the command-line utility and then the command window.

5. Check your statements with the solution.

Introducing Transact-SQL Language

In the early days of relational databases, a number of industry-wide efforts were made to unify different, proprietary query languages. IBM had established an early standard called *Structured English Query Language*. This name was condensed to literally spell the word *SEQUEL*. Another effort resulted in a language called *Select Query Language* (SQL) that included commands allowing data to be read only for reporting and record look-up. This became a popular, product-independent standard to which the "Sequel" acronym was still applied by members of the database community. Eventually, additional commands were added, enabling records to be added, deleted, and modified. This created a quandary. They had worked so hard to create a standard language with a cute name that no longer fit. The word *Select* was finally replaced with the word *Structured*. . . and the universe was once again brought back to a state of balance. Of course, the purists will insist that SQL is pronounced ESS CUE EHL, rather than "SEQUEL." So, how should you pronounce it? Any way you want. Disagree if you like, but I save one syllable and say "SEQUEL."

For the SQL language to survive outside of a specific product or company, the standard was published and held by an independent standards organization. The SQL standard was originally registered with the American National Standards Institute and officially called the *ANSI SQL* standard, established in 1986. This standard has been revised a few times, resulting in revisions known as the following:

- ❑ ANSI SQL-86
- ❑ ANSI SQL-89
- ❑ ANSI SQL-92
- ❑ ANSI SQL-99
- ❑ ANSI SQL-2003

The concept seems quite simple but there is a little more to this story. The ANSI SQL standard is actually no longer held exclusively by the American National Standards Institute. This is a common tale of American-born standards that are later implemented internationally. In 1987, SQL became an international standard and was registered with the International Standards

Organization using its previously copyrighted title, ANSI SQL. This means that the 1992 revision of the SQL standard is actually known *as* ISO ANSI SQL-92. Even though the standard was updated in 1999 and 2003, most SQL-based database products had been established on the ANSI SQL-92 standard and they have not been revised to fully conform to the ANSI SQL-99 or 2003 specifications. Like most of its competition, Transact-SQL does not fully conform to the ANSI SQL-99 or ANSI SQL-2003 standards but does implement selected features.

Finally, the ANSI SQL standard actually defines three conformance levels: Entry, Intermediate, and Full. Most products, including SQL Server, conform entirely to the entry-level standard and partially to the higher levels.

The Nature of SQL

Most folks who work with Transact-SQL have had some experience with other languages. If you've never done any programming, please don't close the book at this point and give up. This is certainly not a prerequisite for writing SQL, but is a reference point for many who have worked with computer systems in other capacities.

Comparing Transact-SQL to a procedural or object-oriented programming language (such as Java, C, C++, C#, or Visual Basic) is like comparing apples to pomegranates. It's not better than or worse than, but quite different than, a true programming language — even though you may see some similarities in the syntax and structure of certain statements. For different types of operations, Transact-SQL may be far superior or much worse than these languages, simply because of what it is designed to accomplish. One of the challenges in making broad statements about the capabilities of different languages is that as they continue to grow and evolve, version after version, additional capabilities are added. The problem with industry standards is that everyone is out to protect and enhance their own product. Over time, the capabilities of each technology (or language, in this case) begin to overlap, leaving us with a number of different options to perform the same tasks.

Is it possible to perform data access or data manipulation (to insert, modify, or delete values in a database) with a procedural programming language without using SQL? Yes, but it's cumbersome and usually inefficient. Can you perform complex mathematical operations, looping, string parsing, or multi-dimensional array management in Transact-SQL? Probably, but it likely won't be a very good experience. Chapter 1 mentioned that SQL Server 2005 gives programmers the capability of writing stored procedures and user-defined functions entirely in object-oriented program code, rather than SQL. This doesn't make Transact-SQL any less capable as SQL Server's native query language. It simply gives programmers another option.

Transact-SQL is designed primarily to work with relational data. No big surprise here. Secondarily, Transact-SQL also has a number of useful capabilities for working with scalar (single value) data, logical operations, mathematics, decision structures, text string parsing, and looping mechanisms. However, compared with most programming languages, SQL is not as powerful or as capable as a true programming language. If your needs call for advanced functionality that may be outside the realm of SQL's native capabilities, you may need to carefully consider using a different approach, such as a custom, extended, stored procedure, application programming interface (API), .NET assembly, or other programming solution. This is why SQL Server's Data Transformation Services (Data Integration Services in SQL Server 2005) can utilize both programming code and Transact-SQL. With that settled, what can you do with Transact-SQL? Quite a lot.

Transact-SQL is the language used to talk to SQL Server, and query expressions are essentially used to ask the server to do things. It's important to know what you can ask for — and what SQL Server can do. Query operations are divided into three different categories. I'll briefly describe them and then take some time to look at specific examples. Like everything else in the technical world, these categories are best known by three-letter abbreviations (that's TLA, for short.) Locally, these fall in the order I've listed here:

❑ **Data Definition Language (DDL)** — Commands are used to create and manage the objects in a database. DDL statements can be used to create, modify, and drop databases, tables, indexes, views, stored procedures, and other objects.

❑ **Data Control Language (DCL)** — Statements control the security permissions for users and database objects. Some objects have different permission sets. You can grant or deny these permissions to a specific user or users who belong to a database role or Windows user group.

❑ **Data Manipulation Language (DML)** — Contains the statements used to work with data. This includes statements to retrieve data, insert rows into a table, modify values, and delete rows.

Where to Begin

Where should we begin? This is one of those chicken and egg questions. Before you can query data, you have to have it stored somewhere. I think it would be a bit distracting to start from the very beginning and step through the entire process to create a new database. For simplicity's sake, I'd like to start out working with data stored in an existing database so we don't get too far off topic. I'll cover DDL and DCL statements, used primarily for database construction and administration, at the end of this chapter.

You'll be working with the Adventure Works Cycles sample database. The versions of this database that Microsoft includes with SQL Server 2000 and SQL Server 2005 are quite different. The SQL Server 2005 version includes some complexity that I felt was unnecessary for this book. This is why the AdventureWorks2000 for both versions of SQL Server is used for the examples. Please double-check that you have this database available to you and, if not, refer to the instructions in Chapter 2.

Because you've already learned the basics of using the Query Analyzer for SQL Server 2000 and the Query Editor in the SQL Server 2005 Management Studio, I'm not going to be giving you specific instructions regarding the use of these tools. The purpose here is to focus on the language. If you need to, review these instructions in Chapter 2. To begin, open Query Analyzer or the SQL Server Management Studio Query Editor and connect to your database server.

Data Manipulation Language (DML)

The basic statements of DML are introduced in this chapter with elaboration to follow in later chapters.

You can do only four things with data. You can *Create* records, *Read* them, *Update* record values, and you can *Delete* records. That spells *CRUD*. . . we do CRUD with data. When SQL was devised, they chose to use different words for these four operations: *Insert, Select, Update*, and *Delete*. Somehow, ISUD isn't quite as easy to remember as CRUD. If you can master these four types of statements, you will be able to do just about anything with data using SQL. Here's the catch: Inserts, Updates, and Deletes are a piece of cake. On the surface, the Select command can also appear simple.

Queries Have Layers

In the movie *Shrek*, Mike Myers' character Shrek the Ogre explains to his friend Donkey that "Ogres are like onions—they have layers." To some degree, the SELECT statement is like an Ogre, or rather it's like an onion—it has layers. On the surface, there isn't that much to it. However, when you start peeling back the layers, there's quite a lot to it. You've likely discovered this fact on your own. Here's the important point: it's not complicated. It's really just layers upon simple layers. The fundamentals are quite simple. I call this principle *compounded simplicity*.

Before I can effectively introduce the next topic, I need to jump the gun a little bit and briefly discuss the SELECT statement. This statement is covered thoroughly in Chapter 5. For now, it's important to understand that to return data from tables in SQL Server, you will use the SELECT statement. In relational databases, information gets transformed into data, typically by storing it in multiple tables. It would stand to reason, then, that to turn data back into useful information it must be retrieved from multiple tables. This is accomplished by using a handful of techniques: joins, subqueries, and unions. You learn more about these topics in future chapters. For now, know that these represent the bulk of the work you will do as you create and use queries.

Here's a simple example. When the following query runs, the query processor parses the query and breaks it down into individual steps.

```
SELECT TOP 10 Product.Name ,SalesOrderDetail.LineTotal
FROM Product INNER JOIN SalesOrderDetail
ON Product.Productid = SalesOrderDetail.ProductID
WHERE SalesOrderDetail.SpecialOfferID = 1
ORDER BY SalesOrderDetail.LineTotal DESC
```

Figure 4-1 shows the execution plan for the preceding query. Reading from right-to-left, the query optimizer chooses to implement each operational step based on available resources and statistical information about the data. The first two steps (at the beginning point of the two branches) show you that clustered index scans were used to initially retrieve data from both of the tables referenced in this query. Subsequent steps are chosen and analyzed for efficiency as the data is handled through the query process.

Figure 4-1

The low-level instructions used to process these steps are compiled into executable instruction code and cached in-memory so that subsequent executions don't require the same degree of preparation and resource overhead. Depending on whether this query is part of an ad-hoc SQL statement or a saved database object, the compiled instructions may also be saved to permanent storage, improving efficiency in the long term.

Set-Based Operations

When SQL Server processes a SELECT command, it builds a structure in memory to return a result set. This structure, essentially a two-dimensional array of rows and columns, is known as a *cursor*. The word cursor is an acronym for **CUR**rent **S**et **O**f **R**ecords. As such, it represents the entire set of rows returned from a table or query. SQL Server's query-processing engine is built on a foundation of cursor processing and is optimized to work with data as a set of records, rather than individual rows.

Row-Based Operations

A technique more popular in other database products is to populate a cursor type variable from a SELECT query and then step through each row. You can do this in SQL Server but it often works against the query-processing engine. Whenever possible, it is advisable to work with this set-based result paradigm rather than trying to process individual rows.

Row-level cursor operations have their place. This technique is discussed in Chapter 10.

Query Syntax Basics

A query is like a sentence; it must to be a complete statement with at least a noun and a verb. The semantic rules of SQL define a simple structure. You start with a clause that states what you intend to do: Select, Insert, Update, or Delete — these are the verbs. You also must define the columns or values to be returned. Usually, you will indicate the table or other database object you want to work with — this is the subject or noun. Depending on the type of operation, there are connecting words such as From and Into.

You'll learn about each of these statements in greater detail later but, for now, some simple examples follow. If you want to retrieve all of the column values from all rows in the Product table, you would execute the following query:

```
SELECT * From Product
```

If you need to raise the cost of all product records by ten percent, this statement would work:

```
UPDATE Product SET StandardCost = StandardCost * 1.1
```

The Transact-SQL language is very forgiving when it comes to formatting statements. The SQL Server query-processing engine doesn't care about whether commands are in upper- or lowercase. It doesn't care about spaces, tabs, and carriage returns as long as they don't interfere with the name of a command or value. This means that you can format your script for readability just about any way you like. For example, the following query returns product sales information for a range of dates, sorted by product category and subcategory. The query could be written like this:

```
SELECT ProductCategory.Name AS Category, ProductSubCategory.Name AS SubCategory,
Product.Name AS ProductName, SalesOrderHeader.OrderDate, SalesOrderDetail.OrderQty,
SalesOrderDetail.UnitPrice FROM SalesOrderHeader INNER JOIN SalesOrderDetail ON
SalesOrderHeader.SalesOrderID = SalesOrderDetail.SalesOrderID INNER JOIN Product ON
SalesOrderDetail.ProductID = Product.ProductID INNER JOIN ProductSubCategory ON
Product.ProductSubCategoryID = ProductSubCategory.ProductSubCategoryID INNER JOIN
ProductCategory ON ProductSubCategory.ProductCategoryID =
ProductCategory.ProductCategoryID WHERE SalesOrderHeader.OrderDate BETWEEN
'1/1/2003' AND '12/31/2003' ORDER BY ProductCategory.Name, ProductSubCategory.Name,
Product.Name
```

Or, it could be written like this:

```
SELECT       ProductCategory.Name AS Category
           , ProductSubCategory.Name AS SubCategory
           , Product.Name AS ProductName
           , SalesOrderHeader.OrderDate
           , SalesOrderDetail.OrderQty
           , SalesOrderDetail.UnitPrice
FROM       SalesOrderHeader
           INNER JOIN SalesOrderDetail
               ON SalesOrderHeader.SalesOrderID = SalesOrderDetail.SalesOrderID
           INNER JOIN Product
               ON SalesOrderDetail.ProductID = Product.ProductID
           INNER JOIN ProductSubCategory
               ON Product.ProductSubCategoryID =
                   ProductSubCategory.ProductSubCategoryID
           INNER JOIN ProductCategory
               ON ProductSubCategory.ProductCategoryID =
                   ProductCategory.ProductCategoryID
WHERE      SalesOrderHeader.OrderDate BETWEEN '1/1/2003' AND '12/31/2003'
ORDER BY ProductCategory.Name, ProductSubCategory.Name, Product.Name
```

Obviously, the second query is easier to read and would be much easier for someone to look at and figure out what's going on. Because both uppercase and lowercase statements are acceptable, a query could be written as follows:

```
select name, standardcost from product
```

Although the preceding statement would execute just fine, it's not quite as easy to read as the following:

```
SELECT Name, StandardCost FROM Product
```

Naming Conventions

There seems to be a universal concept that anything that can be very simple and uncomplicated *must* become confusing and overly complicated. When a database is created, objects should be named according to some kind of sensible naming convention. There is no industry-wide standard, and people have different ideas about appropriate naming conventions. Most folks perceive this as a simple matter of common sense, so they don't put much effort into it. The problem with common sense is that it's not very common and everyone seems to have their own idea about what is sensible.

It would be very convenient to have one simple standard to follow, and if things were that simple, I'd tell you exactly what to do. Most of it is quite easy, but object naming is a bit of an art. There are many considerations. For example, it's a good idea to use names that are descriptive and complete, describing the purpose of each object. On the other hand, you should keep names short and simple so users don't have to do a lot of extra typing. These are conflicting directions.

Be cautious about using any names that duplicate the name of a command or other reserved word. Before deciding upon a table, field, or other object name, review the list of data types, SQL clauses, and function names. Although it is possible to use some of these names, it's never a good idea. Once you have established a name, don't reuse it for something else. For example, the Product table shouldn't contain a Product column. SQL Server will not complain if you do this, but it will be very confusing to someone trying to write queries or read your SQL script.

Some older database products don't support mixed-case names or names containing spaces. For this reason, many database administrators continue to use all lowercase names with words separated by underscores. Personally, I find mixed-case names a little easier on the eyes.

Trends come and go. With Windows 95, Microsoft promoted the use of long file names. Microsoft Access, which was developed at about the same time, also promoted the use of long database object names. From a certain perspective, it makes sense to use friendly, sentence-like, descriptive names. The fact is that SQL Server will have no problem with names containing spaces, but other components of a solution may have issues with this. As values are handled at different levels of an application, they may move from the controls in the user interface to variables in the program code, then to the method parameters or properties of a class. Eventually, these values are passed into a stored procedure as parameters or as field names in a SQL statement. The point is that it is much easier on everyone involved if these items all have the same, or very similar, names. Figure 4-2 shows an example of the data flow through a sample application.

You could argue that there would be no harm in using space-filled field names in the database and similar names, sans spaces, elsewhere — and you'd probably be right. The general belief among database professionals is that spaces don't belong in object names. Frankly, this is probably more of an issue of perception, rather than technical feasibility.

I've done a lot of one-man solution development where I create the database, write the software components, design and develop the user interfaces, and write all the program code to glue the pieces together. Even in these applications, it's easy to get lost if related object names aren't the same. I have always insisted that they be consistent throughout the entire solution. I've also worked on some fairly large, complex projects where the database was designed by someone else long ago. If the names aren't clear and concise in the beginning, I'm faced with a quandary: change the names in my program code to something easier to understand (accepting that they don't match the table and field names), or consistently apply the same cryptic and confusing names throughout the entire solution.

It's not uncommon for a database designer to model and create tables, applying his or her own naming standards to table and field names. After this person has moved on to a different job, another database expert comes in and adds stored procedures. He might disagree with the names applied by the original designer, so he names the procedures and input parameters differently than the fields in the table. Along comes an outside consultant developing software components and he uses abbreviated names for the related class properties that correspond to the fields and parameters. Later, a junior-level software developer is assigned to create a user application for the data. He takes a class or reads a book about appropriate object naming standards and decides to fix the problem by applying his own names in spite of those that already exist. Coincidentally, I just finished modifying some report queries today. I had designed the tables these reports used. In testing, I discovered that performance wasn't ideal and decided to build another table with pre-aggregated data. Another database designer stepped in to help and named some of the columns differently than mine. For example, I have a column named FiscalMonthYearNumber and his was FiscalMonthNum. Is this a big deal? Not really, but it does require that I fix the queries for all of my reports.

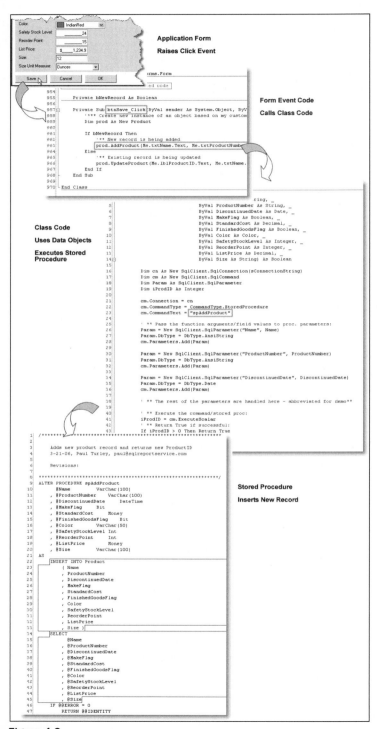

Figure 4-2

There is no easy solution to this common problem. Ideally, the person who designs the database should carefully consider the impact of the names he chooses and document them thoroughly. This sets the standard for all those who follow — and all names should remain consistent. I typically use mixed-case names, capitalizing each word and concatenating them together. In programming circles, this is often referred to as *Pascal Case*, named after the Pascal programming language. The following table shows a few common naming standards with some of the history and pros and cons regarding each.

Naming Standard	Example	Description
Pascal Case	CustomerFirstName	All words are capitalized and concatenated together without delimiting characters.
Camel Case	customerFirstName	All characters are lowercase except the first letter of each word after the first word. This standard is common in XML element names but not as common in database object naming.
Hungarian Notation	VcCustomerFirstName mstrCustomerFirstName	Objects are prefixed with characters used to denote data type and/or scope. This standard is more common in programming code than in database object naming. True Hungarian Notation can be very complicated and verbose.
Lower-case, delimited	customer_first_name	Comes from legacy database products that don't support mixed-case names. Still commonly used due to backward compatibility and tradition.
Long Names	Customer First Name	Promoted in Microsoft products such as Access. Has the advantage of being readable but not commonly used in serious software solutions. Incompatible with related programming code.

Commenting Script

When you write SQL script, it will inevitably be easy to read and understand — at the time you write it. Programming is something we do in a certain context. When I work on a project, my head is in that project and most everything makes perfect sense at the time. I once developed a database application for a consulting client. A few different people had been involved in writing queries and program code over a few months. They asked me to come back in to create some new reports. As I opened the project, reading through the code, I found it difficult to understand the logic. In my frustration, I said, "I don't understand what is going on in this code. Who wrote this?" My customer replied to my dismay, "Paul, that's your code. You wrote it last year." Needless to say, I was embarrassed as well as frustrated.

I learned a valuable lesson: comment everything. No matter how plain the logic seems. No matter how much sense it makes at the time, it probably won't make so much sense to the next person who reads it, especially months or years later. If nothing else reminds you of this simple lesson, just remember this: Every one of us leaves a legacy. Other query designers and programmers will remember you for what you leave behind for them to maintain. They will most likely either remember you for making their job difficult or for making their job easier.

Comments typically are made in two forms that include header blocks and in-line comments. A header block is a formal block of text that precedes every scripted object, such as a stored procedure or user-defined function. It should conform to a standard format and should contain information such as the following:

- ❏ The name of the scripted object
- ❏ The name of the designer or programmer
- ❏ Contact information
- ❏ Creation date
- ❏ Revision dates and notes
- ❏ Information about what the object does and how it's called
- ❏ Validation testing and approval notes

Comments in Transact-SQL can be either in block format or on a single line. Block comments begin with a forward slash and at least one asterisk (/*) and end with an asterisk and a forward slash (*/). Everything in between is treated as a comment and ignored by the query parser. A header block doesn't need to be complicated. It should just be consistent. Here's an example of a simple header block preceding the script for a stored procedure used to insert product records:

```
/*******************************************************************
       spInsProduct - Inserts product records

       Accepts ProductName, StandardPrice, QtyInStock, CategoryID
       Returns new ProductID, Int

       6-12-04 by Paul Turley (paul@sqlreportservices.com)

       Revisions:
       7-10-04 - PT - Added MarkupPercent parameter
       7-12-04 - PT - Changed data type from Int to Decimal
*******************************************************************/
```

In-line comments are placed in the body of the script to document the process and flow along with the actual script. Comments are preceded by two hyphens (--). The query parser ignores the remainder of the line. In-line comments can be placed after executable script on the same line or can be written on a separate line, as you can see in the following example:

```
CREATE PROCEDURE spGetCustomer
-- Define City parameter, set default to Null if parameter not passed
   @City VarChar(25) = NULL
AS
   IF @City IS Null        -- Check for Null (parameter not passed)
     BEGIN
     -- Return all Store records
        SELECT Store.Name AS StoreName, Address.City
        FROM Store
        INNER JOIN Customer
          ON Store.CustomerID = Customer.CustomerID
        INNER JOIN CustomerAddress
          ON Customer.CustomerIDCustomer = Address.CustomerID
```

```
         INNER JOIN Address
           ON CustomerAddress.AddressID = Address.AddressID
     END
   ELSE
     BEGIN
     -- Return Store records only for matching City
       SELECT Store.Name AS StoreName, Address.City
       FROM Store
       INNER JOIN Customer
         ON Store.CustomerID = Customer.CustomerID
       INNER JOIN CustomerAddress
         ON Customer.CustomerID = CustomerAddress.CustomerID
       INNER JOIN Address
         ON CustomerAddress.AddressID = Address.AddressID
       WHERE Address.City = @City
     END
```

If in doubt, add a comment. If not in doubt, add one anyway. Don't worry about overdoing it. Granted, some of your script will make sense without commenting and may be somewhat self-documenting, but don't take a chance. Don't listen to yourself when that little voice says "Don't worry about commenting your code now. You can do it later." Maybe you're more disciplined than I am, but if I don't write comments when I'm writing code, it won't get done.

Another important application of in-line comments is temporary development notes to myself and others. Inevitably, on the first pass through my script, I'm most concerned about getting core functionality working. Exceptions to basic logic, problem workarounds, error-handling, and less-common conditions are usually secondary to just getting the code to work once under ideal conditions. As I consider all of these secondary factors, I make notes to myself that may include to-do items and reminders to go back and add clean-up code and polished features.

Using Templates

Query Analyzer contains a very useful, and often underutilized, feature. Templates provide a starting place for a variety of database object scripts. Several templates come with SQL Server and adding your own is an easy task. In Chapter 3 you learned how to use the script template features in Query Analyzer and the SQL Server Management Studio. In reality, a template is just a text file containing SQL commands and placeholders for object names. Using a template can save considerable time and effort, especially when writing script that you may not use very often. For example, I don't write an Instead Of Trigger very often, so I may not be able to remember the syntax off the top of my head. Rather than scouring Books Online or searching the web for help, I'll simply open this template in a new script window:

```
-- =============================================
-- Create basic Instead Of Trigger
-- =============================================
IF EXISTS (SELECT name
    FROM    sysobjects
    WHERE   name = N'<trigger_name, sysname, trig_test>'
    AND     type = 'TR')
    DROP TRIGGER <trigger_name, sysname, trig_test>
GO

CREATE TRIGGER <trigger_name, sysname, trig_test>
```

```
ON <table_or_view_name, sysname, pubs.dbo.sales>
INSTEAD OF INSERT
AS
BEGIN
 RAISERROR (50009, 16, 10)
 EXEC sp_who
END
GO
```

This script provides a basic pattern to get you started. If you'd like to create your own templates, this is very easy to do. Simply write the script in a new query window and then use the File ⇨ Save As menu to save it to a Template SQL file. In Query Analyzer, templates are saved with a tql extension, but in the SQL Management Studio templates are saved with a sql extension, like other script files.

Template files saved to the standard template folders will be added to the available templates for Query Analyzer and the SQL Management Studio. SQL Server 2000 assigns the extension .TQL to template files. SQL Server 2005 uses the standard .SQL extension. In a default SQL Server installation, these folders are found in the following locations:

Version	Templates Folder Path
SQL Server 2000	C:\Program Files\Microsoft SQL Server\80\Tools\Templates
SQL Server 2005	C:\Program Files\Microsoft SQL Server\90\Tools\Binn\VSShell\Common7\IDE\sqlworkbenchnewitems\Sql

Generating Script

The term *script* simply refers to a bunch of SQL statements typically used together to perform some useful purpose. This could vary from a simple SQL query to a group of several queries and commands used to create an entire database. The SQL Server client and administrative tools (Enterprise Manager, Query Analyzer, Workbench, and Visual Studio) have the ability to generate script for just about any object or combination of objects. You can even generate the script to re-create an entire database. Script is usually saved to a file with a sql extension and is simply plain text. You could easily create or edit a script file with Notepad or any other text editor.

Managing Script

I suggest that you have a designated folder for your script files. I usually create a folder for each database project or application I'm working on. I will also make it a point to back up and archive the script files in these folders. Just like program source code, my scripts are treated like gold. Especially for the programming objects in your database (views, functions, and stored procedures), these objects should be scripted and saved on a CD or protected network folder. This practice will be invaluable in case (make that *when*) something goes wrong.

To keep you and your co-workers on their toes, you may find it helpful to stage a routine fire drill of sorts. On a bi-weekly basis, designate a hard disk or folder as corrupted or deleted and then go in and take inventory of your losses. You can use this exercise to let other team members know how well your recovery plan is working and how it can be improved.

Version Control

One of the greatest challenges in managing scripts is how to keep track of multiple versions of the same file. The natural order of application development involves prototyping a feature, working through iterations of design, testing, and debugging until the feature is stable. At this point, it is important to keep a copy of the working SQL script and program source code before any changes are made. Adding features and capabilities to a query or programming object nearly always has adverse effects, at least in the short term. The secret to success is to script and save your queries and objects to script files after you get them working.

On many occasions, I have been asked to make some minor change or enhancement to a project. It may involve adding a column to a table or just adding a calculation to a query. I do a quick test and then implement the change on the production server the night before flying out to a training engagement. Almost inevitably, the change will have some unforeseen impact. Perhaps my customer calls in a panic to inform me that she's getting an error, it's the end of the month, and they can't print invoices.

Making this minor change often seems like a good idea at the time. Fortunately, if objects were scripted before making changes, it's usually a simple task to either review the original script and make corrections, or to run the original script, returning the query to its previous, working state. Script version management is not complicated, but without having a system in place and making a deliberate effort to follow it, it's easy to lose track of your changes.

A few simple approaches to version control exist. Version control software, such as Microsoft Visual SourceSafe, automates this task by storing files in a central database. As files are checked out and checked in, a separate copy is time-stamped and stored in the SourceSafe database. Any version of the file can then be retrieved at any time. SourceSafe is the best bet if a group of people will be sharing script files and working on different, networked development computers. SQL Server 2000 has no built-in integration with Visual SourceSafe, but SourceSafe is easy enough to use at the file system level. The SQL Server 2005 Workbench does integrate with Visual SourceSafe. Much like Visual Studio, files can be checked out, checked in, and managed from within the Workbench design environment.

A less-sophisticated approach is to simply append file names with the date they are created and the initials of the person creating them. Keep these files in project-related folders and back them up regularly. The following are examples of the script files for a stored procedure called spGetCustomerAccountDetail:

- ❏   Create spGetCustomerAccountDetail – 7-02-04 PT.sql
- ❏   Create spGetCustomerAccountDetail – 7-09-04 PT.sql
- ❏   Create spGetCustomerAccountDetail – 7-11-04 PT.sql
- ❏   Create spGetCustomerAccountDetail – 7-15-04 PT.sql
- ❏   Create spGetCustomerAccountDetail – 8-03-04 PT.sql

Data Definition Language

If you have used Enterprise Manager, Visual Studio, Access, or any other tools to create and design SQL Server databases, you have used Data Definition Language (DDL) — perhaps not directly but by using these user interface tools to manage database objects. Nearly all database maintenance operations are scripted and then that script is executed. This is one reason why there are so many scripting options in the SQL Server management tools. The scripting engine has been there for years in one form or another.

This is a simple topic because you can do only three things with any database object: create it, modify it, or delete it. Subsequently, the corresponding DDL statements are as follows:

Statement	Description
CREATE	Used to create a new object. This applies to many common database objects including Database, Table, View, Procedure, Trigger, and Function.
ALTER	Used to modify the structure of an existing object. The syntax for each of these objects will vary depending on its purpose.
DROP	Used to delete an existing object. Some objects cannot be dropped because they are schema-bound. This means that you may not be able to drop a table if it contains data participating in a relationship or if another object depends on the object you intend to drop.

The syntax of DDL statements is quite simple. A quick tour through each of the common database objects and an example for each follows. Because this isn't a database programming book, it won't be exploring the nuances and uses for these objects, but the syntax used to manage them.

Creating a Table

In its simplest form, to add a new table to the current database, you specify the table name and then list the table's new columns in parentheses, followed by their data type. Here's an example:

```
CREATE TABLE Appointment
  (   AppointmentID    Int
   ,  Description      VarChar(50)
   ,  StartDateTime    DateTime
   ,  EndDateTime      DateTime
   ,  Resource         VarChar(50) Null
  )
```

You can specify several options for each column definition. Briefly, this might include options such as auto-sequencing identity, default values, constraints, and whether the column value may be set to Null. For a complete list of options, check the SQL Server Books Online documentation.

Creating a View

A view is similar to a table in that users can select from a view like a table. Views are stored in the database but they don't really store data. A view is really just a SQL SELECT query that gets optimized to make it execute more efficiently than if you were to make up the query every time you wanted to select data. However, views can do some very interesting things that we're not going to get into (like actually storing data.). They can be indexed and they can be used with other programming objects to make SQL Server do some very powerful things. Enough for now. The finer points of views are discussed in Chapter 10.

When you create a view, you're really just naming a SQL SELECT statement. The syntax looks like this:

```
CREATE VIEW vwProductOrderDetails
AS
SELECT CustomerID
     , OrderDate
     , OrderQty
     , UnitPrice
     , Product.Name AS Product
FROM SalesOrderHeader
     INNER JOIN SalesOrderDetail
        ON SalesOrderHeader.SalesOrderID = SalesOrderDetail.SalesOrderID
     INNER JOIN Product
        ON SalesOrderDetail.ProductID = Product.ProductID
```

Creating a Stored Procedure

Stored procedures can perform a wide range of actions and business functionality. For example, a stored procedure can insert, update, or delete records in a table. By passing parameter values, it can make decisions and either select data or perform other operations accordingly. Because stored procedures can be used in so many unique ways, it's hard to exemplify a "typical" stored procedure. The syntax for creating a stored procedure is similar to that of a view. Note the input parameters defined just before the word AS:

```
/***************************************************
    Checks for existing Product record
    If exists, updates the record.  If not,
    inserts new record
 ***************************************************/
CREATE PROCEDURE spInsertOrUpdateProduct
    -- Input parameters --
    @ProductName nVarChar(50),
    @ProductNumber nVarChar(25),
    @StdCost Money
AS
    IF EXISTS(SELECT * From Product Where ProductNumber = @ProductNumber)
        UPDATE Product SET NAME = @ProductName, StandardCost = @StdCost
        WHERE ProductNumber = @ProductNumber
    ELSE
        INSERT INTO Product (Name, ProductNumber, StandardCost)
        SELECT @ProductName, @ProductNumber, @StdCost
```

Creating a Trigger

Creating a trigger is similar to a stored procedure. Actually, a trigger is a special type of stored procedure that gets executed when specific operations are performed on the records in a table (such as an Insert, Update, or Delete). Business logic similar to that of a standard stored procedure may be performed within a trigger, but it is typically used to apply specialized business rules to ensure data integrity. Some of the unique characteristics of triggers include their assignment to a DML operation (Insert, Update, and/or Delete), implicit transaction control, and virtual table references that are used to represent the record or records involved in the transaction that caused the trigger to fire.

In the following example, note the reference to a virtual table called Deleted. This "table" is actually a virtual set of rows that are in the process of being deleted as the trigger is automatically executed. There is no script to explicitly begin processing a transaction because the trigger execution is the result of a transaction in progress. The Rollback Transaction script affects this inherent transaction and prevents the delete operation from being completed.

```
/*******************************************************
   Checks for existing sales orders using
   the product being deleted.
   Prevents deletion if orders exist.
*******************************************************/
CREATE TRIGGER tr_DelProduct
ON Product
FOR DELETE
AS
   IF (SELECT Count(*) FROM SalesOrderDetail
       INNER JOIN Deleted ON SalesOrderDetail.ProductID = Deleted.ProductID) > 0
   BEGIN
     RAISERROR 50009 'Cannot delete a product with sales orders'
     ROLLBACK TRANSACTION
     RETURN
   END
```

Creating a User-Defined Function

User-defined functions are used to apply custom business logic such as performing calculations, parsing values, and making value comparisons. Functions are often called within views and stored procedures to reduce code redundancy and to encapsulate functionality. The script used to create a new user-defined function is similar to that of a stored procedure. The function is defined on the first executable line of the script (preceded in this example by a comment block). Immediately following the CREATE command, the function name references one or more parameters followed by a data type, in parentheses. The text following the Returns keyword indicates the data type that the function will return. This is a simple scalar (single value) function that returns a DateTime type value. In Chapter 10 you also learn how user-defined functions can return complex, multi-value results and table-type result sets; similar to a view or stored procedure. This function utilizes local variables and system functions to perform its internal logic.

```
/*******************************************************
 Returns a date representing the last date
 of any given month.
*******************************************************/
CREATE Function dbo.fn_LastOfMonth(@TheDate DateTime)
Returns DateTime
AS
BEGIN
 DECLARE @FirstOfMonth  DateTime
 DECLARE @DaysInMonth Int
 DECLARE @RetDate DateTime

 SET @FirstOfMonth = DATEADD(mm, DATEDIFF(mm,0,@TheDate), 0)
 SET @DaysInMonth = DATEDIFF(d, @FirstOfMonth, DATEADD(m, 1, @FirstOfMonth))
 RETURN  DATEADD(d, @DaysInMonth - 1, @FirstOfMonth)
END
```

Scripting Practices

When scripting objects, a common practice is to check for the existence of the object before creating it. Although this isn't necessary when you know the object isn't already in the database, if you generate script using Enterprise Manager, Query Analyzer, or SQL Server Management Studio, logic is typically included to remove the object if it exists and then re-create it. Keep in mind that dropping and re-creating an object will remove any security privileges that have been granted to users. If you simply need to modify an object to add capabilities, it may be advisable to use the ALTER command rather than DROP followed by the CREATE command. A number of different scripting options can be used to customize auto-generated script, and many of the non-default options may be unnecessary.

Every SQL Server 2000 database contains a number of standard system tables. Generally, you need not be concerned with these tables and really ought to leave them alone. However, you can get a lot of useful information about your database from these tables. The following script searches the sysobjects system table to find out if the Product table exists in the current database. If it does exist, the DROP statement is conditionally executed to delete the table. This script will also work on a SQL Server 2005 instance, but sysobjects isn't a table in SQL Server 2005, it is a view. There is no direct access to system tables in SQL Server 2005.

```
IF EXISTS (
SELECT * FROM sysobjects WHERE Name = 'Product'
)
    DROP TABLE Product
GO
```

A line of script may fail for a variety of reasons. Due to referential constraints and other dependencies, tables must be dropped in the right order. In case the table isn't successfully dropped, it may be a good idea to check again for the existence of the table before attempting to create it. This is performed in the following script fragment (shortened for simplicity):

```
IF NOT EXISTS (
SELECT * FROM sysobjects WHERE Name = 'Product'
)
BEGIN
CREATE TABLE Product
(
    ProductID Int Identity
, Name nVarChar(50) Not Null
, ProductNumber nVarChar(25) Null
, DiscontinuedDate DateTime Null
    ...
```

System tables were not designed for ease of use or readability, so they can be somewhat cryptic. Another problem if you use system tables is that there are no guarantees that they won't change in later versions of SQL Server, possibly breaking your code if you were to upgrade and migrate your database. This is the case if you plan to upgrade from SQL Server 2000 to SQL Server 2005. As previously mentioned, there is no direct access to system tables. Microsoft created a number of system views in SQL Server 2005 to replace the system tables from SQL Server 2000. The new views have the same name as the old tables so scripts created on a SQL Server 2000 instance *should* still work. However, Microsoft has been recommending not querying system tables directly for years and there is no guarantee that SQL Server 2000 scripts that ran against system objects will continue to work. In lieu of directly querying system tables, a set of views is provided with both SQL Server 2000 and 2005 to simplify the structure and data in the system tables and the new system views. These *Information Schema* views are stored in the Master database and can be used in any database on the server. Each view is prefixed with the name INFOR-MATION_SCHEMA, followed by a period and a general object type. In place of the script in the previous example, which selects from the sysobjects table, similar script may be used with the INFORMATION_SCHEMA.TABLES view, such as in the following:

```
IF EXISTS (
SELECT * FROM Information_Schema.Tables WHERE Table_Name = 'Product'
)
     DROP TABLE Product
GO
```

Altering Objects

The script used to modify some existing objects is very similar to the syntax used to create objects, using the ALTER command in place of CREATE. This is the case for objects that contain SQL expressions such as views, stored procedures, and user-defined functions. The following script is very similar to the example used to demonstrate how to create a stored procedure. An additional input parameter and a line to handle error conditions have been added.

```
/********************************************************
   Checks for existing Product record
   If exists, updates the record.  If not,
   inserts new record
   Revised: 4-12-06 PT
********************************************************/
ALTER PROCEDURE spInsertOrUpdateProduct
   -- Input parameters --
   @ProductName nVarChar(50),
   @ProductNumber nVarChar(25),
   @StdCost Money,
   @ListPrice Money
AS
  IF EXISTS (SELECT * FROM Product WHERE ProductNumber = @ProductNumber)
     UPDATE Product
     SET Name = @ProductName
       , StandardCost = @StdCost
       , ListPrice = @ListPrice
     WHERE ProductNumber = @ProductNumber
  ELSE
       INSERT INTO Product (Name, ProductNumber, StandardCost, ListPrice)
       SELECT @ProductName, @ProductNumber, @StdCost, @ListPrice
  IF @@Error <> 0
     RAISERROR ('spInsertUpdateProduct execution failed', 15, 1)
```

After the ALTER statement has been executed, the object retains all of its previous properties and security access privileges or restrictions, but its definition is updated with any of the script changes. This includes the comment block before the ALTER statement line.

Some objects require different syntax used to alter their definition than the language used to create them. For example, when creating a table, columns are defined within parentheses after the table name. To alter the design of a table and change the columns, you would use the ADD or DROP keyword before each column definition. Any existing columns that are not addressed in the Alter Table script remain in the table's definition.

```
ALTER TABLE Appointment
ADD   LeadTime SmallInt Null
```

Each column or constraint change must be performed in a separate ALTER TABLE statement. For example, if my goal was to add the LeadTime column and to drop the Resource column, this can be performed using the previous and next statements but can't be done in a single statement.

```
ALTER TABLE Appointment
DROP COLUMN Resource
```

Dropping Objects

Why is it that the most dangerous commands are the easiest to perform? Dropping an object removes it from the database catalog (from the system tables), completely deleting it from the database. Tables containing data and their related indexes are de-allocated, freeing the storage space for other data. To quote a well-known former president of the United States, "let me make one thing perfectly clear". . . There is no Undo command in SQL Server. If you have dropped an object or deleted data, it's gone. However, the storage space occupied by dropped or truncated objects is not actually wiped clean and made available to the operating system unless the database is set to AutoShrink.

The syntax for dropping all objects is the same: DROP *objecttype objectname.* Here are a few examples of script used to drop the objects I previously created:

```
DROP TABLE Appointment

DROP VIEW vwProductOrderDetails

DROP PROCEDURE spInsertOrUpdateProduct

DROP TRIGGER TR_Del_Product

DROP FUNCTION dbo.fn_LastOfMonth
```

Some objects cannot be dropped if there are dependent objects that would be affected if they no longer existed. Examples are tables with foreign key constraints, user-defined types, and rules. This safety feature is called *schema binding.* Some objects don't enforce schema binding by default but it can be created to explicitly enforce this rule. Views, stored procedures, and user-defined functions can optionally be created with schema binding and prevent orphaned dependencies. This feature is discussed in greater detail in Chapter 10.

Data Control Language

This is by far the simplest subset of the SQL language. The goal of Data Control Language (DCL) is to manage users' access to database objects. After the database has been designed and objects are created using DDL, a security plan should be implemented to provide users and applications with an appropriate level of access to data and database functionality, while protecting the system from intrusion. Access privileges can be controlled at the server or database level and groups of privileges can be assigned to individual users and to groups of users who are assigned role membership. Although database security involves simple concepts, it is not a task to be approached in a haphazard manner. It's important to devise a comprehensive plan and to consider all of the business requirements and the organization's security standards when devising a database security plan.

SQL Server recognizes two separate security models. These include SQL Server Security, where roles and users are managed entirely within the database server, and Integrated Windows Security, which maps privileges to groups and users managed in a Windows-based network system. This topic is discussed in greater detail in Chapter 10, but some of the basic principles are explained in this section.

The easiest way to think about permissions is in layers. Because users can have memberships to multiple roles, they may have a mixed set of privileges for different database objects. Like placing multiple locks on a door, a user can only gain access to an object if all restrictive permissions are removed and they have been granted access through at least one role membership. Using the lock analogy, if you had a key to one of three locks, you would not be able to open the door. Likewise, if a user is a member of three roles, two of which are denied access to an object, access won't be allowed even if it is explicitly granted. The user must be either removed from the restrictive roles or these permissions must be revoked.

In short, DCL consists of three commands that are used to manage security privileges for users or roles on specific database objects:

❑ The GRANT command gives permission set to a user or role.

❑ The DENY command explicitly restricts a permission set.

❑ The REVOKE command is used to remove a permission set on an object.

Revoking permissions removes an explicit permission (GRANT or DENY) on an object so that permissions that may have been applied at a less-specific level are used. Before permissions can be applied to objects, users and roles are defined. SQL Server provides a set of standard roles for both the database server and for each database. You learn how to manage permissions for roles and users in Chapter 10.

Following are some examples. This statement grants SELECT permission to the user Paul on the Product table:

```
GRANT SELECT ON Product TO Paul
```

Tables and views have permissions to allow or restrict the use of the four DML statements: Select, Insert, Update, and Delete. Stored procedures and functions recognize the EXECUTE permission. On tables, views, and functions, permissions can also be given or restricted on a user's ability to implement referential integrity, using the DRI permission.

This example grants EXECUTE permission to members of the db_datawriter built-in role but denies this permission to a user named Martha:

```
GRANT EXECUTE ON spAddProduct TO db_datawriter
DENY EXECUTE ON spAddProduct TO Martha
```

Multiple permissions can be applied on an object by placing permissions in a comma-delimited list, as in the following:

```
GRANT SELECT, INSERT, UPDATE ON Product TO Paul
```

An important aspect to remember about SQL Server security is that SQL Server does not enforce logical combinations of permissions. For example, assume that user Paul is a member of a security role called Authors and the following DCL scripts are executed:

```
GRANT UPDATE ON PublishedBooks TO Authors
DENY SELECT ON PublishedBooks TO Paul
```

Because Paul is a member of the Authors role he inherits the UPDATE permission granted to that role. He was also specifically denied the SELECT permission on the table PublishedBooks. The logical assumption would be that Paul could not update the PublishedBooks table, but this assumption would be wrong. Paul cannot update any specific rows due to this permission combination so the following command would fail:

```
UPDATE PublishedBooks SET Author = 'Paul Turley' WHERE BookID = 222
```

However this command would succeed:

```
UPDATE PublishedBooks SET Author = 'Paul Turley'
```

Because the WHERE expression is in essence a select command that is processed prior to the update, Paul is prevented from making the change. Unfortunately, Paul is a savvy SQL user and he knows that by updating all the rows in the table he circumvents the denied select permission and changes all the published book records to show that he is the author. The moral to this story is to use care and planning when applying permissions.

This short discourse should have provided a cursory introduction to the concepts and practices of DCL. As previously mentioned, like database design, security is a matter that should be carefully planned and implemented in a uniform and standard approach. It's usually best to have a small number of database administrators charged with the task of security to keep tight reigns over how privileges are applied for users of a database.

Summary

By now you should have a good understanding about what the Transact-SQL language is used for and how it is implemented with Microsoft SQL Server. You learned that Transact-SQL is a dialect of the Structured Query Language, based on the industry-wide ANSI SQL standard.

Three categories of statements within SQL are used to define and manage a database and the objects contained therein, to control access to data and database functionality, and to manage the data in a database. Data Definition Language (DDL) encompasses the CREATE and ALTER statements, used to define database objects. Data Control Language (DCL) is used to manage security access and user privileges to data and database objects. Finally, Data Manipulation Language (DML) is the subset of SQL you will typically use most often. DML contains the SELECT, INSERT, UPDATE, and DELETE statements and several variations of these statements that you will use to populate tables with records, modify, remove, and read data values. The SELECT statement has several modifiers and additional commands and clauses you will use to do useful things with, and make sense of, the data stored in a database.

The SQL Server database engine uses intelligent logic to process queries as efficiently as possible. The query parser and optimizer translate a SQL query into distinct operations, which are then compiled into low-level machine instructions. This compiled execution plan is cached in memory and can be stored permanently within the database with database programming objects to run more efficiently.

You also learned about the proper way to write SQL script, using comments and naming standards. Script can be saved in script files for safekeeping and templates can be used to save time and effort when writing new queries.

This chapter, along with the first three chapters, is the foundation upon which more specific topics are based. As you move forward, you will be using the scripting techniques discussed here and the tools you learned to use in Chapter 2. The rest of the book focuses on specific types of queries and objects.

Exercises

Exercise 1

Use Query Analyzer or SQL Server Management Studio to create and execute a new query, and view the results:

1. Open a connection to your local or remote test server.

2. Indicate that you want to run queries against the AdventureWorks2000 database.

3. Execute the following SQL statement:

```
SELECT * FROM Contact
```

4. Check the status bar for the numbers of rows returned by the query.

5. Check the results with the solution.

Exercise 2

Insert a row using generated SQL script:

1. Using Query Analyzer or SQL Server Management Studio, expand the AdventureWorks2000 database in the object browser. Right-click the ProductCategory table and select Script Object to New Window As Insert.

2. In the new query editor window, remove the references to the ProductCategoryID column on both lines. On the top line, delete all text from and including the first open square bracket, [, to the first end square bracket,], and the following comma. On the second line, remove all text from and including the first open angled bracket, <, to the first close angled bracket, >, and the following comma.

3. One the second line, replace the placeholders (angled brackets and all text between them) for each of the columns as follows: Replace the Name with 'Widget' (including the single quotes). Replace the ModifiedDate and rowguid with the word DEFAULT (no quotes).

4. Select the AdventureWorks2000 database from the database selection drop-down list on the toolbar and execute the query.

5. Enter the following query to view the contents of the ProductCategory table:

```
SELECT * FROM ProductCategory.
```

6. Highlight this statement and execute this query.

7. Verify that a new row was added to the results. Check the modified SQL expression that you generated with the solution.

Data Retrieval

In Chapter 4 you learned that as the SQL language has evolved, its capabilities have expanded to add more capabilities. In the next two chapters you learn the fundamentals of DML. This chapter introduces the essentials of data retrieval, and Chapter 6 covers data storage and manipulation. Subsequent chapters build on these concepts as you learn about more advanced implementations of these DML components.

Storage and Retrieval

I'm not a particularly organized person by nature. When I am done using an item, my first impulse is to toss it on my dresser or a table. The workbench in my garage hasn't seen the light of day for several months. I tell you this so you can understand my deep appreciation for the orderliness of a relational database. Perhaps this is the element in my life that helps me compensate for the lack of order in other areas. I also love containers of all kinds. The cool thing about having containers is that when you need to put something away, there's always a place for it, but when it comes time to find it, that's often another story.

Retrieving data through queries is really about finding stuff. SQL queries are used to reach into the database and pull out useful information; sometimes you need to get all of the details and sometimes you need only a subset of data based on common characteristics. At times, the value or values you'll want to return are an aggregation of data that tell you something about the data, rather than just returning all of the data in raw form.

I think that the most important statement I can make before diving into the nuts and bolts of SQL is that it's easy. The fundamental mechanics of the language are very straightforward, and this is very much a step-by-step process. Having said that, you will definitely see some complex stuff later on, but it's all based on the same fundamental concepts that are introduced in this chapter.

As you will see later on, queries can be nested within queries and can be saved as programming objects such as functions, stored procedures, and views. Queries can then get their data from these objects. Queries can be joined, nested, and compounded in many different ways. Just remember that it all boils down to the same basic components.

The SELECT Statement

The SELECT statement consists of four clauses or components, as explained in the following table.

Clause	Explanation
SELECT	Followed by a list of columns or an asterisk, indicating that you want to return all columns
FROM	Followed by a table or view name, or multiple tables with join expressions
WHERE	Followed by filtering criteria
ORDER BY	Followed by a list of columns for sorting

The SELECT statement and FROM clause are required. The others are optional. Think of a table as a grid, like an Excel worksheet, consisting of cells arranged in rows and columns. Often, when you want to view the data in a table, you're only interested in seeing some of the information. To control what data gets returned, you can either display a subset of the columns, a subset of the rows, or a combination of the two. In any case, the *result set* is a list of rows, each consisting of the same number of columns.

The first few examples in this chapter show you two different views of the same data. I have pasted the contents of the Product table into an Excel workbook. For each query, you will see the first 66 rows and all 10 columns. As I filter the rows and columns, I'll highlight the selected rows and columns. This will provide a different perspective alongside the filtered result set. Keep in mind that Excel presents values a little differently than the results grid. For example, Null values are displayed as empty cells, whereas the results grid displays the text Null, by default (this can be configured to display anything you like). Figure 5-1 shows a sampling of data from the Product table in an Excel worksheet.

Choosing Columns

Specify the columns you want your query to return immediately after the SELECT statement. The following statement returns two columns and all records in the Product table:

```
SELECT Name, StandardCost, Color FROM Product
```

Even though there may be dozens of columns of data in this table, you're just returning data values for the ProductID and Name columns. You're still going to get all of the rows that exist in the table. Figure 5-2 shows the Excel worksheet with only the selected columns highlighted.

The result set from the previous query will return only three columns, as shown in Figure 5-3.

If you want to return values for all available columns, you can either specify every column by name or use the asterisk (*) to indicate "all columns." This query returns all of the columns in the table, as if you had listed every available column in the SELECT statement:

```
SELECT * FROM Product
```

Occasionally, I hear the asterisk in this context referred to as a *splat*. So if you hear an old-timer DBA say "Select Splat From Products," you'll know what he's talking about.

ProductID	Name	ProductNumber	DiscontinuedDate	MakeFlag	StandardCost	FinishedGoodsFlag	Color	SafetyStockLevel	ReorderPoint	ListPrice
1	Adjustable Race	AR-5381		FALSE		FALSE		1000	750	
2	Bearing Ball	BA-8327		FALSE		FALSE		1000	750	
3	LL Bottom Bracket	BB-7421		TRUE	$39.95	TRUE		500	375	
4	ML Bottom Bracket	BB-8107		TRUE	$74.92	TRUE		500	375	$67.49
5	HL Bottom Bracket	BB-9108		TRUE	$89.90	TRUE		500	375	$126.55
6	BB Ball Bearing	BE-2349		TRUE		FALSE		800	600	$151.86
7	Headset Ball Bearings	BE-2908		FALSE		FALSE		800	600	
8	Mountain-500 Black, 40	BK-M18B-40		TRUE	$399.59	TRUE	Black	100	75	$674.99
9	Mountain-500 Black, 42	BK-M18B-42		TRUE	$399.59	TRUE	Black	100	75	$674.99
10	Mountain-500 Black, 44	BK-M18B-44		TRUE	$399.59	TRUE	Black	100	75	$674.99
11	Mountain-500 Black, 48	BK-M18B-48		TRUE	$399.59	TRUE	Black	100	75	$674.99
12	Mountain-500 Black, 52	BK-M18B-52		TRUE	$399.59	TRUE	Black	100	75	$674.99
15	Mountain-500 Black, 62	BK-M18B-62	12/4/2002	TRUE	$399.99	TRUE	Black	100	75	$674.99
16	Mountain-500 Red, 40	BK-M18R-40	12/4/2002	TRUE	$399.99	TRUE	Red	100	75	$674.99
17	Mountain-500 Red, 44	BK-M18R-44	12/4/2002	TRUE	$399.99	TRUE	Red	100	75	$674.99
19	Mountain-500 Red, 52	BK-M18R-52	12/4/2002	TRUE	$399.99	TRUE	Red	100	75	$674.99
20	Mountain-500 Red, 56	BK-M18R-56	12/4/2002	TRUE	$399.99	TRUE	Red	100	75	$674.99
24	Mountain-500 Silver, 40	BK-M18S-40		TRUE	$418.09	TRUE	Silver	100	75	$706.24
25	Mountain-500 Silver, 42	BK-M18S-42		TRUE	$418.09	TRUE	Silver	100	75	$706.24
26	Mountain-500 Silver, 44	BK-M18S-44		TRUE	$418.09	TRUE	Silver	100	75	$706.24
27	Mountain-500 Silver, 48	BK-M18S-48		TRUE	$418.09	TRUE	Silver	100	75	$706.24
28	Mountain-500 Silver, 52	BK-M18S-52		TRUE	$418.09	TRUE	Silver	100	75	$706.24
32	Mountain-500 Blue, 40	BK-M18U-40	12/4/2002	TRUE	$399.99	TRUE	Blue	100	75	$674.99
34	Mountain-500 Blue, 48	BK-M18U-48	12/4/2002	TRUE	$399.99	TRUE	Blue	100	75	$674.99
36	Mountain-500 Blue, 56	BK-M18U-56	12/4/2002	TRUE	$399.99	TRUE	Blue	100	75	$674.99
37	Mountain-500 Blue, 58	BK-M18U-58	12/4/2002	TRUE	$399.99	TRUE	Blue	100	75	$674.99
40	Mountain-500 Yellow, 40	BK-M18Y-40	12/4/2002	TRUE	$399.99	TRUE	Yellow	100	75	$674.99
41	Mountain-500 Yellow, 44	BK-M18Y-44	12/4/2002	TRUE	$399.99	TRUE	Yellow	100	75	$674.99
42	Mountain-500 Yellow, 48	BK-M18Y-48	12/4/2002	TRUE	$399.99	TRUE	Yellow	100	75	$674.99
43	Mountain-500 Yellow, 52	BK-M18Y-52	12/4/2002	TRUE	$399.99	TRUE	Yellow	100	75	$674.99
44	Mountain-500 Yellow, 56	BK-M18Y-56	12/4/2002	TRUE	$399.99	TRUE	Yellow	100	75	$674.99
48	Mountain-400 Black, 40	BK-M38B-40	12/4/2002	TRUE	$569.99	TRUE	Black	100	75	$961.86
49	Mountain-400 Black, 44	BK-M38B-44	12/4/2002	TRUE	$569.99	TRUE	Black	100	75	$961.86
50	Mountain-400 Black, 48	BK-M38B-48	12/4/2002	TRUE	$569.99	TRUE	Black	100	75	$961.86
51	Mountain-400 Black, 52	BK-M38B-52	12/4/2002	TRUE	$569.99	TRUE	Black	100	75	$961.86
52	Mountain-400 Black, 56	BK-M38B-56	12/4/2002	TRUE	$569.99	TRUE	Black	100	75	$961.86
53	Mountain-400 Black, 58	BK-M38B-58	12/4/2002	TRUE	$569.99	TRUE	Black	100	75	$961.86
55	Mountain-400 Black, 62	BK-M38B-62	12/4/2002	TRUE	$569.99	TRUE	Black	100	75	$961.86
56	Mountain-400 Red, 40	BK-M38R-40	12/4/2002	TRUE	$569.99	TRUE	Red	100	75	$961.86
57	Mountain-400 Red, 44	BK-M38R-44	12/4/2002	TRUE	$569.99	TRUE	Red	100	75	$961.86
58	Mountain-400 Red, 48	BK-M38R-48	12/4/2002	TRUE	$569.99	TRUE	Red	100	75	$961.86
59	Mountain-400 Red, 52	BK-M38R-52	12/4/2002	TRUE	$569.99	TRUE	Red	100	75	$961.86
60	Mountain-400 Red, 56	BK-M38R-56	12/4/2002	TRUE	$569.99	TRUE	Red	100	75	$961.86
61	Mountain-400 Red, 58	BK-M38R-58	12/4/2002	TRUE	$569.99	TRUE	Red	100	75	$961.86
64	Mountain-400-W Silver, 38	BK-M38S-38		TRUE	$569.42	TRUE	Silver	100	75	$961.86
65	Mountain-400-W Silver, 40	BK-M38S-40		TRUE	$569.42	TRUE	Silver	100	75	$961.86
66	Mountain-400-W Silver, 42	BK-M38S-42		TRUE	$569.42	TRUE	Silver	100	75	$961.86

Figure 5-1

ProductID	Name	ProductNumber	DiscontinuedDate	MakeFlag	StandardCost	FinishedGoodsFlag	Color	SafetyStockLevel	ReorderPoint
1	Adjustable Race	AR-5381		FALSE		FALSE		1000	750
2	Bearing Ball	BA-8327		FALSE		FALSE		1000	750
3	LL Bottom Bracket	BB-7421		TRUE	$39.95	TRUE		500	375
4	ML Bottom Bracket	BB-8107		TRUE	$74.92	TRUE		500	375
5	HL Bottom Bracket	BB-9108		TRUE	$89.90	TRUE		500	375
6	BB Ball Bearing	BE-2349		TRUE		FALSE		800	600
7	Headset Ball Bearings	BE-2908		FALSE		FALSE		800	600
8	Mountain-500 Black, 40	BK-M18B-40		TRUE	$399.59	TRUE	Black	100	75
9	Mountain-500 Black, 42	BK-M18B-42		TRUE	$399.59	TRUE	Black	100	75
10	Mountain-500 Black, 44	BK-M18B-44		TRUE	$399.59	TRUE	Black	100	75
11	Mountain-500 Black, 48	BK-M18B-48		TRUE	$399.59	TRUE	Black	100	75
12	Mountain-500 Black, 52	BK-M18B-52		TRUE	$399.59	TRUE	Black	100	75
15	Mountain-500 Black, 62	BK-M18B-62	12/4/2002	TRUE	$399.99	TRUE	Black	100	75
16	Mountain-500 Red, 40	BK-M18R-40	12/4/2002	TRUE	$399.99	TRUE	Red	100	75
17	Mountain-500 Red, 44	BK-M18R-44	12/4/2002	TRUE	$399.99	TRUE	Red	100	75
19	Mountain-500 Red, 52	BK-M18R-52	12/4/2002	TRUE	$399.99	TRUE	Red	100	75
20	Mountain-500 Red, 56	BK-M18R-56	12/4/2002	TRUE	$399.99	TRUE	Red	100	75
24	Mountain-500 Silver, 40	BK-M18S-40		TRUE	$418.09	TRUE	Silver	100	75
25	Mountain-500 Silver, 42	BK-M18S-42		TRUE	$418.09	TRUE	Silver	100	75
26	Mountain-500 Silver, 44	BK-M18S-44		TRUE	$418.09	TRUE	Silver	100	75
27	Mountain-500 Silver, 48	BK-M18S-48		TRUE	$418.09	TRUE	Silver	100	75
28	Mountain-500 Silver, 52	BK-M18S-52		TRUE	$418.09	TRUE	Silver	100	75
32	Mountain-500 Blue, 40	BK-M18U-40	12/4/2002	TRUE	$399.99	TRUE	Blue	100	75
34	Mountain-500 Blue, 48	BK-M18U-48	12/4/2002	TRUE	$399.99	TRUE	Blue	100	75
36	Mountain-500 Blue, 56	BK-M18U-56	12/4/2002	TRUE	$399.99	TRUE	Blue	100	75
37	Mountain-500 Blue, 58	BK-M18U-58	12/4/2002	TRUE	$399.99	TRUE	Blue	100	75
40	Mountain-500 Yellow, 40	BK-M18Y-40	12/4/2002	TRUE	$399.99	TRUE	Yellow	100	75
41	Mountain-500 Yellow, 44	BK-M18Y-44	12/4/2002	TRUE	$399.99	TRUE	Yellow	100	75
42	Mountain-500 Yellow, 48	BK-M18Y-48	12/4/2002	TRUE	$399.99	TRUE	Yellow	100	75
43	Mountain-500 Yellow, 52	BK-M18Y-52	12/4/2002	TRUE	$399.99	TRUE	Yellow	100	75
44	Mountain-500 Yellow, 56	BK-M18Y-56	12/4/2002	TRUE	$399.99	TRUE	Yellow	100	75
48	Mountain-400 Black, 40	BK-M38B-40	12/4/2002	TRUE	$569.99	TRUE	Black	100	75
49	Mountain-400 Black, 44	BK-M38B-44	12/4/2002	TRUE	$569.99	TRUE	Black	100	75
50	Mountain-400 Black, 48	BK-M38B-48	12/4/2002	TRUE	$569.99	TRUE	Black	100	75
51	Mountain-400 Black, 52	BK-M38B-52	12/4/2002	TRUE	$569.99	TRUE	Black	100	75
52	Mountain-400 Black, 56	BK-M38B-56	12/4/2002	TRUE	$569.99	TRUE	Black	100	75
53	Mountain-400 Black, 58	BK-M38B-58	12/4/2002	TRUE	$569.99	TRUE	Black	100	75
55	Mountain-400 Black, 62	BK-M38B-62	12/4/2002	TRUE	$569.99	TRUE	Black	100	75
56	Mountain-400 Red, 40	BK-M38R-40	12/4/2002	TRUE	$569.99	TRUE	Red	100	75
57	Mountain-400 Red, 44	BK-M38R-44	12/4/2002	TRUE	$569.99	TRUE	Red	100	75
58	Mountain-400 Red, 48	BK-M38R-48	12/4/2002	TRUE	$569.99	TRUE	Red	100	75
59	Mountain-400 Red, 52	BK-M38R-52	12/4/2002	TRUE	$569.99	TRUE	Red	100	75
60	Mountain-400 Red, 56	BK-M38R-56	12/4/2002	TRUE	$569.99	TRUE	Red	100	75
61	Mountain-400 Red, 58	BK-M38R-58	12/4/2002	TRUE	$569.99	TRUE	Red	100	75
64	Mountain-400-W Silver, 38	BK-M38S-38		TRUE	$569.42	TRUE	Silver	100	75
65	Mountain-400-W Silver, 40	BK-M38S-40		TRUE	$569.42	TRUE	Silver	100	75
66	Mountain-400-W Silver, 42	BK-M38S-42		TRUE	$569.42	TRUE	Silver	100	75

Figure 5-2

	Name	StandardCost	Color
1	Adjustable Race	NULL	NULL
2	Bearing Ball	NULL	NULL
3	LL Bottom Bracket	39.9526	NULL
4	ML Bottom Bracket	74.9176	NULL
5	HL Bottom Bracket	89.9026	NULL
6	BB Ball Bearing	NULL	NULL
7	Headset Ball Bearings	NULL	NULL
8	Mountain-500 Black, 40	399.5926	Black
9	Mountain-500 Black, 42	399.5926	Black
10	Mountain-500 Black, 44	399.5926	Black
11	Mountain-500 Black, 48	399.5926	Black
12	Mountain-500 Black, 52	399.5926	Black
13	Mountain-500 Black, 62	399.9900	Black
14	Mountain-500 Red, 40	399.9900	Red
15	Mountain-500 Red, 44	399.9900	Red
16	Mountain-500 Red, 52	399.9900	Red
17	Mountain-500 Red, 56	399.9900	Red
18	Mountain-500 Silver, 40	418.0926	Silver
19	Mountain-500 Silver, 42	418.0926	Silver
20	Mountain-500 Silver, 44	418.0926	Silver
21	Mountain-500 Silver, 48	418.0926	Silver
22	Mountain-500 Silver, 52	418.0926	Silver
23	Mountain-500 Blue, 40	399.9900	Blue
24	Mountain-500 Blue, 48	399.9900	Blue
25	Mountain-500 Blue, 56	399.9900	Blue

Figure 5-3

There are advantages of using this technique. If the structure of the table were to change, that is, if a column were added or the name changed, this query would continue to return all of the column values based on the table's current design. Likewise, a disadvantage is that if the table's structure were to change, the results might be less predictable. For example, if an application were developed with a form showing employee information, you might expect to see the employee First Name, Last Name, and Phone Number. Later, if a column was added to the table to store salary information, and if this new information was fed to the form, users might inappropriately see sensitive information. This could also destabilize the application, resulting in errors. For this reason, it may be advisable to list all of the columns you want to return. There are a number of reasons to explicitly list the columns in your query, including the following:

❏   Including columns you don't need produces unnecessary disk I/O and network traffic.

❏   Sensitive information may be available to unauthorized users.

❏   In complex, multi-table queries, including all columns produces redundant column values, confusing users and complicating application development.

❏   Results are more predictable and easier to manage.

Later on, you'll learn about writing queries for multiple tables. In the following Try It Out, you take a look at such a query so you can see how to address columns from more than one table with identical names.

Try It Out

Open SQL Server Query Analyzer or The SQL Server Management Studio and connect to your database server. Select the AdventureWorks2000 database from the selection list on the toolbar. Type the following query into the query editor and execute the query:

```
SELECT CustomerID, SalesPersonID
FROM Customer
```

In the results pane, you should see two columns of values representing customer records — all 19,186 of them. The record count is displayed in the lower status bar, near the right side. Other than possibly the cosmetic differences between SQL Server 2000 Query Analyzer and SQL Server 2005 Management Studio, your results should look something like those shown in Figure 5-4.

Now, expand the query to get sales order information from a related table. Amend the query as in the following example.

Just a quick aside: Although the reason may not be apparent in this example, it's a good idea to get yourself into the habit of formatting your SQL to make it as readable as possible. Note that I have inserted carriage returns before each comma and used tabs and spaces to line up the columns. This is a practice I'll continue to use in the example script, but it is not a requirement.

```
SELECT CustomerID
     , SalesPersonID
     , PurchaseOrderNumber
FROM Customer
    INNER JOIN SalesOrderHeader
        ON Customer.CustomerID = SalesOrderHeader.CustomerID
```

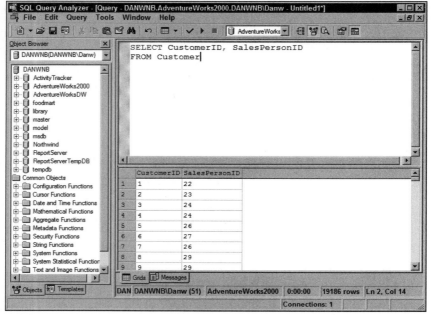

Figure 5-4

Now, when you execute this query, what happens? You get an error that looks like this:

```
Server: Msg 209, Level 16, State 1, Line 1
Ambiguous column name 'CustomerID'.
Server: Msg 209, Level 16, State 1, Line 1
Ambiguous column name 'SalesPersonID'.
```

The query parser is unhappy because you have referred to two different tables that contain columns with identical names. Both the Customer and SalesOrderHeader tables contain columns named CustomerID and SalesPersonID. This problem is easily remedied by prefixing the column names with the table name. The corrected query would look like this:

```
SELECT Customer.CustomerID
    , SalesOrderHeader.SalesPersonID
    , SalesOrderHeader.PurchaseOrderNumber
FROM Customer
    INNER JOIN SalesOrderHeader
        ON Customer.CustomerID = SalesOrderHeader.CustomerID
```

This works as long as you want to see the ID for the salesperson who actually took the order rather than the one assigned to this customer. As you can see in Figure 5-5, the result set doesn't show you the table name, therefore someone looking at this data may not know to which salesperson you are referring.

	CustomerID	SalesPersonID	PurchaseOrderNumber
1	304	31	PO29199294
2	595	302	PO58117793
3	609	27	PO348186287
4	651	29	PO435152332
5	595	302	PO58159451
6	595	302	PO58157962
7	676	29	PO522154989
8	4	24	PO551177057
9	633	35	PO377148431

Figure 5-5

SQL Server 2005 Schemas

In SQL Server 2005, table names are prefixed with a schema name, separating the schema name and object name with a period. This practice is common in other database products. For the examples to remain compatible with SQL Server 2000, I am not using schema names. The purpose for schemas is to categorically group objects and make large, complex databases easier to manage. In SQL Server 2000 objects are identified by the four-part name of *Server.Database.Owner.Object.* SQL Server 2000 does not separate the *owner* from the *schema,* but SQL Server 2005 does. This not only creates a namespace to place objects, but also adds a new layer of security to SQL Server by defining a security scope at the schema level. Users in SQL Server 2005 can be assigned a default schema and granted or denied access to specific schemas. Because it's possible to create objects with duplicate names under different schemas, this practice can also lead to a very complex (and possibly confusing) database design. Using schemas is not much different than the practice of assigning different ownership to objects, a capability available in earlier versions of SQL Server, but discouraged.

Here's how it works: The database designer defines schemas, which are really just category names. These schema names can have associated ownership and permissions, which provides the same capabilities available in earlier SQL Server versions. The implementation is very simple. In the AdventureWorks2000 database, you reference the Product table in a query like this:

```
SELECT * FROM Product
```

If you were using the AdventureWorks database that installs with SQL Server 2005, because the Product table is in the Production schema, you must use this syntax:

```
SELECT * FROM Production.Product
```

In SQL Server 2000 and earlier versions, objects are typically owned by a user called *DBO,* and if you don't prefix an object reference with a username, the DBO user is just assumed. The same is true with schemas in SQL Server 2005. Objects can belong to the DBO schema, and if you don't use a schema name in an object reference, the DBO schema is assumed. However, this is only true if your default schema has not been changed to something other than DBO. If an object is part of any other schema, the schema name must be used in the expression. Here is an example to illustrate this new feature.

User Fred connects to the AdventureWorks database on a SQL Server 2005 instance called Bedrock1. Fred's default schema has not been changed and so it is set to DBO. Fred then executes the following query:

```
SELECT * FROM Product
```

The Query Processor attempts to resolve the Product table name to Bedrock1.AdventureWorks.dbo. Product, but the query fails because the Product table exists in the Production schema and not the DBO schema. Now I change Fred's default schema like this:

```
ALTER USER Fred WITH DEFAULT_SCHEMA = Production
```

When Fred executes the product query again, the Query Processor resolves the product table to Bedrock1.AdventureWorks.Production.Product and the query succeeds.

Now take a look at an opposite example. User Barney connects to the same instance that user Fred did, but he wants to retrieve the contents of the SalesOrder table that exists in the DBO schema. Barney's default schema has also been set to Production. Barney runs the following query:

```
SELECT * FROM SalesOrder
```

The Query Processor first attempts to resolve the SalesOrder table to Barney's default schema; Bedrock1.AdventureWorks.Production.SalesOrder, but the resolution fails. However, because the Query Processor started in a schema other than DBO, it then falls back to the DBO schema and attempts to resolve the table to Bedrock1.AdventureWorks.dbo.SalesOrder. This resolution succeeds and the contents of the table are returned.

Column Aliasing

You may want to change column names in a query for a variety of reasons. These may include changing a column name to make it easier to understand or to provide a more descriptive name. Changing a column name can also provide backward compatibility for application objects if column names were renamed after design.

In a previous example you saw that the Query Processor needs to know what table to retrieve a column from if the column exists in more than one referenced table. The same can also be true for the person reading the results. They might need to know exactly what table the values were extracted from. The following example clarifies the source of an ambiguous column by using an alias:

```
SELECT Customer.CustomerID
     , SalesOrderHeader.SalesPersonID AS OrderSalesPersonID
     , PurchaseOrderNumber
FROM Customer
   INNER JOIN SalesOrderHeader
      ON Customer.CustomerID = SalesOrderHeader.CustomerID
```

In the result set shown in Figure 5-6, you can see that the second column now shows up as OrderSalesPersonID.

Months later, this could save someone a lot of grief and aggravation. Imagine getting a call from the accounting department when they discover that they have been paying commission to the wrong salespeople.

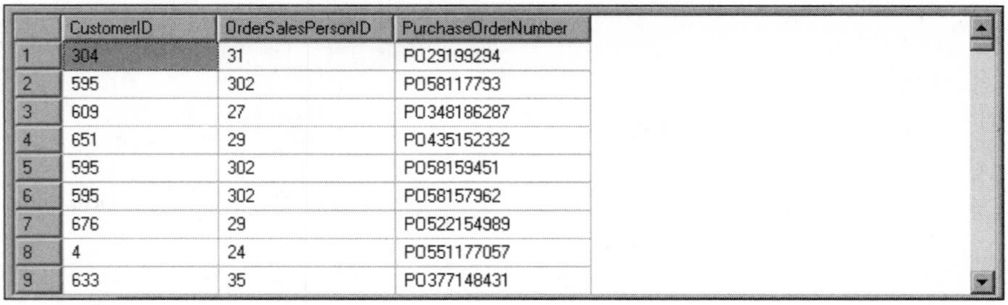

	CustomerID	OrderSalesPersonID	PurchaseOrderNumber
1	304	31	PO29199294
2	595	302	PO58117793
3	609	27	PO348186287
4	651	29	PO435152332
5	595	302	PO58159451
6	595	302	PO58157962
7	676	29	PO522154989
8	4	24	PO551177057
9	633	35	PO377148431

Figure 5-6

You can alias a column in three different ways. The technique used in the preceding example is probably the most descriptive. A popular technique leaves out the AS keyword so the actual column name simply precedes the alias. The following table shows each of these techniques. The last one isn't common, and I don't recommend that you use it. However, this may come in handy if you come across a script containing this syntax.

Syntax	Description
Column AS *Alias*	Most readable technique, however, not popular with SQL purists.
Column Alias	Most common technique. Most auto-generated code is written in this form.
Alias = *Column*	This technique is not common in Transact-SQL.

Here are examples of these three techniques:

```
SELECT FirstName + ' ' + LastName AS FullName
FROM Contact

SELECT FirstName + ' ' + LastName FullName
FROM Contact

SELECT FullName = FirstName + ' ' + LastName
FROM Contact
```

Calculated and Derived Columns

One of the most common types of column aliases is when a new column is created from an expression or calculation. In the following example using the Employee table, the employees' first name and last name are combined (or concatenated) together. Character concatenation can be performed using the plus sign, like so:

```
SELECT FirstName + ' ' + LastName AS EmployeeName
FROM Employee
```

This produces a single column called EmployeeName, which contains the employees' first name, a space, and then their last name, as shown in Figure 5-7.

	EmployeeName
1	Terri Duffy
2	Jian Shuo Wang
3	Michael Sullivan
4	Sharon Salavaria
5	Gail Erickson
6	Jossef Goldberg
7	Ovidiu Crăcium
8	Janice Galvin
9	Thierry D'Hers

Figure 5-7

Character data isn't the only thing you can manipulate to produce new column values. A few examples using various functions and column data types follow. This first simple example uses the UnitPrice and OrderQty columns from the SalesOrderDetail to calculate the purchase amount for a line item by multiplying these two values. The resulting alias column is called PurchasePrice:

```
SELECT SalesOrderID
     , LineNumber
     , ProductID
     , UnitPrice * OrderQty As PurchasePrice
FROM SalesOrderDetail
```

In the result set shown in Figure 5-8, the PurchasePrice column shows the calculated figure.

	SalesOrderID	LineNumber	ProductID	PurchasePrice
1	5001	1	1218	23.3740
2	5002	1	527	534.4920
3	5002	2	558	1749.3840
4	5003	1	1086	440.1742
5	5003	2	661	440.1742
6	5004	1	870	83.2981
7	5005	1	594	1716.5304
8	5005	2	627	236.4300
9	5005	3	1201	140.3740

Figure 5-8

In the following scenario, you need to calculate each employee's age based on their birth date and the current date. Using the DateDiff function, you ask SQL Server to calculate the number of days between the two dates and then divide by 365 to get the approximate result in years. The query would look like this:

```
SELECT FirstName
     , LastName
     , BirthDate
     , DateDiff(Day, BirthDate, GetDate())/365 As Age
FROM Employee
```

The result set should look like that shown in Figure 5-9.

	FirstName	Lastname	BirthDate	Age	
1	Terri	Duffy	9/1/1961 12:00:00 AM	42	
2	Jian Shuo	Wang	12/13/1964 12:00:00 AM	39	
3	Michael	Sullivan	7/17/1969 12:00:00 AM	35	
4	Sharon	Salavaria	6/3/1951 12:00:00 AM	53	
5	Gail	Erickson	10/29/1942 12:00:00 AM	61	
6	Jossef	Goldberg	4/11/1949 12:00:00 AM	55	
7	Ovidiu	Crăcium	2/18/1968 12:00:00 AM	36	
8	Janice	Galvin	6/29/1979 12:00:00 AM	25	
9	Thierry	D'Hers	8/29/1949 12:00:00 AM	54	

Figure 5-9

In this example, the Product table, the SubCategoryID, is related to a column in the ProductSubCategory table. Without using a join between these tables, I would like to see the subcategory name in the output from my query. Because I know that SubCategoryID 1 represents mountain bikes, I can add this description using an alias column. In the WHERE clause, I filter product rows based on the subcategory and then add an alias column called SubCategoryName:

```
SELECT Name, ListPrice, 'Mountain Bike' AS SubCategoryName
FROM Product WHERE ProductSubCategoryID = 1
```

Figure 5-10 shows the results from this query. Note the SubCategoryName column.

	Name	ListPrice	SubCategoryName	
1	Mountain-500 Black, 40	539.9900	Mountain Bike	
2	Mountain-500 Black, 42	539.9900	Mountain Bike	
3	Mountain-500 Black, 44	539.9900	Mountain Bike	
4	Mountain-500 Black, 48	539.9900	Mountain Bike	
5	Mountain-500 Black, 52	539.9900	Mountain Bike	
6	Mountain-500 Black, 62	539.9900	Mountain Bike	
7	Mountain-500 Red, 40	539.9900	Mountain Bike	
8	Mountain-500 Red, 44	539.9900	Mountain Bike	
9	Mountain-500 Red, 52	539.9900	Mountain Bike	

Figure 5-10

I'll come back to this example and expand on it in Chapter 8 when you learn about Union queries.

Filtering Rows

It's safe to say that most of the time you won't want to return every record, especially in your largest tables. Many production databases in business are used to collect and store records for many years of business activity. For small to medium-sized businesses, this is a common practice. In larger-scale systems, data is usually archived yearly or monthly and useful, historical information may be moved into a data warehouse for reporting. Regardless, it often doesn't make sense to return all rows in a table. Two basic techniques exist for returning some of the rows from a query: The WHERE clause is used to qualify each row based on filter criteria, and the TOP clause is used to truncate the list after a certain number of rows are returned.

The WHERE Clause

Filtering is largely the job of the WHERE clause, which is followed by some sort of filtering expression. The syntax of this statement is very natural and should be easy to translate to or from a verbal statement. I'll continue to use the Excel worksheet example that I began using earlier in this chapter. In this example, all columns for product rows where the color is black are returned:

```
SELECT * FROM Product
WHERE Color = 'Black'
```

I'm essentially asking SQL Server to filter the rows for the table only vertically, returning slices that meet only the specified color criteria, as reflected in Figure 5-11.

The result set shows only the matching rows (as much as you can see in the results grid), as shown in Figure 5-12.

Recall that I used this workbook to demonstrate selecting specific columns to be returned from the query. So far, I've selected specific columns and specific rows. Now, I'll combine the two to return a subset of both columns and rows using the following SELECT expressions:

```
SELECT Name, StandardCost, Color
FROM Product
WHERE Color = 'Black'
```

ProductID	Name	ProductNumber	DiscontinuedDate	MakeFlag	StandardCost	FinishedGoodsFlag	Color	SafetyStockLevel	ReorderPoint	ListPrice
1	Adjustable Race	AR-5381		FALSE		FALSE		1000	750	
2	Bearing Ball	BA-8327		FALSE		FALSE		1000	750	
3	LL Bottom Bracket	BB-7421		TRUE	$39.95	TRUE		500	375	$67.49
4	ML Bottom Bracket	BB-8107		TRUE	$74.92	TRUE		500	375	$126.55
5	HL Bottom Bracket	BB-9108		TRUE	$89.90	TRUE		500	375	$151.86
6	BB Ball Bearing	BE-2349		TRUE		FALSE		800	600	
7	Headset Ball Bearings	BE-2908		FALSE		FALSE		800	600	
8	Mountain-500 Black, 40	BK-M18B-40		TRUE	$399.59	TRUE	Black	100	75	$674.99
9	Mountain-500 Black, 42	BK-M18B-42		TRUE	$399.59	TRUE	Black	100	75	$674.99
10	Mountain-500 Black, 44	BK-M18B-44		TRUE	$399.59	TRUE	Black	100	75	$674.99
11	Mountain-500 Black, 48	BK-M18B-48		TRUE	$399.59	TRUE	Black	100	75	$674.99
12	Mountain-500 Black, 52	BK-M18B-52		TRUE	$399.59	TRUE	Black	100	75	$674.99
15	Mountain-500 Black, 62	BK-M18B-62	12/4/2002	TRUE	$399.99	TRUE	Black	100	75	$674.99
16	Mountain-500 Red, 40	BK-M18R-40	12/4/2002	TRUE	$399.99	TRUE	Red	100	75	$674.99
17	Mountain-500 Red, 44	BK-M18R-44	12/4/2002	TRUE	$399.99	TRUE	Red	100	75	$674.99
19	Mountain-500 Red, 52	BK-M18R-52	12/4/2002	TRUE	$399.99	TRUE	Red	100	75	$674.99
20	Mountain-500 Red, 56	BK-M18R-56	12/4/2002	TRUE	$399.99	TRUE	Red	100	75	$674.99
24	Mountain-500 Silver, 40	BK-M18S-40		TRUE	$418.09	TRUE	Silver	100	75	$706.24
25	Mountain-500 Silver, 42	BK-M18S-42		TRUE	$418.09	TRUE	Silver	100	75	$706.24
26	Mountain-500 Silver, 44	BK-M18S-44		TRUE	$418.09	TRUE	Silver	100	75	$706.24
27	Mountain-500 Silver, 48	BK-M18S-48		TRUE	$418.09	TRUE	Silver	100	75	$706.24
28	Mountain-500 Silver, 52	BK-M18S-52		TRUE	$418.09	TRUE	Silver	100	75	$706.24
32	Mountain-500 Blue, 40	BK-M18U-40	12/4/2002	TRUE	$399.99	TRUE	Blue	100	75	$674.99
34	Mountain-500 Blue, 48	BK-M18U-48	12/4/2002	TRUE	$399.99	TRUE	Blue	100	75	$674.99
36	Mountain-500 Blue, 56	BK-M18U-56	12/4/2002	TRUE	$399.99	TRUE	Blue	100	75	$674.99
37	Mountain-500 Blue, 58	BK-M18U-58	12/4/2002	TRUE	$399.99	TRUE	Blue	100	75	$674.99
40	Mountain-500 Yellow, 40	BK-M18Y-40	12/4/2002	TRUE	$399.99	TRUE	Yellow	100	75	$674.99
41	Mountain-500 Yellow, 44	BK-M18Y-44	12/4/2002	TRUE	$399.99	TRUE	Yellow	100	75	$674.99
42	Mountain-500 Yellow, 48	BK-M18Y-48	12/4/2002	TRUE	$399.99	TRUE	Yellow	100	75	$674.99
43	Mountain-500 Yellow, 52	BK-M18Y-52	12/4/2002	TRUE	$399.99	TRUE	Yellow	100	75	$674.99
44	Mountain-500 Yellow, 56	BK-M18Y-56	12/4/2002	TRUE	$399.99	TRUE	Yellow	100	75	$674.99
48	Mountain-400 Black, 40	BK-M38B-40	12/4/2002	TRUE	$569.99	TRUE	Black	100	75	$961.86
49	Mountain-400 Black, 44	BK-M38B-44	12/4/2002	TRUE	$569.99	TRUE	Black	100	75	$961.86
50	Mountain-400 Black, 48	BK-M38B-48	12/4/2002	TRUE	$569.99	TRUE	Black	100	75	$961.86
51	Mountain-400 Black, 52	BK-M38B-52	12/4/2002	TRUE	$569.99	TRUE	Black	100	75	$961.86
52	Mountain-400 Black, 56	BK-M38B-56	12/4/2002	TRUE	$569.99	TRUE	Black	100	75	$961.86
53	Mountain-400 Black, 58	BK-M38B-58	12/4/2002	TRUE	$569.99	TRUE	Black	100	75	$961.86
55	Mountain-400 Black, 62	BK-M38B-62	12/4/2002	TRUE	$569.99	TRUE	Black	100	75	$961.86
56	Mountain-400 Red, 40	BK-M38R-40	12/4/2002	TRUE	$569.99	TRUE	Red	100	75	$961.86
57	Mountain-400 Red, 44	BK-M38R-44	12/4/2002	TRUE	$569.99	TRUE	Red	100	75	$961.86
58	Mountain-400 Red, 48	BK-M38R-48	12/4/2002	TRUE	$569.99	TRUE	Red	100	75	$961.86
59	Mountain-400 Red, 52	BK-M38R-52	12/4/2002	TRUE	$569.99	TRUE	Red	100	75	$961.86
60	Mountain-400 Red, 56	BK-M38R-56	12/4/2002	TRUE	$569.99	TRUE	Red	100	75	$961.86
61	Mountain-400 Red, 58	BK-M38R-58	12/4/2002	TRUE	$569.99	TRUE	Red	100	75	$961.86
64	Mountain-400-W Silver, 38	BK-M38S-38		TRUE	$569.42	TRUE	Silver	100	75	$961.86
65	Mountain-400-W Silver, 40	BK-M38S-40		TRUE	$569.42	TRUE	Silver	100	75	$961.86
66	Mountain-400-W Silver, 42	BK-M38S-42		TRUE	$569.42	TRUE	Silver	100	75	$961.86

Figure 5-11

Figure 5-12

Before showing you the results, Figure 5-13 gives you another look at that workbook data with high-lighted columns and rows.

The result set contains only the values in the intersection of the columns and rows. As you can see in Figure 5-14, only the Name, StandardCost, and Color columns are included, and the only rows are those where the Color value is Black.

Figure 5-13

	Name	StandardCost	Color
1	Mountain-500 Black, 40	399.5926	Black
2	Mountain-500 Black, 42	399.5926	Black
3	Mountain-500 Black, 44	399.5926	Black
4	Mountain-500 Black, 48	399.5926	Black
5	Mountain-500 Black, 52	399.5926	Black
6	Mountain-500 Black, 62	399.9900	Black
7	Mountain-400 Black, 40	569.9900	Black
8	Mountain-400 Black, 44	569.9900	Black
9	Mountain-400 Black, 48	569.9900	Black
10	Mountain-400 Black, 52	569.9900	Black
11	Mountain-400 Black, 56	569.9900	Black
12	Mountain-400 Black, 58	569.9900	Black
13	Mountain-400 Black, 62	569.9900	Black

Figure 5-14

For example, consider the following verbal request: "I would like to see a list of products, including the product name and price that have a price less than $5.00." The SQL version of this request would look like this:

```
SELECT Name, ListPrice
FROM Product
WHERE ListPrice < 5.00
```

Only five products meet these criteria, as shown in Figure 5-15.

	Name	ListPrice
1	Mountain Tire Tube	4.9900
2	Road Tire Tube	3.9900
3	Touring Tire Tube	4.9900
4	water bottle 30 oz	4.9900
5	Patch kit with 8 patches	2.2900

Figure 5-15

Easy, right? Filtering statements should be very natural and easy to read. You just need to get used to the flow.

Comparison Operators

Qualifying values to match a set of criteria is a relatively straightforward proposition, especially when working with numeric and date/time types. Testing a numeric value to see if it is greater than 10 makes sense and there is little room for confusion. However, testing to see if the value Fred is greater than the value Bob may not make much sense.

Comparing and qualifying values generally boils down to this: A value is either equal to, less than, or greater than another value. When matching character values, you can be a little more creative, looking for partial strings of characters to match a value that is "like" another value. Starting with the simplest comparisons, value-matching operators are described in the following table.

Operator	Description
=	Equal to. Matches a value that is exactly equal to another value. Can be used with nearly all data types.
<> or !=	Not equal to.
<	Less than. Typically used with numeric and date/time data types.
>	Greater than.
!<	Not less than.
!>	Not greater than.
<=	Less than or equal to.
>=	Greater than or equal to.
Like	Used to perform wildcard matches with character values.

Logical Comparisons

Using logical comparisons is how we make sense of things and it's how we simplify matters. It's how we dispel the gray area between yes and no or true and false.

It would be convenient if all decisions were based on only one question, but this is rarely the case. Most important decisions are the product of many individual choices. It would also be convenient if each unique combination of decisions led to a unique outcome, but this isn't true either. The fact is that, often, multiple combinations of individual decisions can lead to the same conclusion. This may seem to be very complicated. Fortunately for us, in the 1830s mathematician George Bool boiled all of this down to a few very simple methods for combining outcomes called logical gates. There are only three of them: And, Or, and Not.

It's important to realize that every SQL comparison and logical expression yields only one type of result: True or False. When combining two expressions, there are only three possible outcomes: they are both True, they are both False, or one is True and the other False. With the groundwork laid, let's apply Bool's rules of logic to the SQL WHERE clause and combine multiple expressions.

The AND Operator

The AND operator simply states that for the entire expression to yield a True result, all individual statements must be true. For example, suppose you're looking for product records where the SubCategoryID is 1 (mountain bikes) and the price is less than $1,000. You're not interested in road bikes under $1,000, nor mountain bikes costing $1,000 or more. Both criteria must be met.

Assuming that there are records matching either criterion, the AND operator will always reduce the rows in the result set. For example, the Product table contains 142 mountain bikes and 478 rows with a list price under $1,000. However, only 54 rows match both of these filters. Figure 5-16 shows 9 of them.

	ProductID	Name	ListPrice	
1	8	Mountain-500 Black, 40	539.9900	
2	9	Mountain-500 Black, 42	539.9900	
3	10	Mountain-500 Black, 44	539.9900	
4	11	Mountain-500 Black, 48	539.9900	
5	12	Mountain-500 Black, 52	539.9900	
6	15	Mountain-500 Black, 62	539.9900	
7	16	Mountain-500 Red, 40	539.9900	
8	17	Mountain-500 Red, 44	539.9900	
9	19	Mountain-500 Red, 52	539.9900	

Figure 5-16

The OR Operator

When statements are combined using the OR operator, rows are returned if they match any of the criteria. Using the previous statement, changing the AND to an OR produces a different result:

```
SELECT ProductID, Name, ListPrice
FROM Product
WHERE ProductSubCategoryID = 1 OR ListPrice < 1000
```

Rather than seeing only mountain bikes under $1,000, you see all mountain bikes, regardless of their price, and all products having a price under $1,000. This query returns 521 rows (9 of which are shown in Figure 5-17). Note that even though there would be less expensive mountain bikes in either of the combined results, SQL Server is smart enough to remove the duplicate rows.

	ProductID	Name	ListPrice	
1	3	LL Bottom Bracket	53.9900	
2	4	ML Bottom Bracket	101.2400	
3	5	HL Bottom Bracket	121.4900	
4	8	Mountain-500 Black, 40	539.9900	
5	9	Mountain-500 Black, 42	539.9900	
6	10	Mountain-500 Black, 44	539.9900	
7	11	Mountain-500 Black, 48	539.9900	
8	12	Mountain-500 Black, 52	539.9900	
9	15	Mountain-500 Black, 62	539.9900	

Figure 5-17

The NOT Operator

The NOT operator doesn't stand alone. It's simply a modifier that can precede any logical expression. The job of this operator is to reverse the result. So, if an expression yields True, you get a False. If it's False, you see True. Sometimes it's easier to test for the opposite of what you are looking for. However, the NOT operator is often less efficient because SQL Server actually processes the base expression first (perhaps returning all qualifying rows), and then fetches the rows that were not included in the original result. Depending on the complexity of the statement and the number of rows in the table, using NOT may still be more efficient than having to build an expression that selects everything but the records you want to ignore.

If you wanted to return all product records except for road bikes, you could use this expression:

```
SELECT ProductID, Name, ListPrice
FROM Product
WHERE NOT ProductSubCategoryID = 2
```

In the result set, shown in Figure 5-18, all rows are returned except for those having a SubCategoryID value of 2.

	ProductID	Name	ListPrice
1	3	LL Bottom Bracket	53.9900
2	4	ML Bottom Bracket	101.2400
3	5	HL Bottom Bracket	121.4900
4	8	Mountain-500 Black, 40	539.9900
5	9	Mountain-500 Black, 42	539.9900
6	10	Mountain-500 Black, 44	539.9900
7	11	Mountain-500 Black, 48	539.9900
8	12	Mountain-500 Black, 52	539.9900
9	15	Mountain-500 Black, 62	539.9900

Figure 5-18

The Mighty Null

In the earlier days of databases, designers often found it difficult to consistently express the concept of "no value." For example, if a product invoice line is stored but you don't have the price of the product at the time, do you store a zero? How would you differentiate this row from another where you intended not to charge for the product?

Character data can be particularly strange at times. Within program code, string variables initialize to an empty string. In older file-based databases, what would now be considered to be a field would consist of a designated number of characters in a specific position within the file. If a field wasn't assigned a value, the file stored spaces in place of the data. Programs returned all of the characters including the spaces, which had to be trimmed off. If there wasn't anything left after removing the spaces, the program code concluded that there was no value in the field. So, what if you had intended to store spaces? How would you differentiate between a space and no value at all? Numeric types initialize to zero. The Bit or Boolean data type in some programming languages initializes to zero or False. If you store this value, does this mean that the value is intentionally set to False, or is this just its default state? What about dates that haven't been set to a value? As you can see, there is plenty of room for confusion regarding this topic. For this and other reasons, the ANSI SQL standard for representing the concept of "no value" is to use a special value called *Null*. Internally, Null is actually a real character (on the ANSI character chart, it's character zero — not to be confused with the number zero). It means "nothing," that this field doesn't have a value. Every significant data type supports the use of the Null value.

The Null value has an interesting behavior — it never equals anything, not even itself. To make it stand out, a special operator distinguishes Null from all other values. To test for Null, use the IS operator. So, Null does not equal Null. . . Null *IS* Null.

Some of the product records don't have a standard cost. To intentionally state that the product does not have a cost (or, perhaps, that the cost isn't known), this column is set to Null. Now you'd like to return a list of products with no recorded cost, so you use the following query:

```
SELECT ProductID, Name, StandardCost
FROM Product
WHERE StandardCost IS NULL
```

The results contain no StandardCost values, as shown in Figure 5-19.

	ProductID	Name	StandardCost
1	1	Adjustable Race	NULL
2	2	Bearing Ball	NULL
3	6	BB Ball Bearing	NULL
4	7	Headset Ball Bearings	NULL
5	608	Blade	NULL
6	609	LL Crankarm	NULL
7	610	ML Crankarm	NULL
8	611	HL Crankarm	NULL
9	612	Chainring Bolts	NULL

Figure 5-19

To reverse the logic and return a list of the products with a known cost, you simply add the NOT operator, like so:

```
SELECT ProductID, Name, StandardCost
FROM Product
WHERE StandardCost IS NOT NULL
```

The result should contain all of the rows from this table that were not listed in the previous result, some of which are shown in Figure 5-20.

	ProductID	Name	StandardCost
1	3	LL Bottom Bracket	39.9526
2	4	ML Bottom Bracket	74.9176
3	5	HL Bottom Bracket	89.9026
4	8	Mountain-500 Black, 40	399.5926
5	9	Mountain-500 Black, 42	399.5926
6	10	Mountain-500 Black, 44	399.5926
7	11	Mountain-500 Black, 48	399.5926
8	12	Mountain-500 Black, 52	399.5926
9	15	Mountain-500 Black, 62	399.9900

Figure 5-20

Extended Filtering Techniques

As you've seen, expressions using simple comparison operators can be combined to narrow down results and explicitly return the records you are looking for. Sometimes, even simple filtering expressions can get a little complicated. To simplify common expressions, operators were added to the SQL language. If nothing more, it makes expressions more natural and easier to read. One common example is a query for records in a date range. If you needed to return all employee records for employees born between 1962 and 1985, you would need to specify that the birth date should be greater than or equal to the first day of the first year in the range, January 1, 1962, and that the same column should also be less than or equal to the last day of the last year, December 31, 1985. This query would look like this:

```
SELECT FirstName, LastName, BirthDate
FROM Employee
WHERE BirthDate >= '1-1-62' AND BirthDate <= '12-31-85'
```

The results contain only Employee records where the birth date falls within the specified range, as shown in Figure 5-21.

	FirstName	LastName	BirthDate
1	Jian Shuo	Wang	12/13/1964 12:00:00 AM
2	Michael	Sullivan	7/17/1969 12:00:00 AM
3	Ovidiu	Crăcium	2/18/1968 12:00:00 AM
4	Janice	Galvin	6/29/1979 12:00:00 AM
5	Brian	Welcker	7/8/1967 12:00:00 AM
6	Syed	Abbas	2/11/1965 12:00:00 AM
7	Pamela	Ansman-Wolfe	1/6/1965 12:00:00 AM
8	David	Campbell	12/25/1964 12:00:00 AM
9	Linda	Mitchell	3/30/1970 12:00:00 AM

Figure 5-21

The BETWEEN Operator

Rather than managing the date range, the BETWEEN statement simplifies the range expression, helping state your intentions more explicitly:

```
SELECT FirstName, LastName, BirthDate
FROM Employee
WHERE BirthDate BETWEEN '1-1-62' AND '12-31-85'
```

Granted, the first statement wasn't really that complicated, but if you combine this expression with others in the same query, every attempt to simplify a query helps. Keep in mind that the definition of BETWEEN is actually between and including both extremes of the value range.

When the query is executed, SQL Server's query parser analyzes the expression and reformats the query in more explicit, standardized form. Essentially, if you wrote and executed the second query using the BETWEEN statement, the query that actually runs against the query engine would be similar to the first.

The IN() Function

This function is designed to match a field to any number of values in a list. This is another shortcut to save effort and keep your queries shorter and easier to read. For example, suppose that you're interested in a list of customers in your western sales region. You have no region designation in the database but you know this consists of the following states: Washington, Oregon, California, Idaho, and Nevada. The state/province codes are stored in a table called StateProvince. To keep things simple, I'm going to show you two examples. The first just returns the state names from the StateProvince table. The second example joins several tables together, solving the business problem before you. This expression is necessary due to the complexity of the AdventureWorks2000 database. For the first example, type the following into the query editor:

```
SELECT Name FROM StateProvince
WHERE StateProvinceCode IN ('WA', 'OR', 'CA', 'ID', 'NV')
```

The more realistic example is a little more complex and involves some elements that haven't been covered yet. Don't be concerned with the mechanics of the joins for now. Nevertheless, the following query joins four tables together to return a list of stores and the states in which they reside:

```
SELECT Store.Name, StateProvince.Name
FROM Store
   INNER JOIN CustomerAddress ON Store.CustomerID = CustomerAddress.CustomerID
   INNER JOIN Address ON CustomerAddress.AddressID = Address.AddressID
   INNER JOIN StateProvince ON Address.StateProvinceID =
StateProvince.StateProvinceID
WHERE StateProvince.StateProvinceCode IN ('WA', 'OR', 'CA', 'ID', 'NV')
```

Take a look at these results shown in Figure 5-22. Note that although you are filtering on the StateProvinceCode column, which contains the two-letter state abbreviation, you're returning the StateProvinceName column containing the full name for readability.

	Name	Name
1	Many Bikes Store	California
2	Extreme Riding Supplies	California
3	Imaginary Toys	Washington
4	Metropolitan Manufacturing	California
5	Big-Time Bike Store	California
6	Outstanding Cycles	Washington
7	Bike World	California
8	Roadway Bike Emporium	Oregon
9	Imported and Domestic Cycles	Nevada

Figure 5-22

Note that the column names are the same. This is possible because they came from two different tables. If this were a production query, the next step I'd recommend would be to alias these columns with unique names. Otherwise, it's a little confusing to see two columns called "Name."

Operator Precedence

It's important to consider the order in which multiple operations are carried out. If not, you may not get the results you'd expect. The precedence (order of operations) is determined by a few different factors. The first and most important is whether the precedence is explicitly stated. This is covered shortly. Operations involving different data types may be processed in a different order. Lastly, the operators are considered: NOT is processed first, then AND, then OR operations. Before you look up this topic in Books Online and attempt to memorize the operator precedence for every data type, please read on.

Here's an example. A user says that she would like a list consisting of mountain bikes and road bikes priced over $500 and under $1,000. You know that the product subcategories for mountain bikes and road bikes are 1 and 2, respectively. This query follows the logic of the stated requirement:

```
SELECT Name
      , ProductNumber
      , ListPrice
      , ProductSubCategoryID
FROM Product
WHERE
      ProductSubCategoryID = 1 OR ProductSubCategoryID = 2
  AND  ListPrice > 500 AND  ListPrice < 1000
```

If you run this query, you see that it returns 199 records that appear to meet the requirements (see Figure 5-23).

	Name	ProductNumber	ListPrice	ProductSubCategoryID
111	Mountain-200 Yellow, 60	BK-M68Y-60	2868.7375	1
112	Mountain-200 Yellow, 62	BK-M68Y-62	2868.7375	1
113	Mountain-100 Black, 38	BK-M82B-38	4218.7375	1
114	Mountain-100 Black, 42	BK-M82B-42	4218.7375	1
115	Mountain-100 Black, 44	BK-M82B-44	4218.7375	1
116	Mountain-100 Black, 48	BK-M82B-48	4218.7375	1
117	Mountain-100 Black, 56	BK-M82B-56	4218.7375	1
118	Mountain-100 Black, 58	BK-M82B-58	4218.7375	1
119	Mountain-100 Black, 60	BK-M82B-60	4218.7375	1
120	Mountain-100 Black, 62	BK-M82B-62	4218.7375	1
121	Mountain-100 Red, 40	BK-M82R-40	4218.7375	1
122	Mountain-100 Red, 44	BK-M82R-44	4218.7375	1
123	Mountain-100 Red, 52	BK-M82R-52	4218.7375	1
124	Mountain-100 Red, 58	BK-M82R-58	4218.7375	1
125	Mountain-100 Red, 60	BK-M82R-60	4218.7375	1
126	Mountain-100 Red, 62	BK-M82R-62	4218.7375	1
127	Mountain-100 Silver, 38	BK-M82S-38	4249.9875	1
128	Mountain-100 Silver, 42	BK-M82S-42	4249.9875	1
129	Mountain-100 Silver, 44	BK-M82S-44	4249.9875	1
130	Mountain-100 Silver, 48	BK-M82S-48	4249.9875	1
131	Mountain-100 Silver, 56	BK-M82S-56	4218.7375	1
132	Mountain-100 Silver, 58	BK-M82S-58	4218.7375	1
133	Mountain-100 Silver, 60	BK-M82S-60	4218.7375	1
134	Mountain-100 Silver, 62	BK-M82S-62	4218.7375	1
135	Mountain-100 Blue, 52	BK-M82U-52	4218.7375	1
136	Mountain-100 Blue, 60	BK-M82U-60	4218.7375	1
137	Mountain-100 Blue, 62	BK-M82U-62	4218.7375	1
138	Mountain-100 Yellow, 40	BK-M82Y-40	4218.7375	1
139	Mountain-100 Yellow, 48	BK-M82Y-48	4218.7375	1
140	Mountain-100 Yellow, 52	BK-M82Y-52	4218.7375	1
141	Mountain-100 Yellow, 60	BK-M82Y-60	4218.7375	1
142	Mountain-100 Yellow, 62	BK-M82Y-62	4218.7375	1
143	Road-750 Black, 44	BK-R19B-44	674.9875	2
144	Road-750 Black, 48	BK-R19B-48	674.9875	2

Figure 5-23

However, upon closer examination, you can see that you have $4,000 mountain bikes on the list. Why is that? Go back and take a look at the query. When the query parser has to contend with more than one logical operator, it has to decide how to process them. It will always process an AND expression before an OR expression. The mechanics of query processing are really up to the query optimizer, but the results for a given statement will always be the same. Later on you'll learn how to find out what the query optimizer does when it breaks down and processes a query. Most likely, in this case, it took the first AND expression,

```
ProductSubCategoryID = 2 AND ListPrice
```

processed and buffered the results, and then the next AND expression,

```
AND  ListPrice < 1000
```

and used this to filter the first set of results. So far, so good, but it's the next step that gets you into trouble. Because the query parser processes an OR expression after all of the AND logic, it went back to the beginning of the WHERE clause and processed this statement:

```
ProductSubCategoryID = 1
```

Because this statement preceded the OR operator, it found all of the mountain bike records in the table and appended these to the first set of results. So the query processor did what you told it to do but not necessarily what you wanted it to do.

```
SELECT Name
       , ProductNumber
       , ListPrice
       , ProductSubCategoryID
FROM Product
WHERE
       ListPrice > 500 AND ListPrice < 1000
  AND  ProductSubCategoryID = 1 OR ProductSubCategoryID = 2
```

This query returns 238 rows, including expensive road bikes:

```
SELECT Name
       , ProductNumber
       , ListPrice
       , ProductSubCategoryID
FROM Product
WHERE
       ProductSubCategoryID = 1
  AND  ListPrice > 500 AND ListPrice < 1000
  OR   ProductSubCategoryID = 2
```

Frankly, rearranging these statements will not give you the results you're looking for. Unless you find a way to tell the query-processing engine the order in which you want it to process these operations, you're not going to get a list of affordable bikes.

Using Parentheses

Filter expressions are often combined to return a very specific range and combination of records. When combining the individual expressions, it's often necessary (or at least a good idea) to use parentheses to separate expressions and to specify the operation precedence and order. Making a point to use parentheses when multiple operations are processed makes it unnecessary to be concerned with the complexities of normal operator precedence.

For example, I would like a list consisting of mountain bikes priced over $1,000 and road bikes priced over $500. I know that the product subcategories for mountain bikes and road bikes are 1 and 2, respectively. My query looks like this:

```
SELECT Name
       , ProductNumber
       , ListPrice
       , ProductSubCategoryID
FROM Product
WHERE
       (ProductSubCategoryID = 1 AND ListPrice > 1000)
   OR
       (ProductSubCategoryID = 2 AND ListPrice > 500)
```

The parentheses in this example serve only to clarify the order of operations. Because the AND operator is processed before the OR operator, the parentheses are not actually necessary in this expression. Using the same comparisons with a different combination of operators would yield different results, unless the appropriate application of parentheses was applied. The following queries exemplify this point. This first example (with or without parentheses) returns 272 rows. The following query is the same, only with the parentheses removed:

```
SELECT   Name
       , ProductNumber
       , ListPrice
       , ProductSubCategoryID
FROM Product
WHERE
       ProductSubCategoryID = 1 OR ListPrice > 1000
   AND
       ProductSubCategoryID = 2 OR ListPrice > 500
```

This query returns 563 rows (a sampling of which is shown in Figure 5-24).

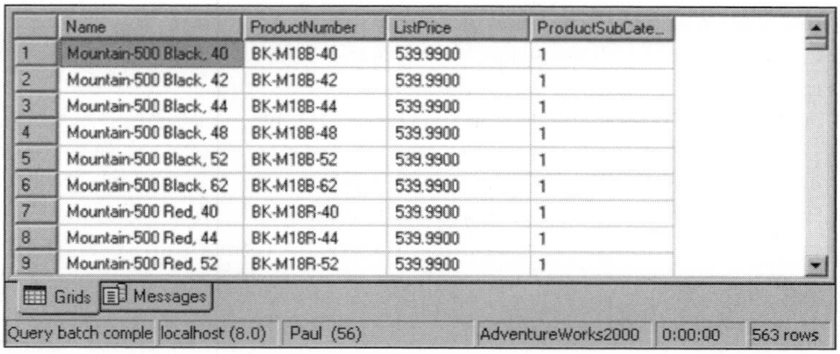

Figure 5-24

With parentheses grouping the two OR operators and separating the AND operators, the same query returns 420 rows:

```
SELECT    Name
     , ProductNumber
     , ListPrice
     , ProductSubCategoryID
FROM Product
WHERE
     (ProductSubCategoryID = 1 OR ListPrice > 1000)
   AND
     (ProductSubCategoryID = 2 OR ListPrice > 500)
```

The results are shown in Figure 5-25.

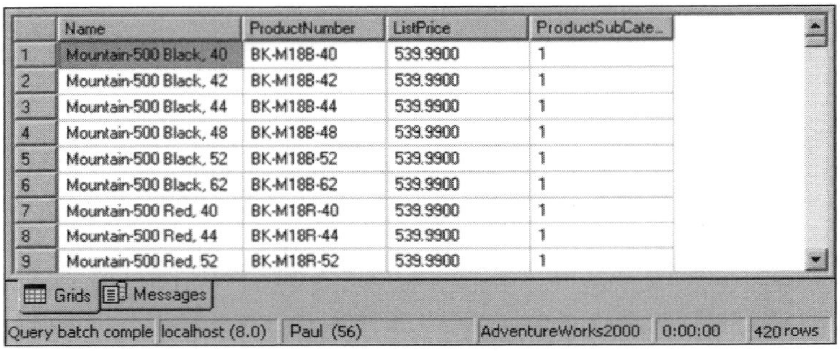

	Name	ProductNumber	ListPrice	ProductSubCate...
1	Mountain-500 Black, 40	BK-M18B-40	539.9900	1
2	Mountain-500 Black, 42	BK-M18B-42	539.9900	1
3	Mountain-500 Black, 44	BK-M18B-44	539.9900	1
4	Mountain-500 Black, 48	BK-M18B-48	539.9900	1
5	Mountain-500 Black, 52	BK-M18B-52	539.9900	1
6	Mountain-500 Black, 62	BK-M18B-62	539.9900	1
7	Mountain-500 Red, 40	BK-M18R-40	539.9900	1
8	Mountain-500 Red, 44	BK-M18R-44	539.9900	1
9	Mountain-500 Red, 52	BK-M18R-52	539.9900	1

Grids | Messages

Query batch comple | localhost (8.0) | Paul (56) | AdventureWorks2000 | 0:00:00 | 420 rows

Figure 5-25

The bottom line is, whether or not parentheses are required, use them to state your intentions and to make your queries easier to read. When multiple operations are combined, it becomes increasingly important to group and separate operations using parentheses. Just as in mathematical expressions, parentheses can be nested any number of levels deep.

Sorting Results

Typically, you will want records to be returned in some sensible order. Rows can be sorted in order of practically any combination of columns. For example, you may want to see employee records listed in order of last name and then by first name. This means that for employees who have the same last name, records would be sorted by first name within that group. When writing and testing queries, you may see that some tables return rows in a specific order even if you don't make it a point to sort them. This may be due to existing indexes on the table, or it may be that records were entered in that order. Regardless, as a rule, if you want rows to be returned in a specific order, you should use the ORDER BY clause to enforce your sorting requirements and guarantee that records are sorted correctly if things change in the table.

The ORDER BY clause is always stated after the WHERE clause (if used) and can contain one or more columns in a comma-delimited list. If not stated otherwise, values will be sorted in ascending order. You can optionally specify ascending order using the ASC keyword. This means that the following two statements effectively do the same thing:

```
SELECT FirstName, LastName
FROM Employee ORDER BY LastName
```

Or

```
SELECT FirstName, LastName
FROM Employee ORDER BYy LastName ASC
```

As you see, records are sorted by the LastName column. In the result set shown in Figure 5-26, I've scrolled down the list to view Brown and Campbell.

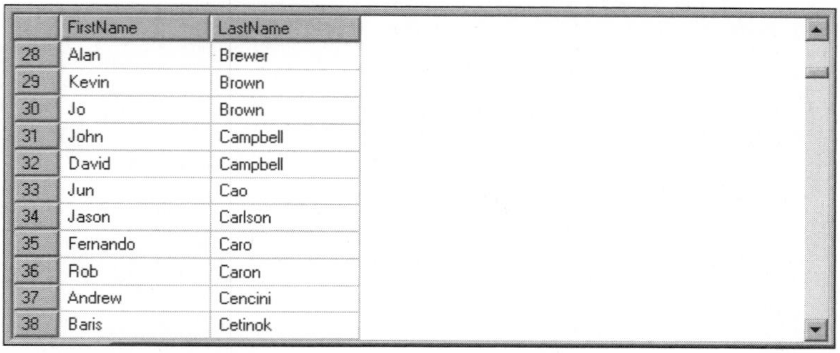

	FirstName	LastName
28	Alan	Brewer
29	Kevin	Brown
30	Jo	Brown
31	John	Campbell
32	David	Campbell
33	Jun	Cao
34	Jason	Carlson
35	Fernando	Caro
36	Rob	Caron
37	Andrew	Cencini
38	Baris	Cetinok

Figure 5-26

Note that the first name values for Kevin and Jo Brown and for John and David Campbell are out of order. As far as we're concerned, this order is completely arbitrary. You can correct this by adding the FirstName column to the ORDER BY list, like so:

```
SELECT FirstName, LastName
FROM Employee ORDER BY LastName, FirstName
```

Now the results show employees sorted in order of LastName and then subsorted by FirstName. Jo, Kevin, David, and John now appear alphabetically, as shown in Figure 5-27.

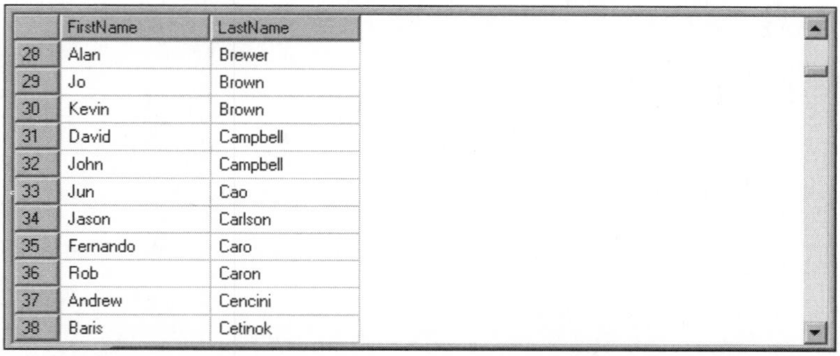

	FirstName	LastName
28	Alan	Brewer
29	Jo	Brown
30	Kevin	Brown
31	David	Campbell
32	John	Campbell
33	Jun	Cao
34	Jason	Carlson
35	Fernando	Caro
36	Rob	Caron
37	Andrew	Cencini
38	Baris	Cetinok

Figure 5-27

One more example shows how rows can be sorted in descending order. Suppose that you want to have your employees listed in order of age, youngest first. This is a simple task. Using the ORDER BY clause, indicate that the BirthDate column should be sorted in descending order:

```
SELECT FirstName, LastName, BirthDate
FROM Employee ORDER BY BirthDate DESC
```

The result shown in Figure 5-28 starts with employees born in 1979.

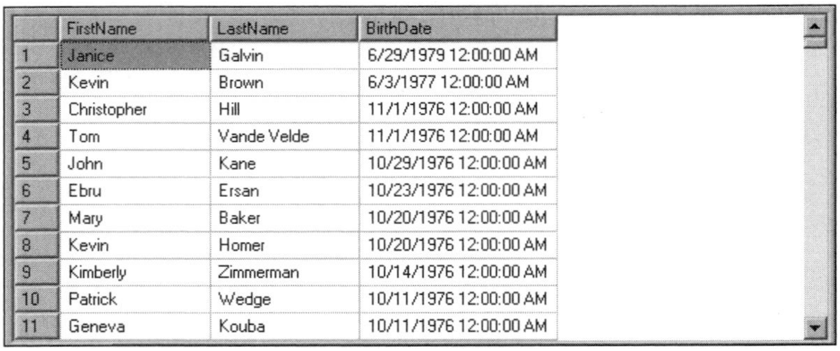

	FirstName	LastName	BirthDate
1	Janice	Galvin	6/29/1979 12:00:00 AM
2	Kevin	Brown	6/3/1977 12:00:00 AM
3	Christopher	Hill	11/1/1976 12:00:00 AM
4	Tom	Vande Velde	11/1/1976 12:00:00 AM
5	John	Kane	10/29/1976 12:00:00 AM
6	Ebru	Ersan	10/23/1976 12:00:00 AM
7	Mary	Baker	10/20/1976 12:00:00 AM
8	Kevin	Homer	10/20/1976 12:00:00 AM
9	Kimberly	Zimmerman	10/14/1976 12:00:00 AM
10	Patrick	Wedge	10/11/1976 12:00:00 AM
11	Geneva	Kouba	10/11/1976 12:00:00 AM

Figure 5-28

Just a side note to clarify what you see here: The DateTime data type stores both the date and time. In this case, the time wasn't actually entered for these birth dates but defaults to 12:00:00 AM, or midnight.

Top Values

So far, you've seen that if you want to return a subset of the rows in a table, it's necessary to filter the results based on some sort of criteria. In some cases, you will want to simply return a specific number of records regardless of the number of qualifying rows. You have two options for returning top values: including a fixed number of rows or a percentage of total rows.

This example also involves the ages of employees in the AdventureWorks2000 database. Like the previous example, the following query returns a list of all employees sorted by their birth date, or age, oldest to youngest (in this case, sorting by birth date in ascending order):

```
SELECT FirstName, LastName, BirthDate
FROM Employee
ORDER BY BirthDate
```

The first few rows in the result set look like those shown in Figure 5-29.

Now, add the TOP statement to indicate that you really only want to see the first five rows in the result set:

```
SELECT TOP 5 FirstName, LastName, BirthDate
FROM Employee
Order By BirthDate
```

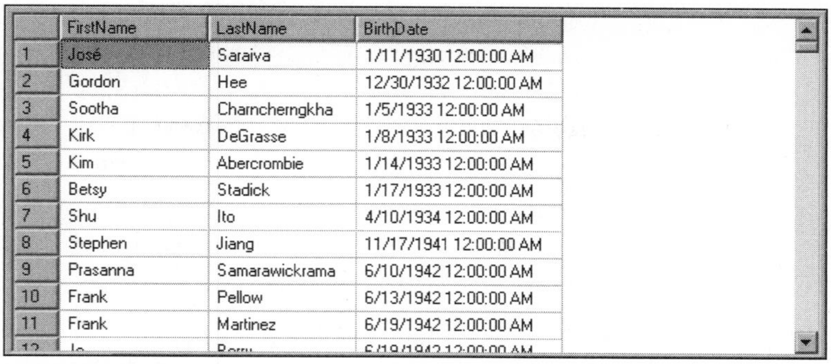

	FirstName	LastName	BirthDate
1	José	Saraiva	1/11/1930 12:00:00 AM
2	Gordon	Hee	12/30/1932 12:00:00 AM
3	Sootha	Charncherngkha	1/5/1933 12:00:00 AM
4	Kirk	DeGrasse	1/8/1933 12:00:00 AM
5	Kim	Abercrombie	1/14/1933 12:00:00 AM
6	Betsy	Stadick	1/17/1933 12:00:00 AM
7	Shu	Ito	4/10/1934 12:00:00 AM
8	Stephen	Jiang	11/17/1941 12:00:00 AM
9	Prasanna	Samarawickrama	6/10/1942 12:00:00 AM
10	Frank	Pellow	6/13/1942 12:00:00 AM
11	Frank	Martinez	6/19/1942 12:00:00 AM
12	Jo	Berry	6/19/1942 12:00:00 AM

Figure 5-29

As you see in the following result set, shown in Figure 5-30, only five rows are returned.

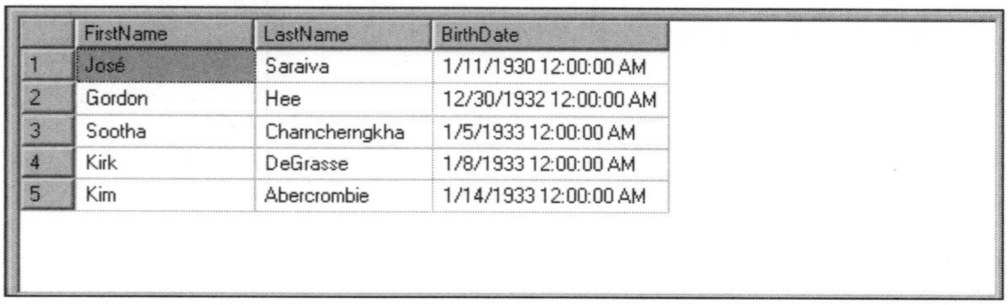

	FirstName	LastName	BirthDate
1	José	Saraiva	1/11/1930 12:00:00 AM
2	Gordon	Hee	12/30/1932 12:00:00 AM
3	Sootha	Charncherngkha	1/5/1933 12:00:00 AM
4	Kirk	DeGrasse	1/8/1933 12:00:00 AM
5	Kim	Abercrombie	1/14/1933 12:00:00 AM

Figure 5-30

SQL Server doesn't try to make much sense out of this data. It doesn't even consider the sorted values when chopping off the list. It simply truncates the results after the fifth row has been returned, regardless of any values. This point is more apparent in the following example. The next query returns products in order of their price. I've made it a point to sort the product list in descending order of list price. This puts the most expensive products at the top of the result list:

```
SELECT Name, ListPrice
FROM Product
ORDER BY ListPrice Desc
```

For the bicycles, a unique product record represents a different color and frame size, so there are actually several rows for the same model. The most expensive bike, the road bike model 150, costs $3,578.27. Given all of the color and frame size combinations, there are 28 products at this price. If you were to ask for the top five list of bikes (and you're sorting only on price), the list is arbitrarily truncated after five records:

```
SELECT TOP 5 Name, ListPrice
FROM Product
ORDER BY ListPrice Desc
```

Keep this in mind when asking for a "top" list.

WITH TIES

There is an easy way to solve the dilemma caused by tied values in the last position of your top list arbitrarily capping the results. First of all, you need to go back and clarify the business rule. Often, this means going back to your users or project sponsor to seek a restatement of requirements. That conversation might go something like this:

"You said that you wanted a report showing the top 25 most expensive products. What if the price of the 25th product were the same as another product — or more — down the list? Do you want to include other products that are tied for the same price as the item in the 25th position?"

If the answer is "Yes," the solution is quite simple. The WITH TIES statement simply continues to populate the list as long as subsequent rows' sorted values are the same as the last item in the Top list. For example, the following requests a list of the top 25 most expensive products using the same statement as before, except using Top 25 WITH TIES:

```
SELECT TOP 25 WITH TIES Name, ListPrice
FROM Product
ORDER BY ListPrice DESC
```

Figure 5-31 shows the complete results for this query.

	Name	ListPrice
1	Road-150 Black, 44	3578.2700
2	Road-150 Black, 48	3578.2700
3	Road-150 Black, 52	3578.2700
4	Road-150 Black, 56	3578.2700
5	Road-150 Red, 40	3578.2700
6	Road-150 Red, 44	3578.2700
7	Road-150 Red, 48	3578.2700
8	Road-150 Red, 52	3578.2700
9	Road-150 Red, 56	3578.2700
10	Road-150 Red, 58	3578.2700
11	Road-150 Red, 60	3578.2700
12	Road-150 Red, 62	3578.2700
13	Road-150 Silver, 40	3578.2700
14	Road-150 Silver, 44	3578.2700
15	Road-150 Silver, 52	3578.2700
16	Road-150 Silver, 58	3578.2700
17	Road-150 Blue, 40	3578.2700
18	Road-150 Blue, 48	3578.2700
19	Road-150 Blue, 52	3578.2700
20	Road-150 Blue, 56	3578.2700
21	Road-150 Blue, 58	3578.2700
22	Road-150 Blue, 60	3578.2700
23	Road-150 Yellow, 44	3578.2700
24	Road-150 Yellow, 52	3578.2700
25	Road-150 Yellow, 56	3578.2700
26	Road-150 Yellow, 58	3578.2700
27	Road-150 Yellow, 60	3578.2700
28	Road-150 Yellow, 62	3578.2700

Figure 5-31

As you can see, 28 rows are returned because rows 26, 27, and 28 have the same ListPrice value as row 25.

Try It Out

To bring this topic full circle, go back to the original example and do the same thing with employee birth dates. Using the same query as before, add the Top 11 statement. Execute this query:

```
SELECT TOP 11 FirstName, LastName, BirthDate
FROM Employee
ORDER BY BirthDate
```

Now add the WITH TIES statement:

```
SELECT TOP 11 WITH TIES FirstName, LastName, BirthDate
FROM Employee
ORDER BY BirthDate
```

How It Works

SQL Server does exactly what you asked it to do: it returns 11 rows. You should get 11 employee records returned with Frank Martinez in the last position when you write the query without WITH TIES. His birth date is 6/19/1942. However, Frank shares his birthday with Jo Berry, who happens to be in the next position. When you use the WITH TIES modifier, Jo shows up in position 12 on your top 11 list. SQL Server will continue to output rows until the sorted value changes.

Note that records 11 and 12 in Figure 5-32 have the same value in the BirthDate column.

	FirstName	LastName	BirthDate
1	José	Saraiva	1/11/1930 12:00:00 AM
2	Gordon	Hee	12/30/1932 12:00:00 AM
3	Sootha	Charncherngkha	1/5/1933 12:00:00 AM
4	Kirk	DeGrasse	1/8/1933 12:00:00 AM
5	Kim	Abercrombie	1/14/1933 12:00:00 AM
6	Betsy	Stadick	1/17/1933 12:00:00 AM
7	Shu	Ito	4/10/1934 12:00:00 AM
8	Stephen	Jiang	11/17/1941 12:00:00 AM
9	Prasanna	Samarawickrama	6/10/1942 12:00:00 AM
10	Frank	Pellow	6/13/1942 12:00:00 AM
11	Frank	Martinez	6/19/1942 12:00:00 AM
12	Jo	Berry	6/19/1942 12:00:00 AM

Figure 5-32

Percent

Rather than specifying a number of records to be returned with the TOP statement, you can also specify a percentage of the entire result set. SQL Server will do the math for you and then round to the nearest whole number. It essentially performs this calculation and then issues a Top X clause in place of the Top X Percent. Do this using the birth date example. If you were to select all employee records, without using the TOP statement, 292 rows would be returned. If you ask for the top 10 percent, a subset of rows is returned. Try it out:

```
SELECT TOP 10 PERCENT FirstName, LastName, BirthDate
FROM Employee
ORDER BY BirthDate
```

As you can see in Figure 5-33, 30 rows are returned. This is because SQL Server rounds up to the nearest whole record.

	FirstName	LastName	BirthDate
1	José	Saraiva	1/11/1930 12:00:...
2	Gordon	Hee	12/30/1932 12:0...
3	Sootha	Charncherngkha	1/5/1933 12:00:0...
4	Kirk	DeGrasse	1/8/1933 12:00:0...
5	Kim	Abercrombie	1/14/1933 12:00:...
6	Betsy	Stadick	1/17/1933 12:00:...
7	Shu	Ito	4/10/1934 12:00:...
8	Stephen	Jiang	11/17/1941 12:0...
9	Prasanna	Samarawickrama	6/10/1942 12:00:...
10	Frank	Pellow	6/13/1942 12:00:...
11	Frank	Martinez	6/19/1942 12:00:...
12	Jo	Berry	6/19/1942 12:00:...
13	Maciej	Dusza	6/28/1942 12:00:...
14	Gail	Erickson	10/29/1942 12:0...
15	JoLynn	Dobney	4/21/1946 12:00:...
16	Matt	Dawson	4/24/1946 12:00:...
17	Barry	Johnson	4/27/1946 12:00:...
18	John	Campbell	4/27/1946 12:00:...
19	Jo	Brown	4/30/1946 12:00:...
20	Diane	Glimp	4/30/1946 12:00:...
21	Taylor	Maxwell	5/3/1946 12:00:0...
22	Doris	Hartwig	5/6/1946 12:00:0...
23	Jeffrey	Ford	5/9/1946 12:00:0...
24	Sidney	Higa	5/15/1946 12:00:...
25	Amy	Alberts	10/22/1947 12:0...
26	Jossef	Goldberg	4/11/1949 12:00:...
27	Thierry	D'Hers	8/29/1949 12:00:...
28	Sharon	Salavaria	6/3/1951 12:00:0...
29	Fernando	Caro	9/29/1952 12:00:...

Figure 5-33

The same rules apply as if you had just used the Top X version of this statement. You can use WITH TIES and sort the result in either ascending or descending order.

Summary

Although you haven't seen a lot of complexity in this introduction to the SELECT statement and its fundamental nuances, it's a very powerful tool. As you continue to build more complex statements, the SELECT statement will be center stage. This chapter started by explaining selecting all rows using the asterisk (*) to return values for all available columns in a table and then moved on to specify selected columns. It is more efficient to return only the columns needed. This is especially the case when standard queries will be called routinely by software code, a report, or an application component. You learned how columns can be aliased to either rename a column or return a new column from a literal value, calculation, or expression based on multiple column values.

Filtering rows is the function of the WHERE clause, using logical comparisons. Values may be equal to, less than, greater than, or the opposite of any of the above by using the NOT operator. Character data types can also be compared using the LIKE operator to perform partial matching, wildcard, and pattern matching. Using Null is the accepted method to indicate that a column value has not been set — and testing for Null gives you an exact method to test for this condition. When combining comparison operators, it's often necessary to indicate the order of operations using parentheses. Not only does this ensure that operations are performed in the appropriate order, but it also makes queries much easier to read and maintain.

Rows can be sorted on any number of columns and can be placed in ascending or descending order. Finally, this chapter discussed the use of the TOP keyword, used to truncate a result set either by a specific number of rows or by a percentage of the entire result set.

Exercises

Exercise 1

Using Query Analyzer or SQL Server Management Studio, write a query to return Employee records from the AdventureWorks2000 database. Include only the FirstName, LastName, and EmailAddress columns in the result set. Execute this query and view the results.

Exercise 2

Return Employee records from the AdventureWorks2000 database. Combine the FirstName and LastName columns separated by a space, to return an aliased column called FullName. Return only the FullName and Title columns. Sort the results by the LastName and then FirstName columns in ascending order.

Exercise 3

Return Product records that have a DiscontinuedDate value greater than or equal to December 4, 2002. Include the Name and ListPrice columns.

Exercise 4

Return a list of Department records including all columns.

Include only departments that have a Name value ending with the word *Control*. These records must also have a Name column value starting with the word *Production*. In addition to these records, include records that have a GroupName value ending in the word *Assurance*.

Sort these records by the Name column in reverse alphabetical order.

SQL Functions

Now that you understand how to formulate SQL queries and return result sets, you need to do something useful with this data. Once you have successfully retrieved values from tables, it's very common to further manipulate values to provide useful and meaningful results. This may involve the following:

❑   Performing calculations and mathematical operations

❑   Conversion

❑   Parsing

❑   Combining values

❑   Aggregation

The purpose of this chapter is to help you learn the mechanics of using functions of all kinds. It introduces you to some of the more common value manipulation functions and some less-common functions to give a sample of these powerful capabilities. You'll also take a look at some new functionality offered in SQL Server 2005.

At the end of the book, you'll find a reference for all of the system-supplied functions and the syntax needed to use them. Additionally, subsequent chapters contain more detailed information about specific groups of functions. For example, Chapter 7 discusses specific uses for aggregate functions in more advanced SQL queries, and Chapter 11 shows you how to use functions to support full-text index searches.

Transact-SQL functions are grouped into the categories described in the following table.

Function Category	Purpose
Aggregation	Aggregate functions return a scalar value representing an aggregation over a range of values, applying a specific aggregate selection or summary.
Configuration Variables	Return information about the SQL Server execution environment that may be useful in programming objects.
Conversion	Used to convert values of one data type to another. Also used to apply formatting characteristics to dates, times, and numeric values.
Cursor	Used to loop through the rows in a result set in a procedural manner when iterating through a cursor.
Date	A set of functions used for parsing the date and time portions of a date value, and for comparing and manipulating date/time values.
Image/Text	Includes both specialized functionality, specific to the Text, nText, and Image types; and functions equivalent to those for standard character types.
Mathematical	Used to perform a variety of common and specialized mathematical operations. Useful in performing algebraic, trigonometric, statistical, approximating, and financial operations.
Metadata	Utility functions that return information about the SQL Server configuration details and details about the server and database settings.
Ranking	New function in SQL Server 2005 used to enumerate sorted and top-valued result sets.
Security	Returns role membership and privilege information for SQL Server users. Also includes a set of functions to manage events and traces.
String Manipulation	Used to parse, replace, and manipulate character values.
System	Utility functions used to perform a variety of tasks. These include value comparisons and value type testing. This category is also a catch-all for other functionality.
System Statistical	Administrative utilities used to discover database system usage and environment information.

The Anatomy of a Function

The purpose of a function is to return a value. Most of the functions you will use return a *scalar* value, meaning a single unit of data, or a simple value. However, functions can return practically any data type, and this includes types such as Table and Cursor, which could be used to return entire, multi-row result sets. I won't take the discussion to that level in this chapter. Chapter 13 explains how to create and utilize user-defined functions to return more complex data.

Functions have been around for a long time, even long before SQL. The pattern used to call functions is the same in nearly all programming languages:

```
Result = Function()
```

In Transact-SQL, values are returned using the SELECT statement. If you just want to return a value in a query, you treat the SELECT as the output operator without using an equals sign:

```
SELECT Function()
```

I'd Like to Have an Argument

When it comes to SQL functions, the term *argument* is used to mean an input variable or placeholder for a value. Functions can have any number of arguments and some arguments are required whereas others are optional. Optional arguments are typically at the end of the comma-delimited argument list, making them easier to exclude if they are not to be provided in the function call.

When you read about functions in SQL Server Books Online or on-line help, you'll see optional arguments denoted in square brackets. In this example for the CONVERT() function, both the length argument for the data type and the style argument for the CONVERT() function are optional:

```
CONVERT ( data_type [ ( length ) ] , expression [ , style ] )
```

I'll simplify this because we're really not discussing how to use data types at the moment:

```
CONVERT ( data_type, expression [ , style ] )
```

According to this, the CONVERT() function will accept either two or three arguments. So, either of these examples would be acceptable:

```
SELECT CONVERT(VarChar(20), 'April 29, 1988')

SELECT CONVERT(VarChar(20), 'April 29, 1988', 101)
```

The first argument for this function is the data type, VarChar(20), and the second argument is the value, 'April 29, 1988'. The third argument in the second statement determines the style for numeric and date types. Even if a function doesn't take an argument, or doesn't require an argument, it is called with a set of empty parentheses. Note that when a function is referred to by name throughout the book, the parentheses are included because this is considered standard form.

Deterministic Functions

Because of the inner-workings of the database engine, SQL Server has to separate functions into two different groups based on what's called *determinism*. This is not a new-age religion. It's simply a statement about whether the outcome of a function can be predicted based on its input parameters or by executing it one time. If a function's output is not dependent on any external factors, other than the value of input parameters, it is considered to be a deterministic function. If the output can vary based on any conditions in the environment or algorithms that produce random or dependent results, the function is *nondeterministic*. Why make a big deal about something that seems so simple? Well, nondeterministic functions and global variables can't be used in some database programming objects such as user-defined functions. This is partially due to the way SQL Server caches and precompiles executable objects. For simple, ad-hoc queries, knock yourself out and use any type of function you like, but if you plan on building more advanced, reusable programming objects, it's important to understand this distinction. As a brief example, these functions are deterministic:

- AVG() (all aggregate functions are deterministic)
- CAST()
- CONVERT()
- DATEADD()
- DATEDIFF()
- ASCII()
- CHAR()
- SUBSTRING()

These functions and variables are nondeterministic:

- GETDATE()
- @@ERROR
- @@SERVICENAME
- CURSORSTATUS()
- RAND()

You can find a complete list of all functions and their determinism in Appendix B.

Using Variables with Functions

Variables can be used for both input and output. In Transact-SQL, a variable is prefixed with the @ symbol, declared as a specific data type, and can then be assigned a value using either the SET or SELECT statements. The following example shows the use of an Int type variable called @MyNumber, passed to the SQRT() function:

```
DECLARE @MyNumber Int
SET @MyNumber = 144
SELECT SQRT(@MyNumber)
```

The result of this call is 12, the square root of 144.

Using SET to Assign Variables

The following example uses another Int type variable, @MyResult, to capture the return value for the same function. This technique is most like the pattern used in procedural programming languages:

```
DECLARE @MyNumber Int, @MyResult Int
SET @MyNumber = 144

-- Assign the function result to the variable:
SET @MyResult = SQRT(@MyNumber)
-- Return the variable value
SELECT @MyResult
```

Using SELECT to Assign Variables

The same result can be achieved using a variation of the SELECT statement. A variable is declared prior to assigning a value. The chief advantage of using the SELECT statement instead of the SET command is that multiple variables can be assigned values in a single operation. The value is assigned using the SELECT statement and then can be used for any purpose after this script has been executed:

```
DECLARE @MyNumber1 Int, @MyNumber2 Int, @MyResult1 Int, @MyResult2 Int
SELECT @MyNumber1 = 144, @MyNumber2 = 121
-- Assign the function result to the variable:
SELECT @MyResult1 = SQRT(@MyNumber1), @MyResult2 = SQRT(@MyNumber2)
-- Return the variable value
SELECT @MyResult1, @MyResult2
```

Functionally, these techniques are identical; however, populating multiple variables with a SELECT statement is a great deal more efficient in regards to server resources than multiple SET commands. The limitation of selecting multiple or even single values into parameters is that the population of variables cannot be combined with data retrieval operations. This is why the preceding example used a SELECT statement to populate the variables followed by a second SELECT statement to retrieve the data in the variables. For example, the following script will not work:

```
DECLARE @ContactName VarChar(65)
SELECT @ContactName = FirstName + ' ' + LastName, Phone
FROM Contact WHERE ContactID = 3
```

This script will generate the following error:

```
Msg 141, Level 15, State 1, Line 2
A SELECT statement that assigns a value to a variable must not be combined with
data-retrieval operations.
```

Using Functions in Queries

Functions are often combined with query expressions to modify column values. This is easily done by passing column names to function arguments. The function reference is inserted into the column list of a SELECT query, like this:

```
SELECT FirstName, LastName, YEAR(BirthDate) AS BirthYear
FROM Employee
```

In this example, the BirthDate column value is passed into the YEAR() function as an argument. The function's result becomes the aliased column BirthYear.

Nested Functions

Often, you will find that the functionality you need doesn't exist in a single function. By design, functions are intended to be simple and focused on providing a specific feature. If functions did a lot of different things, they would be complicated and difficult to use (and some are, but fortunately, not many). For this and other reasons, each function simply does one thing. To get all of the functionality I need, I may pass the value returned from one function into another function. This is known as a *nested function call*. Here's a simple example: The purpose of the GETDATE() function is to return the current date and time. It doesn't return elegantly formatted output; that's the job of the CONVERT() function. To get the benefit of both functions, I pass the output from the GETDATE() function into the value argument of the CONVERT() function, like this:

```
SELECT CONVERT(VarChar(20), GETDATE(), 101)
```

You'll see a few examples of this pattern throughout this chapter.

Aggregate Functions

The essence of reporting is typically to distill a population of data into a value or values representing a trend or summary. This is what aggregation is all about. Aggregate functions answer the questions asked by the consumers of data:

❏   "What were the total sales of chicken gizzard by-products for last month?"

❏   "What is the average price paid for food condiments by male Brazilians between the ages of 19 and 24?"

❏   "What was the longest order-to-shipping time of all orders last quarter?"

❏   "Who is the oldest employee still working in the mail room?"

Aggregate functions return a scalar value (a single value) applying a specific aggregate operation. The return data type is comparable to that of the column or value passed to the function. Aggregates are often used along with grouping, rollup, and pivoting operations to produce results for data analysis. This is covered in greater detail in Chapter 7. The focus here is on some of the more common functions in simple SELECT queries.

Aggregate functions can be used with scalar input values, rather than in a SELECT query, but what's the point? I can pass the value 15 to each of these aggregate functions and each will return the same result:

```
SELECT AVG(15)

SELECT SUM(15)

SELECT MIN(15)

SELECT MAX(15)
```

They all return 15. After all, the average, sum, smallest, and largest value in a range of one value is that value. What happens if I count one value?

```
SELECT COUNT(15)
```

I get 1. I counted one value.

All right, now let's do something useful. Aggregate functions are really only valuable when used with a range of values in a result set. Each function performs its magic on all non-null values of a column. Unless you are applying grouping (which you will see in Chapter 7) you cannot return both aggregated values and regular column values in the same SELECT statement.

AVG()

The AVG() function returns the average for a range of numeric values, for all non-null values. For example, a table contains the following gymnastics meet scores:

Gymnast	Event	Score
Sara	Vault	9.25
Cassie	Vault	8.75
Delaney	Vault	9.25
Sammi	Vault	8.05
Erika	Vault	8.60
Sara	Beam	9.70
Cassie	Beam	9.00
Delaney	Beam	9.25
Sammi	Beam	8.95
Erika	Beam	8.85

The following query is executed with these values:

```
SELECT AVG(Score)
```

The result would be 8.965.

If three girls didn't compete in some events and the table had some missing scores, these might be represented as NULLs:

Gymnast	Event	Score
Sara	Vault	9.25
Cassie	Vault	8.75
Delaney	Vault	NULL

Table continued on following page

165

Gymnast	Event	Score
Sammi	Vault	8.05
Erika	Vault	8.60
Sara	Beam	9.70
Cassie	Beam	NULL
Delaney	Beam	9.25
Sammi	Beam	NULL
Erika	Beam	8.85

In this case, the NULL values are not considered, and the average is calculated based on the existing numerical values. The result would be 8.921429.

However, if the missing scores were counted against the team, and the column contained zero values instead, this would seriously affect the overall score (6.245) and their chances of moving on to state competition.

COUNT()

The COUNT() function returns an integer value for the number of non-null values in the column range. For instance, if the gymnastics data in the previous example were in a table called GymEvent and I wanted to know the number of events that Sammi received a score on, I could execute the following query:

```
SELECT COUNT(Score) FROM GymEvent WHERE Gymnast = 'Sammi'
```

The result would be 1 since the score for Sammi's Beam event was NULL. If you need a count of all rows in a table, regardless of NULL values, use the following syntax:

```
SELECT COUNT(*) FROM table
```

Using the previous example with Sammi, a COUNT(*) query would look like this:

```
SELECT COUNT(*) FROM GymEvent WHERE Gymnast = 'Sammi'
```

Because the COUNT(*) function ignores NULL values, the result of this query would be 2.

MIN() and MAX()

The MIN() function returns the smallest (minimum) non-null value for a column range. The MAX() function returns the maximum or largest value. These functions can be used with most data types and work according to the sorting rules of the type. To make this point, suppose a table contains the following values stored in two different columns, one as an integer type and the other as a character type:

Column1 (Int type)	Column2 (VarChar type)	
2	2	
4	4	
12	12	
19	19	

What will the MIN() and MAX() functions return? You may be surprised.

	Column1 (Int type)	Column2 (VarChar type)	
MIN()	2	12	
MAX()	19	4	

Because values in Column2 are stored as characters rather than numbers, it is sorted according to the ASCII value of each character, from left to right. This is why 12 is less than any other value and 4 is greater than any other value.

SUM()

The SUM() function is one of the most commonly used aggregates and is fairly self-explanatory. Like the AVG() function, it works with numeric data types and returns the additive sum of all non-null values in a column range.

You'll learn to use all of the aggregate functions in Chapter 7, including statistical functions. You'll also see how to create user-defined aggregates with SQL Server 2005.

Configuration Variables

These aren't really functions but they can be used in much the same way as system functions. Each global variable returns scalar information about the SQL Server execution environment. Following are some common examples.

@@ERROR

This variable contains the last error number for the current connection. The default value for @@ERROR is zero. Errors are raised by the database engine when standard error conditions occur. All of the standard error numbers and messages are stored in the sysmessages table and can be queried using the following script:

```
SELECT * FROM master.dbo.sysmessages
```

Custom errors can be raised manually using the RAISERROR statement and can be added to the sysmessages table using the sp_addmessage system stored procedure.

Following is a simple example of the @@ERROR variable. First I try to divide a number by zero. This causes the database engine to raise the standard error number 8134.

```
SELECT 5 / 0
SELECT @@ERROR
```

Successfully retrieving the value of @@ERROR causes the value of @@ERROR to return to zero. This because @@ERROR only holds the error number for the previously executed statement. If I want to retrieve additional error information, I can get it from the sysmessages table (or view it in SQL Server 2005) using the following script:

```
SELECT 5 / 0

SELECT * FROM master.dbo.sysmessages WHERE error = @@ERROR
```

Executing this script returns more detailed error information from the sysmessages table shown in Figure 6-1.

error	severity	dlevel	description	msglangid
8134	16	0	Divide by zero error encountered.	1033

Figure 6-1

If I had installed SQL Server with languages in addition to U.S. English, additional messages would be listed. Each language-specific error message has a language identifier (mslangid), which corresponds to a language in the syslanguages table.

@@SERVICENAME

This is the name of the Windows service used to execute and maintain the current instance of SQL Server. This will typically return the value MSSQLSERVER. Non-default instances (if you were to install SQL Server more than once or choose to install it as a named instance) have uniquely named service names.

@@TOTAL_ERRORS

This is the total number of errors that have occurred since the current connection was opened. Like the @@ERROR variable, this is unique for each user session and is reset when each connection closes.

@@TOTAL_READ

This is a count of the total read operations that have occurred since the current connection was opened.

@@VERSION

This variable contains the complete version information for the current instance of SQL Server.

```
SELECT @@VERSION
```

For example, for an instance of SQL Server 2000, this script returns the following:

```
Microsoft SQL Server  2000 - 8.00.760 (Intel X86)   Dec 17 2002 14:22:05
Copyright (c) 1988-2003 Microsoft Corporation  Developer Edition on Windows NT 5.1
(Build 2600: Service Pack 2)
```

The actual version number, used internally at Microsoft, is a simple integer value, although released products may have other branded names. In this case, SQL Server 2000 is really version 8. Windows XP Professional shows up as Windows NT version 5.1. The build number is used for internal control and reflects changes made in beta and preview product releases, and post-release service packs. Here is an example of the output for SQL Server 2005 running on Windows Server 2003:

```
Microsoft SQL Server 2005 - 9.00.1090 (Intel X86)
   Feb 21 2005 03:39:52
   Copyright (c) 1988-2004 Microsoft Corporation
   Enterprise Edition on Windows NT 5.2 (Build 3790: )
```

Conversion Functions

Data type conversion can be performed using the CAST() and CONVERT() functions. For most purposes, these two functions are redundant and reflect the evolutionary history of the SQL language. The functionality may be similar, however the syntax is different. Not all values can be converted to other data types. Generally speaking, any value that can be converted can be done so with a simple function call.

CAST()

The CAST() function accepts one argument, an expression, which includes both the source value and a target data type separated by the word AS. Here is an example, using the literal string '123' converted to an integer:

```
SELECT CAST('123' AS Int)
```

The return value will be the integer value 123. However, what happens if you try to convert a string representing a fractional value to an integer?

```
SELECT CAST('123.4' AS Int)
```

Neither the CAST() nor the CONVERT() functions will do any guessing, rounding, or truncation for you. Because the value 123.4 can't be represented using the Int data type, the function call produces an error:

```
Server: Msg 245, Level 16, State 1, Line 1
Syntax error converting the varchar value '123.4' to a column of data type int.
```

If you need to return a valid numeric equivalent value, you must use a data type equipped to handle the value. There are a few that would work in this case. If you use the CAST() function with your value to a target type of Decimal, you can specifically define the precision and scale for the decimal value. In this example, the precision and scale are 9 and 2, respectively. Precision is the total number of digits that can be stored to both the left and right of the decimal point. Scale is the number of digits that will be stored to the right of the decimal point. This means that the maximum whole number value would be 9,999,999 and the smallest fractional number would be .01.

```
SELECT CAST('123.4' AS Decimal(9,2))
```

The Decimal data type displays the significant decimal positions in the results grid:

```
123.40
```

The default values for precision and scale are 18 and 0 respectively. Without providing values for precision and scale of the Decimal type, SQL Server effectively truncates the fractional part of the number without causing an error.

```
SELECT CAST('123.4' AS Decimal)
```

The result looks like an integer value:

```
123
```

Applying data type conversions to table data is very easy to do. The next example uses the Employee table, and starts with the following query:

```
SELECT FirstName, LastName, DepartmentID, ShiftID, BirthDate
FROM Employee
ORDER BY LastName
```

Ordering by the last name just gives you some variety in the DepartmentID and ShiftID column values in the first page of the results grid. The results are shown in Figure 6-2.

You'd like to create a new value, made up of the DepartmentID and ShiftID separated by a hyphen. If you use the following expression, you don't get the result you're looking for. In fact, the hyphen isn't even included in the resulting value.

```
SELECT DepartmentID + '-' + ShiftID FROM Employee
```

The problem with this expression is that you're trying to concatenate an integer (the DepartmentID), a character value (the hyphen), and another integer (the ShiftID). Apparently, the query engine perceives the hyphen to be a mathematical operator, rather than a character. Regardless of the outcome, you need to fix the expression and make sure you are working with the appropriate data types. This expression makes the necessary type conversions:

```
SELECT CAST(DepartmentID AS VarChar(5)) + '-' + CAST(ShiftID AS VarChar(5))
FROM Employee
```

	FirstName	LastName	DepartmentID	ShiftID	BirthDate
1	Syed	Abbas	3	1	1965-02-11 00:00:00.000
2	Kim	Abercrombie	7	1	1933-01-14 00:00:00.000
3	Hazem	Abolrous	13	1	1966-01-13 00:00:00.000
4	Humberto	Acevedo	11	1	1966-02-06 00:00:00.000
5	Pilar	Ackerman	15	1	1966-02-06 00:00:00.000
6	Jay	Adams	7	2	1966-03-14 00:00:00.000
7	Osarumwense	Agbonile	7	3	1966-01-25 00:00:00.000
8	François	Ajenstat	11	1	1966-04-07 00:00:00.000
9	Amy	Alberts	3	1	1947-10-22 00:00:00.000
10	Sean	Alexander	13	1	1966-04-07 00:00:00.000
11	Nancy	Anderson	7	3	1966-02-06 00:00:00.000
12	Pamela	Ansman-Wolfe	3	1	1965-01-06 00:00:00.000
13	Zainal	Arifin	12	1	1966-03-02 00:00:00.000
14	Mary	Baker	7	2	1976-10-20 00:00:00.000
15	Angela	Barbariol	7	1	1966-01-13 00:00:00.000
16	David	Barber	10	1	1966-02-06 00:00:00.000
17	Paula	Barreto de Mattos	9	1	1966-03-14 00:00:00.000
18	Shai	Bassli	14	1	1961-09-30 00:00:00.000
19	Wanida	Benshoof	4	1	1965-04-17 00:00:00.000
20	Karen	Berg	11	1	1966-04-19 00:00:00.000
21	Karen	Berge	12	1	1966-01-25 00:00:00.000
22	Andreas	Berglund	13	2	1966-03-02 00:00:00.000
23	Matthias	Berndt	15	1	1966-01-13 00:00:00.000
24	Jo	Berry	14	3	1942-06-19 00:00:00.000
25	Jimmy	Bischoff	15	1	1966-04-19 00:00:00.000

Figure 6-2

Converting the integer values to the VarChar type makes these character values without adding any extra spaces. These values are combined with the hyphen using the plus sign to concatenate string values rather than adding and subtracting the previous numeric values. Now add the first name, last name, and birth date columns:

```
SELECT FirstName
     , LastName
     , CAST(DepartmentID AS VarChar(5)) + '-' + CAST(ShiftID AS VarChar(5)) AS DS
     , BirthDate
FROM Employee
ORDER BY LastName
```

The results are shown in Figure 6-3.

Don't worry about the BirthDate column. I have plans for it in the next section. As you see, the DepartmentID and ShiftID are combined as you wanted them to be.

	FirstName	LastName	DS	BirthDate
1	Syed	Abbas	3-1	1965-02-11 00:00:00.000
2	Kim	Abercrombie	7-1	1933-01-14 00:00:00.000
3	Hazem	Abolrous	13-1	1966-01-13 00:00:00.000
4	Humberto	Acevedo	11-1	1966-02-06 00:00:00.000
5	Pilar	Ackerman	15-1	1966-02-06 00:00:00.000
6	Jay	Adams	7-2	1966-03-14 00:00:00.000
7	Osarumwense	Agbonile	7-3	1966-01-25 00:00:00.000
8	François	Ajenstat	11-1	1966-04-07 00:00:00.000
9	Amy	Alberts	3-1	1947-10-22 00:00:00.000
10	Sean	Alexander	13-1	1966-04-07 00:00:00.000
11	Nancy	Anderson	7-3	1966-02-06 00:00:00.000
12	Pamela	Ansman-Wolfe	3-1	1965-01-06 00:00:00.000
13	Zainal	Arifin	12-1	1966-03-02 00:00:00.000
14	Mary	Baker	7-2	1976-10-20 00:00:00.000
15	Angela	Barbariol	7-1	1966-01-13 00:00:00.000
16	David	Barber	10-1	1966-02-06 00:00:00.000
17	Paula	Barreto de Mattos	9-1	1966-03-14 00:00:00.000
18	Shai	Bassli	14-1	1961-09-30 00:00:00.000
19	Wanida	Benshoof	4-1	1965-04-17 00:00:00.000
20	Karen	Berg	11-1	1966-04-19 00:00:00.000
21	Karen	Berge	12-1	1966-01-25 00:00:00.000
22	Andreas	Berglund	13-2	1966-03-02 00:00:00.000
23	Matthias	Berndt	15-1	1966-01-13 00:00:00.000
24	Jo	Berry	14-3	1942-06-19 00:00:00.000
25	Jimmy	Bischoff	15-1	1966-04-19 00:00:00.000

Figure 6-3

CONVERT()

For simple type conversion, the CONVERT() function does the same thing as the CAST() function, only with different syntax. It requires two arguments: the first for the target data type and the second for the source value. Here are a couple of quick examples similar to those used in the preceding section:

```
SELECT CONVERT(INT, '123')

SELECT CONVERT(Decimal(9,2), '123.4')
```

The CONVERT() function also has some enhanced features making it useful for returning formatted string values. Date values can be formatted in a variety of ways. There are 28 predefined date formats to accommodate international and special-purpose date and time output. The following table shows how these break down.

Format Number	Year Digits	Hour Format	Description	Example
0	2	12	Default	Apr 25 2005 1:05PM
1	2		US	04/25/05
2	2		ANSI	05.04.25
3	2		UK/French	25/04/05
4	2		German	25.04.05

Format Number	Year Digits	Hour Format	Description	Example
5	2		Italian	25-04-05
6	2		Custom - Date Only	25 Apr 05
7	2		Custom - Date Only	Apr 25, 05
8		24	Custom - Time Only	13:05:35
9	4	12	Default, milliseconds	Apr 25 2005 1:05:35:123PM
10	2		US	04-25-05
11	2		Japan	05/04/25
12	2		ISO	050425
13	4	24	Europe	25 Apr 2005 13:05:35:123
14		24	Custom Time, milliseconds	13:05:35:123
100	4	12	Default	Apr 25 2005 1:05PM
101	4		US	04/25/2005
102	4		ANSI	2005.04.25
103	4		UK/French	25/04/2005
104	4		German	25.04.2005
105	4		Italian	25-04-2005
106	4		Custom - Date Only	25 Apr 2005
107	4		Custom - Date Only	Apr 25, 2005
108		24	Custom - Time Only	13:05:35
109	4	12	Default, milliseconds	Apr 25 2005 1:05:35:123PM
110	4		US	04-25-2005
111	4		Japan	2005/04/25
112	4		ISO	20050425
113	4	24	Europe	25 Apr 2005 13:05:35:123
114		24	Custom Time, milliseconds	13:05:35:123

The third argument to this function is optional and accepts the format number integer value. The examples provided in the grid apply to the DateTime data type. When converting from the SmallDateTime data type, the formatting remains the same but some elements will display 0. Here are a few examples of some related script along with formatted date output:

```
SELECT 'Default Date: ' + CONVERT(VarChar(50), GETDATE(), 100)
Default Date: Apr 25 2005 1:05PM
```

```
SELECT 'US Date: ' + CONVERT(VarChar(50), GETDATE(), 101)
US Date: 04/25/2005
```

```
SELECT 'ANSI Date: ' + CONVERT(VarChar(50), GETDATE(), 102)
ANSI Date: 2005.04.25
```

```
SELECT 'UK/French Date: ' + CONVERT(VarChar(50), GETDATE(), 103)
UK/French Date: 25/04/2005
```

```
SELECT 'German Date: ' + CONVERT(VarChar(50), GETDATE(), 104)
German Date: 25.04.2005
```

Format numbers 0, 1, and 2 also apply to numeric types and affect the format of decimal and thousand separators. The effect is different for different data types. In general, using the format number 0 (or no value for this argument) returns a formatted value in the data type's most native form. Using 1 or 2 generally displays a more detailed or precise value. The following example uses 0:

```
DECLARE @Num Money
SET @Num = 1234.56
SELECT CONVERT(VarChar(50), @Num, 0)
```

It returns the following:

```
1234.56
```

Using 1 returns the following:

```
1,234.56
```

And using 2 returns the following:

```
1234.5600
```

This example does the same thing with a Float type:

```
DECLARE @Num Float
SET @Num = 1234.56
SELECT CONVERT(VarChar(50), @Num, 2)
```

Using the value 0 doesn't change the format from what you've provided but using 1 or 2 returns the number expressed in scientific notation, the latter using 15 decimal positions:

```
1.234560000000000e+003
```

The STR() Function

This is a quick-and-easy conversion function that converts a numeric value to a string. The function accepts three arguments: the numeric value, the overall length, and the number of decimal positions. If the integer part of the number and decimal positions is shorter than the overall length, the result is left-padded with spaces. In this first example, the value (including the decimal) is five characters long. I've made it a point to show the results in the grid so you can see any left padding. This call asks for an overall length of eight characters with four decimal positions:

```
SELECT STR(123.4, 8, 4)
```

The result has the decimal value right-filled with 0s, as shown in Figure 6-4.

Figure 6-4

Here I'm passing in a ten-character value and asking for an eight-character result, with four decimal positions:

```
SELECT STR(123.456789, 8, 4)
```

The result must be truncated to meet my requirements. The STR() function rounds the last digit, as shown in Figure 6-5.

Figure 6-5

Now I'll pass in the number 1 for the value and ask for a six-character result with four decimal positions. In this case, the STR() function right-fills the decimal value with zeros, as shown in Figure 6-6.

```
SELECT STR(1, 6, 4)
```

(No column name)
1.0000

Figure 6-6

However, if I specify an overall length greater than the length of the value, decimal point, and the decimal value, the result will be left-padded with spaces, as shown in Figure 6-7.

```
SELECT STR(1, 12, 4)
```

(No column name)
                1.0000

Figure 6-7

Cursor Functions and Variables

Chapter 10 discusses the use of cursors along with some of the pros and cons of using this technique. The short version of this topic is that cursors can provide the ability to process multiple rows of data, one row at a time, in a procedural loop. This ability comes at a cost when compared with more efficient, set-based operations. One function and two global variables are provided to help manage cursor operations.

The CURSOR_STATUS() Function

This function returns an integer indicating the status of a cursor-type variable passed into the function. A number of different types of cursors can affect the behavior of this function. For simplicity, the return value will typically be one of those listed in the following table.

Return Value	Description
1	Cursor contains one or more rows (dynamic cursor contains 0 or more rows)
0	Cursor contains no rows
-1	Cursor is closed
-2	Cursor is not allocated
-3	Cursor doesn't exist

@@CURSOR_ROWS

This variable is an integer value representing the number of rows in the cursor open in the current connection. Depending on the cursor type, this value may or may not represent the actual number of rows in the result set.

@@FETCH_STATUS

This variable is a flag that indicates the state of the current cursor pointer. It is used primarily to determine whether a row still exists and when you have reached the end of the result set after executing a FETCH NEXT statement.

Date Functions

These functions are used for working with DateTime and SmallDateTime type values. Some are used for parsing the date and time portions of a date value and for comparing and manipulating date/time values.

The DATEADD() Function

The DATEADD() function adds a specific number of date unit intervals to a date/time value. For example, to determine the date 90 days after April 29, 1988, the following statement is used:

```
SELECT DATEADD(Day, 90, '4-29-1988')
```

The answer is as follows:

```
1988-07-28 00:00:00.000   (July 28, 1988)
```

Any of the values in the following table can be passed in the Interval argument.

Interval	Interval Argument Values
Year	Year, yyyy, yy
Quarter	quarter, qq, q
Month	Month, mm, m
Day of the year	dayofyear, dy, y
Day	Day, dd, d
Week	Week, wk, ww
Hour	Hour, hh
Minute	minute, mi, n
Second	second, ss, s
Millisecond	millisecond, ms

Using the same date as before, here are some more examples. This time, I'll include the time as well. The results are on the following line:

18 years later:

```
SELECT DATEADD(year, 18, '4-29-1988 10:30 AM')
2006-04-29 10:30:00.000
```

18 years before:

```
SELECT DATEADD(yy, -18, '4-29-1988 10:30 AM')
1970-04-29 10:30:00.000
```

9,000 seconds after:

```
SELECT DATEADD(second, 9000, '4-29-1988 10:30 AM')
1988-04-29 13:00:00.000
```

9,000,000 milliseconds before:

```
SELECT DATEADD(mi, -9000000, '4-29-1988 10:30 AM')
1971-03-20 10:30:00.000
```

I can combine the CONVERT()and the DATEADD() functions to format a return date value nine months before September 8, 1989:

```
SELECT CONVERT(VarChar(20), DATEADD(m, -9, '9-8-1989'), 101)
12/08/1988
```

This returns a variable-length character value, a little easier to read than the default dates you saw in the previous results. This is a nested function call where the results from the DATEADD() function (a DateTime type value) are fed to the value argument of the CONVERT() function.

The DATEDIFF() Function

I think of the DATEADD() and DATEDIFF() functions as cousins — sort of like multiplication and division. There are four elements in this equation: the start date, the interval (date unit), the difference value, and the end date. If you have three, you can always figure out what the fourth one is. I use a start date, an integer value, and interval unit with the DATEADD() function to return the end date value relative to a starting date. The DATEDIFF() function returns the difference integer value if I provide the start and end dates and interval. Do you see the relationship?

To demonstrate, I simply choose any two dates and an interval unit as arguments. The function returns the difference between the two dates in the interval unit provided. I want to know what the difference is between the dates 9-8-1989 and 10-17-1991 in months:

```
SELECT DATEDIFF(month, '9-8-1989', '10-17-1991')
```

The answer is 25 months. How about the difference in days?

```
SELECT DATEDIFF(day, '9-8-1989', '10-17-1991')
```

It's 769 days.

How about the difference in weeks between 7-2-1996 and 8-4-1997?

```
SELECT DATEDIFF(week, '7-2-1996', '8-4-1997')
```

57 weeks.

You can even figure out how old you are in seconds:

```
DECLARE @MyBirthDate DateTime
SET @MyBirthDate = '3-24-1967'
SELECT DATEDIFF(ss, @MyBirthDate, GETDATE())
```

Someone is over 1.3 billion seconds old!

I apply this function to a query by passing a column name to the value argument. This will tell me the approximate age of each employee:

```
SELECT FirstName, LastName, DATEDIFF(year, BirthDate, GETDATE())
FROM Employee
```

Figure 6-8 shows the first 25 rows in the results.

	FirstName	LastName	Age
1	Terri	Duffy	44
2	Jian Shuo	Wang	41
3	Michael	Sullivan	36
4	Sharon	Salavaria	54
5	Gail	Erickson	63
6	Jossef	Goldberg	56
7	Ovidiu	Crăcium	37
8	Janice	Galvin	26
9	Thierry	D'Hers	56
10	Brian	Welcker	38
11	Stephen	Jiang	64
12	Syed	Abbas	40
13	Amy	Alberts	58
14	Pamela	Ansman-Wolfe	40
15	David	Campbell	41
16	Fernando	Caro	53
17	Shu	Ito	71
18	Linda	Mitchell	35
19	Tsvi	Reiter	40
20	José	Saraiva	75
21	Garrett	Vargar	40
22	Ranjit	Varkey Chudukatil	40
23	Rachel	Valdez	40
24	Lynn	Tsoflias	44
25	Jae	Pak	47

Figure 6-8

This may look right at first glance, but it's not accurate to the day. For example, according to the database, Brian Welker's birth date is on July 8 and he would be celebrating his 38th birthday this year (I'm running the query in April). If I were to use the previous calculation to determine when his age changes, I would be sending Brian a birthday card sometime in January, about six months early.

Unless you find the difference between these dates in a more granular unit and then do the math, the result will only be accurate within a year of the employee's actual birth date. This example factors the number of days in a year (including leap year). Converting to an Int type truncates, rather than rounds, the value:

```
SELECT FirstName, LastName
, CONVERT(Int, DATEDIFF(day, BirthDate, GETDATE())/365.25) As Age
FROM Employee
```

Compare the results shown in Figure 6-9 with those of the previous example.

Now Brian is 37 and the rest of the employees' ages should be accurate within a day. The BirthDate column in this table stores the employee's birth date as of midnight (00:00:00 AM). This is the first second of a date. The GETDATE() function returns the current date and time. This means that I'm comparing a two dates with a difference of about eight hours (it's about 8:00 AM as I write this). If you want this calculation to be even more accurate, you need to convert the result of the GETDATE() function to a DateTime value at midnight of the current date.

	FirstName	LastName	Age
1	Terri	Duffy	43
2	Jian Shuo	Wang	40
3	Michael	Sullivan	35
4	Sharon	Salavaria	53
5	Gail	Erickson	62
6	Jossef	Goldberg	56
7	Ovidiu	Crăcium	37
8	Janice	Galvin	25
9	Thierry	D'Hers	55
10	Brian	Welcker	37
11	Stephen	Jiang	63
12	Syed	Abbas	40
13	Amy	Alberts	57
14	Pamela	Ansman-Wolfe	40
15	David	Campbell	40
16	Fernando	Caro	52
17	Shu	Ito	71
18	Linda	Mitchell	35
19	Tsvi	Reiter	40
20	José	Saraiva	75
21	Garrett	Vargar	40
22	Ranjit	Varkey Chudukatil	40
23	Rachel	Valdez	40
24	Lynn	Tsoflias	44
25	Jae	Pak	47

Figure 6-9

The DATEPART() and DATENAME() Functions

These functions return the date part, or unit, for a DateTime or ShortDateTime value. The DATEPART() function returns an integer value and the DATENAME() function returns a string containing the descriptive name, if applicable. For example, passing the date 4-29-1988 to the DATEPART() function and requesting the month returns the number 4:

```
SELECT DATEPART(month, '4-29-1988')
```

Whereas, with the same parameters, the DATENAME() function returns April:

```
SELECT DATENAME(month, '4-29-1988')
```

Both of these functions accept values from the same list of date part argument constants as the DATEADD() function.

The GETDATE() and GETUTCDATE() Functions

Both of these functions return the current date and time as a DateTime type. The GETUTCDATE() function uses the time zone setting on the server to determine the equivalent Universal Time Coordinate time. This is the same as Greenwich Mean Time or what pilots call "Zulu Time." Both functions are accurate to 3.33 milliseconds:

```
SELECT GETDATE()
SELECT GETUTCDATE()
```

Executing these functions returns the unformatted result shown in Figure 6-10.

	(No column name)
1	2005-04-27 17:19:11.303
	(No column name)
1	2005-04-28 00:19:11.303

Figure 6-10

Because I'm in the Pacific time zone, there is a seven-hour difference between the current time and UTC. I can verify this using the following DATEDIFF() function call:

```
SELECT DATEDIFF(hour, GETDATE(), GETUTCDATE())
```

The DAY(), MONTH(), and YEAR() Functions

These three functions return an integer date part of a DateTime or SmallDateTime type value. They serve a variety of useful purposes including the ability to create your own unique date formats. Suppose I need to create a custom date value as a character string. By converting the output from each of these functions to character types and then concatenating the results, I can arrange them practically any way I want:

```
SELECT 'Year: ' + CONVERT(VarChar(4), YEAR(GETDATE()))
    + ', Month: ' + CONVERT(VarChar(2), MONTH(GETDATE()))
    + ', Day: ' + CONVERT(VarChar(2), DAY(GETDATE()))
```

This script produces the following:

```
Year: 2005, Month: 4, Day: 27
```

The next section discusses string manipulation functions and uses a similar technique to build a compact custom time stamp.

String Manipulation Functions

String functions are used to parse, replace, and manipulate character values. One of the great challenges when working with quantities or raw character data is to reliably extract meaningful information. A number of string parsing functions are available to identify and parse substrings (a portion of a larger character type value). As humans, we do this all the time. When presented with a document, an invoice, or written text, we intuitively identify and isolate the meaningful pieces of information. To automate this process can be a cumbersome task when dealing with even moderately complex text values. These functions contain practically all of the tools necessary. The challenge is to find the simplest and most elegant method.

The ASCII(), CHAR(), UNICODE(), and NCHAR() Functions

These four functions are similar because they all deal with converting values between a character and the industry standard numeric representation of a character. The American Standard Code for Information Interchange (ASCII) standard character-set includes 128 alpha, numeric, and punctuation characters. This set of values is the foundation of the IBM PC architecture, and although some of it is now somewhat antiquated, much remains and is still central to modern computing. If you use the English language on your computer, every character on your keyboard is represented in the ASCII character-set. This is great for English-speaking (or at least English typing) computer users, but what about everyone else on the planet?

In the evolution of the computer, it didn't take long for the ASCII set to become obsolete. It was soon extended to form the 256-character ANSI character-set which uses a single byte to store every character. Still an American standard (held by the American National Standards Institute), this extended list of characters meets the needs of many other users, supporting mainly European language characters, but is still founded on the original English-language character-set. To support all printable languages, the Unicode standard was devised to support multiple, language-specific character-sets. Each Unicode character requires 2 bytes of storage space, twice the space as ASCII and ANSI characters, but with 2 bytes more than 65,000 unique characters can be represented. SQL Server supports both ASCII and Unicode standards.

The two ASCII-based functions are ASCII() and CHAR().The fundamental principle here is that every character used on the computer is actually represented as a number. To find out what number is used for a character, pass a single-character string to the ASCII() function:

```
SELECT ASCII('A')
```

This returns 65.

What if I know the number and want to convert it to a character? That's the job of the CHAR() function:

```
SELECT CHAR(65)
```

This returns the letter A.

To get a complete list of ASCII character values, I can populate a temporary table with the values 0 through 127 and then use the CHAR() function to return the corresponding characters. I'll shorten the script but include the entire result set in multi-column format, to save space:

```
-- Create temporary table for numbers:
Create Table #ASCIIVals (ASCIIValue SmallInt)

-- Insert numbers 0 - 127 into table:
Insert Into #ASCIIVals (ASCIIValue) Select 0
Insert Into #ASCIIVals (ASCIIValue) Select 1
Insert Into #ASCIIVals (ASCIIValue) Select 2
Insert Into #ASCIIVals (ASCIIValue) Select 3
Insert Into #ASCIIVals (ASCIIValue) Select 4
...
Insert Into #ASCIIVals (ASCIIValue) Select 123
Insert Into #ASCIIVals (ASCIIValue) Select 124
Insert Into #ASCIIVals (ASCIIValue) Select 125
Insert Into #ASCIIVals (ASCIIValue) Select 126
Insert Into #ASCIIVals (ASCIIValue) Select 127

-- Return all integer values and corresponding ASCII characters:
SELECT ASCIIValue, CHAR(ASCIIValue) As Character FROM #ASCIIVals
```

Here are the results reformatted in a multi-column grid. Note that non-printable control characters show as small squares in the results grid. Depending on a number of factors, such as fonts or languages installed, these may be displayed a little differently.

ASCIIValue	Character	ASCIIValue	Character	ASCIIValue	Character	ASCIIValue	Character
0	□	32		64	@	96	`
1	□	33	!	65	A	97	a
2	□	34	"	66	B	98	b
3	□	35	#	67	C	99	c
4	□	36	$	68	D	100	d
5	□	37	%	69	E	101	e
6	□	38	&	70	F	102	f
7	□	39	'	71	G	103	g
8	□	40	(	72	H	104	h
9	□	41	)	73	I	105	i
10	□	42	*	74	J	106	j
11	□	43	+	75	K	107	k
12	□	44	,	76	L	108	l
13	□	45	-	77	M	109	m
14	□	46	.	78	N	110	n
15	□	47	/	79	O	111	o
16	□	48	0	80	P	112	p
17	□	49	1	81	Q	113	q
18	□	50	2	82	R	114	r
19	□	51	3	83	S	115	s
20	□	52	4	84	T	116	t
21	□	53	5	85	U	117	u
22	□	54	6	86	V	118	v
23	□	55	7	87	W	119	w
24	□	56	8	88	X	120	x
25	□	57	9	89	Y	121	y
26	□	58	:	90	Z	122	z
27	□	59	;	91	[	123	{
28	□	60	<	92	\	124		
29	□	61	=	93	]	125	}
30	-	62	>	94	^	126	~
31	¬	63	?	95	_	127	

The UNICODE() function is the Unicode equivalent of the ASCII() function, and the NCHAR() function does the same thing as the CHAR() function only with Unicode characters. SQL Server's nChar and nVarChar types will store any Unicode character and will work with this function. For extremely large values, the nText type and the new nChar(max) and nVarChar(max) types in SQL Server 2005 also support Unicode characters.

To return extended characters, I'll execute the NCHAR() function with sample character codes:

```
SELECT NCHAR(220)
```

This returns the German U umlaut, Ü.

```
SELECT NCHAR(233)
```

This returns an accented lowercase e, é.

```
SELECT NCHAR(241)
```

This returns a Spanish "enya," or n with a tilde, ñ.

The CHARINDEX() and PATINDEX() Functions

CHARINDEX() is the original SQL function used to find the first occurrence of a substring within another string. As the name suggests, it simply returns an integer that represents the index of the first character of the substring within the entire string. The following script looks for an occurrence of the string 'sh' within the string 'Washington':

```
SELECT CHARINDEX('sh', 'Washington')
```

This returns 3 to indicate that the 's' is the third character in the string 'Washington'. Using two characters for the substring wasn't particularly useful in this example but could be if the string contained more than one letter s.

The PATINDEX() function is the CHARINDEX() function on steroids. It will perform the same task in a slightly different way, but has the added benefit of supporting wildcard characters (such as those you would use with the Like operator). As its name suggests, it will return the index of a pattern of characters. This function also works with large character types such as nText, nChar(max), and nVarChar(max). Note that if PATINDEX() is used with these large data types, it returns a BigInt type rather than an Int type. Here's an example:

```
SELECT PATINDEX('%M_rs%', 'The stars near Mars are far from ours')
```

Note that both percent characters are required if you want to find a string with zero or more characters before and after the string being compared. The underscore indicates that the character in this position is not matched. The string could contain any character at this position.

Compare this to the CHARINDEX() function used with the same set of strings:

```
SELECT CHARINDEX('Mars', 'The stars near Mars are far from ours')
```

Both of these functions return the index value 16. Remember how these functions work. I'll combine this with the SUBSTRING() function in the following section to demonstrate how to parse strings using delimiting characters.

The LEN() Function

The LEN() function returns the length of a string as an integer. This is a simple but useful function that is often used alongside other functions to apply business rules. The following example tests the Month and Day date parts integers, converted to character types, for their length. If just one character is returned, it pads the character with a zero and then assembles an eight-character date string in US format (MMDDYYYY):

```
DECLARE @MonthChar VarChar(2), @DayChar VarChar(2), @DateOut Char(8)

SET @MonthChar = CAST(MONTH(GETDATE()) AS VarChar(2))
SET @DayChar = CAST(DAY(GETDATE()) AS VarChar(2))

-- Make sure month and day are two char long:
IF LEN(@MonthChar) = 1
  SET @MonthChar = '0' + @MonthChar
IF LEN(@DayChar) = 1
  SET @DayChar = '0' + @DayChar

-- Build date string:
SET @DateOut = @MonthChar + @DayChar + CAST(YEAR(GETDATE()) AS Char(4))

SELECT @DateOut
```

The return value from this script will always be an eight-character value representing the date:

```
05012005
```

The LEFT() and RIGHT() Functions

The LEFT() and RIGHT() functions are similar in that they both return a substring of a specified size. The difference between the two is what part of the character string is returned. The LEFT() function returns characters from the left-most part of the string, counting characters to the right. The RIGHT() function does exactly the opposite. It starts at the right-most character and counts to the left, returning the specified number of characters. Take a look at an example that uses the string 'George Washington' to return substrings using these functions.

If I ask to return a five-character substring using the LEFT() function, the function locates the left-most character, counts five characters to the right, and returns the substring shown in Figure 6-11.

```
George Washington
12345678911111111
         01234567
```

Figure 6-11

```
DECLARE @FullName VarChar(25)
SET @FullName = 'George Washington'
SELECT LEFT(@FullName, 5)
Geor
```

If I ask to return a five-character substring using the RIGHT() function, the function locates the right-most character, counts five characters to the left, and returns this substring shown in Figure 6-12.

```
George Washington
111111111987654321
76543210
```

Figure 6-12

```
DECLARE @FullName VarChar(25)
SET @ FullName = 'George Washington'
SELECT RIGHT(@FullName, 5)
ngton
```

Neither of these functions is particularly useful for consistently returning a meaningful part of this string. What if I wanted to return the first name or last name portions of the full name? This takes just a little more work. The LEFT() function may be the right method to use for extracting the first name if I can determine the position of the space in every name I might encounter. In this case, I can use the CHARINDEX() or PATINDEX() functions to locate the space and then use the LEFT() function to return only these characters. The first example here takes a procedural approach, breaking this process into steps:

```
DECLARE @FullName VarChar(25), @SpaceIndex TinyInt
SET @FullName = 'George Washington'

-- Get index of the delimiting space:
SET @SpaceIndex = CHARINDEX(' ', @FullName)

-- Return all characters to the left of the space:
SELECT LEFT(@FullName, @SpaceIndex - 1)
```

I don't want to include the space so it's necessary to subtract one from the @SpaceIndex value to include only the first name.

The SUBSTRING() Function

The SUBSTRING() function starts at a position and counts characters to the right, returning a substring of a specified length. Unlike the LEFT() function, you can tell it at what index position to begin counting. This allows you to extract a substring from anywhere within a character string. This function requires three arguments: the string to parse, the starting index, and the length of the substring to return. If you want to return all text to the end of the input string, you can use a length index larger than necessary. The SUBSTRING() function will return characters up to the last position of the string and will not pad the string with spaces.

The SUBSTRING() function can easily replace the LEFT() function by designating the left-most character of the string (1) as the starting index.

Continuing with the earlier example, I can set the starting position and length, returning a value from the middle of the name string. In this case, I'll start at position 4 and return a 6-character substring, as shown in Figure 6-13.

```
George Washington
12345678911111111
        01234567
  123456
```

Figure 6-13

```
DECLARE @FullName VarChar(25)
SET @FullName = 'George Washington'
SELECT SUBSTRING(@FullName, 4, 6)
rge Wa
```

Now, I'll put it all together and parse the first and last names from the full name in a way that will work for any full name string formatted as FirstName + space + LastName. Using the same logic as before, I'm going to nest the function calls to reduce the number of lines of script and get rid of the @SpaceIndex variable. Instead of the LEFT() function, I'll use SUBSTRING(). I've added a comment below the line that does all the work. Spaces are added to make room for the comment text:

```
DECLARE @FullName VarChar(25)
SET @FullName = 'George Washington'
-- Return first name:
SELECT SUBSTRING(@FullName, 1,      CHARINDEX(' ', @FullName) - 1)
--                ^String   ^Start  ^Returns space index      ^Don't include space
```

Similar logic is used to extract the last name. I just have to change the start index argument to the position following the space. The space is at position seven and the last name begins at position eight. This means that the start index will always be one plus the CHARINDEX() result:

```
DECLARE @FullName VarChar(25)
SET @FullName = 'George Washington'
SELECT SUBSTRING(@FullName, CHARINDEX(' ', @FullName) + 1, LEN(@FullName))
```

The values passed into the SUBSTRING() function are the position of the space plus one as the start index. This will be the first letter of the last name. Because I won't always know the length of the name, I passed in the LEN() function for the length of the substring. The SUBSTRING() function will reach the end of the string when it reaches this position and simply include all characters after the space to the end of the string.

To set up an example, I'll create and populate a temporary table:

```
CREATE TABLE #MyNames (FullName VarChar(50))
GO
INSERT INTO #MyNames (FullName) SELECT 'Fred Flintstone'
INSERT INTO #MyNames (FullName) SELECT 'Wilma Flintstone'
INSERT INTO #MyNames (FullName) SELECT 'Barney Rubble'
INSERT INTO #MyNames (FullName) SELECT 'Betty Rubble'
INSERT INTO #MyNames (FullName) SELECT 'George Jetson'
INSERT INTO #MyNames (FullName) SELECT 'Jane Jetson'
```

Now I'll execute a query using the function calls to parse the first name and last name values as one-line expressions. Note that references to the @FullName variable are replaced with the FullName column in the table:

```
SELECT
    SUBSTRING(FullName, 1, CHARINDEX(' ', FullName) - 1) AS FirstName
  , SUBSTRING(FullName, CHARINDEX(' ', FullName) + 1, LEN(FullName)) AS LastName
FROM #MyNames
```

The results shown in Figure 6-14 display two distinct columns as if the first and last names were stored separately.

	FirstName	LastName
1	Fred	Flintstone
2	Wilma	Flintstone
3	Barney	Rubble
4	Betty	Rubble
5	George	Jetson
6	Jane	Jetson

Figure 6-14

The LOWER() and UPPER() Functions

These functions are pretty easy to figure out. Each simply converts a character string to all lowercase or all uppercase characters. This is most useful when comparing user input or stored strings for comparison. String comparisons are typically case-insensitive, depending on settings chosen during SQL Server setup. Used along with other string manipulation functions, strings can be converted to use proper case for data storage and presentation. This example accounts for mixed-case last names, assuming the name contains a single space before the second capitalized substring. You could argue that some of these names normally wouldn't contain spaces, and I agree. This demonstration could easily be extended to include provisions for other mixed-case names (names beginning with Mc, hyphenated names, and so on).

```
DECLARE @LastName VarChar(25), @SpaceIndex TinyInt
SET @LastName = 'mc donald'              -- Test value

-- Find space in name:
SET @SpaceIndex = CHARINDEX(' ', @LastName)
IF @SpaceIndex > 0                       -- Space: Capitalize first & substring
    SELECT UPPER(LEFT(@LastName, 1))
  + LOWER(SUBSTRING(@LastName, 2, @SpaceIndex - 1))
  + UPPER(SUBSTRING(@LastName, @SpaceIndex + 1, 1))
  + LOWER(SUBSTRING(@LastName, @SpaceIndex + 2, LEN(@LastName)))
ELSE                                     -- No space: Cap only first char.
    SELECT UPPER(LEFT(@LastName, 1))
  + LOWER(SUBSTRING(@LastName, 2, LEN(@LastName)))
```

This script returns Mc Donald. I can also extend the example to deal with last names containing an apostrophe. The business rules in this case expect no space. If an apostrophe is found, the following character is to be capitalized. Note that to test an apostrophe in script, it must be entered twice ('') to indicate that this is a literal, rather than an encapsulating single quote. Last name values are stored with only an apostrophe.

```
DECLARE @LastName VarChar(25), @SpaceIndex TinyInt, @AposIndex TinyInt
SET @LastName = 'o''malley'              -- Test value

-- Find space in name:
SET @SpaceIndex = CHARINDEX(' ', @LastName)
-- Find literal ' in name:
SET @AposIndex = CHARINDEX('''', @LastName)
IF @SpaceIndex > 0                       -- Space: Capitalize first & substring
    SELECT UPPER(LEFT(@LastName, 1))
  + LOWER(SUBSTRING(@LastName, 2, @SpaceIndex - 1))
  + UPPER(SUBSTRING(@LastName, @SpaceIndex + 1, 1))
  + LOWER(SUBSTRING(@LastName, @SpaceIndex + 2, LEN(@LastName)))
ELSE IF @AposIndex > 0                   -- Apostrophe: Cap first & substring
    SELECT UPPER(LEFT(@LastName, 1))
  + LOWER(SUBSTRING(@LastName, 2, @AposIndex - 1))
  + UPPER(SUBSTRING(@LastName, @AposIndex + 1, 1))
  + LOWER(SUBSTRING(@LastName, @AposIndex + 2, LEN(LastName)))
ELSE                                     -- No space: Cap only first char.
    SELECT UPPER(LEFT(@LastName, 1))
  + LOWER(SUBSTRING(@LastName, 2, LEN(LastName)))
```

This script returns O'Malley. For this to be of use, I'll wrap it up into a user-defined function:

```
CREATE FUNCTION dbo.fn_FixLastName ( @LastName VarChar(25) )
RETURNS VarChar(25)
AS
BEGIN
  DECLARE   @SpaceIndex TinyInt
         , @AposIndex TinyInt
         , @ReturnName VarChar(25)
  -- Find space in name:
  SET @SpaceIndex = CHARINDEX(' ', @LastName)
  -- Find literal ' in name:
  SET @AposIndex = CHARINDEX('''', @LastName)
  IF @SpaceIndex > 0                        -- Space: Capitalize first & substring
         SET @ReturnName = UPPER(LEFT(@LastName, 1))
       + LOWER(SUBSTRING(@LastName, 2, @SpaceIndex - 1))
       + UPPER(SUBSTRING(@LastName, @SpaceIndex + 1, 1))
       + LOWER(SUBSTRING(@LastName, @SpaceIndex + 2, LEN(LastName)))
  ELSE IF @AposIndex > 0                    -- Apostrophe: Cap first & substring
         SET @ReturnName =  UPPER(LEFT(@LastName, 1))
       + LOWER(SUBSTRING(@LastName, 2, @AposIndex - 1))
       + UPPER(SUBSTRING(@LastName, @AposIndex + 1, 1))
       + LOWER(SUBSTRING(@LastName, @AposIndex + 2, LEN(LastName)))
  ELSE                                      -- No space: Cap only first char.
         SET @ReturnName =  UPPER(LEFT(@LastName, 1))
       + LOWER(SUBSTRING(@LastName, 2, LEN(LastName)))
  RETURN @ReturnName
END
```

To test my function, I'll populate a temporary table with sample values so that I can query the names from this table:

```
CREATE TABLE #MyIrishFriends (FirstName VarChar(25), LastName VarChar(25) )

INSERT INTO #MyIrishFriends (FirstName, LastName) SELECT 'James', 'O''grady'
INSERT INTO #MyIrishFriends (FirstName, LastName) SELECT 'Nancy', 'o''brian'
INSERT INTO #MyIrishFriends (FirstName, LastName) SELECT 'George', 'MC kee'
INSERT INTO #MyIrishFriends (FirstName, LastName) SELECT 'Jonas', 'mc intosh'
INSERT INTO #MyIrishFriends (FirstName, LastName) SELECT 'Florence', 'MC BRIDE'
```

The results as they are stored are shown in Figure 6-15.

```
SELECT FirstName, LastName
FROM #MyIrishFriends
```

	FirstName	LastName
1	James	O'grady
2	Nancy	O'BRIAN
3	George	MC kee
4	Jonas	mc intosh
5	Florence	MC BRIDE

Figure 6-15

Using the custom function returns the results shown in Figure 6-16.

```
SELECT FirstName, dbo.fn_FixLastName(LastName) AS LastName
FROM #MyIrishFriends
```

	FirstName	LastName
1	James	O'Grady
2	Nancy	O'Brian
3	George	Mc Kee
4	Jonas	Mc Intosh
5	Florence	Mc Bride

Figure 6-16

The LTRIM() and RTRIM() Functions

These two functions simply return a string with white space (spaces) trimmed from either the left or right side of significant characters:

```
DECLARE @Value1 Char(10), @Value2 Char(10)
SET @Value1 = 'One'
SET @Value2 = 'Two'
SELECT @Value1 + @Value2
SELECT CONVERT(VarChar(5), LEN(@Value1 + @Value2)) + ' characters long.'
SELECT RTRIM(@Value1) + RTRIM(@Value2)
SELECT CONVERT(VarChar(5), LEN(RTRIM(@Value1) + RTRIM(@Value2)))
       + ' characters long trimmed.'
```

The abbreviated results in text form follow:

```
--------------------
One        Two
--------------------
13 characters long.


--------------------
OneTwo
----------------------------
6 characters long trimmed.
```

The REPLACE() Function

The REPLACE() function can be used to replace all occurrences of one character or substring with another character or substring. This can be used as a global search and replace utility.

```
DECLARE @Phrase VarChar(1000)
SET @Phrase = 'I aint gunna use poor grammar when commenting script and I aint
gunna complain about it.'
SELECT REPLACE(@Phrase, 'aint', 'isn''t')
```

As you can see, this was quite effective:

```
I isn't gunna use poor grammar when commenting script and I isn't gunna complain
about it.
```

The REPLICATE() and SPACE() Functions

This is a very useful function when you need to fill a value with repeating characters. I'll use the same temporary table I created for the list of names in the SUBSTRING() example to pad each name value to 20 characters. I subtract the length of each value to pass the right value to the REPLICATE() function:

```
SELECT FullName + REPLICATE('*', 20 - LEN(FullName))
FROM #MyNames
```

The result is a list of names padded with asterisk characters, each 20 characters in length:

```
Fred Flintstone*****
Wilma Flintstone****
Barney Rubble*******
Betty Rubble********
George Jetson*******
Jane Jetson*********
```

The SPACE() function does the same thing, only with spaces. It simply returns a string of space characters of a defined length.

The REVERSE() Function

This function reverses the characters in a string. This might be useful if you need to work with single-character values in a concatenated list.

```
SELECT REVERSE('The stars near Mars are far from ours.')
.sruo morf raf era sraM raen srats ehT
```

I'm sure there's a practical application for this.

The STUFF() Function

This function allows you to replace a portion of a string with another string. It essentially will stuff one string into another string at a given position and for a specified length. This can be useful for string replacements where the source and target values aren't the same length. For example, I need to replace the price in this string, changing it from 99.95 to 109.95:

```
Please submit your payment for 99.95 immediately.
```

The price value begins at position 32 and is five characters in length. It really doesn't matter how long the substring is that I want to stuff into this position. I simply need to know how many characters need to be removed.

```
SELECT STUFF('Please submit your payment for 99.95 immediately.', 32, 5, '109.95')
```

The resulting string follows:

```
Please submit your payment for 109.95 immediately.
```

The QUOTENAME() Function

This function is used with SQL Server object names so they can be passed into an expression. It simply returns a string with square brackets around the input value. If the value contains reserved delimiting or encapsulating characters (such as quotation marks or brackets), modifications are made to the string so SQL Server perceives these characters as literals.

Image/Text Functions

The Text, nText, and Image data types define columns that can store up to 2 gigabytes of ANSI text, Unicode text, or binary data, respectively. SQL Server 2005 still has support for these data types, but Microsoft recommends the use of the new VarChar(max) and VarBinary(max) types in their place. These enhanced data types have the same capabilities and storage characteristics as their older counterparts, but they also support all of the string functions like standard character types. Older types may eventually be phased out of future SQL Server versions.

Two functions have specialized functionality specific to the Text, nText, and Image data types. Additionally, the PATINDEX() string function can be used to find a string of text within these columns and return an integer representing the character position of the first occurrence of the string.

Mathematical Functions

The functions listed in the following table are used to perform a variety of common and specialized mathematical operations and are useful in performing algebraic, trigonometric, statistical, approximating, and financial operations.

Function	Description
ABS()	Returns the absolute value for a numeric value.
ACOS()	Computes the arccosine (an angle) in radians.
ASIN()	Computes the arcsine (an angle) in radians.
ATAN()	Computes the arctangent (an angle) in radians.
ATN2()	Computes the arctangent of two values in radians.
CEILING()	Returns the smallest integer value that is greater than or equal to a number.
COS()	Computes the cosine of an angle in radians.
COT()	Computes the cotangent of an angle in radians.
DEGREES()	Converts an angle from radians to degrees.
EXP()	Returns the natural logarithm raised to a specified exponent.
FLOOR()	Returns the largest integer value that is less than or equal to a number.
LOG()	Calculates the natural logarithm of a number using base-2 (binary) numbering.
LOG10()	Calculates the natural logarithm of a number using base-10 numbering.
PI()	Returns the value for PI() as a float type.
POWER()	Raises a value to a specified exponent.
RADIANS()	Converts an angle from degrees to radians.
RAND()	Returns a fractional number based on a randomizing algorithm; accepts an optional seed value.
ROUND()	Rounds a fractional value to a specified precision.
SIGN()	Returns -1 or 1 depending on whether a single argument value is negative or positive.
SIN()	Computes the sine of an angle in radians.
SQRT()	Returns the square root of a value.
SQUARE()	Returns the square (n^2) of a value.
TAN()	Computes the tangent of an angle in radians.

Metadata Functions

These are utility functions that return information about the SQL Server configuration details and details about the server and database settings. This includes a range of general and special-purpose property-related functions that will return the state of various object properties. These functions wrap queries from the system tables in the Master database and a user database. It's recommended that you use these and other system functions rather than creating queries against the system tables yourself, in case schema changes are made in future versions of SQL Server. Some of the information listed in the following table can also be obtained using the INFORMATION_SCHEMA views.

Function	Description
COL_LENGTH()	Returns the length of a column from the column name.
COL_NAME()	Returns the name of a column from the object ID.
COLUMNPROPERTY()	Returns a flag to indicate the state of a column property. Properties include AllowsNull, IsComputed, IsCursorType, IsDeterministic, IsFulltextIndexed, IsIdentity, IsIdNotForRepl, IsIndexable, IsOutParam, IsPrecise, IsRowGuidCol, Precision, Scale, and UsesAnsiTrim.
DATABASEPROPERTY()	This function is maintained for backward compatibility with older SQL Server versions. Returns a flag to indicate the state of a database property. Properties include IsAnsiNullDefault, IsAnsiNullsEnabled, IsAnsiWarningsEnabled, IsAutoClose, IsAutoCreateStatistics, IsAutoShrink, IsAutoUpdateStatistics, IsBulkCopy, IsCloseCursorsOnCommitEnabled, IsDboOnly, IsDetached, IsEmergencyMode, IsFulltextEnabled, IsInLoad, IsInRecovery, IsInStandBy, IsLocalCursorsDefault, IsNotRecovered, IsNullConcat, IsOffline, IsQuotedIdentifiersEnabled, IsReadOnly, IsRecursiveTriggersEnabled, IsShutDown, IsSingleUser, IsSuspect, IsTruncLog, and Version.
DATABASEPROPERTYEX()	Returns a flag to indicate the state of a database property. Properties include Collation, IsAnsiNullDefault, IsAnsiNullsEnabled, IsAnsiPaddingEnabled, IsAnsiWarningsEnabled, IsArithmeticAbortEnabled, IsAutoClose, IsAutoCreateStatistics, IsAutoShrink, IsAutoUpdateStatistics, IsCloseCursorsOnCommitEnabled, IsFulltextEnabled, IsInStandBy, IsLocalCursorsDefault, IsMergePublished, IsNullConcat, IsNumericRoundAbortEnabled, IsQuotedIdentifiersEnabled, IsRecursiveTriggersEnabled, IsSubscribed, IsTornPageDetectionEnabled, Recovery, SQLSortOrder, Status, Updateability, UserAccess, and Version.

Function	Description
DB_ID()	Returns the database ID from the database name.
DB_NAME()	Returns the database name from the database ID.
FILE_ID()	Returns the file ID from the file name.
FILE_NAME()	Returns the file name from the file ID.
fn_listextendedproperty()	Returns a table object populated with extended property names and their settings.
FULLTEXTCATALOGPROPERTY()	Returns a flag to indicate the state of a full-text catalog property. Properties include PopulateStatus, ItemCount, IndexSize, UniqueKeyCount, LogSize, and PopulateCompletionAge.
FULLTEXTSERVICEPROPERTY()	Returns a flag to indicate the state of a full-text service property. Properties include ResourceUsage, ConnectTimeout, IsFulltextInstalled, and DataTimeout.
INDEX_COL()	Returns the name of a column contained in a specified index, by table, index, and column ID.
INDEXKEY_PROPERTY()	Returns a flag to indicate the state of an index key property. Properties are ColumnId and IsDescending.
INDEXPROPERTY()	Returns a flag indicating the state of an index property. Properties include IndexDepth, IndexFillFactor, IndexID, IsAutoStatistics, IsClustered, IsFulltextKey, IsHypothetical, IsPadIndex, IsPageLockDisallowed, IsRowLockDisallowed, IsStatistics, and IsUnique.
OBJECT_ID()	Returns an object ID from the object name.
OBJECT_NAME()	Returns an object name from the object ID.

Table continued on following page

Function	Description
OBJECTPROPERTY()	This function allows you to get property information from several different types of objects. It is advisable to use a function designed to query specific object types if possible. Returns a flag indicating the state of an object property. Properties include CnstIsClustKey, CnstIsColumn, CnstIsDeleteCascade, CnstIsDisabled, CnstIsNonclustKey, CnstIsNotRepl, CnstIsNotTrusted, CnstIsUpdateCascade, ExecIsAfterTrigger, ExecIsAnsiNullsOn, ExecIsDeleteTrigger, ExecIsFirstDeleteTrigger, ExecIsFirstInsertTrigger, ExecIsFirstUpdateTrigger, ExecIsInsertTrigger, ExecIsInsteadOfTrigger, ExecIsLastDeleteTrigger, ExecIsLastInsertTrigger, ExecIsLastUpdateTrigger, ExecIsQuotedIdentOn, ExecIsStartup, ExecIsTriggerDisabled, ExecIsUpdateTrigger, HasAfterTrigger, HasInsertTrigger, HasInsteadOfTrigger, HasUpdateTrigger, IsAnsiNullsOn, IsCheckCnst, IsConstraint, IsDefault, IsDefaultCnst, IsDeterministic, IsExecuted, IsExtendedProc, IsForeignKey, IsIndexable, IsIndexed, IsInlineFunction, IsMSShipped, IsPrimaryKey, IsProcedure, IsQuotedIdentOn, IsReplProc, IsRule, IsScalarFunction, IsSchemaBound, IsSystemTable, IsTable, IsTableFunction, IsTrigger, IsUniqueCnst, IsUserTable, IsView, OwnerId, TableDeleteTrigger, TableDeleteTriggerCount, TableFullTextBackgroundUpdateIndexOn, TableFulltextCatalogId, TableFullTextChangeTrackingOn, TableFulltextKeyColumn, TableFullTextPopulateStatus, TableHasActiveFulltextIndex, TableHasCheckCnst, TableHasClustIndex, TableHasDefaultCnst, TableHasDeleteTrigger, TableHasForeignKey, TableHasForeignRef, TableHasIdentity, TableHasIndex, TableHasInsertTrigger, TableHasNonclustIndex, TableHasPrimaryKey, TableHasRowGuidCol, TableHasTextImage, TableHasTimestamp, TableHasUniqueCnst, TableHasUpdateTrigger, TableInsertTrigger, TableInsertTriggerCount, TableIsFake, TableIsPinned, TableTextInRowLimit, TableUpdateTrigger, and TableUpdateTriggerCount.

Ranking Functions

These are new functions in SQL Server 2005 used to enumerate sorted and top-valued result sets using a specified order, independent from the order of the result set.

The ROW_NUMBER() Function

The ROW_NUMBER() function returns an integer with a running incremental value based on an ORDER BY clause passed to this function. If the ROW_NUMBER's ORDER BY matches the order of the result set, the values will be incremental and in ascending order. If the ROW_NUMBER's ORDER BY clause is different than the order of the results, these values will not be listed in order but will represent the order of the ROW_NUMBER function's ORDER BY clause.

```
SELECT
     ProductCategoryID
   , Name
   , ROW_NUMBER() Over (ORDER BY Name) As RowNum
FROM ProductCategory
ORDER BY Name
```

With the ORDER BY clause on the ROW_NUMBER() call matching the order of the query, these values are listed in order (see Figure 6-17).

ProductCategoryID	Name	RowNum
4	Accessory	1
1	Bike	2
3	Clothing	3
2	Component	4
5	Service	5

Figure 6-17

However, when using a different ORDER BY clause in the function call, these values are not ordered.

```
SELECT
     ProductCategoryID
   , Name
   , ROW_NUMBER() Over (ORDER BY Name) As RowNum
FROM ProductCategory
ORDER BY ProductCategoryID
```

This provides an effective means to tell how the result would have been sorted using the other ORDER BY clause, as shown in Figure 6-18.

ProductCategoryID	Name	RowNum
1	Bike	2
2	Component	4
3	Clothing	3
4	Accessory	1
5	Service	5

Figure 6-18

The RANK() and DENSE_RANK() Functions

Both of these functions are similar to the ROW_NUMBER() function in that they return a value based on an ORDER BY clause, but these values may not always be unique. Ranking values are repeated for duplicate results from the provided ORDER BY clause, and uniqueness is only based on unique values in the ORDER BY list. Each of these functions takes a different approach to handling these duplicate values. The RANK() function preserves the ordinal position of the row in the list. For each duplicate value, it skips the subsequent value so that the next non-duplicate value remains in its rightful position.

```
SELECT
    ProductCategoryID
  , Name
  , RANK() Over (ORDER BY Name) As Rank
FROM ProductCategory
ORDER BY Name
```

Note in the result set shown in Figure 6-19 that the values are repeated for duplicated name values and the skipped values following each tie. For example, both rows for employees named Andrew are ranked number 8, and the following row, Andy, is ranked number 10.

EmployeeID	FirstName	Rank
127	A	1
247	Alan	2
152	Alejandro	3
177	Alex	4
195	Alice	5
21	Amy	6
284	Andreas	7
173	Andrew	8
65	Andrew	8
139	Andy	10
192	Angela	11
108	Anibal	12
50	Annette	13
217	Annik	14
60	Arvind	15
270	Ashvini	16
102	Balaganesan	17
117	Barbara	18
258	Barbara	18
172	Baris	20

Figure 6-19

The DENSE_RANK() function works exactly the same way, but it doesn't skip numbers after each tie. This way, no values are skipped, but the ordinal ranking position is lost whenever there are ties.

```
SELECT
    ProductCategoryID
  , Name
  , DENSE_RANK() Over (ORDER BY Name) As Rank
FROM ProductCategory
ORDER BY Name
```

The result shown in Figure 6-20 repeats ranked values but doesn't skip any numbers in this column.

EmployeeID	FirstName	Rank
127	A	1
247	Alan	2
152	Alejandro	3
177	Alex	4
195	Alice	5
21	Amy	6
284	Andreas	7
173	Andrew	8
65	Andrew	8
139	Andy	9
192	Angela	10
108	Anibal	11
50	Annette	12
217	Annik	13
60	Arvind	14
270	Ashvini	15
102	Balaganesan	16
117	Barbara	17
258	Barbara	17

Figure 6-20

The NTILE(n) Function

This function also ranks results, returning an integer ranking value. However, rather than enumerating the results into uniquely ranked order, it divides the result into a finite number of ranked groups. For example, if a table has 10,000 rows and the NTILE() function is called with an argument value of 1000, as NTILE(1000), the result would be divided into 1000 groups of 10, with each group being assigned the same ranking value. The NTILE() function also supports the OVER (ORDER BY. . .) syntax like the other ranking functions discussed in this section.

Security Functions

The security-related functions return role membership and privilege information for SQL Server users. This category also includes a set of functions to manage events and traces, as described in the following table.

Function	Description
fn_trace_geteventinfo()	Returns a table type populated with event information for a specified trace ID.
fn_trace_getfilterinfo()	Returns a table type populated with information about filters applied for a specified trace ID.
fn_trace_getinfo()	Returns a table type populated with trace information for a specified trace ID.
fn_trace_gettable()	Returns a table type populated with file information for a specified trace ID.
HAS_DBACCESS()	Returns a flag indicating whether the current user has access to a specified database.

Table continued on following page

Function	Description
IS_MEMBER()	Returns a flag indicating whether the current user is a member of a Windows group or SQL Server role.
IS_SRVROLEMEMBER()	Returns a flag indicating whether the current user is a member of a database server role.
SUSER_SID()	Returns either the security ID for a specified user's login name or (if the parameter is omitted) returns the security ID of the current user. Returns either the user ID for a specified username or (if the parameter is omitted) returns the user ID of the current user.
SUSER_SNAME()	Returns the Login name for a specified security ID. If no security ID is provided it returns the login for the current connection.
USER_ID()	Returns either the user ID for a specified username or (if the parameter is omitted) returns the user ID of the current user.
USER_NAME()	Returns a username for a specified user ID.

System Functions and Variables

This section discusses utility functions used to perform a variety of tasks. These include value comparisons and value type testing. This category is also a catch-all for other functionality.

Function	Description
APP_NAME()	Returns the name of the application associated with the current connection.
COALESCE()	Returns the first non-null value from a comma-delimited list of expressions.
COLLATIONPROPERTY()	Returns the value of a specific property for a specified collation. Properties include CodePage, LCID, and ComparisonStyle.
CURRENT_TIMESTAMP()	Returns the current date and time and is synonymous with the GETDATE() function. It exists for ANSI-SQL compliance.
CURRENT_USER()	Returns the name of the current user and is synonymous with the USER_NAME() function.
DATALENGTH()	Returns the numbers of bytes used to store or handle a value. For ANSI string types, this will return the same value as the LEN() function but for other data types the value may be different.
fn_helpcollations()	Returns a table type populated with a list of collations supported by the current version of SQL Server.
fn_servershareddrives()	Returns a table type populated with a list of drives shared by the server.

Function	Description
fn_virtualfilestats()	Returns a table type populated with I/O statistics for database files, including log files.
FORMATMESSAGE()	Returns an error message from the sysmessages table for a specified message number and comma-delimited list of parameters.
GETANSINULL()	Returns the nullability setting for the database, according to the ANSI_NULL_DFLT_ON and ANSI_NULL_DFLT_OFF database settings.
HOST_ID()	Returns the workstation ID for the current session.
HOST_NAME()	Returns the workstation name for the current session.
IDENT_CURRENT()	Returns the last identity value generated for a specified table regardless of the session and scope.
IDENT_INCR()	Returns the increment value specified in the creation of the last identity column.
IDENT_SEED()	Returns the seed value specified in the creation of the last identity column.
IDENTITY()	Used in a SELECT. . . INTO statement to insert an automatically generated identity value into a column.
ISDATE()	Returns a flag to indicate whether a specified value is or is not capable of being converted to a date value.
ISNULL()	Determines whether a specified value is null and then returns a provided replacement value.
ISNUMERIC()	Returns a flag to indicate whether a specified value is or is not capable of being converted to a numeric value.
NEWID()	Returns a newly generated UniqueIdentifier type value. This is a 128-bit integer, globally unique value, usually expressed as an alpha-numeric hexadecimal representation (for example, 89DE6247-C2E2-42DB-8CE8-A787E505D7EA). This type is often used for primary key values in replicated and semi-connected systems.
NULLIF()	Returns a NULL value when two specified arguments have equivalent values.
PARSENAME()	Returns a specific part of a four-part object name.
PERMISSIONS()	Returns an integer whose value is a bit-wise map indicating the permission or combination of permissions for the current user on a specified database object.
ROWCOUNT_BIG()	Like the @@ROWCOUNT variable, returns the number of rows either returned or modified by the last statement. Returns a BigInt type.

Table continued on following page

Function	Description
SCOPE_IDENTITY()	Like the @@IDENTITY variable, this function returns the last Identity value generated but is limited to the current session and scope (stored procedure, batch, or module).
SERVERPROPERTY()	Returns a flag indicating the state of a server property. Properties include Collation, Edition, Engine Edition, InstanceName, IsClustered, IsFullTextInstalled, IsIntegratedSecurityOnly, IsSingleUser, IsSyncWithBackup, LicenseType, MachineName, NumLicenses, ProcessID, ProductLevel, ProductVersion, and ServerName.
SESSION_USER	Returns the current username. Function is called without parentheses.
SESSIONPROPERTY()	Returns a flag indicating the state of a session property. Properties include ANSI_NULLS, ANSI_PADDING, ANSI_WARNINGS, ARITHABORT, CONCAT_NULL_YIELDS_NULL, NUMERIC_ROUNDABORT, and QUOTED_IDENTIFIER.
STATS_DATE()	Returns a date that statistics for a specified index were last updated.
SYSTEM_USER	Returns the current username. Function is called without parentheses.
USER_NAME()	Returns the username for a specified User ID. If no ID number is provided it returns the current database user.

Some examples related to a few of the functions listed in the preceding table follow.

The COALESCE() Function

The COALESCE() function can be very useful, saving quite a lot of IF or CASE decision logic. The following example populates a table of products, showing up to three prices each:

```
CREATE TABLE #ProductPrices (ProductName VarChar(25), SuperSalePrice Money NULL,
SalePrice Money NULL, ListPrice Money NULL)
GO
INSERT INTO #ProductPrices VALUES('Standard Widget', NULL, NULL, 15.95)
INSERT INTO #ProductPrices VALUES('Economy Widget', NULL, 9.95, 12.95)
INSERT INTO #ProductPrices VALUES('Deluxe Widget', 19.95, 20.95, 22.95)
INSERT INTO #ProductPrices VALUES('Super Deluxe Widget', 29.45, 32.45, 38.95)
INSERT INTO #ProductPrices VALUES('Executive Widget', NULL, 45.95, 54.95)
GO
```

All products have a list price, some have a sale price, and others may have a super sale price. The current price of a product is going to be the lowest existing price, or the first non-null value when reading each of the price columns as they are listed:

```
SELECT ProductName, COALESCE(SuperSalePrice, SalePrice, ListPrice) AS CurrentPrice
FROM #ProductPrices
```

This method is far more elegant than using multiple lines of branching and decision logic, and the result is equally simple, as illustrated in Figure 6-21.

	ProductName	CurrentPrice
1	Standard Widget	15.9500
2	Economy Widget	9.9500
3	Deluxe Widget	19.9500
4	Super Deluxe Widget	29.4500
5	Executive Widget	45.9500

Figure 6-21

The DATALENGTH() Function

The DATALENGTH() function returns the number of bytes used to manage a value. This can be used to reveal some interesting differences between data types. It's probably no surprise that when a VarChar type is passed to both the DATALENGTH() and LEN() functions, they return the same value:

```
DECLARE @Value VarChar(20)
SET @Value = 'abc'

SELECT DATALENGTH(@Value)
SELECT LEN(@Value)
```

These statements both return 3 because the VarChar type uses three single-byte characters to store the three-character value. However, if an nVarChar type is used, it takes twice as many bytes to manage a value of the same length:

```
DECLARE @Value nVarChar(20)
SET @Value = 'abc'

SELECT DATALENGTH(@Value)
SELECT LEN(@Value)
```

The DATALENGTH() function returns 6 because 2 bytes are used to store each character using a Unicode character set. The LEN() function returns 3 because this function returns the number of characters, not the number of bytes. Here's an interesting test. How many bytes does it take to store an integer variable set to the value 2? How about an integer a variable set to 2 billion? Let's find out:

```
DECLARE @Value1 Int, @Value2 Int
SET @Value1 = 2
SET @Value2 = 2000000000

SELECT DATALENGTH(@Value1)
SELECT LEN(@Value1)

SELECT DATALENGTH(@Value2)
SELECT LEN(@Value2)
```

The DATALENGTH() function returns 4 in both cases because the Int type always uses 4 bytes, regardless of the value. The LEN() function essentially treats the integer value as if it were converted to a character type, returning the number of digits, in this case, 1 and 10, respectively.

The following global system variables all return an Int type. These may be useful in stored procedures and other programming objects to implement custom business logic.

Variable	Description
@@ERROR	The last error number for the current session.
@@IDENTITY	The last identity value generated in the current session.
@@ROWCOUNT	The row count for the last execution in the current session that returned a result set.
@@TRANCOUNT	The number of active transactions in the current session. This would result from multiple, nested BEGIN TRANSACTION statements before executing corresponding COMMIT TRANSACTION or ABORT TRANSACTION statements.

System Statistical Functions and Variables

The following table describes administrative utilities used to discover database system usage and environment information.

Variable	Description
@@CONNECTIONS	The number of open connections.
@@CPU_BUSY	The number of milliseconds that SQL Server has been working since the service was last started.
@@IDLE	The number of milliseconds that SQL Server has been idle since the service was last started.
@@IO_BUSY	The number of milliseconds that SQL Server has been processing I/O since the service was last started.
@@PACK_RECEIVED	The number of network packets that SQL Server has received since the service was last started.
@@PACK_SENT	The number of network packets that SQL Server has sent since the service was last started.
@@PACKET_ERRORS	The number of network packet errors that SQL Server has received since the service was last started.
@@TIMETICKS	The number of microseconds per tick.
@@TOTAL_ERRORS	The number of disk I/O errors that SQL Server has received since the service was last started.
@@TOTAL_READ	The number of physical disk reads since the SQL Server service was last started.
@@TOTAL_WRITE	The number of physical disk writes since the SQL Server service was last started.

Summary

Functions do the heavy lifting of your business logic and can be used to apply programming functionality to queries. Several useful and powerful functions are standard features of Transact-SQL. You learned that SQL functions, like functions in procedural and object-oriented programming languages, encapsulate programming features into a simple and reusable package. This takes a lot of the work out of the query designer's hands. You know that Transact-SQL is a task-oriented language rather than a procedural language. Although functions give you the option to tread the procedural line, building fairly complex logic into queries, the strength of the language is in allowing the designer to state his intentions rather than the exact steps and methods that must be used to perform a task. Used correctly, functions allow you to do just that.

In Transact-SQL, arguments are used to pass values into a function and most functions return a scalar, or single-value, result. Functions are categorized as either deterministic or nondeterministic. A deterministic function will always return the same value when called with the same argument values. Nondeterministic functions depend on other resources to determine the return value; therefore SQL Server must execute the function explicitly. For this reason, there are some restrictions on the use of nondeterministic functions in custom SQL programming objects.

SQL functions perform a wide variety of important tasks including mathematical operations, comparisons, date parsing and manipulation, and advanced string manipulation. Several categories of specialized functions are introduced along with their related topics in following chapters. A complete function syntax reference is also provided in Appendix B.

Exercises

Exercise 1

Write a query to return the average weight of all touring bikes sold by Adventure Works Cycles that list for over $2,500. Use the ProductSubCategory table to determine how you should filter these products.

Exercise 2

Designate a variable called @ProCount to hold the number of product records on record. Execute a query to return this value and assign it to the variable. Use the variable in an expression to return the value in the phrase "There are X products on record."

Exercise 3

Calculate the square root of the absolute value of the cosine of PI.

Exercise 4

How many days has it been since this book was first published on September 26, 2005? Calculate the answer using Transact-SQL functions.

Exercise 5

Using the Individual table, return the FirstName, LastName, and the three-letter initials of all individuals who have a middle name.

Aggregation and Grouping

Information is meaningful; data is just values stored in a table. Often, the information part of the equation comes from analyzing groups of records and comparing how one range of records relates to another. For example, rather than viewing individual sales records, you may be interested in comparing the total sales of a product in one region to another or, perhaps, the average price of mountain bike sales with the average price of road bike sales.

The term *aggregation* refers to something that is a part of something else. In this context, an aggregate function returns a single value for a group of records. You can use aggregate functions in two different ways. You can "roll up" or summarize all of the rows returned by a query (either all records or use filtering techniques as discussed in Chapter 5). Aggregation can also be applied at a group level, showing summarized values for the rows having the same values in the columns you designate for grouping.

Using Aggregate Functions

The simplest technique is aggregating all rows in a query. Aggregate functions include the means to summarize a range of values in a variety of ways. You may simply want to count the rows that match a criterion or get the sum of a range of numeric values. The following table contains all of the system-supplied aggregate functions supported by Transact-SQL used to summarize column values.

Function	Description
COUNT()	Calculates the count of all non-null values for a specific column. Can also be used as COUNT(*) to return the absolute count of rows regardless of null values. Returns Int data type.
COUNT_BIG()	Same as the COUNT() function but returns the BigInt data type. This would only be necessary if the table contains more than two billion rows.
SUM()	Returns the sum of all non-null values in the range. The return data type is the same as the numeric column data type.
AVG()	Returns the average of all non-null values in the range. The return data type is the same as the numeric column data type.
MIN()	Returns the smallest non-null value in the range. Can be used with any sortable data type.
MAX()	Returns the largest non-null value in the range. Can be used with any sortable data type.
STDEV()	Returns the simple standard deviation for all non-null values in a numeric range. Returns a Float data type regardless of the column type.
STDEVP()	Returns the standard deviation for a population, for all non-null values in a numeric range. Returns a Float data type regardless of the column type.
VAR()	Returns the simple variance for all non-null values in a numeric range. Returns a Float data type regardless of the column type.
VARP()	Returns the variance for a population, for all non-null values in a numeric range. Returns a Float data type regardless of the column type.

The COUNT() Function

The COUNT() function simply counts rows or non-null values in a column's value range. Because the data type of the column isn't considered, it will work with columns of practically any type of data. Consider the following two examples. If you execute this query against the Product table, the total number of rows is returned:

```
SELECT COUNT(*) FROM Product
```

As you can see, the Product table contains 999 rows. Now, count only the values in the ListPrice column using the following expression:

```
SELECT COUNT(ListPrice) FROM Product
```

Because 200 records don't have a ListPrice value (these rows contain the value NULL for this column), only 799 rows get counted. Now add the word DISTINCT before the column reference and execute the query again:

```
SELECT COUNT(DISTINCT ListPrice) FROM Product
```

Because so many of the products have the same prices, only 104 records are counted. The DISTINCT modifier can be used with any of the aggregate functions except when using the CUBE or ROLLUP statements, which are discussed later in this chapter.

The SUM() Function

The SUM() function simply returns the sum of a range of numeric column values. Like the others, this function only considers non-null values. A simple example returns the subtotal for a product order. This query adds up the UnitPrice for each detail line in the order whose SalesOrderID is 5005:

```
SELECT SUM(UnitPrice)
FROM SalesOrderDetail
WHERE SalesOrderID = 5005
```

The result is a single row with a single column just like the previous examples, as shown in Figure 7-1.

	(No column name)
1	1830.4339

Figure 7-1

I have two issues with this result. The first is that the column doesn't have a name. When applying aggregate functions, the resulting column won't be named unless you specifically define an alias for the column name. If you use visual query design tools, such as Access or the Transact-SQL Designer (in Visual Studio or to create a view in Enterprise Manager), these tools will devise column aliases such as SumOfUnitPrice or Expr1. The first order of business is to assign an alias so this column has a sensible name. The other problem with this simple example is that it assumes that the customer purchased one of each product. The fact is that there are three detail rows for this order with respective quantities 1, 3, and 4. To accurately total the order, you'll have to do a little math. This query resolves both of these issues, calculating extended price and defining an alias for the column:

```
SELECT SUM(UnitPrice * OrderQty) As OrderTotalPrice
FROM SalesOrderDetail
WHERE SalesOrderID = 5005
```

The result shown in Figure 7-2 contains the correct amount (the total of all three order detail rows, considering the quantity for the product purchased), and the column has a name.

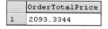

	OrderTotalPrice
1	2093.3344

Figure 7-2

The AVG() Function

The AVG() function returns the calculated average for a range of numeric values. Internally, the query processor calculates the sum of all the values and then divides by the number of rows in the range (containing non-null values.) Optionally, the AVG() function can make a distinct selection of values and then perform the same calculation on this abbreviated set of values. Using a distinct selection can greatly affect the results and is not as common.

I'd like to use the product sales data in the AdventureWorks2000 database to demonstrate the practical application of these functions. In this scenario, the director of marketing has asked for an analysis of road bike sales in 2003. This information exists in three related tables. Pay no attention to the join statements for the time being; they are covered in Chapter 8. The following query uses the SalesOrderHeader table to filter the sales order, the Product table to filter by ProductSubCategoryID (2 is road bikes), and the UnitPrice is retrieved from the SalesOrderDetail table. For simplicity, I'm not considering the quantity of bikes purchased.

I'll start with the lowest price paid for a bike. Using the MIN() function should return only one value:

```
SELECT   MIN(UnitPrice)
FROM     SalesOrderHeader
         INNER JOIN SalesOrderDetail ON
         SalesOrderHeader.SalesOrderID = SalesOrderDetail.SalesOrderID
         INNER JOIN Product ON SalesOrderDetail.ProductID = Product.ProductID
WHERE    Product.ProductSubCategoryID = 2
         AND SalesOrderHeader.OrderDate BETWEEN '1-1-03' And '12-31-03'
```

You can see that the lowest UnitPrice value in this range is $388.79. Just modify the query, substituting the following functions in place of the MIN() function in the example. The following table shows the results.

Question	Function	Result
What was the lowest price paid?	MIN()	388.79
What was the highest price paid?	MAX()	2443.35
What is the average price paid?	AVG()	1116.04

Understanding Statistical Functions

Statistics wasn't my best subject in school. Although I understood the relevance and importance of statistics, my brain just wasn't wired for it. Fortunately, now that I use these functions regularly in consulting and application development work, I no longer struggle with it, but I often need to jog my memory by looking at an example. This section explains these concepts in simple terms and provides some useful examples for those of us who don't think statistically.

The VAR() Function

This function returns the statistical variance for a range of values, that is, a value that indicates how "spread out" the values are in the range. The value returned by this function is actually the measure of how far the extreme low range or high range value is from the middle — or mean value of the range, weighted by the greatest concentration of similar values. For example, given the range of values on a number line, 2, 3, 4, 5, and 6, the number 4 is the mean — it's in the middle of the range. In this simple example, the variance of this range is 2 (from 4 to 2 and from 4 to 6 both have a difference of 2). This is very simple if you have a list of distinct, incremental values but it gets a little more complex as the values are less uniform.

Try It Out

You can do some simple experimenting with values in a single-column table created by running the following query:

```
Create Table MyValues (MyValue Float)
```

Now, insert the values given in the previous example, using this query:

```
Insert Into MyValues (MyValue) SELECT 2
Insert Into MyValues (MyValue) SELECT 3
Insert Into MyValues (MyValue) SELECT 4
Insert Into MyValues (MyValue) SELECT 5
Insert Into MyValues (MyValue) SELECT 6
```

To return the variance of this range, use this query:

```
SELECT VAR(MyValue) FROM MyValues
```

If you insert more values close to the center of the range, you will see that this changes the outcome. This is because the result is computed as the average squared deviation (difference) of each number from its mean. This is done so negative numbers behave appropriately and to weight the equation toward the center of the greatest concentration of values. Regardless, it's a standard statistical function and, fortunately, you probably don't need to concern yourself with the specifics of the internal calculation. Calculating variance is the first step in performing other statistical functions, such as standard deviation.

As you can see, using integer values to keep things simple, you've created a bell-curve around the mean value, 4:

```
INSERT INTO MyValues (MyValue) SELECT 3
INSERT INTO MyValues (MyValue) SELECT 4
INSERT INTO MyValues (MyValue) SELECT 4
INSERT INTO MyValues (MyValue) SELECT 4
INSERT INTO MyValues (MyValue) SELECT 5
```

You then return the deviation for the range again:

```
SELECT VAR(MyValue) FROM MyValues
```

This reduces the value of the standard deviation to indicate that values, on average, are less spread out.

The VARP() Function

The variance over a population is simply another indicator of this same principle, using a different formula. This formula is sometimes called *biased estimate of variance*. Although this method is used in some complex calculations, the other form of variance is more common.

The STDEV() Function

Have you ever taken a class where the teacher graded on a curve? If so, you were the victim of standard deviation (or, perhaps, the benefactor).

The standard deviation is a calculation based on the variance of a numeric range of values. Actually, it's simply the square root of the variance. In a normal distribution, values can be plotted in a bell-curve, the mean value represented by the center of the curve. If you were to slice off the center of the curve, taking about 68% of the most common values, this would represent the standard deviation (or "first standard deviation"). If you were to move outward the same variation of values, you would take off another 27% (a total of 95%), leaving only 5%.

Standard deviation is an effective method for analyzing and making sense of large distributions of data. It is also a common method to calculate risk and probability.

To measure the standard deviation for your sample values table, simply use the following query:

```
SELECT STDEV(MyValue) FROM MyValues
```

The result, 1.1547. . . , tells you that for the values in your table, those values that are in the range from 2.8453 to 5.1547 (within 1.1547 of the mean) are in the first standard deviation.

Using the AdventureWorks sales data, you can apply this analysis to bicycle sales. Suppose that the director of marketing asks "How much did most of our customers pay for road bikes in 2003?" Just modify the query you used before, using the STDEV() function like this:

```
SELECT    STDEV(UnitPrice)
FROM      SalesOrderHeader
          INNER JOIN SalesOrderDetail ON
          SalesOrderHeader.SalesOrderID =SalesOrderDetail.SalesOrderID
          INNER JOIN Product ON SalesOrderDetail.ProductID = Product.ProductID
WHERE     Product.ProductSubCategoryID = 2
          AND SalesOrderHeader.OrderDate BETWEEN '1-1-03' And '12-31-03'
```

The result is 636.54. This means that most of your customers paid between $479.50 and $ 1,752.58 for their road bikes — at least those purchases in the first standard deviation.

The STDDEVP() Function

This function calculates standard deviation based on the variance of a population.

User-Defined Aggregate Functions

SQL Server 2005 allows application developers to add custom aggregate functions to a database. These functions are written in a .NET programming language, such as C# or Visual Basic.NET, and must be compiled into a .NET assembly using the Microsoft .NET Common Language Runtime. As a SQL query designer, all you need to know is that once deployed and correctly configured, you can use these functions in your queries as you would any of the system-supplied aggregate functions.

Grouping Data

So far, your work with aggregate functions has been for a group of records that return a single value. An operation that returns a single value is known as a *scalar* result. Although this may be appropriate for very simple data analysis, aggregate functions can be used in far more sophisticated and useful ways. Groups are used to distill rows with common column values into one row. This gives you the opportunity to perform aggregated calculations on each of the groupings. There are some restrictions and it's important to understand the rules regarding groups. Columns returned by a grouped query must either be referenced in the GROUP BY list or use an aggregate function. Other columns can be used for filtering or sorting but these column values cannot be returned in the result set.

GROUP BY

Grouping occurs after records are retrieved and then aggregated. The GROUP BY clause is added to the query after the WHERE and ORDER BY clauses. Consider that the query runs first without the aggregate functions and grouping to determine which rows will be considered for grouping. After these results are read into memory, SQL Server makes a pass through these records, applying groupings and aggregate calculations.

Consider the following example, using the SUM() function:

```
SELECT SalesOrderID, SUM(OrderQty) FROM SalesOrderDetail
GROUP BY SalesOrderID
```

The SalesOrderID value can be returned because it appears in the GROUP BY list. The query will return one distinct row for each SalesOrderID value. For each group of related records, all of the OrderQty values are added together as the result of the SUM() function. The result should include two columns, the SalesOrderID and the sum of the OrderQty for the related detail rows, as shown in Figure 7-3.

	SalesOrderID	(No column name)
1	5001	4
2	5002	3
3	5003	2
4	5004	1
5	5005	8
6	5006	2
7	5007	149
8	5008	144
9	5009	2
10	5010	148
11	5011	12
12	5012	202
13	5013	33
14	5014	13
15	5015	127
16	5016	1

Figure 7-3

Because detail rows contain multiple quantities, you really can't tell if these rows are aggregated. To get a better view, add another column using the COUNT() function. Also add column aliases to label these values:

```
SELECT  SalesOrderID
      , SUM(OrderQty) As QtySum
      , COUNT(SalesOrderID) As DetailCount
FROM SalesOrderDetail
GROUP BY SalesOrderID
```

The result, shown in Figure 7-4, shows that all but two of the visible rows were grouped and the SUM() function was applied to the OrderQty column value.

	SalesOrderID	QtySum	DetailCount
1	5001	4	1
2	5002	3	2
3	5003	2	2
4	5004	1	1
5	5005	8	3
6	5006	2	2
7	5007	149	37
8	5008	144	33
9	5009	2	2
10	5010	148	35
11	5011	12	3
12	5012	202	51
13	5013	33	21
14	5014	13	4
15	5015	127	43
16	5016	1	1

Figure 7-4

If you were to view the ungrouped records in this table, you could clearly see what's going on. The result shown in Figure 7-5 is just a simple SELECT query on the SalesOrderDetail table showing the first nine rows.

	SalesOrderID	OrderQty
1	5001	4
2	5002	1
3	5002	2
4	5003	1
5	5003	1
6	5004	1
7	5005	1
8	5005	3
9	5005	4
10	5006	1
11	5006	1

Figure 7-5

Sales order 5002 has two detail rows, whose OrderQty values add up to 3, order 5003 also has two detail rows with a total quantity of 3, and order 5005's quantity adds up to 8.

When grouping on more than one column, every unique combination of grouped values produces a row in the result set. Because the SalesOrderDetail table isn't preordered by the two columns you want to group on, you're explicitly ordering the results:

```
SELECT ProductID
     , SpecialOfferID
FROM SalesOrderDetail
GROUP BY ProductID, SpecialOfferID
ORDER BY ProductID, SpecialOfferID
```

The query returns a distinct list of ProductID and SpecialOfferID values (including null values), as shown in Figure 7-6.

	ProductID	SpecialOfferID
1	3	6
2	5	6
3	8	NULL
4	8	6
5	9	NULL
6	9	6
7	10	NULL
8	10	6
9	11	NULL
10	11	6
11	12	NULL
12	12	6
13	24	NULL
14	24	5
15	24	6
16	25	NULL
17	25	5
18	25	6
19	26	NULL
20	26	5
21	26	6
22	27	NULL

Figure 7-6

Although this may be interesting, it's not particularly useful information. Let's find out how many rows are actually being used to produce this list of distinct values. Extending the same query, add two columns that return the count of the ProductID and the SpecialOfferID values:

```
SELECT ProductID, COUNT(ProductID) As ProductIDCount
     , SpecialOfferID, COUNT(SpecialOfferID) As SpecialOfferIDCount
FROM SalesOrderDetail
GROUP BY  ProductID, SpecialOfferID
ORDER BY ProductID, SpecialOfferID
```

In the result set shown in Figure 7-7, you can see that you get the same rows.

	ProductID	ProductIDCount	SpecialOfferID	SpecialOfferIDCount
1	3	150	6	150
2	5	218	6	218
3	8	48	NULL	0
4	8	102	6	102
5	9	49	NULL	0
6	9	146	6	146
7	10	58	NULL	0
8	10	135	6	135
9	11	56	NULL	0
10	11	176	6	176
11	12	41	NULL	0
12	12	105	6	105
13	24	45	NULL	0
14	24	31	5	31
15	24	145	6	145
16	25	45	NULL	0
17	25	37	5	37
18	25	139	6	139
19	26	39	NULL	0
20	26	27	5	27
21	26	129	6	129

Figure 7-7

What you didn't see in the first result set is that the first row is an aggregation of 150 rows where the ProductID was 3 and the SpecialOfferID value was 6. The second row represents 218 rows. In the third row, 48 individual rows had a ProductID value of 8 and the SpecialOfferID was null. The COUNT() function returns 0 because null values are not considered in aggregate function calculations. 102 rows had the same ProductID value but the SpecialOfferID value was 6.

For a more real-world example, due to the complexity of the AdventureWorks database, it's necessary to create a fairly complex query with several table joins. Again, don't be concerned with the statements in the FROM clause, but do pay attention to the column list after the SELECT statement. You'll come back to this query in the next chapter.

The purpose of this query is to find out what products your customers have purchased. The Individual table contains personal information about human being–type customers (rather than stores that buy wholesale products). You've already seen that sales orders have order details, and a sales order detail line is related to a product:

```
SELECT
      Store.Name AS StoreName
    , Product.Name AS ProductName
    , COUNT(SalesOrderDetail.ProductID) AS PurchaseCount
FROM
      Customer INNER JOIN SalesOrderHeader
      ON Customer.CustomerID = SalesOrderHeader.CustomerID
      INNER JOIN SalesOrderDetail
      ON SalesOrderHeader.SalesOrderID = SalesOrderDetail.SalesOrderID
      INNER JOIN Product ON SalesOrderDetail.ProductID = Product.ProductID
      INNER JOIN Store ON Customer.CustomerID = Store.CustomerID
GROUP BY Product.Name, Store.Name
ORDER BY Store.Name, Product.Name
```

Three columns are returned from the query: the StoreName, the ProductName, and the number of product records in each group (PurchaseCount), using the COUNT() function. This returns the number of times a store purchased the same product. You could use the product Name in the COUNT() function but it's usually more efficient to use primary key columns. Note that even though the StoreName and ProductName columns are aliased in the SELECT list, when used in the GROUP BY and ORDER BY statements, the alias name is not used; only the qualified column names are used.

Figure 7-8 shows the first 34 rows in the result set.

Suppose that the purpose of this query was to locate stores that have purchased more than four of any product. Rather than scrolling through 20,531 rows, you can modify the query for rows with a count greater than four.

	StoreName	ProductName	PurchaseCount
1	A Bike Store	LL Road Frame - Black, 52	2
2	A Bike Store	LL Road Frame - Black, 58	1
3	A Bike Store	LL Road Frame - Red, 44	2
4	A Bike Store	LL Road Frame - Red, 48	2
5	A Bike Store	LL Road Frame - Red, 60	1
6	A Bike Store	LL Road Frame - Red, 62	2
7	A Bike Store	long-sleeve logo jersey, M	1
8	A Bike Store	ML Road Frame - Red, 48	2
9	A Bike Store	Road-150 Red, 44	2
10	A Bike Store	Road-150 Red, 48	1
11	A Bike Store	Road-150 Red, 52	1
12	A Bike Store	Road-150 Red, 56	4
13	A Bike Store	Road-150 Red, 62	2
14	A Bike Store	Road-450 Red, 44	3
15	A Bike Store	Road-450 Red, 48	3
16	A Bike Store	Road-450 Red, 52	3
17	A Bike Store	Road-450 Red, 58	3
18	A Bike Store	Road-450 Red, 60	3
19	A Bike Store	Road-650 Black, 44	4
20	A Bike Store	Road-650 Black, 48	2
21	A Bike Store	Road-650 Black, 52	3
22	A Bike Store	Road-650 Black, 58	2
23	A Bike Store	Road-650 Black, 60	2
24	A Bike Store	Road-650 Black, 62	2
25	A Bike Store	Road-650 Red, 44	4
26	A Bike Store	Road-650 Red, 48	3
27	A Bike Store	Road-650 Red, 52	2
28	A Bike Store	Road-650 Red, 58	3
29	A Bike Store	Road-650 Red, 60	2
30	A Bike Store	Road-650 Red, 62	4
31	A Bike Store	Sport-100 helmet, Black	1
32	A Bike Store	Sport-100 helmet, Blue	1
33	A Great Bicycle Company	AWC logo cap	1
34	A Great Bicycle Company	ML Road Pedal	1

Figure 7-8

HAVING

How do you identify these rows? You can't use the WHERE clause because it is processed prior to grouping and aggregation; therefore, you need some way to filter the rows after the grouping has been completed. This is the job of the HAVING clause. The HAVING clause is limited to those columns and aggregate expressions that have already been specified on the SELECT statement. Typically, you will refer to aggregate values by simply repeating the aggregate function expression in the HAVING clause, just like you did in the SELECT statement. Here is the previous query with this expression added:

```
SELECT
      Store.Name AS StoreName
    , Product.Name AS ProductName
    , COUNT(SalesOrderDetail.ProductID) AS PurchaseCount
FROM
      Customer INNER JOIN SalesOrderHeader
      ON Customer.CustomerID = SalesOrderHeader.CustomerID
      INNER JOIN SalesOrderDetail
      ON SalesOrderHeader.SalesOrderID = SalesOrderDetail.SalesOrderID
      INNER JOIN Product ON SalesOrderDetail.ProductID = Product.ProductID
      INNER JOIN Store ON Customer.CustomerID = Store.CustomerID
GROUP BY Product.Name, Store.Name
HAVING COUNT(SalesOrderDetail.ProductID) > 4
ORDER BY Store.Name, Product.Name
```

The result set is now reduced to 2,139 rows, including only the store/product purchases. Examining the results shows something very interesting. In the previous results, you saw that there appeared to be a lot of transactions for the store called A Bike Store. However, when you look at the results in this way, you see that this customer purchased only small quantities of each product. As such, they are not included in these results, shown in Figure 7-9.

This data makes sense because most of the products listed with higher product counts are lower-priced items that tend to sell quickly.

The HAVING clause works much like the WHERE clause in that you can use any combination of comparison expressions and logical operators. Just be mindful that it is processed after the initial record selection (which is filtered by the WHERE clause) and that you are limited to the columns and aggregate expressions in the SELECT statement.

I'll use an example from the AdventureWorks database so you can follow along and work with the data yourself. Chapter 3 pointed out that the SQL Server Product Team had some fun putting the Employee sample data together. You'll see some more evidence of this. I thought it would be fun to see what gender variations there were for first names such as Terry and Pat. It turns out that our friends at Microsoft took this a little further.

Grouping the Employee table on the FirstName and Gender columns will return all the combinations of these values. I'll aggregate the EmployeeID column using the COUNT() function so you can see how many records there are for each FirstName/Gender combination. Here's the SQL expression for this query:

```
SELECT FirstName, Gender, COUNT(EmployeeID)
FROM Employee
GROUP BY  FirstName, Gender
ORDER BY FirstName, Gender
```

	StoreName	ProductName	PurchaseCount
1	Advanced Bike Components	AWC logo cap	12
2	Advanced Bike Components	Half-finger Gloves, M	8
3	Advanced Bike Components	Half-finger Gloves, S	7
4	Advanced Bike Components	LL Road Frame - Black, 52	9
5	Advanced Bike Components	LL Road Frame - Black, 58	8
6	Advanced Bike Components	LL Road Frame - Red, 44	7
7	Advanced Bike Components	LL Road Frame - Red, 60	7
8	Advanced Bike Components	long-sleeve logo jersey, L	11
9	Advanced Bike Components	long-sleeve logo jersey, M	11
10	Advanced Bike Components	long-sleeve logo jersey, XL	11
11	Advanced Bike Components	ML Road Frame-W - Yellow, 38	5
12	Advanced Bike Components	ML Road Frame-W - Yellow, 44	6
13	Advanced Bike Components	Road-250 Black, 44	5
14	Advanced Bike Components	Road-250 Black, 48	6
15	Advanced Bike Components	Road-550-W Yellow, 38	7
16	Advanced Bike Components	Road-550-W Yellow, 40	7
17	Advanced Bike Components	Road-550-W Yellow, 48	7
18	Advanced Bike Components	Road-650 Black, 44	6
19	Advanced Bike Components	Road-650 Black, 52	5
20	Advanced Bike Components	Road-650 Black, 58	7
21	Advanced Bike Components	Road-650 Black, 60	8
22	Advanced Bike Components	Road-650 Red, 44	6
23	Advanced Bike Components	Road-650 Red, 48	6
24	Advanced Bike Components	Road-650 Red, 52	6
25	Advanced Bike Components	Road-650 Red, 60	6
26	Advanced Bike Components	Road-650 Red, 62	6
27	Advanced Bike Components	Sport-100 helmet, Black	11
28	Advanced Bike Components	Sport-100 helmet, Blue	12
29	Advanced Bike Components	Sport-100 helmet, Red	11
30	Adventure WorksCycles Retail	Classic Vest, S	5
31	Affordable Sports Equipment	AWC logo cap	5

Figure 7-9

I've scrolled down a bit to view some of the rows with a higher count. In Figure 7-10, you can see that there are some interesting anomalies in the results. Of the four employees named Brian, three of them are female.

I can't be certain but I think that some of the folks on the SQL Server product team intended for this to be an inside joke and probably wondered if anyone would notice (considering that some of the names in this table are actual product team members). There are also five female employees named David. Apparently someone has a sense humor.

Totals and Subtotals

Before getting into a discussion about the techniques available for totaling grouped aggregates and creating subtotal breaks, a discussion of how you will use this data is needed. SQL Server is typically used as the back-end data store for some type of application or data consumer product. Many data presentation and reporting tools exist that will take care of formatting and totaling values from your queries. The technique you choose will largely depend on the tool or application that will consume this data. A number of products in the Microsoft suite can be used to easily present query results in a readable form. These include Excel, Access, and SQL Server Reporting Services.

	FirstName	Gender	(No column name)
1	Alan	M	1
2	Alejandro	M	1
3	Alex	M	1
4	Alice	M	1
5	Amy	F	1
6	Andreas	F	1
7	Andrew	F	1
8	Andrew	M	1
9	Andy	M	1
10	Angela	M	1
11	Anibal	F	1
12	Annette	M	1
13	Annik	M	1
14	Arvind	M	1
15	Ashvini	M	1
16	Balaganesan	F	1
17	Barbara	F	1
18	Barbara	M	1
19	Baris	F	1
20	Barry	M	2
21	Belinda	F	1
22	Ben	F	1
23	Benjamin	M	1
24	Betsy	F	1
25	Bjorn	F	1
26	Bob	F	1
27	Brandon	F	1
28	Brannon	M	1
29	Brenda	F	1
30	Brian	F	3
31	Brian	M	1
32	Britta	M	1

Figure 7-10

One important consideration is whether you want the data to be grouped, aggregated, and subtotaled by the database server or by the client application after results have been returned from the database. There is little doubt that it is more efficient to let the database server do the work and send less data across the network. However, consider the case where an application allows users to interact with data, choosing different sorting and grouping options. It might make more sense to send raw data to the application one time so it can be manipulated by the client rather than refreshing the result set and resending a different result each time the user chooses a grouping or sorting option. These are decisions that you and solutions designers might need to make on a larger scale. The purpose here is to discuss the options in SQL Server to do the grouping and subtotaling at the database server.

When I use the terms totaling and subtotaling, I use these in a general sense to mean applying whatever aggregate functions you choose at various group levels. So, for example, if I were using the AVG() function to return the average purchase price per product, and per quarter at the quarter level, I would want to see the average calculation for all of the product price averages. I'm loosely using the term subtotal, even though I expect to see an average calculation rather than a sum or total.

Subgrouping

With more than one column referenced in the GROUP BY clause, some interesting things happen. For the sake of simplicity, a hypothetical table follows with simplified values.

ID1	ID2	MyValue
A	X	2
A	X	1
A	Y	2
A	Y	1
B	X	3
B	Y	2
B	Y	2

In a query for my hypothetical table, I include the first two columns, ID1 and ID2, in the GROUP BY clause and use the SUM() function to total the values in the third column:

```
SELECT ID1, ID2, Sum(MyValue)
FROM MyFakeTable
GROUP BY ID1, ID2
```

Multiple rows are returned, one for each unique combination of values, as shown in the following table.

ID1	ID2	MyValue
A	X	3
A	Y	3
B	X	3
B	Y	4

What I don't have in this result set is the sum for all occurrences where ID1 is equal to A or where ID2 is equal to Y. To get the aggregate result of a grouped query, you can use the ROLLUP and CUBE statements. These will essentially take the results from the grouped query and apply the same aggregation to either the first column's values or all combinations of values for each column that appears in the GROUP BY column list.

WITH ROLLUP

This is the simplest option for calculating subtotals and totals on the first column in the GROUP BY column list. In the case of my hypothetical example, in addition to calculating the sum of each unique column value, totals would be tallied for the value A and B in the ID1 column only. Using the same query, I've added WITH ROLLUP after the GROUP BY statement:

```
SELECT ID1, ID2, SUM(MyValue)
FROM MyFakeTable
GROUP BY ID1, ID2
WITH ROLLUP
```

The results would look something like those shown in the following table.

ID1	ID2	MyValue
A	X	3
A	Y	3
B	X	3
B	Y	4
A	(null)	6
B	(null)	7

Null values are used to indicate that the corresponding column was ignored when calculating the aggregate value.

WITH CUBE

The CUBE operator is an expanded version of the ROLLUP operator. Rather than just rolling up the aggregate values for the first column in the GROUP BY list, CUBE performs this rollup for every combination of grouped column values. In the case of the hypothetical tables used in the previous example, three additional rows are added to the result set. Here is the same query using WITH CUBE rather than WITH ROLLUP:

```
SELECT ID1, ID2, SUM(MyValue)
FROM MyFakeTable
GROUP BY ID1, ID2
WITH CUBE
```

The corresponding result set is shown in the following table.

ID1	ID2	MyValue
A	X	3
A	Y	3
B	X	3
B	Y	4
A	(null)	6
B	(null)	7

ID1	ID2	MyValue	
(null)	X	6	
(null)	Y	7	
(null)	(null)	13	

Null values in the first column indicate that this is a rollup on the values in the second column. In this case, these rows contain subtotal values for all rows where ID2 is equal to X or Y. The last row has null values in both grouped columns. This indicates that it is a grand total, the sum of all rows. Be advised that CUBE operations are expensive when it comes to server resources. Carefully consider whether it would be more efficient to just send the simplified aggregate data to the application and let it do the equivalent operations to derive the cubed data.

The GROUPING() Function

Let's go back to the AdventureWorks Product table example used earlier. I made a point not to use this table for the ROLLUP and CUBE examples because it would throw a wrench into the works. Go back and take another look at Figure 7-7; note the null values in the SpecialOfferID column. You'll recall that when using the ROLLUP and CUBE operators, a null is used to indicate a rollup or subtotal row where that column's value isn't being considered. What if a column in the GROUP BY list actually contains null values? Here's the earlier example again, with the added ROLLUP operator:

```
SELECT ProductID, COUNT(ProductID) As ProductIDCount
    , SpecialOfferID, COUNT(SpecialOfferID) As SpecialOfferIDCount
FROM SalesOrderDetail
GROUP BY ProductID, SpecialOfferID
WITH ROLLUP
ORDER BY ProductID, SpecialOfferID
```

In the result set shown in Figure 7-11, additional rows are added with subtotals.

	ProductID	ProductIDCount	SpecialOfferID	SpecialOfferIDCount
1	NULL	121371	NULL	60973
2	3	150	NULL	150
3	3	150	6	150
4	5	218	NULL	218
5	5	218	6	218
6	8	48	NULL	0
7	8	150	NULL	102
8	8	102	6	102
9	9	49	NULL	0
10	9	195	NULL	146
11	9	146	6	146
12	10	58	NULL	0
13	10	193	NULL	135
14	10	135	6	135
15	11	56	NULL	0
16	11	232	NULL	176
17	11	176	6	176

Figure 7-11

Take a close look at rows 6, 7, and 8. Which one contains the subtotal for all products where the ProductID is 8? Two rows have nulls in the SpecialOfferID column. One of them contains NULL because some of this column's values are, in fact, NULL. The answer is row 7, because the count of the ProductID is higher than any other. Row 6 has a SpecialOfferID count of 0 because this row represents those rows where the SpecialOfferID is actually NULL. Do you find this confusing? It certainly can be. Imagine the added confusion if you were grouping on more than two columns, or using the CUBE operator rather than ROLLUP. Imagine taking the results of this query to your software developer and asking him to create a custom report with subtotals and totals and then try to explain this grouping criterion. This is where the GROUPING() function comes in.

The GROUPING() function returns a bit value (1 or 0) to indicate that a row is a rollup. This makes it easy to separate the aggregation of null values. Any application or tool that consumes grouped data can easily distinguish the rolled-up subtotal rows from simple grouped rows. Here's the query with two columns added using the GROUPING() function:

```
SELECT ProductID
    , GROUPING(ProductID) As ProdGroup
    , COUNT(ProductID) As ProductIDCount
    , SpecialOfferID
    , GROUPING(SpecialOfferID) As SO_Group
    , COUNT(SpecialOfferID) As SpecialOfferIDCount
FROM SalesOrderDetail
GROUP BY ProductID, SpecialOfferID
WITH ROLLUP
ORDER BY ProductID, SpecialOfferID
```

In the results shown in Figure 7-12, you can see the two new columns (aliased as ProdGroup and SO_Group). The first row in the result set is the grand total, with rolled-up values for all rows (any combination of ProductID and SpecialOfferID values). This row and each individual rollup row is also flagged with a 1.

	ProductID	ProdGroup	ProductIDCount	SpecialOfferID	SO_Group	SpecialOfferIDCount
1	NULL	1	121371	NULL	1	60973
2	3	0	150	NULL	1	150
3	3	0	150	6	0	150
4	5	0	218	NULL	1	218
5	5	0	218	6	0	218
6	8	0	48	NULL	0	0
7	8	0	150	NULL	1	102
8	8	0	102	6	0	102
9	9	0	49	NULL	0	0
10	9	0	195	NULL	1	146
11	9	0	146	6	0	146
12	10	0	58	NULL	0	0
13	10	0	193	NULL	1	135
14	10	0	135	6	0	135
15	11	0	56	NULL	0	0
16	11	0	232	NULL	1	176
17	11	0	176	6	0	176

Figure 7-12

Because this is a ROLLUP query, only the SpecialOfferID values get rolled up into their respective ProductID combination counterparts. If you substitute CUBE for the ROLLUP function, you will see additional Grouping flags for the ProductID.

Note that if the results of these grouped and aggregated queries will be fed to a custom reporting solution or a similar application, application developers will appreciate the output from the GROUPING() function. This can make life much easier for a custom software developer or report designer.

COMPUTE and COMPUTE BY

Regardless of the data you might work with, SQL Server was designed, and is optimized, to return rows and columns — two dimensions. Likewise, software designed to consume SQL data expects to receive two-dimensional data. All of the components, application programming interfaces (APIs), and connection utilities are engineered to work with two-dimensional result sets.

Why am I making such a big deal out of this two-dimensional result set business? The COMPUTE clause is a very simple means for viewing data with totals and subtotals, but it breaks all the rules when it comes to standard results. It's also important to note that this is a proprietary SQL Server feature and isn't recognized by the ANSI SQL specification. My purpose is not to try to talk you out of using these features entirely but to realize its limitations. This is an effective technique for viewing summary data, but its usefulness may be somewhat limited in many real software solutions because it does not return data in a format that is consumable by any application. Its usefulness is limited to Query Analyzer or SQL Server Management Studio.

Suppose that the sales manager calls you on the phone and asks you to tell her what the total sales were for last month. She doesn't need a formal report, and you're not going to develop a custom application for users to do this themselves. She just wants a list of sales orders with the total. Using this technique may be the best choice.

Here's a simple example of the COMPUTE clause:

```
SELECT ProductID, SalesOrderID, OrderQty
FROM SalesOrderDetail
ORDER BY ProductID, SalesOrderID
COMPUTE SUM(OrderQty)
```

The query editor splits the result into two grids because the result doesn't fit into a standard two-dimensional grid, as shown in Figure 7-13.

I had asked for SQL Server to compute the sum of the OrderQty for the entire result set. This created a grand total for the entire range of data. Because of the formatting restrictions of viewing results in grid view, I'd like to show you the same result in text view.

	ProductID	SalesOrderID	OrderQty
4	3	5092	2
5	3	5134	3
6	3	5139	2
7	3	5163	1
8	3	5174	1
9	3	5189	3
10	3	5204	2
11	3	5217	3
12	3	5221	1
13	3	5230	3
14	3	5236	1
15	3	5331	4
16	3	5362	1
17	3	5416	2
18	3	5421	1
19	3	5433	1
20	3	5467	6
21	3	5468	2

	sum
1	275754

Figure 7-13

Try It Out

To switch the view from grid to text, choose Results in Text from the Query menu in Query Analyzer or Results to Text in the Query Editor. Execute the query from the previous example and scroll all the way down to the bottom of the results. That probably took a while considering that there were more than 120,000 rows. To work with a more manageable set of data, modify the query as follows so it only returns the 23 orders:

```
SELECT ProductID, SalesOrderID, OrderQty
FROM SalesOrderDetail
WHERE SalesOrderID > 43650
ORDER BY ProductID, SalesOrderID
COMPUTE SUM(OrderQty) By ProductID
```

This returns a short result set in the form of monospaced text:

```
ProductID   SalesOrderID OrderQty
----------- ------------ --------
209         43652        1
209         43654        1
209         43655        1
210         43653        1
210         43656        1
211         43657        1
211         43658        1
213         43651        1
1228        43654        1
1273        43658        1
1277        43652        1
1277        43654        1
```

```
1277         43656         1
1277         43657         1
1277         43658         1
1279         43652         1
1279         43654         1
1279         43656         1
1279         43657         1
1279         43658         1
1286         43653         1
1286         43657         1

             sum
             ===========
             22
```

(23 row(s) affected)

This may be useful if you are interested in the grand total following the entire range of values. If you want to see grouped sections of rows with subtotals, it's a simple matter to add the column name or list of columns to the end of the COMPUTE clause. Modify the previous query to group by the ProductID:

```
SELECT ProductID, SalesOrderID, OrderQty
FROM SalesOrderDetail
WHERE SalesOrderID > 43650
ORDER BY ProductID, SalesOrderID
COMPUTE SUM(OrderQty) By ProductID
```

The result set shows the same list of SalesOrderDetail records with a subtotal break after each ProductID. (I've shortened the result text to save space.)

```
ProductID    SalesOrderID OrderQty
-----------  ------------ --------
209          43652         1
209          43654         1
209          43655         1

             sum
             ===========
             3
...


ProductID    SalesOrderID OrderQty
-----------  ------------ --------
1279         43652         1
1279         43654         1
1279         43656         1
1279         43657         1
1279         43658         1

             sum
             ===========
```

```
                          5


  ProductID   SalesOrderID OrderQty
  ----------- ------------ --------
  1286        43653        1
  1286        43657        1

                          sum
                          ===========
                          2


  (31 row(s) affected)
```

The COMPUTE clause is an easy and convenient technique for producing a detailed list of column values with total and grouped subtotal breaks. It doesn't do grouping and aggregation on every row like the GROUP BY clause. Just keep in mind that the output isn't compatible with most standard data consumer software and programming components. If you just need to view or print a quick, ad-hoc report, this may be the easiest way to get there. Otherwise, use the ANSI standard GROUP BY clause with the ROLLUP or CUBE statements.

From a database design standpoint, it is imperative that large tables are indexed on columns that will be used for grouping and aggregation. Few other functions and SQL statements will stress the database engine to the same degree. Consider using a clustered index on a column that is usually used in queries to join to another table or specify the usual sort order. You can find more information about indexing strategies in *Professional SQL Server Programming* from Wrox Press.

As previously mentioned, cube operations can be especially intensive. As you have run some of these queries, you've probably noticed that it takes a little while to perform calculations and return the aggregated results. It's best to use the ROLLUP and CUBE statements with filtered data. If you do need to perform intensive grouping operations on a large volume of data, try to do this at a time when you won't be competing with other large operations.

Although it usually makes sense to let SQL Server do a majority of the work, sometimes returning a larger volume of data that can be reused in the client application, rather than running numerous query operations, is best. This is especially true with dynamic reporting solutions. Make a point to understand your users' needs and try to strike a balance between the flexibility of an application or reporting solution and the efficiency of the whole system. As a rule, don't return any more data than is necessary. Lastly, make a point to order records explicitly using the ORDER BY clause. This will guarantee the sort order of your queries. Even if records in the table already exist in the correct order, using the ORDER BY clause will not cause any processing overhead.

Summary

This chapter introduced nine aggregate functions that can be used in a simple SELECT statement to return summary values for the entire range or with the GROUP BY clause to roll up groups of rows with similar values. The aggregate functions include simple mathematical operations, such as Count and Sum, and statistical functions such as variance and standard deviation.

The GROUP BY clause can be used to reduce the results of a query to distinct combinations of grouped values. When used with aggregate functions, this produces value summaries within the grouping.

The ROLLUP and CUBE statements extend grouping functionality by adding summary rows. Adding WITH ROLLUP to a grouped query will produce summary rows for the first column in the GROUP BY list. Adding WITH CUBE will add summary rows for every possible combination of grouped column values. The GROUPING() function can be used along with these operators to flag summary rows and to avoid confusion.

Use the COMPUTE statement sparingly and only for quick reports in Query Analyzer or the Query Editor. Although it's simple compared to using some of the other techniques discussed in this chapter, it is not ANSI SQL compliant and doesn't work with most software and programming tools. It is, however, a convenient method for viewing summary information quickly.

Exercises

Exercise 1

Write a query to return the first name and the highest ShiftID value for each group of employees named Kevin, Linda, or Mary.

Exercise 2

Return a list of ProductSubCategoryID values from the Product table. Include only subcategories that occur more than 20 times. In addition to the ID value, also return the first product name in alphabetical order and the highest price for products in this subcategory.

Exercise 3

Produce a list of managers from the Employee table using the ManagerID. For each manager, include the average base pay for all employees of each gender. Also include a row for each manager that includes the average base pay for all employees of that manager. This should be done using only one SELECT expression.

Multi-Table Queries

Last week I rented a diesel front loader to level some property and put in a gravel driveway. I had never operated one before, but I figured that it couldn't be too difficult. It was the kind with four wheels and big rubber tires. It had a big lever on each side, for each hand, that controlled power to the wheels on the left and right sides of the vehicle. The hydraulics were controlled using foot pedals that swiveled in each direction. It really felt like a big arcade game — at first. Needless to say, it took coordination that I had yet to develop when I started. It handled a little differently than my Ford Mustang. The first thing I did was ease the throttle forward and try to go forward up a slight incline. The clutches on the traction controls were very sensitive. I pushed the hand levers too quickly, it lunged forward, and I found myself heading nose-up, popping a wheelie on the rear wheels. The thought of rolling over backward in a five-ton, diesel-powered, steel box was not very appealing. Not about to let my wife show me how to operate a big piece of machinery, I eventually got used to the controls and learned to work with it. By the end of the day, I was tearing up the woods like a five-year-old with a Tonka truck.

The key was to learn how this piece of machinery was engineered to work. Like a racehorse, I had to find that middle ground between what *it* wanted to do and what *I* wanted it to do. After I found that space, we got along just fine. Although it's hard to get SQL Server to pop a wheelie, like any other industrial-strength tool, you have to work with it. One of the key factors to achieving this goal is to understand how the tool is designed to work. There are nearly always different ways to approach a problem and different techniques that will ultimately achieve the same end result, but the shortest path will usually be the most efficient.

At the beginning of this book, I briefly discussed some of the concepts of database design. You'll recall that information is often broken down into pieces and stored in several tables to improve accuracy and to reduce redundancy. This leaves you with one of the greatest challenges in relational database work: putting the information back together. When a relational database is designed, tables are typically created with defined relationships between them. When the data is queried, join operations are often used to utilize these relationships and "reassemble" the original information. Although it usually makes sense to join tables using predefined relationships, there are times when you will not use related columns to join tables. If your database has been designed correctly, this should be the rare exception to the rule.

Here's a simple example. I have used the Database Diagram feature of SQL Server to create an entity relation diagram (see Figure 8-1) for part of the AdventureWorks2000 database.

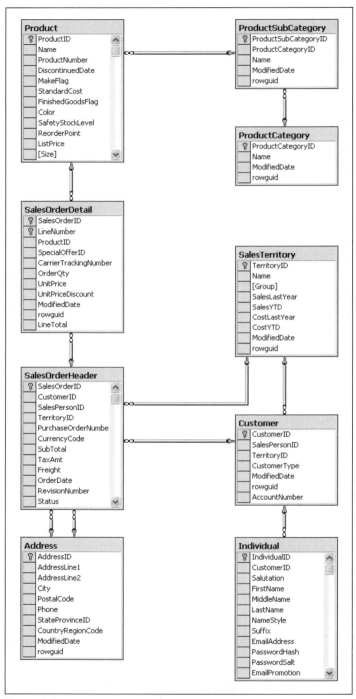

Figure 8-1

You can see that relationships have been defined between these tables that are based in primary and foreign key columns. As you know, primary keys are used to uniquely identify rows in a table and foreign keys are used to relate one table's rows to another. For example, the Customer table's designated primary key is the CustomerID column. Every customer record has a unique value assigned in this column. The SalesOrderHeader table also contains a CustomerID column, but values in this column are not necessarily unique. However, every SalesOrderHeader record with a CustomerID value must have a corresponding CustomerID value in the Customer table. This rule is enforced in the foreign key constraint defined in the SalesOrderHeader table.

Understanding Subqueries and Joins

As the SQL language evolved and was implemented in different products, a few different techniques have been devised for joining tables to match up related records. Although there are a few variations of these techniques, there are essentially three different ways to go about joining records from two different tables. The first two are different forms of join operations within a single SELECT statement. The third technique involves more than one SELECT statement, where one query encompasses a second SELECT statement. This is often called a *subquery* — a query within a query. The tables in a subquery can be independent of each other or can be related through some kind of matching expression. One technique, used to match rows of the subquery to a row or rows of the main query is often referred to as a *correlated subquery*. Subqueries are covered in Chapter 10. For now, I will concentrate on the bread and butter of SQL Server queries: the join operation.

Joining Tables in the WHERE Clause

This is still a popular technique in many other database products and is the most traditional method for joining tables. Because it's an older technique, it's often referred to as a *legacy join*. Although it is supported by SQL Server, this is not part of the recent ANSI-SQL standards and is not the recommended approach for SQL Server. You may encounter this syntax in existing code. In this example, both the Customer and SalesOrderHeader are referenced in the FROM clause, and the join operation is performed in the WHERE clause:

```
SELECT Customer.AccountNumber, SalesOrderHeader.OrderDate
FROM Customer, SalesOrderHeader
WHERE Customer.CustomerID = SalesOrderHeader.CustomerID
```

The query returns 31,519 rows, comprised of a combination of records from the Customer and SalesOrderDetail tables. Figure 8-2 shows the first 24 of these rows.

This query implements an inner join, which is discussed very soon. The equals sign between each of the column references means that this query returns only rows where there are matching records in each of the tables. This is known as an *equijoin*, meaning that the values in two tables compared in the join operation must be equal to one another. In the "Outer Joins" section, you'll also see an example of the legacy version for this type of query.

	AccountNumber	OrderDate
1	304	2003-09-01 00:00:00.000
2	595	2003-09-01 00:00:00.000
3	609	2004-06-01 00:00:00.000
4	651	2003-03-01 00:00:00.000
5	595	2004-06-01 00:00:00.000
6	595	2003-12-01 00:00:00.000
7	676	2002-07-01 00:00:00.000
8	4	2002-10-01 00:00:00.000
9	633	2003-12-01 00:00:00.000
10	4	2003-04-01 00:00:00.000
11	277	2002-12-01 00:00:00.000
12	676	2003-07-01 00:00:00.000
13	647	2002-03-01 00:00:00.000
14	663	2003-08-01 00:00:00.000
15	621	2003-09-01 00:00:00.000
16	654	2002-12-01 00:00:00.000
17	663	2004-05-01 00:00:00.000
18	421	2003-07-01 00:00:00.000
19	128	2002-06-01 00:00:00.000
20	18	2001-08-01 00:00:00.000
21	65	2004-05-01 00:00:00.000
22	128	2002-09-01 00:00:00.000
23	216	2002-03-01 00:00:00.000
24	230	2003-11-01 00:00:00.000

Figure 8-2

Joining Tables in the FROM Clause

The same operation can also be performed using the ANSI standard method. In the FROM clause, the two tables are referenced with a JOIN statement followed by the ON keyword and the same column references used in the preceding example:

```
SELECT Customer.AccountNumber, SalesOrderHeader.OrderDate
FROM Customer INNER JOIN SalesOrderHeader
ON Customer.CustomerID = SalesOrderHeader.CustomerID
```

The result is the same. If you view the execution plan for both of these queries, you'll note that they both cause SQL Server to perform exactly the same operations. There is no difference in time, cost, or efficiency. You can view the execution plan for a query by enabling this option in the Query menu. Run the query and the Execution Plan tab appears below the results window, as shown in Figure 8-3.

Reading from right to left, each icon represents an operation. The records are retrieved from both tables and held in memory. Because each of the columns referenced in the JOIN statement are indexed, the query-processing engine chooses to scan and retrieve records using these indexes. Rows in the Customer table are retrieved using a separate, non-clustered index. Records in the SalesOrderDetail table are physically ordered by the CustomerID column based on a clustered index. The width of the arrows indicates the relative volume of data returned from the respective operation. The rows are combined using a hash join method to produce the final result. If you execute either of these two queries, you will see that the execution plans are the same. Float the mouse pointer over the left-most icon to see statistics for the finished product. The Subtree cost shows the total time in seconds for this and all operations that lead to it.

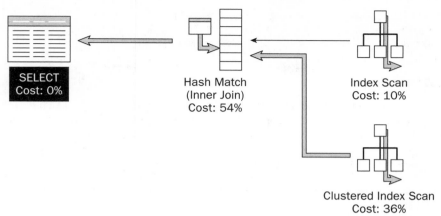

SELECT
Cost: 0%

Hash Match
(Inner Join)
Cost: 54%

Index Scan
Cost: 10%

Clustered Index Scan
Cost: 36%

Figure 8-3

Two major types of joins exist: those that return only corresponding records in two tables or those that return all of the rows in one table and then corresponding rows in the second table.

The AdventureWorks2000 database contains 19,186 customer records. All but 66 have corresponding sales orders rows in the SalesOrderHeader table, where the CustomerID column value is equal to an existing value in the Customer table's CustomerID. There are 31,519 rows in the SalesOrderHeader table.

Inner Joins

This is the most common type of join operation. The purpose of the inner join is to match up rows in one table with corresponding rows in another table where the associated columns contain the same value. If one of these tables' columns has a different value, or no value at all, these rows will not be returned by the query.

Before showing you an example, I'll make this request using common language: I'd like to see all of the customers who have orders — and all of the orders that have corresponding customers. For each customer, show me the customer's account number, and for each order, the order date.

Again, the SQL statement that makes this same request is as follows:

```
SELECT Customer.AccountNumber, SalesOrderHeader.OrderDate
FROM Customer INNER JOIN SalesOrderHeader
ON Customer.CustomerID = SalesOrderHeader.CustomerID
```

You just saw the results from this query in Figure 8-2, so I won't show them to you again. Just remember that it returns 31,519 rows that consist of customers with orders and orders with customers.

The INNER JOIN statement can also be abbreviated by simply using JOIN. Although this is not as explicit, it works just as effectively as the earlier statement:

```
SELECT Customer.AccountNumber, SalesOrderHeader.OrderDate
FROM Customer JOIN SalesOrderHeader
ON Customer.CustomerID = SalesOrderHeader.CustomerID
```

Outer Joins

The job of an outer join is to return all of the rows from one table and then to match those rows in a corresponding table where the joining column has the same value. The difference between this and an inner join is that the unmatched rows in the first table are still returned by the query.

In common language, an outer join request might look like this: I'd like to see all of the customers, and for the customers who have orders, I'd also like to see related order information. Show me the account number for every customer, and if the customer has orders, show me a row for each combination of customers and orders.

Here's the SQL statement for this request:

```
SELECT Customer.AccountNumber, SalesOrderHeader.OrderDate
FROM Customer LEFT OUTER JOIN SalesOrderHeader
ON Customer.CustomerID = SalesOrderHeader.CustomerID
```

Outer joins always favor one table, the table from which you choose all rows. In this case, the table on the left side of the JOIN statement From Customer LEFT OUTER JOIN SalesOrderHeader is the Customer table. This means that all customer rows will be returned from the query and then the corresponding SalesOrderHeader rows. If you think about it, this makes sense because the SalesOrderDetail table has a foreign key constraint that requires a matching CustomerID value. Given the relationship between these tables, it wouldn't make sense to join them the other way around.

When you execute this query, the results will look much the same as before at a glance. However, notice the row count: 31,585 rows — 66 more than before. What's going on here? Go back and look at the numbers I gave you just before I introduced inner joins. The Customer table contains 31,519 rows including 66 without any orders. The outer join returned the customers who don't have orders. When an outer join doesn't have matching rows in the outer table (in a left outer join, the table on the right is the outer table), null values are returned. To find customers without orders, look for a null in the OrderDate column. But can't you use a query to do this? Rather than making you scroll through 31,000 rows looking for those missing an order date, just alter the query, adding a WHERE clause:

```
SELECT Customer.AccountNumber, SalesOrderHeader.OrderDate
FROM Customer LEFT OUTER JOIN SalesOrderHeader
ON Customer.CustomerID = SalesOrderHeader.CustomerID
WHERE SalesOrderHeader.OrderDate IS NULL
```

This query returns 66 rows, customers who have no orders, as shown in Figure 8-4.

	AccountNumber	OrderDate
1	60	NULL
2	526	NULL
3	600	NULL
4	194	NULL
5	374	NULL
6	517	NULL
7	508	NULL
8	42	NULL
9	402	NULL
10	356	NULL
11	619	NULL
12	416	NULL
13	333	NULL
14	347	NULL
15	204	NULL
16	324	NULL
17	158	NULL
18	375	NULL
19	209	NULL
20	329	NULL
21	140	NULL
22	689	NULL
23	463	NULL
24	500	NULL

Figure 8-4

So, what is the purpose of a RIGHT OUTER JOIN? Using a Right in place of Left in this expression would have the same effect as reversing the order of the tables and columns. In most cases, you could choose to use one or the other. However, if you have an outer join on both sides of a table, you may be constrained to use either a left or a right outer join. Fortunately, visual query design tools can be used to create complex queries. This is easy to do using the Transact SQL Query Builder.

Try It Out

One of a few ways to open the Query Builder is to create a new view in Enterprise Manager.

1. Drill down into the AdventureWorks database and right-click the Views icon. From the pop-up menu, click New View. . .

2. Click the right-most button (Add Tables) on the toolbar to add tables to the designer.

3. From the Add Table dialog window, select the Customer table and click Add.

4. Select the SalesOrderHeader table (see Figure 8-5) and click Add. Click Close to close the Add Table dialog window.

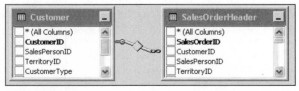

Figure 8-5

The designer always assumes you will want an inner join. The diamond on the join line between these tables represents the join, and the logic is quite simple.

5. Right-click the diamond icon to view a pop-up menu of join operations. From the menu, choose Select All Rows from Customer, as shown in Figure 8-6.

Figure 8-6

The diagram adds a rectangular "cap" to the left side of the join to indicate that all rows will be returned from the table on the corresponding side of the join.

6. Now scroll down or resize the Customer table window and check the box next to the AccountNumber column. Also, for the SalesOrderHeader table, check the OrderDate column (see Figure 8-7).

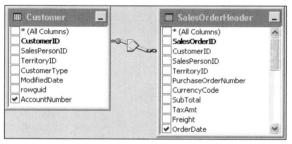

Figure 8-7

Take a look at the SQL statement in the third pane of the designer. It should look like this:

```
SELECT    dbo.Customer.AccountNumber, dbo.SalesOrderHeader.OrderDate
FROM    dbo.Customer LEFT OUTER JOIN
        dbo.SalesOrderHeader ON dbo.Customer.CustomerID =
        dbo.SalesOrderHeader.CustomerID
```

The only real difference between your version of this query and this one is that the designer always adds the dbo user prefix. As far as you're concerned, this doesn't make a difference. This is a great tool for learning join syntax. When in doubt, build your queries this way and examine the SQL. Rather than using the designer as a crutch so you don't have to learn to do it the hard way, use it as a learning tool and then challenge yourself by rewriting the same queries in the Query Editor or Query Analyzer. As I mentioned earlier, there are those purists who refuse to use these design tools to create queries. In my opinion, it all comes down to time, money, and effort. If you can get the job done more effectively using a utility of some kind, then by all means, do so.

There is also shorthand syntax for outer joins. You can abbreviate the join statement by using LEFT JOIN or RIGHT JOIN rather than LEFT OUTER JOIN and RIGHT OUTER JOIN, respectively.

Legacy Outer Joins

Earlier, I showed you how to implement an inner join in the WHERE clause. You'll recall that this technique, often referred to as a legacy join, is not recommended by the ANSI-92 SQL standard. It will, however, work in Transact-SQL and produces the same execution plan. Legacy outer joins are even more discouraged than legacy inner joins. This is because ambiguous results can be returned by a legacy outer join when an expression is placed on the side of the join where all records are to be returned (the "*" side). Microsoft has been threatening for a few years to make the legacy outer join syntax an illegal operation due to this rare anomaly, but as of SQL Server 2005 it has not. I share it with you here because you may encounter it in existing code but you should probably never use this method of creating outer joins. This is the same query as the previous example using the legacy join syntax in the WHERE clause:

```
SELECT Customer.AccountNumber, SalesOrderHeader.OrderDate
FROM Customer, SalesOrderHeader
WHERE Customer.CustomerID *= SalesOrderHeader.CustomerID
```

The asterisk (*) indicates the equivalent of a Left or Right part of a join clause, where *= is a Left Outer Join and =* is a Right Outer Join.

Multicolumn Joins

There is no stated limit to the number of columns that can be used in a join. Typically, you would only need to use more than one joining column to support specific business rules (because joins are usually performed on primary and foreign keys). The logic of a join expression is very similar to that of a WHERE clause. Multiple comparisons can be combined using AND and OR operators.

I'll use this technique to find product sales records (in the SalesOrderDetail table) for products sold at dealer cost. This involves matching the ProductID between the two tables and matching the StandardCost from the Product table to the UnitPrice from the SalesOrderDetail table:

```
SELECT     Product.ProductID
         , Product.Name
         , Product.StandardCost
         , Product.ListPrice
         , SalesOrderDetail.UnitPrice
FROM       Product
           INNER JOIN SalesOrderDetail
           ON  Product.ProductID = SalesOrderDetail.ProductID
           AND Product.StandardCost = SalesOrderDetail.UnitPrice
```

14,574 transactions were recorded without a price markup. The first 24 rows of this result are shown in Figure 8-8.

	ProductID	Name	StandardCost	ListPrice	UnitPrice
1	1086	ML Road Frame-W - Yellow, 48	440.1742	743.5375	440.1742
2	661	ML Road Frame-W - Yellow, 38	440.1742	743.5375	440.1742
3	870	LL Road Rear Wheel	83.2981	140.7063	83.2981
4	627	Front Brakes	78.8100	133.1250	78.8100
5	686	LL Mtn Front Wheel	44.9513	75.9313	44.9513
6	687	ML Mtn Front Wheel	154.6785	261.2813	154.6785
7	867	LL Mtn Rear Wheel	64.9313	109.6813	64.9313
8	868	ML Mtn Rear Wheel	174.6585	295.0313	174.6585
9	869	HL Mtn Rear Wheel	242.1391	409.0188	242.1391
10	690	ML Road Front Wheel	183.8049	310.4813	183.8049
11	691	HL Road Front Wheel	244.2444	412.5750	244.2444
12	1027	LL Road Frame - Red, 44	249.5428	421.5250	249.5428
13	1032	LL Road Frame - Red, 60	249.5428	421.5250	249.5428
14	870	LL Road Rear Wheel	83.2981	140.7063	83.2981
15	620	HL Crankset	299.6926	506.2375	299.6926
16	853	Touring Pedal	59.9326	101.2375	59.9326
17	691	HL Road Front Wheel	244.2444	412.5750	244.2444
18	870	LL Road Rear Wheel	83.2981	140.7063	83.2981
19	1032	LL Road Frame - Red, 60	249.5428	421.5250	249.5428
20	1027	LL Road Frame - Red, 44	249.5428	421.5250	249.5428
21	1033	LL Road Frame - Red, 62	249.5428	421.5250	249.5428
22	690	ML Road Front Wheel	183.8049	310.4813	183.8049
23	697	LL Mtn Handlebars	32.9596	55.6750	32.9596
24	698	ML Mtn Handlebars	45.8208	77.4000	45.8208

Figure 8-8

Non-equijoins

So far, the join operations (in their various forms) you've seen have all used comparisons of equality. In other words, the values compared between two tables must be equal for the query to return matching records. Although far less common, joins can also be performed using any other valid method of comparison. This can include any of those listed in the following table.

Operator	Comparison
<>	not equal
<	less than
>	greater than
<=	less than or equal
>=	greater than or equal

I can modify the previous example to find sales orders for products that were sold below cost:

```
SELECT      Product.ProductID
        , Product.Name
        , Product.StandardCost
        , Product.ListPrice
        , SalesOrderDetail.UnitPrice
```

```
FROM        Product
            INNER JOIN SalesOrderDetail
            ON  Product.ProductID = SalesOrderDetail.ProductID
            AND Product.StandardCost > SalesOrderDetail.UnitPrice
```

This returns 28,959 rows of sales orders that cost the business to sell, some of which are shown in Figure 8-9.

	ProductID	Name	StandardCost	ListPrice	UnitPrice
1	527	Touring-3000 Yellow, 62	549.3390	927.9375	534.4920
2	558	Touring-2000 Blue, 60	898.9890	1518.5625	874.6920
3	594	Touring-1000 Blue, 46	1764.2118	2980.0875	1716.5304
4	602	Touring-1000 Yellow, 46	1764.2118	2980.0875	1716.5304
5	89	Mountain-300 Black, 40	799.1926	1349.9875	777.5928
6	90	Mountain-300 Black, 44	799.1926	1349.9875	777.5928
7	91	Mountain-300 Black, 48	799.1926	1349.9875	777.5928
8	128	Mountain-200 Black, 38	1698.2926	2868.7375	1475.3507
9	129	Mountain-200 Black, 42	1698.2926	2868.7375	1475.3507
10	144	Mountain-200 Silver, 38	1716.7926	2899.9875	1491.4221
11	145	Mountain-200 Silver, 42	1716.7926	2899.9875	1491.4221
12	146	Mountain-200 Silver, 46	1716.7926	2899.9875	1491.4221
13	649	HL Mtn Frame - Silver, 38	1009.7300	1705.6250	917.9363
14	697	LL Mtn Handlebars	32.9596	55.6750	29.9633
15	698	ML Mtn Handlebars	45.8208	77.4000	41.6553
16	699	HL Mtn Handlebars	88.9998	150.3375	80.9089
17	985	HL Mtn Frame - Black, 42	998.7040	1687.0000	907.9127
18	999	HL Mtn Frame - Silver, 42	1009.7300	1705.6250	917.9363
19	249	Road-650 Black, 44	579.4126	978.7375	563.7528
20	250	Road-650 Black, 48	579.4126	978.7375	563.7528
21	251	Road-650 Black, 52	579.4126	978.7375	563.7528
22	253	Road-650 Black, 58	579.4126	978.7375	563.7528
23	254	Road-650 Black, 60	579.4126	978.7375	563.7528
24	255	Road-650 Black, 62	579.4126	978.7375	563.7528

Figure 8-9

Of course, I can easily turn this query around to show profitable sales by changing the comparison expression to read Product.StandardCost < SalesOrderDetail.UnitPrice. This expression returns 77,838 sales order/product rows.

Special-Purpose Join Operations

I think it's safe to say that you have seen 99% of the join operations you will use day-to-day. Two more types of joins are quite rare: full joins and cross joins. Unless you need to do some very unusual things, you will likely not use them. I can think of just three or four times I've used a full join or cross join in the past few years to solve unique problems.

Full Joins

A *full join* or *full outer join* is an outer join that doesn't favor one of the two tables. The result set will return unmatched values on both sides of the join. For example, the Customer table's SalesPersonID column is used to match an employee assigned to the customer. Of the 19,186 customers, 18,485 don't have an assigned salesperson. In a full outer join, you are asking for all customers who have or don't have an assigned salesperson and all employees who are assigned to a customer as well as those who are not. In other words, this query returns all customers, all employees, and combinations of the two based on the joining columns.

Try It Out

Execute the following query and scroll through the results:

```
SELECT CustomerID
     , EmployeeID
FROM Customer
     FULL OUTER JOIN
     Employee ON Customer.SalesPersonID = Employee.EmployeeID
ORDER BY CustomerID, EmployeeID
```

In Figure 8-10, you will notice NULL values in the CustomerID column returned from the Customer table. If you scroll-down, you will also see NULL values in the EmployeeID column returned from the Employee table.

	CustomerID	EmployeeID
266	NULL	293
267	NULL	294
268	NULL	295
269	NULL	296
270	NULL	297
271	NULL	298
272	NULL	299
273	NULL	300
274	NULL	302
275	NULL	303
276	NULL	304
277	NULL	305
278	1	22
279	2	23
280	3	24
281	4	24
282	5	26
283	6	27
284	7	26
285	8	29
286	9	29
287	10	31
288	11	31
289	12	33

Figure 8-10

This query returned 19,463 results. This is essentially every possible combination of distinct values for the two columns participating in the join, including NULL values.

The last time I used this type of join was for a medical patient scheduling application. Business requirements called for the user interface to display the available appointment blocks for all doctors in the clinic. Doctors with appointments scheduled for them were to be displayed in a different color. For example, each of three doctors in the clinic could see patients scheduled for appointments that could begin every 15 minutes. An appointment slot table contained scheduling blocks beginning at 9:00 AM and ending at 4:45 PM. Each row in this table represented a 15-minute block (9:00, 9:15, 9:30, and so on). In the scheduling application, my client wanted to see every possible appointment for each doctor, including those that had appointments scheduled. A full join between the appointment slot table and the appointment table did the trick.

Cross Joins

This is the granddaddy of all joins. When using a CROSS JOIN, you don't designate columns for the join to match values. The query will simply return every possible combination of rows for two tables without regard for matching column values. Needless to say, this can produce a large volume of rows and could be an effective way to populate a test database table with sample data. Frankly I have yet to find a practical use for this technique in a production database.

If you were to implement a cross join between the Customer and SalesOrderHeader tables, this is what you should expect to see: The Customer table contains 19,186 records and the SalesOrderHeader table contains 31,519 rows. This means that for every Customer row, 31,519 rows will be added to the result set. If you do the math, the result will contain 604,723,534 possible combinations. Please do not run this query on a production server. If you do, please don't tell your system administrator what book you were reading when you learned to do this. Joking aside, running this query would take several minutes and would consume a fair amount of server resources.

> As with any query in the Query Analyzer or SQL Server Management Studio query editor utilities, if it is running too long, you can always click the stop button to abort execution.

Here is the syntax for this query:

```
SELECT CustomerID, EmployeeID
FROM Customer CROSS JOIN Employee
ORDER BY CustomerID, EmployeeID
```

In my experience cross joins are more often created by accident than by intent. This is especially true when using the Query Builder. If two tables are added to the diagram that do not have a relationship defined, the Query Builder will generate a cross join query automatically.

Filtering Records in the Join Clause Using a Predicate

This is a lesser-known technique that can be used to filter rows before a join operation is executed. When a traditional multi-table query is executed, the join is processed first and then filtering takes place afterward; at least this is what you're telling SQL Server to do. Fortunately, SQL Server is smart enough to perform filtering ahead of time when it makes sense to do this (as long as indexes and column statistics are up to date, which they should be under normal conditions). Regardless, this technique guarantees that records not matching the filtering criteria will not be considered in the join operation:

```
SELECT CustomerID
     , EmployeeID
     , CustomerType
FROM   Customer
       INNER JOIN Employee ON Customer.SalesPersonID = Employee.EmployeeID
       AND Customer.CustomerID < 10
ORDER BY CustomerID, EmployeeID
```

However unconventional, this method would have the same effect as if the filter criteria (Customer. CustomerID < 10) were specified in the WHERE clause. For readability, I believe that the WHERE clause is the preferred method.

Joining on an Expression

Chapter 10 discusses the idea of using a SELECT statement as a derived table. For the purpose of the current discussion, it's good to know that joins can be used not only for tables, but also for any SELECT expression. An example so you can see how this works follows.

The director of marketing wants to reduce the cost of selling small-ticket items but doesn't want to discontinue low-priced items that are selling well. The director would like to see the accumulative sales for the 10 least-expensive products. This will require two separate SELECT expressions. The first will return the product rows for the 10 least-expensive products, and the second will return the aggregate sales filtered by this product selection. I'm working from the inside out, so the second expression will actually become the first part of the final query. I'll start with the first step and then add the second expression to the beginning.

The first query simply returns the 10 least-expensive products:

```
SELECT TOP 10
        ProductID
    , Name
    , ListPrice
FROM Product
WHERE ListPrice IS NOT NULL
ORDER BY ListPrice ASC
```

The ProductID column is essential but the other two columns shown in Figure 8-11 are included just for reference in the results.

	ProductID	Name	ListPrice
1	1285	Patch kit with 8 patches	2.8625
2	913	Road Tire Tube	4.9875
3	912	Mountain Tire Tube	6.2375
4	914	Touring Tire Tube	6.2375
5	1277	water bottle 30 oz	6.2375
6	1291	Bike wash - dissolver	9.9375
7	1217	Racing Socks, M	11.2375
8	1218	Racing Socks, L	11.2375
9	1228	AWC logo cap	11.2375
10	1279	Road bottle cage	11.2375

Figure 8-11

This expression must be given an alias so I can refer to it in another SELECT expression. The second step is to create another query for the aggregated sales orders. The first query is assigned an alias name and then treated as if it were a physical table:

```
SELECT
        SalesOrderDetail.ProductID
    , CheapProducts.Name
    , CheapProducts.ListPrice
    , SUM(LineTotal) AS SalesTotal
```

```
FROM SalesOrderDetail
    INNER JOIN
        (SELECT TOP 10
             ProductID
         , Name
         , ListPrice
      FROM Product
      WHERE ListPrice IS NOT NULL
      ORDER BY ListPrice ASC) AS CheapProducts
    ON SalesOrderDetail.ProductID = CheapProducts.ProductID
GROUP BY
         SalesOrderDetail.ProductID
    , CheapProducts.Name
    , CheapProducts.ListPrice
```

The alias I created for the derived table is called CheapProducts. The traditional approach is to use a single letter for table aliases. Personally, I find this to be a bit cryptic, so I try to use short and meaningful names. To include columns from the inner products query in the outer result set, they are referenced using the alias, as if this were just another table. Finally, because I'm aggregating the LineTotal column for records sharing the same product, all of the columns except for the aggregate must be included in the GROUP BY column list. This works because each of these column values is unique to a specific product. The results are displayed in Figure 8-12.

	ProductID	Name	ListPrice	SalesTotal
1	1228	AWC logo cap	11.2375	54630.723429995829
2	1291	Bike wash - dissolver	9.9375	18727.560600000699
3	1279	Road bottle cage	11.2375	15390.879999999679
4	1217	Racing Socks, M	11.2375	9965.6307599999091
5	1277	water bottle 30 oz	6.2375	28789.83494000358
6	914	Touring Tire Tube	6.2375	7425.119999999768
7	912	Mountain Tire Tube	6.2375	15444.049999999417
8	1218	Racing Socks, L	11.2375	15157.702773999943
9	913	Road Tire Tube	4.9875	9480.2399999995978
10	1285	Patch kit with 8 patches	2.8625	8233.1362399999016

Figure 8-12

I'll take some more time to cover derived tables and other subquery techniques in the next chapter. This gives you an idea about using joins in creative ways to address unique business rules. What I've learned (and continue to learn) about using SQL to address unique challenges is that there is almost always a method to solve the problem — and there are often several options. The ideal solution is usually not all that complicated. However, the ideal and most elegant solution is often not the one I use on the first attempt.

Multi-Table Joins

Now, let's put it all together. I need a list of all stores and, for those store/customers that have purchased products, details of the order and the product information. In this database, a store is a type of a customer, which requires a join between the Store and Customer tables. Because I want all stores regardless of matching orders, this will require an outer join to the SalesOrderHeader table. All other tables are included through inner joins. Figure 8-13 provides an illustration.

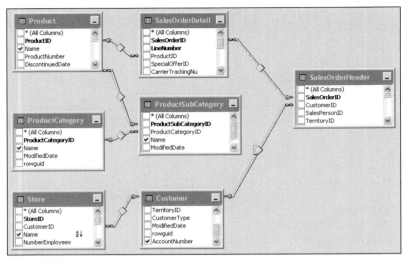

Figure 8-13

This query might be particularly tricky if you were to write it without the help of the designer. Because the SalesOrderHeader table participates in two joins, an inner join with SalesOrderDetail and an outer join with the Customer table, this breaks up the SQL syntax. Note the mispairing of JOIN and related ON statements in the SQL statement for this query:

```
SELECT    Store.Name AS StoreName
        , Customer.AccountNumber
        , SalesOrderHeader.OrderDate
        , ProductCategory.Name AS Category
        , ProductSubCategory.Name AS SubCategory
        , Product.Name AS ProductName
FROM      Store INNER JOIN Customer
            ON Store.CustomerID = Customer.CustomerID
          LEFT OUTER JOIN SalesOrderDetail
          INNER JOIN SalesOrderHeader
            ON SalesOrderDetail.SalesOrderID = SalesOrderHeader.SalesOrderID
          INNER JOIN Product
            ON SalesOrderDetail.ProductID = Product.ProductID
          INNER JOIN ProductSubCategory
            ON Product.ProductSubCategoryID =
               ProductSubCategory.ProductSubCategoryID
          INNER JOIN ProductCategory
            ON ProductSubCategory.ProductCategoryID =
               ProductCategory.ProductCategoryID
            ON Customer.CustomerID = SalesOrderHeader.CustomerID
ORDER BY Store.Name
```

When you need to write a complex query, it may be a good idea to at least start with the graphical query designer. Figure 8-14 shows the result set for this query from the results pane of the SQL Query Designer. Note the NULL values in the first row indicating that the store/customer has no related order records.

StoreName	AccountNumber	OrderDate	Category	SubCategory	ProductName
A Bicycle Association	324	<NULL>	<NULL>	<NULL>	<NULL>
A Bike Store	1	2/1/2002	Bike	Road Bike	Road-650 Black, 44
A Bike Store	1	11/1/2001	Bike	Road Bike	Road-650 Black, 44
A Bike Store	1	5/1/2002	Bike	Road Bike	Road-650 Black, 44
A Bike Store	1	8/1/2001	Bike	Road Bike	Road-650 Black, 44
A Bike Store	1	2/1/2002	Bike	Road Bike	Road-650 Black, 48
A Bike Store	1	5/1/2002	Bike	Road Bike	Road-650 Black, 48
A Bike Store	1	11/1/2001	Bike	Road Bike	Road-650 Black, 52
A Bike Store	1	5/1/2002	Bike	Road Bike	Road-650 Black, 52
A Bike Store	1	8/1/2001	Bike	Road Bike	Road-650 Black, 52
A Bike Store	1	11/1/2001	Bike	Road Bike	Road-650 Black, 58
A Bike Store	1	8/1/2001	Bike	Road Bike	Road-650 Black, 58
A Bike Store	1	2/1/2002	Bike	Road Bike	Road-650 Black, 60
A Bike Store	1	5/1/2002	Bike	Road Bike	Road-650 Black, 60
A Bike Store	1	11/1/2001	Bike	Road Bike	Road-650 Black, 62
A Bike Store	1	5/1/2002	Bike	Road Bike	Road-650 Black, 62
A Bike Store	1	2/1/2002	Bike	Road Bike	Road-650 Red, 44
A Bike Store	1	11/1/2001	Bike	Road Bike	Road-650 Red, 44
A Bike Store	1	5/1/2002	Bike	Road Bike	Road-650 Red, 44

Figure 8-14

Union Queries

Joins expand the result set horizontally. That is, columns are added to the results from multiple tables, essentially widening the result. A UNION query expands the results vertically as records are piled on top of one another. A simple example follows. The Employee table and the Individual table both contain records of people. To shorten the list, I'm just going to select the top five rows from each table:

```
SELECT TOP 5 FirstName, LastName FROM Employee
SELECT TOP 5 FirstName, LastName FROM Individual
```

These two queries, even if executed at the same time, return two different result sets, as shown in Figure 8-15.

	FirstName	LastName
1	Terri	Duffy
2	Jian Shuo	Wang
3	Michael	Sullivan
4	Sharon	Salavaria
5	Gail	Erickson

	FirstName	LastName
1	Jon	Yang
2	Eugene	Huang
3	Ruben	Torres
4	Christy	Zhu
5	Elizabeth	Johnson

Figure 8-15

Now, I'll put them together. A union combines multiple results with the same number of columns. Columns must have compatible data types. To keep things simple, I suggest that columns have the same names and the same data types. Because this is the case with these two queries, combining them is simple.

Try It Out

Enter and execute the following query:

```
SELECT TOP 5 FirstName, LastName FROM Employee
UNION
SELECT TOP 5 FirstName, LastName FROM Individual
```

Note that each SELECT statement could be executed as an independent query. Although not absolutely necessary, all of the columns have the same name. Figure 8-16 shows the results.

	FirstName	LastName
1	Christy	Zhu
2	Elizabeth	Johnson
3	Eugene	Huang
4	Gail	Erickson
5	Jian Shuo	Wang
6	Jon	Yang
7	Michael	Sullivan
8	Ruben	Torres
9	Sharon	Salavaria
10	Terri	Duffy

Figure 8-16

The problem with this result set is that you have no way of knowing what table each of the rows came from. Depending on what you intend to do with this data, this may or may not be important. In case it is, you need to tag each row with a value indicating its source. This is easily accomplished by adding an alias in the individual SELECT statements:

```
SELECT TOP 5 FirstName, LastName, 'I' AS Source FROM Individual
UNION
SELECT TOP 5 FirstName, LastName, 'E' AS Source FROM Employee
```

By creating a Source alias, you provide a literal value. In the results shown in Figure 8-17, this indicates whether the person is an individual customer or an employee.

	FirstName	LastName	Source
1	Christy	Zhu	I
2	Elizabeth	Johnson	I
3	Eugene	Huang	I
4	Gail	Erickson	E
5	Jian Shuo	Wang	E
6	Jon	Yang	I
7	Michael	Sullivan	E
8	Ruben	Torres	I
9	Sharon	Salavaria	E
10	Terri	Duffy	E

Figure 8-17

The UNION operator when used by itself is actually a UNION DISTINCT. This means that the two queries are merged, sorted, and any duplicates removed. Notice the FirstName column in Figure 8-16. The values are in alphabetical order. This is the result of the implied DISTINCT/SORT operation that accompanies the UNION. On the surface this may seem like a good idea, and it may be, but the additional overhead of sorting and removing duplicates can be quite costly when used against large tables. For best performance, use the UNION ALL operator instead. The UNION ALL operator simply concatenates the two results together. Just keep in mind that if the same first name–last name combination existed in both the Employee and Individual table, it would appear twice.

This is kind of a cool trick—I can combine records from multiple tables to produce a unified result set. But what does this really buy me? What is the practical business application of a union? I'll show you a powerful yet simple way to solve what used to be a huge business problem in the following scenario.

Partitioning and Federating Data

In the early days of client/server computing, there were two different approaches to managing data. A database was either managed centrally, in a mainframe or midrange hosted environment; or data was stored in small-scale, file-based data stores. There really wasn't a middle ground between these two options. To compensate for the lack of desktop database scalability, programmers found creative ways to replicate and synchronize data, but none of these work-around solutions provided true concurrency.

Here's a scenario that nearly all of us can relate to: When you make a purchase with a credit card, the store uses a merchant service provider to authorize and transact the purchase. This could be a service offered by their bank, credit card company, or a third-party clearinghouse. Your card number is sent to a data center, a query is executed against a database to retrieve your account information, and then records are added to complete the transaction. Most likely, the bank doesn't have one central data center. A data center is a facility housing a group of computer servers. PC-based servers are often clustered together to form a single, virtual server. Essentially, it's a bunch of PCs lumped together, pretending to be a more powerful computer—almost like a mainframe. The bank probably has a few regional data centers, and merchants connect to one closest to them. For simplicity, assume that my bank has merchant services data centers in Seattle (west coast accounts) and Atlanta (east coast accounts).

I live, and my bank accounts are based, in the Seattle area. If I were to make a purchase at a local store—or a store anywhere in the western United States—the transaction would be processed in the Seattle data center. If someone whose bank account is managed in another data center were to make a purchase in the Seattle area, a connection from the local data center to the customer's home data center would be used to retrieve their account information. Here's how this might work.

If these accounts were managed in SQL Server, a remote server connection may be used to provide on-demand connectivity to a database in another regional data center. In this example, I use the server names EastCoastServer and WestCoastServer to represent the remote servers and LocalHost to represent the respective local server. At each data center, the local database contains a view (a stored SELECT query) called vw_AllAccounts. In the Seattle regional center, the SQL script for the view looks like this:

```
SELECT AccountNumber, Balance, CreditLimit, CustomerName
FROM LocalHost.dbo.AccountDatabase.WestCoastAccounts
UNION
SELECT AccountNumber, Balance, CreditLimit, CustomerName
FROM EastCoastServer.AccountDatabase.dbo.EastCoastAccounts
```

In Atlanta, a view with the same name looks like this:

```
SELECT AccountNumber, Balance, CreditLimit, CustomerName
FROM LocalHost.dbo.AccountDatabase.EastCoastAccounts
UNION
SELECT AccountNumber, Balance, CreditLimit, CustomerName
FROM WestCoastServer.AccountDatabase.dbo.WestCoastAccounts
```

In each of the regional databases, the local accounts table (either WestCoastAccounts or EastCoastAccounts) is used to manage accounts in that region. The account lookup is performed using a stored procedure that accepts the account number as an input parameter and then looks up a record by matching this value to the AccountNumber column. Because there will only ever be one matching record, the stored procedure's SELECT statement uses a TOP 1 modifier that causes the database to stop searching for records after it locates one. The stored procedure script looks like this:

```
CREATE PROCEDURE spGetAccount
      @AccountNumber Int
AS
      SELECT TOP 1 * FROM vw_AllAccounts
```

As you can see, this is just a simple SELECT statement with a parameterized value (@AccountNumber) that gets passed in when it is executed. Chapter 13 uses the views and stored procedure to discuss what happens when the credit card transaction is processed.

Performance and Scaling Considerations

Now, let's look at a smaller-scale implementation to improve performance and efficiently manage a large volume of data. In this scenario, sales records are stored in a single table. Perhaps several thousand records are inserted each month. To report on this data over a period of years, it would be necessary to keep perhaps millions of rows in the sales table. Managing such a large volume of data in an active database will inevitably slow performance and raise administrative costs. At first glance this may seem like a perplexing challenge.

Let's view the facts and consider the options to resolve this quandary. To effectively deal with performance issues, you must first identify the bottlenecks. What's typically the slowest part of a computer system? Nearly all system components are solid-state, route electronic signals moving at near the speed of light and rely on transistors switching pulses at millions of times per second. Computers process data at incredible speeds but continue to store it on spinning disks, using mechanical armatures to write and read values. The hard disk is almost always the slowest part of a system. When retrieving data, other components wait while the disk controller finds and moves the read/write head to the right track and then waits for the disk to rotate to the sectors containing the data bits, assembling interlaced values as the disk rotates multiple times. The head is relocated again until all data is retrieved. You can't speed up the disk, but you can spread data across multiple disks to speed up the overall process.

In a partitioned storage solution, data is split up onto multiple disks. This affords SQL Server the opportunity to retrieve data in parallel and make more efficient use of multiple disk drives. There are actually a few different approaches to multiple-disk storage. In this scenario, I'll present an unsophisticated but very effective technique using multiple tables and a Union query.

At the end of every year, a routine removes year-old sales records from the current sales table and inserts them into a specific archive table containing only that year's sales. Each of these tables is placed on a separate physical disk drive. Over a few years, there may be several tables. Suppose this system has been in place for five years, and the disks and tables are set up as shown in Figure 8-18.

Tables

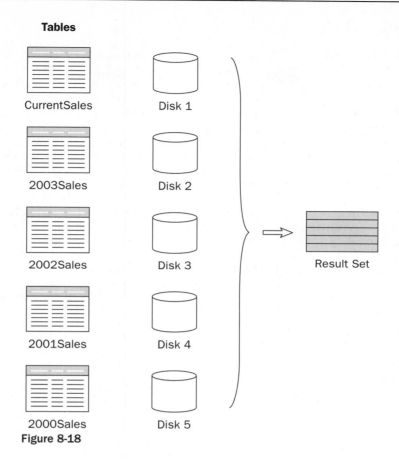

Figure 8-18

For reporting, a view is created that contains a series of UNION statements:

```
SELECT * From CurrentSales
UNION ALL
SELECT * From 2003Sales
UNION ALL
SELECT * From 2002Sales
UNION ALL
SELECT * From 2001Sales
UNION ALL
SELECT * From 2000Sales
```

When this query is executed, all of these disk drives may be accessed at the same time. Assuming there are no other performance barriers, this could theoretically improve performance by a factor of five. Not only is this query going to run faster, but it will also ease the burden on competing operations rather than blocking processes and other users' requests. You'll see some more specific examples of this type of query in the discussion on creating database objects in Chapter 13.

Summary

Dialects of SQL have evolved over the years and SQL Server understands different expressions and techniques that do the same thing. The ANSI-92 SQL standard helps to distill a variety of join techniques to a manageable number. This not only simplifies the choices, but also provides some guidance when maintaining code and scripts written by others. Follow the ANSI standard and use the techniques promoted by SQL Server. This will ensure that your queries will continue to work most efficiently going forward.

Joins provide a means to reassemble data back into meaningful information. The Inner Join matches rows between two tables whereas the Outer Joins select all rows from one side of the join and only matching rows from the other. Cross joins and Full joins, although less common in most applications, provide a means to match up combinations of rows from two tables that may not be related.

Union queries allow records from multiple tables to be combined, rather than joined, bringing rows into a single result set. This is an effective technique for partitioning and federating data in archive tables and databases in different geographic locations.

It's important to understand the impact of multi-table joins and unions. Query performance is significantly impacted by the use of indexes and data types. If done correctly, SQL Server can work very efficiently with a large volume of data. If not, complex queries can demand significant server resources and impede overall system performance and availability. Test your queries with real data, and analyze the execution plans to make sure your queries execute as you expect them to.

Exercises

Exercise 1

Create a list of vendors and the subtotal amounts for their purchase orders, sorted by vendor names. This list should include the vendor name and the subtotal amount for all vendors who have purchase orders recorded in the PurchaseOrderHeader table.

Exercise 2

In Chapter 7, exercise 3, you wrote a query to return the average pay rate for employees by gender for their managers. Extend this query and replace the ManagerID with the manager's name. Concatenate the manager's first and last name, separated with a space, from the employee table. Create an alias for this value called ManagerName. Create an alias to refer to the employee table used to obtain the managers' names called Managers.

Exercise 3

Write a query that returns a list of product subcategories and related products that don't have any sales order detail records. Include two columns, including the subcategory name labeled SubCategoryName and the product name labeled ProductName.

Data Transactions

We live in a transactional world. In the not-too-distant future, some of us may be trying to explain the concept of using cash to our grandchildren: "Most people carried paper and small metal disks around with them, and each one had a different a value. When you wanted to purchase something, you would hand the paper or metal money to a store clerk in exchange for the stuff you bought." What a strange idea. In the physical world, things move from one place to another. Like the money being handed to the store clerk by the customer, this transfer of ownership is a simple concept that even the least sophisticated members of the animal kingdom comprehend. In recent decades, though, mankind has managed to change the mechanics of moving things from one place to another within the information world. For example, on payday, chances are that you don't actually receive money directly from your employer. I don't even get a paycheck. My bank account balance is magically increased as my employer's contracted payroll company posts a credit to my account. Of course, this happens right before the balance decreases due to a similar transaction performed by my mortgage company.

We perceive that things such as money, files, and data move from one place to another. Although the paradigm is the same — modeled after things in the physical world — it's really all made up. We understand that data doesn't *really* move. It gets copied from storage and the new copy is inserted into a new storage location, and then the original copy is deleted from its initial location. Anyone who has worked with computer files or a word processor understands this concept. I think it's important, occasionally, to revisit the facts to fully understand what happens during this process.

Introducing Transactions

When I count money for a purchase and hand it to a store clerk, I have confidence that it's all going to make it to the cash drawer. If the power goes out or the cash register malfunctions, this shouldn't greatly affect our transaction because one of us has the money physically in our hand. As data is processed and moved from one place to another, electronic impulses cause memory registers to "remember" our data. In simple computer processes, this exchange can take place thousands of times. Until it is written to some form of permanent storage, the process can be easily interrupted and the data lost. Most of us have learned that the most effective way to prevent data loss is to make sure you always have at least two copies of your data. For example, if you intend to move an important file from one stand-alone computer's hard disk to another, you copy it from the hard disk to a portable disk or memory device; but you leave the original copy on the hard disk. Only after you verify that it has been copied to the target computer's hard disk would you consider deleting it from the source. And, you always make a backup copy of important files from the hard disk in case it fails, right?

In a database, a transaction is simply a mechanism to ensure and verify that data gets to its intended destination. Just like a purchase or bank transaction, both parties must be satisfied with the results. They must agree on the anticipated outcome. After the transaction has been completed, they should agree that all of the conditions of the transaction have been met and that everything is in the proper place.

Transaction Types

All modifications to data take place in the context of a transaction. SQL Server uses three types of transactions to manage data modification:

1. **Explicit Transaction.** The explicit transaction is defined by the presence of an explicit BEGIN TRANSACTION statement followed by one or more dependent data modification statements and completed with an explicit COMMIT TRANSACTION statement. Error checking is added prior to the COMMIT TRANSACTION statement so that if an error occurred the transaction can be reversed with a ROLLBACK TRANSACTION statement.

2. **Implicit Transaction.** The implicit transaction follows the behavior of some other database products in that whenever a data modification is executed it *implicitly* begins a transaction. However, it does not complete the transaction and release the modified data until an explicit COMMIT TRANSACTION or ROLLBACK TRANSACTION statement is issued. Implicit transactions are enabled on a connection basis with the SET IMPLICIT_TRANSACTIONS ON command.

3. **Auto-Commit Transaction.** If a data modification statement is executed against the database without an explicit or implicit transaction, it is considered an auto-commit transaction. The modification contained in an auto-commit transaction follows the same pattern as other transactions as described in the next section.

The ACID Test

Most of us have been burned enough by data loss problems to realize that steps must be taken to ensure that data gets from one place to another. Although there are a number of benefits, this is what transactions are all about. A bona fide transaction must meet the following criteria:

❑ **Atomic** — All steps and operations that are part of a transaction are treated as an *atomic* unit. Either *all* succeed or *all* fail together.

❑ **Consistent** — The outcome of any transaction is always predictable; all of the operations either fail or succeed. All operations abide by consistency rules and checks to ensure data integrity within the database.

❑ **Isolated** — Any operations performed before, during, or after the transaction will see related data in a consistent state, rather than in a state of partial completion. Any user or operation that queries data affected by a transaction will perceive that the entire transaction was committed instantaneously.

❑ **Durable** — If a transaction succeeds, data is written to disk and does not revert to its previous state. Data can survive system failure.

The Transaction Log

Meeting all of these criteria may seem like a rather tall order, but the way it works is actually quite elegant. SQL Server pulls this off with redundancy. When any data modification is executed, the following actions take place:

1. The appropriate data pages are located in memory. If they are not in memory, they are placed in memory from the disk.

2. The modifications (insert, update, or delete) are made to the applicable pages in memory.

3. The modifications are written to the transaction log.

4. The server issues a checkpoint that causes the changed (dirty) pages in memory to be written back to the hard disk. The pages in memory then have their "dirty" flag removed. If the transaction making the changes has been committed, the pages are released and other requests or transactions have access to them. If the checkpoint occurs prior to the transaction being committed, the pages are still locked until the transaction is committed.

The transaction log is a separate file used to collect all successful data modification requests from all users and applications. During the execution of a data modification request, the transaction exists in the buffer cache and log cache. During the changes to the data pages in memory, the pages (and the pages on disk representing the data to be changed) are locked (or isolated) from access by other requests or transactions. The pages remain locked until they are released from the transaction. Figure 9-1 illustrates the transaction process.

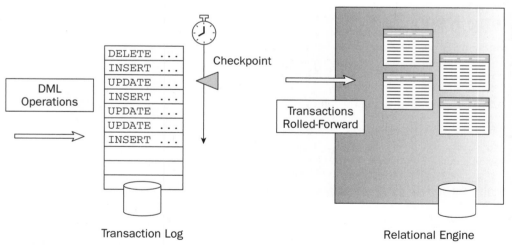

Figure 9-1

Depending on a database setting, the transaction log either continues to fill with archived transaction processes or gets truncated (removing all check-pointed transaction processes by setting the area of the transaction log up for overwrite). In a production database, the transaction log is typically allowed to grow until a scheduled backup cycle. This way, if the main database is damaged or lost, the transaction log becomes a short-term backup solution for new data.

Logged Operations

SQL Server's default behavior is to log all Insert, Update, and Delete operations. For the reasons I explained in the previous section, this generally makes sense. However, the transaction log and its related processes can burden the server with unnecessary work if you don't need this level of protection. For example, if I had exported several thousand records to a text file, intending to load this data into my SQL database, this would be an exception to the day-to-day inserts normally performed by applications. Because I have a copy of the data in the export file and have backed up the data in my database, if this operation failed, I would simply correct the problem and try again. In this case, I could speed things up by performing a non-logged insert and bypass the transaction log. This is usually done using a command-line utility or a feature of Data Transformation Services (DTS). Non-logged operations are really the exception to the rule. Bulk operations are not a core feature of SQL and are beyond the scope of this book. Two options for performing bulk inserts from external files include the bulk copy utility (BCP) and the Bulk Copy Task within Data Transformation Services (DTS), or Data Integration Services in SQL Server 2005. For more information, use the Books Online to read about the BCP utility and DTS.

Let's Do CRUD with Data

As previously mentioned, you can really only do four things with data: Create it, Read it, Update it, and Delete it. These four operations form the basis of what is commonly called CRUD operations. So far, you've been doing a lot of reading using the SELECT statement. Now it's time to work with data in a way that will affect the data in your database.

Adding Records

Adding rows is done using the INSERT statement. Inserts can be performed one row at a time or on multiple rows, depending on the technique, and target only one table. Before attempting to insert data into a table, it is important to know the following:

- ❑   Which columns require values
- ❑   Which columns have data-integrity constraints
- ❑   Which columns are managed by the database through functions
- ❑   Which columns have default values or allow null values
- ❑   What the data types of the destination columns are

To get started, take a look at the Product table in design view (see Figure 9-2).

This table has 27 columns, but only 1 column, the Name, requires a value because every other column either has a default value or accepts NULL. The ProductID column is the primary key. Because it is designated as an identity column, an incremental value will automatically be generated for this column by the database.

Column Name	Data Type	Length	Allow Nulls
ProductID	int	4	
Name	Name (nvarchar)	50	
ProductNumber	nvarchar	25	✓
DiscontinuedDate	datetime	8	✓
MakeFlag	Flag (bit)	1	
StandardCost	money	8	✓
FinishedGoodsFlag	Flag (bit)	1	
Color	nvarchar	15	✓
SafetyStockLevel	smallint	2	✓
ReorderPoint	smallint	2	✓
ListPrice	money	8	✓
[Size]	nvarchar	50	✓
SizeUnitMeasureCode	nchar	3	✓
ProductPhotoID	int	4	✓
WeightUnitMeasureCc	nchar	3	✓
Weight	float	8	✓
DaysToManufacture	int	4	✓
ProductLine	nchar	2	✓
DealerPrice	money	8	✓
Class	nchar	2	✓

Figure 9-2

INSERT Statement

If you only need to provide a value for this column, the statement would be quite simple:

```
INSERT INTO Product (Name)
SELECT 'Widget 1'
```

I'll pick this statement apart in the following sections and show you some variations of this type of query.

The INTO keyword is optional and is often omitted. I like to include it because I think it reads more like natural language. Two different styles are used with the INSERT statement, and each has its own subtleties. Generally, you could select one technique and pretty much use it for all of your insert operations. I'll show you some examples of each and let you decide when to use them.

INSERT. . . Values

The pattern of the INSERT statement is to provide a list of column names and then a list of values in parentheses. If values are provided for all columns or all columns with the exception of the identity column (only one identity column is allowed per table), no column name list is required. This technique is used to insert only one row into the table. The Contact table is one of the simplest in the Adventure Works2000 database so it makes a good example. I'm going to include values for four of the columns. Note that I'm skipping the ContactID column. If I were to include a value for the ContactID column, my INSERT statement would fail, because this column can only be managed by the IDENTITY() function of the database. In the INSERT statement itself, I include the column names and in the Values list, I provide a corresponding value:

```
INSERT INTO Contact (Salutation, FirstName, LastName, Phone)
VALUES ('Ms.', 'Pebbles', 'Flintstone', '123-4567')
```

Note the use of single quotes to denote literal values to be inserted into the table. If I had a numeric value to insert, I would not use the quotes. The order of the values must match the order of the columns in the table if no column list is provided, with the exception of any identity column that is omitted as the following example shows:

```
INSERT INTO Contact
VALUES ( 'Mr.', 'Fred', 'Caveman', 'Flintstone'
        , DEFAULT, '111-123-4567', 'Phd.', 'fredf@bedrock.com'
        , 'ILOveWilm@', 6, DEFAULT, DEFAULT, NULL)
```

NULL and DEFAULT values are covered in the section titled "Inserting NULL, Defaults, and other Column Considerations."

INSERT. . . SELECT

This form of the INSERT statement is similar to the previous values form except it uses a SELECT statement to provide values. As discussed in earlier chapters, the SELECT statement can return scalar literal values, as well as sets of literal values, without even hitting a table in the database. Because SELECT can be used to include a variety of different types of values (from tables, joins, unions, groups, aggregates, and literals), this is a much more flexible technique. Practically anything can be inserted as long as the column count and data types match. Because a SELECT statement can return multiple rows, this would result in multiple rows being inserted into the destination table. Following is the equivalent of the previous example using this technique. In this example, columns and values for the MiddleName and NameStyle columns have been omitted. This insert is successful because NULL will automatically be inserted (because these columns allow the NULL value):

```
INSERT INTO Contact (Salutation, FirstName, LastName, Phone)
SELECT 'Mr.', 'Bam Bam', 'Rubble', '234-5678'
```

Because I've executed the previous two INSERT statements, I'll just return all the records from the Contact table (SELECT * FROM Contact) and scroll down to view the last two rows, shown in Figure 9-3.

	ContactID	Salutation	FirstName	MiddleName	LastName	NameStyle	Phone
988	988	Mr.	Arvid	B.	Ziegler	0	398-087-8579
989	989	Ms.	Karin	NULL	Zimprich	0	183-335-0350
990	990	Ms.	Juanita	J.	Zocchi	0	194-086-6762
991	991	Ms.	Carla	J.	Zubaty	0	516-870-3661
992	992	Ms.	Patricia	M.	Zubaty	0	175-359-1677
993	993	Ms.	Judy	N.	Zugelder	0	611-965-6823
994	994	Mr.	Michael	J.	Zwilling	0	542-788-1394
995	995	Ms.	Cathan	NULL	Cook	0	55-231-8901
996	996	Ms.	Pebbles	NULL	Flintstone	0	123-4567
997	997	Mr.	Bam Bam	NULL	Rubble	0	234-5678

Figure 9-3

You can see that the ContactID column contains an auto-generated, sequential identity value. The MiddleName column is set to NULL and the NameStyle is set to its default value of 0.

Inserting NULL, Defaults, and other Column Considerations

Different settings at the server, database, and user session level for SQL Server can affect the way NULL is available for a particular column. Although not necessarily complicated, this can be a particularly confusing issue because there are a number of variable elements to be considered. Before you read on, please keep in mind that this only becomes an issue if the default settings are altered and, in any case, the situation can be remedied by explicitly defining columns in tables as NULL or NOT NULL.

Database properties can be modified through SQL Server Enterprise Manager or the SQL Server Management Studio or by using SQL script. In Enterprise Manager or Management Studio, right-click the database icon and choose Properties from the menu. For reference, I've included these interfaces. In both examples, the ANSI_NULL_DEFAULT option is set to False.

Figure 9-4 shows the Properties dialog (Options tab) for SQL Server 2000.

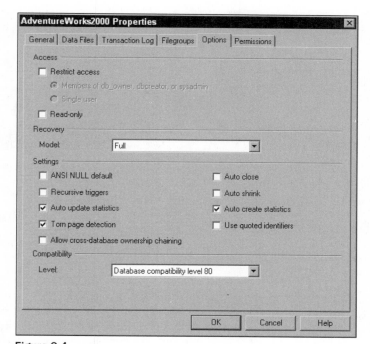

Figure 9-4

Figure 9-5 shows the Properties dialog (Options tab) for SQL Server 2005.

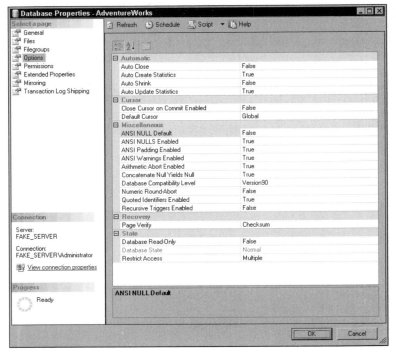

Figure 9-5

The same settings can be applied using script similar to the following:

```
sp_dboption 'AdventureWorks2000','ANSI Null Default','False'
```

The following script will override the database default setting when executed prior to creating or altering a table:

```
SET ANSI_NULL_DFLT_ON ON
```

When a table is created, the database settings apply unless they are explicitly overridden in the session. When ANSI_NULL_DEFAULT is set to ON (True), all user-defined columns and data types that have not explicitly been defined as NOT NULL during the creation or altering process of the table default to allowing NULL values. This is the opposite of the default setting for SQL Server when installed. It is good practice to explicitly define NULL and NOT NULL regardless of the current or eventual resetting of ANSI_NULL_DEFAULT. If this setting has been altered, the INSERT statements assume that the opposite will fail. Note that Constraints (Check and Default) will apply before NULL.

Looking at the Contact table, the columns that are explicitly NOT NULL are as follows:

- ContactID
- LastName
- NameStyle

❑   ModifiedDate

❑   rowguid

Of these, the ContactID value is supplied by the IDENTITY() function. The NameStyle, ModifiedDate, and rowguid are supplied by Default Constraints if no values are explicitly provided (the rowguid's Default Constraint employs the NEWID() function that can be used to generate a Globally Unique Identifier [GUID]). All other columns, as previously stated, are explicitly defined to either prohibit or allow NULL values.

Inserting Rows from Another Table

Using the Insert. . . Select pattern, I can bring data from another table or complex query. Conveniently, the Employee table contains human being–type data I can use to populate the Contact table. Columns in my select list don't have to have the same names but do have to be compatible data types. First, I'll just use a SELECT statement to view the Employee row I intend to insert:

```
SELECT FirstName, LastName, EmergencyContactPhone
FROM Employee
WHERE EmployeeID = 265
```

This returns one record, as shown in Figure 9-6.

	FirstName	LastName	EmergencyContactPhone
1	Jason	Carlson	324-014-2651

Figure 9-6

It is a best practice to always test the SELECT statements that will be used in transaction statements to prevent failures within the Insert, Update, or Delete statement. Step two is to add the INSERT statement to the front of this query and make sure the columns match up between the two lists:

```
INSERT INTO Contact
       (FirstName, LastName, Phone)
SELECT FirstName, LastName, EmergencyContactPhone
FROM Employee
WHERE EmployeeID = 265
```

Finally, execute a SELECT statement against the Contact table and scroll to the bottom of the list to check the result, as shown in Figure 9-7.

	ContactID	Salutation	FirstName	MiddleName	LastName	NameStyle	Phone
989	989	Ms.	Karin	NULL	Zimprich	0	183-335-0350
990	990	Ms.	Juanita	J.	Zocchi	0	194-086-6762
991	991	Ms.	Carla	J.	Zubaty	0	516-870-3661
992	992	Ms.	Patricia	M.	Zubaty	0	175-359-1677
993	993	Ms.	Judy	N.	Zugelder	0	611-965-6823
994	994	Mr.	Michael	J.	Zwilling	0	542-788-1394
995	995	Ms.	Cathan	NULL	Cook	0	55-231-8901
996	996	Ms.	Pebbles	NULL	Flintstone	0	123-4567
997	997	Mr.	Bam Bam	NULL	Rubble	0	234-5678
998	998	NULL	Jason	NULL	Carlson	0	324-014-2651

Figure 9-7

Great care should be taken to limit the size (rows returned) of the SELECT statement with a WHERE clause when querying another table. Each row requested in the SELECT statement will remain locked from changes during the Insert process. This will momentarily block other requests for operations performed on the same table. In an active, multi-user database, nearly every operation carries a statistical possibility of coinciding with a conflicting operation. Most of the time, these operations are simply queued to execute in turn. The database engine will retry a blocked transaction before it times out in error. However, if two competing operations happen to lock the same tables and are waiting for the availability of locked objects before they can continue, this could result in a deadlock situation in the database. The specific behavior will depend on transaction-level locking options and database settings.

SELECT INTO

At times, you may want to populate a new or a temporary table with the results of a query, a technique that can be a real time-saver. Instead of creating a new table the old-fashioned way (by defining all of the columns and data types), and then using an INSERT statement to populate the new table from existing data, this statement simply creates the table on-the-fly using the output and data types from a SELECT statement. Although we try to avoid storing duplicate data when it's not necessary, sometimes it's just easier to copy results into a table for temporary storage — sort of a snapshot of information that alleviates locking of the transactional table by read requests for reports and so on. This might be especially useful to support a complicated report. The results of a complex query may be written to a table either in the current database, a reporting database or warehouse, or the TempDB database, where the data can be reused in other queries. The INSERT INTO statement requires that you target an existing table. If you want to create a new table from the results of the query (from one or multiple tables), use the SELECT INTO statement. In this example, I select a subset of contact records and create a new table called MyContacts:

```
SELECT * INTO MyContacts
FROM Contact WHERE Salutation = 'Sr.'
```

Keep in mind that the new table is a permanent member of the database like any other table, unless you have placed it in the TempDB database as a temporary table. Typically, in a production environment, a database administrator wouldn't grant the privilege to create new tables to all users. If you only need to use the data for a short time, you can create a temporary table by starting the table name with a pound sign (#) or double pound sign (##). A single pound sign denotes a local temporary object that is only visible from the current connection. A double pound sign denotes a global temporary object that is visible to all connections as long as the connection that created it is still active. Here is the same statement that creates a temporary table:

```
SELECT * INTO #MyContacts
FROM Contact WHERE Salutation = 'Sr.'
```

The difference between this and the previous example is that the table will be created in the TempDB database. When the connection used to create this table is closed, SQL Server automatically removes the table and reclaims the storage space. The local temporary table is often used in a stored procedure where cursors are inefficient. The stored procedure first creates the temporary table using a SELECT INTO statement and then returns rows from this table as a result set. When the stored procedure completes and the connection is closed, the local temporary table in TempDB is dropped.

Managing Inserts Using Stored Procedures

In a large-scale, production environment, administrators often limit users' ability to insert, update, and delete records directly. Implementing such restrictions while accommodating all user and application needs requires careful planning and can be a lot of work. One popular approach is to deny users all transactional activity against tables and create stored procedures to manage the inserts, updates, and deletes. For each major entity in the database, there will typically be at least three stored procedures: to insert, update, and delete records in that table. Using stored procedures offers the added benefit of enforcing any special business rules, simplifying complex tables and returning custom error messages.

Earlier you looked at the design of the Product table and should recall that several columns don't require values. For the sake of simplicity, I will create a stored procedure to insert rows into the Product table, providing values for just a few of these columns. Chapter 13 takes a comprehensive look at stored procedures. For now, I'll keep this simple.

```
CREATE PROCEDURE spIns_Product
    @ProductName    nVarChar(50),
    @ProductNumber  nVarChar(25),
    @StandardCost   Money
AS
    INSERT INTO Product (name, ProductNumber, StandardCost)
    SELECT @ProductName, @ProductNumber, @StandardCost
RETURN @@Identity
```

This procedure accepts three input parameters: @ProductName, @ProductNumer, and @StandardCost. These parameters are used to pass values to the INSERT statement. The global constant @@Identity is used to obtain the last identity value, in this case, the new ProductID value generated by this INSERT statement. To test this procedure, execute the following SQL statement:

```
spIns_Product 'Gadget', '23456', 49.95
```

Modifying Records

When any data in a record or group of records is modified, the user or application making the changes must have exclusive access to the record or records for a short period of time. This locking mechanism is an important part of SQL Server's transaction management model. So, what exactly gets locked? This depends on different factors. SQL Server supports row-level locking and, when feasible, will lock a single row so that neighboring rows don't get locked, affecting other users. This was an issue in earlier versions of SQL Server that supported only page-level locking. In truth, SQL Server will sometimes lock all of the records in an 8KB page, SQL Server's native storage allocation unit. It may do this because it deems this method to be faster or more efficient than locking individual records. Based on inter-table relationships, when a row is modified in one table, locks may be placed on dependent rows in the related table. It may also choose to lock an entire table, groups of tables, or even the entire database, under certain circumstances.

The database engine must make decisions about how it will process each transaction. Based on the scope or number of records involved in a transaction, different locking options may be invoked to manage the transaction as efficiently as possible. With rare exception, this should be completely transparent to all users and operations. Any concurrent or conflicting requests are simply queued and executed in turn. Only after a transaction request has waited several seconds will it time-out and return an error. Fortunately, SQL Server manages record-locking and data modification automatically. Understanding the fundamentals of SQL Server's locking behavior will help you work with the database engine as you modify data. Multi-table updates and other conditions where you should be mindful of these issues are discussed at the end of this chapter.

UPDATE Command

Data is modified one table at a time. A single UPDATE statement can affect one, many, or all records in a table depending on filtering criteria. The syntax is uncomplicated. Column values are modified using the SET keyword.

Filtering Updates

There is no undo feature in SQL Server, short of restoring a backup. Because an update can affect many records, it's important to be absolutely sure of the records you intend to modify. To be cautious, a trial is advisable using only a SELECT query. Inspect the rows returned and then, after you verify that these are the rows you want to change and that the target values are correct, add the UPDATE command to your query. Here's an example. My objective is to raise the standard cost for all mountain bikes by 10 percent. I'm going to break this down into steps to verify the records and my calculation before actually performing the update.

The first step is to perform a simple SELECT query. This query returns the product name and current cost:

```
SELECT Name, StandardCost
FROM Product
WHERE ProductSubCategoryID = 1
```

In the results, shown in Figure 9-8, I verify that these are all mountain bikes and that the StandardCost column contains the values I want to modify.

	Name	StandardCost
1	Mountain-500 Black, 40	399.5926
2	Mountain-500 Black, 42	399.5926
3	Mountain-500 Black, 44	399.5926
4	Mountain-500 Black, 48	399.5926
5	Mountain-500 Black, 52	399.5926
6	Mountain-500 Black, 62	399.9900
7	Mountain-500 Red, 40	399.9900
8	Mountain-500 Red, 44	399.9900
9	Mountain-500 Red, 52	399.9900
10	Mountain-500 Red, 56	399.9900

Figure 9-8

The next step is to calculate the new value for the StandardCost column. I'll create an additional column with the calculated value:

```
SELECT Name, StandardCost, StandardCost * 1.1
FROM Product
WHERE ProductSubCategoryID = 1
```

Now, I check the calculated value and take a quick look over the entire list to make sure everything is in order (see Figure 9-9).

	Name	StandardCost	
1	Mountain-500 Bl...	399.5926	439.55186
2	Mountain-500 Bl...	399.5926	439.55186
3	Mountain-500 Bl...	399.5926	439.55186
4	Mountain-500 Bl...	399.5926	439.55186
5	Mountain-500 Bl...	399.5926	439.55186
6	Mountain-500 Bl...	399.9900	439.98900
7	Mountain-500 R...	399.9900	439.98900
8	Mountain-500 R...	399.9900	439.98900
9	Mountain-500 R...	399.9900	439.98900
10	Mountain-500 R...	399.9900	439.98900

Figure 9-9

The calculated value is correct — a 10 percent increase — and the row selection is correct, so I'll move on to the next step and prepare to modify these rows.

The FROM clause gets moved to the top and becomes the UPDATE statement. I'm dropping the Name column because it's not affected by this query and then I'm using the remaining two references to the StandardCost column to form the SET statement:

```
UPDATE Product
SET StandardCost = StandardCost * 1.1
WHERE ProductSubCategoryID = 1
```

When this statement is executed in Query Analyzer or the Query Editor, no results are returned. The following message is displayed on the Messages tab:

```
Command(s) completed successfully
```

To verify the results, I'll execute the first query again:

```
SELECT Name, StandardCost
FROM Product
WHERE ProductSubCategoryID = 1
```

This time, the StandardCost values have increased by 10 percent, as shown in Figure 9-10.

	Name	StandardCost
1	Mountain-500 Black, 40	439.5519
2	Mountain-500 Black, 42	439.5519
3	Mountain-500 Black, 44	439.5519
4	Mountain-500 Black, 48	439.5519
5	Mountain-500 Black, 52	439.5519
6	Mountain-500 Black, 62	439.9890
7	Mountain-500 Red, 40	439.9890
8	Mountain-500 Red, 44	439.9890
9	Mountain-500 Red, 52	439.9890
10	Mountain-500 Red, 56	439.9890

Figure 9-10

When working with important data, I try to make it a point to test my queries in this way before actually performing the update. Often, I won't if it's a simple query and I'm certain that I have it right the first time. However, I've learned that it's better to err on the side of caution. In any case, make sure you have a current backup copy of the data just in case things don't go as planned.

Now, let's look at some variations of the UPDATE statement. In the previous example, I updated one column value. Modifying multiple values is quite easy. Each column value assignment is included in a comma-delimited list in the SET statement. This statement shows how to update a product record with multiple column values:

```
UPDATE Product
SET  Name = 'Trail Bike-500 Grey, 40mm'
   , StandardCost = 489.00
   , Color = 'Grey'
WHERE ProductID = 8
```

I can view all mountain bikes with this query:

```
SELECT ProductID, Name, StandardCost, Color
FROM Product
WHERE ProductSubCategoryID = 1
```

This, of course, includes my new grey trail bike with the inflated price, as shown in Figure 9-11.

	ProductID	Name	StandardCost	Color
1	8	Trail Bike-500 Grey, 40mm	489.0000	Grey
2	9	Mountain-500 Black, 42	439.5519	Black
3	10	Mountain-500 Black, 44	439.5519	Black
4	11	Mountain-500 Black, 48	439.5519	Black
5	12	Mountain-500 Black, 52	439.5519	Black
6	15	Mountain-500 Black, 62	439.9890	Black
7	16	Mountain-500 Red, 40	439.9890	Red
8	17	Mountain-500 Red, 44	439.9890	Red
9	19	Mountain-500 Red, 52	439.9890	Red
10	20	Mountain-500 Red, 56	439.9890	Red

Figure 9-11

Updating Rows Based on Multiple Tables

Sometimes you will need to modify records in one table based on conditions in another table. This can be accomplished using a join or subquery. The rule is that you can only update column values in one table. In the following example, I join the SalesOrderHeader and SalesOrderDetail tables. Based on criteria in the header table, I modify the order quantity value in the related detail row:

```
UPDATE  SalesOrderDetail
SET     OrderQty = 10
FROM    SalesOrderDetail INNER JOIN SalesOrderHeader
        ON SalesOrderDetail.SalesOrderID = SalesOrderHeader.SalesOrderID
WHERE   SalesOrderHeader.PurchaseOrderNumber = 'PO29199294'
```

In this case, there is only one related detail row but there could be multiple detail rows related to the header row.

When setting values, it's common to derive those values from various system functions. One of the simplest and most common of these functions is GETDATE(), which returns the current date and time. Using this function, I'll stamp an order record to indicate that it has been shipped. First, I'll set the stage for this scenario. In the AdventureWorks2000 database, all of the order records have already been marked as having been shipped. Suppose that a customer calls your customer service department asking about their order. You look up the order and see that it is marked as having been shipped to the customer. Upon careful investigation, you discover that the package was returned because the customer's address was incorrect. Your first order of business is to update the record to indicate that it was not shipped (or at least not received by the customer). The order in question is SalesOrderID 5005. This statement will remove the ship date, setting it to null:

```
UPDATE SalesOrderHeader
SET ShipDate = Null
WHERE SalesOrderID = 5005
```

Now you obtain the correct address and schedule the package for shipment. Once confirmed, you update the order record with the current data and time using the GETDATE() function:

```
UPDATE SalesOrderHeader
SET ShipDate = GETDATE()
WHERE SalesOrderID = 5005
```

Updating Using Views

Most database professionals agree that the traditional purpose for views is to provide a read-only view of data from tables. One of the most compelling capabilities is that sensitive data can be secured and protected — both selected rows and columns hidden from the user's view. Complicated queries and joins can be represented as if they were a single table. We don't normally think of these "virtual tables" as being updatable but it is possible to update records through views under certain conditions. Updates can only affect the columns of one table at a time. Further, values created by grouping and aggregation cannot be updated. As a rule, if you intend to create a view to support updates, it should either reference only one table or multiple tables through inner joins. All required columns must be included, and update statements must include only references to a single table within the view.

Updating Records Using Stored Procedures

Probably the most comprehensive and secure method for managing record updates is to allow updates only through stored procedures. When this approach is taken, a separate stored procedure is typically used to modify the records for each major entity in the database. The following example is a stored procedure to modify a record in the Product table. I've made a point to include all of the columns in this table just to demonstrate what this would normally look like:

```
ALTER PROCEDURE spUpd_Product
    @ProductID              Int
  , @ProductName            nVarChar(50)
  , @ProductNumber          nVarChar(25)
  , @DiscontinuedDate       DateTime = Null
  , @MakeFlag               Bit = 1
```

```
  , @StandardCost            Money = Null
  , @FinishedGoodsFlag       Bit = 1
  , @Color                   nVarChar(15) = Null
  , @SafetyStockLevel        SmallInt = Null
  , @ReorderPoint            SmallInt = Null
  , @ListPrice               Money = Null
  , @Size                    nVarChar(50) = Null
  , @SizeUnitMeasureCode     nChar(3) = Null
  , @ProductPhotoID          Int = Null
  , @WeightUnitMeasureCode   nChar(3) = Null
  , @Weight                  Float = Null
  , @DaysToManufacture       Int = Null
  , @ProductLine             nChar(2) = Null
  , @DealerPrice             Money = Null
  , @Class                   nChar(2) = Null
  , @Style                   nChar(2) = Null
  , @ProductSubCategoryID    SmallInt = Null
  , @ProductModelID          Int = Null
  , @SellStartDate           DateTime = Null
  , @SellEndDate             DateTime = Null
AS
UPDATE Product
SET
  Name = @ProductName
, ProductNumber = @ProductNumber
, DiscontinuedDate = @DiscontinuedDate
, MakeFlag = @MakeFlag
, StandardCost = @StandardCost
, FinishedGoodsFlag = @FinishedGoodsFlag
, Color = @Color
, SafetyStockLevel = @SafetyStockLevel
, ReorderPoint = @ReorderPoint
, ListPrice = @ListPrice
, Size = @Size
, SizeUnitMeasureCode = @SizeUnitMeasureCode
, ProductPhotoID = @ProductPhotoID
, WeightUnitMeasureCode = @WeightUnitMeasureCode
, Weight = @Weight
, DaysToManufacture = @DaysToManufacture
, ProductLine = @ProductLine
, DealerPrice = @DealerPrice
, Class = @Class
, Style = @Style
, ProductSubCategoryID = @ProductSubCategoryID
, ProductModelID = @ProductModelID
, rowguid = NEWID()
, SellStartDate = @SellStartDate
, SellEndDate = @SellEndDate
WHERE ProductID = @ProductID
```

Note that most of the parameters in the list of input parameters (the variable names preceded with @) are assigned default values. Some accept Null whereas others, such as the @MakeFlag and @FinishedGoodsFlag, are set to the bit value 1, or True. This is so these parameters are optional when executing the procedure. The rowguid column is set using the NEWID() function to generate a unique value. This may or may not be appropriate logic in an update procedure. I've included this just to demonstrate a variety of techniques for setting values.

This stored procedure is actually simplified. In production, procedures typically include some conditional business logic and error-handling code. These scripts can be time-consuming and cumbersome to write. However, once written and debugged, using stored procedures can significantly simplify data management going forward. Chapter 10 revisits this stored procedure when discussing the finer points of database programming.

To test the procedure, I'm going to update the record I inserted using the insert stored procedure, spIns_Product. The first thing I need to do is get the ProductID value for this record. I select all product records and find that the ProductID value is 1302. The following script can be used to modify this record using the procedure:

```
spUpd_Product 1302, 'Super Gadget Deluxe', '98765'
```

Because all of the input parameters after the first three have values set in the body of the procedure, I must supply values only for the first three. All other columns will be set to these default values.

Removing Records

Removing records from a table is very easy to do — maybe too easy. Depending on your viewpoint, this convenience could be a blessing or a curse. Take caution before you start practicing your deleting skills on production data. Having said that, I'm going to ask SQL Server to delete all of the product records in the AdventureWorks2000 database.

DELETE Command

As you can see, this is a simple statement. There is no need to address specific columns because the DELETE statement removes entire rows of data:

```
DELETE FROM Product
```

The FROM clause is actually optional. Personally, I find it a little easier to read this statement with the FROM clause but that's a minor point. This statement does the same thing:

```
DELETE Product
```

Did it work? No. SQL Server returned an error — fortunately:

```
Server: Msg 547, Level 16, State 1, Line 1

DELETE statement conflicted with COLUMN REFERENCE constraint
'FK_Product_BillOfMaterials_ComponentID'. The conflict occurred in database
'AdventureWorks2000', table 'BillOfMaterials', column 'ComponentID'.

The statement has been terminated.
```

Due to the foreign key constraint displayed in the error the statement failed. The database won't allow rows to be deleted if there are related rows in another table. What about the product records that do not have related records in another table? That's not going to happen either, because every Insert, Update, and Delete statement is automatically wrapped into a transaction. You'll recall that transactions are an all-or-nothing proposition; either all the records are affected or none of them are. In this case, no records are affected.

Embrace the WHERE Clause

Just as when updating records, it's important to test the water and make sure you delete the records you intend to. The Product table has foreign key constraints defined with several tables, which make it difficult to delete existing records. For demonstration purposes, I'll add a few products that we can play with:

```
INSERT INTO Product (Name, ProductNumber, StandardCost, ListPrice)
SELECT 'Widget 2002', 'wi002', 50.05, 49.99

INSERT INTO Product (Name, ProductNumber, StandardCost, ListPrice)
SELECT 'Widget 2003', 'wi003', 55.97, 54.99

INSERT INTO Product (Name, ProductNumber, StandardCost, ListPrice)
SELECT 'Widget 2004', 'wi004', 42.97, 49.99

INSERT INTO Product (Name, ProductNumber, StandardCost, ListPrice)
SELECT 'Widget 2005', 'wi005', 45.97, 49.99
```

Your objective is to remove all product records for products that would be unprofitable to sell, where the ListPrice is less than the StandardCost. Before actually deleting any records, test your criteria using a SELECT statement:

```
SELECT ProductID, Name, ProductNumber, ListPrice, StandardCost
FROM Product
WHERE StandardCost > ListPrice
```

Two rows meet these criteria, as shown in Figure 9-12.

	ProductID	Name	ProductNumber	ListPrice	StandardCost
1	1312	Widget 2002	wi002	49.9900	50.0500
2	1313	Widget 2003	wi003	54.9900	55.9700

Figure 9-12

After verifying that these are the records you intend to delete, write the DELETE statement, appending this WHERE clause to the end to affect the same records:

```
DELETE FROM Product
WHERE StandardCost > ListPrice
```

These two records are deleted.

Deleting Records Based on Another Table

You may need to remove records from one table based on conditions in another table. Usually there will be a relationship of some kind between these tables. Deletes can be facilitated using any type of join or subquery expression between multiple tables.

How It Works

In this scenario, suppose that one of your salespeople, Amy Alberts, has left the company and you want to archive all of the related sales orders and detail records. You've already copied these records to their respective archive tables so now all you need to do is delete them. Amy was the salesperson for 39 sales order records with 586 related order detail records.

Try It Out

Before you continue I'm going to recommend that you back up the AdventureWorks2000 database just in case things don't go as planned. In this exercise, you should only remove a small number of records but it's better to be safe than sorry.

Figure 9-13 shows the relationship between the tables involved. By specifying an EmployeeID (on the left side of the diagram), you can delete related SalesOrderDetail rows. The SalesOrderHeader, which defines orders, is related to the SalesPerson table through the SalesPersonID foreign key. This is a many-to-many intersect table between Employee and SalesOrderHeader. Order details, in the SalesOrderDetail table, are related to orders through the SalesOrderID foreign key column. Because it's on the outer side of the relationships and nothing else depends on it, begin by deleting rows from this table first.

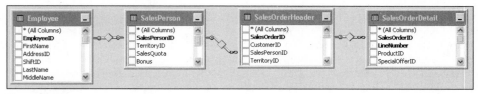

Figure 9-13

There are a few techniques and this is one of the easiest. Earlier you saw how the IN() function is used to compare a value to a comma-delimited list of values. The same function can be used to compare a value with a single-column result set. The mechanics are simple: create any SELECT query that returns a single column. Pass this query to the IN() function used in the WHERE clause of a DELETE statement:

```
DELETE FROM SalesOrderDetail
WHERE    SalesOrderID IN(
         SELECT SalesOrderDetail.SalesOrderID
         FROM SalesOrderHeader
           INNER JOIN SalesPerson
             ON SalesOrderHeader.SalesPersonID = SalesPerson.SalesPersonID
           INNER JOIN Employee
             ON SalesPerson.SalesPersonID = Employee.EmployeeID
           WHERE Employee.FirstName = 'Amy' And Employee.LastName = 'Alberts' )
```

This deletes the 586 order detail records. Removing the sales order records is easy and requires only a simple change. Because the SalesOrderID is also the identifying column for records in the SalesOrderHeader table, all you need to do is change the table name in the DELETE statement:

```
DELETE FROM SalesOrderHeader
WHERE     SalesOrderID IN(
            SELECT SalesOrderDetail.SalesOrderID
            FROM SalesOrderHeader
              INNER JOIN SalesPerson
                ON SalesOrderHeader.SalesPersonID = SalesPerson.SalesPersonID
              INNER JOIN Employee
                ON SalesPerson.SalesPersonID = Employee.EmployeeID
            WHERE Employee.FirstName = 'Amy' And Employee.LastName = 'Alberts' )
```

This deletes the 39 sales orders. It was necessary to delete the order detail rows first because these records depend on the existence of the sales order records in the SalesOrderHeader table.

TRUNCATE TABLE

The DELETE command is a logged operation. For deletes on a small number of rows or manual operations, there may be a negligible difference in performance. However, for repeated and automated deletes, or on a large volume of records, skipping the transaction logging can improve performance dramatically.

The TRUNCATE TABLE command does only one thing—it removes all of the records in a table without logging a transaction. It performs the deletes in a manner far more efficiently than the DELETE command. You cannot filter specific rows to delete or use any kind of selection criteria. Please do not execute the following query. This statement will very efficiently remove all order detail records:

```
TRUNCATE TABLE SalesOrderDetail
```

I'm going to perform a performance test, comparing the Delete and Truncate techniques. I don't intend for you to follow along because it would take a bit of work to set this up. I've created two additional databases, called AW_1 and AW_2. Using a DTS package, I've copied all of the objects and data from AdventureWorks2000 into these two databases. The following script gets the current time before and after performing each of these two operations. After each, I compare the two times and display the number of milliseconds that it took to complete the operation.

```
DECLARE @starttime DateTime
DECLARE @endtime DateTime
DECLARE @totaltime Int

USE AW_1 -- Copy 1 of AdventureWorks2000 DB
SET @starttime = GetDate()
DELETE FROM SalesOrderDetail
SET @endtime = GetDate()

SET @totaltime = DateDiff(ms, @starttime, @endtime)
PRINT 'Time to Delete:   ' + CONVERT(VarChar(10), @totaltime)

USE AW_2 -- Copy 2 of AdventureWorks2000 DB
SET @starttime = GetDate()
TRUNCATE TABLE SalesOrderDetail
```

```
SET @endtime = GetDate()

SET @totaltime = DateDiff(ms, @starttime, @endtime)
PRINT 'Time to Truncate: ' + CONVERT(VarChar(10), @totaltime)
```

The results are as follows:

```
(121371 row(s) affected)

Time to Delete:    14030
Time to Truncate: 130
```

The Truncate technique takes less than 1 percent of the time it took to process the DELETE statement. The Delete operation took about 14 seconds and the Truncate operation took about 1/7th of a second. That's a big difference! This is because transactional operations are physically written to the transaction log and then rolled forward into the table, one row at a time. The TRUNCATE statement doesn't do all of this. It simply deallocates all of the data pages for a table. In reality, data in these pages is not actually changed, but the pointer entries in the index allocation map for these pages are removed. Eventually, data left in the pages gets overwritten but is not really removed.

The only limitation of the TRUNCATE command is that it is a privileged command and only database owners or system administrators can execute it, even if it is encapsulated in a stored procedure.

Explicit Transactions

You saw how all insert, update, and delete statements are automatically wrapped into an auto-commit transaction. This means that each of these operations creates a unique entry in the transaction log.

With the exception of the TRUNCATE command, all data modifications are performed in two steps. The two steps are not necessarily sequential and in fact they occur independently of one another. One step is to write all transactions sequentially to the transaction log. This happens quickly because the disk heads don't have to be repositioned and it's not necessary to find free data pages as if writing to a table. The database engine then considers all of the constraints defined for the target table and simply checks to see if the operation would violate those constraints. If not, the transaction succeeds even though the data hasn't been physically written to the table. Any operations that are waiting behind this one are allowed to proceed and users perceive that the database has completed their request.

The second step that occurs is completed by a background process called the *checkpoint*. The checkpoint occurs at dynamic intervals depending on the amount of data modifications occurring in the database. The more modifications and thus transactions that occur, the more checkpoints are issued by the database engine. A checkpoint can occur anywhere in a transaction or at the end of a transaction. Whenever SQL Server detects that a predetermined amount of data pages have been modified, it executes a checkpoint. This setting is adjustable but is beyond the scope of this book. It's the database server's job to balance new transaction requests with pending transactions that have been committed but not yet written to disk by the checkpoint process. When the checkpoint runs, it writes all dirty pages (pages modified by transactions) to disk, but does not release them. The pages are freed when released by a completed transaction. Checkpoints are recorded in the transaction log so SQL Server knows where it left off. When SQL Server is restarted, such as in the case of a power failure or during a database restore, SQL Server finds the last checkpoint in the transaction log and rolls all transactions that committed after the checkpoint forward, writing them to disk. All incomplete transactions that were written to disk during the checkpoint are rolled back, or "undone" so that the database is in a consistent state.

Different operations that need to be processed as a unit should be executed within a stated transaction. For example, if you plan to move a group of records from one table to another, you don't want to insert rows into one table if the corresponding delete doesn't take place for the other table. To create an explicit transaction, begin the script with the BEGIN TRANSACTION statement. Any operations that follow will only be completed when the COMMIT TRANSACTION statement is issued.

Explicit transactions should be used whenever multiple modifications are dependent on each other. The chief advantage that explicit transactions bring to data modifications is that you can check for any errors in your operations prior to committing the transaction. If any errors are present you rollback the transaction. If no errors are detected you commit the transactions. A common misconception is that transactions automatically supply this error detection. Nothing could be further from the truth. As an example I will create a Savings account table and a Checking account table and then place a check constraint on the checking account table that enforces a minimum balance of $100.00. I will then populate the tables with data:

```
CREATE TABLE MySavings
(AccountNum Int NOT NULL,
 Amount Money NOT NULL)

CREATE TABLE MyChecking
(AcountNum Int NOT NULL,
 Amount Money NOT NULL)

ALTER TABLE MyChecking ADD CONSTRAINT ckMinBalance
CHECK (Amount > $100.00)

INSERT MySavings
VALUES
(12345, $1000.00)

INSERT MyChecking
VALUES
(12345, $1000.00)
```

Now that I have my two bank accounts set up I will try to transfer $990.00 from my checking account to my savings account inside an explicit transaction:

```
BEGIN TRANSACTION

  UPDATE MyChecking SET Amount = Amount - $990.00
  WHERE AccountNum = 12345

  UPDATE MySavings SET Amount = Amount + $990.00
  WHERE AccountNum = 12345

COMMIT TRANSACTION
```

The result of this transaction looks like this:

```
Msg 547, Level 16, State 0, Line 2
The UPDATE statement conflicted with the CHECK constraint "ckMinBalance". The
conflict occurred in database "AdventureWorks2000", table "MyChecking", column
'Amount'.
The statement has been terminated.

(1 row(s) affected)
```

The "1 row(s) affected" indicates that something unintended has happened. A query of the savings account and checking account table reveal an interesting outcome:

```
SELECT Amount AS CheckingAmount FROM MyChecking WHERE AccountNum = 12345
SELECT Amount AS SavingsAmount FROM MySavings WHERE AccountNum = 12345

CheckingAmount
--------------------
1000.00

SavingsAmount
--------------------
1990.00
```

The checking account still has its original balance, but the savings account balance is now increased by $990.00. This is because the update to the checking account was aborted when it violated the minimum balance constraint. However, because I did not do anything about the error SQL Server continued with the next update and obediently modified the savings account balance, then committed the transaction, just like I told it to. Good for me, bad for the bank. To prevent this from happening you must add error checking to your transactions.

Chapter 13 covers error handling in greater detail, but for now it is important to see how error handling must be included in transactions to guarantee their consistency. I will demonstrate two different error checking methods. The first is the SQL Server 2000 method and the second is the new improved SQL Server 2005 method:

```
/************************************************
 *                                              *
 *        SQL SERVER 2000 Error Handling        *
 *                                              *
 ************************************************/
BEGIN TRANSACTION
  UPDATE MyChecking SET Amount = Amount - $990.00
  WHERE AccountNum = 12345
    IF @@ERROR != 0
      BEGIN
        ROLLBACK TRANSACTION
        RETURN
      END
    ELSE
  UPDATE MySavings SET Amount = Amount + $990.00
  WHERE AccountNum = 12345
    IF @@ERROR != 0
      BEGIN
        ROLLBACK TRANSACTION
```

```
         RETURN
      END
   ELSE
COMMIT TRANSACTION


/**************************************************
*                                                 *
*         SQL SERVER 2005 Error Handling          *
*                                                 *
**************************************************/
BEGIN TRANSACTION
  BEGIN TRY
    UPDATE MyChecking SET Amount = Amount - $90.00
    WHERE AccountNum = 12345
    UPDATE MySavings SET Amount = Amount + $990.00
    WHERE AccountNum = 12345
    COMMIT TRANSACTION
  END TRY

  BEGIN CATCH
    RAISERROR('Transaction Aborted',16,1)
    ROLLBACK TRANSACTION
  END CATCH
```

You can also use the shorthand version of these statements, substituting TRAN for the word
TRANSACTION:

```
BEGIN TRAN
COMMIT TRAN
ROLLBACK TRAN
```

Summary

Whether you explicitly declare a transaction or not, all data inserts, updates, and deletes are managed as
transactional operations. SQL Server uses the transaction log to queue requested operations and to test
validation rules prior to completing the physical operations on rows in the tables. Transactions provide
the mechanism to guarantee that all operations either complete successfully or fail all together. Multiple
operations can be explicitly included in a single transaction to ensure that they are managed as an
autonomous unit.

Chapter 13 discusses how inserts, updates, and deletes can be managed in secured stored procedures.
The INSERT statement supports two different syntax forms, either using the VALUES keyword or
SELECT. Using SELECT is more flexible and allows values to be retrieved from other tables and sources.

When updating data, the database engine will lock data at various levels, depending on the scope of the
operation and user concurrency. Locking may occur at the row, page, table, or database level. Updates
and deletes should always be tested using a SELECT statement before they are performed. These operations may be irreversible without a backup of the database.

The DELETE command allows affected rows to be filtered, based on practically any criteria. For large-scale delete operations, this comes at the cost of transaction management. The TRUNCATE command offers a far more efficient method to effectively remove all rows in a table without the overhead of having to log and manage the deletions as transactions, but can only be executed by a user with elevated privileges.

Exercises

Exercise 1

Create a new product category for Snorkels. Demonstrate two methods to add a record to this table using the SELECT and VALUES statements.

Exercise 2

Populate a new table called RoadBikes with the contents of product records of this sub category. Your query must filter on the value 'Road Bike'.

Exercise 3

Write a query that will delete product records for products that do not have sales order detail records and where the SubCategoryID is 5. Also write a query that will add a new record to the ProductSubCategory table with the Name column value set to *Accessory*. Include both of these statements in a single transaction and execute them in a batch. Check the row count of the Product table before and after to determine whether records were deleted.

Advanced Queries and Scripting

Writing queries is like driving to work. There are probably 18 different ways to get there, and most likely, some routes are clearly better than others. Under different conditions, different choices may be preferable. This might depend on variable traffic conditions, the time of day, or whether you need to stop by the grocery store to pick up milk and flowers. In my case, the route I choose depends largely on the ferry schedule. If I can't make the ferry, I save time by driving a much greater distance rather than waiting for the next boat. Some opt for consistency, choosing to take the same route, regardless of changing conditions, while others weave through traffic to find the fastest lane, and shave-off a few seconds here and there.

Similarly, many queries can be written more than one way. Traditional SQL statements, written for other database products, often use subqueries whereas SQL Server leans toward ANSI-standard join expressions. Most SQL Server professionals will tell you that if you have the option to choose between using a subquery and a join, the joins will execute faster. Generally speaking, I think this is true, but it depends on the expression and other conditions. Using joins gives the database engine more leeway to implement the best type of operations for a query, whereas subqueries may not afford SQL Server as many options.

Depending on the query, the same results can be achieved using either technique. Graphical design tools, such as the Query Designer, build ANSI join statements. This is considered to be SQL Server's native form for combining column data from more than one table. To implement some business logic, joins simply may not give you the flexibility you need and a subquery may be the only answer.

Subqueries

A subquery is simply a SELECT query within a SELECT query. Several forms of subqueries exist, ranging from expressions that return a single, or scalar, value to a multi-row result set. I'm going to show you several examples of each type, beginning with scalar expressions.

Chapter 10

Scalar Expressions

Within the column selection list of a SELECT statement, embedded SELECT statements can be used to return a single-column value. One of the most common examples of a scalar expression is to use an aggregate function to return a value based on the scope of multiple rows.

How It Works

Here's an example. I'd like to compare the price paid for a product with the average price of all product sales. This can be done by using a simple SELECT statement that uses the AVG() function to produce a column in the query's result set given the alias AvgPrice:

```
SELECT    ProductID
        , UnitPrice
        , (SELECT AVG(UnitPrice) FROM SalesOrderDetail)
     AS AvgPrice
  FROM SalesOrderDetail
```

In the results shown in Figure 10-1, you can see that the values in this column are constant. This is because the subquery expression has no correlation or dependency on the outer query. It simply calculates the average price for all product sales again and again, and returns this value in every row of the result.

	ProductID	UnitPrice	AvgPrice
1	1218	5.8435	514.2045
2	527	534.4920	514.2045
3	558	874.6920	514.2045
4	1086	440.1742	514.2045
5	661	440.1742	514.2045
6	870	83.2981	514.2045
7	594	1716.5304	514.2045
8	627	78.8100	514.2045
9	1201	35.0935	514.2045
10	602	1716.5304	514.2045
11	1201	35.0935	514.2045
12	89	777.5928	514.2045
13	90	777.5928	514.2045
14	91	777.5928	514.2045

Figure 10-1

Fortunately, SQL Server is smart enough to perform the calculation once and then simply return a cached value for each request. Can you imagine how wasteful it would be to recalculate the average of 121 thousand values, and then repeat the same calculation 121 thousand times? It's important to note that the database engine doesn't just do exactly what you ask it to. It has intelligence built in to find shortcuts like this one.

Speaking of intelligence, I'll do something a little more intelligent with this data. Rather than showing the average price of all sales on each row, I'll use this value to calculate the difference between this row's sale price and the average for all sales:

```
SELECT    ProductID
        , UnitPrice
        , UnitPrice - (SELECT Avg(UnitPrice) FROM SalesOrderDetail)
      As AvgPriceDifference
  FROM SalesOrderDetail
```

Now the result shows the difference between the value returned by the subquery and the sale price in the UnitPrice column (see Figure 10-2).

	ProductID	UnitPrice	AvgPriceDifference
1	1218	5.8435	-508.3610
2	527	534.4920	20.2875
3	558	874.6920	360.4875
4	1086	440.1742	-74.0303
5	661	440.1742	-74.0303
6	870	83.2981	-430.9064
7	594	1716.5304	1202.3259
8	627	78.8100	-435.3945
9	1201	35.0935	-479.1110
10	602	1716.5304	1202.3259
11	1201	35.0935	-479.1110
12	89	777.5928	263.3883
13	90	777.5928	263.3883
14	91	777.5928	263.3883

Figure 10-2

As you can see, subqueries can be used to add dimension to data in flat tables. I'm going to build on this query to show some variations.

Try It Out

Rather than getting a scalar value from an aggregate on the same table, you can also use another table. Try out the following query. Use the ProductID value to join the SalesOrderDetail and Product tables and get the ListPrice for the corresponding product:

```
SELECT    ProductID
        , UnitPrice AS SalePrice
        , (SELECT ListPrice FROM Product
            WHERE Product.ProductID = SalesOrderDetail.ProductID)
            AS ProductListPrice
  FROM SalesOrderDetail
```

In Figure 10-3, the results show the list price in the third column.

	ProductID	SalePrice	ProductListPrice
1	1218	5.8435	8.9900
2	527	534.4920	742.3500
3	558	874.6920	1214.8500
4	1086	440.1742	594.8300
5	661	440.1742	594.8300
6	870	83.2981	112.5650
7	594	1716.5304	2384.0700
8	627	78.8100	106.5000
9	1201	35.0935	53.9900
10	602	1716.5304	2384.0700
11	1201	35.0935	53.9900
12	89	777.5928	1079.9900
13	90	777.5928	1079.9900
14	91	777.5928	1079.9900

Figure 10-3

Now take it one step further. Use this value to calculate the difference between the product's list price and price charged. By adding the expression, UnitPrice – , before the subquery, you can tell whether the sale price is inflated or discounted from the list price:

```
SELECT    ProductID
       , UnitPrice AS SalePrice
       , UnitPrice - (SELECT ListPrice FROM Product
         WHERE Product.ProductID = SalesOrderDetail.ProductID)
           AS PriceDifference
FROM SalesOrderDetail
```

The results are shown in Figure 10-4.

	ProductID	SalePrice	PriceDifference
1	1218	5.8435	-3.1465
2	527	534.4920	-207.8580
3	558	874.6920	-340.1580
4	1086	440.1742	-154.6558
5	661	440.1742	-154.6558
6	870	83.2981	-29.2669
7	594	1716.5304	-667.5396
8	627	78.8100	-27.6900
9	1201	35.0935	-18.8965
10	602	1716.5304	-667.5396
11	1201	35.0935	-18.8965
12	89	777.5928	-302.3972
13	90	777.5928	-302.3972
14	91	777.5928	-302.3972

Figure 10-4

The negative values in the third column indicate that these products were sold for less than the list price in the product table. Apparently, Adventure Works Cycles makes it a point to sell all of their products below list price (too bad that this is a fictitious business).

Alternate Join Operations

Before I show you the following examples, I want to answer an obvious question: Why learn to use subqueries that do the same thing as join operations when joins are preferable? All by themselves, it probably doesn't make sense to use subqueries in place of joins. So why take this route? As you will see, some business rules are best implemented using a subquery expression. Under the right conditions join-type subqueries used in concert with specialized business logic subqueries may be the right choice. Although the exception rather than the rule, sometimes you may need more flexibility than an ANSI join will offer.

Inner Join Subqueries

An inner join subquery is a simple expression. The main difference between this technique and the ANSI-SQL INNER JOIN statement is that this join is performed in the WHERE clause rather than the FROM clause. Note that two tables are referenced in the FROM clause as a comma-delimited list:

```
SELECT SalesOrderHeader.OrderDate
    , SalesOrderDetail.ProductID
    , SalesOrderDetail.UnitPrice
FROM SalesOrderHeader, SalesOrderDetail
WHERE SalesOrderHeader.SalesOrderID = SalesOrderDetail.SalesOrderID
ORDER BY SalesOrderHeader.OrderDate
```

There are no surprises in the result set shown in Figure 10-5. Just like an inner join, you will only see matching records between the SalesOrderHeader and SalesOrderDetail tables.

	OrderDate	ProductID	UnitPrice
1	2001-07-01 ...	169	2429.9928
2	2001-07-01 ...	170	2429.9928
3	2001-07-01 ...	171	2429.9928
4	2001-07-01 ...	184	2447.9928
5	2001-07-01 ...	185	2447.9928
6	2001-07-01 ...	186	2447.9928
7	2001-07-01 ...	187	2447.9928
8	2001-07-01 ...	1195	31.2437
9	2001-07-01 ...	1197	31.2437
10	2001-07-01 ...	1215	6.1750
11	2001-07-01 ...	1228	5.6187
12	2001-07-01 ...	1286	20.1865
13	2001-07-01 ...	257	503.3507
14	2001-07-01 ...	339	1049.7528

Figure 10-5

Before adding anything to the script in this example, I'd like to compare this query to its ANSI-SQL equivalent:

```
SELECT SalesOrderHeader.OrderDate
    , SalesOrderDetail.ProductID
    , SalesOrderDetail.UnitPrice
FROM SalesOrderHeader INNER JOIN SalesOrderDetail
ON SalesOrderHeader.SalesOrderID = SalesOrderDetail.SalesOrderID
ORDER BY SalesOrderHeader.OrderDate
```

There is no reason to show the result set because it's going to look exactly as that for the previous example.

You can compound join operations for more than two tables very easily. I'll add the Product table so you can see the product name for each sales record:

```
SELECT SalesOrderHeader.OrderDate
    , SalesOrderDetail.ProductID
    , SalesOrderDetail.UnitPrice
    , Product.Name
FROM    SalesOrderHeader, SalesOrderDetail, Product
WHERE   SalesOrderHeader.SalesOrderID = SalesOrderDetail.SalesOrderID
        AND SalesOrderDetail.ProductID = Product.ProductID
ORDER BY SalesOrderHeader.OrderDate
```

Using the AND operator, you can extend the WHERE clause with the join between the SalesOrderDetail and Product tables. The result (shown in Figure 10-6) shows the OrderDate column from the SalesOrderHeader table, the ProductID and UnitPrice from SalesOrderDetail, and the Name column from the table.

	OrderDate	ProductID	UnitPrice	Name
1	2001-07-01 ...	169	2429.9928	Mountain-100 Black, 42
2	2001-07-01 ...	170	2429.9928	Mountain-100 Black, 44
3	2001-07-01 ...	171	2429.9928	Mountain-100 Black, 48
4	2001-07-01 ...	184	2447.9928	Mountain-100 Silver, 38
5	2001-07-01 ...	185	2447.9928	Mountain-100 Silver, 42
6	2001-07-01 ...	186	2447.9928	Mountain-100 Silver, 44
7	2001-07-01 ...	187	2447.9928	Mountain-100 Silver, 48
8	2001-07-01 ...	1195	31.2437	long-sleeve logo jersey, M
9	2001-07-01 ...	1197	31.2437	long-sleeve logo jersey, XL
10	2001-07-01 ...	1215	6.1750	Mountain Bike Socks, M
11	2001-07-01 ...	1228	5.6187	AWC logo cap
12	2001-07-01 ...	1286	20.1865	Sport-100 helmet, Blue
13	2001-07-01 ...	257	503.3507	Road-650 Red, 44
14	2001-07-01 ...	339	1049.7528	Road-450 Red, 52

Figure 10-6

Outer Join Subqueries

An outer join can be performed in a few different ways. A simple outer join without complex business rules is performed as a simple variation of an inner join subquery. Note the LEFT OUTER JOIN operator (*=) used for matching key values between the two tables:

```
SELECT SalesOrderHeader.OrderDate
     , SalesOrderDetail.ProductID
     , SalesOrderDetail.UnitPrice
FROM SalesOrderHeader, SalesOrderDetail
WHERE SalesOrderHeader.SalesOrderID *= SalesOrderDetail.SalesOrderID
ORDER BY SalesOrderHeader.OrderDate
```

Like the LEFT OUTER JOIN statement, this means that all rows will be selected from the left side of the expression and then matching rows are returned from the right side. I'm not going to show the results because they will be the same as the inner join example. In the AdventureWorks database, there are no SalesOrderHeader records without matching SalesOrderDetail records, so the outer join doesn't produce any orphaned records.

The following example does expose unmatched records. Let's see if there are any products that haven't been purchased:

```
SELECT    Product.ProductID, SalesOrderDetail.SalesOrderID
FROM      Product, SalesOrderDetail
WHERE     Product.ProductID *= SalesOrderDetail.ProductID
```

Again, the *= comparison operator instructs SQL Server to retrieve all of the products first and then the matched sales records. The results are shown in Figure 10-7.

	ProductID	SalesOrderID
1	1	NULL
2	2	NULL
3	3	5015
4	3	5081
5	3	5087
6	3	5092
7	3	5134
8	3	5139
9	3	5163
10	3	5174
11	3	5189
12	3	5204
13	3	5217
14	3	5221

Figure 10-7

The null value in the SalesOrderID column indicates that there are no order detail records matching these products.

I have included the *= and =* syntax here because you may encounter it, but a very important note to remember about this syntax is that in the future it may become an illegal operation. In some very specific scenarios the *= and =* syntax may return ambiguous results. As a result, the preferred method for outer joins is using the ANSI-SQL syntax of LEFT OUTER JOIN and RIGHT OUTER JOIN.

Table Aliasing 101

The mechanics of subqueries are sometimes considerably different than standard join operations. The need to refer to columns from one table within an expression using a different table often requires that tables be aliased. In Chapter 5 you learned how to alias columns. This is the same concept but now you're just giving a table an alternate name. Here's a simple example to introduce the technique:

```
SELECT ProductID, Name FROM Product AS P
```

The alias in this query doesn't really accomplish anything in its basic form, but it would be useful if this query were used as a nested subquery, within another SELECT statement.

Using Aggregate Functions in Subqueries

In Chapter 7 you saw how aggregate functions are used to return summary values over a group of rows rolled up using the GROUP BY clause. In subqueries, a similar result can be achieved by using aggregate function in a filtered SELECT expression. In a scalar expression, you use the AVG() function to return a single column value and then use that value to perform calculations with other column values.

In row set queries, aggregate functions can be used along with various filtering and matching techniques to achieve more flexible results. For example, I can simulate a top values query by using the COUNT() function. I'll introduce some other techniques first. Aggregate functions allow you to do some very powerful things in correlated subqueries, which are discussed later in the chapter.

The HAVING Clause

Chapter 7 also showed you how to use the HAVING clause to filter aggregated rows when using the GROUP BY statement. Similar results can be achieved using subquery techniques. Until we have a chance to discuss the mechanics of correlated subqueries, it may not seem to make sense to use the HAVING clause without a GROUP BY. For example, the following expression serves only to include or exclude all rows from this query:

```
SELECT SUM(UnitPrice) FROM SalesOrderDetail
HAVING SUM(UnitPrice) > 100000
```

In this example, one value is returned if the UnitPrice sum for the entire range meets this criterion; otherwise, the query returns nothing. In effect, the HAVING statement does the same thing as a WHERE clause, but only after the aggregate value has been calculated. The WHERE clause is used to qualify records before they are fed to the aggregate SUM() function within the subquery. This query returns the name of products that have generated sales exceeding two million dollars:

```
SELECT Name FROM Product
WHERE EXISTS
  (
    SELECT SUM(UnitPrice) FROM SalesOrderDetail
    WHERE SalesOrderDetail.ProductID = Product.ProductID
    HAVING SUM(UnitPrice) > 2000000
  )
```

When you need to use an aggregated value within a subquery, this technique can be quite useful.

Creating a Derived Table

Sometimes you may need to build values into a query that are not obtained from a table. You've seen that the SELECT statement allows you to return literal values that are just part of an expression. For example, the following statement returns a single row result as if it were read from a table:

```
SELECT 'Fred' As FirstName, 'Flintstone' As LastName
```

Because tables can be aliased, an expression-type result set can also be aliased and then treated as if it were a table:

```
SELECT * FROM (SELECT 'Fred' As FirstName, 'Flintstone' As LastName)
AS CartoonCharacter
```

Derived tables can be used in joins and subqueries. As far as the query processor is concerned, the CartoonCharacter alias is a table, like any other table, and can be joined or used in expressions like a physical table. Extending the previous example, a UNION statement is used to create two records, returned as an aliased table. This table is then joined to the physical Department table:

```
SELECT FirstName, LastName, Department.Name As DeptName FROM
  (SELECT 'Fred' As FirstName, 'Flintstone' As LastName, 1 As DepartmentID
   UNION ALL
   SELECT 'Barney' As FirstName, 'Rubble' As LastName, 4 As DepartmentID)
As CartoonCharacter
Inner Join Department On CartoonCharacter.DepartmentID = Department.DepartmentID
```

The result, shown in Figure 10-8, returns the department name based on the join to the Department table and the DepartmentID provided for each of these records.

	FirstName	LastName	DeptName
1	Barney	Rubble	Marketing
2	Fred	Flintstone	Engineering

Figure 10-8

Using the IN() Function

In Chapter 5 you saw how the IN() function can be used to match a column to any value in a comma-delimited list of values. This function has a dual purpose in that it also knows how to match a column to the results of a SELECT statement when this statement returns a single column of values. Here's a simple example that returns all products that have been used in orders:

```
SELECT ProductID, Name
FROM Product
WHERE ProductID IN
     ( SELECT ProductID
       FROM SalesOrderDetail )
```

Subqueries can be nested. Extending the previous example, I can return products that were ordered in March 2003. The OrderDate is stored in the SalesOrderHeader table and the ProductID for the order is in the SalesOrderDetail table. This requires three expressions—a query within a query within a query, like this:

```
SELECT ProductID, Name
FROM Product
WHERE ProductID IN
     ( SELECT ProductID
       FROM SalesOrderDetail
       WHERE SalesOrderID IN
           ( SELECT SalesOrderID
             FROM SalesOrderHeader
             WHERE OrderDate BETWEEN '3-1-03' AND '3-31-03')
     )
```

The first product/order example returns a large number of rows. Reversing the logic using the NOT operator will return a list of all the products that haven't sold:

```
SELECT ProductID, Name
FROM Product
WHERE ProductID NOT IN
        (SELECT ProductID FROM SalesOrderDetail)
```

Perhaps my purpose is to clean up the product inventory and remove those product records that haven't generated revenue. To this end, I can delete products that haven't sold by applying the DELETE command:

```
DELETE FROM Product
WHERE ProductID NOT IN
        (SELECT ProductID FROM SalesOrderDetail)
```

Using the EXISTS() Function

The EXISTS() function is used to return a row in the outer query when any records are returned by a subquery. The subquery can be any SELECT statement, directly related or not, to the main SELECT statement. The EXISTS() function is often used in correlated subqueries to either mimic the behavior of a join or to implement business rules that wouldn't be possible with a standard join.

It doesn't really matter what column or columns are returned in the subquery because you don't actually use these values. For this reason, it's common to use the asterisk rather than column names. The asterisk is typically used to return all column values from a query but, in this case, it simply allows the query engine to test for the presence of any rows without unnecessarily wasting system resources.

Here's a simple example of this type of subquery:

```
SELECT EmployeeID, FirstName, LastName
FROM Employee
WHERE EXISTS
        (SELECT * FROM Customer
         WHERE SalespersonID = Employee.EmployeeID)
```

Note the correlation between the inner and outer query using a reference to the Employee table from the subquery based on the Customer table. The results, shown in Figure 10-9, return only employee records where the employee is assigned as a salesperson for a customer.

	EmployeeID	FirstName	LastName
1	22	Pamela	Ansman-Wolfe
2	23	David	Campbell
3	24	Fernando	Caro
4	26	Shu	Ito
5	27	Linda	Mitchell
6	29	Tsvi	Reiter
7	31	José	Saraiva
8	33	Garrett	Vargar
9	34	Ranjit	Varkey Chudukatil
10	35	Rachel	Valdez
11	36	Lynn	Tsoflias
12	37	Jae	Pak
13	38	Michael	Blythe

Figure 10-9

NOT EXISTS()

To reverse the logic for this query (in this, to return all of the unassigned employees), simply add the NOT operator before the EXISTS statement:

```
SELECT EmployeeID, FirstName, LastName
FROM Employee
WHERE NOT EXISTS
        (SELECT * FROM Customer
        WHERE SalespersonID = Employee.EmployeeID)
```

The result set shown in Figure 10-10 returns all of the employees that were excluded in the previous example.

	EmployeeID	FirstName	LastName
1	1	Terri	Duffy
2	2	Jian Shuo	Wang
3	55	Ben	Miller
4	56	Linda	Meisner
5	57	Fukiko	Ogisu
6	58	Frank	Pellow
7	59	Mikael	Sandberg
8	60	Arvind	Rao
9	61	Dylan	Miller
10	62	Diane	Margheim
11	63	Gigi	Matthew
12	64	James	Hamilton
13	65	Andrew	Hill

Figure 10-10

Correlated Subqueries

You've just seen some examples of subqueries where the outer query refers to, and conditionally filters rows based on, the inner query. A correlated subquery is a subquery where the selection criterion of the inner query refers to values in the outer query. Correlated subqueries can be a bit tricky. One of the restrictions is that the inner query cannot return more than one row matching the outer row. In the following example, I am looking for mountain bike products (where the SubCategoryID is 1) that have been purchased (where there is an existing SalesOrderDetail record). This query contains the proper logic but returns an error because the inner query returns multiple results for some of the products:

```
SELECT ProductID
   , Name
FROM Product AS P
WHERE 1 =
     (SELECT ProductSubCategoryID
      FROM SalesOrderDetail As SD
      WHERE P.ProductID = SD.ProductID)
```

The problem is easily corrected by adding a TOP 1 statement:

```
-- Correlated subquery using TOP 1:
SELECT ProductID
   , Name
FROM Product AS P
WHERE 1 =
     (SELECT TOP 1 ProductSubCategoryID
      FROM SalesOrderDetail As SD
      WHERE P.ProductID = SD.ProductID)
```

The first few rows of the result set are shown in Figure 10-11.

	ProductID	Name
1	8	Mountain-500 Black, 40
2	9	Mountain-500 Black, 42
3	10	Mountain-500 Black, 44
4	11	Mountain-500 Black, 48
5	12	Mountain-500 Black, 52
6	24	Mountain-500 Silver, 40
7	25	Mountain-500 Silver, 42
8	26	Mountain-500 Silver, 44
9	27	Mountain-500 Silver, 48
10	28	Mountain-500 Silver, 52
11	64	Mountain-400-W Silver, 38

Figure 10-11

The same result could also be achieved using SELECT DISTINCT or a GROUP BY statement in the inner query, as shown in the following two examples:

```
-- Correlated subquery using Distinct:
SELECT ProductID
   , Name
FROM Product AS P
```

```
WHERE 1 =
    (SELECT DISTINCT ProductSubCategoryID
     FROM SalesOrderDetail As SD
     WHERE P.ProductID = SD.ProductID)

-- Correlated subquery using Group By:
SELECT ProductID
  , Name
FROM Product AS P
WHERE 1 =
    (SELECT ProductSubCategoryID
     FROM SalesOrderDetail As SD
     WHERE P.ProductID = SD.ProductID
     GROUP BY ProductSubCategoryID)
```

Just an aside: I've always found this logic a little awkward because the value comparison (1 = ...) seems backward. But this is a good example of where it's sometimes necessary to think outside the box. This might not be the way you would typically make a value comparison, putting the expression on the right side of the result, but it's an accurate, logical expression that provides one more way to solve a problem.

One of the significant differences between the outer query value matching (using IN or EXISTS) and correlated techniques is in how the query processor builds the execution plan. In the case of a correlated subquery, a row is selected from the outer query and then a row is selected from the inner query. Value comparisons are made to determine if an outer row should be output and, if so, the row is typically sent to an output buffer. This process is repeated, processing each of the inner rows for every one of the outer rows until all combinations have been considered. This process is more rigorous than subqueries that use the IN or EXISTS functions and don't match outer query column values within the inner query.

Benchmarking and Best Practices

Several subquery techniques can be used to return the same kind of results you would get from an INNER JOIN or OUTER JOIN query. I don't want to beat the proverbial dead horse, but I'll say it one more time: Using ANSI standard join expressions gives the query processor the opportunity to make intelligent decisions about your stated intentions and then to build an optimal execution plan. Using explicit subquery expressions to achieve the same result doesn't.

Don't just take my word for it. Let's test it out. Using either the SQL Server 2005 Management Studio or SQL Server 2000 Query Analyzer, enable the feature to show the actual execution plan. In either tool, you will find this option on the Query menu. Execute the first correlated subquery example using the AdventureWorks database and then view the execution plan (see Figure 10-12). You can do this by selecting the Execution Plan tab in the query results pane.

The first thing to note is that this query was executed in seven steps. From right to left, you see all of the activities performed by the query-processing engine to process this query. The join was processed using an operation called a *Nested Loop Inner Join*. This is exactly what you told the query processor to do: perform an inner join by matching records in two nested loops. Now, place the mouse pointer over the leftmost icon. A pop-up window displays statistical performance information about the execution. Take note of the Subtree Cost value. In my case, it was about 3.1. Also, note that the vast majority of time was spent processing an Index Seek operation on the SalesOrderDetails table's index. According to the execution statistics, 266 rows were processed 1004 times.

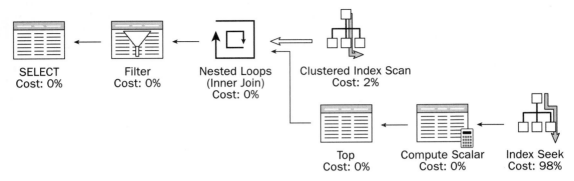

SELECT
Cost: 0%

Filter
Cost: 0%

Nested Loops
(Inner Join)
Cost: 0%

Clustered Index Scan
Cost: 2%

Top
Cost: 0%

Compute Scalar
Cost: 0%

Index Seek
Cost: 98%

Figure 10-12

Now, type the following ANSI Join version of the same query, highlight the query text, and execute the query:

```
-- ANSI Join:
SELECT DISTINCT Product.ProductID
    , Name
FROM Product INNER JOIN SalesOrderDetail
    ON Product.ProductID = SalesOrderDetail.ProductID
WHERE ProductSubCategoryID = 1
```

Again, view the execution plan shown in Figure 10-13.

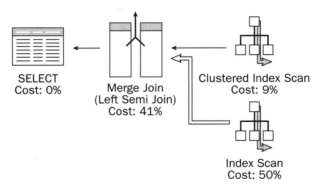

SELECT
Cost: 0%

Merge Join
(Left Semi Join)
Cost: 41%

Clustered Index Scan
Cost: 9%

Index Scan
Cost: 50%

Figure 10-13

This time it only took four steps. Note the total Subtree Cost in the statistics for the left-most icon. In my case, this is only .67. It took almost one-fifth of the time to process this query as it did before. Note that instead of spending nearly all of this time reprocessing the same rows using the index scan, it only scanned the index once. The query optimizer decided that it made more sense to scan all 121,371

SalesOrderDetail rows using this index, matching 12,826 in the next operation. It also chose to use a Merge Join instead of the less-efficient Nested Loop Join. This time it spent a greater percentage of time processing the join but achieved a much more efficient result overall.

The real question is when do you really need to use a subquery instead of a join? So far you've seen that it usually makes sense to use a join wherever you can. However, business doesn't always follow simple rules. The next section looks at some examples of unique business rules that can be solved using various forms of subqueries.

Business Cases for Subqueries

Creating subqueries to solve unique business problems is a fine art, and a source of pride among true database professionals. Often an evolutionary process, queries may progress from crude data selections based on other views or queries, or multi-step inserts and updates to populate temporary tables, finally arriving at a short and elegant solution. This process can take days to years in the life of a database solution. I've learned to think twice before making statements such as "that *can't* be done in a single query," only to later discover otherwise. The following examples, with one exception, use the AdventureWorks database so you can follow along.

Top Sales by Territory

The Director of Sales at Adventure Works Cycles would like to see a report showing the top 5 sales in each sales territory and the salespeople responsible for those sales. The trick here is that I want to see five sales records in the result for every territory so a top values query won't help unless it is nested in a subquery. I can use a different technique to achieve a similar result. This is done by ordering the SalesOrderHeader rows by the SubTotal column in descending order. This places the largest sales records at the top of the list. The MIN() function is just a trick used to enable the HAVING() function to work. The HAVING expression used in this correlated subquery essentially returns the top 5 values from matching records within the inner query:

```
SELECT TerritoryID, SubTotal, SalesPersonID, SalesOrderID
FROM SalesOrderHeader AS SO1
WHERE SubTotal >=
 (
   SELECT Min(SubTotal)
   FROM SalesOrderHeader AS SO2
   WHERE SO1.TerritoryID = SO2.TerritoryID
   AND SO1.SubTotal <= SO2.SubTotal
   HAVING Count(*) <= 5
 )
ORDER BY TerritoryID, SubTotal Desc
```

Figure 10-14 shows the first few records in the result set.

	TerritoryID	SubTotal	SalesPersonID	SalesOrderID
1	1	135653.7237	23	6558
2	1	135620.8741	14	7676
3	1	127361.5271	302	7057
4	1	124079.9878	302	8117
5	1	123118.9525	23	5554
6	2	179754.1225	38	6265
7	2	129038.6978	24	6300
8	2	127012.8505	24	6262
9	2	125373.5743	38	6799
10	2	121699.3439	38	6261
11	3	147176.2415	24	8240
12	3	140191.9196	24	6446
13	3	130638.8047	24	6410
14	3	129359.2821	38	8671
15	3	127702.94	24	7996
16	4	224356.4831	26	7578

Figure 10-14

Unshipped Product Orders

In this scenario, I want a list of sales order records and products where part of the order has been shipped and part has not been shipped. In the outer query, I ask for records from the SalesOrderDetail table (sales order line items) that don't have a tracking number. This indicates that this item has not shipped. For these rows to be output, there must be records with the same SalesOrderID (related to the same SalesOrderHeader record) that do have a tracking number:

```
SELECT SalesOrderID, ProductID
FROM SalesOrderDetail As SD1
WHERE CarrierTrackingNumber IS NULL
AND SalesOrderID IN
  (SELECT SalesOrderID FROM SalesOrderDetail AS SD2
   WHERE CarrierTrackingNumber IS NOT NULL
   AND SD1.SalesOrderID = SD2.SalesOrderID)
```

Figure 10-15 shows the results.

Consulting Billing Time

One of the quandaries in the software development consulting business is just what we should bill our customers for. Inevitably, projects require ramp-up time and, sometimes, projects get cancelled before they really get started. With new clients, the process usually progresses from the sales stage to initiation meetings, specification forming, requirement gathering, and then finally to the development work. We certainly can't bill our customers for the sales calls and all the schmoozing that goes on when building a new business relationship, prior to getting started on a billable project. So, when does the billing clock actually begin to run? Customers want assurance that we can deliver results and we don't want to waste our time on dead-end projects that we won't get paid for.

For this example, I've created a table called ConsultingActivity with columns containing a description of consulting activities, the number of hours, and the activity type. In a production solution, this data may exist in multiple tables but in this simplified example, I've used only one table. The data looks like that shown in Figure 10-16.

	SalesOrderID	ProductID
1	5007	128
2	5030	1032
3	5031	1206
4	5042	187
5	5053	1196
6	5064	1032
7	5078	170
8	5087	965
9	5096	145
10	5108	1225
11	5114	460
12	5121	211
13	5124	25
14	5127	699
15	5132	65

Figure 10-15

	CustProject	Hours	ActivityType
1	Inventory	2	Investigation
2	Inventory	2	Investigation
3	Inventory	5	Requirement Gathering
4	Invoice	1	Investigation
5	Invoice	3	Requirement Gathering
6	Document Manager	2	Requirement Gathering
7	Inventory	8	Development
8	Inventory	6	Development
9	Inventory	2	Investigation
10	Document Manager	8	Development
11	Inventory	7	Development
12	Inventory	8	Development
13	Document Manager	7	Investigation
14	Document Manager	8	Development
15	Inventory	9	Development
16	Scheduling	3	Investigation
17	Scheduling	4	Investigation
18	Scheduling	6	Requirement Gathering

Figure 10-16

This is the only example in this chapter that doesn't use the AdventureWorks sample database. If you would like to see these results, you will need to create this table and populate it with these values. The ActivityType column may contain a number of different values. The business rule is that if our consultants have performed any development work, we will bill the customer for all activities. Otherwise, we don't bill on this project at all.

```
SELECT CustProject, Hours
FROM ConsultingActivity as ca1
WHERE CustProject IN (SELECT CustProject
        FROM ConsultingActivity as ca2
        WHERE ActivityType = 'Development'
        AND ca1.CustProject = ca2.CustProject)
ORDER BY CustProject
```

Of the four projects in various stages of progress, only two have had any development consulting activity performed. The results of this query, shown in Figure 10-17, include all of the activities for these two projects.

	CustProject	Hours
1	Document Manager	2
2	Document Manager	8
3	Document Manager	7
4	Document Manager	8
5	Inventory	9
6	Inventory	7
7	Inventory	8
8	Inventory	2
9	Inventory	2
10	Inventory	5
11	Inventory	8
12	Inventory	6
13	Inventory	2

Figure 10-17

Cursors

The definition of the word *cursor* can actually be a little confusing. This is because there are several meanings that have similar context. Before going any further, I'd like to clarify our use of this word. If asked, most computer users would likely tell you that the little blinking bar in a text editor is a cursor. It's a placeholder or position pointer. You could reason that after a SQL query is executed, the cursor would be a pointer to the current record. As much as this makes sense, this isn't the definition of a cursor in the SQL world. In this context, the word cursor is an acronym for *CURrent Set Of Rows*. A cursor is a set of records returned from a query.

Unfortunately, it can get a little more confusing than that. It is true that when a SELECT statement is executed, the database engine returns a cursor — or set of records — held in memory or streamed across a network connection. This type of cursor is the basis for programming objects such as recordsets and datasets. In Transact-SQL, when you declare a cursor-type variable, a result set is read into the memory managed by this object for the purpose of iterating through each record. I know, this actually takes us back to the original definition of a cursor as a single record pointer. The fact is that the cursor represents the entire set of records and supports navigation, one record at a time.

Rowset Versus Cursor Operations

Probably one of the greatest challenges for programmers learning to use SQL is the different approach usually taken to handling data. In procedural and object-oriented programming, developers typically work with objects one at a time. Groups of objects are organized into collections, structures, or arrays that support looping and enumeration. So far, you've seen that SQL Server returns sets of rows, all at once, and is optimized to support this paradigm rather than one record at a time. SQL Server performs best when using native set-based operations. There may be times when you will need to loop through a set of individual records, but be forewarned that cursor operations are typically the worst performing operations that occur in T-SQL. If there is a set-based solution than can provide the same functionality as the cursor, choose the set-based solution.

T-SQL cursors' default behavior is forward-only and updatable, unlike their counterparts used in other programming languages, which typically default to forward-only read-only. This makes the T-SQL cursor even more expensive as far as performance is concerned. When a cursor is updatable it means that the cursor maintains a link to the underlying data that it is built from. If the underlying data changes, so will the contents of the cursor. To prevent this behavior the cursor can be declared with an INSENSITIVE option that makes it read-only and decreases the amount of resources needed to maintain it. Another method of mitigating the cost of a cursor is to mark only specific columns in the cursor as updatable rather than the default of all the columns. If you must use a cursor, keep this in mind and use the least expensive cursor possible. The examples used in this chapter follow these performance guidelines.

Creating and Navigating a Cursor

The first order of business is to declare a cursor-type variable. Because this is a special type of non-scalar object, the variable name isn't prefixed with an at symbol (@). The cursor variable can be declared and defined on the same line with the SELECT statement used to populate the cursor:

```
DECLARE curProduct INSENSITIVE CURSOR FOR SELECT ProductID, Name FROM Product
```

To create a cursor that allows updates only to and from the Name column of the Product table, declare the cursor like this:

```
DECLARE curProduct CURSOR FOR SELECT ProductID, Name FROM Product
FOR UPDATE OF Name
```

The cursor isn't actually populated until it is opened. Executing the OPEN command loads the cursor structure and data into memory:

```
OPEN curProduct
```

At this point, the record pointer is positioned before the first row. The FETCH NEXT command navigates the pointer to the next record and returns a comma-delimited list of column values. In this case, the pointer is moved to the first row. Individual variables can be used to capture the values of the current row's column values:

```
DECLARE @ProdID Int
DECLARE @ProdName VarChar(100)

FETCH NEXT FROM curProduct INTO @ProdID, @ProdName
```

After FETCH NEXT is executed, one of two things will happen: the record pointer will either be positioned on a valid record or it will navigate beyond the last row. The state of the pointer can be determined using the global variable @@Fetch_Status. On a valid row, it returns 0, otherwise it returns –1 or –2. It returns –1 if there is no next row to fetch. If a –2 is returned it means that the next row was deleted in the underlying table when using an updatable cursor. Using this variable, create a simple loop, navigating to the next record as long as @@Fetch_Status is equal to 0:

```
WHILE @@Fetch_Status = 0
   BEGIN
      PRINT @ProdName
      FETCH NEXT FROM curProduct INTO @ProdID, @ProdName
   END
```

In this example, you're simply printing one of the variable values to the query results window. In production, you could use conditional statements to decide whether to perform related operations, such as inserting or deleting records. The real power of using cursors is in using them to conditionally call stored procedures. This way you can use conditional logic to call different procedures under different conditions, and then a stored procedure can perform practically any combination of operations.

Finally, after navigating past the last record, it's necessary to do some clean up. Use the CLOSE command to close the cursor and then use the DEALLOCATE command to recover the memory used by the cursor:

```
CLOSE curProduct
DEALLOCATE curProduct
```

Putting it all together, here's the entire script:

```
DECLARE curProduct INSENSITIVE CURSOR
FOR SELECT ProductID, Name FROM Product
DECLARE @ProdID Int
DECLARE @ProdName VarChar(100)

OPEN curProduct
FETCH NEXT FROM curProduct INTO @ProdID, @ProdName
WHILE @@Fetch_Status = 0
   BEGIN
      PRINT @ProdName
      FETCH NEXT FROM curProduct INTO @ProdID, @ProdName
   END
CLOSE curProduct
DEALLOCATE curProduct
```

A list of product names is displayed in the query results pane, as shown in Figure 10-18.

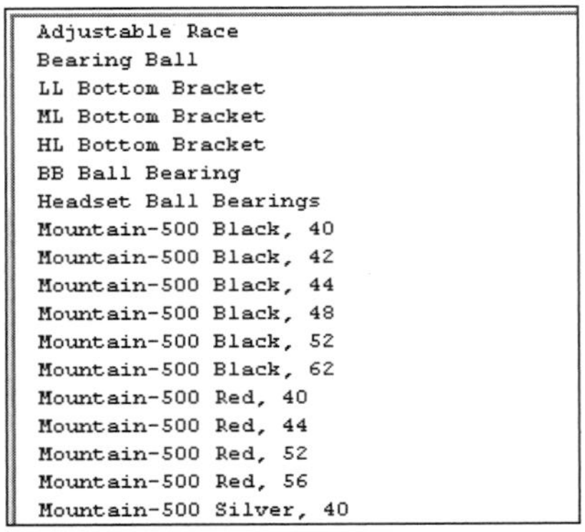

```
Adjustable Race
Bearing Ball
LL Bottom Bracket
ML Bottom Bracket
HL Bottom Bracket
BB Ball Bearing
Headset Ball Bearings
Mountain-500 Black, 40
Mountain-500 Black, 42
Mountain-500 Black, 44
Mountain-500 Black, 48
Mountain-500 Black, 52
Mountain-500 Black, 62
Mountain-500 Red, 40
Mountain-500 Red, 44
Mountain-500 Red, 52
Mountain-500 Red, 56
Mountain-500 Silver, 40
```

Figure 10-18

Summary

There may be several ways to write some queries. Although there are some basic rules and guidelines to follow, the best approach will often depend on a number of factors including the volume of data, complexity of the database, and your business rules. Subqueries allow a SELECT statement to feed values or rows to another query. Subqueries can be scalar, single-value expressions, or nested rowset expressions. Joins can be implemented using subqueries rather than ANSI join syntax. Although often more complex and less efficient than standard joins, subquery joins can be used to process specialized business logic. If given the choice between standard join syntax and subqueries, you should typically favor standard joins. In any case, you can test your queries for performance and efficiency using graphical execution plans, SQL Profiler, System Monitor, and other benchmarking and tuning tools. The results are often surprising. Overall, be open to different ways to solve business problems. Try different forms of queries and explore various query expressions and techniques. Taking time to experiment, you will either confirm that you are using the best approach or find a better way to solve the problem.

Exercises

Exercise 1

Write a query to return a list of products in order of the product name, the list price, and the highest price for which that product has sold. Use an in-line, scalar query to calculate the highest sales price for the product. Columns in the result set should be labeled ProductName, ProductListPrice, and MaxSalesPrice.

Exercise 2

The following query returns the top 10 employee pay rates and employee names:

```
SELECT TOP 10 FirstName + ' ' + LastName AS Name
  , BaseRate FROM Employee ORDER BY BaseRate DESC
```

This query returns the average pay for all other employees as one summary row labeled '(other)' in-place of the employee's name. A subquery is used to join the all employee rows to the results of the top 10 expression and then to eliminate these from the aggregated group:

```
SELECT '(Other)' AS Name, AVG(Employee.BaseRate) AS BaseRate FROM Employee
    LEFT OUTER JOIN
    (SELECT TOP 10 EmployeeID, BaseRate FROM Employee ORDER BY BaseRate DESC) AS E
    ON Employee.EmployeeID = E.EmployeeID
    WHERE E.EmployeeID IS NULL
```

These two queries need to be combined into a UNION query to return a single result set. However, simply adding the UNION statement between them raises errors due to restrictions of the UNION statement. You can work around these limitations by creating two alias tables similar to the one in the join statement of the second query, and selecting columns from them. Rewrite these statements so the final query has three alias table subqueries. Call them E1, E2, and E3. The existing subquery should be renamed from E to E2. Execute the query to verify that it returns 11 rows.

Full-Text Index Queries

In the late 1980s, I worked as the Tech Support Manager for a growing medical billing software company. We had written most of our own internal support systems, accounting, payroll, and tech support incident management, not to mention our own software products. After a few years and hundreds of thousands of support calls later, we had accumulated what we considered to be a huge repository of support call notes and history. We found ourselves taking calls from customers whose issues seemed vaguely familiar. When a support technician received a call, he or she would page through support incident screens, looking for old records to help find resolutions to repeat problems, often to no avail. Our system didn't store data in a relational database so we couldn't use SQL or any other standard language to query data. All of our data lived in flat text files. While attending Comdex in Las Vegas, I found a company with an interesting product that did indexing over large volumes of text. This software could build searchable indexes for practically anything: encyclopedias, dictionaries, religious books, or hundreds of files in your file system. We quickly built this into our support system and it changed everything. When a customer called and told one of our support technicians they were getting error 3204 when they entered a new patient diagnosis, the technician could instantly find all incidents related to the same problem by simply typing a few keywords.

Free-form text indexing has been around for many years and has improved and matured since my experience as a Tech Support Manager. Relational databases have largely replaced old flat-file systems, but with that transition, we've actually lost some useful functionality—namely the ability to simply store a large volume of searchable text. Systems evolve to fill gaps and to meet users' needs. Today, most relational database products support the ability to store large volumes of data in a structure called *binary large objects (BLOBs)*. SQL Server offers three different implementations of BLOB types in the data types *Text*, *nText*, and *Image*. When the Text and Image types were originally added to the SyBase and Microsoft SQL Server products in the early 1990s, they didn't support indexing or ordering. Even today, you cannot use these columns with a standard WHERE or ORDER BY clause—and for good reason. Can you imagine sorting rows using all of the text in a 15-page document?

Transact-SQL includes some simple tools for inexact text comparisons. This includes functionality such as Soundex phonetic and approximate word matching. By contrast, full-text indexing includes built-in logical operators, "near" matching, and ranked results. Whether you should choose to use full-text searches or standard SQL techniques depends on your specific needs.

Microsoft Search Service

To compensate for this shortcoming, Microsoft implemented a flexible, free-form text indexing technology very similar to the product I used to index our support call system. The Microsoft Search Service was originally adopted to index newsgroup servers and web sites. Because it was capable of indexing practically any volume of text stored in files, it was integrated into SQL Server several versions ago. Today, any SQL data type capable of storing text characters can be indexed for free-form searches using full-text indexing and the Microsoft Search Service. Keep in mind that this is not a capability of SQL Server, rather a separate service made accessible through extensions in both the SQL Server product and the Transact-SQL language. Because text in practically any form can be indexed, SQL Server can be used as a storage repository for content such as Office documents that can then be indexed and searched using full-text indexing. Word documents, for example, contain both text and binary markup information. This poses no problem because the non-textual data is simply ignored.

Full-text indexing works much differently than standard indexes in SQL Server. Indexed data is not stored in the database. Full-text catalogs store index data in separate catalog files on the server. When the index is populated, the search service weeds out all of the noise words such as "and" and "of." All of the remaining words are added to a table-specific index stored within a catalog. Multiple columns can be added to the same index within a catalog.

Most of us use full-text searching every day. Although the Microsoft Search Service is not implemented on the same scale as the Google and Yahoo web search engines, the fundamental technology is the same. If you have used any of the leading web search services on-line, then you're already familiar with some of the things you can do with the Microsoft Search Service and full-text indexing.

Soundex Matching

One of the great challenges when mixing the nuance of language with the exactness of computing is to make sense of things that are similar to other things, but not exactly the same. My friend, Steve, who writes a humorous newspaper column, says that there are people who like things to be black and white, and there are other people who are OK with things in that gray area in between. For the gray people, driving 70 on a 60-mile-per-hour road is perfectly acceptable for the surgeon on his way to the hospital. This is not to say that the gray people are all about breaking rules and cheating their employers, they just have a different way of looking at things. Likewise, at times you may need to match a word or phrase that is similar to another, in that gray area between equal to and not equal to. One of the great challenges, for those of us who spend our lives in the world of Boolean logic, is to cope with the concept of inexact comparisons.

Soundex, as applied in SQL Server, is a standard used to compare words based on their phonetic equivalents, using a mathematical algorithm. This standard is based on the *Consensus Soundex,* developed by Robert Russell and Margaret Odell in the early 1900s. It was used by the United States Census in the 19th and early 20th centuries and in genealogical research to index and deal with spelling variations in surnames. Although the rules are based on English language phonetic rules, it does work with many words in different languages. Here's something to keep in mind: Just as the rules of spoken language can be a bit arbitrary, so is this. Soundex matching is pretty accurate, most of the time, but on occasion some exceptions may occur. Use it for search and matching features to be validated by a user, but don't bet the farm on every result.

The sound of a word is represented by a letter, representing the first sound, followed by a three-digit integer, each numeral representing adjacent consonant sounds. Before processing a word, the letters A, E, I, O, U, H, W, and Y are ignored unless they have a phonetic significance when combined with another letter. The first three prominent consonant sounds (after the first letter, if it's a consonant) are translated as shown in the following table.

Letters	English Phonetic Description	Represented By
B, F, P, V	labials and labio-dentals	1
C, G, J, K, Q, S, X, Z	gutterals and sibilants	2
D, T	dental-mutes	3
L	palatal-fricative	4
M, N	labio-nasal and lingua-nasal	5
R	dental fricative	6

The resulting value is padded with zeros, if necessary. Here are some simple examples. The words "Two," "To," and "Too" all have the same pronunciation. I'll pass each to the Soundex function:

```
SELECT SOUNDEX('Two')

SELECT SOUNDEX ('To')

SELECT SOUNDEX ('Too')
```

The result is the same for each word, T000, as shown in Figure 11-1.

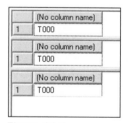

Figure 11-1

Because there are no consonants after the "T," zeros are added. This happens to be the same value returned for Tea, Tee, Tow, Toe, and Toy. Using a more complex word, the result is more precise. For example, the Soundex value for the word "Microsoft" is M262: 2 for C, 6 for R, and 2 for S.

Try a few different words. Generally, I've found this to work reasonably well for comparing the close-ness of words, but using the Soundex function for this purpose is not an exact science. For example, the word Seattle has a Soundex value of S340, which is the same for the word Settle. However, the word Subtle has a Soundex value of S134 because the algorithm missed the fact that the B is silent. This con-firms what I've known all along, that people from Seattle are not very subtle.

The SOUNDEX() function returns a character string. With the exception of an exact match, you would need to parse this string and convert the numeric value to a numeric type. This would allow you to make quantitative comparisons. In this example, I use variables to hold the input and output values. The

SOUNDEX() function output is parsed using the SUBSTRING() function to return only the numerical value. The difference is calculated and converted to a positive value using the ABS() function. Using this approach, I'll compare Redmond and Renton, two neighboring Washington State cities that many people (including my wife) often confuse:

```
DECLARE @Word1 VarChar(100)
DECLARE @Word2 VarChar(100)
DECLARE @Value1 Int
DECLARE @Value2 Int
DECLARE @SoundexDiff Int

SET @Word1 = 'Redmond'
SET @Word2 = 'Renton'
SELECT @Value1 = CONVERT(Int, SUBSTRING(SOUNDEX(@Word1), 2, 3))
SELECT @Value2 = CONVERT(Int, SUBSTRING(SOUNDEX(@Word2), 2, 3))
SET @SoundexDiff = ABS(@Value1 - @Value2)

PRINT @SoundexDiff
```

According to the SOUNDEX() function, these two words are quite different phonetically. My query returns a difference of 180. If you don't want to go to this much work and don't need such a granular comparison, all this effort isn't necessary.

The DIFFERENCE() Function

The DIFFERENCE() function is really just a wrapper around two SOUNDEX() function calls and some business logic to compare the values. It simplifies the comparison, reducing the result to a scale from 0 to 4, where the value 4 indicates a very close or exact match.

I'll use the DIFFERENCE() function to compare the words To and Two:

```
SELECT DIFFERENCE('To', 'Two')
```

The result is 4, indicating a very close or exact match.

Using the DIFFERENCE() function to compare Redmond with Renton, as follows,

```
SELECT DIFFERENCE ('Redmond', 'Renton')
```

returns 3, meaning a similar but not-so-close match.

Managing and Populating Catalogs

Even though the task of managing full-text indexes belongs to the Microsoft Search Service, rather than SQL Server, all of the management work can be performed within the SQL Server management tools. These tasks are similar in SQL Server 2000 and SQL Server 2005. I'll start with the SQL Server 2000 Enterprise Manager and then move on to the SQL Server 2005 Management Studio. I'll briefly show you how to create and populate a full-text catalog. For detailed information on managing full-text indexes and catalogs, please refer to *Professional SQL Server 2000 Programming* and *Professional SQL Server 2005* from Wrox Press.

SQL Server 2000

A few different methods are used to create a catalog and indexes. If you are using Enterprise Manager, you can use one of these methods to create a new full-text catalog:

- ❑ Right-click a database and choose New Full-Text Catalog to open the New Full-Text Catalog dialog window (see Figure 11-2).

- ❑ From the Tools menu, choose Full-Text Indexing to open the Full-Text Index Wizard.

- ❑ Right-click a table and, from the pop-up menu, select Full-Text Index Table ➪ Define Full-Text Indexing. If a catalog doesn't currently exist, you will be prompted to create one and then to define an index for the table.

Figure 11-2

This launches the Full-Text Indexing Wizard dialog shown in Figure 11-3.

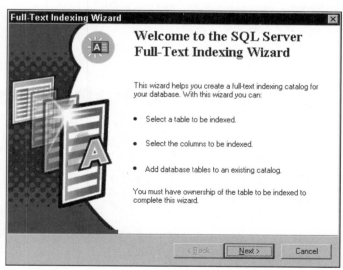

Figure 11-3

Enter a name for the new catalog and finish the wizard, accepting all other default settings, as shown in Figure 11-4.

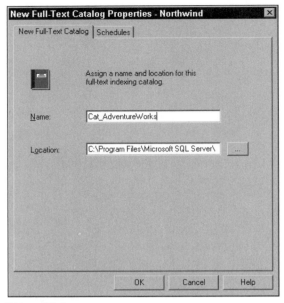

Figure 11-4

After a full-text catalog has been created, the console tree will have an icon added enabling you to manage full-text indexing for the database. Indexes can be created in a number of ways. One simple technique is to right-click a table icon in Enterprise Manager and then select Full-Text Index Table from the menu, choosing the Define Full-Text Indexing on a Table. . . option, as shown in Figure 11-5.

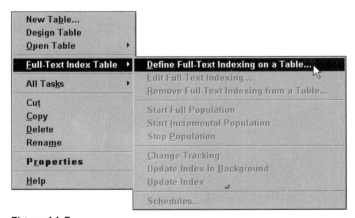

Figure 11-5

SQL Server 2005

Probably the most significant enhancement to full-text indexing in SQL Server 2005 is that the database engine can update indexes as data changes. This can make full-text indexing behave more like standard indexing and greatly reduce data latency. Just keep in mind that this feature can have a significant impact on overall server performance. This may not be a wise option in a busy transactional database environment unless you have a very capable server.

Implementing catalogs and indexes in the SQL Server Management Studio is very similar to using Enterprise Manager. The Full-Text Indexing Wizard contains several pages, and I'm not going to show them all. Begin by defining a new catalog for the AdventureWorks2000 database. Under the database, expand the Storage node and right-click Full-Text Catalogs. From the menu, select New Full-Text Catalog. . ., as shown in Figure 11-6.

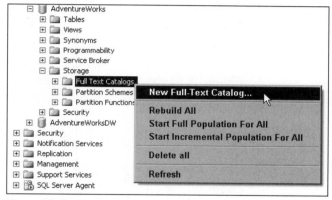

Figure 11-6

The New Full-Text Catalog dialog is used to name, specify a file location, and set options for the new catalog file, as shown in Figure 11-7.

After creating a catalog, indexes can be created for tables. To create a new index, right-click a table icon and choose Full-Text Index ⇨ Define Full-Text Index. . . , as shown in Figure 11-8.

When the Full-Text Indexing Wizard opens, navigate past the opening page. Because the wizard was launched from the Product table, it polls the table for a list of indexes. A unique index must exist in order to build a full-text index. Accept the default selection, which is the primary key for this table, as shown in Figure 11-9.

Next, a list of columns is displayed. These are candidates for full-text indexing. Check any columns that you would like to have included in the full-text index, as demonstrated in Figure 11-10.

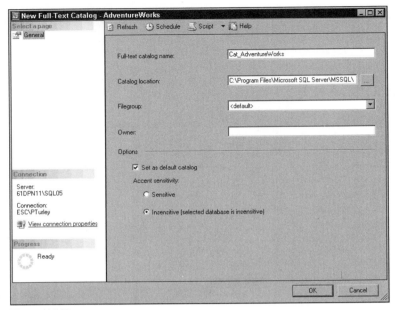

Figure 11-7

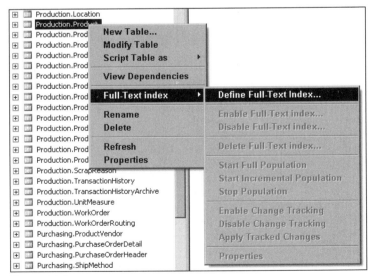

Figure 11-8

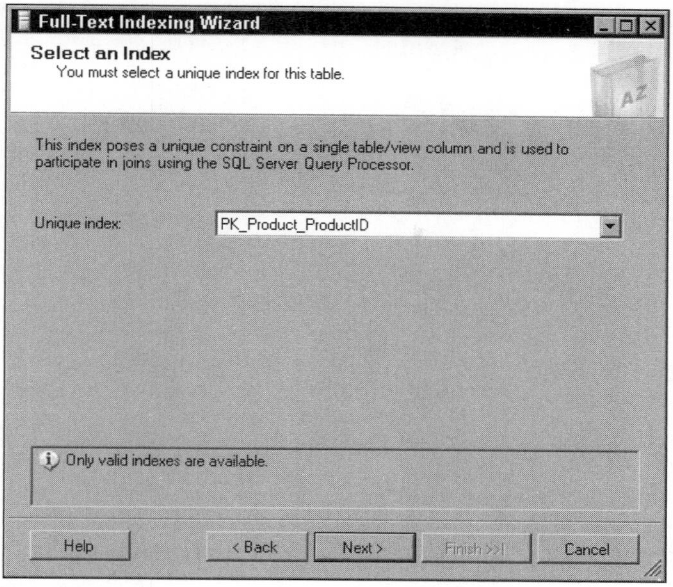

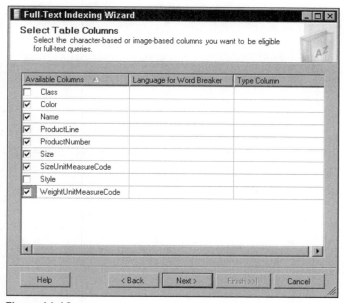

Figure 11-9

Figure 11-10

If you would like to have SQL Server track and automatically update this full-text index as data is modified, leave the Change Tracking option set to Automatically, as shown in Figure 11-11.

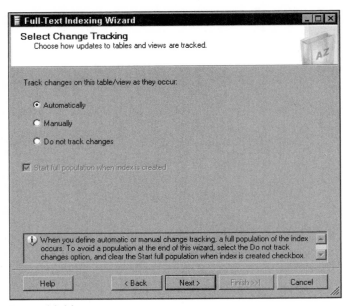

Figure 11-11

The page gives you the option to select an existing catalog or to create a new catalog. Because I created a catalog to store full-text indexes for this database, select the existing catalog, as shown in Figure 11-12.

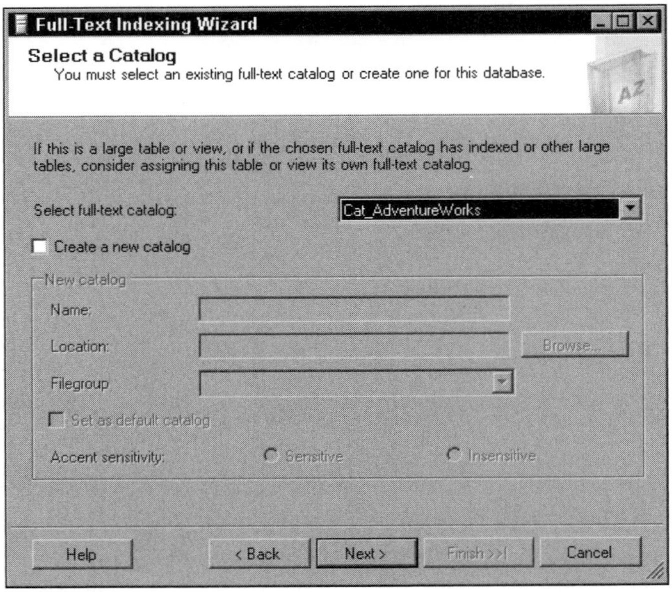

Figure 11-12

The next page allows you to manage full-text catalog population schedules. Creating a schedule invokes the SQL Server Agent service, which must be running for this option to function properly. Click Next to skip this page.

The following page displays summary information (see Figure 11-13). Using this dialog, you can review your selections and options. Because no settings have yet been applied, you can use the Next and Previous buttons to navigate to any page to make changes. Click the Finish button to apply your selections and build the next full-text index.

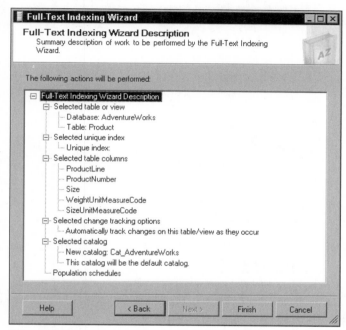

Figure 11-13

The final wizard page, shown in Figure 11-14, displays the progress of each step, as it is applied by the wizard.

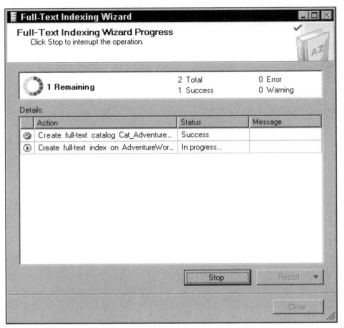

Figure 11-14

Later in this chapter, I'm going to use some examples of full-text queries on the ProductReview table. Rather than using the wizard, create this index using the following script:

```
CREATE FULLTEXT INDEX
ON ProductReview(Comments, ReviewerName)
KEY Index PK_ProductReview_ProductReviewID
```

An optional statement can be used to explicitly control whether SQL Server tracks changes and whether it automatically populates and updates the index. You may want to disable change tracking to conserve server resources or to give yourself more control over this process.

To explicitly populate the index using change tracking, add this line to the end of the prior script:

```
WITH Change_Tracking Auto
```

To explicitly turn off change tracking, use this option:

```
WITH Change_Tracking OFF
```

In case you want to manually populate a full-text index that has not been set up for automatic population, use this option of the sp_fulltext_table system stored procedure:

```
sp_fulltext_table 'ProductReview', 'start_full'
```

This stored procedure can be used in place of the Create FullText Index expression used previously and includes several related maintenance options.

Full-Text Query Expressions

Full-text indexing in SQL Server extends the Transact-SQL feature set by adding four languages predicates:

- ❑   CONTAINS
- ❑   FREETEXT
- ❑   CONTAINSTABLE
- ❑   FREETEXTTABLE

You'll recall that a predicate is simply a functional statement that yields a Boolean result. Predicates always return a true or false value. Functionally, these are really only two predicate statements with each having an alternate implementation that returns a SQL Server table object — rather than a standard result set — from the query. A predicate is simply an extension to the SQL language, used in a WHERE clause, that provides a conduit from SQL Server to the Microsoft Search Service. As far as you are concerned, you are working with SQL and communicating to the database engine. The reality is that these statements take your request outside of SQL Server and make requests against the search service. The only real evidence of this is in the way you must pass string values.

Quotes in Quotes

This is an interesting idiosyncrasy of the full-text query syntax. As you know, when passing text string values to Transact-SQL, these values are encapsulated in single quotes. This is still the case when using full-text predicates, however, these string values are then passed from SQL to the search service, which requires that values are passed within double quotes. This means that when you need to pass values to a full-text query expression (if the value contains spaces) you must pass a double-quoted value within single quotes, like this:

```
'"My Value"'
```

This may seem a little strange but let me explain why this is necessary. Transact-SQL requires literal string values to be passed in single quotes. Before SQL Server reroutes the statement to the search service, it strips off the single quotes, passing values in the proper format for the search service, which requires literal values that include spaces to be enclosed in double quotes. When using logical operators within a full-text predicate call, you may need to pass multiple quoted values between operators, all of which are enclosed within single quotes for SQL to handle them, and each value in double quotes, as follows:

```
'"My Value" OR "Your Value"'
```

Examples of the entire call syntax follow shortly, but I want to make sure you're comfortable with this requirement to pass double-quoted values (required by the Microsoft Search Service) within single quotes (required by SQL Server).

The CONTAINS Predicate

The CONTAINS predicate lets you find and return rows where one or any combination of indexed column values contains a specified value, or optionally a form of a specified word. The features of this predicate are as follows:

- ❑ Search criterion can apply to values in one or any number of specified column(s) contained in the full-text index.

- ❑ Search criterion can apply to values in all columns contained in the full-text index.

- ❑ The columns' text includes a word or string of characters located anywhere within the text. Matching text can include wildcards indicating that a word starts with, ends with, or contains a string of characters.

- ❑ Match may be based on a form of a specified word. For example, the text may include a plural, singular, different gender form, or different tense of the word.

The full-text indexing engine includes a vast thesaurus of words in different forms and inflections. This supports multiple languages if different language packs have been installed. To be able to apply language rules to the text, the engine needs to know what language to use. The language parameter for all predicates will accept either the language alias (friendly name) or the LCID, an integer value used internally. Full-text indexing recognizes the languages listed in the following table.

Alias	LCID
Arabic	1025
Brazilian	1046
British English	2057
Bulgarian	1026
Croatian	1050
Czech	1029
Danish	1030
Dutch	1043
English	1033
Estonian	1061
Finnish	1035
French	1036
German	1031
Greek	1032
Hungarian	1038
Italian	1040
Japanese	1041

Alias	LCID	
Korean	1042	
Latvian	1062	
Lithuanian	1063	
Norwegian	2068	
Polish	1045	
Portuguese	2070	
Romanian	1048	
Russian	1049	
Simplified Chinese	2052	
Slovak	1051	
Slovenian	1060	
Spanish	3082	
Swedish	1053	
Thai	1054	
Traditional Chinese	1028	
Turkish	1055	

If the language parameter is omitted, the language will be derived from the column, table, or database.

I'll start with a simple example. I'm interested in returning all Product records where any indexed column contains the value "Black." The first parameter to this function-like statement indicates the indexed columns I want to include in the search. The asterisk (*) represents all available columns. The second parameter is my search criteria:

```
SELECT * FROM Product
WHERE CONTAINS(*, '"Black"')
```

The results are shown in Figure 11-15.

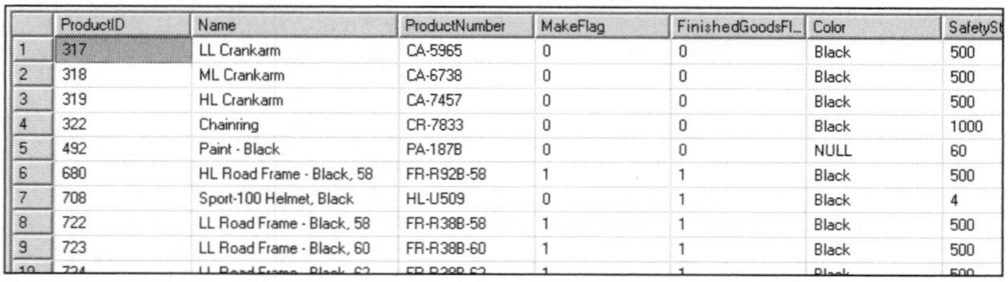

	ProductID	Name	ProductNumber	MakeFlag	FinishedGoodsFl...	Color	SafetySt
1	317	LL Crankarm	CA-5965	0	0	Black	500
2	318	ML Crankarm	CA-6738	0	0	Black	500
3	319	HL Crankarm	CA-7457	0	0	Black	500
4	322	Chainring	CR-7833	0	0	Black	1000
5	492	Paint - Black	PA-187B	0	0	NULL	60
6	680	HL Road Frame - Black, 58	FR-R92B-58	1	1	Black	500
7	708	Sport-100 Helmet, Black	HL-U509	0	1	Black	4
8	722	LL Road Frame - Black, 58	FR-R38B-58	1	1	Black	500
9	723	LL Road Frame - Black, 60	FR-R38B-60	1	1	Black	500
10	724	LL Road Frame - Black, 62	FR-R38B-62	1	1	Black	500

Figure 11-15

As you can see, rows are returned where the word "Black" is contained in both the Name and Color columns. However, you may be wondering why the word "Black" was found in the middle of a field value when I didn't use any wildcard characters. Something to get used to when using full-text queries are the differences in behavior from this and the SQL *LIKE* operator. Full-text queries match whole words anywhere within a field without using wildcards. Wildcard matching is performed to match a substring, or part of a word. For example, I'll look for any rows that contain text beginning with the letters "crank":

```
SELECT * FROM Product
WHERE CONTAINS(*, '"crank*"')
```

Note that the wildcard character isn't the percent symbol, %, as it is in Transact-SQL. It's the asterisk, *. The results are shown in Figure 11-16.

	ProductID	Name	ProductNumber
1	317	LL Crankarm	CA-5965
2	318	ML Crankarm	CA-6738
3	319	HL Crankarm	CA-7457
4	949	LL Crankset	CS-4759
5	950	ML Crankset	CS-6583
6	951	HL Crankset	CS-9183

Figure 11-16

You can also specify a list of columns you want to include in the search by specifying a comma-delimited column list within parentheses:

```
SELECT * FROM Product
WHERE CONTAINS((ProductNumber, Name, Color), '"Black"')
```

The full-text indexing engine includes an internal thesaurus of words and their variations. This enables the CONTAINS predicate to match different forms of a word. This might include past-, future-, or present-tense, or different gender inflections. For example, performing a full-text search on the Product table for the word "tour" returns records containing the word "touring," as shown in Figure 11-17.

```
SELECT * FROM Product
WHERE CONTAINS(*, 'FORMSOF(Inflectional, "Tour")')
```

	ProductID	Name
1	330	Touring End Caps
2	513	Touring Rim
3	520	LL Touring Seat Assembly
4	521	ML Touring Seat Assembly
5	522	HL Touring Seat Assembly
6	821	Touring Front Wheel
7	829	Touring Rear Wheel
8	842	Touring-Panniers, Large
9	885	HL Touring Frame - Yellow, 60
10	886	LL Touring Frame - Yellow, 62

Figure 11-17

Weighting Values

You can affect the outcome of word matching, and relative ranking of rows, by designating relative weight values for different words. A weight value is a numeric value between 0.0 and 1.0, accurate to one decimal position. Because these values are actually passed as a text string along with the rest of the search criteria, SQL Server doesn't really see this as a numerical type. These values are used only for relative comparison, so it's not necessary to make them add up to anything in particular. A weighted-value word list is passed to the ISABOUT() function, within the CONTAINS predicate expression:

```
ISABOUT (<word> weight (.75), <word> weight (.25))
```

The result of this weighting will affect whether or not some rows are included in the result set but may not otherwise be apparent when using the CONTAINS predicate. This is apparent, however, in the value of the calculated Rank column returned by the CONTAINSTABLE and FREETEXTTABLE predicates.

Ranked Results

Internally, the CONTAINS predicate calculates a qualifying ranking value for each row, based on exact and approximate word matching, logical operators, and explicit weighting value factors. Because the CONTAINS and FREETEXT predicates are only used to qualify selected rows returned in the result set, these techniques can't expose the ranking of each row. The CONTAINSTABLE and FREETEXTTABLE predicates do create a new result set, returned as a SQL table object. A new column, called Rank, is added to the result with the relative ranking value of each row.

The CONTAINSTABLE Predicate

Functionally, this is the CONTAINS predicate, wrapped by functionality that returns a SQL table object. Two additional columns are added to the result. The Key column is just a duplicate of the full-text index key column, which was specified when the full-text index was created. The Rank column appears, as I mentioned previously.

```
SELECT ProductID, Name, ProductNumber, Color, Rank
FROM Product INNER JOIN
CONTAINSTABLE(Product, *
    , 'ISABOUT (Black weight (.2), Blue weight (.8))') AS ConTbl
    ON Product.ProductID = ConTbl.[Key]
ORDER BY Rank DESC
```

Take a look at another example. Full-text queries are ideal for searching large volumes of text. The first thing I'll do is create a full-text index on the ProductReview table. This table contains a Comments column used to hold verbose text. After populating the index, the following query can be executed. Note the weight values for the two words:

```
SELECT Comments, Rank
FROM ProductReview INNER JOIN
CONTAINSTABLE(ProductReview, Comments
    , 'ISABOUT (terrible weight(.9), advertised weight(.1))') AS ConTbl
    ON ProductReview.ProductReviewID = ConTbl.[Key]
ORDER BY Rank DESC
```

When the query is executed, a rank value is calculated based on these words found in the Comments column and the relative weight values. Note the values in the Rank column shown in Figure 11-18.

	Comments	Rank
1	Maybe it's just because I'm new to mountain biking, but I had a terrible time getting use t...	61
2	The Road-550-W from Adventure Works Cycles is everything it's advertised to be. Finally...	2

Figure 11-18

Now I'll change the weight values (reversing .9 and .1) and execute the query again:

```
SELECT Comments, Rank
FROM ProductReview INNER JOIN
CONTAINSTABLE(ProductReview, Comments,
   'ISABOUT (terrible weight(.1), advertised weight(.9))') AS ConTbl
  ON ProductReview.ProductReviewID = ConTbl.[Key]
ORDER BY Rank DESC
```

The FREETEXT Predicate

Can a computer really understand what you want rather than simply give you exactly what you asked it for? The FREETEXT predicate attempts to do just that — to understand the meaning of a phrase or sentence. It does this by breaking a phrase down into individual words and then using the full-text indexing thesaurus to match all forms of these words, applying language rules. It may choose to return text that only contains forms of some of these words. As each row is considered for selection, an algorithm calculates a relative ranking value, used to qualify each record against the matching phrase.

The FREETEXT predicate takes few parameters, and the only optional parameter is the language. As with the CONTAINS predicate, if omitted, the language will be derived from the database. The ranking is not exposed in the result, and the order of records is unaffected by the ranking.

```
SELECT * FROM Product
WHERE FREETEXT (*, 'Yellow road bike')
```

Not only are records returned where indexed columns contain the words "yellow," "road," and "bike," but those records that contain any one of these words or forms of these words are also returned, as shown in Figure 11-19.

	ProductID	Name	ProductNumber	MakeFlag	FinishedGoodsFl...	Color
1	329	Road End Caps	EC-R098	1	0	NULL
2	496	Paint - Yellow	PA-823Y	0	0	NULL
3	510	LL Road Rim	RM-R436	0	0	NULL
4	511	ML Road Rim	RM-R600	0	0	NULL
5	512	HL Road Rim	RM-R800	0	0	NULL
6	517	LL Road Seat Assembly	SA-R127	1	0	NULL
7	518	ML Road Seat Assembly	SA-R430	1	0	NULL
8	519	HL Road Seat Assembly	SA-R522	1	0	NULL
9	680	HL Road Frame - Black, 58	FR-R92B-58	1	1	Black
10	706	HL Road Frame - Red, 58	FR-R92R-58	1	1	Red

Figure 11-19

Logical Operators

Multiple words or text strings can be specified applying three different forms of logic, as explained in the following table.

Operator	Logic
AND	Criteria on both sides of the operator must match. If two values were provided with the AND operator, a single column value in each qualifying row must match both of the values.
OR	Criteria on either side of the operator must match. If two values were provided with the OR operator, a single column value in each qualifying row must match any provided value.
NEAR	Like the AND operator, both values must match text in a single column value for qualifying rows.

The FREETEXTTABLE Predicate

Like the CONTAINSTABLE predicate, FREETEXTTABLE is functionally the same as the FREETEXT predicate, but it returns a table with ranking values. Using the same technique as before, this table can be joined with the base table to return matching rows and the ranking values.

In this example, I've used a phrase that doesn't match any text exactly but several of the words may be found in the column text:

```
SELECT Comments, Rank
FROM ProductReview INNER JOIN
FREETEXTTABLE(ProductReview, Comments
   , 'mountain biking is new for me') AS FtTbl
   ON ProductReview.ProductReviewID = FtTbl.[Key]
ORDER BY Rank DESC
```

The result returns two rows with one row ranked significantly higher than the other, as shown in Figure 11-20.

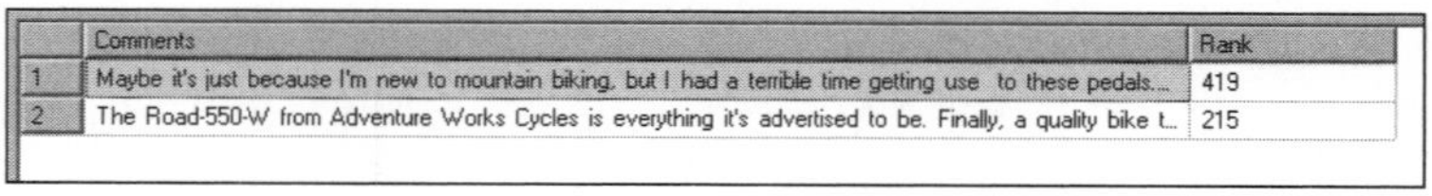

	Comments	Rank
1	Maybe it's just because I'm new to mountain biking, but I had a terrible time getting use to these pedals...	419
2	The Road-550-W from Adventure Works Cycles is everything it's advertised to be. Finally, a quality bike t...	215

Figure 11-20

The goal of free-text matching is to loosen the matching rules and provide some level of flexibility. Inevitably, this will return some rows that are simply not all that similar to the search text. To make the FREETEXT or FREETEXTTABLE predicate behave in a more predictable manner, you can force it to match the text exactly as it is presented by encapsulating the entire search text in double quotes:

```
SELECT Comments
FROM ProductReview
WHERE FREETEXT (Comments, '"new to mountain biking"')
```

Only one row matches this text exactly, as shown in Figure 11-21.

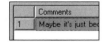

Figure 11-21

Summary

Often in our world of computer-managed precision and rigid logic, it's important to see past exact values and look for information with similar meaning and context. The SOUNDEX() and DIFFERENCE() functions were designed help you make inexact comparisons, matching words with the same or similar phonetic patterns. Using the SOUNDEX() function is actually an older and fairly unsophisticated technique for matching words based on basic phonetic language rules. It's simple and often useful for matching words that sound similar.

Full-text indexing is a very capable resource for searching and matching content within any text, large or small. The CONTAINS and FREETEXT predicates work very effectively where you may be storing very large volumes of notes, comments, or document content. The CONTAINS predicate gives you fairly precise control over matching logic but will also let you find words, text, and phrases that are grammatically similar to the words you search for. The FREETEXT predicate is generally used for soft-matching a phrase when you don't need text to match exactly, but to find text with similar meaning and content. The CONTAINSTABLE and FREETEXTTABLE predicates expand on their base predicates by returning SQL table types capable of presenting a ranked listing of qualifying values and integrating these features into more sophisticated queries.

Creating and Managing Database Objects

My friend Eric said that I should have titled this chapter "Going Fishing." I commute and do much of my writing on the Washington State ferries and I get a lot of input from my fellow commuters. When I asked Eric "Why Going Fishing," he said that managing database objects is boring and that people would be more interested in fishing stories than creating tables. The fact is that creating and managing database objects is pretty simple (and, yes, mundane) stuff. However, there is little doubt that this is an essential part of the process. After all, how can you use a database until it's been designed and created?

Anything you can do with SQL Server's graphical or console management tools can be done with script. Many of the menu options in Enterprise Manager and Management studio actually use the Transact-SQL script you'll be using in this chapter.

Data Definition Language

You can do only three things with any database object, other than actually use it; you can create it, alter it, or drop it to get rid of it. Every type of database object at least supports the CREATE and DROP statements. Of course, there is actually a little more to this story. Depending on the object type, there are a number of options affecting certain capabilities and settings. You've already seen a number of these statements, because it would have been difficult to cover earlier topics without first showing you how to create some objects.

Unless permissions are explicitly assigned, only members of the following roles can execute these statements:

❑   sysadmin
❑   dbcreator
❑   db_ddladmin
❑   db_owner

It's a good idea to use role assignments rather than changing permissions for individual users. In the long run, this creates a more manageable environment.

SQL Server 2005 introduces several new objects that have corresponding CREATE and DROP statements. Many of these objects also have a corresponding ALTER statement. Managing all of these special-purpose objects is beyond the scope of this book. This chapter covers the use of these statements related to tables, views, stored procedures, and user-defined functions.

Creating Objects

The basic pattern of the CREATE statement is the same for all objects. However, due to the unique characteristics of different objects, each statement may have a number of different options. To keep things simple, this chapter does not include examples of every incarnation of CREATE statements, but it does includes the most common.

Altering Objects

Generally, any options or changes that can be applied with the CREATE statement can be applied to an existing object using the ALTER statement. If security permissions have been granted or denied for an object, it's a good idea to use the ALTER statement to make changes to an object rather than dropping and re-creating it. This way, the security settings are preserved and the database doesn't make a new entry into the sysobjects system table. A consequence of dropping and re-creating some objects is that this may affect related dependencies. For example, dropping a table with indexes is a cumbersome task and any dependent objects created with schema binding will cause errors to be raised. Altering tables instead wouldn't have the same impact, especially if you didn't make changes to columns that would affect other objects.

Dropping Objects

The syntax for dropping most any object is pretty much the same. You cannot drop objects that would render schema-bound dependencies invalid. For example, you cannot drop a table if it is referenced in a dependent foreign key constraint. In this case, you must either drop the related table or alter the table and remove the constraint.

Names

The rules for naming objects in SQL Server are extraordinarily flexible. They are so flexible, in fact, that it becomes very easy to create objects with names that will cause pain and suffering from the moment you create them. The following sections explain two naming guidelines. The first I would consider more a set of rules than a guideline, and the second is strictly a naming convention. You can disagree with it if you like, but examine the merits of the convention and then come up with your own.

Naming Rules

SQL Server limits the maximum number of characters in any object's name to 128 with the exception of local temporary tables, which are limited to 116 characters. If you choose to create data objects in SQL Server that push this limitation, I can guarantee that you will not be very popular with anyone who must write queries against your objects. For maximum compatibility, all permanent SQL objects should begin with a letter, should not contain any embedded spaces, and should not use any reserved words. After the first letter the name can contain any combination of numbers and letters. It can also contain some special characters, but these should be avoided like the plague. SQL Server's loose naming rules actually allow you to create an object with the same name as a reserved word, but if you do you will have to use delimiter characters. If, for some reason, you actually wanted to create a table called Select with columns called From, Insert, and Delete, SQL Server would let you as long as you delimit the names so that SQL Server does not recognize the reserved words as reserved words, as the following example illustrates:

```
CREATE TABLE [Select]
([From] Int,
[Insert] nVarChar(50),
[Delete] nVarChar(50))
```

There are two different delimiter characters: the square bracket and the double quote. The square bracket delimiter is the default in SQL Server, as illustrated in the previous example. The ANSI standard, however, designates the double quote as the standard delimiter. To use double quotes as delimiters, the database or connection-specific QUOTED_IDENTIFIER option must be set to ON. The .NET Native SQL Client, Microsoft OLE DB Provider for SQL Server, and the SQL Server ODBC driver set the QUOTED_IDENTIFIER option to ON by default when they connect:

```
SET QUOTED_IDENTIFIER ON
CREATE TABLE "Select"
(
"From" Int,
"Insert" nVarChar(50),
"Delete" nVarChar(50)
)
```

An object's name should be as short as practical but still identify what the object is all about. A table that is used to store data about an employee could simply be called Employee. It's simple and descriptive. The Northwind and Pubs sample databases that ship with SQL Server 7 and 2000 are actually very good examples of how not to name objects. Both Northwind and Pubs use reserved words to define objects, which should never be done. Northwind also contains a few objects with embedded spaces in their names. Order Details is a prime example. This anti-example actually uses a reserved word and an embedded space.

Here is a simple and effective way of checking your names: If you type the name in Query Analyzer and it shows up blue, don't use it as an object name. As mentioned in Chapter 3, Query Analyzer automatically changes the color of any reserved word to blue by default. Query Analyzer is a bit aggressive on what it considers a reserved word because it includes both SQL and ODBC keywords, but discretion is not just the better part of valor, it is also the better part of SQL programming. If it turns blue, choose a different name. When it comes to embedded spaces, they are not prohibited; they are just, in the opinion of this author, stupid. Remember that Database object names are limited to 128 characters, so you could conceivably create a table using the following script:

```
CREATE TABLE [This is my table that contains employee data]
(
[My primary key to uniquely track employees] Int,
[The employee's last name goes here] nVarChar(50),
[The employee's First name goes here] nVarChar(50)
)
```

However, I am sure you would not want to write queries against a database that adhered to this type of naming, and, in fact, many database and database application tools do not support embedded spaces.

Sometimes even I want to give an object a name that contains more than one word so I, like many database developers, avoid the embedded space problem by using either underscores or what is known as "camel case." If you choose underscores, just replace the embedded spaces with an underscore. As a result the Order Details table in Northwind would end up as Order_Details. I prefer camel case, probably because I am not a very good typist and having to use the Shift key unnecessarily causes me discomfort. My official public reason for using "camel case" is that underscores disappear in hyperlinks. Camel case avoids both spaces and underscores by pushing multiple words together and capitalizing each individual word. In this way Order Details becomes OrderDetails. There is no hard and fast rule concerning underscores and camel case so it really comes down to personal preference or company coding guidelines. The most important aspect of naming objects is to avoid reserved words, embedded spaces, and to be consistent.

Naming Guidelines

The basic rules outlined previously will prevent a large amount of pain and frustration. The following naming guideline is just one of many. I prefer it, but I know of many developers who do not. What naming guidelines or conventions boil down to are naming rules, best practices, and personal preference. As a general rule, when I name a table or view I express them in the singular. A view and table represent a single instance of the entity described by the table. Therefore, the table that describes an employee is called Employee, not Employees. This may seem a bit picky, but when you do a great deal of data modeling with Entity Relationship Diagram (ERD) tools, Object Relational Modeling (ORM) tools, or United Modeling Language (UML), it becomes rather significant. These tools typically enforce singularity for the object and plurality with the relationship.

Most of the organizations I have worked with have had some sort of established naming convention that dictated the use of a prefix on all objects so that they were identifiable in their own right without database context. This is another one of those areas where some developers cringe and others celebrate. The following table is an example of a typical naming convention.

Object Type	Name
Table	tblEmployee
View	vwOpsEmployee
Stored Procedure	spInsertEmployee
Function	fnNewEmployees
Trigger	trVerifyEmployee
Check Constraint	ckPhoneNumber
Foreign Key Constraint	fkSalesEmployeeLink
Primary Key Constraint	pkEmployeeID
Default	dfRegion
Clustered Index	clRegionID
Non-Clustered Index	ncLastName

As the table illustrates, data objects take on the name of a single instance of their data. Programming objects, such as stored procedures, triggers, and functions, take on the name of what they do.

Now armed with information about the name of objects, the following sections look at how to actually create, alter, and drop them.

CREATE TABLE

In its simplest form, the CREATE TABLE statement contains the name of the new table followed by its column definitions in parentheses. For each column, a name, data type specification, and NULL specification are provided, as in the following example:

```
CREATE TABLE MyTable (MyID Int NOT NULL, MyDescription nVarChar(50) NULL)
```

This example script creates a table called MyTable that is made up of two columns. The first column is called MyID, which has a data type of integer and cannot hold a NULL. The second column is called MyDescription. It has a Unicode variable character data type and can be NULL. This may be sufficient to get started, but it certainly isn't comprehensive. Tables are typically a little more sophisticated than this. Several options are available to us as this partial syntax for CREATE TABLE suggests:

```
CREATE TABLE
    [ database_name.[ owner ] . | owner. ] table_name
    ( { < column_definition >
        | column_name AS computed_column_expression
        | < table_constraint > ::= [ CONSTRAINT constraint_name ] }

          | [ { PRIMARY KEY | UNIQUE } [ ,...n ]
    )
```

Most of the time when a table is created the options that are defined are the table name, the column names, whether or not the columns are nullable, and what column is the primary key. Chapters 1 and 2 reviewed all the possible data types that can be assigned to a column and briefly explained the concept of NULLs and primary keys, so I won't repeat them here except as it applies to the CREATE TABLE statement.

Nullability

You can enable a column to optionally not require a value by designating it as a nullable column. This simply means that if no value is provided it defaults to NULL. NULL is defined as the absence of data, so it does not have any real value. To enable a column to be nullable, the NULL keyword is added immediately after the data type. To prevent nulls, the NOT NULL keywords are added. NOT NULL is actually considered a column constraint, which is covered later in this chapter. If NULL or NOT NULL is not specified, the default setting is to allow nulls, as the next two examples show. However, it is a best practice to always designate the nullability of a column when creating or altering a table.

```
CREATE TABLE MyTable
    ( Category nVarChar(50) NOT NULL
    , MyDescription nVarChar(50)
    )
```

```
CREATE TABLE MyTable
```

```
       ( Category nVarChar(50) NOT NULL
       , MyDescription nVarChar(50) NULL
)
```

With either of the two preceding examples the MyTable table only requires the value for Category to be provided for an insert operation:

```
INSERT MyTable (Category)
VALUES ('Category1')

SELECT * FROM MyTable

Category                MyDescription
----------------------  -----------------------------------------------
Category1               NULL
```

Identity

Very often the database developer will want to have a numerical value automatically assigned to a row any time a new row is added. This is the purpose of a column assigned the IDENTITY property. It is very similar to Microsoft Access's AutoNumber feature, which automatically assigns an integer to every new row. However, the IDENTITY property is much more powerful and flexible. Typically what happens is that a table is created with the default values, which is equivalent to how Access functions:

```
CREATE TABLE MyTable (MyID Int IDENTITY(1, 1) NOT NULL
                      , MyDescription nVarChar(50) NOT NULL)
```

```
CREATE TABLE MyTable (MyID Int IDENTITY NOT NULL
                      , MyDescription nVarChar(50) NOT NULL)
```

Both of the preceding examples cause an incremental value to be assigned starting at 1 and incrementing by 1. The actual syntax for the IDENTITY property is as follows:

```
IDENTITY [ (seed , increment ) ]
```

As the syntax infers, the seed and increment values are not restricted to 1, and they are not strictly limited to integers. Supported data types for the IDENTITY property are TinyInt, SmallInt Int, BigInt, Decimal, and Numeric. However, the decimal and numeric data types are of limited usefulness because they can only be assigned a scale of 0. The scale of these data types defines how many digits are supported to the right of the decimal point. Specifying a decimal or numeric data type with a scale of 0 makes the data type behave like an integer.

The increment value of the IDENTITY property is restricted to whole numbers regardless of the data type used, but it is not limited to a value of 1 or even to positive numbers. A table could be created with an IDENTITY property that is set to start at 1,000,000 and decrement by 100 for every row added. The CREATE statement would look like this:

```
CREATE TABLE MyTable (MyID Int IDENTITY(1000000, -100) NOT NULL
                      ,MyDescription NVarChar(50) NOT NULL )
```

If you were designing a database that tracked ticket sales for a venue that could seat 3000 people, you could conceivably seed a tracking table at 3000 with an incremental value of −1 and not allow the number to go negative (through the use of a constraint). This way, every sale could also return the number of tickets remaining without writing an expression to calculate the value.

A table could also be created so that the seed value was negative and the increment was positive:

```
CREATE TABLE MyTable (MyID Int IDENTITY(-1000000, 100) NOT NULL
                     ,MyDescription NVarChar(50) NOT NULL)
```

A column with an IDENTITY property is probably the most common form of primary key value, but be aware that the IDENTITY property by itself does not guarantee uniqueness. If a value is explicitly inserted in the IDENTITY column, SQL Server will not prevent a duplicate unless a constraint has been added to the column to prevent duplicates. Also, keep in mind that a table can have only one IDENTITY column defined.

By default, once a column has been assigned the IDENTITY property, SQL Server does not allow explicit values to be inserted into it. Any attempt to manually enter a value will result in the following error:

```
INSERT MyTable (MyID, MyDescription)
VALUES (5, 'This will not work')
```

```
Server: Msg 544, Level 16, State 1, Line 1
Cannot insert explicit value for identity column in table 'MyTable' when
IDENTITY_INSERT is set to OFF.
```

Although SQL Server by default doesn't allow explicit values to be inserted into an IDENTITY column, there may very well be times when you need to do exactly that. To do so, the IDENTITY property must be temporarily turned off. This can be done by using a SET option on the connection to the database that will be used for the explicit insert:

```
SET IDENTITY_INSERT MyTable ON
INSERT MyTable (MyID, MyDescription)
VALUES (5, 'This will work')
SET IDENTITY_INSERT MyTable OFF
```

It is very important to turn IDENTITY_INSERT off after the transaction is complete because any normal insertions into the table (by not specifying the INDENTITY value) within the same connection context will fail if the IDENTITY column is not explicitly identified and options can only be enabled on one table at a time. The SET IDENTITY_INSERT option is only effective on the connection on which it is used and will be terminated if the connection is closed, even if the option is not reset. Best practices in database design, however, are a lot like the rules our parents tried to teach us: If you use or borrow something, put it back where you found it. So, if you alter a database or connection setting and you do not intend for the change to be permanent, put it back the way you found it. All other connections will continue to work normally by having the IDENTITY value automatically supplied.

It may be a goofy way of remembering how the IDENTITY property works, but for me, I just make a mental note to remember that it is the opposite of what it sounds like. SET IDENTITY_INSERT *tablename* ON actually turns the IDENTITY property off. SET IDENTITY_INSERT *tablename* OFF turns the IDENTITY property back on.

Another aspect of explicitly entering a value into an IDENTITY column is the impact on the IDENTITY property's current value. For instance, you create a table with the following script:

```
CREATE TABLE MyTable (MyID Int IDENTITY(1, 10) NOT NULL
                    , MyDescription nVarChar(50) NOT NULL)
```

After the table is created you add two records:

```
INSERT MyTable (MyDescription)
VALUES ('Auto Record 1')
INSERT MyTable (MyDescription)
VALUES ('Auto Record 2')
```

A query of the table reveals the following data:

```
MyID        MyDescription
----------- -------------------------------------------------
1           Auto Record 1
11          Auto Record 2

(2 row(s) affected)
```

Now you explicitly enter a MyID value with the following script:

```
SET IDENTITY_INSERT MyTable ON
INSERT MyTable (MyID, MyDescription)
VALUES (5, 'Manual Record 1')
SET IDENTITY_INSERT MyTable OFF
```

What is the next value that SQL Server will automatically assign for MyID? Will it be 15 (incrementing 10 from 5) or will it be 21? The answer is that SQL Server will always choose the highest number as its current seed for a positive increment value or the lowest for a negative increment value, so the results will look like this:

```
INSERT MyTable (MyDescription)
VALUES ('Auto Record 3')

SELECT * FROM MyTable
```

```
MyID        MyDescription
----------- -------------------------------------------------
1           Auto Record 1
11          Auto Record 2
5           Manual Record 1
21          Auto Record 3

(4 row(s) affected)
```

Often, when working with IDENTITY values, you will want to know what the last value supplied was. SQL Server provides the @@IDENTITY global variable to hold that value. Retrieving the IDENTITY value is as simple as selecting the variable:

```
INSERT MyTable (MyDescription)
VALUES ('Auto Record 4')
SELECT * FROM MyTable
SELECT @@IDENTITY AS LastIdentity
```

```
MyID         MyDescription
-----------  -------------------------------------------------
1            Auto Record 1
11           Auto Record 2
5            Manual Record 1
21           Auto Record 3
31           Auto Record 4


LastIdentity
----------------------------------------
31
```

Because @@IDENTITY is a global variable, it will work on every connection, but it will only return the last IDENTITY value issued on the connection that the variable is retrieved. If you need to discover what the last IDENTITY value for a table is regardless of your current scope, you can use the IDENT_CURRENT function. So opening a different connection from that used in the previous example would return results like this:

```
SELECT @@IDENTITY AS LastIdentity

SELECT IDENT_CURRENT(MyTable) AS CurrentIdentity
```

```
LastIdentity
----------------------------------------
NULL

CurrentIdentity
----------------------------------------
31
```

Defaults

In its simplest form, a default is simply a hard-coded value that is assigned to a column if it isn't specified in an INSERT statement. Chapter 1 mentioned that I have a deep-rooted prejudice against NULL. Whenever possible I avoid allowing nulls in my table designs. However, there are many times when I need to allow for a value not to be provided in a table insert. In these instances a default is very handy. For example, let's go back to my MyTable example. This time I will add a new column called Region. This column will contain a three-character region code. Because I live in the Seattle area, I want this value to be PNW, for Pacific Northwest, if no value is provided. Here is the script to create my new table:

```
CREATE TABLE MyTable (MyID Int IDENTITY(1, 1) NOT NULL
          , MyDescription nVarChar(50) NOT NULL
          , MyRegion nChar(3) NOT NULL DEFAULT 'PNW')
```

Now if an insert is made to my table and a region is not provided, the value PNW will automatically be used.

This is the preferred method for using defaults, but it is not the only way. A default can also be created as a stand-alone object in the database and then bound to any number of columns in any number of tables in the database:

```
CREATE DEFAULT df_Region AS 'PNW'
GO
CREATE TABLE MyTable (MyID Int IDENTITY(1, 1) NOT NULL
            , MyDescription nVarChar(50) NOT NULL
            , MyRegion nChar(3) NOT NULL)
GO
sp_bindefault df_Region, MyTable.MyRegion
```

UniqueIdentifier

A problem with using an auto-incrementing IDENTITY is that this system only works when any users or clients that create records are concurrently connected to the same database server. This introduces problems for replicated systems or off-line applications that need to synchronize data from other sources. For example, I was recently involved with a project where user data needed to be joined from a SQL Server database and an Active Directory domain. Microsoft's Active Directory uniquely identifies all of its resident objects with a Globally Unique Identifier (GUID, pronounced "goo-id"). As a result, a column needed to be defined in the database that could hold this GUID. To complicate matters even more, part of the application design specified that not all of the system's users would reside in Active Directory. Some would exist only in SQL Server. A method was needed to either use existing GUIDs or to generate new ones. That is where SQL Server's UniqueIdentifier data type and NEWID() function come into play. The UniqueIdentifier type stores a 128-bit integer value that is usually displayed as an alpha-numeric representation of its hexadecimal form. These values are not intended for human consumption, because they are quite large and fairly random in composition.

> I'm proud to say that I am responsible for creating a new acronym to describe the category for these values. It's a BUN, which stands for Big Ugly Number.

In SQL Server, UniqueIdentifier values are either explicitly provided or they are generated by the NEWID() system function. To define a new table with an ID of this type, I'll use the following script:

```
CREATE TABLE MyTable (MyID UniqueIdentifier NOT NULL DEFAULT NewID()
                    , MyDescription nVarChar(50) NOT NULL)
```

Once the table is created I can either specify a GUID to be inserted or allow a new GUID to be generated by the NEWID() function, which has been specified as the default value. The NEWID() function only works as a default value for a table's UniqueIdentifier column when no value is provided, as demonstrated in the following:

```
INSERT MyTable (MyID, MyDescription)
VALUES ('2BD9307D-5AAD-417C-AE3A-C1ACDCA0F6C9', 'Explicitly provided GUID')

INSERT MyTable (MyID, MyDescription)
VALUES (DEFAULT, 'SQL Server generated GUID')

SELECT * FROM MyTable
```

```
MyID                                MyDescription
------------------------------      -------------------------------
2BD9307D-5AAD-417C-AE3A-C1ACDCA0F6C9 Explicitly provided GUID
30D618FC-8179-436D-9A7E-3E3032A72C09 SQL Server generated GUID
```

Keep in mind that like the IDENTITY property, the UniqueIdentifier type does not in and of itself guarantee uniqueness. A unique or primary key constraint must be used in conjunction with the UniqueIdentifier data type. The NEWID() function, however, will never generate the same value twice on any database server in the world (at least that is the theory).

Constraints

SQL Server constraints fall into one of five categories, as described in the following table.

Constraint Type	Description
Not Null	Ensures that the column has a defined non-null value.
Primary Key	Enforces uniqueness for the purpose of identifying a row. Doesn't accept Null values.
Check	Validates a row based on the value of a column. Uses a clause, similar to that following a WHERE statement, to identify acceptable values.
Unique	Requires each value in a column to have a unique value. Column will accept a single Null value unless used in conjunction with Not Null.
Foreign Key	Enforces referential integrity rules by checking the value of a column against that of the primary key value in a related table. Null values are allowable unless explicitly restricted.

The Not Null constraint was explained earlier. Just remember that to prevent null values the key words NOT NULL must follow the data type declaration in the column definition.

Primary Key Constraint

The Primary Key object was introduced in Chapter 1, but I will review it here in more detail. A table's primary key is the primary value that is used to uniquely identify every row in the table. The primary key designation is specified as a constraint on the table. Although we often think of constraints as being applied to a specific column, they are defined at the table level and really apply to each row. Constraints can be created during the initial CREATE TABLE statement or can be added later with an ALTER TABLE statement. A couple of different ways exist to designate a primary key during the table creation process:

```
CREATE TABLE MyTable (MyID Int IDENTITY(1,1) NOT NULL CONSTRAINT PK_ID PRIMARY KEY
                , Description nVarChar(50) NOT NULL
                , Region nVarChar(10) NOT NULL DEFAULT 'PNW' )
```

```
CREATE TABLE MyTable (MyID Int IDENTITY(1,1) NOT NULL
                    , Description nVarChar(50) NOT NULL
                    , Region nVarChar(10) NOT NULL DEFAULT 'PNW'
                    , CONSTRAINT PK_ID PRIMARY KEY (MyID))
```

In the preceding examples PK_ID is the name of the constraint and PRIMARY KEY is the type of constraint. You can omit the name attribute of the constraint for a primary key constraint if the constraint is defined in the column definition. SQL Server will automatically assign the primary key constraint the name PK_TableName_xxxxxxxx. In the first example, for instance, SQL Server would assign a name very similar to PK__MyTable2__3C69FB99. At this point, the name of the constraint is also the name of the supporting index.

To enforce uniqueness, SQL Server builds an index on the key column. This makes perfect sense if you think about it. If I gave you a deck of cards and told you that I wanted to ensure that there were no duplicate cards in the deck, what would you do? Most likely you would sort the cards so that you could easily identify if any duplicates existed. SQL Server does the same thing, except it keeps the column values sorted to prevent a duplicate from occurring in the first place. The index that SQL Server creates to support a primary key will be either a clustered or non-clustered index. If you do not specify one way or the other, SQL Server will create the index as a clustered index if one does not already exist. This is by no means a recommendation that all of your primary key columns also be the clustered index column. The decision on what column to define as the primary key and what column a clustered index is ordered on are very separate design decisions. To specify a non-clustered index, add the keyword NONCLUSTERED to the constraint definition immediately following the PRIMARY KEY keywords:

```
CREATE TABLE MyTable (
      MyID Int IDENTITY(1,1) NOT NULL CONSTRAINT PK_ID PRIMARY KEYNONCLUSTERED
    , Description nVarChar(50) NOT NULL
    , Region nVarChar(10) NOT NULL DEFAULT 'PNW' )
```

```
CREATE TABLE MyTable (
      MyID Int IDENTITY(1,1) NOT NULL
    , Description nVarChar(50) NOT NULL
    , Region nVarChar(10) NOT NULL DEFAULT 'PNW'
    , CONSTRAINT PK_ID PRIMARY KEY NONCLUSTERED (MyID))
```

You can also apply the primary key constraint to multiple columns by including the columns in a comma-delimited list. This is often the case for bridge tables used to join two tables and form a many-to-many relationship. A unique constraint is defined using similar syntax:

```
CREATE TABLE MyTable (
      MyID Int IDENTITY(1,1) NOT NULL
    , CategoryID Int NOT NULL
    , Description nVarChar(50)
    , Region nVarChar(10) DEFAULT 'PNW'
    , CONSTRAINT MyTable_PK PRIMARY KEY NONCLUSTERED (MyID,CategoryID))
```

If the table has already been created without a primary key, the table will have to be altered to add the constraint, as shown in the following example:

```
ALTER TABLE MyTable
ADD CONSTRAINT PK_ID PRIMARY KEY NONCLUSTERED (MyID))
```

The syntax is fairly straightforward.

1. After the ALTER statement you specify what it is you want to add: a constraint.
2. Specify the name of what you want to add: PK_ID.
3. Specify what type of constraint it is: Primary Key.
4. Specify what column the constraint is being applied to: MyID.

The syntax is the same regardless of what type of constraint it is you add.

Unique Constraint

Primary keys enforce uniqueness and are very often used to manage relationships as briefly explained in Chapter 1. Sometimes, however, you need to enforce uniqueness on a column that is not the column used to primarily identify each row. Chapter 1 used the Employee table as an example, so let's return to that. In the following example the script creates a table called Employee. The table's primary key is an integer that is automatically generated by the IDENTITY function, but the table also contains the employee's social security number:

```
CREATE TABLE Employee (
       EmployeeID Int IDENTITY(1,1) NOT NULL
     , LastName nVarChar(50) NOT NULL
     , FirstName nVarChar(50) NOT NULL
     , SSN Char(9) NOT NULL)
```

It will probably be very important for the company not to have any duplicate social security numbers so you need to find a way to enforce that uniqueness without making the column your primary key. The answer is the unique constraint. Unique constraints are very similar to primary keys with a couple of distinct differences. A unique constraint also requires an index to enforce the uniqueness so SQL Server automatically creates one, but it doesn't create a clustered index by default. Unique constraints will also allow one NULL, whereas primary keys will not. If a NULL is not appropriate, a NOT NULL constraint must be added to the column. Unique constraints, like all other constraints, can be created when initially creating the table or added after, as the following two examples show:

```
CREATE TABLE Employee (
       EmployeeID Int IDENTITY(1,1) NOT NULL
     , LastName nVarChar(50) NOT NULL
     , FirstName nVarChar(50) NOT NULL
     , SSN Char(9) NOT NULL
     , CONSTRAINT U_SSN UNIQUE NONCLUSTERED (SSN))
```

```
ALTER TABLE Employee
ADD CONSTRAINT U_SSN UNIQUE NONCLUSTERED (SSN)
```

Check Constraint

A *check constraint* uses an expression to qualify records that are acceptable for any Inserts or Updates performed on the table:

```
CREATE TABLE MyTable
    ( MyID Int IDENTITY(1, 1) NOT NULL
    , MyDescription nVarChar(50) NOT NULL
    , Region nVarChar(10) NOT NULL DEFAULT 'PNW'
    , CONSTRAINT PK_ID PRIMARY KEY CLUSTERED (MyID)
    , CONSTRAINT CK_Region CHECK (Region
                             IN('PNW','SW','MT','CENTRAL','EAST','SOUTH'))
    )
```

If a record were inserted with a Region value other than those in the list, an error would be raised and the insert would be aborted. If an update were performed on the table that attempted to modify the value of Region and make it any value other than those on the list, it would also fail.

Check constraints, like primary key constraints, can be added to a table after the table is created. Unlike primary key constraints, the data in the table does not have to conform to the check constraint. For example, I create the table MyTable with the following script:

```
CREATE TABLE MyTable
    ( MyID Int IDENTITY(1, 1) NOT NULL
    , MyDescription nVarChar(50) NOT NULL
    , Region nVarChar(10) NOT NULL DEFAULT 'PNW'
    , CONSTRAINT PK_ID PRIMARY KEY CLUSTERED (MyID)
    )
```

Shortly after creating the table I find that rows are being added with Region values I did not expect or want. I want to add a check constraint to the table to prevent additional rows being added that don't conform to my business rules, but when I try to add a constraint I get the following error:

```
ALTER TABLE MyTable
ADD CONSTRAINT ckRegion CHECK
(REGION IN ('PNW','SW','MT','CENTRAL','EAST','SOUTH'))
```

```
Server: Msg 547, Level 16, State 1, Line 1
ALTER TABLE statement conflicted with COLUMN CHECK constraint 'ckRegion'. The
conflict occurred in database 'Pubs', table 'MyTable', column 'Region'.
```

When I tried to add the constraint, there were already records that did not conform to the constraint, so the ALTER TABLE command failed. However, if I modify my ALTER statement to specify that SQL Server should not check existing data, I can add the constraint and prevent any additional bad rows from being added:

```
ALTER TABLE MyTable WITH NOCHECK
ADD CONSTRAINT ckRegion CHECK
(REGION IN ('PNW','SW','MT','CENTRAL','EAST','SOUTH'))
```

Foreign Key Constraint

Foreign key constraints are used to enforce relationships between tables. Chapters 1 and 2 explained one-to-many, one-to-one, and many-to-many relationships. These relationships between tables can exist without the use of foreign key constraints, and I have seen many databases where this was the case. In my experience, the reason for not using foreign key constraints was because the database design was intentionally made complex to prevent organizations from developing internal tools to examine the data. Columns that linked tables would have different names and even different data types. This process is euphemistically called *obfuscation*, which is a developer's way of saying "made confusing on purpose." The problem with this approach is that inconsistencies in the data can appear because of an application bug or the data being manipulated outside of the application. The preferred method of managing table relationships is through Declarative Relational Integrity (DRI). Foreign keys are an implementation of DRI. The *Declarative* part means that the constraint is a declared part of the table's structure. Foreign keys are a part of the child table's structure.

Let's return to the employee example. I have for this example, two tables (shown in Figure 12-1): the Employee table and the Department table.

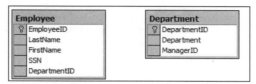

Figure 12-1

I want to ensure that I can identify every employee by the department they work in so I add the department ID to my employee table. I also want to ensure that when an ID for a department is added to my employee table that the department ID actually exists. I can do this declaratively through the use of a foreign key constraint when creating the employee table or after the creation by altering the employee table:

```
CREATE TABLE Employee (
      EmployeeID Int IDENTITY(1,1) NOT NULL
    , LastName nVarChar(50) NOT NULL
    , FirstName nVarChar(50) NOT NULL
    , SSN Char(9) NOT NULL
    , DepartmentID Int NOT NULL
    , CONSTRAINT PK_Employee PRIMARY KEY CLUSTERED (EmployeeID)
    , CONSTRAINT FK_Employee_Department FOREIGN KEY (DepartmentID)
  REFERENCES Department (DepartmentID))
```

```
ALTER TABLE Employee
ADD CONSTRAINT fk_Employee_Department FOREIGN KEY (DepartmentID)
REFERENCES Department (DepartmentID)
```

Foreign key constraints also prevent the parent record from being modified or deleted if it is referenced by a child record. For example, it is decided to change a department's identifier. If the foreign key has been created in the default manner and employees exist that are in the respective department, the update will fail:

```
UPDATE Department
SET DepartmentID = 25
WHERE DepartmentID = 1
```

```
Server: Msg 547, Level 16, State 1, Line 1
UPDATE statement conflicted with COLUMN REFERENCE constraint
'FK_Employee_Department'. The conflict occurred in database 'Sales', table
'Employee', column 'DepartmentID'.
The statement has been terminated.
```

SQL Server allows for the creation of the constraint in such a way that any changes to the parent table, instead of causing an error, will make the same changes to the child table. All that is required is to create the foreign key constraint with the CASCADE option. The CASCADE option can be configured so that an update and/or delete made to the parent table are reflected in the child table, as shown in the following example:

```
ALTER TABLE Employee
ADD CONSTRAINT fk_Employee_Department FOREIGN KEY (DepartmentID)
REFERENCES Department (DepartmentID) ON DELETE CASCADE ON UPDATE CASCADE
```

Overriding Constraints

Foreign key and check constraints are very effective at maintaining data in a consistent state by enforcing all insert and update operations to conform to a set of rules. However, they do not come without cost. Any insert or update must be compared to the rules that were established for the constraint, and that takes time and CPU resources, especially for large inserts. I often load a large number of rows into an existing table with a check or foreign key constraint and I know that the data being loaded already conforms to the constraint. In these instances I will disable the constraint before I add the data and then re-enable the constraint after the load is complete. An example of this is provided here:

```
ALTER TABLE Employee
NOCHECK CONSTRAINT FK_Employee_Department

INSERT Employee
SELECT LastName, FirstName, SSN, DepartmentID
FROM NewEmployee

ALTER TABLE Employee
CHECK CONSTRAINT FK_Employee_Department
```

CREATE VIEW

Views are the simplest of all the SQL programming objects. The basic syntax is little more than that of a query preceded by an object definition:

```
CREATE VIEW view_name [ ( column [ ,...n ] ) ]
[ WITH [ENCRYPTION | SCHEMABINDING | VIEW_METADATA] ]
AS
select_statement
[ WITH CHECK OPTION ]
```

To create a view, simply write a query that returns the data you want to expose with the view:

```
SELECT P.Name AS ProductName, S.Name AS CategoryName
, P.ProductNumber, P.ListPrice
FROM Product P INNER JOIN ProductSubCategory S
ON P.ProductSubCategoryID = S.ProductSubCategoryID
INNER JOIN ProductCategory C
ON S.ProductCategoryID = C.ProductCategoryID
WHERE FinishedGoodsFlag = 1
```

Then insert the object definition before the SELECT statement:

```
CREATE VIEW vwFinishedProductsAndCategories
As
SELECT P.Name AS ProductName, S.Name AS CategoryName
, P.ProductNumber, P.ListPrice
FROM Product P INNER JOIN ProductSubCategory S
ON P.ProductSubCategoryID = S.ProductSubCategoryID
INNER JOIN ProductCategory C
ON S.ProductCategoryID = C.ProductCategoryID
WHERE FinishedGoodsFlag = 1
```

If the column names are not defined in the SELECT statement or if different column names are desired and aliases in the SQL statement are not desired, then the column names can be defined in the CREATE statement:

```
CREATE VIEW vwFinishedProductsAndCategories
(ProductName, CategoryName, ProductNumber, ListPrice)
As
SELECT P.Name, S.Name, P.ProductNumber, P.ListPrice
FROM Product P INNER JOIN ProductSubCategory S
ON P.ProductSubCategoryID = S.ProductSubCategoryID
INNER JOIN ProductCategory C
ON S.ProductCategoryID = C.ProductCategoryID
WHERE FinishedGoodsFlag = 1
```

Views have a couple of limitations. The first is that they must be static, so they cannot contain any variables in the WHERE clause. The second is that they cannot be sorted with ORDER BY unless the TOP command is also used. For example, if I wanted to pre-sort my finished products view, the query would have to be written like this:

```
CREATE VIEW vwFinishedProductsAndCategories
As
SELECT TOP 100 PERCENT P.Name AS ProductName, S.Name AS CategoryName
, P.ProductNumber, P.ListPrice
FROM Product P INNER JOIN ProductSubCategory S
ON P.ProductSubCategoryID = S.ProductSubCategoryID
INNER JOIN ProductCategory C
ON S.ProductCategoryID = C.ProductCategoryID
WHERE FinishedGoodsFlag = 1
ORDER BY ProductName
```

Four common options are used to modify the default behavior of views in the CREATE VIEW statement:

❑ WITH CHECK OPTION

❑ SCHEMABINDING

❑ ENCRYPTION

❑ VIEW_METADATA

The last option is used by programming components to return information about the view.

WITH CHECK OPTION

In Chapter 9, you learned that data can be modified through a view using an UPDATE statement just as you would with a table. For views that filter results, the WITH CHECK OPTION keeps the results synchronized with the table(s). This line of script is added to the end of the view definition. To demonstrate with the same view I just created, I can either drop the view and re-create it or use the ALTER statement, like so:

```
ALTER VIEW vwFinishedProductsAndCategories
As
SELECT P.Name AS ProductName, S.Name AS CategoryName
, P.ProductNumber, P.ListPrice
FROM Product P INNER JOIN ProductSubCategory S
ON P.ProductSubCategoryID = S.ProductSubCategoryID
INNER JOIN ProductCategory C
ON S.ProductCategoryID = C.ProductCategoryID
WHERE FinishedGoodsFlag = 1
WITH CHECK OPTION
```

The rest of the options are specified immediately after the view name, in the CREATE VIEW statement.

SCHEMABINDING

By default, views employ a feature called delayed name resolution. This means that any changes to an object that other objects depend on are allowed. Of course, this means that it's possible to create problems that won't be revealed until later. When I first learned about delayed name resolution, I thought it was a bit silly to promote this as a feature rather than a shortcoming of SQL Server; but the reason for it is to enable you to make changes to a database design. Much like trying to delete a record in a highly normalized database, it's difficult to make changes or delete objects in a large database when so many objects (typically views, functions, and stored procedures) are dependent on each other.

After the database design has been stabilized, you can consider altering views so that the database engine prevents changes to underlying tables or other dependent objects, which would break the view:

```
CREATE VIEW vwProductList
WITH SCHEMABINDING
As
SELECT ProductID, Name As ProductName
FROM dbo.Product
```

This view is created using the WITH SCHEMABINDING option. If I were to try to make changes to the dependent table, an error would be raised and the action would be aborted. To schemabind a view, the objects referenced in the SELECT statement must be referenced with their two-part name.

The SCHEMABINDING option is also required to support indexed views.

WITH ENCRYPTION

When a view is created using the WITH ENCRYPTION option, the view is defined and stored within the sysobjects system table in encrypted form. This would make it impossible, even for a system administrator, to see the view's syntax. Encrypted objects cannot be decrypted by anyone, regardless of their permissions. If you decide to encrypt a view, you should probably save the script in a safe place so you can make changes or regenerate the view later on. Encrypting a view doesn't affect performance to a noticeable degree.

The following examples show the effects of definition encryption. The first example shows the result of an sp_helptext stored procedure on a view created in the clear. The sp_helptext procedure returns the statement used to create the object. The second example shows the result of encryption on the availability of the definition information.

Try It Out

To see the effects of encryption on an object's definition, first create a view without the encryption option:

```
CREATE VIEW vwProductList
As
SELECT ProductID, Name As ProductName
FROM dbo.Product
```

Next, use the system stored procedure sp_helptext to retrieve the views definition from the sysobjects table:

```
EXEC sp_helptext vwProductList
```

Notice that the results are the same as the original statement used to create the view.

Now alter the view to add the encryption option to the view definition:

```
ALTER VIEW vwProductList
WITH ENCRYPYION
As
SELECT ProductID, Name As ProductName
FROM dbo.Product
```

Run the system stored procedure sp_helptext again to retrieve the view definition from the sysobjects table. Observe that no results are returned other than a statement letting you know that the object was encrypted.

> *Using a system stored procedure to retrieve the definition of an object is preferable over directly querying the system tables. Direct access to the system tables is strongly discouraged in SQL Server 2000 and impossible in SQL Server 2005.*

Indexed Views

At first, the idea of indexing views may seem to be a bit unusual. After all, isn't a view just a SELECT query on one or more tables, and don't indexes really just apply to a table? From a performance and efficiency standpoint, designing a relational database is about finding the right balance between optimizing for transactional performance and data retrieval queries. This feature tips the scales heavily into the data retrieval camp.

I'd like to revisit the topic of indexes briefly. An index is more than just something you tack onto a table to make it find data more efficiently. Indexes contain the actual values for one or more specific columns, stored in presorted order. If an index were to contain all of the column values to support a query, there would be no need for SQL Server to read data from the table pages. All of the necessary data already exists in the data pages allocated to the index. This condition is known as "covering a query" with an index.

If a covering index could be associated with a view, the query optimizer would not only benefit from the caching and stored execution plan for the view, but it wouldn't need to analyze the query to decide which indexes should be used. Such is the case with indexed views. This is by far the most efficient method for returning a subset of sorted data from one or more large tables. The trade-off is that for every Insert, Update, or Delete operation performed on related rows, values in the index must be maintained in real time. In highly transactional systems on a busy server, this performance cost can be quite significant.

A view is indexed using a unique clustered index. This actually creates an index object a little different than a clustered index defined for a table. The underlying tables aren't modified, but the index itself contains a separate copy of all the data.

Try It Out

The first order of business in creating an indexed view is to create (or alter) a view using the WITH SCHEMABINDING option:

```
CREATE VIEW vwFinishedProductsAndCategories
WITH SchemaBinding
As
SELECT ProductID
    , P.Name As ProductName
    , ProductNumber
    , SC.Name As SubCategoryName
    , ListPrice
FROM dbo.Product P Inner Join dbo.ProductSubCategory SC
ON P.ProductSubCategoryID = SC.ProductSubCategoryID
WHERE FinishedGoodsFlag = 1
```

After the view has been schema bound, to index the view, a unique clustered index is created on the view. Remember that a clustered index is the actual data organized in the order of the column the index is created on.

```
CREATE UNIQUE CLUSTERED INDEX CL_FinishedProducts
ON vwFinishedProductsAndCategories (ProductID)
```

Additional non-clustered indexes can then be created on additional columns of the view, if desired.

CREATE PROCEDURE

The basic syntax for creating a stored procedure looks like this:

```
CREATE PROCEDURE procedure_name
    [ { @parameter data_type }[ OUTPUT ]
    ] [ ,...n ]
[ WITH
    { RECOMPILE | ENCRYPTION } ]
AS sql_statement [ ...n ] >
```

Stored procedures are the principle method by which changes are made to the database. Any time you want to insert, update, or delete rows in a table you should use a stored procedure. Stored procedures are also very useful for filtering tables or views by limiting the rows returned through the use of parameters. There are two primary reasons why stored procedures are the preferred method for making changes to a database. The first is security. When a stored procedure is created to make changes, only the changes programmed into the procedure can be executed. Users or even application developers do not need to have any permission granted to the underlying table or tables to make changes to them. The second reason you always want to use stored procedures is efficiency. Stored procedures are compiled and cached on the server upon initial execution. Subsequent executions will be very fast because the compiled version of the stored procedure is being used. The compiled plan stays in cache until SQL Server ages it out or SQL Server is restarted. Typically, SQL Server will leave an active stored procedure in cache indefinitely unless SQL Server runs out of available memory.

Using Parameters

Input and output parameters are declared after the CREATE PROCEDURE statement. Parameter names begin with the @ symbol and are followed by any number of spaces and then the data type. The Input or Output keywords can be used to designate the direction for each parameter. If not specified otherwise, it's assumed that parameters are used for input.

In this SQL script fraction, all four parameters are used for input. The third and fourth parameters are optional because default values are provided:

```
  @WidgetID        Int
, @Description     nVarChar(100)
, @Category        VarChar(20) = Null
, @StatusCode      Char(2) = Null
```

If a procedure is to return one single (scalar) value, whether you should use an output parameter or the return value of the procedure may just be a matter of preference. However, there is one argument for using the return value rather than an output parameter. Because all stored procedures are equipped to return a value by default, using an output parameter can add a slight degree of additional overhead. The following examples demonstrate both of these techniques:

```
/**************************************
        Stored procedure returning value
        using an Output parameter
**************************************/
CREATE PROCEDURE spCalculateOutput
    @Value1      Float
  , @Value2      Float
  , @Operator    Char(10)
  , @Result      Float        Output
As
  IF @Operator = 'Add'
        SET @Result = @Value1 + @Value2
  ELSE IF @Operator = 'Subtract'
        SET @Result = @Value1 - @Value2
  ELSE IF @Operator = 'Multiply'
        SET @Result = @Value1 * @Value2
  ELSE IF @Operator = 'Divide'
        SET @Result = @Value1 / @Value2
```

To test this procedure in the Query Editor or Query Analyzer, first declare a variable to hold the output value. This value is assigned in reverse order compared to a typical value assignment statement (remember, you've changed the direction using the Output statement). After executing the procedure, print the result using the variable:

```
-- Declare a variable for the result value
Declare @Out Float
-- Execute the procedure & assign the result
Execute spCalculate_Output 123, 456, 'Add', @Result = @Out Output
-- Print the result value
Print @Out
```

The logic for the return-value technique is the same but the syntax varies slightly. Instead of declaring an output parameter, a private variable is declared after the As keyword. This variable simply holds the calculated value until it is returned at the end of the procedure script. Another valid technique would be to use the Return keyword in each of the branch expressions (that is, Return @Value1 + @Value2), rather than using the variable at all.

```
/**************************************
        Stored procedure returning value
        using Return value
**************************************/
CREATE PROCEDURE spCalculateReturn
  @Value1       Float
, @Value2       Float
, @Operator     Char(10)
As
 Declare @Result Float
 IF @Operator = 'Add'
        SET @Result = @Value1 + @Value2
 ELSE IF @Operator = 'Subtract'
        SET @Result = @Value1 - @Value2
 ELSE IF @Operator = 'Multiply'
        SET @Result = @Value1 * @Value2
 ELSE IF @Operator = 'Divide'
        SET @Result = @Value1 / @Value2
RETURN @Result
```

To test the return value procedure the syntax is slightly different:

```
-- Declare a variable for the result value
Declare @Out AS Float
-- Execute the procedure by assigning it to the variable
EXECUTE @Out = spCalculateReturn 123, 456, 'Add'
-- Print the result value
Print @OutPrint @Out
```

The ability to capture the value of a stored procedure's return value is built into Visual Studio, but to capture it with T-SQL you must again declare a variable to hold the output, in this case, the return value:

```
DECLARE @Result AS Float
exec @Result = spCalculateReturn 10,10,'Add'
SELECT @Result AS 'spCalculateReturn Return Value'
```

WITH ENCRYPTION

The definition of a stored procedure can be encrypted just like the view definition previously discussed by using the WITH ENCRYPTION option. Remember that an encrypted procedure cannot be decrypted, so it is advisable to keep a copy of the script used to create it for safekeeping.

WITH RECOMPILE

The first time a stored procedure executes, the query optimizer builds an execution plan based on the conditions present in the database. This means that decisions are made based upon the volume, selectivity, density, and distribution of data values in tables accessed by the stored procedure. This execution plan is compiled and then cached with the stored procedure. Rather than repeating the process when the procedure is subsequently called, the same execution plan is used to save time and resources. However, as the data changes in the tables, the efficiency of the execution plan also changes. Over a period of time, a stored procedure's execution plan could become very inefficient, especially if indexes are added to the tables to optimize data access after the stored procedure is created. A stored procedure execution plan does not become invalid if an index is added because the original plan will still work. However, if an index that is referenced by a query plan is dropped, SQL Server will invalidate the execution plan and cause the stored procedure to be recompiled.

If the database has been optimized with additional indexes after the creation of the stored procedures or a lot of changes have occurred to indexed values, it is generally a good idea to recompile the affected stored procedures or to clear out the procedure cache. Stored procedures can be recompiled in one of three ways. One way is to use the WITH RECOMPILE statement when executing the procedure, like this:

```
EXECUTE spGetCustomers WITH RECOMPILE
```

This method really isn't that useful in a production environment because the stored procedures are almost always called from an application. It wouldn't make much sense to redesign your applications to force procedure recompilation. The second way is to create or alter the stored procedure so that a compiled plan is never cached:

```
CREATE PROC spDeletePurchaseOrder WITH RECOMPILE
 @PurchaseOrderID Int
AS
DELETE PurchaseOrderDetail
WHERE PurchaseOrderID = @PurchaseOrderID
```

Every time this stored procedure is executed a new plan will be compiled and used and then immediately discarded. This method is also of limited usefulness and would be implemented in an environment where the database structure was expected to change frequently.

The last and most frequently used method is to execute the sp_recompile stored procedure against any table where a new index or other structure was added. This system stored procedure marks the cached plan of all the stored procedures that reference the table invalid, which causes them to be recompiled at their next execution:

```
EXECUTE sp_recompile PurchaseOrderDetail
```

When a table or view is specified as the object in sp_recompile, only those compiled plans that reference the table or view are affected. The sp_recompile procedure can also be executed against individual stored procedures or triggers:

```
EXECUTE sp_recompile spDeletePurchaseOrder
```

To globally clear all cached plans you can either restart SQL Server or execute the DBCC FREEPROC-CACHE command.

EXECUTE AS

This new feature in SQL Server 2005 allows a stored procedure to be executed within an explicit security context. Regardless of the user or login used to execute the procedure, all contained script will execute with the permissions provided in this statement.

Valid options for this statement are described in the following table.

Option	Description
Caller	Executes all script or objects called by the procedure in the context of the user executing the procedure.
Self	Executes all script or objects called by the procedure with default permissions.
Owner	Executes all script or objects called by the procedure in the context of the owner of the procedure.
'user_name'	Executes all script or objects called by the procedure in the context of a specific user or login.

When using the Execute As option, it is very important to control access to the procedure. This could enable users to execute statements that they would otherwise not be granted the ability to execute.

CREATE FUNCTION

User-defined functions are built using the CREATE FUNCTION statement, much like any other type of object. In Chapter 10, you looked at the syntax for creating each of the three different types of UDFs. Like views and procedures, the CREATE FUNCTION statement accepts the WITH ENCRYPTION, WITH SCHEMABINDING, and EXECUTE AS options.

Remember that a function cannot call any nondeterministic functions. This means that any function that doesn't consistently return the same value every time can't be used in the body of a user-defined function.

Securing Database Objects

SQL Server's security mechanism is both elegant and flexible. When SQL Server first came to be, it included a role-based security model where all roles and logins were defined within the database server. Users are similar to logins but defined at the database level. Users could be made members of a role and then permissions for various database objects could be assigned at the individual or role level. This approach met all of the necessary requirements except that it duplicated much of the security assignments managed by the network system. As SQL Server was integrated into the Windows platform, it made sense to integrate the existing Windows security model. Today, you have the option to use either Windows Integrated Security or both Windows and SQL Server security mechanisms to secure database objects. Whether or not you choose to utilize the Windows security integration is up to you, but this option is always enabled.

Typically, it makes sense to use Windows Integrated Security if you have the luxury of managing the network security as well. This is convenient considering you don't have to create duplicate login names and groups. There are some situations where it may not be feasible to use integrated security. On a departmental database server, where the server is managed separately from the corporate network, this can be a challenge. Another common exception is the Internet service provider that creates accounts for its customers to manage their databases on a common server. In this scenario, there may be no reason to allow access to any other network resources.

The coverage of this topic focuses on the language rather than the administrative tasks and practices. In brief, SQL Server defines eight fixed server roles that can be used to map various server and database object permissions. Logins defined at the server level may have membership in these roles. Logins can be defined using the SQL Server security model or can map to a user or group in Windows. At the database level, custom roles can be defined that may also be used to grant or deny object permissions. Users are defined at the database level that map to a login at the server level. This may seem a little complicated at first, but it really isn't. The short version is that users, in one form or another, are grouped into roles so that you don't have to assign permissions for every individual user. Ideally, all permissions are assigned to a role with the occasional exception for the user who needs to have special permissions or restrictions.

New in SQL Server 2005 is the ability to enforce complex passwords and password expiration on SQL Server logins. SQL Server retrieves the password policy from the local security policy on the server and uses it. If complex passwords are required on the server, then, by default, they will also be required for SQL Server logins. The same goes for password expirations.

Managing Security Objects

In SQL Server 2005, logins, users, and roles have their own corresponding CREATE and DROP statements. In SQL Server 2000, this administrative task is handled by system stored procedures.

The syntax for creating a new login is slightly different depending on whether the new login is a Windows login or a SQL Server login, as the following examples illustrate.

SQL Server 2005 SQL Server login:

```
/**************************************************
*      ********SQL SERVER 2005**************
* Creates a new SQL Server login and then maps
* that login to a new database user
***************************************************/
USE Master
GO
CREATE LOGIN Paul WITH Password = 'P@ssword1'

USE AdventureWorks2000
GO
CREATE USER Paul FOR Login Paul
SQL Server 2005 Windows login./***********************************************************
*      ********SQL SERVER 2005**************
* Creates a new Windows login and then maps
* that login to a new database user
***************************************************/
```

```
USE Master
GO
CREATE LOGIN Adventureworks\Paul

USE AdventureWorks2000
GO
CREATE USER WindowsPaul FOR Login AdventureWorks\Paul
```

SQL Server 2000 SQL Server login:

```
/***************************************************
*      ********SQL SERVER 2000**************
* Creates a new SQL Server login and then maps
* that login to a new database user
***************************************************/
USE Master
GO
sp_addlogin 'Paul', 'P@ssword1'

USE AdventureWorks2000
GO
sp_grantdbaccess 'Paul', 'Paul'
```

SQL Server 2000 Windows login:

```
/***************************************************
*      ********SQL SERVER 2000**************
* Creates a new Windows login and then maps
* that login to a new database user
***************************************************/
USE Master
GO
sp_grantlogin 'AdventureWorks\Paul'

USE AdventureWorks2000
GO
sp_grantdbaccess 'AdventureWorks\Paul', 'WindowsPaul'
```

In SQL Server 2000, Windows logins are removed with the sp_revokelogin system stored procedure. Users are removed with the sp_revokedbaccess procedure. In SQL Server 2005, the DROP LOGIN and DROP USER commands are used.

Data Control Language

Three SQL statements are used to control permission to all database objects and securable user resources (that is, users and roles). Each statement accepts the permission type (Select, Insert, Update, Delete, Execute, and so on), the object name, and the user or role to which the setting applies.

GRANT

To *grant* permission is to give or allow permission to perform a type of operation on an object. The following are examples:

```
GRANT INSERT ON Product TO Paul
GRANT EXEC ON spDeletePurchaseOrders TO Paul
```

DENY

The DENY statement is used to explicitly prohibit a user or role members from performing a specific action on an object. Even if a user is a member of a role or is otherwise granted permission, they will not be able to perform the action if they are denied permission explicitly or through any role membership:

```
DENY INSERT ON Product TO Paul
DENY EXEC ON spDeletePurchaseOrders TO Paul
```

REVOKE

This statement is often misunderstood, as the term revoke means to take away. Revoking a permission doesn't necessarily mean that a user loses the ability to perform an action. To revoke permission means to remove the current set of permissions for an object and user or role. This could have the effect of removing an explicit GRANT or DENY, if either exists. This would cause the permission set for a user to revert to those applied through a role membership or to the default permissions.

```
REVOKE INSERT ON Product TO Paul
REVOKE EXEC ON spDeletePurchaseOrders TO Paul
```

Summary

After you get past the fine points, managing all database objects is a fairly simple matter of using the CREATE, ALTER, and DROP statements for each type of object. These three SQL statements comprise Data Definition Language (DDL), which is the most common method used by administrative tools to design a database and its objects.

Many types of database objects exist, some of which are specialized, and others are more common. In this chapter, you learned to create and manage tables, views, stored procedures, and user-defined functions.

Security permissions are applied for a combination of an object and a user or role. Roles allow groups of users with similar requirements to be managed as a cohesive unit, rather than as individuals. Because SQL Server lets you define logins and users separately or integrated with existing Windows users and groups, security can be managed at a very granular level. This provides a great deal of flexibility for both simple database applications and complex enterprise solutions. Applicable, object-specific actions can be enabled or restricted on each object for individual users or those belonging to a defined role. Permissions to perform an action (such as Insert, Update, Delete, Select, or Execute) may be explicitly granted or denied, and revoking a permission removes that permission, whether it be a grant or deny.

There is much to consider when planning the security requirements for your system. This is one of a database administrator's most important tasks. This chapter just scratched the surface of this important topic in focusing only on the SQL language related to this topic.

Exercises

Exercise 1

Write the SQL script to define a new table to track customers buying wristbands from an on-line store. Decide upon an appropriate name, data type, and nullability option for each column. Due to strict storage requirements, use the most conservative data types possible. Guidelines for the columns in this table are as follows:

Define a single column for the customer's name. It should allow between 1 and 200 characters and is a required entry. Some customer's may have foreign names.

Four columns are needed to store the customer's address, city, state and zip code. All addresses and cities will contain only U.S. domestic names, and none of these columns require a value. The address column should allow up to 200 characters, the city should allow up to 100 characters, the state will always be a two-character abbreviation, and the postal code will always be five characters in length.

A column is needed to store the quantity of wristbands purchased. This column will store a whole number value up to 10,000 and should be automatically set to 1 for new records.

A column is needed to store the price paid. This is a required entry and should store values up to $100,000.

Exercise 2

Wristbands are sold on two separate web sites that use two copies of the database. Sales records will be merged together on occasion into one database.

Using the query you created in Exercise 1, add a column to serve as a primary key and to uniquely identify each sales record. Records should not be stored in physical order using this value.

We're currently only licensed to sell wristbands in three states. Constrain the State column so it only accepts customers in Washington, Oregon, and California (WA, OR, and CA).

Transact-SQL Programming Objects

SQL Server 2000 is an enormously capable relational data store. SQL Server 2005 is even more powerful. Both versions do a good job of storing large volumes of data. SQL Server in general manages transactions and enforces checks and rules to protect the integrity of related records and values. You've seen how the query optimizer makes intelligent decisions and uses indexes to make queries run fast and efficiently. Now we're going to take SQL Server to the next level. Most data is accessed through business applications. SQL Server can be more than just an idle medium for storing this data. A well-designed business solution uses the capabilities of an active database server, programming objects, and other components to distribute the workload and minimize unnecessary network traffic.

I want to take you on a brief tour of history so that you can appreciate the impact of the features we're about to discuss. In the 1980s and early 1990s, PC-based applications ran only on the desktop. If data could be shared across networks, it was simply stored in files managed by the file system. Applications supported a small number of users and quickly choked low-bandwidth networks as they moved all of their data to each desktop for processing. Desktop database applications sprang up like weeds in a new garden as inexpensive business applications became available — but the industry quickly hit the technology wall. In the past decade, the PC platform came of age with the advent of client/server database systems. In a nutshell, the enabling technology behind client/server applications was the cutting-edge concept of running application code on a database server. Products like SQL Server enabled this capability using database programming objects such as views and stored procedures.

I could stop there and keep things quite simple, but the current state of the industry has moved forward in recent years. Most enterprise database solutions have progressed beyond simple client/server technology. Now it's easier than ever before to distribute program components across two, three, or more different computers. These may include desktop computers, web servers, application servers, and database servers.

Sophisticated database applications use complicated queries. For this reason, it is important that queries and other SQL logic are protected and run as efficiently as possible. If SQL statements are managed in server-side database objects rather than in applications, this reduces the overall complexity of a solution. This separation of client-side applications and databases enables programmers and database professionals to each do what they do best, rather than having to write both program code and complex SQL, not to mention the fact that application programmers, unless they have a background in database technologies, have traditionally written very bad SQL.

The very first rule of developing database applications is to avoid the ad-hoc query at all costs. Ad-hoc queries create great efficiency issues, and when it comes to web applications, great security issues as well. The best practice when creating database-centric applications is to use database programming objects. In SQL Server, these objects include views, stored procedures, functions, and triggers. This chapter covers each of these objects in turn.

Views

This is one of the simplest database objects (at least views can be simple). On the surface, a view is nothing more than a SELECT query that is saved with a name in a database. Ask any modern-day programmer what they believe to be the most important and fundamental concept of programming. They will likely tell you that it is code reuse. Writing every line of code, every object, every script, and every query represents a cost or risk. One risk is that there could be a mistake (a bug) in the code. The cost of a bug is that it must be fixed (debugged) and tested. Buggy applications must be redeployed, shipped, installed, and supported. Undiscovered bugs pose a risk to productivity, business viability, and perhaps even legal exposure. One of the few constants in the software universe is change. Business rules will change, program logic will change, and the structure of your databases will also change. For all of these and other reasons, it just makes sense to reduce the number of objects that you create and use in your solutions. If you can create one object and reuse it in several places rather than duplicating the same effort, this limits your exposure to risk. Views promote this concept of code reuse by allowing you to save common queries into a uniform object. Rather than rewriting queries, complex queries can be created and tested and then reused without the added risk of starting over the next time you need to add functionality to an application.

Virtual Tables

One of the great challenges facing users is dealing with the complexity of large business databases. Many tools are available for use by casual database consumers for browsing data and building reports. Applications such as Microsoft Excel and Access are often used by information workers, rather than programmers, to obtain critical business management and operational information. A typical mid-scale database can contain scores of tables that contain supporting or special-purpose data. To reassemble the information stored in a large database, several tables must be joined in queries that take even skilled database professionals time and effort to create effectively. As you've seen in many examples, this is often not a trivial task. From the user's perspective, views are tables. They show up in most applications connecting to a SQL Server, along with the tables. A view is addressed in a SELECT statement and exposed columns, just like a table.

From the developer or database designer's perspective, a view can be a complex query that is exposed as if it were a simple table. This gives you an enormous amount of flexibility and the ability to hide all of the query logic, exposing a simple object. Users simply see a table-like object from which they can select data.

Creating a View

Defining a view is quite simple. First of all, a database user must be granted permission to create database objects. This is a task that you may want to have performed only by a database administrator or a select number of trusted users. Because creating most views isn't particularly complicated, you may want certain users to be granted this ability.

Several simplified tools are available that you can use to create views. Microsoft Access, Enterprise Manager, and Visual Studio all leverage the Transact-SQL Query Designer interface to create and manage views. The process is just about the same in all of these tools because they all actually expose the same components. The following section steps through creating a view using Microsoft Access. I will not demonstrate each tool because the process is nearly identical.

Creating a View in Microsoft Access

Microsoft Access is a popular tool that can be used to manage and query a SQL Server database. I don't intend for this example to serve as a full-blown Access tutorial so it's just going to demonstrate some of the basics. The following example is an Access Data Project (ADP) connected to the AdventureWorks2000 database.

In the database window shown in Figure 13-1, you can see that the database contains a stored procedure and two views, all listed on the Queries tab.

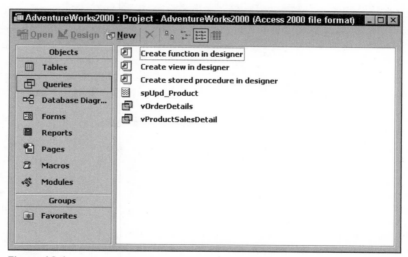

Figure 13-1

Click the New button on the toolbar to create a new query. The New Query window opens, allowing you to create a few different types of objects. Choose Design View, as shown in Figure 13-2, to create a new view and then click OK.

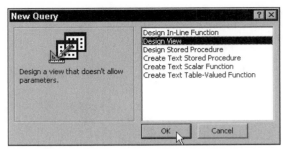

Figure 13-2

The next window should look familiar. Access uses a version of the Transact-SQL query designer window. In the default view, the table diagramming pane and the columns grid are displayed. The Access product designers made this tool appear as much as they could like the original Access SQL query designer by hiding the actual SQL script. The Add Table window, shown in Figure 13-3, is automatically opened. Use this to select and add three tables: Product, ProductCategory, and ProductSubCategory. Because of the relationships that exist between these tables, inner joins are automatically defined in the query.

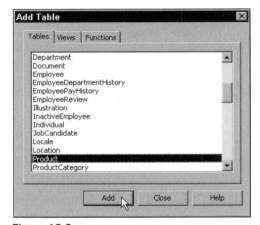

Figure 13-3

Select the Name column from the ProductCategory table (using the checkboxes in the table windows), the Name column from the ProductSubCategory table, and the columns you see in Figure 13-4, from the Product table. Using the Alias column in the columns grid, define aliases for the following three columns:

Table.Column	Alias
ProductCategory.Name	CategoryName
ProductSubCategory.Name	SubCategoryName
Product.Name	ProductName

Also, designate these three columns for sorting in the order listed by dropping down and selecting the word Ascending in the Sort Type column. Check your results against Figure 13-4 and make any adjustments necessary.

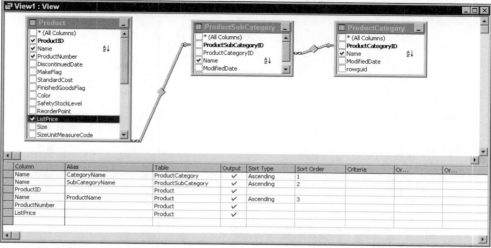

Figure 13-4

If you close the window, using the Close button in the top-right corner, Access will prompt you to save the view. Enter a name for the new view in the Save As dialog, as demonstrated in Figure 13-5. I've always made it a point to prefix view names with v, vw, or vw_ and to use Pascal-case (no spaces, with the first letter of each word capitalized).

> *Naming standards are discussed in more detail in Chapter 11. Just ensure that whatever you name your views is consistent and agreeable to those who will use it within your organization.*

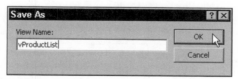

Figure 13-5

After saving the view, it appears in the list of objects on the Queries list. If you double-click the new item, it will open and display data just like a table, as you can see in Figure 13-6.

Creating Views in Visual Studio

All database objects are managed in the Server Explorer window. To create a view, it is first necessary to establish a connection to a SQL Server data source. After that, expand the connection and then right-click the node labeled Views. Select the New View menu item to launch the Transact-SQL Query Builder, as demonstrated in Figure 13-7.

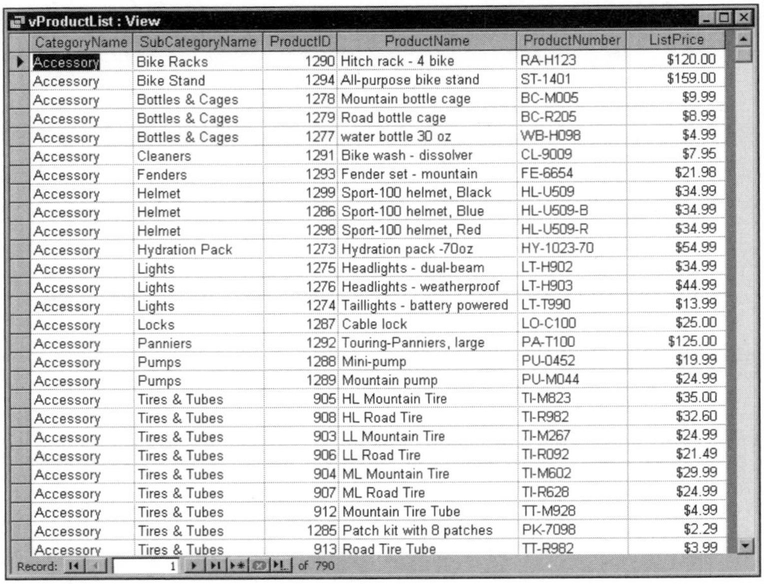

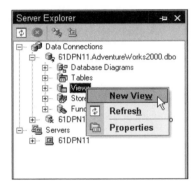

Figure 13-6

Figure 13-7

After the query is completed, close the Query Builder window. When prompted, provide a name for the new view.

When naming tables and other database objects it is important to consider the long-term implications. Keep in mind that individual views can be created to support a variety of application or reporting features. With so many views on the same entities, it becomes important to use unique, descriptive names.

Creating a View Using SQL Script

Regardless of the tool or product used to create a view, SQL script runs in the background and the result will be the same as handwriting without the use of an automated tool. The syntax for creating a new view is quite simple. The pattern is the same whether the query is very simple or extremely complex. I'll start with a simple view on a single table:

```
CREATE VIEW vProductCosts
AS
SELECT ProductID, Name, StandardCost
FROM Product
```

To continue working with this same view and extend its capabilities, I can either use the ALTER command to make modifications to the existing view or drop and create it. Using the ALTER statement rather than dropping and re-creating a view has the advantage of keeping any existing properties and security permissions intact.

Here are examples of these two statements. The ALTER statement is issued with the revised view definition:

```
ALTER VIEW vProductCosts
AS
SELECT ProductID, Name, ProductNumber, StandardCost
FROM Product
```

Using the DROP statement will wipe the slate clean, so to speak, reinitializing properties and security permissions:

```
DROP VIEW vProductCosts
```

What happens if there are dependencies on a view? I'll conduct a simple experiment by creating another view that selects data from the view previously created:

```
CREATE VIEW vProductCosts2
AS
Select Name, StandardCost From vProductCosts
```

For this view to work the first view has to exist and it must support the columns it references. Now, what happens if I try to drop the first view? I'll execute the previous DROP command. Here's what SQL Server returns:

```
Command(s) completed successfully.
```

My view is gone? What happens if I execute a query using the second view?

```
SELECT * FROM vProductCosts2
```

SQL Server returns this information:

```
Msg 208, Level 16, State 1, Procedure vProductCosts2, Line 1
Invalid object name 'vProductCosts'.
Msg 4413, Level 16, State 1, Line 1
Could not use view or function 'vProductCosts2' because of binding errors.
```

Why would SQL Server allow me to do something so silly? I may not be able to answer this question to your satisfaction because I can't address the question to my own satisfaction. This ability to drop an object and break something else is actually documented as a feature call *delayed resolution*. It's actually a holdover from the early days of SQL Server. To a degree it makes some sense. The perk of this feature is that if you needed to write script to drop all of the objects in the database and then create them again, this would be difficult to pull off with a lot of complex dependencies. If you're uncomfortable with this explanation, there is good news. An optional directive on the CREATE VIEW statement called SCHEMA BINDING tells SQL Server to check for dependencies and disallow any modifications that would violate them. To demonstrate, the first thing I'll do is drop both of these views and then re-create them:

```
CREATE VIEW vProductCosts WITH SCHEMABINDING
AS
SELECT ProductID, Name, ProductNumber, StandardCost
FROM Product
GO

CREATE VIEW vProductCosts2 WITH SCHEMABINDING
AS
SELECT Name, StandardCost
FROM dbo.vProductCosts
```

Some unique requirements are apparent in the example script. First of all, for a view to be schema-bound, any objects it depends on must also be schema-bound. Tables inherently support schema binding, but views must be explicitly schema-bound.

Any dependent objects must exist in the database before they can be referenced. For this reason, it's necessary to use batch delineation statements between dependent CREATE object statements. This example used the GO statement to finalize creating the first view.

When referring to a dependent view, you must use a two-part name. This means that in SQL Server 2000, use the owner and object name (dbo, by default), and in SQL Server 2005, use the schema name (which, as you can see in this example, is also dbo). A schema-bound view also cannot use the SELECT * syntax. All columns must be explicitly referenced.

Ordering Rows

Back when the original ANSI SQL specification was written, the authors wanted to make sure that database designers wouldn't do dumb things in their SQL queries that would waste server resources. Keep in mind that this was at a time when production servers had 32MB of memory. One memory-intensive operation is reordering a large result set. So, in their infinite wisdom, the authors imposed a rule that views cannot support the ORDER BY clause unless the results are restricted using a Top Values statement.

I run into this restriction all of the time. I'll spend some time creating some big, multi-table join or subquery with ordered results. After it's working, I think, "Hey, I ought to make this into a view." So I slap a CREATE VIEW vMyBigGnarlyQuery AS statement on the front of the script and execute the script with this result:

```
The ORDER BY clause is invalid in views, inline functions, derived tables,
subqueries, and common table expressions, unless TOP or FOR XML is also specified.
```

Then I remember I have to use a TOP statement. This is a no-brainer and is easily rectified using the following workaround:

```
CREATE VIEW vProductCosts
AS
SELECT TOP 100 PERCENT ProductID, Name, ProductNumber, StandardCost
FROM Product
ORDER BY Name
```

Now that most database servers have 50 times the horsepower and 10 times the memory of those 10 to 15 years ago, ordering a large result set is of little concern.

Partitioned Views

Every system has its limits. Performance-tuning and capacity planning is the science of identifying these gaps and formulating appropriate plans to alleviate them. To partition data is to place tables or other objects in different files and on different disk drives to improve performance and organize data storage on a server. One of the most common methods to increase the performance and fault-tolerance of a database server is to implement RAID storage devices. I know this isn't a book on server configuration, but I bring this up for a good reason. In teaching classes on database design and talking about partitioning data across multiple hard disks, I've often heard experienced students ask, "Why don't you just use a RAID device? Doesn't this accomplish the same thing?" Yes, to a point, disk arrays using RAID 5 or RAID 10 simply spread data across an array of physical disks, improving performance and providing fault-tolerance. However, data partitioning techniques and using RAID are not necessarily mutually exclusive. Categorically, there may be three scenarios for server size and scale:

❑ Small-scale servers

❑ Medium-scale servers

❑ Large-scale servers

Small-scale servers will have system files and data on physical disks. You can implement data partitioning by placing objects in different database files residing on different disks, as depicted in Figure 13-8.

Moderate-scale servers may implement a RAID device where an array of identical physical disk drives is treated by the operating system as a single, logical volume. From the database designer's standpoint, the server has one disk, as illustrated in Figure 13-9. The fact that what we perceive to be a single hard disk drive is actually a bank of parallel disks is completely transparent and may have little impact on how we design our database. One could argue that there is no need to be concerned with partitioning because the RAID device does this for us — as long as we have ample disk space.

In a large-scale server environment, we generally take RAID technology for granted and may have several RAID devices, each acting as if it were an individual disk drive. This brings us back to the same scenario as the first example given where the server has a number of physical disks. In this case, we can partition our data across multiple disks, only each "disk" is actually a RAID device, as shown in Figure 13-10.

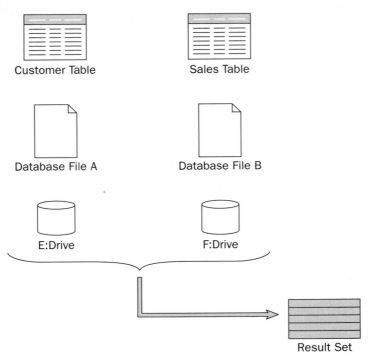

Figure 13-8

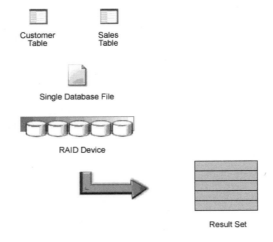

Figure 13-9

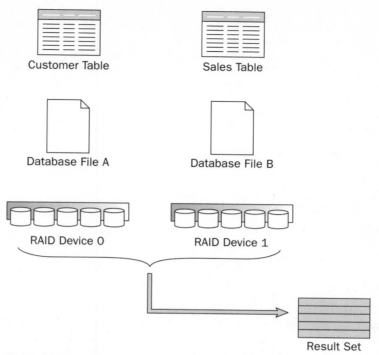

Figure 13-10

For this discussion, I'd like to put the RAID option aside and treat disks as if they are all physical disks, when in fact, each may be a RAID device.

So what does all of this have to do with views? You'll remember that one of the main reasons for views is to treat complex data as if it were a simple table. Partitioning takes this concept to the next level. Here's an example: Suppose that your product marketing business has been gathering sales order data for five years. Business has been good and, on average, you're storing 500,000 sales detail rows each year. At the end of each month your sales managers and executives would like to run comparative sales reports on all of this data but you certainly don't want to keep nearly three million rows of data in your active table. When database performance began to slow down a couple of years ago, you decided to archive older records by moving them to a different table. This improved transactional performance because the active sales detail table stored less data. As long as you only accessed the most current records for reporting, performance was fine. However, when you combined the archive tables with the current detail, you were back to where you started and, once again, the server ground to a snail's pace. This is because all of these tables resided on the same physical disk.

Here's a quick computer trivia question: What's the slowest component of almost any computer system? The user? OK, besides that. The memory? How about the CPU? Typically not. It's the hard disk. Aside from the cooling fans, the hard disk is the only critical component that is still mechanical. The industry hasn't yet found a cost-effective replacement without moving parts. The platter can only spin so fast and the read/write heads can only move back and forth so fast. In earlier chapters you learned that the greatest cost-affecting query performance is disk I/O — the time it takes for the system to position the heads and read data from a physical disk. If the system has one disk, it must find a page of data, reposition the heads, read the next page, and so on until it reads all of the data to return a complete result set. Because one disk has one set of heads, this happens in a linear fashion, one page at a time. If you were able to able to spread data across multiple disks, SQL Server could retrieve data from each disk simultaneously. The query execution plan makes this possible as it maps out those operations that are dependent and those that can be performed in parallel. This is depicted in Figure 13-11.

The view that makes all of this possible is actually quite simple. Using your successful marketing business as an example, the view definition might look like this:

```
SELECT * FROM SalesDetail_1999
UNION ALL
SELECT * FROM SalesDetail_2000
UNION ALL
SELECT * FROM SalesDetail_2001
UNION ALL
SELECT * FROM SalesDetail_2002
UNION ALL
SELECT * FROM SalesDetail_2004
UNION ALL
SELECT * FROM SalesDetail_Current
```

Because these tables are all addressable within the database, they can be referenced in joins, subqueries, or any type of SQL expression. It may not make sense to put every table on its own disk, but if you did, each of these SELECT statements could be processed in parallel. Assuming that each drive had its own independent controller, the data on each of these disks could be read simultaneously.

As you can see, many factors can contribute to the effectiveness of a partitioned view. You would likely choose this route when system performance became an issue. The best indicator that an approach solves a performance or resource problem would be to use performance-tuning tools such as analyzing query execution plans, using the Windows system monitor and SQL Server Profiler.

Federated Views

Federated views are close cousins of partitioned views. The term *federated* means working together, so a federated server solution consists of more than one independent database server working together to solve a business problem. This is not to be confused with a server cluster, where multiple servers appear as a single server on the network. Federated servers may be in close proximity or could be a great distance apart. In fact, one of the significant advantages to a federated server solution is that the database servers are geographically located in close proximity to the users and applications that will use them. With database servers in regional or satellite business locations, the majority of the region's supporting data is typically stored on the local server. Federated views may be used to access data stored on remote servers and in exceptional cases, connecting over the Internet or corporate wide-area network (see Figure 13-12).

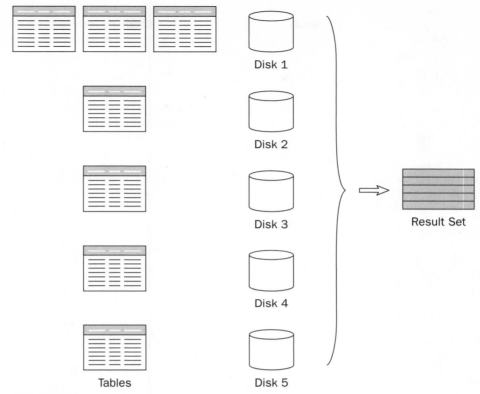

Figure 13-11

Figure 13-12

You could take a few different approaches to make data accessible from one server to another. One of the most common choices is to configure a *linked server* connection. A linked server maintains a connection to a database on another server as if the remote database were local. Once a linked server connection is established, tables are referenced using a four-part name, as follows:

```
LinkedServer.SalesDatabase.dbo.SalesDetail
```

What does this accomplish? Suppose I have designed the database infrastructure for a banking system. Let's say that credit card transactions may be processed in one of two data centers: one in Atlanta for east coast accounts, and one in San Francisco for west coast accounts. All U.S. customers have their account records managed in one of these two data centers. If I live in Seattle and make a purchase anywhere in the western United States, the merchant system sends my transaction to the San Francisco data center where it locates my account record and processes the transaction. However, the system must also be prepared to locate east coast account records stored in the Atlanta data center. The view used to locate all accounts (from the west coast server) may be defined like this:

```
CREATE VIEW vAllAccounts
AS
SELECT * FROM Accounts      -- (local West coast)
UNION ALL
SELECT * FROM EastCoastServer.SalesDatabase.dbo.Accounts -- (remote East coast)
```

The query issued from the client would look like this:

```
SELECT TOP 1 * FROM vAllAccounts WHERE CardNumber = @CardNumber
```

The TOP 1 statement tells the query-processing engine to stop looking after it finds one record. If the record is located in the first table (on the local server), no request is made on the remote server. Otherwise, the connection is used to pass the request to the other server, which processes the query until it locates the account record. Figure 13-13 demonstrates this scenario.

Figure 13-13

Now suppose that I travel to New York and buy a stuffed animal for my daughter's birthday. I find a great deal on a Teddy bear wearing a Yankees baseball cap and pay with my credit card, which sends a request to the Atlanta data center to Select Top 1 from a view defined as follows:

```
CREATE VIEW vAllAccounts
AS
SELECT * FROM Accounts        -- (local East coast)
UNION ALL
SELECT * FROM WestCoastServer.SalesDatabase.dbo.Accounts -- (remote West coast)
```

In this example, the east coast server doesn't find my account record in the local Accounts table so it moves to the remote server, which begins searching in its Accounts table. This part of the query is actually processed on the west coast server so data isn't unnecessarily transferred across the network connection. After finding one record (my account), it stops looking and terminates the query execution. This scenario is depicted in Figure 13-14.

Figure 13-14

Securing Data

Another useful offering of views is to provide a layer for user data access without giving users access to sensitive data or other database objects. A common security practice is for the database administrator to lock down all of the tables, denying access to all regular users. Views are then created to explicitly expose selected tables, columns, and/or rows for all or selected users. When the select permission is granted on a view, users gain access to the view's underlying data even if the same user is explicitly denied the select permission on the underlying table(s).

Hiding Complexity

One of the most common, and arguably one of the most important reasons to use views is to simplify data access. In a normalized database, even the most basic queries can involve many different tables. Views make it possible for programmers, report writers, and users to gain access to data at a reasonably low level without having to contend with the complexities of relationships and database schema. A practical transactional database is broken down into many tables and related information is spread out across these tables to maintain data integrity and to reduce unnecessary redundancy. Reassembling all of these elements can be a headache for someone who doesn't fully understand the data or who may not be versed in relational database design. Even for the experienced developer or DBA, using a view can save time and minimize errors. The following is an example to demonstrate this point. To do something as fundamental as return employee contact information can be a relatively complex proposition.

In this example, I want to return the name, address, city, state or province, country, shift, and department information for all my employees. Because this information could be common to more than one employee, the address, state or province, country, shift, and department details are all stored in their own tables. For security reasons, I also don't want users to have access to an employee's pay rate or other private information. Using a view, users are not even aware that the columns containing this restricted information exist.

```
CREATE VIEW vEmployeeContactDetail
AS
SELECT Employee.EmployeeID
     , Employee.FirstName
     , Employee.LastName
     , Employee.Title
     , Employee.EmailAddress
     , Employee.BirthDate
     , Employee.Gender
     , Address.AddressLine1
     , Address.AddressLine2
     , Address.City
     , StateProvince.Name AS StateProvinceName
     , CountryRegion.Name AS CountryName
     , Address.PostalCode
     , Department.Name AS DepartmentName
     , Employee.FirstName + ' ' + Employee.LastName AS ManagerName
     , Shift.Name AS ShiftName
     , Employee.HireDate
FROM    Employee
        INNER JOIN Shift
          ON Employee.ShiftID = Shift.ShiftID
        INNER JOIN Address
          ON Employee.AddressID = Address.AddressID
        INNER JOIN Department
          ON Employee.DepartmentID = Department.DepartmentID
        INNER JOIN Employee AS Manager_Employee
          ON Employee.ManagerID = Manager_Employee.EmployeeID
        INNER JOIN StateProvince
          ON Address.StateProvinceID = StateProvince.StateProvinceID
        INNER JOIN CountryRegion
          ON StateProvince.CountryRegionCode = CountryRegion.CountryRegionCode
```

Here's one more example of a very lengthy view. This view will be used a little later in the discussion on processing business logic in stored procedures. What I like about this view is that it contains several columns that could easily be used for reporting purposes, to sort, group, or filter the resulting data.

```
CREATE VIEW vProductSalesDetail
AS
SELECT TOP 100 Percent
      ProductCategory.Name AS CategoryName
    , ProductSubCategory.Name AS SubCategoryName
    , Product.Name AS ProductName
    , SalesOrderDetail.OrderQty
    , SalesOrderDetail.UnitPrice
    , SalesOrderHeader.OrderDate
    , SalesOrderHeader.TaxAmt
    , SalesOrderHeader.SubTotal
    , Customer.AccountNumber
    , Address.AddressLine1
    , Address.City
    , Address.PostalCode
    , StateProvince.StateProvinceCode
    , StateProvince.Name AS StateProvinceName
    , CountryRegion.Name AS CountryRegionName
FROM  CountryRegion
      RIGHT OUTER JOIN StateProvince
        ON CountryRegion.CountryRegionCode = StateProvince.CountryRegionCode
      RIGHT OUTER JOIN Address
        ON StateProvince.StateProvinceID = Address.StateProvinceID
      INNER JOIN CustomerAddress
        ON Address.AddressID = CustomerAddress.AddressID
      RIGHT OUTER JOIN Customer
        ON CustomerAddress.CustomerID = Customer.CustomerID
      LEFT OUTER JOIN Individual
        ON Individual.CustomerID = Customer.CustomerID
      INNER JOIN SalesOrderHeader
        ON SalesOrderHeader.CustomerID = Customer.CustomerID
      INNER JOIN SalesOrderDetail
        ON SalesOrderHeader.SalesOrderID = SalesOrderDetail.SalesOrderID
      INNER JOIN Product
        ON Product.ProductID = SalesOrderDetail.ProductID
      INNER JOIN ProductSubCategory
        ON Product.ProductSubCategoryID = ProductSubCategory.ProductSubCategoryID
      INNER JOIN ProductCategory
        ON ProductSubCategory.ProductCategoryID = ProductCategory.ProductCategoryID
```

Modifying Data through Views

Can data be modified through a view? Perhaps a better question is should data be modified through a view? The definitive answer is maybe. Yes, you can modify some data through views. Because a view can expose the results of a variety of query techniques, some results may be updatable, some may not, and others may allow some columns to be updated. This all depends on various join types, record-locking conditions, and permissions on the underlying tables.

As a rule, I don't think views are for updating records—that's my opinion. After all, doesn't the word view suggest that its purpose is to provide a read-only view of data? I think so, but I've also worked on enough corporate production databases where this was the only option. The fact of the matter is that over time, databases evolve. Over the years, people come and go, policies are implemented with little evidence of their purpose, and political culture dictates the methods we use. If I were king of the world, no one would have access to data directly through tables; views would provide read-only data access and support all related application features, and stored procedures would be used to perform all transactional operations and filtered data retrieval. These are the guidelines I follow when designing a system from the ground up. However, I acknowledge that this is not always possible in the typical circumstance where one database designer isn't given free license.

In simple terms, these are the most common rules governing the conditions for updating data through views:

❑   In an inner join, columns from one table at a time may be modified. This is due to the record-locking restrictions on related tables. Updates generally cannot be performed on two related tables within the same transaction.

❑   In an outer join, generally columns only for the inner table are updatable.

❑   Updates can't be performed through a view containing a UNION query.

Stored Procedures

If views raise the bar of database functionality, then stored procedures take it to the next level. Unlike views, stored procedures can be used for much more than reading data. They provide a wide range of programming functionality. Categorically, stored procedures can be used to do the following:

❑   Implement parameterized views

❑   Return scalar values

❑   Maintain records

❑   Process business logic

In the following examples, I've prefixed the names with the letters sp for stored procedure. If you use the Object Browser to view system stored procedure names, you'll see that most of these existing procedures are prefixed with sp_. It's not a good idea to use the same prefix as the system procedures because this is an indicator to the database engine to try to locate this procedure in the system catalog before it looks in your database. Although there are no specific compatibility issues with this prefix, this can degrade performance and cause potential confusion.

Stored Procedures as Parameterized Views

Like views, stored procedures can be used to return a result set based on a SELECT statement. However, I want to clarify an important point about the difference between views and stored procedures. A view is used in a SELECT statement as if it were a table. A stored procedure is executed, rather than selected from. For most programming APIs, this makes little difference. If a programmer needs to return a set of rows to an application or report, ActiveX Data Objects (ADO) or ADO.NET can be used to obtain results from a table, a view, or a stored procedure.

A stored procedure can be used in place of a view to return a set of rows from one or more tables. Earlier in this chapter, I used a simple view to return selected columns from the Product table. Again, the script looks like this:

```
CREATE VIEW vProductCosts
AS
SELECT ProductID, ProductSubcategoryID, Name, ProductNumber, StandardCost
FROM Product
```

Contrast this with the script to create a similar stored procedure:

```
CREATE PROCEDURE spProductCosts
AS
SELECT ProductID, ProductSubcategoryID, Name, ProductNumber, StandardCost
FROM Product
```

To execute the new stored procedure, the name is preceded by the EXECUTE statement:

```
EXECUTE spProductCosts
```

Although this is considered the most proper syntax, the following are also examples of acceptable syntax.

The shorthand version of EXECUTE:

```
EXEC spProductCosts
```

No EXECUTE statement:

```
spProductCosts
```

Using Parameters

A parameter is a special type of variable used to pass values into an expression. Named parameters are used for passing values into and out of stored procedures and user-defined-functions. Parameters are most typically used to input, or pass values into, a procedure, but can also be used to return values.

Parameters are declared immediately after the procedure definition and before the term AS. Parameters are declared with a specific data type and are used as variables in the body of a SQL statement. I will modify this procedure with an input parameter to pass the value of the ProductSubCategoryID. This will be used to filter the results of the query. This example shows the script for creating the procedure. If the procedure already exists, the CREATE statement may be replaced with the ALTER statement:

```
ALTER PROCEDURE spProductCosts
@SubCategoryID Int
AS
SELECT ProductID, Name, ProductNumber, StandardCost
FROM Product
WHERE ProductSubCategoryID = @SubCategoryID
```

To execute the procedure and pass the parameter value in SQL Query Analyzer or the Query Editor, simply append the parameter value to the end of the statement, like this:

```
EXECUTE spProductCosts 1
```

Alternatively the stored procedure can be executed with the parameter and assigned value like this:

```
EXECUTE spProductCosts @SubCategory = 1
```

Stored procedures can accept multiple parameters and the parameters can be passed in either by position or by value similar to the previous example. Suppose I want a stored procedure that filters products by subcategory and price. It would look something like this:

```
CREATE PROCEDURE spProductsByCost
@SubCategoryID Int, @Cost Money
AS
SELECT ProductID, Name, ProductNumber, StandardCost
FROM Product
WHERE ProductSubCategoryID = @SubCategoryID
AND StandardCost > @Cost
```

Using SQL, the multiple parameters can be passed in a comma-delimited list in the order they were declared:

```
EXECUTE spProductsByCost 1, $1000.00
```

Or the parameters can be passed explicitly by value. If the parameters are supplied by value it doesn't matter in what order they are supplied:

```
EXECUTE spProductsByCost @Cost = $1000.00, @SubCategoryID = 1
```

If a programmer is using a common data access API such as ADO or ADO.NET, separate parameter objects are often used to encapsulate these values and execute the procedure in the most efficient manner.

Although views and stored procedures do provide some overlap in functionality, they each have a unique purpose. The view used in the previous example can be used in a variety of settings where it may not be feasible to use a stored procedure. However, if I need to filter records using parameterized values, a stored procedure will allow me to do this where a view will not. So, if the programmer building the product browse screen needs an unfiltered result set and the report designer needs a filtered list of products based on a subcategory parameter, do I create a view or a stored procedure? That's easy, both. Use views as the foundation upon which to build stored procedures. Using the previous example, I select from the view rather than the table:

```
ALTER PROCEDURE spProductCosts
@SubCategoryID Int
As
SELECT ProductID, Name, ProductNumber, StandardCost
FROM vProductCosts
WHERE ProductSubCategoryID = @SubCategoryID
```

The benefit may not be so obvious in this simple, one-table example. However, if a procedure were based on the seven-table vEmployeeContactDetail view, the procedure call might benefit from optimizations in the view design and the lower maintenance cost of storing this complex statement in only one object.

Returning Values

The parameter examples shown thus far demonstrate how to use parameters for passing values into a stored procedure. One method to return a value from a procedure is to return a single-column, single-row result set. Although there is probably nothing grossly wrong with this technique, it's not the most effective way to handle simple values. A result set is wrapped in a cursor, which defines the rows and columns, and may be prepared to deal with record navigation and locking. This kind of overkill reminds me of a digital camera memory card I recently ordered from a discount electronics supplier. A few days later, a relatively large box arrived and at first appeared to be filled with nothing more than foam packing peanuts. I had to look carefully to find the postage-size memory card inside.

In addition to passing values into a procedure, parameters can also be used to return values for output. Stored procedure parameters with an OUTPUT direction modifier are set to store both input and output values by default. Additionally, the procedure itself is equipped to return a single integer value without needing to define a specific parameter. The return value is also called the return code and defaults to the integer value of 0. Some programming APIs such as ADO and ADO.NET actually create a special output parameter object to handle this return value. Suppose I want to know how many product records there are for a specified subcategory. I'll pass the SubCategoryID using an input parameter and return the record count using an output parameter:

```
CREATE PROCEDURE spProductCountBySubCategory
  @SubCategoryID Int,
  @ProdCount Int OUTPUT
AS
  SELECT @ProdCount = COUNT(*)
  FROM Product
  WHERE ProductSubCategoryID = @SubCategoryID
```

To test a stored procedure with output parameters in the Management Studio or Query Analyzer environments, it is necessary to explicitly use these parameters by name. Treat them as if they were variables but you don't need to declare them. When executing a stored procedure using SQL, the behavior of output parameters can be a bit puzzling because they also have to be passed in. In this example, using the same stored procedure, a variable is used to capture the output parameter value. The curious thing about this syntax is that the assignment seems backwards. Remember that the OUTPUT modifier affects the direction of the value assignment — in this case, from right to left:

```
DECLARE @Out Int

EXECUTE spProductCountBySubCategory
@SubCategoryID = 2,
@ProdCount = @Out OUTPUT

SELECT @Out AS ProductCountBySubCategory

ProductCountBySubCategory
-------------------------
184
```

It is critical that the OUTPUT modifier also be added to the output parameter when it is passed in to the stored procedure. If you don't, the stored procedure will still execute, but it will not return any data.

```
DECLARE @Out Int

EXECUTE spProductCountBySubCategory
@SubCategoryID = 2,
@ProdCount = @Out --Missing the OUTPUT directional modifier

SELECT @Out AS ProductCountBySubCategory
```

```
ProductCountBySubCategory
-------------------------
NULL
```

There is no practical limit to the number of values that may be returned from a stored procedure. The stated limit is 2,100, including input and output parameters.

If you need to return only one value from the procedure, this can be done without the use of an output parameter using the return code of the procedure as long as the value being returned is an integer. Here is the same stored procedure showing this technique:

```
CREATE PROCEDURE spProductCountBySubCategory
   @SubCategoryID Int
AS
   DECLARE @Out Int
   SELECT @Out = Count(*)
   FROM Product
   WHERE ProductSubCategoryID = @SubCategoryID
RETURN @Out
```

The RETURN statement does two things: it modifies the return value for the procedure from the default value, 0, and it terminates execution so that any statements following this line do not execute. This is significant in cases where there may be conditional branching logic. Typically the capture of the return value must be done with a programming API. Executing this stored procedure in Query Analyzer or Management Studio will not return any results because these interfaces don't display the procedure's return value by default.

Record Maintenance

Using stored procedures to manage the insert, update, and delete operations for each major database entity can drastically reduce the cost of data maintenance tasks down the road. Any program code written to perform record operations should do so using stored procedures and not ad-hoc SQL expressions. As a rule of thumb, when I design a business application, every table that will have records managed through the application interface gets a corresponding stored procedure to perform each of these operations. These procedures are by far the most straightforward in terms of syntax patterns. Although simple, writing this script can be cumbersome due to the level of detail necessary to deal with all of the columns. Fortunately, the SQL Server 2000 Query Analyzer and the SQL Server 2005 Management Studio include scripting tools that will generate the bulk of the script for you. Beyond creating the fundamental Insert, Update, Delete, and Select statements, you need to define and place parameters into your script.

Insert Procedure

The basic pattern for creating an Insert stored procedure is to define parameters for all non-default or auto-populated columns. In the case of the Product table, the ProductID primary key column will automatically be incremented because it's defined as an identity column; the rowguid and ModifiedDate columns have default values assigned in the table definition. The MakeFlag and FinishedGoodsFlag columns also have default values assigned in the table definition, but it may be appropriate to set these values differently for some records. For this reason, these parameters are set to the same default values in the procedure. Several columns are nullable and the corresponding parameters are set to a default value of null. If a parameter with a default assignment isn't provided when the procedure is executed, the default value is used. Otherwise, all parameters without default values must be supplied:

```
CREATE PROCEDURE spProduct_Insert
       @Name                     nVarChar(50)
     , @ProductNumber            nVarChar(25)
     , @MakeFlag                 Bit            = 1
     , @FinishedGoodsFlag        Bit            = 1
     , @Color                    nVarChar(15)   = Null
     , @SafetyStockLevel         SmallInt
     , @ReorderPoint             SmallInt
     , @StandardCost             Money
     , @ListPrice                Money
     , @Size                     nVarChar(5)    = Null
     , @SizeUnitMeasureCode      nChar(3)       = Null
     , @WeightUnitMeasureCode    nChar(3)       = Null
     , @Weight                   Decimal        = Null
     , @DaysToManufacture        Int
     , @ProductLine              nChar(2)       = Null
     , @Class                    nChar(2)       = Null
     , @Style                    nChar(2)       = Null
     , @ProductSubcategoryID     SmallInt       = Null
     , @ProductModelID           Int            = Null
     , @SellStartDate            DateTime
     , @SellEndDate              DateTime       = Null
     , @DiscontinuedDate         DateTime       = Null
AS
INSERT INTO Product
     (   Name
       , ProductNumber
       , MakeFlag
       , FinishedGoodsFlag
       , Color
       , SafetyStockLevel
       , ReorderPoint
       , StandardCost
       , ListPrice
       , Size
       , SizeUnitMeasureCode
       , WeightUnitMeasureCode
       , Weight
       , DaysToManufacture
       , ProductLine
       , Class
       , Style
```

```
        , ProductSubcategoryID
        , ProductModelID
        , SellStartDate
        , SellEndDate
        , DiscontinuedDate  )
    SELECT
          @Name
        , @ProductNumber
        , @MakeFlag
        , @FinishedGoodsFlag
        , @Color
        , @SafetyStockLevel
        , @ReorderPoint
        , @StandardCost
        , @ListPrice
        , @Size
        , @SizeUnitMeasureCode
        , @WeightUnitMeasureCode
        , @Weight
        , @DaysToManufacture
        , @ProductLine
        , @Class
        , @Style
        , @ProductSubcategoryID
        , @ProductModelID
        , @SellStartDate
        , @SellEndDate
        , @DiscontinuedDate
```

It's a lot of script but it's not complicated. Executing this procedure in SQL is quite easy. This can be done in comma-delimited fashion or by using explicit parameter names. Because the majority of the fields and corresponding parameters are optional, they can be ommitted. Only the required parameters need to be passed; the optional parameters are simply ignored:

```
EXECUTE spProduct_Insert
      @Name                = 'Widget'
    , @ProductNumber       = '987654321'
    , @SafetyStockLevel    = 10
    , @ReorderPoint        = 15
    , @StandardCost        = 23.50
    , @ListPrice           = 49.95
    , @DaysToManufacture   = 30
    , @SellStartDate       = '10/1/04'
```

The procedure can also be executed with parameter values passed in a comma-delimited list. Although the script isn't nearly as easy to read, it is less verbose. Even though this may save you some typing, it often becomes an exercise in counting commas and rechecking the table's field list in the Object Browser until the script runs without error.

```
EXECUTE spProduct_Insert 'Widget', '987654321', 1, 1, Null, 10, 15, 23.50, 49.95,
Null, Null, Null, Null, 30, Null, Null, Null, Null, Null, '10/1/04'
```

When using this technique, parameter values must be passed in the order they are declared. Values must be provided for every parameter up to the point of the last required value. After that, the remaining parameters in the list can be ignored.

A useful variation of this procedure may be to return the newly generated primary key value. The last identity value generated in a session is held by the global variable, @@Identity. To add this feature, simply add this line to the end of the procedure. This would cause the Insert procedure to return the ProductID value for the inserted record.

```
RETURN @@Identity
```

Of course, if you have already created this procedure, change the CREATE keyword to ALTER, make changes to the script, and then re-execute it.

Update Procedure

The Update procedure is similar. Usually when I create these data maintenance stored procedures, I write the script for the Insert procedure and then make the modifications necessary to transform the same script into an Update procedure. As you can see, it's very similar:

```
CREATE PROCEDURE spProduct_Update
        @ProductID              Int
    ,   @Name                   nVarChar(50)
    ,   @ProductNumber          nVarChar(25)
    ,   @MakeFlag               Bit             = 1
    ,   @FinishedGoodsFlag      Bit             = 1
    ,   @Color                  nVarChar(15)    = Null
    ,   @SafetyStockLevel       SmallInt
    ,   @ReorderPoint           SmallInt
    ,   @StandardCost           Money
    ,   @ListPrice              Money
    ,   @Size                   nVarChar(5)     = Null
    ,   @SizeUnitMeasureCode    nChar(3)        = Null
    ,   @WeightUnitMeasureCode  nChar(3)        = Null
    ,   @Weight                 Decimal         = Null
    ,   @DaysToManufacture      Int
    ,   @ProductLine            nChar(2)        = Null
    ,   @Class                  nChar(2)        = Null
    ,   @Style                  nChar(2)        = Null
    ,   @ProductSubcategoryID   SmallInt        = Null
    ,   @ProductModelID         Int             = Null
    ,   @SellStartDate          DateTime
    ,   @SellEndDate            DateTime        = Null
    ,   @DiscontinuedDate       DateTime        = Null
AS
UPDATE Product
SET     Name                = @Name
    ,   ProductNumber       = @ProductNumber
    ,   MakeFlag            = @MakeFlag
    ,   FinishedGoodsFlag   = @FinishedGoodsFlag
    ,   Color               = @Color
    ,   SafetyStockLevel    = @SafetyStockLevel
    ,   ReorderPoint        = @ReorderPoint
```

```
      , StandardCost           = @StandardCost
      , ListPrice              = @ListPrice
      , Size                   = @Size
      , SizeUnitMeasureCode     = @SizeUnitMeasureCode
      , WeightUnitMeasureCode   = @WeightUnitMeasureCode
      , Weight                 = @Weight
      , DaysToManufacture       = @DaysToManufacture
      , ProductLine            = @ProductLine
      , Class                  = @Class
      , Style                  = @Style
      , ProductSubcategoryID    = @ProductSubcategoryID
      , ProductModelID          = @ProductModelID
      , SellStartDate           = @SellStartDate
      , SellEndDate             = @SellEndDate
      , DiscontinuedDate        = @DiscontinuedDate
 WHERE ProductID = @ProductID
```

The parameter list is the same as the Insert procedure with the addition of the primary key, in this case, the ProductID column.

Delete Procedure

In its basic form, the Delete procedure is very simple. The only necessary parameter is for the ProductID column value:

```
CREATE PROCEDURE spProduct_Delete
     @ProductID    Int
AS
     DELETE FROM Product
     WHERE ProductID = @ProductID
```

Handling and Raising Errors

A common choice you may need to make in many data maintenance procedures is how you will handle errors. Attempting to insert, update, or delete a record that violates constraints or rules will cause the database engine to raise an error. If this is acceptable behavior, you don't need to do anything special in your procedure code. When the procedure is executed, an error is raised and the transaction is aborted. You simply need to handle the error condition in the client program code. Another, often more desirable, approach would be to proactively investigate the potential condition and then raise a custom error. This may have the advantage of offering the user or client application more useful error information or a more graceful method to handle the condition. In the case of the Delete procedure, I could check for existing dependent records and then raise a custom error without attempting to perform the delete operation. This also has the advantage of not locking records while the delete operation is attempted.

Error Handling in SQL Server 2000

For many years, the ability to handle errors in Transact-SQL script has been limited to the same type of pattern used in other scripting languages. The query-processing engine is not equipped to respond to error conditions in the same way that an event-driven run-time engine would. What this boils down to is that if you suspect that an error might be raised after a specific line of script, you can check for an error condition and respond to it. The downside to this approach is that you have to be able to guess where an error might occur and be prepared to respond to it.

There are two general approaches to raising errors. One is to raise the error on-the-fly. This is done using a single statement. The other approach is to add custom error codes and message text to the system catalog. These messages can then be raised from script in any database on the server. Custom errors are added to the system catalog using the sp_AddMessage system stored procedure. Here's an example:

```
sp_AddMessage @msgnum=50010
            , @severity=16
            , @msgtext='Cannot delete a product with existing sales order(s).'
            , @with_log='True'
            , @replace='Replace'
```

Three parameters are required: the message number, message severity, and message text. There are also three additional optional parameters: one to specify logging the error in the server's application log, one for replacing a current error with the same message number, and one to specify the language of the error if multiple languages are installed on the server. Custom error numbers begin at 50,001. This is user-assigned and has no special meaning. It's just a unique value. The system recognizes severity values within specified numeric ranges and may respond by automatically logging the error or sending alerts. Alerts are configurable within the SQL Server Agent. Messages and errors are distinguished by the Severity Level flag. Those with a severity level from 0 to 10 are considered to be informational messages and will not raise a system exception. Those with a severity level from 11 to 18 are non-fatal errors, and those 19 or above are considered to be most severe. This scale was devised for Windows service error logging. The following table shows the system-defined error severity levels.

Severity Level	Description
1	Misc. System Information
2 - 6	Reserved
7	Notification: Status Information
8	Notification: User Intervention Required
9	User Defined
10	Information
11	Specified Database Object Not Found
12	Unused
13	User Transaction Syntax Error
14	Insufficient Permission
15	Syntax Error in SQL Statements
16	Misc. User Error
17	Insufficient Resources
18	Fatal Error in Resource
19 *	Fatal Error in Resource

Table continued on following page

Severity Level	Description
20 *	Fatal Error in Current Process
21 *	Fatal Error in Database Processes
22 *	Fatal Error: Table Integrity Suspect
23 *	Fatal Error: Database Integrity Suspect
24 *	Fatal Error: Hardware Error
25 *	Fatal Error

* Messages with a severity level 19 or above will automatically be logged in the server's application log. When an error is raised in the procedure, you also have the option to explicitly log the message regardless of the severity level.

When logging an error in the application log, errors with a severity level less than 14 will be recorded as informational. Level 15 is recorded as a warning, and levels greater than 15 are issued the error status.

This example demonstrates raising a previously declared error:

```
RAISERROR (50010, 16, 1)
```

The output from this expression returns the message defined earlier:

```
Msg 50010, Level 16, State 1, Line 1
Cannot delete a product with existing sales orders.
```

The severity level is actually repeated in the call. I know, this seems like a strange requirement, but that's the way it works. It also does not have to be the same as the defined severity level. If I want to raise the error as a severity level 11 instead of the 16 I created it with, I can. The last parameter is the state. This value is user-defined and has no inherent meaning to the system, but it is a required argument. State can be a signed integer between –255 and +255. State can be used for internal tracking, for example, to track all "State 3" errors.

Here is an example of an ad-hoc message that has not been previously defined:

```
RAISERROR ('The sky is falling', 16, 1)
```

The resulting output is as follows:

```
Msg 50000, Level 16, State 1, Line 1
The sky is falling
```

Note that ad-hoc messages use the reserved message id of 50000. Raising an ad-hoc message with a severity level of 19 or higher requires elevated privileges and must be performed with explicit logging. If you need to raise an error of this type, it's advisable to define these messages ahead of time.

When an error occurs, the global variable, @@ERROR, changes from its default value of 0 to an integer type standard error number. SQL Server 2000 can return more than 3800 standard errors and SQL Server 2005 includes more than 6800 unique errors. All of these error numbers and messages are stored in the Master database.

This example is a simple stored procedure using a generic approach to error handling:

```
CREATE PROCEDURE spRunSQL
 @Statement VarChar(2000)
AS
DECLARE @StartTime DateTime
     , @EndTime DateTime
     , @ExecutionTime Int
 SET @StartTime = GetDate()
 EXECUTE (@Statement)
 IF @@Error = 0
     BEGIN
       SET @EndTime = GetDate()
       SET @ExecutionTime = DateDiff(MilliSecond, @StartTime, @EndTime)
       RETURN @ExecutionTime
     END
```

Without the error-checking script, the remaining statements would be executed after the erroneous EXCUTE. . . line. The following example uses a more specific approach. This assumes that I want to replace the default error message and numbers with my own:

```
CREATE PROCEDURE spRunSQL
   @Statement VarChar(2000) -- Input param. accepts any SQL statement.
AS
   DECLARE   @StartTime DateTime
           , @EndTime DateTime
           , @ExecutionTime Int
           , @ErrNum Int
   SET @StartTime = GetDate()
   EXECUTE (@Statement)
   SET @ErrNum = @@Error
     IF @ErrNum = 207          -- Bad column
       RAISERROR ('Bad column name', 16, 1)
     ELSE IF @ErrNum = 208     -- Bad object
       RAISERROR ('Bad object name', 16, 1)
     ELSE IF @ErrNum = 0       -- No error. Resume.
       BEGIN
         SET @EndTime = GetDate()
         SET @ExecutionTime = DateDiff(MilliSecond, @StartTime, @EndTime)
         RETURN @ExecutionTime -- Return execution time in milliseconds
       END
```

Just a note about this example: I chose to use this scenario because it was easy to demonstrate. Under the right conditions, and with appropriate security constraints, this can be a very useful procedure. However, you should be very cautious about enabling a stored procedure that allows users to execute any SQL statements they choose. Otherwise, users who are otherwise restricted from executing certain statements could work around these restrictions.

Error Handling in SQL Server 2005

One of the most significant enhancements to Transact-SQL is its new error-handling capability. In the previous discussion, you saw how it was necessary to check for errors after each statement. In SQL Server 2005, error handling is much like some modern programming languages (such as C#, Java, and VB.NET). The new pattern is quite easy to implement and will be familiar to you if you have worked with newer programming languages. Any statements that could possibly cause an error to be raised are wrapped within a TRY block. The error-handling script is located in a separate CATCH block. When an error condition occurs in the TRY block, execution is moved to the first line within the CATCH block. The limitation of SQL Server 2005 error handling is that it can only be used to retrieve error information and to significantly reduce the amount of error code required, but it cannot in a true sense of the word "handle" errors. Once an error occurs inside a transaction the transaction enters a Doomed state. The error can only be recorded and maybe some other event code executed, but the transaction will have to be reissued.

```
BEGIN TRY
    ... Transaction
END TRY
BEGIN CATCH
    ... error-handing script
END CATCH
```

This is an example using this form of error handling:

```
CREATE PROCEDURE spDeleteProduct @Productid int
AS
BEGIN TRY
  BEGIN TRANSACTION
  DELETE Product WHERE ProductID = @ProductID
  COMMIT TRANSACTION
END TRY
BEGIN CATCH
  DECLARE @Err AS int
  DECLARE @Msg AS varchar(max)
  SET @Err = @@Error
  SET @Msg = Error_Message()
  ROLLBACK TRANSACTION
  INSERT ErrorTable
  VALUES (@err, @msg)
END CATCH
```

Processing Business Logic

Handling business rules is all about making decisions. The decision structures in Transact-SQL are uncomplicated. When I need to write a decision statement, the first thing I typically do is state the logic using natural language. Transact-SQL's roots are in the English language. You'll recall from Chapter 1 that IBM's predecessor to SQL was actually called SEQUEL, which stood for Structured English Query Language. You should be able to break down any process into a decision tree. Even complex logic, once distilled into fundamental components, is just a series of simple logical combinations. This concept is what I call compounded simplicity — each individual piece is simple, there just may be a lot of pieces.

Using logical operators within SQL statements, you should be able to handle quite a lot of relatively complex business logic. I find that my first attempt to address a complex problem is usually a bit convoluted. After taking some time to approach the problem from different angles, I'm usually more successful in using a simpler technique. It takes a little patience and a few iterations to get to the optimal solution.

In the previous section on views, I created a complex view called vProductSalesDetail. This view is an excellent example of the kind of data my sales manager may want to see in a report. Suppose I plan to use SQL Server Reporting Services to design a sales detail report. Users have asked for the ability to provide a variety of parameter values to be used for filtering. As a rule, if a parameter is provided, the report data is filtered accordingly. If the parameter value is not provided, the parameter is ignored and no related filtering takes place. The report parameters are listed in the following table.

Parameters	Logic
Sales Order From Date and **Sales Order To Date**	The user is prompted to type a date value for each of these parameters. If both parameters contain a value, the sales order data is filtered within the given range of order dates. If either of the parameters is not provided, this criterion is ignored.
Account Number	The user is prompted to type a customer's account number. If this value is not provided, this criterion is ignored.
Product Category	The product category is selected from a drop-down list. The first item of the list displays the word "All." If this value is selected, records are not filtered by the product category.

Combining logical operators may seem to be very complicated but it's actually quite simple when broken down into core components. Each branch of logic must be isolated from others that it shouldn't affect. Using parentheses, group these statements together. For example, if the account number parameter is not provided (the value is Null), you need not consider the value of the corresponding column. In SQL, this logic would look like this:

```
((@ProductCategory IS NULL) OR (CategoryName = @ProductCategory))
```

The inner parentheses, surrounding each individual statement, just make this statement easier to read and could be omitted. The outer parentheses isolate this logic from any other statements. If the value of the parameter @ProductCategory is NULL, then it doesn't matter whether the CategoryName column value matched the parameter value or not. One side of the OR expression has already been satisfied so the expression on other side need not be true as well.

Because I want to filter the entire result set based on combinations of multiple parameters, each group of parameters-related statements are combined using the AND operator. This is because one of the two statements on the OR statement must be true to return any records for that part of the WHERE clause. Combining the logic for two parameters looks like this:

```
((@ProductCategory IS NULL) OR (CategoryName = @ProductCategory))
AND
((@ProductCategory = 'All') OR (CategoryName = @ProductCategory))
```

I changed the logic for the product category to check for the word "All" just to mix this up a little. It would be convenient if all parameters were compared in the same way, but this is a very realistic scenario. Putting it all together, the stored procedure might look like the following. Notice how the actual selection and column referencing is very simple. This is because I've already handled the complexity of the query in the view. The procedure simply leverages this investment.

```
CREATE PROCEDURE spProductSalesDetail
  @SalesOrderDateFrom  DateTime = Null,
  @SalesOrderDateTo    DateTime = Null,
  @ProductCategory     nVarChar(50) = 'All',
  @AccountNumber       VarChar(10) = Null
AS
SELECT * FROM vProductSalesDetail
WHERE
  ((@SalesOrderDateFrom Is Null) OR (@SalesOrderDateTo Is Null))
  OR
  (OrderDate BETWEEN @SalesOrderDateFrom AND @SalesOrderDateTo)
  AND
  ((@ProductCategory = 'All') OR (CategoryName = @ProductCategory))
  AND
  ((@AccountNumber Is Null) OR (AccountNumber = @AccountNumber))
```

Try It Out

Test this procedure by supplying some parameters and not others. You should be able to use any combination of parameters. You can even leave off the product category because this parameter defaults to the value All. For example:

```
EXECUTE spProductSalesDetail
@SalesOrderDateFrom    = '12-1-03',
@SalesOrderDateTo      = '12-31-03',
@ProductCategory       = 'Bike'
```

Conditional Logic

At the very core of all logic is the simple word "If" in the English language. All other decision structures are variations or extensions of the same basic if concept. Before I show you the specific SQL syntax, take a look at some simple phrases that are examples of conditional logic:

> *If* a product record exists, update it.

> *If* a product record doesn't exist, create one.

> *If* a backorder record exists *and* sufficient inventory exists, delete the backorder and ship the product.

What happens if this condition is not met? That's easy. This is done using an Else statement:

> *If* an account balance is current, calculate the new total.

> ...or *else if* the account balance is past due, add a late fee and calculate the new total.

> ...or *else if* the account is seriously past due, add a late fee, close the account, and calculate the new total.

Most programming languages include some other forms of logical branching statements that extend the If statement paradigm. For example, the Visual Basic Select Case command just consolidates what would otherwise be several if. . . else statements. Transact-SQL contains a Select Case structure that is quite different, which will be introduced shortly.

IF

In SQL, the IF statement is not followed by the word Then. If a condition is met (if the outcome is True), script beginning on the next line is simply executed. This stored procedure checks for the named table in the database catalog:

```
CREATE PROCEDURE spTableExists
  @TableName VarChar(128)
AS
  IF EXISTS(SELECT * FROM sysobjects WHERE name = @TableName)
    PRINT @TableName + ' exists'
```

The ELSE statement, in this case, simply allows me to execute another line of script when the condition is not met:

```
CREATE PROCEDURE spTableExists
  @TableName VarChar(128)
AS
  IF EXISTS(SELECT * FROM sysobjects WHERE name = @TableName)
    PRINT @TableName + ' exists'
  ELSE
    PRINT @TableName + ' doesn''t exist'
```

When multiple lines of code follow an IF statement it is best to wrap the lines in a BEGIN. . . END block. Although this is not strictly required, it makes the code much simpler to read and debug.

Try It Out

Using the AdventureWorks database, create a stored procedure to return product information. An optional parameter will be used to determine when records will be filtered. The query uses the Product and ProductSubCategory tables so you can pass the subcategory name for filtering. This is a lot of script to type so you might consider using the Query Builder to create the basic SELECT statement. The input parameter, @Category, is set to Null so it becomes optional.

```
CREATE PROCEDURE spGetProductByCategory
 @Category nVarChar(50) = NULL
AS
IF @Category IS NULL
 BEGIN
    SELECT PC.Name AS ProductCategory
        , P.ProductID
        , P.Name AS ProductName
    FROM   Product AS P
    INNER JOIN ProductSubCategory AS PSC
    ON P.ProductSubCategoryID = PSC.ProductSubCategoryID
    INNER JOIN ProductCategory AS PC
    ON PSC.ProductCategoryID = PC.ProductCategoryID
```

```
      END
   ELSE
    BEGIN
       SELECT PC.Name AS ProductCategory
            , P.ProductID
            , P.Name AS ProductName
       FROM   Product AS P
       INNER JOIN ProductSubCategory AS PSC
       ON P.ProductSubCategoryID = PSC.ProductSubCategoryID
       INNER JOIN ProductCategory AS PC
       ON PSC.ProductCategoryID = PC.ProductCategoryID
       WHERE PC.Name = @Category
    END
```

If the procedure is executed without a category name value, all product records are returned. Otherwise, the results are filtered. Now, try this out. Execute the procedure with and without a category parameter value:

```
EXECUTE spProductGetByCategory 'Bikes'
```

By passing the category 'Bikes', only 97 product records are returned because the results are filtered by this category, as shown in Figure 13-15.

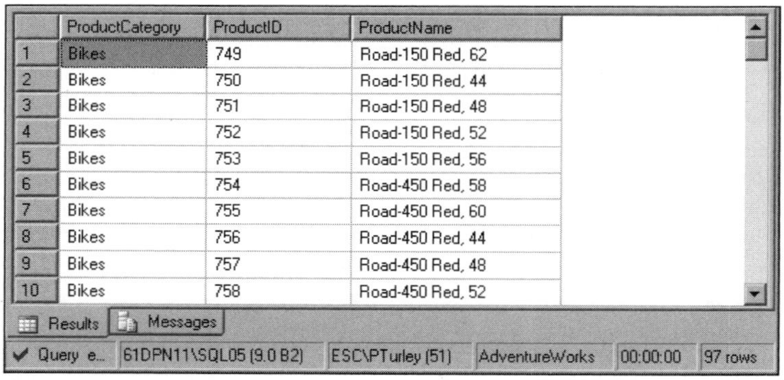

	ProductCategory	ProductID	ProductName	
1	Bikes	749	Road-150 Red, 62	
2	Bikes	750	Road-150 Red, 44	
3	Bikes	751	Road-150 Red, 48	
4	Bikes	752	Road-150 Red, 52	
5	Bikes	753	Road-150 Red, 56	
6	Bikes	754	Road-450 Red, 58	
7	Bikes	755	Road-450 Red, 60	
8	Bikes	756	Road-450 Red, 44	
9	Bikes	757	Road-450 Red, 48	
10	Bikes	758	Road-450 Red, 52	

Results | Messages

✓ Query e... 61DPN11\SQL05 (9.0 B2)   ESC\PTurley (51)   AdventureWorks   00:00:00   97 rows

Figure 13-15

Now execute the procedure without a category value:

```
EXECUTE spProductGetByCategory
```

This time, 295 rows (give or take a few depending on other sample queries you may have run) are returned because the products are unfiltered, as shown in Figure 13-16.

CASE

The purpose of the CASE statement is to return a specified value based on a set of business logic. A variety of useful applications for the CASE statement include translating abbreviations into descriptive values and simulating look-up table joins.

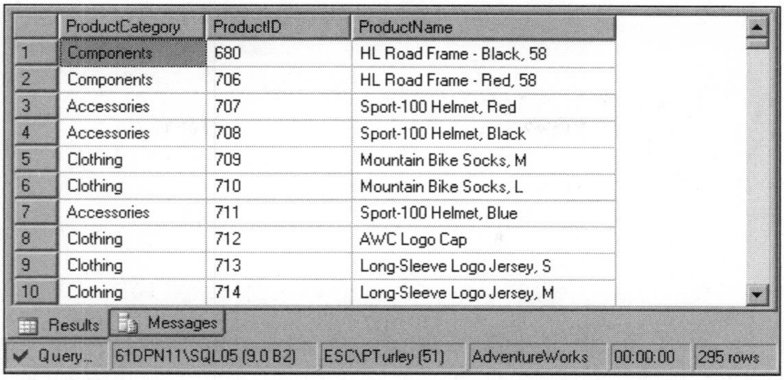

	ProductCategory	ProductID	ProductName
1	Components	680	HL Road Frame - Black, 58
2	Components	706	HL Road Frame - Red, 58
3	Accessories	707	Sport-100 Helmet, Red
4	Accessories	708	Sport-100 Helmet, Black
5	Clothing	709	Mountain Bike Socks, M
6	Clothing	710	Mountain Bike Socks, L
7	Accessories	711	Sport-100 Helmet, Blue
8	Clothing	712	AWC Logo Cap
9	Clothing	713	Long-Sleeve Logo Jersey, S
10	Clothing	714	Long-Sleeve Logo Jersey, M

Figure 13-16

The syntax pattern looks like this:

```
SELECT CASE value to evaluate
WHEN literal value 1 THEN return value
WHEN literal value 2 THEN return value
...
END
```

Here's a simple example that could be applied to a status indicator value:

```
DECLARE @Status Int
SET @Status = 1

SELECT CASE @Status
  WHEN 1 THEN 'Active'
  WHEN 2 THEN 'Inactive'
  WHEN 3 THEN 'Pending'
END
```

Now, I'll plug the same logic into a query, replacing what would otherwise be an outer join to a related table, with a CASE expression:

```
SELECT ProductID
   , Name
   , ListPrice
   , CASE ProductSubCategoryID
       WHEN 1 THEN 'Mountain Bike'
       WHEN 2 THEN 'Road Bike'
       WHEN 3 THEN 'Touring Bike'
       WHEN Null THEN 'Something Else'
       ELSE '(No Subcategory)'
     END As SubCategory
FROM Product
```

This script effectively creates an alias column called SubCategory. You can use it with a different aliasing technique, in this case, using the column = . . . syntax:

```
SELECT ProductID
    , Name
    , ListPrice
    , SubCategory = CASE ProductSubCategoryID
        WHEN 1 THEN 'Mountain Bike'
        WHEN 2 THEN 'Road Bike'
        WHEN 3 THEN 'Touring Bike'
        WHEN Null THEN 'Something Else'
        ELSE '(No Subcategory)'
      END
FROM Product
```

Either way, the results are the same. Note that I've filtered these results to show a variety of values by adding WHERE ListPrice > 2000. You don't need to do the same because you can scroll through the results as shown in Figure 13-17.

	ProductID	Name	ListPrice	SubCategory
1	749	Road-150 Red, 62	3578.27	Road Bike
2	750	Road-150 Red, 44	3578.27	Road Bike
3	751	Road-150 Red, 48	3578.27	Road Bike
4	752	Road-150 Red, 52	3578.27	Road Bike
5	753	Road-150 Red, 56	3578.27	Road Bike
6	771	Mountain-100 Silver, 38	3399.99	Mountain Bike
7	772	Mountain-100 Silver, 42	3399.99	Mountain Bike
8	773	Mountain-100 Silver, 44	3399.99	Mountain Bike
9	774	Mountain-100 Silver, 48	3399.99	Mountain Bike
10	775	Mountain-100 Black, 38	3374.99	Mountain Bike
11	776	Mountain-100 Black, 42	3374.99	Mountain Bike
12	777	Mountain-100 Black, 44	3374.99	Mountain Bike
13	778	Mountain-100 Black, 48	3374.99	Mountain Bike
14	779	Mountain-200 Silver, 38	2319.99	Mountain Bike

Figure 13-17

Looping

Statements can be repeated in a conditional looping structure. Looping is performed with the WHILE statement and an expression returning a Boolean result. In the following example, a separate WHERE statement is executed for each iteration of the loop, filtering on the corresponding product subcategory ID.

Try It Out

Switch the query results from grid to text and execute the following:

```
DECLARE @Counter Int
SET @Counter = 1
WHILE @Counter < 4
  BEGIN
      PRINT ''
      PRINT 'SubCategory '
          + CONVERT(VarChar(10), @Counter) + ':'
```

```
        SELECT Name, ProductSubCategoryID, ListPrice
        FROM Product
        WHERE ProductSubCategoryID = @Counter

        SET @Counter = @Counter + 1
    END
```

The results show three separate lists for each of the subcategories:

```
SubCategory 1:
Name                                               ProductSubCategoryID ListPrice
-------------------------------------------------- -------------------- ----------
Mountain-100 Silver, 38                            1                    3399.99
Mountain-100 Silver, 42                            1                    3399.99
Mountain-100 Silver, 44                            1                    3399.99
...
Mountain-500 Silver, 52                            1                    564.99
Mountain-500 Black, 40                             1                    539.99
Mountain-500 Black, 42                             1                    539.99
Mountain-500 Black, 44                             1                    539.99
Mountain-500 Black, 48                             1                    539.99
Mountain-500 Black, 52                             1                    539.99

(32 row(s) affected)

SubCategory 2:
Name                                               ProductSubCategoryID ListPrice
-------------------------------------------------- -------------------- ----------
Road-150 Red, 62                                   2                    3578.27
Road-150 Red, 44                                   2                    3578.27
Road-150 Red, 48                                   2                    3578.27
...
Road-350-W Yellow, 44                              2                    1700.99
Road-350-W Yellow, 48                              2                    1700.99
Road-750 Black, 58                                 2                    539.99
Road-750 Black, 44                                 2                    539.99
Road-750 Black, 48                                 2                    539.99
Road-750 Black, 52                                 2                    539.99

(43 row(s) affected)

SubCategory 3:
Name                                               ProductSubCategoryID ListPrice
-------------------------------------------------- -------------------- ----------
Touring-2000 Blue, 60                              3                    1214.85
Touring-1000 Yellow, 46                            3                    2384.07
Touring-1000 Yellow, 50                            3                    2384.07
...
Touring-1000 Blue, 60                              3                    2384.07
Touring-2000 Blue, 46                              3                    1214.85
Touring-2000 Blue, 50                              3                    1214.85
Touring-2000 Blue, 54                              3                    1214.85
Touring-3000 Blue, 44                              3                    742.35
Touring-3000 Blue, 50                              3                    742.35

(22 row(s) affected)
```

During the loop, you may need to modify the logic of some operations. The BREAK statement exits the WHILE structure, resuming execution after the END statement. The CONTINUE statement doesn't exit the loop but sends execution back up to the WHILE statement to repeat the loop:

```
/* If the avg price for all products is below $1200,
   raise all prices by 25% until avg is $1200 or higher
   or highest price is over $4000.
*/
WHILE (SELECT AVG(ListPrice) FROM Product) < $1200
BEGIN
    UPDATE Product SET ListPrice = ListPrice * 1.25
    SELECT MAX(ListPrice) FROM Product
    IF (SELECT MAX(ListPrice) FROM Product) > $4000
        -- Greatest price is too high, quit.
        BREAK
    ELSE
        -- Prices are within range, continue to loop.
        CONTINUE
END
PRINT 'Done.'
```

User-Defined Functions

When user-defined functions were introduced in SQL Server 2000, this opened the door to a whole new level of functionality. Until then, nearly all business logic had to be in compound expressions with little opportunity to reuse code. In traditional programming languages, functions typically accept any number of values and then return a scalar (single) value. Functions are typically used to perform calculations, to compare, parse, and manipulate values. This describes one of the capabilities of user-defined functions (UDFs), but they can also be used to return sets of data.

Set-based functions can be parameterized like a stored procedure but are used in a SELECT expression like a view. In some ways this makes UDFs the best of both worlds. Three different categories of user-defined functions exist, two of which return result sets. These categories include the following:

❑   Scalar functions

❑   Multi-statement table-valued functions

❑   Inline table-valued functions

> One important thing to keep in mind when designing user-defined functions is that other functions called within the script must be deterministic. In other words, the value returned must be dependent only on the value(s) passed to it, and not based on external resources. For example, a UDF cannot call a nondeterministic GetDate() function. Instead, to deal with this limitation, you would pass the date value into the function as a parameter.

Scalar Functions

A scalar function accepts any number of parameters and returns one value. The term *scalar* differentiates a single, "flat" value from more complex structured values, such as arrays or result sets. This pattern is much like that of traditional functions written in common programming languages.

The script syntax is quite simple. Input parameters are declared within parentheses followed by the return value declaration. All statements must be enclosed in a BEGIN. . . END block. In this simple example, I calculate the age by getting the number of days between the birth date and today's date. Because my function can't call the nondeterministic GETDATE() function, this value must be passed into the function using the @Today parameter. The number of days is divided by the average number of days in a year to determine the result:

```
CREATE FUNCTION fnGetAge (@BirthDate DateTime, @Today DateTime)
 RETURNS Int
AS
 BEGIN
     RETURN DateDiff(day, @BirthDate, @Today) / 365.25
 END
```

When a scalar function is called without specifying the owner or schema, SQL Server assumes it to be a built-in function in the system catalog. For this reason, user-defined scalar functions are always called using multi-part names, prefixed at least with the owner or schema name:

```
SELECT dbo.fnGetAge('1/4/1962', GetDate())
```

Before writing the next sample function, I'd like to create a set of data to use. Assume that you are in charge of preparing invitations to your annual company picnic. The HR department manager has exported a list of employees from the personnel system to a text file. You have used DTS to import this data into SQL Server and now you need to format the data for the invitations. Names are in a single column in the form: LastName, FirstName. You need to separate the first name and last name values into two columns.

The business logic for parsing the last name and first name values is very similar. The logic for extracting the last name is as follows:

1. Find the position of the delimiting comma.

2. Identify the last name value from the first character through the character one position before the comma.

3. Return this value from the function.

Translating this logic into SQL, the function definition looks like this:

```
CREATE FUNCTION fnLastName (@FullName VarChar(100))
 RETURNS VarChar(100)
AS
 BEGIN
     DECLARE @CommaPosition Int
     DECLARE @LastName VarChar(100)
     SET @CommaPosition = CHARINDEX(',', @FullName)
     SET @LastName = SUBSTRING(@FullName, 1, @CommaPosition - 1)
     RETURN @LastName
 END
```

Two built-in functions are used. The CHARINDEX() function returns the position of a character string within another character string, in this case, the position of the comma within the full name. The SUBSTRING() function returns part of a character string from one character position to another. This will be used to carve the last name value from the full name. Because the last name ends one position before the comma, you subtract one from the value returned by the CHARINDEX() function.

If you execute this script, only the last name is returned, as shown in Figure 13-18.

```
SELECT dbo.fnLastName('Washington, George')
```

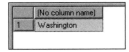

Figure 13-18

Try It Out

Create two functions, one to parse the last name and another to parse the first name. Start by executing the script in the previous example. Next, create a new table and populate it with employee records:

```
CREATE TABLE EmployeeList
  (EmployeeName VarChar(100))
GO
INSERT INTO EmployeeList (EmployeeName) SELECT 'Flintstone, Fred'
INSERT INTO EmployeeList (EmployeeName) SELECT 'Flintstone, Wilma'
INSERT INTO EmployeeList (EmployeeName) SELECT 'Flintstone, Pebbles'
INSERT INTO EmployeeList (EmployeeName) SELECT 'Rubble, Barney'
INSERT INTO EmployeeList (EmployeeName) SELECT 'Rubble, Betty'
INSERT INTO EmployeeList (EmployeeName) SELECT 'Rubble, BamBam'
```

The easiest way to create the first name function is to copy and paste the script and make a few modifications. The logic is similar to the first function but you want to start two characters after the comma to omit the space character. The SUBSTRING() function returns characters up to the end of the text. This means that if you provide a value greater than the remaining length of text, all characters to the right of the start position will be returned. The LEN() function ensures that this value always exceeds the number of available characters:

```
CREATE FUNCTION fnFirstName (@FullName VarChar(100))
 RETURNS VarChar(100)
AS
 BEGIN
    DECLARE @CommaPosition Int
    DECLARE @FirstName VarChar(100)
    SET @CommaPosition = CHARINDEX(',', @FullName)
    SET @FirstName = SUBSTRING(@FullName, @CommaPosition + 2, LEN(@FullName))
    RETURN @FirstName
 END
```

Test the new function like before:

```
SELECT dbo.fnFirstName('Washington, George')
```

The result is shown in Figure 13-19.

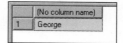

Figure 13-19

Finally, use both of these functions in a SQL statement, selecting rows from the table you already created. Remember that the table has only one column. Using each function, you will define two alias columns:

```
SELECT dbo.fnLastName(EmployeeName) As LastName
   , dbo.fnFirstName(EmployeeName) As FirstName
FROM EmployeeList
```

In the result set shown in Figure 13-20, the last and first names are separate and may be used in a form letter.

	LastName	FirstName
1	Flintstone	Fred
2	Flintstone	Wilma
3	Flintstone	Pebbles
4	Rubble	Barney
5	Rubble	Betty
6	Rubble	BamBam

Figure 13-20

Taking this example just one step further, these two functions can be combined into one by passing in a second parameter to indicate the name to extract:

```
CREATE FUNCTION fnGetName (@FullName VarChar(100)
                        , @FirstOrLast VarChar(5))
 RETURNS VarChar(100)
AS
 BEGIN
    DECLARE @CommaPosition Int
    DECLARE @TheName VarChar(100)
    IF @FirstOrLast = 'First'
       BEGIN
          SET @CommaPosition = CHARINDEX(',', @FullName)
          SET @TheName = SUBSTRING(@FullName, @CommaPosition + 2, LEN(@FullName))
       END
    ELSE IF @FirstOrLast = 'Last'
       BEGIN
          SET @CommaPosition = CHARINDEX(',', @FullName)
          SET @TheName = SUBSTRING(@FullName, 1, @CommaPosition - 1)
       END
    RETURN @TheName
 END
```

The new function is called just like before but with the addition of a second parameter, like this:

```
SELECT dbo.fnFirstName('Washington, George', 'First')
```

Inline Table-Valued Functions

This type of function returns a result set, much like a view. However, unlike a view, functions can accept parameters. The inline function's syntax is quite simple. In the function definition, the return type is set to a Table. A RETURN statement is used with a SELECT query in parentheses:

```
CREATE FUNCTION fnProductListBySubCategory (@SubCategoryID Int)
 RETURNS Table
AS
 RETURN
 (
    SELECT ProductID, Name, ListPrice FROM Product
    WHERE ProductSubCategoryID = @SubCategoryID
 )
```

The function is treated almost like a table using the syntax Select ... From *(function name)*:

```
SELECT * FROM fnProductListBySubCategory(1)
```

An added benefit is the ability to process business logic, as you would if using a stored procedure. This example shows the same function as before with an optional parameter and related conditional logic. If a subcategory ID value is provided, products are filtered by this value; otherwise, all products are returned.

```
CREATE FUNCTION fnProductListBySubCategory (@SubCategoryID Int = Null)
 RETURNS Table
AS
BEGIN
 IF @SubCategoryID Is Null
    BEGIN
      RETURN
        (
        SELECT ProductID, Name, ListPrice
        FROM Product
        )
    END
 ELSE
    BEGIN
      RETURN
        (
        SELECT ProductID, Name, ListPrice
        FROM Product
        WHERE ProductSubCategoryID = @SubCategoryID
        )
    END
END
```

For returning a result set from a function, the inline table-valued function is likely the best choice. It's the most elegant blend of SELECT-compatible syntax with stored procedure style input parameters. Aside from these powerful capabilities, the syntax is simple and easy to manage.

Multi-Statement Table-Valued Functions

Multi-statement functions can be used to do some very unique things outside the context of a standard SELECT statement. Like the preceding inline function, this type of function also returns a table-type result set, but the table is explicitly constructed in script. This can be used to accomplish one of two things: either to process some very unique business logic by assembling a virtual table on-the-fly, or to duplicate the functionality of an inline function in a more verbose and complicated way. In short, if you need to select records from an existing table to return a result set, use an inline table-valued function.

The following is an example of the same function demonstrated in the previous section, as a multi-statement function. In the declaration, a table-type variable is used to define the return structure. In this case, the variable @ProdList defines a virtual table with three columns. The fact that these columns are the same as the corresponding columns in the Product table is purely a matter of choice. You can see that in the body of the function, I've inserted rows into the variable as if it were a physical table. Finally, the RETURN statement terminates execution and returns the result set:

```
CREATE FUNCTION fnProductListBySubCategory (@SubCategoryID Int)
 RETURNS @ProdList Table
     (   ProductID Int
       , Name nVarChar(50)
       , ListPrice Money
     )
AS
 BEGIN
     IF @SubCategoryID IS NULL
       BEGIN
         INSERT INTO @ProdList (ProductID, Name, ListPrice)
         SELECT ProductID, Name, ListPrice
         FROM Product
       END
     ELSE
       BEGIN
         INSERT INTO @ProdList (ProductID, Name, ListPrice)
         SELECT ProductID, Name, ListPrice
         FROM Product
         WHERE ProductSubCategoryID = @SubCategoryID
       END
     RETURN
 END
```

Now, I'll step out of the mainstream and show you a more unique application for this type of function. This function doesn't select data from a table. The records returned by this function are entirely manufactured within the script contained by the function. The filtering logic, implemented by the @Category parameter, accepts three relevant values: Mainframe, Micro, or All. If the value All is passed, rows for both of the previous categories are returned.

```
CREATE FUNCTION fnComputerTypes(@Category VarChar(15))
 Returns @CompType Table
    (  Year Int
     , BrandName VarChar(50)
     , ModelName VarChar(50)
     , Category VarChar(25)
    )
AS
 BEGIN
    IF @Category IN ('MainFrame', 'All')
      BEGIN
        INSERT INTO @CompType (Year, BrandName, ModelName, Category)
        SELECT 1945, 'US Ordinance Dept.', 'ENIAC', 'Mainframe'

        INSERT INTO @CompType (Year, BrandName, ModelName, Category)
        SELECT 1951, 'Remington Rand', 'Univac', 'Mainframe'

        INSERT INTO @CompType (Year, BrandName, ModelName, Category)
        SELECT 1952, 'IBM', '701', 'Mainframe'

        INSERT INTO @CompType (Year, BrandName, ModelName, Category)
        SELECT 1964, 'IBM', 'System/360', 'Mainframe'

        INSERT INTO @CompType (Year, BrandName, ModelName, Category)
        SELECT 1988, 'IBM', 'AS/400', 'Mainframe'
      END

  IF @Category IN ('Micro', 'All')
      BEGIN
        INSERT INTO @CompType (Year, BrandName, ModelName, Category)
        SELECT 1977, 'Tandy Radio Shack', 'TSR-80', 'Micro'

        INSERT INTO @CompType (Year, BrandName, ModelName, Category)
        SELECT 1981, 'Commodore ', 'VIC-20', 'Micro'

        INSERT INTO @CompType (Year, BrandName, ModelName, Category)
        SELECT 1982, 'Commodore', 'Commodore 64', 'Micro'

        INSERT INTO @CompType (Year, BrandName, ModelName, Category)
        SELECT 1981, 'IBM', 'PC', 'Micro'

        INSERT INTO @CompType (Year, BrandName, ModelName, Category)
        SELECT 2004, 'Dell', 'PowerEdge 1855', 'Micro'
      END
    RETURN
END
```

I'll test the function using the value All:

```
SELECT * FROM dbo.fnComputerTypes('All')
```

The result is shown in Figure 13-21.

	Year	BrandName	ModelName	Category
1	1945	US Ordinance Dept.	ENIAC	Mainframe
2	1951	Remington Rand	Univac	Mainframe
3	1952	IBM	701	Mainframe
4	1964	IBM	System/360	Mainframe
5	1988	IBM	AS/400	Mainframe
6	1977	Tandy Radio Shack	TSR-80	Micro
7	1981	Commodore	VIC-20	Micro
8	1982	Commodore	Commodore 64	Micro
9	1981	IBM	PC	Micro
10	2004	Dell	PowerEdge 1855	Micro

Figure 13-21

As far as the consumer of this data is concerned, it behaves like, and appears to have been selected from, a table in the database.

Transaction Management

You'll recall that in Chapter 9, you learned how to explicitly control transactions. I'll briefly review this topic as it applies to database programming objects. Transaction statements (BEGIN, ROLLBACK, and COMMIT TRANSACTION) are used to queue up a set of statements and control the sequence and dependency of a group of operations. For example, if a stored procedure or user-defined function were to update several sales records and then delete sales records based on some criteria that may have been modified in the UPDATE statement, it would be important to let the update operation finish before deleting any records. In its ever-zealous quest to be efficient, SQL Server may perform operations in parallel, thus working against important business logic. In such cases, it would be important to serialize these dependent operations into separate transactions.

Another important purpose for transactions is to manage the atomicity of a group of operations. If multiple operations are grouped into a single transaction, they are executed as a unit. The outcome of the entire transaction is dependent upon the success of all statements. If they all succeed, the transaction is rolled forward from the transaction log and succeeds. If any operations are unsuccessful, or an error is otherwise raised; the transaction is rolled back, and none of the operations result in committed (inserted, updated, or deleted) records.

Stored procedures are the ideal environment for transactional management. Using the techniques demonstrated in Chapter 9, it's a simple matter to wrap groups of statements into a transactional batch. You can also use error-handling script with transaction management to make your procedures even more bulletproof.

Locking Options

One of the database engine's important jobs is to balance the task of record locking (to protect data as it's modified) and to present consistent result sets of data to queries. This behavior is performed automatically and usually requires no intervention. SQL Server implements locking at various levels based on requested operations and concurrent users sharing the same or adjacent data. On rare occasions, it may be necessary to override the default locking behavior within a transaction. This is done using the SET TRANSACTION ISOLATION LEVEL statement. The locking options described in the following table are supported in SQL Server 2000.

Locking Option	Description
READ UNCOMMITTED	Records are read from the transaction log if they have been modified. This includes "dirty" records that have yet to be rolled forward into table data pages.
READ COMMITTED	This is the default behavior. Records are read only from data pages after newly committed rows have been rolled forward into the database. This option prevents inaccurate dirty reads of data within the context of the current transaction. However, concurrent statements could modify records between operations creating an anomaly known as a *phantom read*. This typically only happens in cases where multiple users are frequently modifying multiple records.
REPEATABLE READ	This option locks the transaction unconditionally so that no other operations can modify records. This is an extreme measure that can cause increased locking contention, and is recommended only in rare cases.
SERIALIZABLE	This option serializes transactions so that no concurrent operations can be performed that would affect the state of records within the current transaction. This is done by locking records within a range of key values or other search criteria. This has the advantage of simplifying locking contention problems; however, it can impair functionality and performance.

SQL Server 2005 introduces a new isolation level called SNAPSHOT. Snapshot isolation allows users to access the last committed version of data even if that data is undergoing modification. With Snapshot isolation, when data is modified a copy of the data is written to TempDB. Any other transaction that attempts to read the data being modified will be redirected automatically to the copy stored in TempDB.

The behavior of these options may appear to be easily predictable. However, the actual locking behavior of individual rows, tables, and other objects is a result of the locking options specified by the combined transactions as multiple operations are performed on the same data. The following example serializes these other users' operations on the same data. This way, no modifications would be allowed to these records between the two UPDATE statements:

```
SET TRANSACTION ISOLATION LEVEL SERIALIZABLE
GO
BEGIN TRANSACTION
GO
    UPDATE Product SET StandardCost = StandardCost * 1.15
    WHERE ProductSubCategoryID = 1
GO
    UPDATE Product SET ListPrice = ListPrice * 1.15
    WHERE ProductSubCategoryID = 1
```

```
            AND StandardCost < 1000
    GO
    COMMIT TRANSACTION
```

Summary

When designing a database solution, it is important to see the bigger picture. Ideally, queries and other database operations should be contained in manageable database objects. In the long run, views, stored procedures, and user-defined functions provide improved security, performance, and simplicity. In most databases, this is a significant investment and may take time and considerable effort.

Views are SELECT statements that can be treated as a table. By organizing complex queries into views, users and programmers don't have to contend with the complexities of a database design and can focus on their pertinent data and business problems. Federated and partitioned views allow data to be stored on different physical media and in different locations, all of which may be transparent to the consumer.

Stored procedures can simplify common operations, providing a standard approach for managing records and high-level data entities. Complex business logic can be processed in a stored procedure, complete with decision branching and error handling. Stored procedures are reusable objects that run efficiently because the SQL script is compiled and optimized.

User-defined functions can provide the same functionality as views and have a lot of the same capabilities as stored procedures. In some ways, UDFs are the best of both approaches because they support the more common SELECT statement rather than having to be executed like a stored procedure.

Each of these three objects still has its place in SQL programming. Views are far more common than UDFs and under certain conditions may be more efficient. Stored procedures can use nondeterministic functions, which are not allowed in UDFs. The one thing that functions provide that views and procedures do not is the ability to encapsulate the logic to return scalar values. Use UDFs to simplify parsing, calculations, and value manipulation.

Exercises

Exercise 1

Define a new view called vwSalesEmployees. It should return the EmployeeID, FirstName, LastName, and Title columns from the Employee table for all employees who are sales persons. Results should be sorted by last name and then by first name.

Exercise 2

Create a stored procedure called spEmployeeAddUpdate. This procedure accepts three parameters: FirstName, LastName, and LoginID. The data types are nVarChar(50), nVarChar(50), and nVarChar(256), respectively. Define logic in this procedure to check for an existing employee record with the same first and last name values. If the employee record exists, update the LoginID. Otherwise, insert a new employee record.

Exercise 3

Add a comment header block and error handling logic to the procedure you created in exercise 2. The block should contain a description of the procedure, parameters, your contact information, the date created, and revision information.

Add error-handling logic to catch the errors that would occur if a parameter were omitted or if a null value were passed into a parameter. If an error is caught, raise a custom error message.

Exercise 4

If you have completed all previous exercises, use the following script to produce a message. Analyze each statement so you understand how each value is produced.

```
USE AdventureWorks2000
GO
--
ALTER FUNCTION dbo.fnProperCase (@In VarChar(255))
    RETURNS VarChar(255)
AS
BEGIN
    RETURN  UPPER(SUBSTRING(@In, 1, 1)) + LOWER(SUBSTRING(@In, 2, 254))
END
GO
-- Execute query from here if function has already been created --
-- Assemble message from string fragments:
DECLARE @Message VarChar(255)
SELECT @Message = dbo.fnProperCase(REVERSE(SUBSTRING(LastName, 4, 3))) FROM
Employee WHERE EmployeeID = 199
SET @Message = @Message + ' ' + CHAR(73) + CHAR(39) + CHAR(109) + ' ' + CHAR(97)
SELECT @Message = @Message + ' ' + dbo.fnProperCase(SUBSTRING(Description, 61, 5))
FROM ProductDescription WHERE ProductDescriptionID = 1586
SELECT @Message = @Message  + SUBSTRING(Name, 6, 3) FROM ProductSubCategory WHERE
ProductSubCategoryID = 38
SELECT @Message = @Message + CHAR(45) + SUBSTRING(@@SERVICENAME, 3, 3)
SELECT @Message = @Message  + ' ' + LOWER(SUBSTRING(Description, 1, 3)) FROM
ProductDescription WHERE ProductDescriptionID = 847
SELECT @Message = @Message + SUBSTRING(LastName, 4, 3) FROM Employee WHERE
EmployeeID = 21
SELECT @Message = @Message + CHAR(33)
-- Print the entire string:
PRINT @Message
```

Transact-SQL in Applications and Reporting

I've always been a firm believer in the principle that any learning experience should lead to a tangible and usable end product. I remember taking a Visual Basic 3.0 programming class at a local college. It was a daytime class so most of the students were typical first-year college kids, just trying to pass the class and get their credits. I, on the other hand, was working in the industry as a database programmer with Hewlett Packard and was in need of a particular skill. Students would raise their hands and ask questions like, "Will this be on the test?" When I asked questions about user-input validation and concurrent database access, others would grimace because these topics weren't covered in the textbook.

This chapter is all about turning theory into reality. I'd like to share some experience (and the experience of others) with you about building applications and database solutions on the concepts you've learned in previous chapters. Throughout this book, I've mentioned that Transact-SQL isn't really a programming language, although in many ways it acts like one. Structured Query Language is best suited for returning and manipulating data and database objects. When it comes to processing complex business logic and interacting with users, the SQL language usually doesn't do the job — that's not what it's for. Fortunately, SQL Server integrates extremely well with many programming languages and application development environments. It's probably more accurate to say that a number of application development environments work well with SQL Server and other database products that use the SQL query language.

Application Programming Models

An application programming model is a high-level guide, the foundation upon which all of the components of a solution rest. It's also a set of standards and practices that apply to the finer points of application design. This encompasses the concept of *design patterns*, which are repeatable practices and methods for building solutions. There really isn't one application programming model that fits all user and business needs. In fact, it's really hard to say that any one approach is typical. Every software developer, over time, adopts their own toolkit of coding habits, naming conventions, and program code and script snippets to reuse in subsequent projects. This is great for small projects architected and built by one developer. However, larger projects need a more disciplined approach requiring standards applied across the project team or organization.

To appreciate this idea of design patterns, you need only to look around and make some observations. Have you ever noticed how so many cars from different manufacturers are so similar? Why do you think this is? Likely, it's because each company has fed off of the other's success. For example, in the 1980s, the Honda Accord became an icon of style and efficiency. In the 1990s, several competing models suddenly became very similar, including the Toyota Camry, the Nissan Maxima, and others. Someone found a design that worked well and the industry followed. Innovation is occasionally the result of starting over and applying a pattern radically different than the status quo, but is more often obtained through a series of incremental improvements. In simple terms, the software industry, although relatively young, has matured quickly over the past few decades. Developing software and database solutions is arduous and expensive. The best approach is to build upon the experiences and success of others with a cautious eye toward improvement.

The business of defining usable software programming and design models is not a lightweight topic by any means. Many large businesses have invested millions in defining their own strategies, and a number of industry-wide standards have evolved. The need for reliable and auditable processes has spawned many related, industry, and project type-specific standards. In manufacturing and production, the ISO-9000:9002 standards have prompted businesses of all kinds to maintain specific standards of quality control. Information Technology–related industries have adopted methodologies for better understanding requirements, deliverables, and project lifecycles. Specific methodologies exist for this purpose. These include the Unified Modeling Language (UML) for object-oriented application design and modular solution architecture, and Object Role Modeling (ORM) for high-level data entity modeling and database design. Software project management approaches vary from high-level, principle-centered strategies such as the Microsoft Solutions Framework (MSF) to more rigid, rules-based standards rooted in the top-down waterfall approach. Fully engaged project management deals with core issues and challenges people across different areas of business. For a methodology to work, it requires participants to share a unified belief system. This treads on culture, communication, and trust. It's hard to get two people outside of the same organization to agree on some specifics, but there are a number of principles and practices most of us who have been down this bumpy road can agree upon.

Selecting a Model

The selection of a programming model should be driven by the user and system requirements. When I am enlisted to design and implement a new system, I often go in with preconceived ideas about the size and scope of the final solution. Although it's important to start somewhere, I've learned to keep my mind open to changing requirements. Projects that start small can soon reveal a much larger scope and growth potential, and problems that seemed expansive might be easily solved with small, simple solutions. Likewise, shrink-wrapped commercial applications often need to be customized to such a degree that it is most cost-effective to build the system from scratch; and large, expensive custom applications can sometimes be replaced with off-the-shelf software. In short, an ounce of careful planning and design can be far more beneficial than a pound of brute-force application development.

Database application programming models roughly fall into the following categories:

❑   Desktop Database Applications

❑   Client/Server Database Solutions

- ❏ Three-tier Component Solutions
- ❏ Web Server Applications
- ❏ Multi-tier Web Service Solutions
- ❏ Multi-system Integrated Solutions

Additionally, database systems generally fall into these categories:

- ❏ On-Line Transaction Processing Databases
- ❏ On-Line Analytical Processing Databases
- ❏ Hybrid Database Systems

A database solution is going to involve some combination of application model and database system. Before discussing the finer points of each of these models, I'd like to put some questions in your head. In many database applications, the business requirements aren't always cut-and-dried. You can reason that there may be some opportunity to incorporate pieces of these different models and that a system may need to evolve from one type to another. That's the beautiful thing about modern tools. If you design a system correctly, it can grow and evolve. Ask yourself the following questions about your project or application:

- ❏ **How many users need access to data?**

  How many users do you have now and how many users will you have in a year, or in five years? Are they employees, customers, or vendors? The volume of concurrent users is a significant factor. After you establish the answer to this question, you also need to know something about the needs of these users. For example, 10 users who will consistently enter and modify records can be far more demanding than a thousand users who will occasionally browse data or view reports. It's often difficult to predict the size or profile of your user base years into the future, but this will have a large bearing on your scalability needs — how much the system will need to grow in the future.

  Modular, multi-tier applications are more scalable but also more complex and expensive to build.

- ❏ **Where are users located?**

  Are users situated in the same building or on the local-area network (LAN)? Perhaps they are at multiple sites or they need access to the system when they travel. Geographic boundaries have typically been one of the most significant factors in overall solution design.

- ❏ **What is your current infrastructure investment?**

  Implementing a new software solution involves more than installing a database and writing software. Any solution requires a significant investment in server and network infrastructure. Many companies have already made a sizable investment and are committed to a specific platform, operating system, and maybe even the database product.

  Does your company currently manage database servers, web servers, component hosting services, and a corporate network? Do you have available bandwidth for the increased load? Do you use server clustering or replication? Not only do these services and the related hardware represent a cost, but so do trained and capable personnel. It's important to consider the existing infrastructure and to decide whether you can design a compatible system, or whether it makes sense to take on this additional investment.

❑ **What are your security requirements and restrictions?**

How sensitive is the data you are managing? How costly would a security breach be to your business? Consider the legal and regulatory risks and restrictions. If you need a high level of security protection, this represents a greater cost in terms of coding standards, auditing, and testing. Encryption components and certificates are reasonably affordable, but encrypted data slows the system and requires more bandwidth.

❑ **How current does the data need to be?**

It's not particularly difficult for a simple database system to let all users see and manipulate current data, but this becomes an issue when the system approaches its capacity limits. If data won't change that often or if data concurrency isn't a big issue, one database may suffice for both data entry and reporting applications. Otherwise, it may be necessary to use two separate databases: one for entry and another for reporting and analysis.

❑ **What data volumes do you anticipate?**

Databases grow. That's inevitable. How much storage space will your database require in the next year, or five years? Very large databases have a higher maintenance overhead and need a more capable server. Historical data can be managed by archiving or partitioning portions of the database.

❑ **What are the system availability requirements?**

Although allowing a database server to run around the clock isn't very expensive, guaranteeing that it will always be running can be very expensive. When does the data need to be available? During business hours? Week days? 24/7? Unless you invest in redundant, fail-over systems, you must plan for some downtime — both scheduled and unscheduled. A data maintenance and recovery plan will help but cannot guarantee 100% uptime unless you have redundancy and measures to mitigate every risk of failure.

❑ **What are your delivery time constraints?**

Writing software and building a solution takes time, typically months to years. Usually 20%–30% of the total time will be spent gathering requirements and designing the system. Another 20%–30% is required for testing and debugging. After installation, deployment, and training, this leaves only 30%–50% of the time for the actual system development. Many projects fail because of unexpected schedule overruns because these factors aren't considered or estimated realistically. Pre-built, shrink-wrapped systems can usually be delivered faster, but custom-built solutions often offer greater flexibility.

❑ **What are your budget constraints?**

The more complex the project, the more difficult it may be to estimate the final cost. Custom solutions are often budgeted based on the return on investment (ROI) rather than the initial cost. This is because, quite frankly, it's often difficult to justify the cost without considering the long-term benefit.

Desktop Database Applications

This is the most traditional type of database application. Several file-based database products have been around for many years. When I began working with medical billing software in the late 1980s, our application stored data in flat text files and the programmers wrote code that did a lot of the low-level work performed by database engines today. Most desktop database applications, even as early as the 1980s, used integrated database tools such as dBase, Clipper, Clarion, Paradox, FileMaker, and FoxPro. The most popular desktop database for Windows is Microsoft Access. Most modern database products, like Access, support variations of the SQL language.

Access will support a handful of concurrent network users. Because the database engine doesn't run as a server-hosted service, large data volumes and complex queries can easily create excessive network traffic. Even if the database file is located on a server, data is processed on the user's computer. The advantage of this option is its simplicity and low initial cost. The disadvantage is its lack of scalability and less-efficient query processing.

Microsoft Access includes a forms design environment to create data-centric user interfaces. More sophisticated and lighter-weight applications can also be created using Microsoft Visual Studio or other application development suites.

The Access database engine incorporates an application programming interface (API) called Data Access Objects (DAO). In recent years, Microsoft has all but discouraged the use of the Access JET database engine and DAO for programming. In its place, it has promoted the Microsoft SQL Server 2000 Desktop Engine (MSDE), a lightweight client/server database distributed with Access and Microsoft Office. The MSDE is being replaced by the SQL Server 2005 Express Edition. Even though the use of the traditional Access database is being deemphasized, the fact remains that it can actually be simpler and easier to use for creating small database solutions. Figure 14-1 shows an Access form opened from the Access database window. This form may be used for data entry, viewing, or modifying existing records.

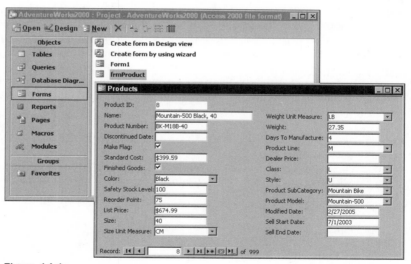

Figure 14-1

Client/Server Database Solutions

The most significant difference between this and the desktop database is that the database engine runs as a service on a file server. Requests sent to the database are processed on the server and only results are returned from queries. All query and database processing occurs on the database server. As previously mentioned, the MSDE database and SQL Server 2005 Express Edition are inexpensive options for getting started and running a small database on a desktop computer. MSDE databases have a hard limit of 10 concurrent connections.

When client/server databases came onto the scene in the mid 1990s, it was a common practice to pass ad-hoc SQL strings from the client application to the server. Although this practice causes a significant performance improvement over the client-side processing of desktop databases, it doesn't take advantage of some of SQL Server's query execution optimizations. By using stored procedures with views and user-defined functions, applications benefit from improved security and compiled execution plan caching.

This model takes advantage of the processing capabilities of two computers: the client and server. That's why it is also known as a *two-tier* solution. This is typically an effective solution for mid-size applications with users connected to a LAN. The client-side application is installed entirely on each user's desktop computer. Data access code routines connect directly to the back-end database server through an API layer, such as ActiveX Data Objects (ADO) or ADO.NET. The first native API for SQL Server was introduced for SQL Server 6.0. Roughly modeled after the existing DAO object model designed for Access/JET databases, Remote Data Objects (RDO) was built on top of Open Database Connectivity (ODBC), Microsoft's first database connectivity and driver standard. In the late 1990s, Microsoft introduced ADO, an upgraded API engineered to work more efficiently with SQL Server 7.0 and above, using the OLEDB connectivity standard. DAO, RDO, and ADO, along with their corresponding connectivity components, implemented Microsoft's original object-oriented programming and execution standard, known as the Component Object Model (COM). Microsoft's latest program execution model is the .NET Common Language Runtime (CLR). This supports updated objects used to connect through ODBC, OLEDB, and the .NET native SQL Server data provider (for SQL Server 7.0 and up).

Client/server applications exist at the entry-level of distributed solution models and have limited scalability. One common practice today is to design the system with three tiers and then deploy the middle-tier components on either the client or server computers, as illustrated in Figure 14-2. This way, if the solution needs to be scaled into a larger environment, it may simply be a matter of reconfiguring existing components to run on three computers. Although this option comes at an elevated initial cost, it may spare the additional cost of rewriting large portions of the application if the solution needs to be scaled up.

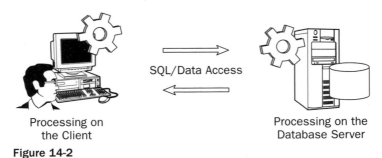

SQL/Data Access

Processing on
the Client

Processing on the
Database Server

Figure 14-2

The client application contains the user interface. Figure 14-3 shows a Windows form in design view. Using Visual Studio, a variety of application types can be created to be used on the Windows desktop, in a web browser, at the command prompt, or on portable mobile devices.

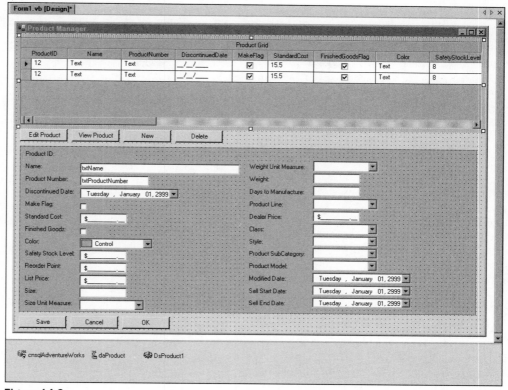

Figure 14-3

Specialized user interface controls give users a rich, interactive experience for entering and modifying record data. In this example, you can see a variety of controls that may be appropriate for different data types and fields. These include the following:

- Drop-down list combo boxes
- Check boxes
- Masked currency text boxes
- A color-picker drop-down list box
- Date-picker drop-down list boxes

Some of these controls have associated event-handling code, which runs when certain activities are performed by the user. The most common example is the click event of a button. Programmers can write program logic using a programming language of their preference, such as C#, Visual C++, or Visual Basic.NET. The following simplified Visual Basic code might run when the Save button is clicked after a user enters or modifies a product record:

```vb
Private Sub btnSave_Click(ByVal sender As System.Object, _
                          ByVal e As System.EventArgs) Handles btnSave.Click

    '** Determine whether new or existing record
    If bNewRecord Then
        '** New record is being added
        '** Define and open a connection:
        Dim cn As New SqlClient.SqlConnection("Data Source= " _
            & "Corp_DatabaseServer;Initial Catalog=AdventureWorks")
        cn.Open()
        '** define a command object for the Insert SQL:
        Dim cm As New SqlClient.SqlCommand
        cm.Connection = cn
        cm.CommandType = CommandType.Text
        cm.CommandText = "INSERT INTO Product (Name, ProductNumber, " _
                    & "DiscontinuedDate, MakeFlag, StandardCost) " _
            & "SELECT '" _
            & Me.txtName.Text & "', '" _
            & Me.txtProductNumber.Text & "', '" _
            & Me.dtpkDiscontinuedDate.Value & "', " _
            & Me.chkMakeFlag.Checked.ToString & ", " _
            & Me.txtcurStandardCost.Value.ToString
        '** Execute the SQL:
        cm.ExecuteNonQuery()
        '** Close the connection
        cn.Close()
    Else
        '** Existing record is being updated
        '** Define and open a connection:
        Dim cn As New SqlClient.SqlConnection("Data Source= " _
            & "Corp_DatabaseServer;Initial Catalog=AdventureWorks")
        cn.Open()
        '** define a command object for the Insert SQL:
        Dim cm As New SqlClient.SqlCommand
        cm.Connection = cn
        cm.CommandType = CommandType.Text
        cm.CommandText = "UPDATE Product SET " _
            & "Name = '" & Me.txtName.Text & "' ,'" _
            & "ProductNumber = '" & & Me.txtProductNumber.Text & "', '" _
            & "DiscontinuedDate = '" & Me.dtpkDiscontinuedDate.Value & "', " _
            & "MakeFlag = " & Me.chkMakeFlag.Checked.ToString & "', " _
            & "StandardCost = " & Me.txtcurStandardCost.Value.ToString _
            & "WHERE ProductID = " & me.lblProductID.Text
        '** Execute the SQL:
        cm.ExecuteNonQuery()
        '** Close the connection
        cn.Close()
    End If
End Sub
```

In this example, the actual Transact-SQL statements are assembled in the client code. This may seem to have the advantage of keeping all of the business logic in one place. However, this approach passes uncached ad-hoc SQL statements to the database server that will likely not perform as well as precompiled stored procedures. Allowing queries to be passed to the server on external connections can also be a security risk. This code is simple and relatively easy to maintain, but it may not be a very scalable solution.

n-tier Component Solutions

As two-tier solutions grew and began to run out of steam, many software designers looked for a way to take their applications to the next level. The great challenge was that Windows was designed to primarily run user-interactive applications on the desktop. Developing server-based components has long been difficult and expensive, using capabilities in the hands of large product vendors, not IT application developers. It took a few years for that to change. Visual Basic version 5.0 and 6.0 used COM and ActiveX technology, enabling software developers to create middle-tier components. Although writing components is pretty easy, configuring them to run on a server was quite a hassle in the beginning.

At first, software systems with this added component layer were known as *three-tier* solutions because the entire solution runs on three different physical layers: the database on the database server, middle-tier components on an application server, and the client application running on the desktop. Along with the capability to distribute the workload beyond two layers came the ability to extend the solution to four, five, or more separate computers (thus the term *n-tier*, rather than three-tier). One could argue that regardless of the number of servers or desktop computers, there are still conceptually only three tiers. Figure 14-4 depicts an n-tier component solution.

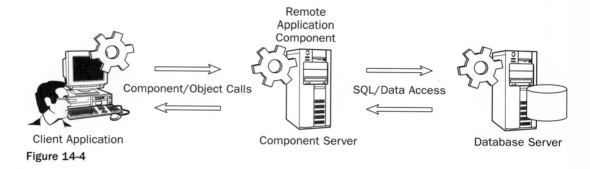

Figure 14-4

Compared with the client-server example you looked at previously, the following demonstrates a more elegant solution. The three following samples are code snippets from a three-tier application. Using Figure 14-4 as a reference, we'll move from right to left. Note that not all fields are used just to keep these examples small and simple. I've made it a point to simplify this code to make it more readable.

Server-Side SQL Objects

In this model, all Transact-SQL is isolated to the database server as stored procedures, user-defined functions, and views. This provides a layer of security, keeps business logic close to the data, and is a very efficient use of database services and network resources.

```
/****************************************************************

Adds new product record and returns new ProductID
    3-21-06, Paul Turley


Revisions:
    3-23-06    Added error-handling script


****************************************************************/
```

```
CREATE PROCEDURE spAddProduct
  @Name                 nVarChar(50)
, @ProductNumber nVarChar(25)
, @DiscontinuedDate       DateTime
, @MakeFlag             Bit
, @StandardCost           Money
, @FinishedGoodsFlag     Bit
, @Color                nVarChar(15)
, @SafetyStockLevel      Int
, @ReorderPoint          Int
, @ListPrice           Money
, @Size                 nVarChar(50)
AS
  INSERT INTO Product
    ( Name
    , ProductNumber
    , DiscontinuedDate
    , MakeFlag
    , StandardCost
    , FinishedGoodsFlag
    , Color
    , SafetyStockLevel
    , ReorderPoint
    , ListPrice
    , Size )
  SELECT
    @Name
    , @ProductNumber
    , @DiscontinuedDate
    , @MakeFlag
    , @StandardCost
    , @FinishedGoodsFlag
    , @Color
    , @SafetyStockLevel
    , @ReorderPoint
    , @ListPrice
    , @Size
  IF @@ERROR = 0
  RETURN @@IDENTITY
  ELSE
  RETURN -1
```

Middle-Tier Component

The component code, written in Visual Basic.NET in this example, serves as a broker between the presentation layer and the database objects. In this layer, I focus entirely on business logic and don't concern myself with the details of the user interface or the implementation of data storage. Programming objects provide an abstract representation for data access objects such as connections, queries, parameters, and results. This way, application programmers don't concern themselves with different dialects of SQL or other specific requirements of any single data provider.

```
'*****************************************************************
    Product class provides object definition to work with
    product records and product-related maintenance.
```

```
          Methods:
                  AddProduct()
                  UpdateProduct()
                  DeleteProduct()
                  GetProductList()
                  GetProductsByType()
                  GetProducts()

        3-23-06, Paul Turley
        Revisions:

'****************************************************************
Public Class Product
    Public Function AddProduct(ByVal Name As String, _
                          ByVal ProductNumber As String, _
                          ByVal DiscontinuedDate As Date, _
                          ByVal MakeFlag As Boolean, _
                          ByVal StandardCost As Decimal, _
                          ByVal FinishedGoodsFlag As Boolean, _
                          ByVal Color As Color, _
                          ByVal SafetyStockLevel As Integer, _
                          ByVal ReorderPoint As Integer, _
                          ByVal ListPrice As Decimal, _
                          ByVal Size As String) As Boolean

        Dim cn As New SqlClient.SqlConnection(sConnectionString)
        Dim cm As New SqlClient.SqlCommand
        Dim Param As SqlClient.SqlParameter
        Dim iProdID As Integer

        cm.Connection = cn
        cm.CommandType = CommandType.StoredProcedure
        cm.CommandText = "spAddProduct"

        ' ** Pass the function arguments/field values to proc. parameters:
        Param = New SqlClient.SqlParameter("Name", Name)
        Param.DbType = DbType.AnsiString
        cm.Parameters.Add(Param)

        Param = New SqlClient.SqlParameter("ProductNumber", ProductNumber)
        Param.DbType = DbType.AnsiString
        cm.Parameters.Add(Param)

        Param = New SqlClient.SqlParameter("DiscontinuedDate", DiscontinuedDate)
        Param.DbType = DbType.Date
        cm.Parameters.Add(Param)

        ' ** The rest of the parameters are handled here - abbreviated for demo**

        ' ** Execute the command/stored proc:
        iProdID = cm.ExecuteScalar
        ' ** Return True if successful:
        If iProdID > 0 Then Return True
```

```
         cn.Close()
    End Function

    '*** Other Functions to Update, Delete, Get products, etc.:
         Function UpdateProduct() As Boolean
             '***
    End Function

    '*** DeleteProduct()
    '*** GetProductList()
    '*** GetProductsByType()
    '*** GetProducts()

End Class
```

Presentation Layer

Compare the following code sample with that from the client-server sample. Rather than handling all of the data access and business logic in one chunk, I simply create objects based on the class defined in my middle-tier component. Using this object, I call methods (defined in Visual Basic as functions) and pass necessary values. The class method code performs data access and executes stored procedures in the database.

```
    Private Sub btnSave_Click(ByVal sender As System.Object, _
                              ByVal e As System.EventArgs) Handles btnSave.Click
        '*** Create new instance of an object based on my custom Product class:
        Dim prod As New Product

        If bNewRecord Then
            '** New record is being added
            prod.AddProduct(Me.txtName.Text, Me.txtProductNumber.Text, _
                    Me.dtpkDiscontinuedDate.Value, Me.chkMakeFlag.Checked, ...)
        Else
            '** Existing record is being updated
            prod.UpdateProduct(Me.lblProductID.Text, Me.txtName.Text, _
                    Me.txtProductNumber.Text, Me.dtpkDiscontinuedDate.Value, ...)
        End If
    End Sub
```

Overall it takes a little more work to design a multi-tier application, but the result is a flexible, scalable solution that is easier to maintain as it grows.

Resource Pooling

Why is a three-tier solution so much more capable than a client/server application? If you have the same number of users running just about the same desktop application connected to the same database, what's the big advantage of having this middle layer? Adding the middle-tier doesn't just raise system capacity by one-third. The middle-tier becomes a broker for pooling and recycling resources. Between the database server and component layer, it enables *connection-pooling*, a feature that was built into ODBC years ago (but largely unused until component technology matured). The database server-side network library keeps a pool of connections active. Each connection will stay open, unused, for a few minutes at a time. When a client or component makes a new connection request, it simply recycles one of the existing idle connections in the pool. Because most operations only take a few seconds at most, this is an effective way to allow lots of clients to utilize a relatively small number of database connections. The catch is that every client has to use the same connection settings and security credentials.

Between the client and component layer, the application server enables *object-pooling*. In a similar way to connection-pooling, after a call is made to run the code (known as a *method call*) in a hosted business object component, a cached copy of the executable code remains in the application server's memory. There it waits for additional requests. Between object-pooling on the application server and connection-pooling on the database server, it's all just a matter of timing. As thousands of users use a few hundred pooled business objects, the business object code uses just a few dozen connections. . . You do the math.

Component Transaction Management

Large-scale applications not only use multiple components but may also use data stored in multiple databases. The ADO and ADO.NET programming objects contain hooks to SQL Server's Distributed Transaction Coordinator (DTC) service. This lets programmers manage and synchronize transactions between different data sources. The benefit is that even with data in separate databases, on separate servers, and even using different database products, application code can have transactional control over multiple operations. Imagine an application that manages the transfer of funds between two different banking systems. After verifying that the interrelated debits and credits are all successfully processed on each separate system, either all operations are explicitly rolled forward or all operations are rolled back.

With the capability to take advantage of all this computer horsepower, one significant barrier remained. COM technology (extended in the network-capable implementations, DCOM and COM+) was designed to run only on Microsoft Windows and Windows networks. These applications would support any number of users, so long as they were all clients on the same network, running Windows applications and components.

Today, both component development and component hosting are much easier than ever before. Microsoft's .NET Framework, integrated server, and development environments have improved upon all of the original features of COM and COM+. Though it's true that this style of large-scale application development takes a fair amount of application development expertise, now it's fairly easy to deploy and configure an enterprise-class component server.

Web Server Application

Desktop applications give users tactile control of data. Generally, applications respond quickly and users can see an immediate response when they perform an action. We've become accustomed to a variety of sophisticated user interface controls that are relatively universal across different systems. For example, most users know what to do when they are presented with a list box, drop-down combo box, a scrollbar, or grill control. However, one of the significant limitations to building custom Windows desktop applications is they must be preinstalled on each user's Windows computer. To share data, they must be connected through a LAN.

Web server applications can make data accessible to users across the Internet. User interface options include web pages or custom Windows components. Web services make data and application functionality available to custom applications from server to server or desktop to server, across the Internet. Web-based applications have improved significantly over the past few years, and although desktop applications continue to be more responsive and flexible than browser-based solutions, this gap continues to narrow as the Web has become a common medium for business applications. The unique characteristic of a web server application is that it runs on a web server, rather than on the user's desktop computer. All, or at least the vast majority, of the processing takes place on a central server running web server components. The user sees data and changing options as they interact with a user interface that is dynamically regenerated on the web server and sent back down to the user's web browser.

The advantage is that users need only a web browser and a connection to the Internet to use the application. Several challenges continue to be somewhat costly for solution developers. Compared to desktop solutions, performance and response time is slow. Web server applications typically display web pages using HTML, the mark-up language displayed by web browsers like Microsoft Internet Explorer. When a user clicks a button on a web page to retrieve a record, for example, this request is sent across the Internet to the web server, where code interacts with the database and server-side components. Code on the server modifies the HTML tags for the copy of the user's web page in the server's memory and then sends it back across the Internet to the user's browser, displaying a response to the user's request.

Programming web solutions is still a little more cumbersome than traditional applications but this has improved in recent years. Microsoft's web application programming standard matured significantly in 2001 when Active Server Pages (ASP) graduated to ASP.NET. Now using Visual Studio.NET, creating web server-based applications is a matter of dragging and dropping controls on a design surface and writing event code much like we've been doing to create desktop application interfaces using products such as Access and Visual Basic.

Data-bound web server components do much of the work of transforming data into an HTML-based user interface. To create a simple data sheet page to display records in a table format, the developer needs only to set properties for a few components and write a minimal amount of code. More sophisticated web applications may require more advanced-level coding. ASP.NET web components offer developers the flexibility of working at a lower level when they need to have more control or at a higher level to let the components do more of the work, to develop common applications rapidly. Many of the data access components generate volumes of Transact-SQL script for common operations. For example, when using drag-and-drop tools to generate a DataAdaptor object, a wizard dialog prompts the developer for a database table. From this, Transact-SQL script is generated to manage Select, Insert, Update, and Delete operations that are implemented using auto-generated programming code. The DataAdaptor wizard will also generate parameterized stored procedures in the database for managing these operations.

Multi-tier Web Service Solutions

In a web server model, the web server application really becomes the client to the database. Like a desktop application, the client can participate in a number of different application models. Simple web server applications may use a file-based database or a client/server database. A web server application can also execute code and use the features exposed by middle-tier components, making it a true three-tier application, with the client code running on the web server. Additionally, web applications can run script or separate components in the web browser, adding yet another layer to the model. To some degree it doesn't make a lot of sense to run custom components in the browser, because this really defeats the core objectives of a browser-based solution. However, using common client-side components can enhance the user experience and add more compelling content to web pages. It's common for web applications to make use of preinstalled client components such as Macromedia Flash, Windows Media Player, and the Adobe Reader.

Web servers can also act as application servers to host middle-tier components. One of the most exciting recent developments in component technology is the XML Web Service. Like a COM-based component, a web service can expose functionality for network clients. It can be used as a data source broker to route database requests and return results. The most compelling feature that makes this option so unique is that requests and results are sent as text using the Hypertext Transfer Protocol (HTTP). This means that a web service can be hosted by a web server and can communicate with different types of clients using the plumbing of the World Wide Web. Web services are based on industry-wide standards that finally make it a simple matter for applications running on one platform, or type of computer system, to work with those on a different platform.

The magic behind web services is a programming abstraction layer called Simple Object Application Protocol (SOAP). SOAP's job is to provide a standard for translating programming object calls into XML-formatted data on one end of the conversation and then back into objects on the other end. This means that programmers just write program code to work with objects. From a programmer's perspective, working with web services is much like working with earlier types of components.

Multi-system Integrated Solutions

In a perfect world (at least from a software architect and developer's point of view), all of our business systems should be designed from the ground up to integrate with each other, to exchange information efficiently, and to provide a seamless, unified experience for business users. This just doesn't happen in most businesses. Different systems serve different business users and processes. As business grows and processes evolve, users eventually need to access applications and systems designed for different groups in the organization. This leads to requirements for these systems to interoperate. The almost inevitable outcome is the realization that similar data stored in disparate systems is not stored or used in the same way. This presents a situation common in nearly all large businesses today: To support isolated users and processes, data gets transformed and reshaped in very specific ways, eventually creating scores of special-purpose and incompatible data stores and systems designed to meet some unique business need.

This organic growth of data-related systems can be better managed if database system architects can create flexibly designed databases that can serve multiple business applications. Applications may be designed to share functionality and data through standardized data interfaces and components. Application functionality and data can now be shared by different systems using data-exchange standards such as SOAP, RSS, and XML web services. Architecting an enterprise-wide application architecture may seem to be a daunting task, especially when integrating commercial application packages, but there are many options today that can make this much easier than before. If applications can't use shared data from a single database, moving and synchronizing copies of similar data can be achieved using resources such as Data Transformation Services, SQL Server 2005 Integration Services, and Biztalk Server.

Database professionals should keep a tight reign on systems that transform multiple copies of the same data for application and reporting use. Remember that information is the context of data — it's what it means and its significance to the business. When people start pushing copies of this data around, it will be easy to lose that context as this data is transformed back into information. This process should be carefully controlled and managed. The control and limitation of access to information is one thing. Every business has to have its own standards regarding information access (that are hopefully not unnecessarily restrictive). However, controlling the ability to change data and information is an entirely different matter. Ensuring that nothing is lost in the translation as data moves around the business will only serve to empower informed information users. This is often best achieved through IT-managed data marts and data warehouse databases that are accessible to all systems and users, who would otherwise be granted access to isolated data sources.

System Integration and Data Exchange

Large organizations manage lots of data. One common reason that large solutions may consist of different databases and applications is that each serves a specific purpose. Dividing data stores between transactional and decision-support systems is a common practice in large business environments. Different systems, each with its own databases, are designed to perform different business functions. Applications may use different database products.

Unfortunately, for system integrators, most specialized business systems aren't intended to integrate or share data with others. In a perfect world, all software would be designed to work together and share common data sources. The reality is that this ideal continues to be a far-off dream in most businesses. As we continue to reengineer disparate systems, we may inch a little closer to this objective in each iteration. For now, the best most of us can hope for are methods to ease the burden of exchanging data between systems.

In recent years, eXtensible Markup Language (XML) has evolved to become a common medium to help connect different databases and applications. XML is not a standard structure for data but a flexible set of standards to define almost any type of data. Unlike rigid data formatting standards of the past (such as EDS) XML allows data to be defined, stored, and documented in the same structure. This makes the data highly portable and easier to transform into that of another system. A number of supporting standards and products are now available to connect systems and synchronize data through the use of XML. Microsoft BizTalk Server allows multiple systems to easily interconnect and exchange data. Databases and specialized business systems can be integrated without cumbersome, manual intervention.

Project Management Challenges

I recently read that the FBI had commissioned a project to consolidate its many disparate databases and computer systems. After more than a billion dollars in expenses and consulting fees, the project is in shambles. Many business requirements had been revised and the project scope has been adjusted and expanded to accommodate changing needs and business practices. Budget constraints now threaten efforts to complete the work. Fingers are being pointed and bureaucrats are covering their tracks to avoid blame. Under public scrutiny and executive control, dark clouds of failure are looming.

On a slightly smaller scale, this is all too common. One of the greatest threats to the success of an IT project is time. The larger the scope of the project, the more time it takes to complete. This allows more opportunity for business rules to change. Even if a project is completed to the satisfaction of the original requirements, if it takes too long, requirements will have changed and the product may not address the current needs of the business.

On a recent consulting assignment, I experienced numerous challenges due to ever-changing scope and requirements. The client is a large technology company with plenty of project experience. In the grand scheme of the product, my component was consistently put on hold as requirements changed in other areas. Although beyond my control, the lack of finite deliverables can be a bit disconcerting.

The ideal solution for managing larger-scale projects is to break them down into manageable pieces with a manageable-sized project team. According to the Microsoft Solutions Framework, Microsoft's internal project management guidelines, teams should consist of no more than eight individuals. If a project requires more people than this, it should be broken down into smaller components. Teams may be divided by features, discipline, or release versions. The larger the project, often the less decision-making control each team member will have over individual components and requirements. This can be demoralizing and frustrating — all the more reason to establish clear requirements and avoid making changes until completing each stage.

SQL Server Reporting Services

Database reporting solutions are really applications with a user interface, query components, and a data source. Generally speaking, these fit into the client/server application model. Until recently, enterprise-level reporting products were only offered by third-party companies such as Crystal and Business Objects. A number of specialized reporting products, such as Brio and Hyperion, are also available for multi-dimensional, decision-support databases. Microsoft has offered desktop reporting capabilities in Access and Excel, but it wasn't until 2003 that Microsoft released a serious, enterprise-ready reporting extension for SQL Server 2000 called SQL Server Reporting Services. It was originally intended to ship with SQL Server 2005 (which it does) but was completed ahead of the rest of the SQL Server 2005 components. Reporting Services is for serious reporting but it's pretty easy to use.

A brief tour of SQL Server Reporting Services is provided here. You'll see how to use some of the query techniques you've learned to support report features. This will be an opportunity to apply some of the techniques and practices you've learned earlier in this book. I'll use Reporting Services to show you how to create and use parameterized queries.

Reporting Services Architecture

Reporting Services is really quite different from other products for a number of significant reasons. The reporting engine runs as a Windows service on a computer configured as a web server. The core component is an XML web service sitting on top of ASP.NET and the .NET Common Language Runtime (CLR). This is a highly scalable and extensible architecture, meaning that features and additional capabilities can be added and that it can be expanded to more capable hardware and to multiple servers to handle increased workload. Reports can be integrated into a variety of application types and viewers, but it is most commonly used from a web browser. Out of the box, Reporting Services can render reports to different formats including variations of the following:

- ❏ HTML
- ❏ Adobe PDF
- ❏ Excel
- ❏ TIFF bitmap
- ❏ XML
- ❏ CSV text

Reports can be viewed on demand or saved to a file. User can subscribe to reports, resulting in the report being sent by email or to a file share at scheduled intervals.

In addition to these standard features, Reporting Services is programmable. Application developers can add additional capabilities for report rendering, data access, security, and delivery. They can also programmatically manage the report server and render reports, embedding report content into custom applications. In a nutshell, Reporting Services has an enormous feature set and with a little custom programming, can be made to do most anything imaginable.

To acquaint you with the Reporting Services design environment, I will walk you through the steps to create a simple report with basic features.

Because our focus is using SQL queries to drive reports, you will create two queries that utilize a parameter to filter report data. Before getting started, here is a quick disclaimer. The book you are reading is not a book on Reporting Services or Visual Studio, so I will not provide an in-depth explanation of all the features you're about to see. Because Visual Studio and Reporting Services are large, complex products, I can't guarantee that I can cover every detail in this short tutorial to get you completely up-to-speed on designing reports with Reporting Services.

> *The Wrox book, Professional SQL Server Reporting Services (Wiley Publishing, Inc.), provides an excellent explanation of SQL Server Reporting Services. The first edition is based on SQL Server 2000, and the second edition includes SQL Server 2005. If you would like to have a comprehensive guide to Reporting Services and report design, I recommend that you pick up this book.*

The Report Designer

The Report Designer is an ad-on design environment that integrates into the Microsoft Development Environment. This means that it can be used in Visual Studio 2003 and 2005. The Report Designer is opened when you create or open a report project. Aside from some minor cosmetic differences, your experience creating simple reports should be similar whether you use Visual Studio 2003 with SQL Server 2000 Reporting Services or Visual Studio 2005 for SQL Server 2005 Reporting Services.

To begin, open Visual Studio and create a new project. Depending on the installation options, different project types may be available. Select Business Intelligence from the Project Types list. For you to see the mechanics of report design, I don't want to use the report project or report wizards. Select the Report Project icon from the Templates list on the left. I originally created this demonstration using the Report Designer for SQL Server 2000 and then re-created it for SQL Server 2005. I've included screen captures from both. As you work through these screens, note that there are only subtle, cosmetic differences between those in the Visual Studio 2003 Report Designer (used with Reporting Services for SQL Server 2000) and the Visual Studio 2005 Report Designer, for SQL Server 2005. The 2005 New Project dialog is pictured in Figure 14-5.

The Name and Location values can be set as you deem appropriate. A report project places data-source and report definition files into a single folder, and this folder can be stored pretty much anywhere you like. Unless you have another location for your projects, just append a folder name to the default path in the Location box and then enter a project name in the Name box.

Along the left and right edges of the Visual Studio window are a number of dockable utility windows. Each of these windows can be "pinned" in place or moved. The default behavior is for each of these windows to auto show and hide as the mouse is moved over the icon and then off of the window. Although this nifty feature effectively conserves screen real estate, it can be a bit annoying when the window you are working with suddenly goes away. To show the Solution Explorer (if it's not already pinned out), just float the mouse pointer over the Solution Explorer icon. To pin down a window so it doesn't perform this disappearing act, click the little pushpin icon so it becomes oriented vertically rather than horizontally. Depending on whether or not windows are pinned, the window icons will either be along the edge of an auto-hidden window, displayed on either side of the design environment, or along the top of each window if it is shown.

Visual Studio 2005 has added window-docking aids that show up when you drag a dockable window around. This new feature allows you to see exactly where a window will be docked before you let go of it.

The Solution Explorer window is shown in Figure 14-6. Begin by adding a new shared data source. Right-click the Shared Data Sources folder and then choose Add New Data Source from the pop-up window.

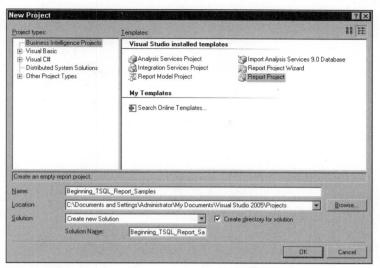

Figure 14-5

Figure 14-6

The concept of a data source is quite simple. A shared data source is actually a small XML file with an RDS extension, containing the connection information. Enter or select the name of your SQL Server in the first box. If you are using Reporting Services with SQL Server 2000, select the AdventureWorks2000 database, as shown in Figure 14-7. If you are using Reporting Services with SQL Server 2005, select the AdventureWorks database.

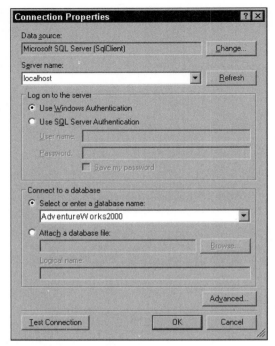

Figure 14-7

That's all there is to it. After entering the server name, verifying your authentication options (you can leave this alone if your server is configured for Windows authentication), and selecting the database name, just click the OK button.

The next step is to add a new report. From the Solution Explorer, right-click the Reports folder. From the pop-up menu, select Add and then Add New Item. . . , as shown in Figure 14-8.

There are two options for creating new reports, which include using the report wizard or building the report from scratch. You won't learn as much by using the wizard so I'm not going to have you use this method. You may want to go back and use the report wizard on your own. This will automate the process for creating a few styles of canned reports.

In the Add New Item dialog, select the Report icon on the right and give the new report file a name, as shown in Figure 14-9. This report will list products grouped by category and subcategory. Name the report Products by Category. Click the OK button when this is done.

Now step back and take a look at the Report Designer screen. Again, if you are not seeing the same thing as that shown in Figure 14-10, namely the utility windows along the left and right; just float the mouse pointer over the corresponding icons to make these windows appear.

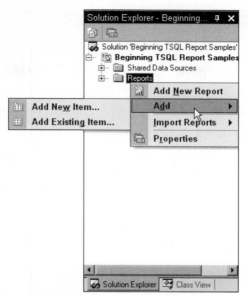

Figure 14-8

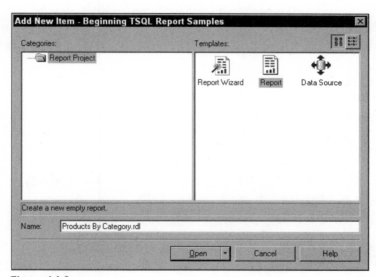

Figure 14-9

The Report Designer has three tabs along the top, which represent three distinct design surfaces. The first tab is the data set designer, used to create and work with queries. In just a bit, you'll see how to use the report Layout and Preview tabs. Again, there are only a few cosmetic differences between the Visual Studio 2003 and 2005 versions.

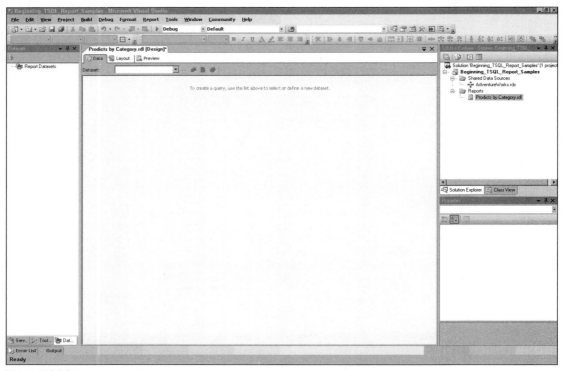

Figure 14-10

Report Queries

In Reporting Services, a query is called a dataset (not to be confused with an ADO.NET dataset, used in .NET programming). To create a new dataset or query, drop down the Dataset list and select <New Dataset. . . >. This opens a dialog box for setting up the dataset, shown in Figure 14-11.

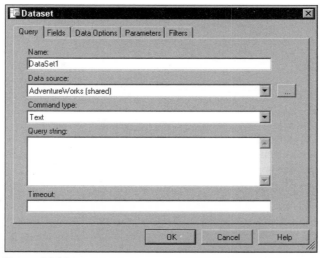

Figure 14-11

Replace the default dataset name with something meaningful. I typically like to use a name that describes the data. This may be the same as, or similar to, the name of the report. Note that the shared data source is selected for you. For the command type, I will typically either choose Text if I plan to create an ad-hoc SQL query or Stored Procedure if I will use an existing SQL Server stored procedure. You can type a SQL expression directly into the Query string box or leave it blank for now. Either way, the query can be designed or modified after closing this dialog. After changing the dataset name to Products_And_Categories and making no other changes, click the OK button.

The default query view is the generic query builder. This is a simple interface with few features. You can simply type a SQL expression into this window. The generic designer doesn't offer much help. You can switch to the graphical query designer view using the third icon from the left. This button is in the "pushed" position while in the generic query view and in the "up" position when using the graphic query designer, as shown in Figure 14-12.

Because you're already familiar with the graphic query designer, I'm going to give you only high-level instructions. Begin creating the query by adding these three tables to the diagram pane: ProductCategory, ProductSubCategory, and Product. If you are using SQL Server 2005, these three tables are all in the Production schema. When you add these three tables, inner joins are added because of the referential constraints defined in the database, as depicted in Figure 14-13.

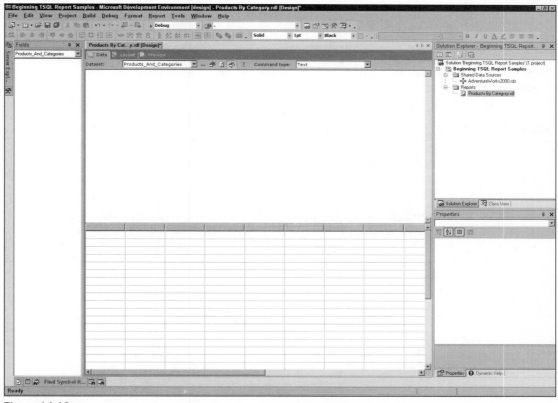

Figure 14-12

Figure 14-13

Add columns to the SELECT statement by checking them in the diagram pane in the following order:

1. ProductCategory.Name

2. ProductSubCategory.Name

3. Product.Name

4. Product.Color

5. Product.ListPrice

The query should look like that shown in Figure 14-14 in the graphical query designer.

Creating a Parameterized Query

This query is completely unconstrained and will return all records. Unless you have a controlled set of low-value data, you will typically want to limit the result set. I'd like to build some logic into my query so that if a category value is selected and passed into the query only product records matching the selection will be returned. I also want some way of indicating that I want to ignore the category and return all rows. A few different ways exist to approach this common requirement. I want to filter on the key value for categories, the CategoryID column. Because this is an Int data type, I want to limit all of the values I work with to numeric types. Whenever possible, I try to avoid the use of Null values to perform business logic. I need to have a special value that doesn't occur in the result set to indicate that I want to return all rows. Rather than mixing data types or using a Null value, I'll designate –1 as my magic number for all records.

Using the graphic query design tools, modify the query so the CategoryID column has two conditions: the column value must either match the @CategoryID parameter or the @CategoryID parameter is equal to –1. Now that you have mastered Transact-SQL, you might feel like using this technique is beneath your abilities. However, I want you to see how the query designer behaves (just in case you forget something and need to go back to it some day). Note the placement of these two conditions before you move the cursor to another cell. Figure 14-15 shows the graphical query designer environment completed to this point.

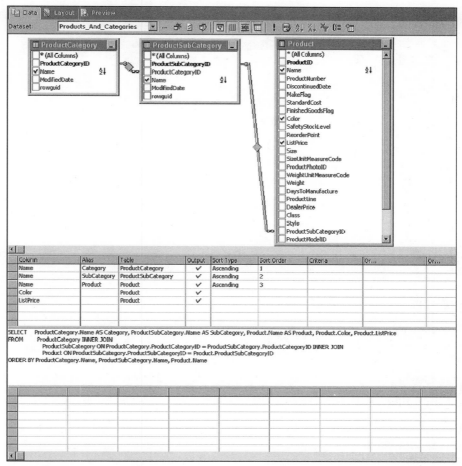

Figure 14-14

Now click another cell in the column designer grid. Observe both the column design grid and the SQL pane, as shown in Figure 14-16.

The designer moved the second parameter reference into the Columns area along with the corresponding equation. This is a very simple example but keep this in mind when you are building more complex parameterized queries. This is a common scenario in the reporting world. Imagine a report query with five or six parameters, each with similar logic. You could have dozens of possible combinations of literal values and "all record" indicators. At some point, I find that the graphical query designer begins to work against me, and will often mess up my logic expressions. In such cases, I typically use the graphical tools to get to this point, switch back to the generic designer, and then write the rest of the WHERE clause by hand. Remember to make explicit use of parentheses to clarify and control the grouping of operations when nesting and combining AND and OR logic.

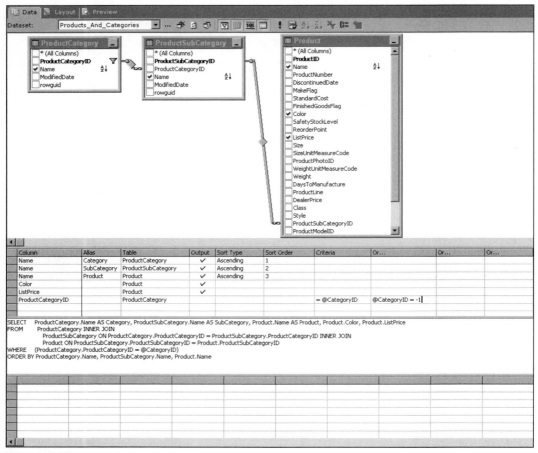

Figure 14-15

The main query is done. To test this query and view results, click the Execute button on the toolbar (the dark red exclamation mark). You will be prompted for the parameter value. Enter a low, positive integer value to see products for a specific category or enter –1 to see all product records, regardless of the category, as shown in Figure 14-17.

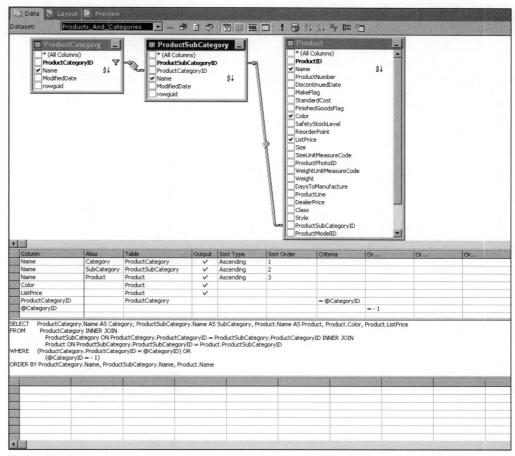

Figure 14-16

Figure 14-17

Creating a Parameter Lookup List

To test the product query and filter by a category, you used to either have to know the category primary key values or take a wild guess until you found the one you were looking for. Entering –1 for all records isn't particularly intuitive either. To make this a better experience for users, it helps to provide a lookup list of product categories for selection. This list will include an item to select all products as well.

Begin by creating a new dataset. Drop down the dataset list on the data design tab and select <New Dataset. . . Just like before, the Dataset dialog opens. Just change the name to Category_List, as shown in Figure 14-18, and then click OK.

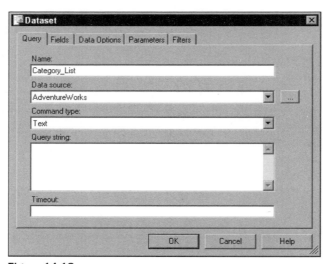

Figure 14-18

After the Dataset dialog is closed, the designer window is cleared and takes you to the generic query designer. This will be a simple query, so I'll just type the script directly into the SQL pane. Here's my query:

```
SELECT     - 1 AS ProductCategoryID, '(All Categories)' AS Name
UNION
SELECT     ProductCategoryID, Name
FROM       Production.ProductCategory
ORDER BY Name
```

If you are using Reporting Services for SQL Server 2005, the query designer displays a special grid for the UNION query, showing the literal values for the first expression and then the table selection for the second SELECT expression, as shown in Figure 14-19.

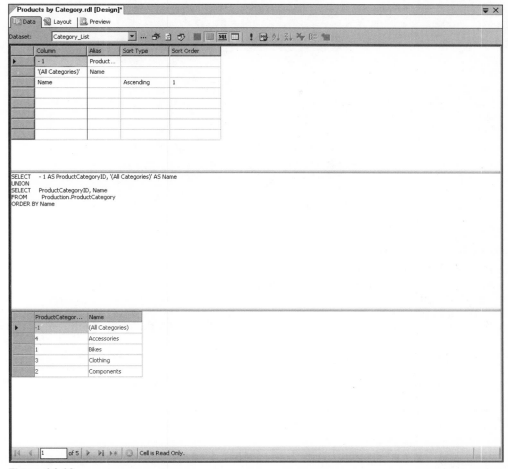

Figure 14-19

The results for the query are displayed in the lower pane of the designer. Note that the first row displays the special value, –1, to indicate that product records are not to be filtered by category.

The tools for SQL Server 2000 don't handle the UNION query quite as gracefully. The first thing the query designer does is show a warning dialog that, if you didn't read carefully, might appear to be an error. This dialog simply explains that the graphical query designer isn't equipped to display the design of a UNION query (see Figure 14-20).

This is fine. Just click the Yes button to make the warning go away and keep your changes. The designer window will show the results but makes no attempt to represent the query in any other form except SQL text.

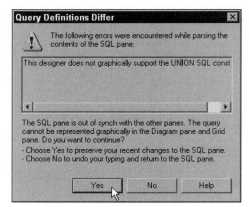

Figure 14-20

Designing the Report Layout

Think of the report layout as a canvas representing the body of the report. There are three dockable utility windows on the left side of the Report Designer in Visual Studio. These include the Toolbox, which contains report items (similar to controls in application development projects), the Dataset window, and the Server Explorer. The Dataset window, pictured in Figured 14-21, differs between Reporting Services for SQL Server 2000 and 2005. As you see in the Visual Studio 2005 designer, multiple datasets are displayed on a tree view. In Visual Studio 2003 (the designer for Reporting Services 2000), this window presents a drop-down list and iconized list of fields for only one dataset at a time.

Switch tabs or hover over the Toolbox icon to show the Toolbox window shown in Figure 14-22.

In design, standard report items are placed on the body and these items may be bound to the fields in a dataset. These are known as scalar report items because an instance represents a single value. Report items include the following:

- ❑ Textbox
- ❑ Rectangle
- ❑ Line
- ❑ Image

There is another class of report items called data range items. These items render repeated sections for every row returned from a dataset query. Scalar report items are placed into cells or sections of data range items. These include the following:

- ❑ Table
- ❑ List
- ❑ Matrix

Additionally, subreports and charts are special-purpose and although they are often categorized as data range items, they have unique behaviors.

Reports are rendered from top to bottom, and items placed on the report body will be rendered only once unless they are placed within a data range object. For this reason, if a text box in the body of the report references a dataset field, the expression must use an aggregate function to resolve to a scalar value. To keep things simple, examples will work with just a few report items. Tables are the most common data range item used in basic reporting and text boxes are the item of choice for scalar values.

Start by resizing the report body. Use the mouse pointer to find the right edge of the report body. The pointer will change to an east-west pointer icon (that is the official name). Use this to drag the edge and resize the body to a width of 8 inches. If your machine is configured to a different locale than mine, your scale may be in centimeters. In that case, make the report body 20cm wide.

Next, place a text box in the upper-left corner of the report body by either dragging and dropping the text box from the Toolbox window or by selecting the text box item and then drawing it on the report body. This text box will not be bound to data but will display the name of the report. Type **=Globals!ReportName** into the text box.

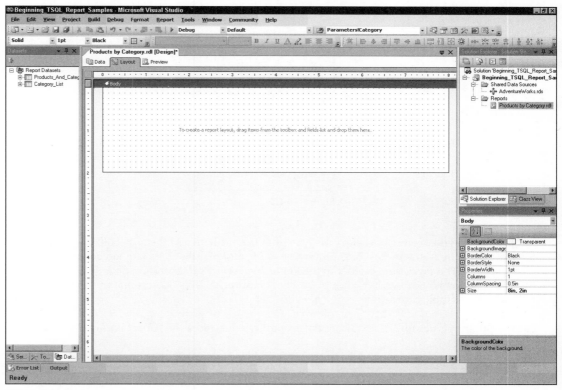

Figure 14-21

Figure 14-22

For more help with expressions, you can also right-click the item and then select Expression. . . to open the Expression Builder window. This is one area of the designer that has changed between the 2000 and 2005 versions. The expression builder in the Reporting Services 2005 designer has several enhancements over the 2000 version shown in Figure 14-23. For our purposes, this doesn't matter because we're only adding a very simple expression.

Set the font properties for the text using the properties window or the Report Formatting toolbar.

So far, your report should look like that shown in Figure 14-24.

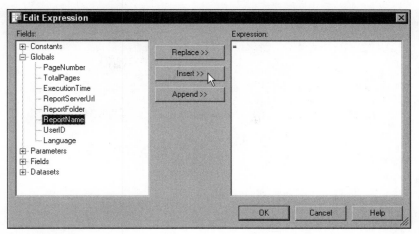

Figure 14-23

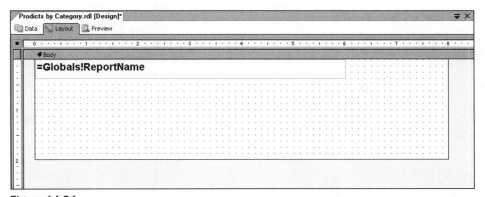

Figure 14-24

This report will display a list of products in rows and columns, grouped by category and subcategory. A columnar report calls for a table data range item. Drag a table from the Toolbox and drop it onto the report body just below the text box. Your report designer should look similar to Figure 14-25.

I need five columns and a table has three by default. The easiest method to add columns is to right-click a column header and then use the menu options to add columns to the right or left of the current column. Before you do that, resize the existing columns to make room. The table designer behaves much like Excel. In the column header, grab the border separating two columns or the right edge of the rightmost column in the table. Add two additional columns. It's very common while designing a table to make it too wide. This pushes the report body out to fit. This is no problem. Just resize the columns and then the report body accordingly.

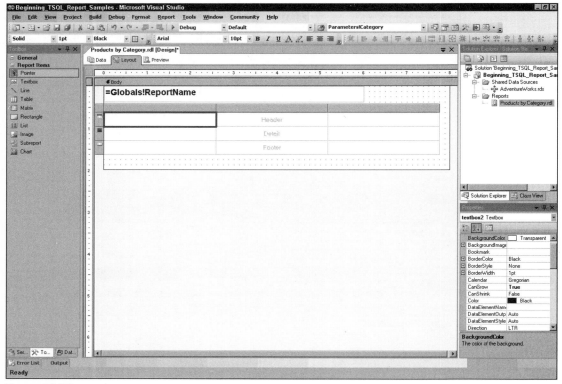

Figure 14-25

Adding Fields

This is the easy part. Show the fields list in the Dataset window and drag and drop fields into cells in the detail section of the table. Figure 14-26 shows the mouse pointer just prior to dropping the first field.

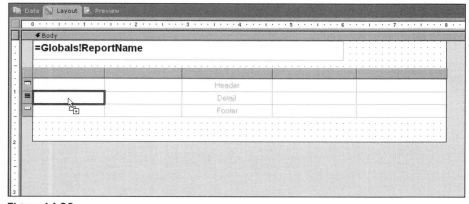

Figure 14-26

When using this technique, the designer not only sets the value of the text boxes in the detail row to the right field expression, but it also sets the text in the header row text boxes. As you see in Figure 14-27, fields with mixed-case names (such as SubCategory) are converted to title case. Every cell in a table contains a text box unless you replace it with a different report item. Different types of values should be formatted appropriately. I would like the currency value for the ListPrice field to be right-aligned and formatted as currency. Select the last column in the table by clicking the column header and then use the Report Formatting toolbar to right-align all of the cells in this column. I've also made the headers bold. The easiest method to set the properties for all cells in a row (in this case, the header text) is to use the row selector. Use this method to select the entire header row and then click the Bold button on the Report Formatting toolbar. To see the row and column selectors, you must first click on any cell in the table.

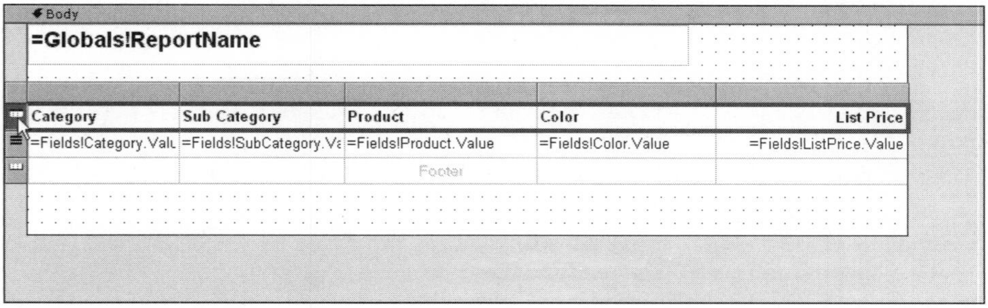

Category	Sub Category	Product	Color	List Price
=Fields!Category.Valu	=Fields!SubCategory.Va	=Fields!Product.Value	=Fields!Color.Value	=Fields!ListPrice.Value

Body — =Globals!ReportName

Footer

Figure 14-27

Setting Format Properties

To set the format for the ListPrice text box, select the text box and then right-click to open the Textbox Properties dialog. In Figure 14-28, you can see the table with the ListPrice cell selected prior to opening the Properties dialog.

All of an item's properties may be set using the properties utility window as well. In the Textbox Properties dialog, shown in Figure 14-29, indicate that this item is to be formatted as currency by selecting the Currency format from the Standard format list box. Click the OK button to return to the designer.

Configuring Report Parameters

The last step in completing the first iteration of the working report is to configure the CategoryID parameter I defined in the main dataset. By default, the user would have to type the CategoryID value into a text box in the report parameter bar. I'd like to make things a little easier for my user by listing the available product categories by name, along with the option to view products for all categories. You'll recall that I created a dataset for this purpose using a UNION expression.

With the Report Designer in layout view, drop down the Report menu on the Report Designer toolbar and select Report Parameters. . . , as shown in Figure 14-30. The Report Parameters dialog opens and you will see that the CategoryID query parameter is now listed as a report parameter.

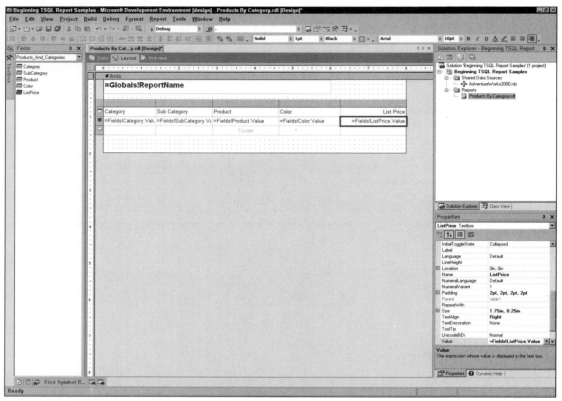

Figure 14-28

Figure 14-29

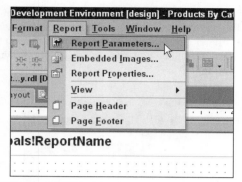

Figure 14-30

You defined a parameter in the query by prefixing the name with the @ symbol. This query parameter is now a report parameter. Just to clarify, a parameter defined in a query is known as a query parameter. Parameters can also be defined within the report, separate from query parameters. All query parameters are part of the report parameters collection.

Not all report parameters are necessarily query parameters. I won't go into this any more in this book, but you can do a lot of very creative things with report parameters that go way beyond the scope of simple, query-based filtering.

In the Report Parameters dialog, change the Prompt for this parameter to a friendly label. This is the text displayed in the parameter bar for the drop-down list containing the parameter values. I want to feed the Available Values list from a query. Choose this option and then select the dataset name, Category_List, from the Dataset drop-down. I defined two columns, the CategoryID and the Name. I want the CategoryID value to feed the actual parameter value so this become the Value Field selection, and I want my user to see only the Name field value in the list, so this becomes my Label Field selection.

Click the OK button when your selections look like that shown in Figure 14-31.

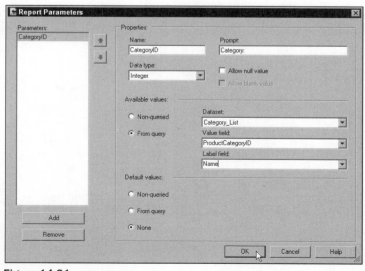

Figure 14-31

The report should be ready for testing. Switch to the Preview tab. Because the parameter wasn't configured with a default value, the report won't render until a parameter value is selected. At the top of the report preview pane the parameter drop-down list is displayed next to the label you defined. Drop down the list and select the first item, labeled (All Categories), as shown in Figure 14-32, and then click the View Report button on the right.

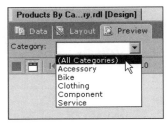

Figure 14-32

As the report begins to render, an animated icon is displayed. After a few seconds, you should see the first page of the report, as shown in Figure 14-33.

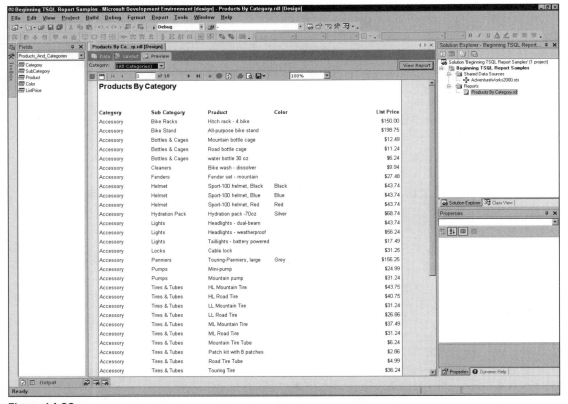

Figure 14-33

Notice the page count displayed just below the parameter list. If you navigate through the pages, you will see products for all of the categories. Now select one category from the list and click the View Report button again. This time, only products for the selected parameter are displayed, and the page count should be considerably less than before. The report should look similar to Figure 14-34.

It's not an elegant report by any means, and you can dress it up a bit by adding a shaded background to the header row. Switch back to the Layout tab, as shown in Figure 14-35, and select the header row as you did when you set the text to bold.

In the Properties window, find the BackgroundColor property and click the down arrow button to open the color selection list. From the list, select the color Silver, as demonstrated in Figure 14-36.

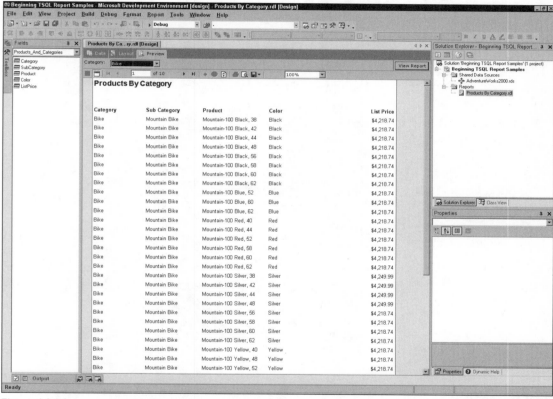

Figure 14-34

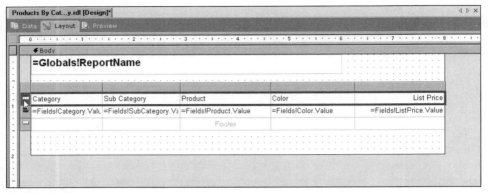

Figure 14-35

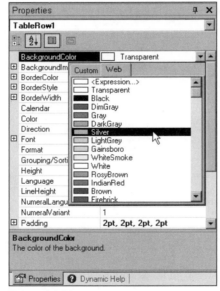

Figure 14-36

Adding Groups

Now you can begin grouping the data in the table. If you've worked with other reporting products, you may be accustomed to the idea of the report having banded sections used to group and sort the data. The same pattern applies here but this is a feature of the table rather than the report. Suppose you want to create two groups for category and for subcategory. Groups are created top-down, in order of their hierarchy. Begin by using the right mouse button to click the detail row selector. The pop-up menu displays several options that apply to the table row. Select Insert Group to open the Grouping and Sorting Properties dialog, as shown in Figure 14-37.

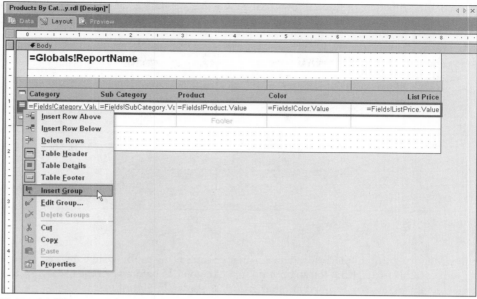

Figure 14-37

Like report items, a group is given a name. Drop-down the list in the first row of the Group on: expression list box, shown in Figure 14-38. You will see a list of field expressions. From this list, select =Fields!Category.Value and then click the OK button.

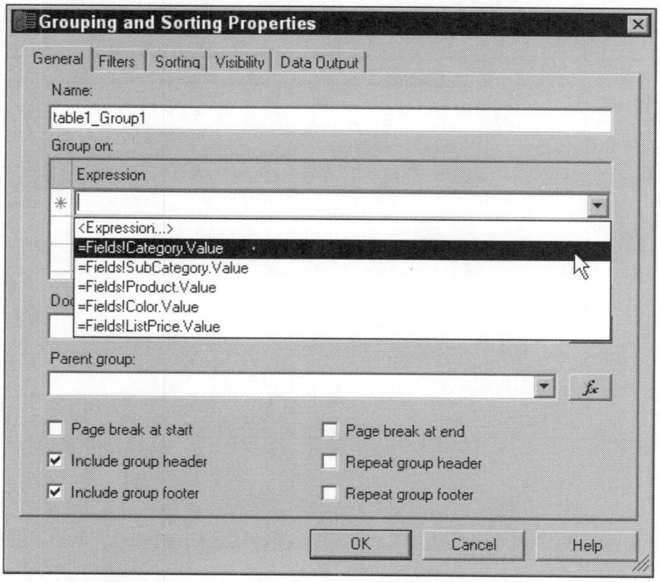

Figure 14-38

As you see, this adds two additional rows to the table that will be repeated for each instance of grouped values. As in Figure 14-39, you'll use the group header and footer rows to show the product category and subcategory headings and subtotals.

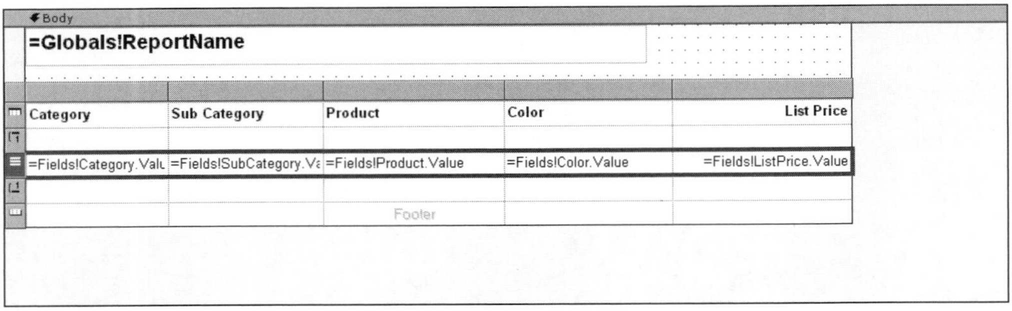

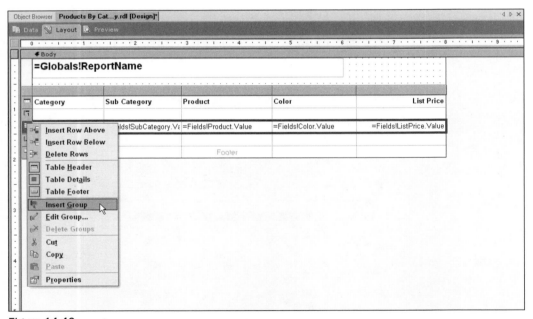

Figure 14-39

With the category group in place, also add another group for the product subcategory. Groups must be added in hierarchal order, from top to bottom. Just like you did before with the category group, right-click the detail row selector and add another group, as shown in Figure 14-40.

Figure 14-40

Select the SubCategory field expression, as shown in Figure 14-41, and then click the OK button.

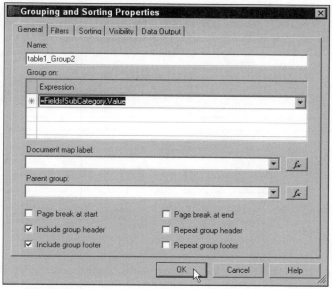

Figure 14-41

As you can see in Figure 14-42, when you click the OK button, a group header and footer appears in the table.

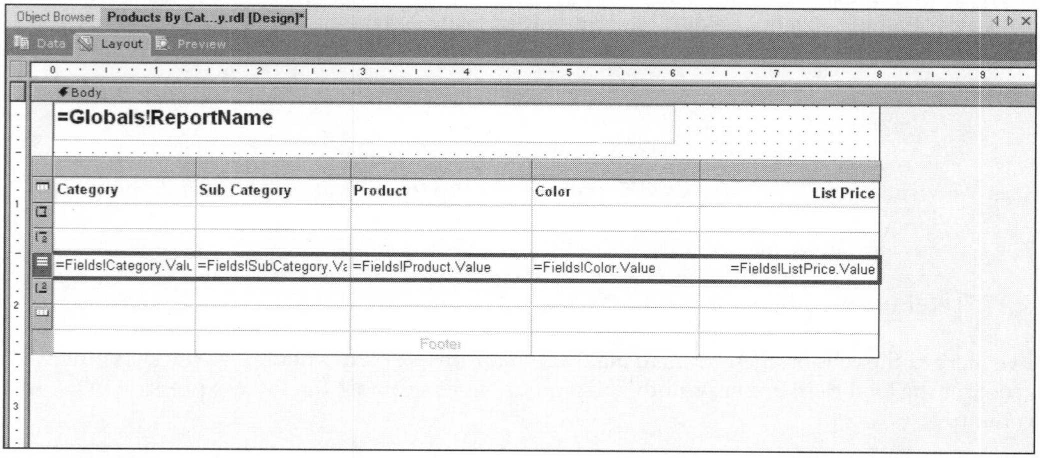

Figure 14-42

You can drag and drop the existing text boxes to different cells within the table. Do this with the Category and SubCategory fields. In the same column, place the Category text box in the group one header row and place the SubCategory text box in the group two header row, within the second column.

Make some additional room for these values. Because the category and subcategory fields don't have to share space on the same row with any other fields, you can set a cell to span adjacent cells to the right. This works much the same way as Excel and HTML tables. Begin with the Category field and drag across the other cells in the row to select them as a group. Right-click the selection and choose Merge Cells from the menu, as shown in Figure 14-43.

	Category	Sub Category	Product	Color		List Price
	=Fields!Category.Valu					
		=Fields!SubCategory.Va				
			=Fields!Product.Value	=Fields!Color.Value		
			Footer			

Figure 14-43

Repeat these steps with the SubCategory field, starting with the second cell in the group two header row. Group-select the remainder of the row, right-click and choose Merge Cells from the menu. Change the font size and weight for each of these headings. Go ahead and experiment with these properties to adjust the headings to your own liking. Report design is a little bit of an artistic endeavor. You'll need to try out ideas and test them by switching to the Preview tab.

I won't lead you through the rest of the process step by step. By now you should have a good feel for the basics of report design. In Figure 14-44, you can see the final design. In the group footers for the SubCategory and Category fields, I have added summaries using the Avg aggregate function with the ListPrice field. You'll also notice that I have labeled the SubCategory group footer (Group 2) with the expression:

```
=Fields!SubCategory.Value & " average price:"
```

This is a Visual Basic expression used to prefix the group footer for the SubCategory field value.

The Category group footer is similar:

```
=Fields!Category.Value & " average price:"
```

I've merged the cells on these rows to make room for this text. I did not merge the last column to make room for the ListPrice summary. Both of the group footers contain the same expression in the ListPrice column.

```
=Avg(Fields!ListPrice.Value)
```

Now it's finally time for some cosmetic touch-ups: Note the leading space in front of the footer label text. This is accomplished by using the padding properties of these cells. Select one of these cells (before or after it has been merged) and use the properties window to select the Padding properties group. Use the plus sign to expand the group and increase the Left Padding property to about 15 points (15pt.).

Now modify the borders to for the text boxes and table row. Group-select the cells in the table and then use the properties window to view the BorderStyle properties. Expand this group to reveal the Left, Right, Top, and Bottom properties. Set the Bottom border to Solid. You can also experiment with any of these properties to get different results.

To add a page footer section to the report, select this option from the Report menu. I've added a gray line and two text boxes to the page footer. The text boxes will display the date and time the report was executed and the page number (Page X of Y) at the bottom of each page.

My finished report design looks like that shown in Figure 14-44.

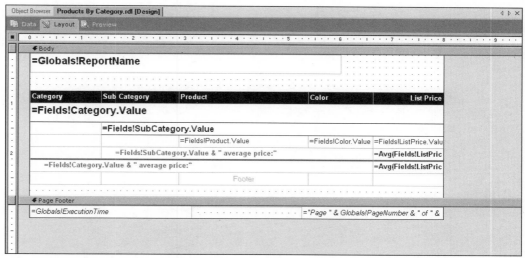

Figure 14-44

The final product, when rendered to the Preview pane, looks like that shown in Figure 14-45.

Deploying the report to the report server is actually very easy. Before this can be done from the Report Designer, Visual Studio needs to know where your report server is located. If you have a standard installation of Reporting Services on your local computer, do the following.

Using the Solution Explorer window on the right side of Visual Studio, right-click the project icon. This opens the project Property Pages dialog. Make sure that the TargetServerURL property is valid. The path shown in Figure 14-46 is correct for a default development workstation configuration.

In the Solution Explorer, right-click the report icon and choose Deploy from the menu. Assuming that there are no errors in the report design, the report will be deployed to your local server ready for use.

Chapter 14

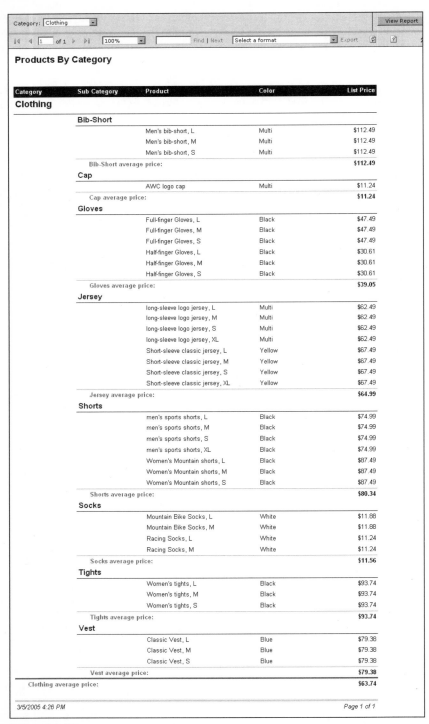

Figure 14-45

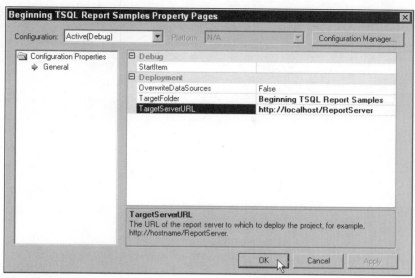

Figure 14-46

Viewing Report with the Report Manager

When Reporting Services is installed a shortcut is created in the SQL Server group for the Report Manager page. This shortcut can be found under Start ➪ All Programs ➪ Microsoft SQL Server ➪ Reporting Services ➪ Report Manager. This opens a page located at http://localhost/Reports, as shown in Figure 14-47.

Report Data Caching

Possibly one of the most compelling features of Reporting Services is its ability to cache report data so that subsequent requests don't require the database to be re-queried. There are a number of ways that reports can be cached and that parameters can be used in combination to refresh cached data and filter cached results.

Report snapshots are a form of cached reports that are completely static. Snapshots are lightweight and simple. This may be an appropriate option for common reports that are produced at regular intervals and usually don't contain parameterized options. Snapshots can be placed into history so that one snapshot doesn't overwrite a previously cached rendering of the same report. Each snapshot is marked with a date and time stamp, and a specific number are typically held in history before they are overwritten. Snapshots are typically generated on a predefined schedule and users don't need to wait while queries run against live data.

Cached instance reports are more flexible than snapshots but take a little planning and design effort. When a report is configured for instance caching, each unique combination of query parameters causes a separate cached copy of the report data to be stored in the report server database. Further, non-query report parameters may be used to filter the data stored in the cache. A cached instance may be configured to "live" for a specific period of time or to expire on a regular schedule. Because the cache is populated when a report is requested, the first user who views the report must wait for the query to run. Subsequent users or requests run against the cache until it expires.

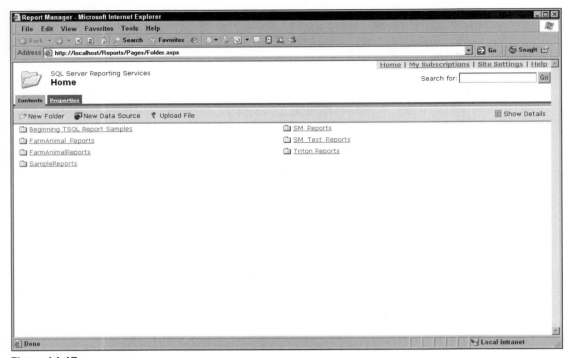

Figure 14-47

Report Application Integration

Reporting Services can be integrated into applications in several ways. These range from a simple hyperlink to fully embedded reports within custom and commercial applications. Using a hyperlink to open a report is uncomplicated. The following URL opens a report in a web browser window:

```
http://localhost/ReportServer?/FarmAnimal_Reports/Farm Animal
Sales_BW&rs:Command=Render
```

Parameters can either be left to be filled with default values, be provided by users, or may be provided in the URL request:

```
http://localhost/ReportServer?/FarmAnimal_Reports/Farm Animal
Sales_BW&rs:Command=Render&DateFrom='1/1/2005'&DateTo='3/5/2005'&GroupBy=AnimalName
&Animals='Cow','Horse','Chicken','Llama'
```

This URL opens a browser with the report displayed below a parameter bar, pre-filled with the parameter values supplied in the URL string, as shown in Figure 14-48.

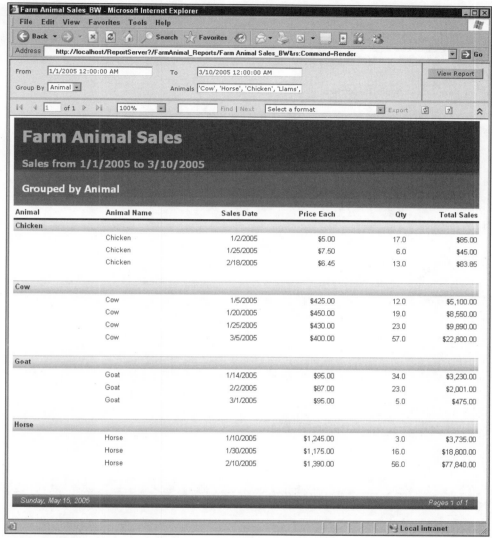

Figure 14-48

This approach is simple and provides a great deal of functionality. However, this may not be an ideal interface for all reporting solutions. A more customized approach uses an ASP.NET Web Form, such as that shown in Figure 14-49. Sophisticated web controls may be used to prompt users for parameter values.

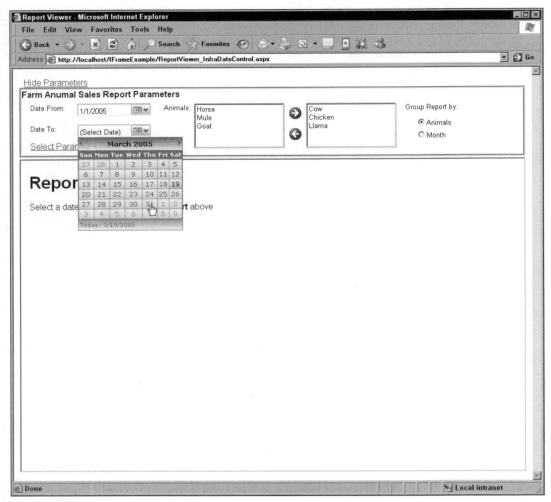

Figure 14-49

Parameter values are gathered from these controls and then concatenated into a URL like the previous example. A hyperlink control uses this URL to target an HTML frame on the Web Form. After using the custom parameter interface to choose a user's selection criteria, the link renders the report to the in-line frame embedded in the web page. As far as the user is concerned, this is simply a feature of a web browser-based custom business application (see Figure 14-50).

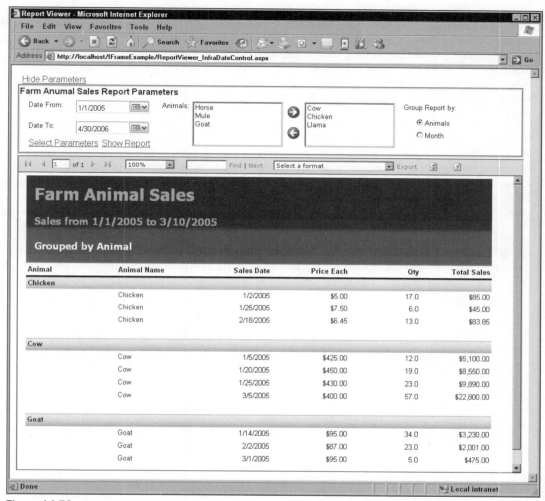

Figure 14-50

Summary

This chapter looked at how Transact-SQL is used in common applications and reporting solutions. A wide range of options are available for architecting and building database application solutions. Programming models vary in purpose and complexity. It's senseless to overengineer a solution with capabilities that won't ever be used — but it's also important to plan for future requirements. Striking the appropriate balance between these two principles is often the greatest challenge in database solution design.

Scalable solutions can accommodate a larger number of users without redesigning the fundamental application architecture. Scalable solutions make appropriate use of program components to separate the user interface from business logic and data access. How you implement Transact-SQL in an application plays an important role in its ability to handle whatever requirements may be discovered or imposed after the fact. Isolating database connections to separate reusable application components can simplify ongoing application design. Keeping SQL queries in database server objects, such as views, stored procedures, and user-defined functions, not only offers improved performance, but is also much more secure.

Finding the optimal balance between an application architecture that just gets the job done quickly and being able to adapt to any needs that could potentially arise is often a challenge. Ultimately, it is the long-term business requirements and objectives that should lead to choosing an application model that meets these needs. Fortunately, building scalable solutions is less costly using more capable programming objects and development tools.

Reporting is an important part of many business applications. SQL Server Reporting Services makes use of ad-hoc Transact-SQL statements, views, and stored procedures. These queries can include parameters to filter results and modify business logic. Reporting Services takes this concept to a level beyond SQL queries by allowing reports to filter cached data results and to provide rich, dynamic reporting capabilities, using report parameters and other advanced Reporting Services features.

Command Syntax Reference

SQL Server recognizes up to four parts of object names. Depending on the context of an expression, some parts may or may not be necessary when referencing an object. When script runs on a different server or when using a different database, related object names may be required. Note that SQL Server 2005 recognizes the schema name in the third position, whereas SQL Server 2000 recognizes the object owner name in the same position. If you are using SQL Server 2000, substitute the owner for the schema.

Object Reference	Use and Context
object	In the context of the local database, on the same server. Object is owned by the dbo user (SQL Server 2000) or part of the dbo schema (SQL Server 2005) and there are no duplicate object names.
schema.object	In the context of the local database, on the same server. Object may be owned by a user other than dbo (SQL Server 2000) or part of a specific schema. Duplicate object names that have different owners or schema names are permitted. Also uses a standard convention for clarity.
database..object	In the context of the same or different database on the same server. Without specifying the owner or schema, assumes the dbo owner or schema.
database.schema.object	A three-part name fully describes an object on the same server, in the same or different database.
server.database.schema.object	A four-part name is valid in the context of a remote server or the local server, in the local or a different database, and for any user or schema.
server.database..object	The database owner or schema in the third position can be omitted to use the default dbo owner or schema.
server..schema.object	The database name can be omitted to use the default database on that server. This is a not a typical practice.
server...object	Omitting the database and owner or schema name uses the default database and the default dbo user or schema. This is not a typical practice.

Transact-SQL Commands, Clauses, and Predicates

Following are the core components of the Transact-SQL language. New commands for SQL Server 2005 are explicitly called out in this section.

WITH

This is a new method in SQL Server 2005 for defining an alias for the result set returned by a SELECT expression.

```
WITH MyCTE
AS
( SELECT * FROM Product WHERE ListPrice < 1000 )
```

Optionally, column aliases can be defined in parentheses following the Common Table Expression (CTE) name:

```
WITH MyCTE ( ID, ProdNumber, ProdName, Price )
AS
( SELECT
    ProductID
  , ProductNumber
  , Name
  , ListPrice
  FROM Product WHERE ListPrice < 1000
)
```

SELECT

Return all columns from a table or view:

```
SELECT * FROM table_name
```

Return specific columns from a table or view:

```
SELECT Column1, Column2, Column3 FROM table_name
```

Column alias techniques:

```
SELECT Column1 AS Col1, Column2 AS Col2 FROM table_name
SELECT Column1 Col1, Column2 Col2 FROM table_name
SELECT Col1 = Column1, Col2 = Column2 FROM table_name
```

Literal values:

```
SELECT 'Some literal value'
SELECT 'Some value' AS Col1, 123 AS Col2
```

Returning an expression value:

```
SELECT (1 + 2) * 3
```

Returning the result of a function call:

```
SELECT CONVERT( VarChar(20), GETDATE(), 101 )
```

TOP

Return a fixed number of rows:

```
SELECT TOP 10 * FROM table_name ORDER BY Column1
SELECT TOP 10 Column1, Column2 FROM table_name ORDER BY Column2
```

Return a fixed number of rows with the ties for last position:

```
SELECT TOP 10 WITH TIES Column1, Column2 FROM table_name ORDER BY Column2
```

Return a percentage of all available rows:

```
SELECT TOP 25 PERCENT * FROM table_name ORDER BY Column2
SELECT TOP 25 PERCENT Column1, Column2 FROM table_name ORDER BY Column2
```

For SQL Server 2005 only, substitute a variable or expression for a top values number:

```
DECLARE @TopNumber Int
SET @TopNumber = 15
SELECT TOP @ TopNumber * FROM table_name ORDER BY Column2
```

Top values based on an expression:

```
SELECT TOP (SELECT a_column_value FROM some_table) * FROM another_table
```

SELECT INTO

Create and populate a table from a result set:

```
SELECT Column1, Column2 INTO new_table_name FROM existing_table_or_view_name
```

FROM

Single table query:

```
SELECT * FROM table_name
```

Multi-table join query:

```
SELECT *
FROM table1.key_column INNER JOIN table2 ON table1.key_column = table2.key_column
```

Derived table:

```
SELECT DerTbl.Column1, DerTbl.Column2
FROM
    ( SELECT Column1, Column2 FROM some_table ... ) AS DerTbl
```

WHERE

Exact match:

```
SELECT ... FROM ...
WHERE Column1 = 'A literal value'
```

Not NULL:

```
SELECT ... FROM ...
WHERE Column1 IS NOT NULL
```

Any trailing characters:

```
SELECT ... FROM ...
WHERE Column1 LIKE 'ABC%'
```

Any leading characters:

```
SELECT ... FROM ...
WHERE Column1 LIKE '%XYZ'
```

Any leading or trailing characters:

```
SELECT ... FROM ...
WHERE Column1 LIKE '%MNOP%'
```

Placeholder wildcard:

```
SELECT ... FROM ...
WHERE Column1 LIKE '_BC_EF'
```

Criteria using parentheses to designate order:

```
SELECT ... FROM ...
WHERE
    (Column1 LIKE 'ABC%' AND Column2 LIKE '%XYZ')
    OR
    Column3 = '123'
```

GROUP BY

All non-aggregated columns in the SELECT list must be included in the GROUP BY list:

```
SELECT COUNT(Column1), Column2, Column3
FROM ... WHERE ...
GROUP BY Column2, Column3
```

Designating order:

```
SELECT COUNT(Column1), Column2, Column3
FROM ... WHERE ...
GROUP BY Column2, Column3
ORDER BY Column2 DESC, Column3 ASC
```

HAVING

Filter results based on values available after the aggregations and groupings are performed:

```
SELECT COUNT(Column1), Column2, Column3
FROM ... WHERE ...
GROUP BY Column2, Column3
HAVING COUNT(Column1) > 5
```

UNION

Combine multiple results with the same column count:

```
SELECT Column1, Column2 FROM table1_name
UNION
SELECT Column1, Column2 FROM table2_name
```

Combine literal values and query results:

```
SELECT -1 AS Column1, 'A literal value' AS Column2
UNION
SELECT Column1, Column2 FROM table1_name
```

Include non-distinct selection (UNION performs SELECT DISTINCT by default):

```
SELECT Column1, Column2 FROM table1_name
UNION ALL
SELECT Column1, Column2 FROM table2_name
```

EXCEPT and INTERSECT

Select the differences (EXCEPT) or common values (INTERSECT) between two queries:

```
SELECT * FROM TableA EXCEPT SELECT * FROM TableB

SELECT * FROM TableA INTERSECT SELECT * FROM TableB
```

ORDER BY

Order a result set by one or more column values. The default order is ascending. If ordering by more than one column, each column can have a different order.

```
SELECT * FROM table_name ORDER BY Column1

SELECT * FROM table_name ORDER BY Column1 DESC, Column2 ASC
```

COMPUTE (BY)

The COMPUTE and COMPUTE BY clauses generate totals that are appended to the end of an aggregate query result set. These clauses are not very useful in applications because the aggregated results are not in relational form and cannot be utilized in a dataset.

```
SELECT * FROM table_name ORDER BY Column1

SELECT * FROM table_name ORDER BY Column1 DESC, Column2 ASC
```

FOR Clause

The FOR clause is used with either the XML or BROWSE option in a SELECT statement. However, the BROWSE and XML options are completely unrelated. FOR XML specifies that the result set is returned in XML format. FOR BROWSE is used when accessing data through the DB-Library so that rows can be browsed and updated one row at a time in an optimistic locking environment. There are several requirements when using the FOR BROWSE option. For more information consult the SQL Server Books Online under the topic "Browse Mode."

```
SELECT * FROM table_name FOR XML {XML Option}

SELECT * FROM table_name FOR BROWSE
```

OPTION Clause

The OPTION clause is used in a SELECT statement to provide a query hint that will override the query optimizer and specify an index or specific join mechanism to be used along with other hint options.

CASE

CASE evaluates one or more expressions and returns one or more specified values based on the evaluated expression:

```
SELECT expression = CASE Column
WHEN value THEN resultant_value
WHEN value2 THEN resultant_value2
. . .
ELSE alternate_value
END
FROM table

SELECT value =
       CASE
       WHEN column IS NULL THEN value
```

```
                    WHEN column {expression true} THEN different_value
                    WHEN column {expression true} and price {expression true} THEN other_value
                    ELSE different_value
                    END,
                column2
        FROM table
```

INSERT

Adds a new row to a table:

```
INSERT table (column list)
VALUES
(column values)

INSERT table
SELECT columns FROM source expression

INSERT table
EXEC stored_procedure
```

UPDATE

Updates selected columns in a table:

```
UPDATE table SET column1 = expression1, column2 = expression2
WHERE filter_expression
```

Update a table based on the contents of another table:

```
UPDATE table SET column1 = expression
FROM table INNER JOIN table2
ON table.column = table2.column
WHERE table.column = table2.column
```

DELETE

Deletes selected rows from a table:

```
DELETE table
WHERE filter_expression
```

Deletes rows from a table based on the contents of a different table:

```
DELETE table
FROM table INNER JOIN table2
ON table.column = table2.column
WHERE column = filter_expression
```

DECLARE @local_variable

This creates a named object that temporarily holds a value with the data type defined in the declaration statement. Local variables have scope only within the calling batch or stored procedure. The value of a local variable can be set with either a SET or SELECT operation. SELECT is more efficient and has the advantage of populating multiple variables in a single operation, but the SELECT operation cannot be confined with any data retrieval operation.

```
DECLARE @local_variable AS int
SET @local_variable = integer_expression

DECLARE @local_variable1 AS int, @local_variable2 AS varchar(55)
SELECT @local_variable1 = integer_column_expression, @local_variable2 =
character_column_expression FROM table
```

SET

The SET operator has many functions, from setting the value of a variable to setting a database or connection property. The SET operator is divided into the categories listed in the following table.

Category	Alters the Current Session Settings For
Date and time	Handling date and time data
Locking	Handling Microsoft(r) SQL Server locking
Miscellaneous	Miscellaneous SQL Server functionality
Query execution	Query execution and processing
SQL-92 settings	Using the SQL-92 default settings
Statistics	Displaying statistics information
Transactions	Handling SQL Server transactions

LIKE

LIKE is a pattern-matching operator for comparing strings or partial strings.

Compare a string value where the compared string is anywhere in the string:

```
SELECT * FROM table WHERE column1 LIKE '%string%'
```

Compare a string value where the compared string is at the beginning of the string:

```
SELECT * FROM table WHERE column1 LIKE 'string%'
```

Compare a string value where the compared string is at the end of the string:

```
SELECT * FROM table WHERE column1 LIKE '%string'
```

Compare a string value where a specific character or character range is in the string:

```
SELECT * FROM table WHERE column1 LIKE '[a-c]'
SELECT * FROM table WHERE column1 LIKE '[B-H]olden'
```

Compare a string value where a specific character or character range is not in the string:

```
SELECT * FROM table WHERE column1 LIKE '[M^c]%' -Begins with M but not Mc
```

ALTER TABLE

Alter the structure of a table by adding or removing table objects such as Constraints, Columns, and Partitions or enabling and disabling Triggers:

```
ALTER TABLE table_name ADD new_column int NULL
ALTER TABLE table_name ADD CONSTRAINT new_check CHECK (check expression)
ALTER TABLE table_name DISABLE TRIGGER trigger_name
ALTER TABLE table_name ENABLE TRIGGER trigger_name
```

CREATE DATABASE

Create a database and all associated files:

```
CREATE DATABASE new_database
ON (
    NAME = 'logical_name',
    FILENAME = 'physical_file_location',
    SIZE = initial_size_in_MB,
    MAXSIZE = max_size_in_MB, --If no MAXSIZE specified unlimited growth is assumed
    FILEGROWTH = percentage_OR_space_in_MB)
LOG ON
( NAME = 'logical_log_name',
    FILENAME = 'physical_file_location',
    SIZE = initial_size_in_MB,
    MAXSIZE = max_size_in_MB, --If no MAXSIZE specified unlimited growth is assumed
    FILEGROWTH = percentage_OR_space_in_MB)
COLLATE database_collation
```

CREATE DEFAULT

Create a database-wide default value that can then be bound to columns in any table to provide a default value:

```
CREATE DEFAULT default_name AS default_value
--bind the default to a table column
sp_bindefault default_name, 'table.column'
```

CREATE PROCEDURE

Create a new stored procedure:

```
CREATE PROC proc_name @variable variable_data_type ...n
AS
...procedure code
```

CREATE RULE

Create a database-wide rule, much like a Check Constraint, that can then be bound to individual columns in tables throughout the database:

```
CREATE RULE rule_name AS rule_expression
--bind the Rule to a table column
sp_bindrule rule_name, 'table.column'
```

CREATE TABLE

Create a new table:

```
CREATE TABLE table_name (
Column1 data_type nullability column_option,
Column2 data_type nullability column_option,
Column3 data_type nullability column_option,

--Column_option = Collation, IDENTITY, KEY...
```

Create a new partitioned table:

```
CREATE TABLE partitioned_table_name (col1 int, col2 char(10))
Column1 data_type nullability column_option,
Column2 data_type nullability column_option,
Column3 data_type nullability column_option

ON partition_scheme_name (column)
```

CREATE TRIGGER

Create a new trigger on a table that fires AFTER a DML event or INSTEAD OF a DML event:

```
CREATE TRIGGER trigger_name
ON table_name FOR dml_action -INSERT, UPDATE or DELETE
AS
...trigger_code
CREATE TRIGGER trigger_name
ON view_or_table_name INSTEAD OF dml_action -INSERT, UPDATE or DELETE
AS
...trigger_code
```

CREATE VIEW

Creates a new view:

```
CREATE VIEW view_name
AS
...Select Statement
```

CREATE SCHEMA

Creates a new schema in SQL Server 2005 with the option of specifying a non-dbo owner with the AUTHORIZATION clause:

```
CREATE SCHEMA schema_name AUTHORIZATION user_name
```

CREATE PARTITION FUNCTION

Creates a partition function in SQL Server 2005 to use in physically partitioning tables and indexes:

```
CREATE PARTITION FUNCTION partition_function_name ( input_parameter_type )
AS RANGE LEFT --or RIGHT
FOR VALUES (value1, value2, value3, ...n)
```

CREATE PARTITION SCHEME

Creates a partition scheme in SQL Server 2005 to use in physically partitioning tables and indexes:

```
CREATE PARTITION SCHEME partition_scheme_name
AS PARTITION partition_function_name
TO (filegroup1, filefroup2, filefroup3, ...n)
```

Script Comment Conventions

In-line comment:

```
SELECT ProductID, Name AS ProductName    -- Comment text
```

Single-line comment:

```
/* Comment text */
-- Comment text
```

Comment block:

```
/*****************************************************
     spProductUpdateByCategory
     Created by Paul Turley, 5-21-06
     nospam@sqlreportservices.com
     Updates product price info for a category

     Revisions:
     5-22-06 - Fixed bug that formatted C:
               drive if wrong type was passed in.
*****************************************************/
```

Reserved Words

Chapter 12 gave some recommendations and guidance around the naming of objects in SQL Server. One of the recommendations was that reserved words should not be used as names of objects. Reserved words are typically easy to see in both Query Analyzer and SQL Server Management Studio. Both these tools change the color of reserved words to blue, but for whatever reason, not all reserved words are recognized by Query Analyzer and Management Studio and color-coded. To make matters worse, some words are color-coded blue even when they are not really reserved words. Also, if the object names are delimited with double-quotes or square brackets, which they often are if using a graphical tool to create queries, then they won't show up color-coded at all. However, use of a non-delimited reserved word, whether or not it is blue, will always cause a syntax error to be raised. You will know when you have placed a non-delimited reserved word in your script when you receive the error "Incorrect syntax near the keyword *'keyword'*." Keep in mind that if the decision is made to use a keyword in an object name, you will be forced to delimit that keyword every time it is used in the future.

The following keywords have significant meaning within Transact-SQL and should be avoided in object names and expressions. If any of these words must be used in a SQL expression, they must be contained within square brackets [ ].

ADD	EXCEPT	PERCENT
ALL	EXEC	PLAN
ALTER	EXECUTE	PRECISION
AND	EXISTS	PRIMARY
ANY	EXIT	PRINT
AS	FETCH	PROC
ASC	FILE	PROCEDURE
AUTHORIZATION	FILLFACTOR	PUBLIC
BACKUP	FOR	RAISERROR
BEGIN	FOREIGN	READ
BETWEEN	FREETEXT	READTEXT
BREAK	FREETEXTTABLE	RECONFIGURE
BROWSE	FROM	REFERENCES
BULK	FULL	REPLICATION
BY	FUNCTION	RESTORE
CASCADE	GOTO	RESTRICT
CASE	GRANT	RETURN
CHECK	GROUP	REVOKE
CHECKPOINT	HAVING	RIGHT
CLOSE	HOLDLOCK	ROLLBACK
CLUSTERED	IDENTITY	ROWCOUNT
COALESCE	IDENTITY_INSERT	ROWGUIDCOL
COLLATE	IDENTITYCOL	RULE
COLUMN	IF	SAVE
COMMIT	IN	SCHEMA
COMPUTE	INDEX	SELECT

CONSTRAINT	INNER	SESSION_USER
CONTAINS	INSERT	SET
CONTAINSTABLE	INTERSECT	SETUSER
CONTINUE	INTO	SHUTDOWN
CONVERT	IS	SOME
CREATE	JOIN	STATISTICS
CROSS	KEY	SYSTEM_USER
CURRENT	KILL	TABLE
CURRENT_DATE	LEFT	TEXTSIZE
CURRENT_TIME	LIKE	THEN
CURRENT_TIMESTAMP	LINENO	TO
CURRENT_USER	LOAD	TOP
CURSOR	NATIONAL	TRAN
DATABASE	NOCHECK	TRANSACTION
DBCC	NONCLUSTERED	TRIGGER
DEALLOCATE	NOT	TRUNCATE
DECLARE	NULL	TSEQUAL
DEFAULT	NULLIF	UNION
DELETE	OF	UNIQUE
DENY	OFF	UPDATE
DESC	OFFSETS	UPDATETEXT
DISK	ON	USE
DISTINCT	OPEN	USER
DISTRIBUTED	OPENDATASOURCE	VALUES
DOUBLE	OPENQUERY	VARYING
DROP	OPENROWSET	VIEW
DUMMY	OPENXML	WAITFOR
DUMP	OPTION	WHEN
ELSE	OR	WHERE
END	ORDER	WHILE
ERRLVL	OUTER	WITH
ESCAPE	OVER	WRITETEXT

ODBC Reserved Words

Although ODBC keywords are not strictly prohibited, as a best practice to prevent driver inconsistencies, they should be avoided. These are listed in the following table.

ABSOLUTE	EXEC	OVERLAPS
ACTION	EXECUTE	PAD
ADA	EXISTS	PARTIAL
ADD	EXTERNAL	PASCAL
ALL	EXTRACT	POSITION
ALLOCATE	FALSE	PRECISION
ALTER	FETCH	PREPARE
AND	FIRST	PRESERVE
ANY	FLOAT	PRIMARY
ARE	FOR	PRIOR
AS	FOREIGN	PRIVILEGES
ASC	FORTRAN	PROCEDURE
ASSERTION	FOUND	PUBLIC
AT	FROM	READ
AUTHORIZATION	FULL	REAL
AVG	GET	REFERENCES
BEGIN	GLOBAL	RELATIVE
BETWEEN	GO	RESTRICT
BIT	GOTO	REVOKE
BIT_LENGTH	GRANT	RIGHT
BOTH	GROUP	ROLLBACK
BY	HAVING	ROWS
CASCADE	HOUR	SCHEMA
CASCADED	IDENTITY	SCROLL
CASE	IMMEDIATE	SECOND
CAST	IN	SECTION
CATALOG	INCLUDE	SELECT
CHAR	INDEX	SESSION
CHAR_LENGTH	INDICATOR	SESSION_USER

CHARACTER	INITIALLY	SET
CHARACTER_LENGTH	INNER	SIZE
CHECK	INPUT	SMALLINT
CLOSE	INSENSITIVE	SOME
COALESCE	INSERT	SPACE
COLLATE	INT	SQL
COLLATION	INTEGER	SQLCA
COLUMN	INTERSECT	SQLCODE
COMMIT	INTERVAL	SQLERROR
CONNECT	INTO	SQLSTATE
CONNECTION	IS	SQLWARNING
CONSTRAINT	ISOLATION	SUBSTRING
CONSTRAINTS	JOIN	SUM
CONTINUE	KEY	SYSTEM_USER
CONVERT	LANGUAGE	TABLE
CORRESPONDING	LAST	TEMPORARY
COUNT	LEADING	THEN
CREATE	LEFT	TIME
CROSS	LEVEL	TIMESTAMP
CURRENT	LIKE	TIMEZONE_HOUR
CURRENT_DATE	LOCAL	TIMEZONE_MINUTE
CURRENT_TIME	LOWER	TO
CURRENT_TIMESTAMP	MATCH	TRAILING
CURRENT_USER	MAX	TRANSACTION
CURSOR	MIN	TRANSLATE
DATE	MINUTE	TRANSLATION
DAY	MODULE	TRIM
DEALLOCATE	MONTH	TRUE
DEC	NAMES	UNION
DECIMAL	NATIONAL	UNIQUE
DECLARE	NATURAL	UNKNOWN
DEFAULT	NCHAR	UPDATE

Table continued on following page

DEFERRABLE	NEXT	UPPER
DEFERRED	NO	USAGE
DELETE	NONE	USER
DESC	NOT	USING
DESCRIBE	NULL	VALUE
DESCRIPTOR	NULLIF	VALUES
DIAGNOSTICS	NUMERIC	VARCHAR
DISCONNECT	OCTET_LENGTH	VARYING
DISTINCT	OF	VIEW
DOMAIN	ON	WHEN
DOUBLE	ONLY	WHENEVER
DROP	OPEN	WHERE
ELSE	OPTION	WITH
END	OR	WORK
END-EXEC	ORDER	WRITE
ESCAPE	OUTER	YEAR
EXCEPT	OUTPUT	ZONE
EXCEPTION		

Future Reserved Words

The following table contains keywords that may be reserved in future editions of SQL Server.

ABSOLUTE	FOUND	PRESERVE
ACTION	FREE	PRIOR
ADMIN	GENERAL	PRIVILEGES
AFTER	GET	READS
AGGREGATE	GLOBAL	REAL
ALIAS	GO	RECURSIVE
ALLOCATE	GROUPING	REF
ARE	HOST	REFERENCING
ARRAY	HOUR	RELATIVE
ASSERTION	IGNORE	RESULT

AT	IMMEDIATE	RETURNS
BEFORE	INDICATOR	ROLE
BINARY	INITIALIZE	ROLLUP
BIT	INITIALLY	ROUTINE
BLOB	INOUT	ROW
BOOLEAN	INPUT	ROWS
BOTH	INT	SAVEPOINT
BREADTH	INTEGER	SCROLL
CALL	INTERVAL	SCOPE
CASCADED	ISOLATION	SEARCH
CAST	ITERATE	SECOND
CATALOG	LANGUAGE	SECTION
CHAR	LARGE	SEQUENCE
CHARACTER	LAST	SESSION
CLASS	LATERAL	SETS
CLOB	LEADING	SIZE
COLLATION	LESS	SMALLINT
COMPLETION	LEVEL	SPACE
CONNECT	LIMIT	SPECIFIC
CONNECTION	LOCAL	SPECIFICTYPE
CONSTRAINTS	LOCALTIME	SQL
CONSTRUCTOR	LOCALTIMESTAMP	SQLEXCEPTION
CORRESPONDING	LOCATOR	SQLSTATE
CUBE	MAP	SQLWARNING
CURRENT_PATH	MATCH	START
CURRENT_ROLE	MINUTE	STATE
CYCLE	MODIFIES	STATEMENT
DATA	MODIFY	STATIC
DATE	MODULE	STRUCTURE
DAY	MONTH	TEMPORARY
DEC	NAMES	TERMINATE
DECIMAL	NATURAL	THAN

Table continued on following page

DEFERRABLE	NCHAR	TIME
DEFERRED	NCLOB	TIMESTAMP
DEPTH	NEW	TIMEZONE_HOUR
DEREF	NEXT	TIMEZONE_MINUTE
DESCRIBE	NO	TRAILING
DESCRIPTOR	NONE	TRANSLATION
DESTROY	NUMERIC	TREAT
DESTRUCTOR	OBJECT	TRUE
DETERMINISTIC	OLD	UNDER
DICTIONARY	ONLY	UNKNOWN
DIAGNOSTICS	OPERATION	UNNEST
DISCONNECT	ORDINALITY	USAGE
DOMAIN	OUT	USING
DYNAMIC	OUTPUT	VALUE
EACH	PAD	VARCHAR
END-EXEC	PARAMETER	VARIABLE
EQUALS	PARAMETERS	WHENEVER
EVERY	PARTIAL	WITHOUT
EXCEPTION	PATH	WORK
EXTERNAL	POSTFIX	WRITE
FALSE	PREFIX	YEAR
FIRST	PREORDER	ZONE
FLOAT	PREPARE	

System Variables and Functions Reference

Variables and functions are often used interchangeably. SQL Server Books Online documents some variables as if they were functions. However it's important to note that variables return a value whereas functions process specific business logic and many functions accept input arguments. Optional arguments are denoted using square brackets.

System Global Variables

The system-supplied global variables are organized into these categories:

❑ Configuration

❑ Cursor

❑ System

❑ System Statistics

Configuration

Variable Name	Return Type	Description
@@DATEFIRST	TinyInt	Returns the system setting for the first day of the week. 1 = Monday, 2 = Tuesday, 3 = Wednesday, 4 = Thursday, 5 = Friday, 6 = Saturday, 7 = Sunday. U.S. default is 7.
@@DBTS	VarBinary	The last assigned unique TimeStamp value.
@@LANGID	SmallInt	The current language ID for the server. (US English = 0, German = 1, French = 2, and so on)

Table continued on following page

Variable Name	Return Type	Description
@@LANGUAGE	nVarChar	The current language string for the server. Returns the language name in the native language form (us_english, Deutsch, Français, Dansk, Español, Italiano, and so on).
@@LOCK_TIMEOUT	Int	Lock time-out setting for the current session in milliseconds.
@@MAX_CONNECTIONS	Int	The maximum concurrent connections setting for the server.
@@MAX_PRECISION	TinyInt	The maximum precision setting for decimal and numeric types. Default is 38 significant digits (total to the left and right of the decimal point).
@@MICROSOFTVERSION	Int	Returns an internal tracking number used by product development and support groups at Microsoft.
@@NESTLEVEL	Int	The current number of nested stored procedure or trigger calls. This may be used to limit cascading and/or recursive calls prior to reaching the system limit of 32 recursive calls.
@@OPTIONS	Int	The set of query-processing options for the current user session. Multiple options are combined mathematically using bitwise addition (that is, If SELECT @@OPTIONS & (512 + 8192) > 0 ...). Any combination of option values can be added to determine whether all these options are enabled. Option values: 1 = DISABLE_DEF_CNST_CHK 2 = IMPLICIT_TRANSACTIONS 4 = CURSOR_CLOSE_ON_COMMIT 8 = ANSI_WARNINGS 16 = ANSI_PADDING 32 = ANSI_NULLS 64 = ARITHABORT 128 = ARITHIGNORE 256 = QUOTED_IDENTIFIER 512 = NOCOUNT 1024 = ANSI_NULL_DFLT_ON

Variable Name	Return Type	Description
		2048 = ANSI_NULL_DFLT_OFF
		4096 = CONCAT_NULL_YIELDS_NULL
		8192 = NUMERIC_ROUNDABORT
		16384 = XACT_ABORT
@@REMSERVER	nVarChar	Name of the remote server if executing remote procedures.
@@SERVERNAME	nVarChar	Name of the current server.
@@SERVICENAME	nVarChar	Name of the Windows service for the current SQL Server instance.
'ID	Int	The process/session ID assigned to the current user's connection.
@@TEXTSIZE	Int	The current value of the TEXTSIZE option for a query returning data from a Text, nText, or Image type. The default setting is 4096 (4 K bytes).
@@VERSION	nVarChar	Returns a text string with detailed information about the current version of SQL Server. This includes the major version, build number, sevice pack, and copyright information.

Cursor

Variable Name	Return Type	Description
@@CURSOR_ROWS	Int	The row count for the currently open cursor. Used for explicit cursor processing following an OPEN command. If an asynchronous cursor is opened, the row count will not be known and this variable returns –1.
@@FETCH_STATUS	Int	Used as a flag to indicate whether the open cursor has navigated past the last row (EOF). Status values include:
		0 = Normal fetch operation
		–1 = Fetch past last row or unsuccessful
		–2 = Fetched row has been removed

System

Variable Name	Return Type	Description
@@ERROR	Int	Value of the most recent error within the current user session. Error numbers (from the sysmessages table) are used to determine the status of an error condition.
@@IDENTITY	Numeric	Value of the most recently generated identity value. This is typically the result of an identity column insert.
@@ROWCOUNT	Int	Number of rows affected by, or returned by, the last operation.
@@TRANCOUNT	Int	Number of currently active transactions. Used to determine the number of nested transactions. The maximum number of nested transactions is 11.

System Statistical

Variable Name	Return Type	Description
@@CONNECTIONS	Int	The total connects that have been opened or attempted since the SQL Server service was last started.
@@CPU_BUSY	Int	The total time in milliseconds that the server has not been idle since the SQL Server service was last started.
@@IDLE	Int	The total time in milliseconds that the server has been idle since the SQL Server service was last started.
@@IO_BUSY	Int	The total time in milliseconds that the server has performed physical disk I/O operations since the SQL Server service was last started.
@@PACK_RECEIVED	Int	The total number of network packets received by the server since the SQL Server service was last started.
@@PACK_SENT	Int	The total number of network packets sent by the server since the SQL Server service was last started.

Variable Name	Return Type	Description
@@PACKET_ERRORS	Int	The total number of network packet errors that have occurred since the SQL Server service was last started.
@@TIMETICKS	Int	The number of milliseconds per CPU tick. Each tick takes 1/32 of a second.
@@TOTAL_ERRORS	Int	The total number of disk read/write errors that have occurred, while performing physical disk I/O, since the SQL Server service was last started.
@@TOTAL_READ	Int	The total number of physical disk reads that have occurred since the SQL Server service was last started.
@@TOTAL_WRITE	Int	The total number of physical disk writes that have occurred since the SQL Server service was last started.

System Functions

The system functions are organized into these categories:

- ❏ Aggregation
- ❏ Checksum
- ❏ Conversion
- ❏ Cursor
- ❏ Date
- ❏ Image/Text
- ❏ Mathematical
- ❏ Metadata
- ❏ Ranking
- ❏ Security
- ❏ System
- ❏ System Statistics

Aggregation

Function Name	Return Type	Description
AVG()	(numeric — depends on input)	Calculates the arithmetic average for a range of column values. Internally, this function counts rows and calculates the sum for all non-null values in the column and then divides the sum by the count. Returns the same numeric data type as the column.
COUNT()	Int	Counts all non-null values for a column. The row count is returned using COUNT(*) regardless of null values.
COUNT_BIG()	BigInt	Same as COUNT() but returns a BigInt type rather than an Int type.
GROUPING()	Int	Used in conjunction with ROLLUP and CUBE operations in a GROUP BY query, this function returns 0 to indicate that it is on a detail row and 1 to indicate a summary row.
MAX()	(numeric or date — depends on input)	Returns the largest value in a range of column values.
MIN()	(numeric or date — depends on input)	Returns the smallest value in a range of column values.
STDEV()	Float	Calculates the standard deviation for a range of non-null column values.
STDEVP()	Float	Calculates the standard deviation over a population for a range of non-null column values.
SUM()	(numeric — depends on input)	Calculates the arithmetic sum for a range of non-null column values. If all values are NULL, returns NULL.
VAR()	Float	Calculates the statistical variance for a range of non-null column values. If all values are NULL, returns NULL.
VARP()	Float	Calculates the statistical variance over a population for a range of non-null column values. If all values are NULL, returns NULL.

Checksum

Function Name	Return Type	Description
CHECKSUM()	Int	Calculates a checksum value for a row or range of column values. This function accepts a single column name, a comma-delimited list of columns, or '*' to use the entire row. Accepts columns of all types except Text, nText, Image, Cursor, and Sql_Variant. The returned value itself is meaningless but will consistently yield the same result for a column or row unless a value changes. String comparisons are case-insensitive.
BINARY_CHECKSUM()	Int	Calculates a checksum value for a row or range of column values. This function accepts a single column name, a comma-delimited list of columns, or '*' to use the entire row. Accepts columns of all types except Text, nText, Image, Cursor, and Sql_Variant. The returned value itself is meaningless but will consistently yield the same result for a column or row unless a value changes. String comparisons are case-sensitive.
CHECKSUM_AGG()	Int	Calculates a single checksum value for a range of Int type column values. When applied to the result of the CHECKSUM() or BINARY_CHECKSUM() functions, returns a scalar (single value) checksum value for the entire range of values. Can be used to detect value changes over a table or range of column values.

Conversion

Function Name	Return Type	Description
CAST()	(returns a specified type)	Converts a value to a specified data type. CAST(*the_value* AS *the_type*)
CONVERT()	(returns a specified type)	Converts (and optionally formats) a value to a specified data type. Formatting can be applied to numeric and date types.
		CONVERT(the_type, the_value) or CONVERT(*the_type, the_value, format_number*)

Cursor

Function Name	Return Type	Description
CURSOR_STATUS()	SmallInt	Returns the status of a previously opened cursor. 1 = Open and populated, 0 = Contains no records, −1 = Closed −2 = no cursor or deallocated, −3 = Doesn't exist

Date

Function Name	Return Type	Description
DATEADD()	DateTime or SmallDateTime (depending on input type)	Returns a date value (DateTime or SmallDateTime) from a date value added by X number of date interval units. Units may be Year, Quarter, Month, DayOfYear, Day, Hour, Minute, Second, or Millisecond.
DATEDIFF()	Int	Returns an integer representing the difference between two date values (DateTime or SmallDateTime) in specified date interval units. Units may be Year, Quarter, Month, DayOfYear, Day, Hour, Minute, Second, or Millisecond.
DATENAME()	nVarChar	Similar to DATEPART(). Returns a character string representing the specified date part for a date value. Datepart parameter is the same as the DATEDIFF() interval and includes Year, Quarter, Month, DayOfYear, Day, Hour, Minute, Second, or Millisecond.
DATEPART()	Int	Similar to DATENAME(). Returns an integer representing the specified date part for a date value. Datepart parameter is the same as the DATEDIFF() interval and includes Year, Quarter, Month, DayOfYear, Day, Hour, Minute, Second, or Millisecond.
DAY()	Int	Returns the day date part for a date as an integer.
GETDATE()	DateTime	Returns the current date and time value.
GETUTCDATE()	DateTime	Returns the current date and time value, for the Universal Time Zone, based on the server's time zone settings. UTC is the same as Greenwich Mean Time (GMT).
MONTH()	Int	Returns the month part for a date as an integer.
YEAR()	Int	Returns the year part for a date as an integer.

Image/Text

Function Name	Return Type	Description
PATINDEX()	Int	Returns the character index (first position) for a character string pattern occurring within another character string. Similar to CHARINDEX() but supports wildcards.
TEXTPTR()	VarBinary	Returns a VarBinary text pointer handle to be used with the READTEXT(), WRITETEXT(), and UPDATETEXT() functions. Used for performing special operations on Text, nText, and Image type column data.
TEXTVALID()	Int	Used to verify a VarBinary text pointer value, obtained from the TEXTPTR() function.

Mathematical

Function Name	Return Type	Description
ABS()	(numeric — same type as input)	Returns the absolute value for a numeric value.
ACOS()	Float	Computes the arccosine (an angle) in radians.
ASIN()	Float	Computes the arcsine (an angle) in radians.
ATAN()	Float	Computes the arctangent (an angle) in radians.
ATN2()	Float	Computes the arctangent of two values in radians.
CEILING()	(numeric — same type as input)	Returns the smallest integer value that is greater than or equal to a number.
COS()	Float	Computes the cosine of an angle in radians.
COT()	Float	Computes the cotangent of an angle in radians.
DEGREES()	(numeric — same type as input)	Converts an angle from radians to degrees.
EXP()	Float	Returns the natural logarithm raised to a specified exponent. Result is in exponential form.
FLOOR()	(numeric — same type as input)	Returns the largest integer value that is less than or equal to a number.
LOG()	Float	Calculates the natural logarithm of a number using base-2 (binary) numbering.
LOG10()	Float	Calculates the natural logarithm of a number using base-10 numbering.

Table continued on following page

Function Name	Return Type	Description
PI()	Float	Returns the value for PI.
POWER()	Float	Raises a value to a specified exponent as FLOAT(the_value, the_exponent).
RADIANS()	(numeric — same type as input)	Converts an angle from degrees to radians.
RAND()	Float	Returns a fractional number based on a randomizing algorithm. Accepts an optional seed value.
ROUND()	(numeric — same type as input)	Rounds a fractional value to a specified precision.
SIGN()	Float	Returns –1 or 1 depending on whether a single argument value is negative or positive.
SIN()	Float	Computes the sine of an angle in radians.
SQRT()	Float	Returns the square root of a value.
SQUARE()	Float	Returns the square (n^2) of a value.
TAN()	Float	Computes the tangent of an angle in radians.

Metadata

Function Name	Return Type	Description
COL_LENGTH()	Int	Returns the length of a column from the column name.
COL_NAME()	sysname (nVarChar)	Returns the name of a column from the object ID.
COLUMNPROPERTY()	Int	Returns a flag to indicate the state of a column property.
DATABASEPROPERTY()	Int	This function is maintained for backward compatibility with older SWL Server versions. Returns a flag to indicate the state of a database property.
DATABASEPROPERTYEX()	SqlVariant	Returns a numeric flag or string to indicate the state of a database property.
DB_ID()	SmallInt	Returns the database ID from the database name.
DB_NAME()	nVarChar	Returns the database name from the database ID.
FILE_ID()	SmallInt	Returns the file ID from the file name.
FILE_NAME()	nVarChar	Returns the file name from the file ID.

Function Name	Return Type	Description
fn_listextendedproperty()	Table	Returns a table object populated with extended property names and their settings.
FULLTEXTCATALOGPROPERTY()	Int	Returns a flag to indicate the state of a full-text catalog property.
FULLTEXTSERVICEPROPERTY()	Int	Returns a flag to indicate the state of a full-text service property.
INDEX_COL()	nVarChar	Returns the name of a column contained in a specified index, by table, index, and column ID.
INDEXKEY_PROPERTY()	Int	Returns a flag to indicate the state of an index key property.
INDEXPROPERTY()	Int	Returns a flag indicating the state of an index property.
OBJECT_ID()	Int	Returns an object ID from the object name.
OBJECT_NAME()	nChar	Returns an object name from the object ID.
OBJECTPROPERTY()	Int	This function allows you to get property information from several different types of objects. It is advisable to use a function designed to query specific object types, if possible. Returns a flag indicating the state of an object property.

Ranking (SQL Server 2005)

Function Name	Return Type	Description
DENSE_RANK()	Int	Returns a running incremental value based on an ORDER BY clause passed into the function. Doesn't preserve the ordinal position of the row in the list if there are ties.
NTILE(n)	Int	Returns an evenly distributed ranking value, dividing the result into a finite number of ranked groups.
RANK()	Int	Returns a running incremental value based on an ORDER BY clause passed into the function. Preserves the ordinal position of the row in the list with duplicate values for ties followed by subsequent skips.
ROW_NUMBER()	Int	Returns a running incremental value based on an ORDER BY clause passed into the function.

Security

Function Name	Return Type	Description
fn_trace_geteventinfo()	Table	Returns a table type populated with event information for a specified trace ID.
fn_trace_getfilterinfo()	Table	Returns a table type populated with information about filters applied to a trace, for a specified trace ID.
fn_trace_getinfo()	Table	Returns a table type populated with trace information for a specified trace ID.
fn_trace_gettable()	Table	Returns a table type populated with file information for a specified trace ID.
HAS_DBACCESS()	Int	Returns a flag indicating whether the current user has access to a specified database.
IS_MEMBER()	Int	Returns a flag indicating whether the current user is a member of a Windows group or SQL Server role.
IS_SRVROLEMEMBER()	Int	Returns a flag indicating whether the current user is a member of a database server role.
SUSER_SID()	VarBinary	Returns the security ID for a specified username.
SUSER_SNAME()	nVarChar	Returns the username for a specified security ID.
USER_ID()	SmallInt	Returns a username for a specified user ID.
fn_trace_geteventinfo()	Table	Returns a table type populated with event information for a specified trace ID.

String Manipulation

Function Name	Return Type	Description
ASCII()	Int	Returns the numeric ASCII character value for a standard character.
CHAR()	Char	Returns the ASCII character for a numeric ASCII character value.
CHARINDEX()	Int	Similar to PATINDEX(), returns the index (character position) of the first occurrence of a character string within another character string.
DIFFERENCE()	Int	Returns the numeric difference between two character strings based on the consensus Soundex values.
LEFT()	VarChar	Returns the left-most X characters from a character string.
LEN()	Int	Returns the length of a character string.
LOWER()	VarChar	Converts a character string to all lowercase characters.

Function Name	Return Type	Description
LTRIM()	VarChar	Removes leading spaces from the left side of a character string.
NCHAR()	nChar	Like the CHAR() function, returns the Unicode character for a numeric character value.
PATINDEX()	Int	Returns the index (first character position) for the first occurrence of characters matching a specified pattern within another character string. Wildcard characters may be used.
QUOTENAME()	nVarChar	Returns a character string with square brackets around the input value. Used with SQL Server object names so they can be passed into an expression.
REPLACE()	(character or binary types—depending on input)	Returns a character string with all occurrences of one character or substring replaced with another character or substring.
REPLICATE()	VarChar	Returns a character string consisting of a specified number of repeated characters.
REVERSE()	VarChar	Returns a character string with all characters in reverse order.
RIGHT()	VarChar	Returns a specific number of characters from the right-most side of a character string.
RTRIM()	VarChar	Removes trailing spaces from the right side of a character string.
SOUNDEX()	Char	Returns a four-character alphanumeric string representing the approximate phonetic value of a word, based on the U.S. Census Soundex algorithm.
SPACE()	Char	Returns a character string consisting of a specified number of spaces.
STR()	Char	Returns a character string value that represents a converted numeric data type. Three arguments include the value, the overall length, and the number of decimal positions.
STUFF()	(character or binary types—depending on input)	Returns a character string with one string placed into another string at a given position and for a specified length.
SUBSTRING()	(character or binary types—depending on input)	Returns a portion of a character string from a specified position and for a specified length.
UNICODE()	Int	Returns the numeric Unicode character value for a specified character.
UPPER()	VarChar	Converts a character string to all uppercase characters.

System

Function Name	Return Type	Description
APP_NAME()	nVarChar	Each session is associated with an application name, passed to the database server by explicit program code or by the driver or data provider.
COALESCE()	(same type as input)	Returns the first non-null value from a comma-delimited list of expressions.
COLLATIONPROPERTY()	Sql_Variant	Returns the value of a specific property for a specified collation. Properties include CodePage, LCID, and ComparisonStyle.
CURRENT_TIMESTAMP()	DateTime	Returns the current date and time and is synonymous with the GETDATE() function. It exists for ANSI-SQL compliance.
CURRENT_USER()	Sysname (VarChar)	Returns the name of the current user and is synonymous with the USER_NAME() function.
DATALENGTH()	Int	Returns the number of bytes used to store or handle a value. For ANSI string types, this will return the same value as the LEN() function, but for other data types, the value may be different.
ENCRYPT()	VarChar	Returns a hexadecimal value as a character string from a character string value. The result is a one-way encrypted value. This value can be read by the database engine (in the case of an object script definition) but cannot be decrypted.
fn_Get_SQL()	Table	Returns a table populated with the full text of a query based on a process handle. This value is stored in the sysprocesses table referencing a SPID. This function was introduced with SQL Server 2000 SP3.
fn_HelpCollations()	Table	Returns a table type populated with a list of collations supported by the current version of SQL Server.
fn_ServerSharedDrives()	Table	Returns a table type populated with a list of drives shared by the server.
fn_VirtualFileStats()	Table	Returns a table type populated with I/O statistics for database files, including log files.
FORMATMESSAGE()	nVarChar	Returns an error message from the sysmessages table for a specified message number and comma-delimited list of parameters.
GETANSINULL()	Int	Returns the nullability setting for the database, according to the ANSI_NULL_DFLT_ON and ANSI_NULL_DFLT_OFF database settings.

Function Name	Return Type	Description
HOST_ID()	Char	Returns the workstation ID for the current session.
HOST_NAME()	nChar	Returns the workstation name for the current session.
IDENT_CURRENT()	Sql_Variant	Returns the last identity value generated for a specified table regardless of the session and scope.
IDENT_INCR()	Numeric	Returns the increment value specified in the creation of the last identity column.
IDENT_SEED()	Numeric	Returns the seed value specified in the creation of the last identity column.
IDENTITY()	(same as input)	Used in a SELECT. . . INTO statement to insert an explicitly generated identity value into a column.
ISDATE()	Int	Returns a flag to indicate whether a specified value is, or is capable of being converted to, a date value.
ISNULL()	(same as input)	Determines whether a specified value is null and then returns a provided replacement value.
ISNUMERIC()	Int	Returns a flag to indicate whether a specified value is, or is capable of being converted to, a numeric value.
NEWID()	UniqueIdentifier	Returns a newly generated UniqueIdentifier type value. This is a 128-bit integer, globally unique value, usually expressed as an alphanumeric hexadecimal representation (such as 89DE6247-C2E2-42DB-8CE8-A787E505D7EA). This type is often used for primary key values in replicated and semi-connected systems.
NULLIF()	(same as input)	Returns a NULL value when two specified arguments have equivalent values.
PARSENAME()	nChar	Returns a specific part of a four-part object name.
PERMISSIONS()	Int	Returns an integer whose value is a bit-wise map indicating the permission or combination of permissions for the current user on a specified database object.
PWDCONPARE()	Int	Compares an encrypted value with an unencrypted character string value. May be used to compare the encrypted and unencrypted forms of a password to determine whether they match. Returns 1 for a match and 0 for no match.

Table continued on following page

Function Name	Return Type	Description
PWDENCRYPT()	VarChar	Returns the encrypted form of a character string in hexadecimal form. May be used to encrypt a password for storage. This value cannot be decrypted using SQL Server tools or Transact-SQL commands.
ROWCOUNT_BIG()	BigInt	Like the @@ROWCOUNT variable, returns the number of rows either returned by or modified by the last statement. Returns a BigInt type.
SCOPE_IDENTITY()	Sql_Variant	Like the @@IDENTITY variable, this function returns the last Identity value generated but is limited to the current session and scope (stored procedure, batch, or module).
SERVERPROPERTY()	Sql_Variant	Returns a flag indicating the state of a server property. Properties include Collation, Edition, Engine Edition, InstanceName, IsClustered, IsFullTextInstalled, IsIntegratedSecurityOnly, IsSingleUser, IsSyncWithBackup, LicenseType, MachineName, NumLicenses, ProcessID, ProductLevel, ProductVersion, and ServerName.
SESSION_USER	nChar	Returns the current username. Function is called without parentheses.
SESSIONPROPERTY()	Sql_Variant	Returns a flag indicating the state of a session property. Properties include ANSI_NULLS, ANSI_PADDING, ANSI_WARNINGS, ARITHABORT, CONCAT_NULL_YIELDS_NULL, NUMERIC_ROUNDABORT, and QUOTED_IDENTIFIER.
STATS_DATE()	DateTime	Returns the date that statistics for a specified index were last updated.
SYSTEM_USER	nVarChar	Returns the current username. Function is called without parentheses.
USER_NAME()	nVarChar	Returns the username for a specified User ID.

System Statistical

Function Name	Return Type	Description
fn_virtualfilestats	Table	Returns a table type populated with I/O statistics for database files, including log files.

System Stored Procedure Reference

SQL Server 2000 and 2005 support the following system and extended stored procedures. Procedures introduced with SQL Server 2005 are so indicated.

Active Directory

Procedure Name	Return Type	Description
sp_ActiveDirectory_Obj	Int	Adds, updates, or removes the registration record of a SQL Server database in the Active Directory.
sp_ActiveDirectory_SCP	Int	Adds, updates, or removes the registration record of a SQL Server instance in the Active Directory.

Catalog

Procedure Name	Return Type	Description
sp_column_privileges	Table	Returns column privileges for a table in the current session.
sp_column_privileges_ex	Table	Returns column privileges for a table on a linked or remote server.
sp_columns	Table	Returns column information for a table or view.
sp_columns_ex	Table	Returns column information for a table or view on a linked or remote server.

Table continued on following page

Procedure Name	Return Type	Description
sp_databases	Table	Returns information about databases on the local server.
sp_fkeys	Table	Returns foreign key information for a table.
sp_pkeys	Table	Returns primary key information for a table.
sp_server_info	Table	Returns server attributes for the server on a specified connection.
sp_special_columns	Table	Returns columns used to uniquely identify a row (that is, primary key and unique constraints) and columns with programmatically updated values and defaults.
sp_sproc_columns	Table	Returns column information for a stored procedure or user-defined function.
sp_statistics	Table	Returns information about indexes and statistics for a table.
sp_stored_procedures	Table	Returns information about all stored procedures matching a name or wildcard pattern.
sp_table_privileges	Table	Returns information about permissions for a table or tables matching a wildcard pattern in the current session.
sp_table_privileges_ex	Table	Returns information about permissions for a table or tables matching a wildcard pattern on a linked or remote server.
sp_tables	Table	Returns information about all tables matching a name or wildcard pattern.

Cursor Management

Procedure Name	Return Type	Description
sp_cursor_list	Cursor	Returns attributes and information about currently open cursor(s).
sp_describe_cursor	Cursor	Returns attributes and information about a specific cursor.
sp_describe_cursor_columns	Cursor	Returns information about columns used to populate a cursor.
sp_describe_cursor_tables	Cursor	Returns information about tables used to populate a cursor.

Database Engine

Procedure Name	Return Type	Description
sp_add_data_file_recover_suspect_db	Int	Adds a database file to a file group after a disk full error. Similar to ALTER DATABASE ADD FILE.
sp_add_log_file_recover_suspect_db	Int	Adds a transaction log file to a file group after a disk full error. Similar to ALTER DATABASE ADD LOG FILE.
sp_addextendedproc	Int	Adds and registers an extended stored procedure to the server meta data.
sp_addextendedproperty	Int	Adds an extended property to the server metadata.
sp_addmessage	Int	Adds a custom error message to the server messages meta data.
sp_addtype	Int	Adds a user-defined data type to a database.
sp_addumpdevice	Int	Adds a backup device (file, tape drive, or other device) to the server.
sp_altermessage	Int	Modifies an existing error message (number, severity, category, or message text).
sp_attach_db	Int	Attaches a database file to a SQL Server instance and makes it available as an active database.
sp_attach_single_file_db	Int	Similar to sp_attach_db but only for single-file databases. Builds new transaction log file.
sp_autostats	Int	Returns or modifies the UPDATE STATISTICS setting for a table's index or statistics in the current database.
sp_bindefault	Int	Associates a defined default with a table's column as a shared default.
sp_bindrule	Int	Associates a defined rule with a table's column as a default check constraint.
sp_bindsession	Int	Allows multiple connections to participate in a single transaction by associating them to an established session.
sp_certify_removable	Int	Verifies (certifies) that a database may be actively used on removable media.
sp_configure	Int	Returns or modifies server configuration settings.

Table continued on following page

Procedure Name	Return Type	Description
sp_create_removable	Int	Creates a set of files and a new database to be used on removable media.
sp_createstats	Int	Generates statistics for all tables and candidate columns in the current database.
sp_cycle_errorlog	(none)	Closes the current error log and initiates a new error log with a default name and settings (as if for a server restart).
sp_datatype_info	Table	Returns detailed information about all current data types or information for a specific data type (system and user-defined data types).
sp_dbcmptlevel	Int	Sets the SQL Server version database compatibility level. Setting the level to an older version number disables certain product features to emulate the capabilities of an older SQL Server version.
sp_dboption	Int & Table	Sets user database options similar to those set using ALTER DATABASE.
sp_dbremove	Int	Removes a database and associated files.
sp_delete_backuphistory	Int	Removes backup history information for a database.
sp_depends	Int & Table	Lists the dependent objects for a database object.
sp_detach_db	Int	Detaches a database's file(s) from the server.
sp_dropdevice	Int	Removes a database or backup device record from the server.
sp_dropextendedproc	Int	Drops an extended stored procedure from the server.
sp_dropextendedproperty	Int	Drops an extended property from the server.
sp_dropmessage	Int	Removes an error message record from the server.
sp_droptype	Int	Removes a user-defined data type from the server.
sp_executesql	Int	Executes a parameterized Transact-SQL statement.
sp_getapplock	Int	Places a lock on an application or system resource outside of SQL Server for the duration of a transaction or session.

Procedure Name	Return Type	Description
sp_getbindtoken	(none)	Uses a VarChar type output parameter to return a unique ID for a transaction.
sp_help	Int & Table	Returns descriptive help information specific to a database object.
sp_helpconstraint	Int & Table	Returns help information for a specified constraint.
sp_helpdb	Int & Table	Returns help information for a specified database.
sp_helpdevice	Int & Table	Returns help information for a specified device.
sp_helpextendedproc	Int & Table	Returns help information for a specified extended stored procedure.
sp_helpfile	Int & Table	Returns help information for a specified database file.
sp_helpfilegroup	Int & Table	Returns help information for a specified database file group.
sp_helpindex	Int & Table	Returns help information for a specified index.
sp_helplanguage	Int & Table	Returns help information for a specified server language.
sp_helpserver	Int & Table	Returns help information for a specified server (local or remote).
sp_helpsort	Int & Table	Returns a description of the server's collation and sort order.
sp_helpstats	Int & Table	Returns help information regarding the statistics associated with the indexes for a specified table.
sp_helptext	Int & Table	Returns the definition of a rule, default, stored procedure, user-defined function, trigger, or view.
sp_helptrigger	Int & Table	Returns information about the triggers associated with a specified table.
sp_indexoption	Int	Allows default level-locking options (that is, row, page, table) to be overridden for a specified index.
sp_invalidate_textptr	Int	Invalidates a specified in-row text pointer, or all in-row text pointers in a transaction.

Table continued on following page

Procedure Name	Return Type	Description
sp_lock	Int & Table	Returns information about all active locks.
sp_monitor	Int & Table	Returns the results from several system functions to show the status of server and system resources.
sp_procoption	(none - uses error codes)	Enables one of several procedure options to be set.
sp_recompile	Int	Recompiles a stored procedure or trigger.
sp_refreshview	Int	Updates the metadata for a specified view.
sp_releaseapplock	Int	Removes a lock set on an application or external system resource that may have been set using sp_getapplock.
sp_rename	Int	Renames a database object.
sp_renamedb	Int	Renames a database.
sp_resetstatus	Int	Resets the suspect status of a database back to normal status.
sp_serveroption	Int	Sets specified server options for a remote and linked server.
sp_setnetname	Int	Sets the network name for a linked or remote server.
sp_settriggerorder	Int	Sets a specified trigger for a table to execute first or last.
sp_spaceused	Int & Table	Returns information about the disk space used by rows, table, and a database.
sp_tableoption	Int	Sets one of several table options.
sp_unbindefault	Int	Removes a specified default from a column or user-defined data type.
sp_unbindrule	Int	Removes a specified rule from a column or user-defined data type.
sp_updateextendedproperty	Int	Updates the value of a specified extended property.
sp_updatestats	Int	Updates all index statistics in the database.
sp_validname	Int	Checks a specified character string for validity as an object name. If invalid, raises an option error.
sp_who	Int	Returns information about current connections and user sessions on a server.

Database Maintenance

Procedure Name	Return Type	Description
sp_add_maintenance_plan	Int	Adds a maintenance plan to the server and returns the plan ID.
sp_add_maintenance_plan_db	Int	Associates a database with a maintenance plan. (A maintenance plan is added using sp_add_maintenance_plan.)
sp_add_maintenance_plan_job	Int	Associates a maintenance plan with an existing job.
sp_delete_maintenance_plan	Int	Deletes a maintenance plan based in the specified plan ID.
sp_delete_maintenance_plan_db	Int	Removes an associated maintenance plan from the specified database.
sp_delete_maintenance_plan_job	Int	Removes an associated maintenance plan from the specified job.
sp_help_maintenance_plan	Int & Table	Returns information about maintenance plans on the server.

Distributed Queries

Procedure Name	Return Types	Description
sp_addlinkedserver	Int	Adds a linked server to the current server, allowing persistent access to a remote SQL Server from the current server.
sp_addlinkedsrvlogin	Int	Adds the association of a local login to a linked server login for user connectivity to a linked server.
sp_catalogs	Table	Returns the list of databases on a linked server.
sp_column_privileges_ex	Table	Returns column-level security access privilege information for a specified table on a linked server.
sp_columns_ex	Table	Returns column information for a table or view on a linked server.
sp_droplinkedsrvlogin	Int	Removes the association of a local login to the login on a linked server.
sp_foreignkeys	Table	Returns information about foreign key columns related to a specified primary key for tables on a linked server.

Table continued on following page

Procedure Name	Return Types	Description
sp_indexes	Table	Returns index information for a remote or linked server table.
sp_linkedservers	Table	Returns information about all linked servers.
sp_primarykeys	Table	Returns information about primary key columns for a specified remote or linked server table.
sp_serveroption	Int	Sets server options for remote servers and linked servers.
sp_table_privileges_ex	Table	Returns information about column and table-level security privileges for a specified remote or linked table.
sp_tables_ex	Table	Returns information about tables on a remote or linked server.

External Systems and Extended Procedures

Procedure Name	Return Types	Description
xp_cmdshell	Int	Executes an operating system shell command, as if entered at the command prompt on the server.
xp_enumgroups	Int & Table	Returns information about Windows domain groups.
xp_findnextmsg	Int	Uses an output parameter to return a MAPI message ID from the SQL Server Inbox.
xp_grantlogin	Int	Calls sp_grantlogin for backward compatibility. Creates a SQL Server login for an associated Windows user or group.
xp_logevent	Int	Logs a message to the SQL Server log file without raising a SQL Server error.
xp_loginconfig	Int & Table	Returns SQL Server security configuration information.
xp_logininfo	Int & Table	Returns detailed information about a SQL Server login and related privileges.
xp_msver	Table	Returns detailed information about the instance of SQL Server and the operating system environment.
xp_revokelogin	Int	Calls sp_revokelogin for backward compatibility. Revokes permissions of a SQL Server login.

Procedure Name	Return Types	Description
xp_sprintf	Int	Uses an output parameter to return a character string. Used to assemble a character string from parameterized values.
xp_sqlmaint	(none)	Calls the SQLMAIN command-line tool to set SQL Server maintenance options.
xp_sscanf	Int	Uses an output parameter to return a character string. Used to dissassemble a character string into corresponding parameterized values. This is the converse of the xp_sprintf procedure.

Full-Text Index/Search

Procedure Name	Return Types	Description
sp_fulltext_catalog	Int	Creates or maintains a full-text catalog to be used to store and maintain full-text indexes.
sp_fulltext_column	Int	Indicates whether a specified column should be included in a full-text index.
sp_fulltext_database	Int	Enables or disables full-text indexing for a database.
sp_fulltext_service	Int	Used to manage full-text indexing services on a server.
sp_fulltext_table	Int	Manages and enables actions for full-text indexing on a specific table.
sp_help_fulltext_catalogs	Int & Table	Returns information about the tables and attributes for a full-text catalog.
sp_help_fulltext_catalogs_cursor	Int & Table	Returns information about the tables and attributes for a full-text catalog.
sp_help_fulltext_columns	Int & Table	Returns information about the columns contained in a full-text index for a table.
sp_help_fulltext_columns_cursor	Int & Cursor	Returns information about the columns contained in a full-text index for a table.
sp_help_fulltext_tables	Int & Table	Returns information about the tables contained in a full-text catalog.
sp_help_fulltext_tables_cursor	Int & Cursor	Returns information about the tables contained in a full-text catalog.

Log Shipping

Procedures added in SQL Server 2005.

Procedure Name	Return Type
sp_add_log_shipping_alert_job	Int
sp_add_log_shipping_primary_database	Int
sp_add_log_shipping_primary_secondary	Int
sp_add_log_shipping_secondary_database	Int
sp_add_log_shipping_secondary_primary	Int
sp_change_log_shipping_primary_database	Int
sp_change_log_shipping_secondary_database	Int
sp_change_log_shipping_secondary_primary	Int
sp_cleanup_log_shipping_history	Int
sp_delete_log_shipping_alert_job	Int
sp_delete_log_shipping_primary_database	Int
sp_delete_log_shipping_primary_secondary	Int
sp_delete_log_shipping_secondary_database	Int
sp_delete_log_shipping_secondary_primary	Int
sp_help_log_shipping_alert_job	Table
sp_help_log_shipping_monitor_primary	Table
sp_help_log_shipping_monitor_secondary	Table
sp_help_log_shipping_primary_database	Table
sp_help_log_shipping_primary_secondary	Table
sp_help_log_shipping_secondary_database	Table
sp_help_log_shipping_secondary_primary	Table
sp_refresh_log_shipping_monitor	Int
sp_resolve_logins	Int

Mail

The xp_readmail and xp_sendmail procedures are valid in SQL Server 2000. All others procedures are new in SQL Server 2005.

Procedure Name	Return Type	
sp_send_dbmail	Int	
sysmail_add_account_sp	Int	
sysmail_add_principalprofile_sp	Int	
sysmail_add_profile_sp	Int	
sysmail_add_profileaccount_sp	Int	
sysmail_configure_sp	Int	
sysmail_delete_account_sp	Int	
sysmail_delete_principalprofile_sp	Int	
sysmail_delete_profile_sp	Int	
sysmail_delete_profileaccount_sp	Int	
sysmail_help_account_sp	Table	
sysmail_help_configure_sp	Table	
sysmail_help_principalprofile_sp	Table	
sysmail_help_profile_sp	Table	
sysmail_help_profileaccount_sp	Table	
sysmail_start_sp	Int	
sysmail_stop_sp	Int	
sysmail_update_account_sp	Int	
sysmail_update_principalprofile_sp	Int	
sysmail_update_profile_sp	Int	
sysmail_update_profileaccount_sp	Int	
xp_readmail	Int & Table	
Xp_sendmail	Int	

Notification Services

Procedures added in SQL Server 2005.

Procedure Name	Return Type	
NSAdministrationHistory	Table	
NSDiagnosticDeliveryChannel	Table	
NSDiagnosticEventClass	Table	

Table continued on following page

Procedure Name	Return Type
NSDiagnosticEventProvider	Table
NSDiagnosticFailedNotifications	Table
NSDiagnosticNotificationClass	Table
NSDiagnosticSubscriptionClass	Table
NSEventBatchDetails	Table
NSEventBeginBatch	Table
NSEventFlushBatch	Table
NSEventSubmitBatch	Table
NSEventWrite	Int
NSExecuteRuleFiring	Table
NSNotificationBatchDetails	Table
NSPrepareRuleFiring	Table
NSQuantumDetails	Table
NSQuantumExecutionTime	Table
NSQuantumFailures	Table
NSQuantumList	Table
NSQuantumPerformance	Table
NSQuantumsSkipped	Table
NSScheduledSubscriptionDetails	Table
NSScheduledSubscriptionList	Table
NSSetQuantumClock	Int
NSSetQuantumClockDate	Int
NSSnapshotApplications	Int
NSSnapshotDeliveryChannels	Table
NSSnapshotEvents	Table
NSSnapshotProviders	Table
NSSnapshotSubscriptions	Table
NSVacuum	Table

OLE Automation

Using these OLE automation stored procedures, it's possible to execute certain application code from SQL queries to perform actions and automate applications outside of SQL Server. Using custom-created COM components; practically any programmatic interaction is possible.

Procedure Name	Return Type	Description
sp_OACreate	Int	Instantiates an OLE object from a specified class using either the ProgID or CLSID. If stopped, starts the OLE automation execution process on the server.
sp_OADestroy	Int	Destroys a previously instantiated OLE object.
sp_OAGetErrorInfo	Int & Table	Returns the error information associated with an OLE object instance and actions.
sp_OAGetProperty	Int & Table	Uses either an output parameter or a result set to return the value(s) or structured information for a specified object property.
sp_OAMethod	Int & Table	Calls a method of an OLE object. Uses either an output parameter or a result set to return the value(s) or structured information returned by the method call.
sp_OASetProperty	Int	Sets an object property to a specified value.
sp_OAStop	Int	Stops the OLE automation execution process environment on the server. Immediately terminates all OLE automation activity for all sessions.

Profiler

Procedure Name	Return Type	Description
sp_trace_create	Int	Creates a new Profiler trace.
sp_trace_generateevent	Int	Creates a new Profiler event.
sp_trace_setevent	Int	Adds an existing event to a trace. These items may be created using the sp_trace_create and sp_trace_generateevent procedures.
sp_trace_setfilter	Int	Adds a filter to an existing trace.
sp_trace_setstatus	Int	Modifies an existing trace.

Replication

Procedure Name	Return Type
sp_add_agent_parameter	Int
sp_add_agent_profile	Int
sp_addarticle	Int
sp_adddistpublisher	Int
sp_adddistributiondb	Int
sp_adddistributor	Int
sp_addmergealternatepublisher	Int
sp_addmergearticle	Int
sp_addmergefilter	Int
sp_addmergepublication	Int
sp_addmergepullsubscription	Int
sp_addmergepullsubscription_agent	Int
sp_addmergesubscription	Int
sp_addpublication	Int
sp_addpublication_snapshot	Int
sp_addpublisher70	Int
sp_addpullsubscription	Int
sp_addpullsubscription_agent	Int
sp_addscriptexec	Int
sp_addsubscriber	Int
sp_addsubscriber_schedule	Int
sp_addsubscription	Int
sp_addsynctriggers	Int
sp_addtabletocontents	Int
sp_adjustpublisheridentityrange	Int
sp_article_validation	Int
sp_articlecolumn	Int
sp_articlefilter	Int
sp_articlesynctranprocs	Int
sp_articleview	Int

Procedure Name	Return Type	
sp_attachsubscription	Int	
sp_browsemergesnapshotfolder	Table	
sp_browsereplcmds	Table	
sp_browsesnapshotfolder	Table	
sp_change_agent_parameter	Int	
sp_change_agent_profile	Int	
sp_change_subscription_properties	Int	
sp_changearticle	Int	
sp_changedistpublisher	Int	
sp_changedistributiondb	Int	
sp_changedistributor_password	Int	
sp_changedistributor_property	Int	
sp_changemergearticle	Int	
sp_changemergefilter	Int	
sp_changemergepublication	Int	
sp_changemergepullsubscription	Int	
sp_changemergesubscription	Int	
sp_changepublication	Int	
sp_changesubscriber	Int	
sp_changesubscriber_schedule	Int	
sp_changesubscriptiondtsinfo	Int	
sp_changesubscriptiondtsinfo	Int	
sp_changesubstatus	Int	
sp_check_for_sync_trigger	Int	
sp_copymergesnapshot	Int	
sp_copysnapshot	Int	
sp_copysubscription	Int	
sp_deletemergeconflictrow	Int	
sp_disableagentoffload	Int	
sp_drop_agent_parameter	Int	

Table continued on following page

Procedure Name	Return Type
sp_drop_agent_profile	Int
sp_dropanonymouseagent	Int
sp_droparticle	Int
sp_dropdistpublisher	Int
sp_dropdistributiondb	Int
sp_dropdistributor	Int
sp_dropmergealternatepublisher	Int
sp_dropmergearticle	Int
sp_dropmergefilter	Int
sp_dropmergepublication	Int
sp_dropmergepullsubscription	Int
sp_dropmergesubscription	Int
sp_droppublication	Int
sp_droppullsubscription	Int
sp_dropsubscriber	Int
sp_dropsubscription	Int
sp_dsninfo	Int & Table
sp_dumpparamcmd	Int
sp_enableagentoffload	Int
sp_enumcustomresolvers	Int & Table
sp_enumdsn	Int & Table
sp_enumfullsubscribers	Int & Table
sp_expired_subscription_cleanup	Int
sp_generatefilters	Int
sp_get_distributor	Int
sp_getagentoffloadinfo	Int & Table
sp_getmergedeletetype	Int
sp_getqueuedrows	Int
sp_getsubscriptiondtspackagename	Int
sp_grant_publication_access	Int
sp_help_agent_default	Table

Procedure Name	Return Type	
sp_help_agent_parameter	Table	
sp_help_agent_profile	Table	
sp_help_publication_access	Table	
sp_helparticle	Table	
sp_helparticlecolumns	Table	
sp_helparticledts	Table	
sp_helpdistpublisher	Table	
sp_helpdistributiondb	Table	
sp_helpdistributor	Table	
sp_helpmergealternatepublisher	Table	
sp_helpmergealternatepublisher	Table	
sp_helpmergearticle	Table	
sp_helpmergearticlecolumn	Table	
sp_helpmergearticleconflicts	Table	
sp_helpmergeconflictrows	Table	
sp_helpmergedeleteconflictrows	Table	
sp_helpmergefilter	Table	
sp_helpmergepublication	Table	
sp_helpmergepullsubscription	Table	
sp_helpmergesubscription	Table	
sp_helppublication	Table	
sp_helppullsubscription	Table	
sp_helpreplfailovermode	Table	
sp_helpreplicationdboption	Table	
sp_helpreplicationoption	Table	
sp_helpsubscriberinfo	Table	
sp_helpsubscription	Table	
sp_helpsubscription_properties	Table	
sp_ivindexhasnullcols	Int	
sp_link_publication	Int	

Table continued on following page

Procedure Name	Return Type
sp_marksubscriptionvalidation	Int
sp_mergearticlecolumn	Int
sp_mergecleanupmetadata	Int
sp_mergedummyupdate	Int
sp_mergesubscription_cleanup	Int
sp_publication_validation	Int
sp_refreshsubscriptions	Int
sp_reinitmergepullsubscription	Int
sp_reinitmergesubscription	Int
sp_reinitpullsubscription	Int
sp_reinitsubscription	Int
sp_removedbreplication	Int
sp_repladdcolumn	Int
sp_replcmds	Table
sp_replcounters	Table
sp_repldone	Int
sp_repldropcolumn	Int
sp_replflush	Int
sp_replication_agent_checkup	Int
sp_replicationdboption	Int
sp_replqueuemonitor	Int
sp_replsetoriginator	Int
sp_replshowcmds	Table
sp_repltrans	Table
sp_restoredbreplication	(none)
sp_resyncmergesubscription	Int
sp_revoke_publication_access	Int
sp_script_synctran_commands	Int & Table
sp_setreplfailovermode	Int
sp_showrowreplicainfo	Table
sp_subscription_cleanup	Int

Procedure Name	Return Type	
sp_table_validation	Int	
sp_update_agent_profile	Int	
sp_validatemergepublication	Int	
sp_validatemergesubscription	Int	
sp_vupgrade_replication	Int	

Security

Procedure Name	Return Type	Description
sp_addalias	Int	Matches a server login to a database user. This is an older alternative to using role-based security.
sp_addapprole	Int	Adds an application role to a database to be used for programmatic access from an application component.
sp_addgroup	Int	Adds a user group to a database. This is an older alternative to using role-based security.
sp_addlinkedsrvlogin	Int	Matches a local server login to a linked server login for access to a remote database server.
sp_addlogin	Int	Adds a new server login.
sp_addremotelogin	Int	Adds a login to the local server for use by remote users.
sp_addrole	Int	Adds a new database role.
sp_addrolemember	Int	Adds a SQL Server user, role, Windows user, or group to a SQL Server role.
sp_addserver	Int	Obsolete. Similar to sp_addlinkedserver, adds the metadata representing a registered linked server with persistent access from the local server.
sp_addsrvrolemember	Int	Adds a server login to a server role.
sp_adduser	Int	Obsolete. Similar to sp_grantdbaccess, adds a SQL Server user, role, Windows user, or group to a database.
sp_approlepassword	Int	Modifies the password for an application role.

Table continued on following page

Procedure Name	Return Type	Description
sp_change_users_login	Int & Table	Modifies the association between a server login and a database user.
sp_changedbowner	Int	Modifies the owner of a database.
sp_changegroup	Int	Obsolete. Similar to sp_addrolemember, modifies the role membership for a user.
sp_changeobjectowner	Int	Modifies the owner of any database object.
sp_dbfixedrolepermission	Int & Table	Returns permission information for all fixed database roles.
sp_defaultdb	Int	Modifies the default database setting for a login.
sp_defaultlanguage	Int	Modifies the default language setting for a login.
sp_denylogin	Int	Denies access to the server for a Windows user or group.
sp_dropalias	Int	Obsolete. Drops an alias associated with a database user. This is an older technique used before SQL Server role-based security. sp_droprolemember provides similar functionality as a recommended practice.
sp_dropapprole	Int	Drops an application role.
sp_dropgroup	Int & Table	Removes a database role. This is an older procedure provided for compatibility.
sp_droplinkedsrvlogin	Int	Removes the association between a local server login and a linked server login.
sp_droplogin	Int	Drops a local server login.
sp_dropremotelogin	Int	Drops a remote login from the local server.
sp_droprolemember	Int	Removes a user, login, Windows user, or group from a database role.
sp_dropserver	Int	Removes the record of a linked or remote server from a local server.
sp_dropsrvrolemember	Int	Removes a server login, Windows user, or group from a server role.
sp_dropuser	Int	Obsolete. Similar to sp_revokedbaccess, removes access to a database for a SQL Server user, Windows user, or group.
sp_grantdbaccess	Int	Adds access to a database for a server login, Windows user, or group.

Procedure Name	Return Type	Description
sp_grantlogin	Int	Adds access for a Windows user of group to the database server using Windows Integrated Security.
sp_helpdbfixedrole	Table	Returns information about fixed database roles.
sp_helpgroup	Table	Obsolete. Returns information about database groups.
sp_helplinkedsrvlogin	Table	Returns information about linked server logins.
sp_helplogins	Table	Returns information about local server logins.
sp_helpntgroup	Table	Returns information about Windows groups.
sp_helpremotelogin	Table	Returns information about remote logins registered with the local server.
sp_helprole	Table	Returns information about fixed database roles.
sp_helprolemember	Table	Returns information about the roles for a database.
sp_helprotect	Table	Returns permissions information related to a specified database object.
sp_helpsrvrole	Table	Returns information about server roles.
sp_helpsrvrolemember	Table	Returns information about the logins, Windows user, and groups that are members of a specified server role.
sp_helpuser	Table	Returns information about database users, Windows users, groups, and database roles in a database.
sp_MShasdbaccess	Int & Table	Returns database information accessible to a user.
sp_password	Int	Adds or modifies the password for a login.
sp_remoteoption	Int & Table	Returns or modifies option settings for a remote login.
sp_revokedbaccess	Int	Removes a database user, Windows user, or group from a database.
sp_revokelogin	Int	Removes a login associated with a Windows user or group.

Table continued on following page

Procedure Name	Return Type	Description
sp_setapprole	Int	Enables an application role for a database. Used to allow programmatic access from an application component.
sp_srvrolepermission	Int & Table	Returns permission information for a server role.
sp_validatelogins	Int & Table	Returns Windows user and group entries in the database server that no longer exist in the operating system or Windows domain.

SQL Agent

Procedure Name	Return Type	Description
sp_add_alert	Int	Creates a new alert.
sp_add_category	Int	Creates a new category that may be associated with jobs, operators, and so on.
sp_add_job	Int	Creates a new job to contain steps.
sp_add_jobschedule	Int	Creates a new schedule for an existing job.
sp_add_jobserver	Int	Changes the server that will run a job.
sp_add_jobstep	Int	Adds a step to an existing job.
sp_add_notification	Int	Creates and adds a notification for an alert.
sp_add_operator	Int	Creates an operator associated with a job and an alert.
sp_add_proxy	Int	(SQL Server 2005) Creates a proxy account for users and roles to execute jobs with elevated permissions, without administrative role membership.
sp_add_schedule	Int	(SQL Server 2005) Creates a schedule for use with a job.
sp_add_targetservergroup	Int	Creates a server group to associate a job with a group of servers.
sp_add_targetsvrgrp_member	Int	Adds a server to a target server group.
sp_apply_job_to_targets	Int	Associates a job with one or more target servers.
sp_attach_schedule	Int	(SQL Server 2005) Associates a schedule with a job.
sp_cycle_agent_errorlog	Int	(SQL Server 2005) Closes the agent error log and initializes a new log file.

Procedure Name	Return Type	Description
sp_cycle_errorlog	Int	Closes the current error log and starts a new log file.
sp_delete_alert	Int	Deletes an alert.
sp_delete_category	Int	Deletes a category.
sp_delete_job	Int	Deletes a job.
sp_delete_jobschedule	Int	Deletes the schedule for a job.
sp_delete_jobserver	Int	Deletes the association between a job and a server.
sp_delete_jobstep	Int	Deletes a specified job step.
sp_delete_jobsteplog	Int	(SQL Server 20005) Deletes a specified job step, all job steps for a specified job, or those that meet other criteria.
sp_delete_notification	Int	Deletes notifications for an operator and an alert.
sp_delete_operator	Int	Deletes a specified operator.
sp_delete_proxy	Int	(SQL Server 20005) Removes a user proxy.
sp_delete_schedule	Int	(SQL Server 2005) Deletes a job schedule.
sp_delete_targetserver	Int	Removes a target server designation for a job.
sp_delete_targetservergroup	Int	Deletes a target server group.
sp_delete_targetsvrgrp_member	Int	Removes a target server from a group.
sp_detach_schedule	Int	(SQL Server 2005) Associates a schedule to a job.
sp_enum_login_for_proxy	Table	(SQL Server 2005) Returns logins associated with a proxy.
sp_enum_proxy_for_subsystem	Table	(SQL Server 2005) Returns proxy users that have access to a specified subsystem.
sp_enum_sqlagent_subsystems	Table	Returns the subsystems (process threads) for SQL Agent.
sp_grant_login_to_proxy	Int	(SQL Server 2005) Grants a login, user, Windows user, or group access to a proxy.
sp_grant_proxy_to_subsystem	Int	(SQL Server 2005) Assigns a DTS/Integration Services subsystem to a proxy user.
sp_help_alert	Table	Returns information about an alert or alerts.

Table continued on following page

Procedure Name	Return Type	Description
sp_help_category	Table	Returns information about a category or categories.
sp_help_downloadlist	Table	Returns information about queued target server download instructions.
sp_help_job	Table	Returns information about a job or jobs.
sp_help_jobactivity	Table	Returns information about job activities.
sp_help_jobcount	Int	(SQL Server 2005) Returns the count of jobs for an associated schedule.
sp_help_jobhistory	Table	Returns information about jobs for associated servers.
sp_help_jobs_in_schedule	Table	(SQL Server 2005) Returns the information about jobs for an associated schedule.
sp_help_jobschedule	Table	Returns information about automated job scheduling.
sp_help_jobserver	Table	Returns information about a server associated with a job.
sp_help_jobstep	Table	Returns information about the steps for a job.
sp_help_notification	Table	(SQL Server 2005) Returns information about notifications.
sp_help_operator	Table	Returns information about an operator or operators.
sp_help_proxy	Table	(SQL Server 2005) Returns information about a proxy user or proxies.
sp_help_schedule	Table	Returns information about a schedule or schedules.
sp_help_targetserver	Table	Returns information about a job target server or servers.
sp_help_targetservergroup	Table	Returns information about a job target server group or groups.
sp_manage_jobs_by_login	Int	Removes or modifies jobs for a specified login.
sp_msx_defect	Int	Modifies the system registry to remove the server from target multiserver operations.
sp_msx_enlist	Int	Modifies the system registry to add the server to the available multiserver target list.

Procedure Name	Return Type	Description
sp_msx_get_account	Table	Returns credentials information for a target server, used to log into a master server.
sp_msx_set_account	Int	Sets credentials for a target server to log into a master server.
sp_notify_operator	Int	Sends an e-mail message to an operator by using SQLiMail.
sp_post_msx_operation	Int	Inserts job information into the sysdownloadlist table for target servers to execute.
sp_purge_jobhistory	Int	Removes history metadata associated with a job.
sp_remove_job_from_targetss	Int	Removes the association between a job and a target server.
sp_resync_targetserver	Int	Synchronizes all job metadata from remote servers to the target server.
sp_revoke_login_from_proxy		(SQL Server 2005)
sp_revoke_proxy_from_subsystem		(SQL Server 2005) Removes access to a subsystem for a proxy.
sp_start_job	Int	Starts executing a job regardless of its schedule.
sp_stop_job	Int	Stops executing a job.
sp_update_alert	Int	Modifies the settings for an alert.
sp_update_category	Int	Modifies the name of a category.
sp_update_job	Int	Modifies the settings for a job.
sp_update_jobschedule	Int	Modifies the settings for a job's schedule.
sp_update_jobstep	Int	Modifies the settings for a step.
sp_update_notification	Int	(SQL Server 2005) Modifies the settings for a notification.
sp_update_operator	Int	Modifies the information for an operator.
sp_update_proxy		(SQL Server 2005) Modifies the information for a proxy user.
sp_update_schedule	Int	(SQL Server 2005) Modifies an agent schedule.
sp_update_targetservergroup	Int	Modifies the name of a target server group.

XML

Procedure Name	Return Type	Description
sp_xml_preparedocument	Int	Uses an output parameter to return a numeric handle to a cached copy of a well-formed and prepared XML document structure. The initial XML document is passed into this procedure as a VarChar type.
sp_xml_removedocument	Int	Removes data from the server's XML cache.

Information Schema Views Reference

The following views can be used in any database to obtain metadata about database objects. Select from each view as if it were a table in the database, prefixing the view with "INFORMATION_SCHEMA." as in the following example:

```
SELECT * FROM INFORMATION_SCHEMA.CHECK_CONSTRAINTS
```

Information schema views are stored in the Master database. Note that the SysName(256) user-defined data type is equivalent to nVarChar(128).

CHECK_CONSTRAINTS

Column Name	Data Type
CONSTRAINT_CATALOG	nVarChar(256)
CONSTRAINT_SCHEMA	nVarChar(256)
CONSTRAINT_NAME	SysName(256)
CHECK_CLAUSE	nVarChar(8000)

COLUMN_DOMAIN_USAGE

Column Name	Data Type
DOMAIN_CATALOG	nVarChar(256)
DOMAIN_SCHEMA	nVarChar(256)
DOMAIN_NAME	SysName(256)
TABLE_CATALOG	nVarChar(256)

Table continued on following page

Column Name	Data Type
TABLE_SCHEMA	nVarChar(256)
TABLE_NAME	SysName(256)
COLUMN_NAME	SysName(256)
DOMAIN_CATALOG	nVarChar(256)

COLUMN_PRIVILEGES

Column Name	Data Type
GRANTOR	nVarChar(256)
GRANTEE	nVarChar(256)
TABLE_CATALOG	nVarChar(256)
TABLE_SCHEMA	nVarChar(256)
TABLE_NAME	SysName(256)
COLUMN_NAME	SysName(256)
PRIVILEGE_TYPE	VarChar(10)
IS_GRANTABLE	VarChar(3)

COLUMNS

Column Name	Data Type
TABLE_CATALOG	nVarChar(256)
TABLE_SCHEMA	nVarChar(256)
TABLE_NAME	SysName(256)
COLUMN_NAME	SysName(256)
ORDINAL_POSITION	SmallInt(2)
COLUMN_DEFAULT	nVarChar(8000)
IS_NULLABLE	VarChar(3)
DATA_TYPE	SysName(256)
CHARACTER_MAXIMUM_LENGTH	Int(4)
CHARACTER_OCTET_LENGTH	Int(4)
NUMERIC_PRECISION	TinyInt(1)
NUMERIC_PRECISION_RADIX	SmallInt(2)

Column Name	Data Type	
NUMERIC_SCALE	Int(4)	
DATETIME_PRECISION	SmallInt(2)	
CHARACTER_SET_CATALOG	nVarChar(256)	
CHARACTER_SET_SCHEMA	nVarChar(256)	
CHARACTER_SET_NAME	nVarChar(256)	
COLLATION_CATALOG	nVarChar(256)	
COLLATION_SCHEMA	nVarChar(256)	
COLLATION_NAME	SysName(256)	
DOMAIN_CATALOG	nVarChar(256)	
DOMAIN_SCHEMA	nVarChar(256)	
DOMAIN_NAME	nVarChar(256)	

CONSTRAINT_COLUMN_USAGE

Column Name	Data Type	
TABLE_CATALOG	nVarChar(256)	
TABLE_SCHEMA	nVarChar(256)	
TABLE_NAME	nVarChar(256)	
COLUMN_NAME	nVarChar(256)	
CONSTRAINT_CATALOG	nVarChar(256)	
CONSTRAINT_SCHEMA	nVarChar(256)	
CONSTRAINT_NAME	nVarChar(256)	

CONSTRAINT_TABLE_USAGE

Column Name	Data Type	
TABLE_CATALOG	nVarChar(256)	
TABLE_SCHEMA	nVarChar(256)	
TABLE_NAME	SysName(256)	
CONSTRAINT_CATALOG	nVarChar(256)	
CONSTRAINT_SCHEMA	nVarChar(256)	
CONSTRAINT_NAME	SysName(256)	

DOMAIN_CONSTRAINTS

Column Name	Data Type
CONSTRAINT_CATALOG	nVarChar(256)
CONSTRAINT_SCHEMA	nVarChar(256)
CONSTRAINT_NAME	SysName(256)
DOMAIN_CATALOG	nVarChar(256)
DOMAIN_SCHEMA	nVarChar(256)
DOMAIN_NAME	SysName(256)
IS_DEFERRABLE	VarChar(2)
INITIALLY_DEFERRED	VarChar(2)

DOMAINS

Column Name	Data Type
DOMAIN_CATALOG	nVarChar(256)
DOMAIN_SCHEMA	nVarChar(256)
DOMAIN_NAME	SysName(256)
DATA_TYPE	SysName(256)
CHARACTER_MAXIMUM_LENGTH	Int(4)
CHARACTER_OCTET_LENGTH	Int(4)
COLLATION_CATALOG	nVarChar(256)
COLLATION_SCHEMA	nVarChar(256)
COLLATION_NAME	SysName(256)
CHARACTER_SET_CATALOG	nVarChar(256)
CHARACTER_SET_SCHEMA	nVarChar(256)
CHARACTER_SET_NAME	nVarChar(256)
NUMERIC_PRECISION	TinyInt(1)
NUMERIC_PRECISION_RADIX	SmallInt(2)
NUMERIC_SCALE	Int(4)
DATETIME_PRECISION	SmallInt(2)
DOMAIN_DEFAULT	nVarChar(8000)

KEY_COLUMN_USAGE

Column Name	Data Type	
CONSTRAINT_CATALOG	nVarChar(256)	
CONSTRAINT_SCHEMA	nVarChar(256)	
CONSTRAINT_NAME	nVarChar(256)	
TABLE_CATALOG	nVarChar(256)	
TABLE_SCHEMA	nVarChar(256)	
TABLE_NAME	nVarChar(256)	
COLUMN_NAME	nVarChar(256)	
ORDINAL_POSITION	Int(4)	

PARAMETERS

Column Name	Data Type	
CONSTRAINT_CATALOG	nVarChar(256)	
CONSTRAINT_SCHEMA	nVarChar(256)	
CONSTRAINT_NAME	nVarChar(256)	
TABLE_CATALOG	nVarChar(256)	
TABLE_SCHEMA	nVarChar(256)	
TABLE_NAME	nVarChar(256)	
COLUMN_NAME	nVarChar(256)	
ORDINAL_POSITION	Int(4)	

REFERENTIAL_CONSTRAINTS

Column Name	Data Type	
CONSTRAINT_CATALOG	nVarChar(256)	
CONSTRAINT_SCHEMA	nVarChar(256)	
CONSTRAINT_NAME	SysName(256)	
UNIQUE_CONSTRAINT_CATALOG	nVarChar(256)	
UNIQUE_CONSTRAINT_SCHEMA	nVarChar(256)	
UNIQUE_CONSTRAINT_NAME	SysName(256)	

Table continued on following page

Column Name	Data Type
MATCH_OPTION	VarChar(4)
UPDATE_RULE	VarChar(9)
DELETE_RULE	VarChar(9)

ROUTINE_COLUMNS

Column Name	Data Type
TABLE_CATALOG	nVarChar(256)
TABLE_SCHEMA	nVarChar(256)
TABLE_NAME	SysName(256)
COLUMN_NAME	SysName(256)
ORDINAL_POSITION	SmallInt(2)
COLUMN_DEFAULT	nVarChar(8000)
IS_NULLABLE	VarChar(3)
DATA_TYPE	SysName(256)
CHARACTER_MAXIMUM_LENGTH	Int(4)
CHARACTER_OCTET_LENGTH	Int(4)
NUMERIC_PRECISION	TinyInt(1)
NUMERIC_PRECISION_RADIX	SmallInt(2)
NUMERIC_SCALE	Int(4)
DATETIME_PRECISION	SmallInt(2)
CHARACTER_SET_CATALOG	nVarChar(256)
CHARACTER_SET_SCHEMA	nVarChar(256)
CHARACTER_SET_NAME	nVarChar(256)
COLLATION_CATALOG	nVarChar(256)
COLLATION_SCHEMA	nVarChar(256)
COLLATION_NAME	SysName(256)
DOMAIN_CATALOG	nVarChar(256)
DOMAIN_SCHEMA	nVarChar(256)
DOMAIN_NAME	nVarChar(256)

ROUTINES

Column Name	Data Type	
SPECIFIC_CATALOG	nVarChar(256)	
SPECIFIC_SCHEMA	nVarChar(256)	
SPECIFIC_NAME	nVarChar(256)	
ROUTINE_CATALOG	nVarChar(256)	
ROUTINE_SCHEMA	nVarChar(256)	
ROUTINE_NAME	nVarChar(256)	
ROUTINE_TYPE	nVarChar(40)	
MODULE_CATALOG	nVarChar(256)	
MODULE_SCHEMA	nVarChar(256)	
MODULE_NAME	nVarChar(256)	
UDT_CATALOG	nVarChar(256)	
UDT_SCHEMA	nVarChar(256)	
UDT_NAME	nVarChar(256)	
DATA_TYPE	nVarChar(256)	
CHARACTER_MAXIMUM_LENGTH	Int(4)	
CHARACTER_OCTET_LENGTH	Int(4)	
COLLATION_CATALOG	nVarChar(256)	
COLLATION_SCHEMA	nVarChar(256)	
COLLATION_NAME	nVarChar(256)	
CHARACTER_SET_CATALOG	nVarChar(256)	
CHARACTER_SET_SCHEMA	nVarChar(256)	
CHARACTER_SET_NAME	nVarChar(256)	
NUMERIC_PRECISION	TinyInt(1)	
NUMERIC_PRECISION_RADIX	SmallInt(2)	
NUMERIC_SCALE	Int(4)	
DATETIME_PRECISION	SmallInt(2)	
INTERVAL_TYPE	nVarChar(60)	
INTERVAL_PRECISION	SmallInt(2)	
TYPE_UDT_CATALOG	nVarChar(256)	

Table continued on following page

Column Name	Data Type
TYPE_UDT_SCHEMA	nVarChar(256)
TYPE_UDT_NAME	nVarChar(256)
SCOPE_CATALOG	nVarChar(256)
SCOPE_SCHEMA	nVarChar(256)
SCOPE_NAME	nVarChar(256)
MAXIMUM_CARDINALITY	bigInt(8)
DTD_IDENTIFIER	nVarChar(256)
ROUTINE_BODY	nVarChar(60)
ROUTINE_DEFINITION	nVarChar(8000)
EXTERNAL_NAME	nVarChar(256)
EXTERNAL_LANGUAGE	nVarChar(60)
PARAMETER_STYLE	nVarChar(60)
IS_DETERMINISTIC	nVarChar(20)
SQL_DATA_ACCESS	nVarChar(60)
IS_NULL_CALL	nVarChar(20)
SQL_PATH	nVarChar(256)
SCHEMA_LEVEL_ROUTINE	nVarChar(20)
MAX_DYNAMIC_RESULT_SETS	SmallInt(2)
IS_USER_DEFINED_CAST	nVarChar(20)
IS_IMPLICITLY_INVOCABLE	nVarChar(20)
CREATED	DateTime(8)
LAST_ALTERED	DateTime(8)

SCHEMATA

Column Name	Data Type
CATALOG_NAME	SysName(256)
SCHEMA_NAME	nVarChar(256)
SCHEMA_OWNER	nVarChar(256)
DEFAULT_CHARACTER_SET_CATALOG	nVarChar(256)
DEFAULT_CHARACTER_SET_SCHEMA	nVarChar(256)
DEFAULT_CHARACTER_SET_NAME	SysName(256)

TABLE_CONSTRAINTS

Column Name	Data Type	
CONSTRAINT_CATALOG	nVarChar(256)	
CONSTRAINT_SCHEMA	nVarChar(256)	
CONSTRAINT_NAME	SysName(256)	
TABLE_CATALOG	nVarChar(256)	
TABLE_SCHEMA	nVarChar(256)	
TABLE_NAME	SysName(256)	
CONSTRAINT_TYPE	VarChar(11)	
IS_DEFERRABLE	VarChar(2)	
INITIALLY_DEFERRED	VarChar(2)	

TABLE_PRIVILEGES

Column Name	Data Type	
GRANTOR	nVarChar(256)	
GRANTEE	nVarChar(256)	
TABLE_CATALOG	nVarChar(256)	
TABLE_SCHEMA	nVarChar(256)	
TABLE_NAME	SysName(256)	
PRIVILEGE_TYPE	VarChar(10)	
IS_GRANTABLE	VarChar(3)	

TABLES

Column Name	Data Type	
TABLE_CATALOG	nVarChar(256)	
TABLE_SCHEMA	nVarChar(256)	
TABLE_NAME	SysName(256)	
TABLE_TYPE	VarChar(10)	

VIEW_COLUMN_USAGE

Column Name	Data Type
VIEW_CATALOG	nVarChar(256)
VIEW_SCHEMA	nVarChar(256)
VIEW_NAME	SysName(256)
TABLE_CATALOG	nVarChar(256)
TABLE_SCHEMA	nVarChar(256)
TABLE_NAME	SysName(256)
COLUMN_NAME	SysName(256)

VIEW_TABLE_USAGE

Column Name	Data Type
VIEW_CATALOG	nVarChar(256)
VIEW_SCHEMA	nVarChar(256)
VIEW_NAME	SysName(256)
TABLE_CATALOG	nVarChar(256)
TABLE_SCHEMA	nVarChar(256)
TABLE_NAME	SysName(256)

VIEWS

Column Name	Data Type
TABLE_CATALOG	nVarChar(256)
TABLE_SCHEMA	nVarChar(256)
TABLE_NAME	nVarChar(256)
VIEW_DEFINITION	nVarChar(8000)
CHECK_OPTION	VarChar(7)
IS_UPDATABLE	VarChar(2)

Answers to Exercises

Chapter 3 Exercises

In the exercises for Chapters 3 and 4, I will provide numbered step-by-step instructions. The solutions for these chapters are the final query, commands, or result. In the exercises for subsequent chapters, I will provide less detailed instructions. You should use the material in each chapter to determine the appropriate steps and to find the solution.

Exercise 1

1. Using Enterprise Manager or SQL Server Management Studio, create a new view in the AdventureWorks2000 database. You won't actually save the view but use this option to open the graphical query designer.

2. Add the Product table to the designer.

3. Select the ProductID, Name, and ListPrice columns by checking the corresponding boxes in the table window.

4. Sort the results by the Name column in Ascending order using the Sort Type option.

5. Check the SQL expression in the third pane of the graphical query designer with the solution.

Solution

The SQL Expression in the third pane of the graphical query designer should be as follows:

```
SELECT     TOP 100 PERCENT ProductID, Name, ListPrice
FROM       dbo.Product
ORDER BY Name
```

Exercise 2

1. Using Enterprise Manager or SQL Server Management Studio, create a new view in the AdventureWorks2000 database as you did in Exercise 1.

2. Add two tables: The Product table and the ProductSubCategory table.

3. For the ProductSubCategory table, select the Name column and create an alias for it as SubCategory. For the Product table, select the Name column and create an alias for it as ProductName. Also select the ListPrice column from this table.

4. Sort the query by the ProductSubCategory Name column and then the Product table Name column, both in Ascending order.

5. Execute the query and then scroll through the results using the fourth pane in the designer. Check the SQL expression displayed in the third pane of the designer with the solution.

Solution

The SQL expression in the third pane of the graphical query designer should be as follows (formatting may vary):

```
SELECT     TOP 100 PERCENT dbo.ProductSubCategory.Name AS SubCategory,
           dbo.Product.Name AS ProductName, dbo.Product.ListPrice
FROM       dbo.Product INNER JOIN dbo.ProductSubCategory
           ON dbo.Product.ProductSubCategoryID =
           dbo.ProductSubCategory.ProductSubCategoryID
ORDER BY dbo.ProductSubCategory.Name, dbo.Product.Name
```

Exercise 3

Write a simple query using the query editor window in Query Analyzer or the SQL Server Manager Studio using the following steps:

1. Open Query Analyzer or SQL Server Management Studio.

2. If using Query Analyzer for SQL Server 2000, you will be prompted for connection information. Enter **localhost** for the server name or the name of your server if connecting remotely. If using SQL Server 2005, create a new query and provide this same connection information.

3. Select the AdventureWorks2000 database from the database selection list in the toolbar.

4. Enter the following SQL script in the query window:

```
Select * From Product Where ListPrice > 4000
```

5. To find out how many products have a list price greater than $4,000, execute this query and check the row count in the status bar.

Solution

This query returns 58 rows. These are all of the products with a list price greater then $4,000.

Exercise 4

Execute a simple query using command-line utilities:

1. If using SQL Server 2000, open a command prompt and execute the OSQL utility to utilize Windows Integrated (Enterprise) security. If using SQL Server 2005, use the SQLCMD utility to utilize Windows Integrated (Enterprise) security. Each statement should be followed by a batch delineation command.

2. Indicate that you want run statements using the AdventureWorks2000 database.

3. Execute the following SQL statement and view the results:

```
SELECT ProductCategoryID, Name FROM ProductCategory
```

4. Exit the command-line utility and then the command window.

5. Check your statements with the solution.

Solution

Command-line statements should resemble the following:

```
> OSQL -E     (or SQLCMD -E)
> USE AdventureWorks2000
> GO
> SELECT ProductCategoryID, Name FROM ProductCategory
> GO
> EXIT
> EXIT
```

For simple Transact-SQL commands, the OSQL and SQLCMD command-line query utilities are nearly identical. The SQLCMD tool supports additional enhancements for SQL Server 2005.

The –E switch indicates that the database query engine should open a new connection using Windows Integrated, or *Enterprise*, security; using the current user's Windows credentials.

The session will be opened using the default database, typically the Master database, so it is necessary to explicitly name the target database for this session. Commands are executed in batch mode, and no commands are actually processed until a batch directive statement (GO) is issued.

The first EXIT command is processed by the query utility, which exits the session, closes the connection, and returns control to the command shell prompt. The second EXIT statement is processed by the command shell. This closes the command prompt window and terminates the command session.

Chapter 4 Exercises

Exercise 1

Use Query Analyzer or SQL Server Management Studio to create and execute a new query, and view the results.

1. Open a connection to your local or remote test server.

2. Indicate that you want to run queries against the AdventureWorks2000 database.

3. Execute the following SQL statement:

```
SELECT * FROM Contact
```

4. Check the status bar for the numbers of rows returned by the query.

5. Check the results with the solution.

Solution

This query returns 996 rows. All columns are returned for all rows in the Contact table.

Exercise 2

Insert a row using generated SQL script:

1. Using Query Analyzer or SQL Server Management Studio, expand the AdventureWorks2000 database in the object browser. Right-click the *ProductCategory* table and select **Script Object to New Window As Insert**.

2. In the new query editor window, remove the references to the ProductCategoryID column on both lines. On the top line, delete all text from and including the first open square bracket; [, to the first end square bracket;], and the following comma. On the second line, remove all text from and including the first open angled bracket; <, to the first close angled bracket; >, and the following comma.

3. On the second line, replace the placeholders (angled brackets and all text between them) for each of the columns as follows: Replace the Name with 'Widget' (including the single quotes). Replace the ModifiedDate and rowguid with the word DEFAULT (no quotes).

4. Select the AdventureWorks2000 database from the database selection drop-down list on the toolbar and execute the query.

5. Enter the following query to view the contents of the ProductCategory table:

```
SELECT * FROM ProductCategory.
```

6. Highlight this statement and execute this query.

7. Verify that a new row was added to the results. Check the modified SQL expression that you generated with the solution.

Solution

The modified script should resemble the following:

```
INSERT INTO [AdventureWorks2000].[dbo].[ProductCategory] ([Name], [ModifedDate],
[rowguid])
VALUES ('Widget', Default, Default)
```

The INSERT command script contains some unnecessary details that can be eliminated. Using this technique can help you to get started to learn the basic structure of certain Transact-SQL statements. After you've done this a few times, you will likely find it easier to write statements without assistance.

Generated script typically uses multi-part object references with names in square brackets to handle spaces and reserved words.

The Default key word is used to fill these two columns with the default values specified in the table definition.

Chapter 5 Exercises

Exercise 1

Using Query Analyzer or SQL Server Management Studio, write a query to return Employee records form the AdventureWorks2000 database. Include only the FirstName, LastName, and EmailAddress columns in the result set. Execute this query and view the results.

Solution

```
SELECT FirstName, LastName, EmailAddress
FROM Employee
```

This query should return approximately 290 employee records.

Exercise 2

Return Employee records from the AdventureWorks2000 database. Combine the FirstName and LastName columns separated by a space, to return an aliased column called FullName. Return only the FullName and Title columns. Sort the results by the LastName and then FirstName columns in ascending order.

Solution

```
SELECT FirstName + ' ' + LastName AS FullName, Title
FROM    Employee
ORDER BY LastName, FirstName
```

There are multiple techniques for defining a column alias. This query returns two columns: FullName and Title. Note that the ORDER BY clause may contain columns that are not included in the result set.

Exercise 3

Return Product records that have a DiscontinuedDate value greater than or equal to December 4, 2002. Include the Name and ListPrice columns.

Solution

```
SELECT Name, DiscontinuedDate
FROM    Product
WHERE DiscontinuedDate >= '12-4-2002'
```

Multiple date formats may be used. I chose to use the standard U.S. short date. Others include the ANSI and European standard formats.

This query returns 495 rows.

Exercise 4

Return a list of Department records including all columns.

Include only departments that have a Name value ending with the word *Control*. These records must also have a Name column value starting with the word *Production*. In addition to these records, include records that have a GroupName value ending in the word *Assurance*.

Sort these records by the Name column in reverse alphabetical order.

Solution

```
SELECT * FROM Department
WHERE
(Name Like '%Control' AND Name Like 'Production%')
OR
(GroupName Like '%Assurance')
ORDER BY Name Desc
```

The WHERE expression contains three criteria. Since the first two statements are enclosed in parentheses, these are processed before the third statement. The AND operator is restrictive and will only return the one record where the Name is *Production Control*.

The OR statement makes the result additive: results are added where the GroupName column ends with the text Assurance. All together, this query returns three rows.

Chapter 6 Exercises

Exercise 1

Write a query to return the average weight of all touring bikes sold by Adventure Works Cycles that list for over $2,500. Use the ProductSubCategory table to determine how you should filter these products.

Solution

```
SELECT   AVG(Weight)
FROM Product
WHERE ProductSubCategoryID = 3 AND ListPrice > 2500
```

In the ProductSubCategory, the sub category named 'Touring Bike' has a ProductSubCategoryID value of 3. This column is related to the foreign key column with the same name in the Product table. Using this key value, you will find touring bike records.

Twenty-eight rows match this criterion with an average weight of approximately 25.4 pounds.

Exercise 2

Designate a variable called @ProCount to hold the number of product records on record. Execute a query to return this value and assign it to the variable. Use the variable in an expression to return the value in the phrase: "There are X products on record."

Solution

```
DECLARE @ProdCount Int
SELECT @ProdCount = COUNT(*) FROM Product
SELECT 'There are ' + CONVERT(VarChar(5), @ProdCount) + ' products on record.'
```

The SELECT statement is used to assign a variable to an aggregated value. In order to concatenate an integer value with a literal character string, it is necessary to first convert the numeric value to a compatible string. This may be done using a few different conversion functions, including CAST(), STR(), or CONVERT().

Exercise 3

Calculate the square root of the absolute value of the cosine of PI.

Solution

```
SELECT SQRT(ABS(COS(PI())))
```

The result is one. The cosine is an angle in degrees converted to radians by a factor equal to the value of PI. Therefore, the cosine of PI is equal to –1. The absolute value changes the sign to positive one. The square root of one is one.

Exercise 4

How many days has it been since this book was first published on September 26, 2005? Calculate the answer using Transact-SQL functions.

Solution

```
SELECT DATEDIFF(Day, '9-26-2005', GETDATE())
```

Exercise 5

Using the *Individual* table, return the FirstName, LastName, and the three-letter initials of all individuals who have a middle name.

Solution

```
SELECT   FirstName
       , LastName
       , LEFT(FirstName, 1) + LEFT(MiddleName, 1) + LEFT(LastName, 1) AS Initials
FROM Individual
WHERE MiddleName IS NOT NULL
```

Chapter 7 Exercises

Exercise 1

Write a query to return the first name and the highest ShiftID value for each group of employees named Kevin, Linda, or Mary.

Solution

```
SELECT FirstName, MAX(ShiftID)
FROM Employee
WHERE FirstName IN('Kevin', 'Linda', 'Mary')
GROUP BY FirstName
```

The IN() function provides the most concise method to match a column to a list of values. The MAX() aggregate is used to return the largest value for a column based on the sort order of the column's data type.

This query returns one row for each name, which represent multiple employees sharing these names. The ShiftID values are 3, 2, and 2 respectively.

Exercise 2

Return a list of ProductSubCategoryID values from the Product table. Include only subcategories that occur more than 20 times. In addition to the ID value, also return the first product name in alphabetical order and the highest price for products in this subcategory.

Solution

```
SELECT ProductSubCategoryID, MIN(Name) AS Name, MAX(ListPrice)
FROM Product
GROUP BY ProductSubCategoryID
HAVING COUNT(ProductSubCategoryID) > 20
ORDER BY Name
```

Exercise 3

Produce a list of managers from the Employee table using the ManagerID. For each manager, include the average base pay for all employees of each gender. Also include a row for each manager that includes the average base pay for all employees of that manager. This should be done using only one SELECT expression.

Solution

```
SELECT ManagerID, Gender, AVG(BaseRate)
FROM Employee
GROUP by ManagerID, Gender
WITH ROLLUP
```

Chapter 8 Exercises

Exercise 1

Create a list of vendors and the subtotal amounts for their purchase orders, sorted by vendor names. This list should include the vendor name and the subtotal amount for all vendors who have purchase orders recorded in the PurchaseOrderHeader table.

Solution

```
SELECT Name, SubTotal
FROM Vendor INNER JOIN PurchaseOrderHeader
ON Vendor.VendorID = PurchaseOrderHeader.VendorID
ORDER BY Name
```

Exercise 2

In Chapter 7, exercise 3; you wrote a query to return the average pay rate for employees by gender for their managers. Extend this query and replace the ManagerID with the manager's name. Concatenate the manager's first and last name, separated with a space, from the employee table. Create an alias for this value called ManagerName. Create an alias to refer to the employee table used to obtain the managers' names called Managers.

Solution

```
SELECT
    Managers.FirstName + ' ' + Managers.LastName AS ManagerName
    , Employee.Gender, AVG(Employee.BaseRate)
FROM Employee INNER JOIN Employee AS Managers
ON Employee.ManagerID = Managers.EmployeeID
GROUP BY
    Managers.FirstName + ' ' + Managers.LastName
    , Employee.Gender
WITH ROLLUP
```

Exercise 3

Write a query that returns a list of product subcategories and related products that don't have any sales order detail records. Include two columns including the subcategory name labeled SubCategoryName and the product name labeled ProductName.

Solution

```
SELECT
    ProductSubCategory.Name AS SubCategoryName
    , Product.Name AS ProductName
FROM ProductSubCategory
    INNER JOIN Product
        ON ProductSubCategory.ProductSubCategoryID = Product.ProductSubCategoryID
    LEFT OUTER JOIN SalesOrderDetail
        ON Product.ProductID = SalesOrderDetail.ProductID
WHERE SalesOrderDetail.ProductID IS NULL
```

Chapter 9 Exercises

Exercise 1

Create a new product category for Snorkels. Demonstrate two methods to add a record to this table using the SELECT and VALUES statements.

Solution

```
INSERT INTO ProductCategory (Name) SELECT 'Snorkels'

INSERT INTO ProductCategory (Name) VALUES ('Snorkels')
```

Exercise 2

Populate a new table called RoadBikes with the contents of product records of this sub category. Your query must filter on the value 'Road Bike'.

Solution

```
SELECT Product.* INTO RoadBikes
FROM Product
   INNER JOIN ProductSubCategory
      ON Product.ProductSubCategoryID = ProductSubCategory.ProductSubCategoryID
WHERE ProductSubCategory.Name = 'Road Bike'
```

Exercise 3

Write a query that will delete product records for products that do not have sales order detail records and where the SubCategoryID is 5. Also write a query that will add a new record to the ProductSubCategory table with the Name column value set to *Accessory*. Include both of these statements in a single transaction and execute them in a batch. Check the row count of the Product table before and after to determine whether records were deleted.

Solution

```
BEGIN TRANSACTION

DELETE FROM Product
WHERE ProductID IN
 (
     SELECT Product.ProductID
     FROM Product LEFT OUTER JOIN SalesOrderDetail
        ON Product.ProductID = SalesOrderDetail.ProductID
     WHERE SalesOrderDetail.ProductID IS NULL
     AND Product.ProductSubCategoryID = 5
 )
INSERT INTO ProductCategory (Name) SELECT 'Accessory'

COMMIT TRANSACTION
```

No product records were deleted because the second query raised an error, causing the transaction to roll-back.

Chapter 10 Exercises

Exercise 1

Write a query to return a list of products in order of the product name, the list price, and the highest price for which that product has sold. Use an in-line, scalar query to calculate the highest sales price for the product. Columns in the result set should be labeled ProductName, ProductListPrice, and MaxSalesPrice.

Solution

```
SELECT
      Name AS ProductName
    , ListPrice AS ProductListPrice
    , (SELECT MAX(UnitPrice) AS MaxSalesPrice FROM SalesOrderDetail
       WHERE ProductID = Product.ProductID
       GROUP BY ProductID) AS MaxSalesPrice
FROM Product
ORDER BY Name
```

Exercise 2

The following query returns the top 10 employee pay rates and employee names:

```
SELECT TOP 10 FirstName + ' ' + LastName AS Name
, BaseRate FROM Employee ORDER BY BaseRate DESC
```

This query returns the average pay for all other employees as one summary row labeled '(other)' in place of the employee's name. A subquery is used to join all employee rows to the results of the top 10 expression and then to eliminate these from the aggregated group:

```
SELECT '(Other)' AS Name, AVG(Employee.BaseRate) AS BaseRate FROM Employee
    LEFT OUTER JOIN
    (SELECT TOP 10 EmployeeID, BaseRate FROM Employee ORDER BY BaseRate DESC) AS E
    ON Employee.EmployeeID = E.EmployeeID
    WHERE E.EmployeeID IS NULL
```

These two queries need to be combined into a UNION query to return a single result set. However, simply adding the UNION statement between them raises errors due to restrictions of the UNION statement. You can work around these limitations by creating two alias tables similar to the one in the join statement of the second query, and selecting columns from them. Rewrite these statements so the final query has three alias table subqueries. Call them E1, E2, and E3. The existing subquery should be renamed from E to E2. Execute the query to verify that it returns 11 rows.

Solution

```
SELECT Name, ListPrice FROM
    (SELECT TOP 10 Name, ListPrice FROM Product ORDER BY ListPrice DESC) AS E1
UNION
SELECT Name, ListPrice FROM
    ( SELECT 'Other' AS Name, AVG(Product.ListPrice) AS ListPrice FROM Product
      LEFT OUTER JOIN
        (SELECT TOP 10 ProductID, ListPrice FROM Product ORDER BY ListPrice DESC) AS E2
```

```
      ON Product.ProductID = E2.ProductID
      WHERE E2.ProductID IS NULL
  ) AS E3
```

Chapter 12 Exercises

Exercise 1

Write the SQL script to define a new table to track customers buying wristbands from an on-line store. Decide upon an appropriate name, data type, and nullability option for each column. Due to strict storage requirements, use the most conservative data types possible. Guidelines for the columns in this table are as follows:

Define a single column for the customer's name. It should allow between 1 and 200 characters and is a required entry. Some customers may have foreign names.

Four columns are needed to store the customer's address, city, state, and zip code. All addresses and cities will contain only U.S. domestic names, and none of these columns require a value. The address column should allow up to 200 characters, the city should allow up to 100 characters, the state will always be a two-character abbreviation, and the postal code will always be five characters in length.

A column is needed to store the quantity of wristbands purchased. This column will store a whole number value up to 10,000 and should be automatically set to 1 for new records.

A column is needed to store the price paid. This is a required entry and should store values up to $100,000.

Solution

```
CREATE TABLE WristBandSales
  (  CustomerName    nVarChar(200)   NOT NULL
  ,  Address         VarChar(200)    NULL
  ,  City            VarChar(100)    NULL
  ,  State           Char(2)         NULL
  ,  ZipCode         VarChar(5)      NULL
  ,  Quantity        SmallInt        NOT NULL    DEFAULT 1
  ,  Price           SmallMoney      NOT NULL
  )
```

Although it's considered good practice to define a primary key column, the requirements didn't specify this. The CustomerName column is defined as an nVarChar type so it can store Unicode characters using an international character set. This doubles the storage requirement but meets this need as effectively as possible.

The Address and City columns don't require Unicode capability so they use a VarChar data type. The State column uses a fixed-length type because of the overhead associated with the VarChar type uses 2 bytes even if the column is empty. The ZipCode column could be defined as either Char(5) or VarChar(5). There are slight performance improvements using the Char type for smaller values but an empty value in a Char will use five characters of storage. Although it's probably more practical to use the Char type in this example, the requirement was to reduce store space.

The SmallMoney type, although not common, reduces storage requirements and meets the maximum value requirement.

Exercise 2

Wristbands are sold on two separate web sites that use two copies of the database. Sales records will be merged together on occasion into one database.

Using the query you created in exercise 1, add a column to serve as a primary key and to uniquely identify each sales record. Records should not be stored in physical order using this value.

We're currently only licensed to sell wristbands in three states. Constrain the State column so it only accepts customers in Washington, Oregon, and California (WA, OR, and CA).

Solution

```
CREATE TABLE WristBandSales
(  SalesID          UniqueIdentifier  NOT NULL   DEFAULT NEWID()
                    CONSTRAINT PK_ID PRIMARY KEY NONCLUSTERED
,  CustomerName     nVarChar(200)     NOT NULL
,  Address          VarChar(200)      NULL
,  City             VarChar(100)      NULL
,  State            Char(2)           NULL
,  ZipCode          VarChar(5)        NULL
,  Quantity         SmallInt          NOT NULL   DEFAULT 1
,  Price            SmallMoney        NOT NULL
,  CONSTRAINT CK_State CHECK (State IN('WA', 'OR', 'CA'))
)
```

The SalesID column was defined as a UniqueIdentifier type to ensure uniqueness. Unlike using the Identity attribute with the Int type, this column will not automatically generate a value when a record is inserted. The NEWID() function is used to do this when referenced in a default attribute.

Chapter 13 Exercises

Exercise 1

Define a new view called vwSalesEmployees. It should return the EmployeeID, FirstName, LastName, and Title columns from the Employee table for all employees who are sales persons. Results should be sorted by last name and then by first name.

Solution

```
CREATE VIEW vwSalesEmployees
AS
SELECT TOP 100 Percent
       EmployeeID
     , FirstName
     , LastName
     , Title
FROM Employee
WHERE SalesPersonFlag = 1
ORDER BY LastName, FirstName
```

Exercise 2

Create a stored procedure called spEmployeeAddUpdate. This procedure accepts three parameters: FirstName, LastName, and LoginID. The data types are nVarChar(50), nVarChar(50), and nVarChar(256), respectively. Define logic in this procedure to check for an existing employee record with the same first and last name values. If the employee record exists, update the LoginID. Otherwise, insert a new employee record.

Solution

```
CREATE PROCEDURE spEmployeeAddUpdate
(
    @FirstName    nVarChar(50)
  , @LastName     nVarChar(50)
  , @LoginID      nVarChar(256)
)
AS
IF EXISTS
    (
     SELECT * FROM Employee
     WHERE FirstName = @FirstName
           AND
           LastName = @LastName
    )
    UPDATE Employee
    SET LoginID = @LoginID
     WHERE FirstName = @FirstName
           AND
           LastName = @LastName
ELSE
    INSERT INTO Employee
    (FirstName, LastName, LoginID)
    SELECT @FirstName, @LastName, @LoginID
```

Exercise 3

Add a comment header block and error handling logic to the procedure you created in exercise 2. The block should contain a description of the procedure, parameters, your contact information, the date created, and revision information.

Add error-handling logic to catch the errors that would occur if a parameter were omitted or if a null value were passed into a parameter. If an error is caught, raise a custom error message.

Solution

SQL Server 2000 error handling style:

```
/*****************************************************
    Adds or updates an employee record.
    If the first and last name match an existing
    record, updates the LoginID.
```

```
    6-15-05 Paul Turley
    nospan@mydomain.com

    Revisions:
    6-18-05 - Added comment block
            and error handling.
***************************************************/
CREATE PROCEDURE spEmployeeAddUpdate
(
   @FirstName    nVarChar(50)
 , @LastName     nVarChar(50)
 , @LoginID      nVarChar(256)
)
AS
IF EXISTS
    (
     SELECT * FROM Employee
     WHERE FirstName = @FirstName
           AND
           LastName = @LastName
    )
    UPDATE Employee
    SET LoginID = @LoginID
     WHERE FirstName = @FirstName
           AND
           LastName = @LastName
ELSE
    INSERT INTO Employee
    (FirstName, LastName, LoginID)
    SELECT @FirstName, @LastName, @LoginID
IF @@ERROR IN (515, 2601)
    RAISERROR 'FirstName, LastName & LoginID parameter values are required', 16, 1
```

SQL Server 2005 error handling style:

```
/**************************************************
    Adds or updates an employee record.
    If the first and last name match an existing
    record, updates the LoginID.

    6-15-05 Paul Turley
    nospam@mydomain.com

    Revisions:
    6-18-05 - Added comment block
            and error handling.
***************************************************/
CREATE PROCEDURE spEmployeeAddUpdate
(
   @FirstName    nVarChar(50)
 , @LastName     nVarChar(50)
 , @LoginID      nVarChar(256)
)
```

```
AS
BEGIN TRY
  IF EXISTS
    (
      SELECT * FROM Employee
      WHERE FirstName = @FirstName
            AND
            LastName = @LastName
    )
    UPDATE Employee
    SET LoginID = @LoginID
     WHERE FirstName = @FirstName
            AND
            LastName = @LastName
  ELSE
    INSERT INTO Employee
    (FirstName, LastName, LoginID)
    SELECT @FirstName, @LastName, @LoginID
END TRY

BEGIN CATCH
  IF @@ERROR IN (515, 2601)
      RAISERROR 'FirstName, LastName & LoginID parameter values are required'
               , 16, 1
  ELSE
      RAISERROR ERROR_MESSAGE(), @ERROR, 16, 1
END CATCH
```

Exercise 4

If you have completed all previous exercises, use the following script to produce a message. Analyze each statement so you understand how each value is produced.

```
USE AdventureWorks2000
GO
--
ALTER FUNCTION dbo.fnProperCase (@In VarChar(255))
    RETURNS VarChar(255)
AS
BEGIN
    RETURN  UPPER(SUBSTRING(@In, 1, 1)) + LOWER(SUBSTRING(@In, 2, 254))
END
GO
-- Execute query from here if function has already been created --
-- Assemble message from string fragments:
DECLARE @Message VarChar(255)
SELECT @Message = dbo.fnProperCase(REVERSE(SUBSTRING(LastName, 4, 3))) FROM
Employee WHERE EmployeeID = 199
SET @Message = @Message + ' ' + CHAR(73) + CHAR(39) + CHAR(109) + ' ' + CHAR(97)
SELECT @Message = @Message + ' ' + dbo.fnProperCase(SUBSTRING(Description, 61, 5))
FROM ProductDescription WHERE ProductDescriptionID = 1586
SELECT @Message = @Message  + SUBSTRING(Name, 6, 3) FROM ProductSubCategory WHERE
ProductSubCategoryID = 38
```

```
SELECT @Message = @Message + CHAR(45) + SUBSTRING(@@SERVICENAME, 3, 3)
SELECT @Message = @Message  + ' ' + LOWER(SUBSTRING(Description, 1, 3)) FROM
ProductDescription WHERE ProductDescriptionID = 847
SELECT @Message = @Message + SUBSTRING(LastName, 4, 3) FROM Employee WHERE
EmployeeID = 21
SELECT @Message = @Message + CHAR(33)
-- Print the entire string:
PRINT @Message
```

Solution

The message returned from this statement is:

```
Now I'm a Transact-SQL expert!
```

Index

budget constraints, 400
buffer cache, 44
BULK (reserved word), 460
business cases for subqueries, 293–296
Business Intelligence Development Studio, 73, 97–98
business logic, processing, 378–380
BY (reserved word), 460, 462

C

calculated columns, 135–137
CALL (reserved word), 465
CALLER option, 344
Camel Case naming standard, 112
CASCADE (reserved word), 460, 462
CASCADED (reserved word), 462, 465
CASE command, 382–384, 454–455
CASE (reserved word), 460, 462
CAST() function, 169–171, 473
CAST (reserved word), 462, 465
catalog procedures
  sp_column_privileges, 483
  sp_column_privileges_ex, 483
  sp_columns, 483
  sp_columns_ex, 483
  sp_databases, 484
  sp_fkeys, 484
  sp_pkeys, 484
  sp_server_info, 484
  sp_special_columns, 484
  sp_sproc_columns, 484
  sp_statistics, 484
  sp_stored_procedures, 484
  sp_table_privileges, 484
  sp_table_privileges_ex, 484
  sp_tables, 484
CATALOG (reserved word), 462, 465
CATALOG_NAME view, 516
catalogs, managing and populating, 304–313
categories of application programming models, 398–399
CEILING() function, 193, 475

CHAR() function, 182, 478
CHAR (reserved word), 462, 465
CHARACTER (reserved word), 463, 465
CHARACTER_LENGTH (reserved word), 463
CHARACTER_MAXIMUM_LENGTH view, 510, 512, 514, 515
CHARACTER_OCTET_LENGTH view, 510, 512, 514, 515
CHARACTER_SET_CATALOG view, 511, 512, 514, 515
CHARACTER_SET_NAME view, 511, 512, 514, 515
CHARACTER_SET_SCHEMA view, 511, 512, 514, 515
CHARINDEX() function, 184–185, 478
CHAR_LENGTH (reserved word), 462
check constraints, 324, 333–334
CHECK (reserved word), 460, 463
CHECK_CONSTRAINTS views
  CONSTRAINT_CATALOG view, 509
  CONSTRAINT_CLAUSE view, 509
  CONSTRAINT_NAME view, 509
  CONSTRAINT_SCHEMA view, 509
CHECK_OPTION view, 518
checkpoint, 273–274
CHECKPOINT (reserved word), 460
checksum functions
  BINARY_CHECKSUM() function, 473
  CHECKSUM() function, 473
  CHECKSUM_AGG() function, 473
CLASS (reserved word), 465
client/server database solutions
  application programming models, 401–404
  event-handling code, 403–404
  overview, 401–402
  user interface, 402–403
client/server processes, 42
CLOB (reserved word), 465
CLOSE (reserved word), 460, 463
clustered index, 324
CLUSTERED (reserved word), 460
COALESCE() function, 200, 202–203, 480
COALESCE (reserved word), 460, 463